Therapeutic Feedback and Treatment Planning with the MMPI-3

This book is the first to introduce empirically informed yet empathically framed language for MMPI-3 users communicating findings to clients. It integrates interpretive guidance with evidence-based therapeutic strategies and structured self-help recommendations, thereby enriching the clinical utility of the instrument in therapeutic assessment.

Therapeutic Feedback and Treatment Planning with the MMPI-3 provides a clear set of guidelines for using this comprehensive personality/psychopathology instrument, for sharing productive, non-judgmental feedback with clients who are entering therapy, and identifying treatment plans based on clients' MMPI-3 results. Following an introduction that includes the history and evolution of the MMPI instruments and therapeutic assessment, readers will be guided through the steps of therapeutic assessment and feedback, and an exploration of the MMPI-3 scales. These include Validity Scales, Higher-Order Scales, Restructured Clinical Scales, Specific Problems Scales consisting of Somatic/Cognitive Scales, Internalizing Scales, Externalizing Scales, and Interpersonal Scales, and the Personality Psychopathology Five Scales. Each scale is interpretively described for feedback and descriptive purposes for patients. By focusing on clients' subjective experiences, the book guides and facilitates therapeutic engagement. The authors provide case studies to clearly illustrate the updated psychometric standard for psychological assessment.

This book is a must-have resource for psychologists who practice psychotherapy. It will support MMPI-3 users of all levels; enriching personality assessment, strengthening the therapeutic alliance, and informing treatment planning. It will also assist researchers working with this instrument and educate students in training.

Dr. Richard W. Levak has co-authored seven books on the MMPI/MMPI-2 and is a Fellow of the San Diego Psychological Association, the Society for Personality Assessment, and a diplomate of the American Board of Assessment Psychology.

Dr. Alan F. Friedman is a licensed clinical psychologist in full-time independent practice in Chicago, IL. He is an associate clinical professor in the Department of Psychiatry and Behavioral Sciences at the Feinberg School of Medicine, Northwestern University, Chicago, IL. He is also a fellow in the Society for Personality Assessment.

Dr. Yossef S. Ben-Porath is an emeritus professor of Psychological Sciences at Kent State University, OH. He has been involved extensively in MMPI research for the past 40 years and is a co-developer of the MMPI-3.

Therapeutic Feedback and Treatment Planning with the MMPI-3

Richard W. Levak, Alan F. Friedman, and
Yossef S. Ben-Porath

Routledge
Taylor & Francis Group
NEW YORK AND LONDON

Designed cover image: Biod © Getty Images

First published 2026
by Routledge
605 Third Avenue, New York, NY 10158

and by Routledge
4 Park Square, Milton Park, Abingdon, Oxon, OX14 4RN

Routledge is an imprint of the Taylor & Francis Group, an informa business

ISBN: 978-1-032-90426-9 (hbk)
ISBN: 978-1-032-89213-9 (pbk)
ISBN: 978-1-003-55792-0 (ebk)

DOI: 10.4324/9781003557920

Typeset in Times New Roman
by Newgen Publishing UK

"As a co-author of *Therapeutic Feedback with the MMPI-2*, I have witnessed firsthand how deeply validating feedback can be and the way it reduces defensiveness and encourages openness in clients. This has been especially important in my assessment work on *Survivor* and other reality television programs where people want to look their best. Given this, I have long been curious about the MMPI-3, particularly its suitability for younger individuals who struggle with a lengthy test battery. This book clearly demonstrates the ways that person-centered and compassionate feedback can be used with the MMPI-3. It gives the clinician a deeper understanding of the scales and the implications for family background and potential pitfalls in the course of work with the client. This will undoubtedly be a must-have manual for psychologists who aim to integrate therapeutic feedback into their MMPI-3 assessment practice."

Liza Siegel, Ph.D., *Consulting Psychologist*

"Over 20+ years of teaching assessment courses to doctoral students, I've found that the process of giving feedback is grossly overlooked in the available resources. The majority of the literature focuses on how to write a report, rather than how to communicate the results to clients in a productive manner. With this new text Levak, Friedman, and Ben-Porath have filled that void, at least with regard to the MMPI-3. This text provides abundant feedback examples that can not only help clients understand their results but may also assist them in gaining self-insight and engaging in the treatment process. This new book will be assigned reading in my next MMPI-3 class."

P. Kevin Bolinskey, Ph.D., HSPP, *Professor, Department of Psychology, Indiana State University, Terre Haute, IN*

"Leading experts guide readers in interpreting the MMPI-3 with clarity and precision. They show how to translate complex test correlations into meaningful statements that psychotherapy clients can truly use to understand themselves and make productive changes in their lives. Because unaccepted truths yield nothing, this book focuses on insights that are both accurate and usable – helping therapists frame results in ways that might yield real transformation in their clients. Without a doubt: a powerful new resource to clinicians doing clinical personality assessment."

Professor Dr. Jan H. Kamphuis, *University of Amsterdam, Netherlands; Clinical Psychology President, Society for Personality Assessment*

To Rachel and Linda
Richard W. Levak

For Ben, Marco, and Emily
Alan F. Friedman

To my wife Denise, with love and gratitude for all that you do
Yossef S. Ben-Porath

Contents

Figures and Tables

Figures

Tables

About the Authors

Richard W. Levak, Ph.D., is recognized as an authority on the Minnesota Multiphasic Personality Inventory and has co-authored seven books on the subject. Over the course of his career, Dr. Levak has evolved a unique framework for providing accurate, empathic feedback using the MMPI and its revisions. This approach has been informed by more than four decades of experience providing personality assessment feedback to well over 10,000 patients, business executives, and reality TV applicants. He is a fellow of the San Diego Psychological Association, the Society for Personality Assessment, and a diplomate and founding member of the American Board of Assessment Psychology. Dr. Levak has lectured extensively in academic, professional, and community settings and teaches MMPI feedback workshops.

Alan F. Friedman, Ph.D., is a licensed clinical psychologist in full-time independent practice in Chicago, IL, and an associate clinical professor in the Department of Psychiatry and Behavioral Sciences at the Feinberg School of Medicine, Northwestern University. Dr. Friedman specializes in litigation consulting, forensic assessments, and provides consultations to mental health professionals, security and human resource professionals, managers, executives, and attorneys interested in crisis prevention and management strategies for critical incidents. He regularly performs fitness-for-duty evaluations and threat assessments for law enforcement agencies and organizations as well as designing workplace violence prevention programs. He is a fellow of the Society of Personality Assessment and a member of the American and Illinois Psychological Associations. He has served as a consulting editor of the journals *Assessment*, *Journal of Personality Assessment*, and *Professional Psychology: Research and Practice.* He acts as a litigation consultant and expert witness in cases of employment, criminal, personal injury, and disability matters, and child custody disputes.

Yossef S. Ben-Porath, PhD., is an emeritus professor of Psychological Sciences at Kent State University, OH. He has been involved extensively in MMPI research for the past 40 years and is a co-developer of the MMPI-3.

Foreword

Radhika Krishnamurthy

Clinical personality assessment has historically been used to aid treatment planning, albeit previously in a manner that confined the obtained information to the professional's realm and with findings rarely communicated to the recipients of assessment and therapeutic services. Indeed, this approach undoubtedly contributed to impressions of psychological testing as an impersonal and detached procedure riddled with the use of esoteric psychological verbiage and generally inaccessible to persons other than assessment psychologists. Arguably, even treatment providers likely overlooked the bulk of findings presented in a psychological assessment report, attending largely to the provided diagnosis and general recommendations for treatment. Thus, there was tremendous underutilization, even wastage, of test results.

Fortunately, the tide has turned in recent decades. Influenced by the framework of Constance Fischer's (1994, 2000) expositions of individualized, collaborative assessment, Stephen Finn (1996) applied his emerging test feedback model to the MMPI-2, demonstrating how to systematically organize and communicate MMPI-2 results in a meaningful, sensitive, and digestible manner. His method has since been elaborated to a comprehensive model of therapeutic assessment, with numerous published empirical studies demonstrating its efficacy and case studies exemplifying its clinical applications. Therapeutic assessment and feedback practices have become a mainstay of good assessment practice today, with applications shown for various personality assessment instruments and in clinical, neuropsychological, forensic, and medical settings. Test feedback methods are currently incorporated into the personality assessment courses of many clinical and counseling psychology programs, with instructors and students alike eager for resources to guide their teaching and learning of these methods.

The predecessor to the current text is an impressive work by Levak, Siegel, and Nichols (with Stolberg) (2011) titled *Therapeutic Feedback with the MMPI-2: A Positive Psychology Approach*. Using a different paradigm (shaped by Lewak, Marks, & Nelson's 1990 guide to providing MMPI/MMPI-2 feedback and treatment) than the one proposed by Finn, their text provided the language for communicating MMPI-2 test results to clients in an empathic and easily understood manner, along with prognostic statements and treatment suggestions to benefit treatment providers. The current text by Levak, Friedman, and Ben-Porath updates the earlier work to the MMPI-3, which has a vastly different structure and set of scales than the MMPI-2. These authors are well-established experts of MMPI instruments, which is evident in the nuanced interpretations they offer for scores in different T score brackets. Importantly, they contextualize the interpretations to lifestyle and family background, thereby positioning the descriptions within clients' lived experiences, along with *translating* test score correlates and their implications into everyday language. For example, "hypersensitivity" and "persecutory ideation" associated with a high RC6 score is translated to "feeling very vulnerable to being mistreated, criticized, judged, even physically attacked" and finding it "hard to know whom to trust." Accompanying such descriptions are an important reminder to the assessor that there may be a real basis for the client's persecutory ideation, as well as provision of guidelines to use non-threatening language to avoid eliciting defensiveness. Such an approach is particularly valuable when providing feedback to persons from culturally disadvantaged groups who have likely experienced the negative effects of bigotry and discrimination and/or at least not felt understood. Such compassion is woven into the very fabric of this text.

In teaching therapeutic test feedback methods to my students, I often ask them to consider how they would phrase their communications when talking with a family member or friend. In doing so, phrases such as "interpersonal relationships," "internalizing patterns," "somatic manifestations" and "anhedonic tendencies" disappear from their rehearsed scripts. Levak and colleagues provide both the road map and the specific phrasing for assessment students and practitioners to convey their feedback, which has the added benefit of bringing clarity on the constructs measured by the MMPI-3. My students will love this!

This book contains manifold gifts for multiple professionals. In addition to the features I mentioned earlier, MMPI-3 users will greatly appreciate the authors' discussion of profile patterns to consider, reviewed under the "Clarifying Scales" section associated with each MMPI-3 scale, and will find the case examples illuminating. Treatment providers will relish the therapist's notes, therapy guidelines, and therapeutic pitfalls discussed for each MMPI-3 scale and pattern of results. Notably, this text will help to further advance the recognition that personality characteristics influence treatment response, that psychological assessment and intervention are fundamentally intertwined, and that assessment is, in itself, a therapeutic intervention.

It has been my great pleasure and honor to be invited to write the Foreword to this excellent text. This book will definitely be a valuable addition to the resource libraries of students, instructors, and practitioners of personality assessment and therapeutic practices.

Radhika Krishnamurthy, Psy.D, ABAP
Professor, Clinical Psychology
Florida Institute of Technology

Preface

In 2011, Philip Marks, a distinguished authority on the MMPI, remarked in his endorsement of *Therapeutic Feedback with the MMPI-2* (Levak, Siegel, Nichols, & Stolberg, 2011) that feedback had long been the "forgotten stepchild" of personality assessment with the MMPI. Since that time, both assessment feedback in general and collaborative assessment in particular have emerged as central themes in annual presentations of the Society for Personality Assessment (SPA). While feedback can no longer be considered the stepchild, and may, in fact, have become the favorite child, there remains a notable scarcity of resources offering detailed, practical guidance on the specific language clinicians might use when delivering feedback about potentially distressing personality traits and psychological symptoms. Existing texts on feedback tend to emphasize structure and methodology over therapeutic communication.

Restructuring of the MMPI, first with the MMPI-2-RF and most recently with the MMPI-3, has retained the core constructs assessed by the original MMPI Clinical Scales while introducing numerous new, psychometrically refined scales. These additions have enhanced diagnostic clarity by reducing item overlap and linking the scales of the inventory to contemporary constructs that are the focus of research in the areas of personality and psychopathology. The MMPI-3 scales assess a broad array of clinical concerns relevant to contemporary psychological practice, increasing the test's applicability for both therapeutic and forensic contexts. Despite these advancements, there are currently no publications devoted specifically to feedback language and therapeutic application of the MMPI-3. This book seeks to fill that gap by offering clinicians a structured approach to using the MMPI-3 as a tool for both feedback and therapeutic intervention. The guidance provided herein is intended to enrich the clinician's understanding of the examinee and offer language that articulates the individual's psychological and existential experience.

Acknowledgments

Richard W. Levak, Ph.D.: I extend my sincere thanks to my teachers, mentors, and colleagues – Lowell Storms, Ph.D., Alex Caldwell, Ph.D., Phil Marks, Ph.D., and Peter Briggs, Ph.D. – who nurtured my passion for the MMPI by generously sharing their clinical expertise. I am especially indebted to Phil Marks, Ph.D., for encouraging me to write the first feedback-focused book using the MMPI. I am also profoundly thankful to my friend and mentor, Gerald Nelson, M.D., who challenged me to present assessment results directly to his patients. His insistence compelled me to develop a language that is both empirically grounded and non-judgmental. Steve Bierman, M.D., through his insightful lectures on hypnosis, revealed the power of language that bypasses resistance. Al Assad, a gifted and self-taught philosopher-psychologist, was an invaluable and exacting sounding board whose insights helped me refine and deepen my thinking. We are grateful to Radhika Krishnamurthy for her willingness to write our Foreword. Finally, I owe special thanks to my wife, who not only undertook much of the typing for this book but also served as a relentless and vigilant editor.

Alan F. Friedman, Ph.D.: Many thanks to Micki Kowalik who not only kept me on track throughout this project but was invaluable in editing and organizing the materials for the book. Her dedication to this project exceeded what I could have ever hoped for. My appreciation to my friends who support me in all endeavors including my academic projects: Larry Barton, Richard Pechter, Richard Grossman, and Paul Shafer, thanks for always "being there." And, to my early assessment mentors and teachers, Phil Marks, Hans Eysenck, William Seeman, Grant Dahlstrom, James Butcher, Goldine Gleser, and James A. Wakefield, Jr.: your influence has been so valuable to me in my career. And, to Yossef Ben-Porath, for showing me new ways to understand personality through the MMPI-3.

Yossef S. Ben-Porath, Ph.D.: I would like to thank my co-authors, Richard Levak and Alan Friedman, for inviting me to collaborate with them on this important project. And express my heartfelt appreciation for my wife, Denise, for her decades-long support and steadfast encouragement of my work on the MMPI.

1 Introduction

History and Evolution of the MMPI Instruments and Therapeutic Assessment

The original Minnesota Multiphasic Personality Inventory (**MMPI**) was developed as a differential diagnostic instrument in the 1930s and early 1940s (Hathaway & McKinley, 1943). The developers, Starke Hathaway (a clinically experienced physiological psychologist) and J. C. McKinley (a neuropsychiatrist) brought to MMPI development the objective eyes and methods of scientists (Lindzey, 1989). Hathaway was known to be a rigorous and meticulous researcher but also a man who was humane and empathic (APA, 1978). The MMPI reflects his astute understanding of personality and psychopathology. It was a breakthrough in the field of empirical psychology, but the power of the instrument as a measure of the richness of personality was developed over time through the contributions of clinicians and researchers. Detailed reviews of the development of the original MMPI and its five successor versions are provided in Nichols (2011), Friedman et al. (2015), Ben-Porath & Sellbom (2023), and McCord & Veltri (2024).

In a 1956 *American Psychologist* article, Paul Meehl called for a good "cookbook" that would provide an actuarial description of the MMPI (Meehl, 1956). Philip Marks and his colleagues responded and empirically generated personality and psychopathology descriptors for the individual scales and commonly occurring codetypes of the MMPI. After Marks and Seeman's work was published (1963), a proliferation of studies was published, adding an enormous amount of empirical and clinical data for the correlates of MMPI scales for various populations.

The MMPI further evolved as researchers and clinicians continued to adapt and refine the test (Butcher, 2000; Weed & Butcher, 1992). Numerous studies added richness and depth to personality descriptions across various settings. However, the original MMPI had several limitations that required modifications. The MMPI was revised and published as the MMPI-2 in 1989 (Butcher et al., 1989). The main reasons for its revision included the following:

- **Outdated norms**: The original MMPI normative group consisted of a relatively small and homogeneous sample of primarily White, working-class, rural Minnesotans, possessing an average of eight years of education, who were visiting friends and relatives at the university hospital at the time the test was developed. The MMPI-2, introduced in 1989, included a then-contemporary sample of individuals tested throughout the United States who matched the adult population on demographics of the 1989 U.S. Census intended to improve its validity and generalizability to a variety of settings.
- **Eliminating obsolete/biased items and adding new items**: Many items from the original test were outdated, sexist, culturally biased, poorly worded, or no longer relevant to contemporary society. Outdated MMPI items were eliminated, such as asking the respondent if they liked playing the game "Drop the Handkerchief." Items asking about medical issues such as bowel movements were also deleted since they were deemed as irrelevant and/or an invasion of privacy in a psychological test. Other controversial items that were eliminated dealt with test takers' religious beliefs and practices. The removal or revisions of items ensured compliance

DOI: 10.4324/9781003557920-1

with then-contemporary standards to modernize the language of the MMPI-2. Non-scored items were also deleted allowing for space to add new items related to clinically relevant topics, such as drug usage, suicidal ideation, Type A behavior, work-related difficulties, and treatment readiness.

- **New T scores – improved metrics**: The MMPI-2 Re-Standardization Committee modified the ways raw scores were converted to T scores by utilizing uniform rather than linear T scores for 8 of the clinical scales. The traditional validity scales (L, F, and K) continued to use linear T scores. The purpose of using uniform T scores was to make the percentile values of the T scores comparable across the 8 clinical scales and 15 content scales.

The MMPI-2 aimed to improve measurement accuracy by refining test scales, reducing ambiguous or confusing wording, and adding new validity scales to detect response inconsistencies, overreporting, and underreporting. The revision also included new content scales to better assess both personality variables and test-taking attitudes, enhancing the MMPI-2's utility in clinical, forensic, and research settings. While the MMPI-2 was a significant improvement over the MMPI, it did not address the fundamental problems with the MMPI clinical scales, including significant item overlap between the clinical scales; heterogenous symptom sets within the scales; and a demoralization factor that was common to each of the scales reducing the specificity of the scales' meanings.

One of the more sweeping revisions to the standard MMPI-2 emerged in 2003 with the introduction of the Restructured Clinical (RC) Scales (Tellegen et al., 2003). The RC Scales constituted the core set of scales that subsequently carried over to the MMPI-2 – Restructured Form (**MMPI-2-RF**) and to the MMPI-3. The RC Scales comprise eight independent "restructured" original clinical scales and one scale measuring demoralization. They are described as "restructured" because they were designed to measure the core component of each of the original clinical scales (not including MMPI-2 Scales 5 and 0) without the confounding effects of demoralization, which Tellegen et al. believed saturated each clinical scale, attenuating their discriminant validity. In essence, the main reason for creating the MMPI-2 RC Scales was to correct the longstanding problem of extensive co-variation among the clinical scales of the original MMPI impeding clinical interpretation. The demoralization factor pervasive among the original clinical scales served to inflate the correlations among many, if not most, of the scales and, in turn, compromised their discriminant validity. Tellegen et al. (2003) also recommended that the RC Scales not be combined with each other into RC Scale-based codetypes because the clinical scale codetype literature could not be applied to the RC Scales.

A strategic decision by the MMPI-2 Re-Standardization Committee had been to keep the clinical scales essentially intact in order to allow for continuation and reliance on the reported empirical correlates of codetypes. Over the years, codetypes had become the primary interpretive method, even though the scales' high intercorrelations rendered the MMPI-2 diagnostically weak.

After almost 20 years, it became apparent that the MMPI-2 needed revision, so in 2008 the MMPI-2-RF was introduced to further refine and modernize the test. In a much faster-paced world, and with immediate gratification from social media available, it became clear that a test of 567 items was too lengthy. The MMPI-2-RF reduced the number of items from 567 to 338 and improved the discriminant validity of the scales by eliminating item overlap among scales within each of the three measurement tiers of the test. New scales reflecting contemporary concerns were added resulting in improved efficiency in assessing a broad range of psychological conditions.

The MMPI-2-RF was composed of 51 scales organized into several scale sets. There were 9 Validity Scales designed to provide information about the test-taker's approach to the assessment, with measures focused on inconsistent responding, overreporting, and underreporting. The remaining 42 Substantive Scales were organized in a three-tiered hierarchical structure that included, at its broadest level, 3 Higher-Order (H-O) Scales, the 9 MMPI-2 RC Scales carried over intact to the MMPI-2-RF, and 25 Specific Problems (SP) Scales that represented more narrow constructs. An additional 5 Personality Psychopathology Five (PSY-5) Scales focused on manifestations of personality disorder. No new items were added to the MMPI-2-RF and the 1980s MMPI-2 norms were used to develop standard MMPI-2-RF scores. These two features of the MMPI-2-RF were among the primary goals for developing the MMPI-3.

The goals in developing the MMPI-3 included enhancing the item pool, updating normative data, optimizing existing scales, and introducing new scales where necessary. Focus was placed on creating a well-validated, psychometrically up-to-date instrument that reflects current societal demographics and psychological understanding. The MMPI-3 is designed to evaluate personality structure and psychopathology, and its robustness means it is suitable for diverse settings, including mental health, medical, forensic, and public safety environments.

The restandardization of the MMPI-3 with a new, nationally representative normative sample closely matched the 2020 U.S. Census projections concerning race, ethnicity, education, and age, ensuring the assessment's applicability across diverse populations. Additionally, for the first time, Spanish-language norms were developed for the U.S. Spanish translation of the MMPI-3, enhancing its utility among Spanish-speaking individuals.

New MMPI-3 scales to assess disordered eating, compulsivity, impulsivity, self-importance, and dominance added interpretive richness. Several existing scales were also refined to improve their psychometric properties and clinical relevance. These revisions aimed to enhance the scales' convergent and discriminant validity, ensuring that they accurately reflect the constructs they intend to measure. Ben-Porath and Sellbom (2023) provide detailed information about the MMPI-3 scale development process, revisions made to existing MMPI-2-RF scales, and the new scales added to the MMPI-3. Table 1.1 provides a list of the 52 MMPI-3 scales and the constructs they assess.

Table 1.1 The MMPI-3 scales

Validity Scales	
CRIN	Combined Response Inconsistency – Combination of random and fixed inconsistent responding
VRIN	Variable Response Inconsistency – Random responding
TRIN	True Response Inconsistency – Fixed responding
F	Infrequent Responses – Responses infrequent in the general population
Fp	Infrequent Psychopathology Responses – Responses infrequent in psychiatric populations
Fs	Infrequent Somatic Responses – Somatic complaints infrequent in medical patient populations
FBS	Symptom Validity Scale – Noncredible somatic and cognitive complaints
RBS	Response Bias Scale – Exaggerated memory complaints
L	Uncommon Virtues – Rarely claimed moral attributes or activities
K	Adjustment Validity – Claims of uncommonly high level of psychological adjustment
Higher-Order (H-O) Scales	
EID	Emotional/Internalizing Dysfunction – Problems associated with mood and affect
THD	Thought Dysfunction – Problems associated with disordered thinking
BXD	Behavioral/Externalizing Dysfunction – Problems associated with under-controlled behavior
Restructured Clinical (RC) Scales	
RCd	Demoralization (DEM) – General unhappiness and dissatisfaction
RC1	Somatic Complaints (SOM) – Diffuse physical health complaints
RC2	Low Positive Emotions (LPE) – Lack of positive emotional responsiveness
RC4	Antisocial Behavior (ASB) – Rule breaking and irresponsible behavior

(*Continued*)

Table 1.1 (Continued)

RC6	Ideas of Persecution (PER) – Self-referential beliefs that others pose a threat
RC7	Dysfunctional Negative Emotions (DNE) – Maladaptive anxiety, anger, irritability
RC8	Aberrant Experiences (ABX) – Unusual perceptions of thoughts associated with thought dysfunction
RC9	Hypomanic Activation (HPM) – Overactivation, aggression, impulsivity, and grandiosity
Specific Problems (SP) Scales	
Somatic/Cognitive Scales	
MLS	Malaise – Overall sense of physical debilitation, poor health
NUC	Neurological Complaints – Dizziness, weakness, paralysis, loss of balance, etc.
EAT	Eating Concerns – Problematic eating behaviors
COG	Cognitive Complaints – Memory problems, difficulties concentrating
Internalizing Scales	
SUI	Suicidal/Death Ideation – Direct reports of suicidal ideation and recent attempts
HLP	Helplessness/Hopelessness – Belief that goals cannot be reached or problems solved
SFD	Self-Doubt – Lack of self-confidence, feelings of uselessness
NFC	Inefficacy – Belief that one is indecisive and inefficacious
STR	Stress – Problems involving stress and nervousness
WRY	Worry – Excessive worry and preoccupation
CMP	Compulsivity – Engaging in compulsive behaviors
ARX	Anxiety-Related Experiences – Multiple anxiety-related experiences such as catastrophizing, panic, dread, and intrusive ideation
ANP	Anger Proneness – Becoming easily angered, impatient with others
BRF	Behavior-Restricting Fears – Fears that significantly inhibit normal behavior
Externalizing Scales	
FML	Family Problems – Conflictual family relationships
JCP	Juvenile Conduct Problems – Difficulties at school and at home, stealing
SUB	Substance Abuse – Current and past misuse of alcohol and drugs
IMP	Impulsivity – Poor impulse control and nonplanful behavior
ACT	Activation – Heightened excitation and energy level
AGG	Aggression – Physically aggressive, violent behavior
CYN	Cynicism – Non-self-referential beliefs that others are bad and not to be trusted
Interpersonal Scales	
SFI	Self-Importance – Beliefs related to having special talents and abilities
DOM	Dominance – Being domineering in relationships with others
DSF	Disaffiliativeness – Disliking people and being around them
SAV	Social Avoidance – Not enjoying and avoiding social events
SHY	Shyness – Feeling uncomfortable and anxious in the presence of others
Personality Psychopathology Five (PSY-5) Scales	
AGGR	Aggressiveness – Instrumental, goal-directed aggression
PSYC	Psychoticism – Disconnection from reality
DISC	Disconstraint – Under-controlled behavior
NEGE	Negative Emotionality/Neuroticism – Anxiety, insecurity, worry, and fear
INTR	Introversion/Low Positive Emotionality – Social disengagement and anhedonia

The MMPI/MMPI-2/MMPI-3 and Feedback

The original MMPI evolved, in part, according to the medical model that views diagnosis of malfunction and disease as the first step in treatment (Barron, 1998). Its focus was on psychopathology. Historically, clinical psychology has assumed that human nature is largely motivated by aggressive, self-serving impulses, negative emotions, and unconscious self-defeating drives (Domino & Conway, 2001; Freud, 1930; James, 1902; Levak et al., 2011; Seligman, 2002). Assessment psychologists have traditionally focused on diagnosing psychopathology and suggesting treatment strategies (Tallent, 1992; Vaillant, 2000). Clinicians, perhaps due to Freud's notion of resistance, assumed that clients would reject feedback, especially if it was perceived as negative. The traditional models of psychotherapy were based on the idea that the clinician knew what was "wrong" with the client. It was believed that the client had to discover what was wrong themselves, prompted by wise clinician interventions or questions. The assumption was that clients would resist interpretation and the model was "top-down," with the clinician "in the know," and the client blinded by their own self-deception and ego defenses. According to this traditional paradigm, ego defenses were labeled as "maladaptive," "immature," or "regressive," and the role of treatment was to increase "adaptive" higher-order defenses.

The various MMPI versions were not developed with the goal of feedback in mind. In fact, the test and personality correlates were developed because of a firm belief in empiricism and the actuarial method in an era when a clinician's judgment was highly suspect (Meehl, 1996). Consequently, the concept of using feedback as a collaborative data-gathering and therapeutic tool was antithetical to the actuarial method. Although actuarial personality descriptors were an improvement from the vague, intuitively based methods practiced earlier, there were some costs and some early critics (Fischer, 1985/1994). Reports written about clients were, at times, so judgmental and potentially pejorative that they were often stamped, "Do not share with the client." Psychologists trained in the 1980s will recall when it was considered unethical to share records with clients because the content was potentially too distressing, as it was written in judgmental language. A manifestation of the Freudian belief was that people with psychopathology resist interpretation of their symptoms and that the work of the therapist is to circumvent their defenses (Eagle, 1999; Grossman, 1993). Traditional models of assessment assumed that the client's resistance was inevitable (Engle & Arkowitz, 2006; Rosenthal, 1987) and, therefore, the process of insight had to be circuitous to avoid it. Research, however, suggests that clients can be open to feedback, even concerning negative attributes, if it is presented in a balanced, non-judgmental way (El-Shaieb, 2005; Finn & Tonsager, 1992, Veilleux et al., 2024).

Although there were numerous books and articles on MMPI/MMPI-2 interpretation, there was no guidance book on how to provide feedback until 1990. Lewak et al.'s (1990) therapeutic feedback paradigm described individuals' MMPI-2 test results in a way that reflected the client's existential experience. From their perspective, resistance is not inevitable but is the result of feedback that is poorly articulated. Consequently, in this book we do not follow one aspect of the Collaborative Assessment Model (Finn, 1996) – that the therapist needs to divide client feedback into three levels. According to that model, Level 1 feedback gives feedback about issues, dynamics, and symptoms that are clearly recognized and accepted by the client. Level 2 feedback amplifies what the client already knows about themselves. And Level 3 feedback is about issues the client will likely resist due to being perceived as threatening. According to that model, the therapist makes the decision about the client's receptiveness and adjusts their feedback level accordingly.

Lewak's experience is that clients can accept psychological test feedback if it is given from an adaptation paradigm. According to Lewak, feedback, even potentially distressing feedback, can be accepted by the client if it is presented empathically as an understandable adaptation to adverse circumstances. Using a similar approach, Veilleux and colleagues (2024) developed a protocol that minimized resistance to receiving feedback by a client with a diagnosis of borderline personality disorder. They focused upon feedback to an individual with a borderline personality disorder as they knew that this was a diagnosis that most people would find difficult to accept. An empathic approach can create a rapid therapeutic alliance because the feedback statements validate the client's inner experiences. Since one aim of this book's feedback model is to create a collaborative discussion that avoids the hierarchical model of the "therapist knows best," trust is enhanced by honest and sensitively presented feedback.

A mandate for providing feedback on psychological test data has evolved over time, influenced by ethical guidelines, professional standards, and legal considerations.

- **Early views (pre-1970s)**: Psychologists often withheld test results from clients, believing that only trained professionals could properly interpret them. The emphasis was on protecting clients from potential misunderstandings or distress. Since most reports were written in clinical, judgmental language, the potential for misunderstanding and distress by sharing client results was great.
- **Shift in the 1970s and 1980s**: The humanistic and client-centered movements pushed for greater transparency, arguing that clients had a right to access and understand their psychological test results (Finn & Tonsager, 2002). Test results and reports, however, were often stamped "Do not share with the client."
- **Current ethical standards** (APA, 2017): Psychologists are now ethically required to ensure that explanations of results are given to individuals, unless the nature of the relationship precludes provision of an explanation of findings (e.g., forensic evaluations, security screenings.)
- **American Psychological Association Guidelines**: The most recent *APA Guidelines for Psychological Assessment and Evaluation* (APA, 2020) state that psychologists strive to provide assessment feedback and test findings in a manner suitable for the recipient to comprehend the information as well as to understand how the recommendations can be used to accomplish the purpose of the assessment.

These standards and guidelines allow clients the right to their assessment results and even, in some cases, the right to the actual test protocols (but not the actual copyrighted test materials), unless a psychologist can show that harm would result from the disclosure. Accordingly, there is a need for assessment psychologists to continue developing feedback language that is both empirically informed and at the same time comprehensible and useful. There is also a continuing need for research to determine the efficacy of different feedback approaches.

Although traditional assessment was hierarchical, authoritarian, and assumed the assessor had the answers and the client did not, some researchers in university settings attempted to describe positive adaptive correlates for many of the MMPI scales (Duckworth & Barley, 1988; Kunce & Anderson, 1976; Newman & Greenway, 1997). There were also attempts to reformulate the clinical language of the MMPI into more user-friendly terms. The *Therapist Guide to the MMPI and the MMPI-2* (Lewak et al., 1990) was published within a year of the MMPI-2's release so it was limited in its MMPI-2 descriptors. It provided an empirical–phenomenological framework for giving MMPI feedback to clients in non-judgmental, jargon-free language. In this approach, the therapist is seen as a guide rather than an authority, and the process is collaborative instead of hierarchical. Research (Finn & Tonsager, 2002; Poston & Hanson, 2010) has demonstrated that a collaborative assessment feedback approach can produce positive therapeutic effects even after one session.

Over the past 20 years, the number of people seeking some kind of counseling has grown exponentially. During the COVID-19 pandemic, the demand for psychological intervention grew enormously. Many clients not suffering serious psychopathology, but seeking help with life transition, work and school, family, or marital issues, began to use psychotherapy.

We believe that psychological assessment can be useful in providing personality feedback and expediting issue-specific, short-term therapeutic strategies. The language of psychopathology does not lend itself to creating a therapeutic alliance, whether clients are seriously disturbed or merely seeking help with a transitional issue. We believe the large increase in the profession of "coaching" (Williams & Davis, 2002), usually practiced by individuals with less formal clinical training and who rely on a "non-diagnostic" mentality, is a manifestation of how much psychology has fallen behind in developing a positive, non-judgmental paradigm to help people with reactive problems by providing personality feedback.

The Influence of Positive Psychology

A positive psychology approach to the client and the process of assessment looks to interpret what appears as dysfunctional behavior as adaptation instead. Martin Seligman and his colleagues (Seligman & Maier, 1967) were conducting tests of learning theory in the University of Pennsylvania Psychology Department, where dogs in a shuttle box were repeatedly exposed to a mild, inescapable electric shock. Eventually, most dogs gave up the effort to escape, even when provided an easy opportunity to do so. The researchers explained that the dogs had "learned" to be helpless. The extrapolation was that both the helpless dog and a depressed person have learned that escape actions are useless (Seligman et al., 1968). However, there were exceptions to the learned helplessness paradigm (Seligman & Weiss, 1980). About one in four dogs, even after they had been exposed to the "helpless situation," did not develop learned helplessness. The same thing happened in human experiments when people were given unsolvable tasks or inescapable noise; about one in four did not behave in a manner consistent with the learned helplessness paradigm.

Eventually, it became evident that the early theory of learned helplessness was "half-baked" (Seligman, 1990) and that some people manifest a buffering strength, a core resilience or hardiness that inoculates them against depression and other symptoms of severe stress. Seligman theorized that people could also learn to be optimistic and he continued to write several books on optimism and wellbeing (1990, 1993, 1996, 2002), thereby spawning a new field of interest: positive psychology.

In 1996, when he was elected president of the APA, Seligman made it his mission to encourage psychologists to study the positive as well as the negative aspects of human response to stress. Since then, positive psychology has evolved to encompass the study of positive emotions (joy, resilience, happiness), positive traits (strengths and virtues), and positive institutions (Foster & Lloyd, 2007; Fredrickson, 2001; Gable & Haidt, 2005; Seligman, 2002). It aims to complement the traditional focus on understanding, preventing, and curing negative psychological states by gaining a better understanding of human strengths (Aspinwall & Staudinger, 2003). Contributions from the field of positive psychology have shifted the paradigm away from pathology and mental illness and toward cultivating the qualities that benefit health, relationships, and careers.

Treatment paradigms of positive psychology draw on research about how people exposed to severe risk factors maintain positive mental health and live a full life (Bonanno, 2004, 2019, 2021; Bonanno et al., 2004; Peterson & Park, 2003). By attempting to understand how some people survive and even thrive after being exposed to traumatic events, psychologists hope to shed light on learnable resilience skills and are now empirically testing the therapeutic applications of positive psychology (Linley & Joseph, 2004). The study of post-traumatic growth after exposure to adverse events has shed much light on the adaptive abilities of individuals not only to recover from toxic situations but also, in fact, to flourish and grow as a result of their experiences. Richard

Tedeschi and his colleagues have published numerous studies on human resilience and post-traumatic growth (Calhoun & Tedeschi, 1991; Tedeschi, 1990, 2020, 2023; Tedeschi & Calhoun, 1995; Tedeschi et al., 2020).

Many see the assessment of psychological health as a future trend in treatment paradigms (Borgen & Betz, 2008; Lopez & Snyder, 2003; Naglieri & Graham, 2003). Positive psychology has made an impact on the field of assessment in general (Jiang & Shen, 2007; Park & Peterson, 2007) but has had a relatively small impact in the realm of traditional assessment tools like the MMPI-3. While it is important not to ignore human vulnerabilities, bringing balance into assessment by recognizing strengths is essential in order to understand and treat the individual. According to this book's therapeutic feedback model, we identify which possible conditioning experiences may have led to an understandable adaptive response that initially appears maladaptive. We interpret what is seen as maladaptive as, in fact, an adaptive defense given the events that precipitated it. Therapeutic intervention can reshape the defense structure given that the conditioning event is no longer present.

History of Therapeutic Models of Assessment

Therapeutic models of assessment developed from disparate roots: some based in philosophy, some accidental, and some humanistic. Fischer's collaborative model (Fischer, 1985/1994, 2000, 2006), was based on existential/phenomenological philosophy with an inherent respect for the individual. Craddick (1972, 1975) and Dana (1982, 1984) came from a humanistic multicultural perspective, recommending that clients be more involved in the assessment process through discussions with the testing psychologist about the purpose of their psychological assessment. Therapeutic assessment (Finn, 1996, 2007; Finn & Tonsager, 1992; Newman & Greenway, 1997) developed when Finn became curious about the fact that some clients appeared to have life-changing experiences as a result of the psychological testing (Finn, 2007). Incorporating these traditions, Beutler & Groth-Marnat (2003) called for a more integrated approach to the reporting of assessment data, avoiding the use of jargon and the rote reporting of test scores. Though grounded empirically, all these approaches aimed to provide a more complete, existential, and therapeutically oriented assessment of the individual.

Therapeutic models of assessment can be viewed as consonant with the humanistic model (Poston & Hanson, 2010), positing that human nature is creative, active, and purposeful in shaping a response to the environment (Adler, 1964; Allport, 1950/1975; Maslow, 1987; May, 1989; Rogers 1951; Vaillant, 1977). Carl Rogers' (1961) interest in the intrinsic value of the therapeutic relationship encourages therapists to accept clients "unconditionally," and views the therapeutic process as "client centered."

Integrative assessment (Groth-Marnat, 2009), the individualized/collaborative approach (Fischer 2000, 2006; Purves, 2002), therapeutic assessment (Finn 1996, 2007; Finn and Tonsager, 1992), and the feedback approach developed by Levak and colleagues (Lewak et al., 1990; Levak et al., 2011) all reflect roots in existential/phenomenological and humanistic perspectives. In all these approaches, the focus is client- rather than test-centered, with the aim of describing the unique individual tested, rather than a "typical individual" with "similar test scores" in the hope of providing a better focused, balanced, and therapeutically useful assessment. This is consistent with interpretive guidelines for the MMPI-3, which focus on what the test-taker reports and the empirical correlates of their self-report, rather than classifying individuals into "types" based on what is known about individuals with similar scores.

Levak and his colleagues view assessment feedback as therapeutic rather than being a sterile and unidirectional endeavor (Riddle et al., 2002). The therapeutic/collaborative/integrative assessment models have become important paradigms in the field of assessment psychology.

Basics of Therapeutic Assessment

Although therapeutic assessment (TA) is a blanket term for humanistically based assessment methods in general, Finn and Tonsager (1997) developed a structured approach and distinguished their own brand of TA (Finn & Kamphuis, 2006). Their approach was based on the principle that clients become most engaged in taking the MMPI-2 when they fully understand how the information can be used and are treated as collaborators (Butcher, 1990; Butcher & Finn, 1984). They noted that TA shares a great deal of its philosophy and background with "collaborative" and "individualized" assessment (Fischer, 2000; Beutler & Groth-Marnat, 2003; Purves, 2002).

Although many of the original studies of TA were conducted with participants from college and university counseling centers (Finn & Tonsager, 1992; Newman & Greenway, 1997), a growing body of literature has established the effectiveness of TA (Poston & Hanson, 2010) in diverse populations such as inpatients with eating disorders (Michel, 2002); families, children, and adolescents (Handler, 2007; Tharinger et al., 2008); patients undergoing neuropsychological evaluation (Engelman, et al., 2016; Gorske & Smith, 2009); and even inpatients diagnosed with severe mental illness (Peters et al., 2008; Smith et al., 2015).

Therapeutic assessment appears to be effective, as the process of psychological testing creates empathy in the assessor for the clients and their challenges, which in turn allows the assessor to help the clients develop more accurate and empathic stories about themselves. The collaborative technique allows clients to "review" their stories so that, for example, rather than a client defining himself as an angry person, he may realize through the assessment that he is fearful, anxious, and feels inefficacious. This is a more accurate, less negative description that points to specific corrective steps.

Therapeutic Feedback with the MMPI-3

We believe the next significant advance in assessment builds on the previously described therapeutic assessment process and incorporates the concept of therapeutic feedback first outlined by Levak (Lewak et al., 1990; Levak et al., 2011). In this paradigm, the MMPI-3 is used as a therapeutic feedback tool where the client's current symptoms and personality traits are seen from an adaptive perspective. We see the MMPI-3 as a road map, the therapist as the navigator, feedback statements in this book as the directions, and the lifestyle and family background experiences as possible areas to discover conditioning experiences. The client provides the motivation to travel, determines the destination and speed, and is the driver in the treatment adventure.

Therapeutic feedback presents the data in a way that creates a human picture devoid of jargon and judgment. This approach describes a client's pain, internal conflicts, and anxieties in a way that promotes self-empathy and modifies negative self-talk. It seeks to give suffering an understandable, non-blaming cause and provides strategies that have potential for prompt or eventual relief. The approach attempts to normalize a client's experiences wherever possible, and the feedback provides a road map for a collaborative, exploratory therapeutic dialogue.

The feedback component of existing assessment models and textbooks relies on traditional language. Currently, in the field of MMPI-3 assessment there are no guides that describe personality in accurate, empirically based, non-judgmental, empathic terms. Rather, the MMPI-3 literature to date primarily describes personality traits, symptoms, and states through the lens of psychopathology. Our book is intended to provide the therapeutic assessment tools and language for delivering collaborative/therapeutic feedback to clients.

Through the process of providing thousands of people feedback using the MMPI-2/MMPI-2-RF, Levak has developed an understanding of personality and psychopathology consistent with the model described in this book. This book seeks to describe clients' existential experience as reflected in their MMPI-3 scores. Our aim is to aid clinicians in developing a rapid therapeutic alliance and effective therapeutic suggestions.

The process begins with alliance-building through rapport and collaboration. The clinician obtains a psychosocial and therapeutic history and provides therapeutic feedback, resulting in a more insightful client who is more hopeful, with an empirically based treatment plan and self-help strategies. In this book many of the scale descriptors are based on available empirical data. A sizable proportion of the statements are clinically based, derived from Levak's years of experience with feedback from earlier MMPI versions.

Three contributions of positive psychology shape the therapeutic assessment and MMPI-3 feedback process described in this book. First, all behavior can be viewed as potentially adaptive; behaviors that are traditionally viewed as pathological and maladaptive may be reframed as understandable responses to the particular stressors that precipitated them. Second, therapeutic feedback is empathic, non-judgmental, and mostly jargon free. This type of feedback is not blindly positive; rather, it assumes that humans respond to overwhelming stress in understandable ways and that the therapist seeks to give coherence and meaning to their client's narrative. Third, therapeutic feedback stresses self-esteem and resilience-building through self-awareness as a goal of the assessment and feedback process. Self-esteem increases if the feedback helps clients positively reframe their current suffering in the context of understandable adaptation, given their life story.

We believe that conceptualizing the client's defenses as adaptive and providing specific language for guiding the clinician's feedback will add to the utility of training clinicians in the art of therapeutic assessment. For example, in their national survey of psychologists regarding feedback training, supervision, and practice, Curry and Hanson (2010) noted that approximately one-third of respondents indicated that their pre-doctoral coursework, practica, and internship were of little utility in preparing them to give clients feedback. However, more recent studie s (Goosse et al., 2025; Jacobson et al., 2015; Smith & Egan, 2017) show that psychology trainees and practitioners have, in fact, embraced the value of providing psychological test feedback to clients.

We see the field of therapeutic feedback as an exciting new opportunity to build on the MMPI-3, with its rich empirical data. We encourage clinicians to appreciate human capacities and potentials and view their clients' current functioning as the best available adaptation given their genetic makeup, history, and precipitating circumstances. Feedback framed in this manner will be therapeutic and help establish a collaborative treatment plan.

Conditioning Experiences and Feedback

We think of the MMPI-3 as a key to the understanding of how personality and psychopathology are structured and how they are linked. We view therapeutic feedback as a collaborative process during which a client's current fears, symptoms, and defenses are described in the context of the events that shaped them. In the guidelines provided in this book, we emphasize the use of empathic language to provide feedback to clients about their test results; this language is both empirically and clinically based but purged of judgmental content. The framework was derived from an approach first formulated by Alex Caldwell in his written papers and lectures at the University of California at Los Angeles (UCLA) in the 1970s (Caldwell 1976, 1977). He and others (Kunce, 1979; Kunce & Anderson, 1976) suggested that, as all behavior is adaptive, psychopathology could be understood as an adaptational adjustment to a painful or frightening conditioning event. We conceptualize that a particular defensive pattern and the cluster of symptoms and defensive behaviors associated with it can be understood in the context of the possible conditioning experiences that led to it.

The MMPI-3 Higher-Order, Restructured Clinical, Specific Problems, and Personality Psychopathology Five Scale scores provide information about defenses, symptoms, and traits associated with each scale. For example, an individual with an elevation on Low Positive Emotions

(RC2) is described as pessimistic, lacking energy, and socially withdrawn (Ben-Porath & Tellegen, 2020a/2020b). A possible conditioning experience that leads to such an understandable response would be some type of perceived or actual loss (Bowlby, 1983; Harris & Bifulco, 1991; Tyrka et al., 2008). Negative and avoidant behavior would make sense against the backdrop of loss and the need to defend against further loss. Actively avoiding hope, engaging in negative self-talk, and reducing desire-driven behavior could be seen as an adaptation to avoid further loss.

Using MMPI-3 generated data, therapeutic feedback is communicated with compassion for a client's current feelings, symptoms, and painful or frightening losses that may have shaped their functioning and current outlook. The assessment builds on a client's strengths by helping them understand the adaptive and understandable nature of their current behavior given their early experiences and current stressors. The purpose of the therapeutic feedback is to validate their feelings and provide understanding about why a particular current stressor is destabilizing, putting it in the context of past trauma and emotional scar tissue. Levak defines *emotional scar tissue* as the result of past trauma that has not been fully integrated or resolved and is, therefore, more likely to be restimulated by current triggers of similar quality or intensity. Using the example of an individual with an elevated score on RC2, the feedback would explore current feelings, symptoms, and concerns about possible recent losses. Past losses, that could have predisposed the client to a vulnerability to destabilization associated with loss, are explored in the feedback process, and healing and prophylactic strategies are agreed upon.

In our view, elevated MMPI-3 scales are associated with a cluster of emotions, thoughts, and predominant ways of responding that reflect a set of primary fears or concerns. For example, people who have elevated scores on Antisocial Behavior (RC4), Ideas of Persecution (RC6), Self-Importance (SFI), and Dominance (DOM) could be described as argumentative, hostile, self-indulgent, and demanding. They approach the world defensively and see themselves as victims. Using our empathic reformulation, we describe these clients as approaching the world fearful that others will take advantage of them. Being suspicious of others' motives and vigilant for unfairness makes adaptive sense given that particular fear. The reasons for the development of that current fear are further explored as part of the therapeutic feedback dialogue. Possible past emotional scar tissue around being taken advantage of and treated unfairly is discussed, validating why current reactions are particularly intense and disturbing.

It has been argued that we are products of a combination of our genetic makeup and environmental factors that comprise our core personality (Brendgen et al., 2006; Dickens & Flynn, 2001; McLafferty, 2006). From our perspective, defensive behavior is a product of stress (fear) operating within individuals who have a predisposition or vulnerability. We hypothesize that a traumatic event or series of events interacts with individuals' core personalities and leaves them vulnerable to experiencing later similar stress as disorganizing and distressing. We assume that people develop a repertoire of available psychological defenses against stress. Studies over 30 years, which began at birth, have revealed that character traits are recognizable very early and tend to persist into adulthood (Chess & Thomas, 1977; Durbin et al., 2007; Juffer et al., 2004). Certain personality types are more vulnerable to stress; others are naturally more resilient. Regardless of personality type, under increased stress the defenses that serve to reduce tension become fixed and maintained in accordance with their reinforcement value. Thus, any defense needs to be understood in the context of the stress that initially activated it. Figure 1.1 illustrates the diathesis-stress model as it relates to therapeutic feedback.

Integral to this empathic approach is the language used in communicating MMPI-3 results to clients. Traditional terms used in interpreting personality tests tend to be technical (e.g., introjecting, dissociating, ideas of reference), strongly negative or pejorative (e.g., obnoxious, incompetent, hostile), highly evaluative (e.g., personality disorder, psychotic, has a poor prognosis), imprecise (e.g., imbalanced, insecure, immature), or obscure (e.g., calculated, refractory). These are terms

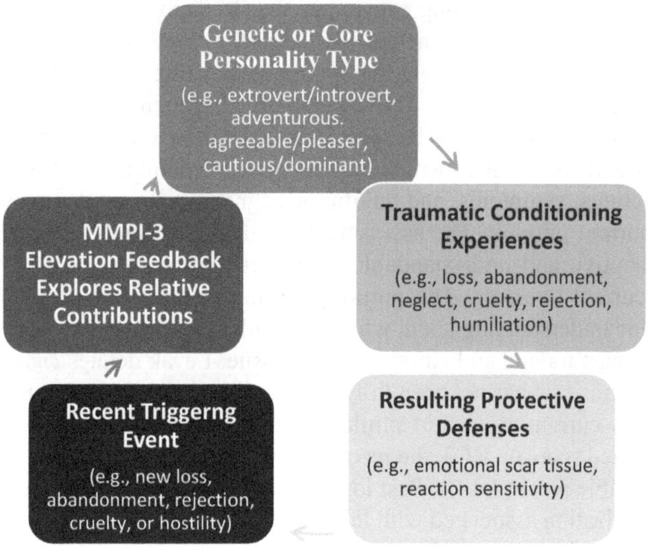

Figure 1.1 Diathesis-stress model and therapeutic feedback.

that, in our experience, often threaten and confuse clients or are far removed from their everyday thoughts, feelings, and experiences. Many of the test correlates, though informative to the clinician, are simply ill-suited for the purpose of feedback as they are antithetical to the paradigm of therapeutic assessment. However, these correlates do form the basis of our system. We recognize that they were the psychometrically defensible starting point to construct our way of characterizing a person.

For MMPI-3 feedback to be of therapeutic value, the correlates needed to be reformulated in terms that are understandable for clients and can be presented in a therapeutic manner. Thus, we approached the correlates from a phenomenological perspective and, in talking with clients, conceptualized the correlates in terms of complaints, cognitions, emotions, and traits or behaviors. Each of these descriptor correlates can be translated into formulations suitable for therapeutic feedback. In this manner, for example, the distrust and confusion of Thought Dysfunction (THD), Aberrant Experiences (RC8), and Psychoticism (PSYC) elevations suggest the feedback, "The world may be a somewhat frightening place because it is hard for you to read people and know how they feel and think about you. Currently, you seem to be knocked off balance and confused." The alienation and depersonalization of RC8 suggests the feedback statement, "You may be disconnected from others, as if you are looking at the world from a distance."

Some feedback statements are relatively simple and straightforward. For example, the correlate "pessimistic" could be communicated as, "Right now it is hard for you to have much hope in the future, which currently feels bleak." Whereas other feedback statements are more complex. For example, the following feedback statements represent multiple RC4 correlates (impulsivity, selective reporting, and manipulation), "Your profile suggests you are a rebel and dislike being told what to do by authority figures. You can be impulsive, acting on an impulse and not taking time to think through consequences. If your behavior gets you into trouble, you are likely to selectively report and manipulate your way out of it."

Interpreting correlates associated with various MMPI-3 scale scores can be confusing because the same descriptor is often used for different scales. For example, one descriptor of people scoring high on Somatic Complaints (RC1) is "fatigue," but individuals with elevations on Malaise

(MLS) can also be described as experiencing fatigue (Ben-Porath & Tellegen, 2020a/2020b). By understanding each of the RC Scales as resulting from a particular conditioned fear/avoidance response, the clinician can conceptualize the source of the various defensive behaviors. According to this paradigm, individuals scoring high on RC1 are fatigued because of their fear of body damage and their physical complaints generally serve to elicit caregiving behavior from supportive others and medical personnel. Elevations on MLS would also predict demands of attention and reassurance about one's physical wellbeing, such as sleep hygiene and easy fatiguability. In each case, these individuals can be described as concerned or even frightened about their physical health. Interactive therapeutic feedback based on the MMPI-3 should help the clinician determine the relative contribution of personality, past conditioning events, basic fears or concerns, and current stressors leading to the scale elevations.

How to Use this Book

In the following chapters, we provide for each set of MMPI-3 scales:

- *General Descriptors*: Including complaints, cognitions, emotions, and traits and behavior.
- *Therapist's Notes*: Conceptual formulations of the construct assessed by the scale informed by the therapeutic assessment framework just described.
- *Lifestyle and Family Background*: Clinically informed hypotheses about genetic predispositions and childhood experiences that may have shaped the individual's personality.
- *Clarifying Scales*: Discussion of how scores on other MMPI-3 scales may help sharpen the focus or provides elaborations on the interpretation of a given scale.
- *Therapy and Therapeutic Pitfalls*: Guidance on how the information provided by the scale can be translated into therapeutic actions, and potential pitfalls to avoid.
- *Feedback Statements*: Suggested language for translating the correlates of MMPI-3 scale scores (including combinations of scale scores) into therapeutically beneficial feedback.
- *Lifestyle and Family Background Feedback*: Suggested ways to convey hypotheses about how the interplay between the individual's predispositions and childhood experiences may have shaped their current psychological functioning.
- *Treatment and Self-Help Suggestions*: A list of specific actions the individual can take to obtain and maintain the benefits of therapy.

The reader will find considerable redundancy in the information provided across MMPI-3 scales. This redundancy is a product of several factors. First, as a hierarchically structured instrument, the MMPI-3 measures psychological functioning at three different levels of depth; with the H-O Scales providing a global assessment of functioning in the domains of emotion, thinking, and behavior, the RC Scales reflecting a more granular assessment of subdomains within each of the broad H-O domains, and the SP Scales conveying the most narrowly focused and detailed information about the individual's psychological makeup, including their interpersonal functioning. As with any hierarchically structured instrument, redundancy occurs (by definition) across the different levels of the structure. For example, the H-O Scale Emotional/Internalizing Dysfunction (EID) provides a global assessment of the individual's emotional functioning; the RC Scales break down emotional functioning into associated (but distinct) manifestations of Demoralization or dysphoria (RCd), Low Positive Emotions or anhedonia (RC2), and various Dysfunctional Negative Emotions or negative affectivity (RC7); and the Internalizing SP Scales provide a further breakdown of demoralization as it relates to suicidal/death ideation, helplessness/hopelessness, self-doubt, and inefficacy, and the dysfunctional negative emotions into stress, worry, compulsivity, anxiety-related experience, anger proneness, and behavior-restricting fears. The more granular manifestations of emotional dysfunctions are not mutually exclusive, and most likely reflect common predispositions and childhood experiences, leading to redundancy across scales.

A second source of MMPI-3 scale redundancy is the PSY-5 Scales, which represent a specific dimensional model of personality disorder-related experiences that links the test to contemporary conceptualizations of personality disorder included in both the *Diagnostic and Statistical Manual of Mental Disorders, Fifth Edition, Text Revision* (DSM-5-TR) (American Psychiatric Association, 2022) and the World Health Organization's (WHO's) *International Classification of Diseases, Eleventh Edition* (ICD-11) (WHO, 2019/2021) frameworks. The PSY-5 Scales are an accompaniment to, rather than a part of, the test's hierarchical structure, resulting in redundancies of scale score correlates and our hypotheses about their origins and therapeutic recommendations.

A third source of redundancy is a product of how we structured this book. For each scale we provide interpretive guidance for the scale on its own and in combination with other MMPI-3 scale scores. Consequently, interpretations are discussed for various scale score combinations more than once.

In the final chapter of this book (Chapter 10) we describe and illustrate an interpretive strategy that integrates the scale-by-scale guidance provided in earlier chapters, including how to compose and deliver feedback results to the client. This step in the therapeutic assessment process involves non-redundant integration of the MMPI-3 results (and possibly extra-test information) and the therapist's formulation of predispositions and childhood experiences that have shaped and continue to impact the individual's psychological functioning. Two case studies are provided to illustrate our recommended approach to translating MMPI-3 results into therapeutically beneficial feedback.

2 Validity Scales

Introduction

This chapter covers the MMPI-3 validity measures that, in some cases, are refinements of the MMPI-2-RF version of these scales. Readers interested in a thorough explanation of the development and assessment of each of the MMPI-3 Validity Scales should refer to the textbook *Interpreting the MMPI-3* (Ben-Porath & Sellbom, 2023). Because there are differences between the responses of the MMPI-2-RF and the MMPI-3 normative samples, the recommended cut scores associated with several of the MMPI-3 Validity Scales have changed, most notably the Infrequent Responses (F) Scale, Symptom Validity (FBS) Scale, and Response Bias (RBS) Scale (Ben-Porath & Sellbom, 2023). Detailed MMPI-2-RF interpretive guidance was included in updated versions of previous MMPI textbooks (Friedman et al., 2015; Graham, 2012; Greene, 2011; and McCord, 2018).

Determining the manner in which an individual responds to the MMPI-3 items is an essential step prior to interpreting the individual's scores on the instrument. It is important to investigate Validity Scales, as a measure of threat to protocol validity, prior to the interpretation of a profile. Determining validity is a multivariate process. It involves examining all the Validity Scales scores, taking into consideration the setting and the client's motivation to employ various response sets, such as positive or negative impression management.

Cannot Say (CNS) Score

General Descriptors

Complaints

Reading difficulties; irritation with the testing procedure.

Cognitions

Possible confusion; obsessiveness; concentration and memory difficulties.

Emotions

Possible anxiety; anger; severe despondency and malaise.

Traits and behaviors

Possible resistance to the testing; cognitive impairment; serious psychological disturbance; lacking insight or self-awareness to respond to items.

DOI: 10.4324/9781003557920-2

Therapist's Notes – CNS Score

Every MMPI-3 item provides an opportunity for communication between a client and the clinician. Occasionally, clients provide unscorable responses to items, defined as leaving an item unanswered or double marked both True and False. (However, double marking is only possible when paper-and-pencil administration is used. It is not an option when the MMPI-3 is administered using the software from the distributor, Pearson Assessments.) Even in these situations a therapeutic dialogue may be possible. By providing unscorable responses, the client is communicating about their approach to the test, whether it be confusion, reading difficulties, comprehension/attentional problems, or disorganized or suspicious thinking. Feedback will provide an opportunity to explore the meaning of unscorable responses.

The CNS score is a count of the unscorable responses. The MMPI-3 manual suggests that 15 or more items in this category may compromise MMPI-3 test interpretation because unscorable responses artifactually lower scores, as the scoring method only counts items answered in the keyed direction. It is suggested that when 15 or more items are unscorable, the psychologist should examine these items to discern possible themes or areas of concern for the test-taker. Unscorable responses could be due to confusion, reading difficulties, or severe cognitive impairment. A range of 1–14 unanswered items may reflect selective non-responsiveness. These unanswered items should be examined for possible themes. At least 90% of any scale's items need to be endorsed to allow for interpretation.

Feedback Statements – CNS Score

Unanswered items

You answered many of the items on this test, but not all. It is hard to know your motivation without checking in with you. As you were taking the test, were you aware that you did not answer either True or False to certain items, mostly to do with particular problem areas? It appears that many of the unanswered items deal with … (e.g., somatic, anxiety, depression, drug use [determine the content]. What made it difficult to answer items about these issues? You avoided answering an item about … [go to a specific item] – tell me what concerned you about that item?

Double marked items

You answered both True and False to a number of items. Were you unsure about the answer or did you have mixed emotions about certain areas of inquiry? For example, on item … [go to a specific item], you answered both True and False. Were you confused about that item, or did you have mixed feelings about it? Help me understand what you were thinking. Would you be open to answering those items this time responding with how you feel?

Combined Response Inconsistency (CRIN) Scale

General Descriptors

Complaints

Reading difficulties.

Cognitions

Confusion; anxiety; carelessness due to attention and memory problems.

Emotions

Impulsivity; overarousal; anger; depressed mood.

Traits and behaviors

Concentration difficulties; possible fatigue; disordered thinking.

Therapist's Notes – CRIN Scale

The CRIN Scale measures all inconsistent responding, whether it is the tendency to say "yea" or "nay" or the tendency to give contradictory responses in general. It includes the 86 item pairs that comprise the Variable Response Inconsistency (VRIN) Scale and the True Response Inconsistency (TRIN) Scale and gives a global measure of inconsistency.

Although a highly inconsistent profile is not valid, nevertheless, it may contain useful clinical data. Cognitive impairment could be one reason for scores elevated above a T score of 80, but people with reading difficulties or people from a different cultural and language background could also elevate the CRIN score. Explore the reasons for a high score and use the inconsistent responses as talking points to engage the client in explaining their inconsistent responding. If possible, have them retake the test.

T score 30–38

The individual answered the test carefully and consistently.

T score 39–69

The profile is consistent, and the items were understood.

T score 70–79

Some evidence of inconsistency exists, which could be due to reading difficulties, carelessness, or a foreign background leading to idiosyncratic understanding of the items. The profile should be interpreted with caution, especially if the inconsistent responses are not all in one content area.

T score ≥80

This suggests invalidity. It could be due to reading difficulties, mental disturbance confusion, or random responding.

Feedback Statements – CRIN Scale

T score 30–38

You were very thoughtful and consistent in answering the items. Your profile is likely to be valid.

T score 39–69

You answered the test thoughtfully and consistently, clearly reading the items carefully.

T score 70–79

The way you answered the test items suggests that on a few occasions you might have been confused or had mixed feelings about the way to answer an item. You may have found some items hard to understand or you may have become distracted by your thoughts. Sometimes we all have confusing thoughts and feelings. For example, we may love someone but still see them as a bad person. I may explore with you some of the answers you gave that appear inconsistent as you may have an important reason why you answered the way you did.

T score ≥80

It is hard to give you feedback about your results as your responses were difficult to interpret. You answered a number of items in a way that suggests you were either confused or distracted as you completed the test. It is also possible that you have mixed and confused feelings right now so you may have found it hard to be consistent. As you read the test, were you aware that you occasionally answered two similar items in a contradictory way? Did the test items upset you in any way? Were you able to stay focused or did you find the items hard to understand or offensive? I might ask you to retake the test so we can get an accurate picture of you.

Variable Response Inconsistency (VRIN) Scale

General Descriptors

Complaints

Lack of motivation for testing.

Cognitions

Marked confusion due to cognitive impairment such as attentional problems.

Emotions

Frustration with testing process.

Traits and behaviors

Possible fatigue; carelessness.

Therapist's Notes – VRIN Scale

The VRIN score is based on the test-taker's responses to 53 item pairs, selected so that members of each pair are similar in content. Elevated VRIN scores reflect the number of item pairs answered inconsistently. While high scores can invalidate the protocol, they do not always reflect intentional uncooperativeness. It is important for the test interpreter to consider other factors outside of the testing to understand possible elevated VRIN scores.

T score 30–38

The client answered with an almost perfect level of consistency, suggesting a careful, thoughtful approach to the test.

T score 39–69

Scores in this range reflect consistent responding. The client answered thoughtfully, carefully, and consistently so there are no concerns about invalidity due to a lack of consistency.

T score 70–79

The profile shows some evidence of inconsistency which may be due to language or reading difficulties or cognitive impairment. It could also be due to occasional carelessness from fatigue. Clinicians should examine which responses were inconsistent and explore them with the client.

T score ≥80

This protocol may be invalid because of a high number of inconsistent responses. This may have occurred because of reading or language difficulties (as can occur with someone from a different country). It could also reflect a cognitive impairment or the episodic intrusion of psychotic processes. Examine which items were inconsistently marked and explore with the client possible reasons.

Feedback Statements – VRIN Scale

T score 30–38

You were extremely consistent in taking the test, revealing that you thoughtfully and carefully read the items. This approach suggests that you wanted to give me a true picture of your current situation.

T score 39–69

You answered the test consistently, suggesting that you read all the items carefully and gave much thought to being accurate about how you feel.

T score 70–79

You answered some items in an inconsistent way. We may want to explore some of these inconsistent responses since they may be reflecting some of your mixed feelings. Sometimes occasional inconsistent responding could be valid. After we have explored some of these inconsistent responses, I may be able to interpret some of your other scores more accurately. Please share with me if there were some items you didn't fully understand or whether you got tired and occasionally careless when you took the test.

T score ≥80

It is difficult to interpret your profile because you answered a number of items in an inconsistent way. We should explore the inconsistent answers since there may be a logical explanation. However, until this is resolved as to why this happened, it will be hard to give you a lot of feedback about the meaning of your test results. It is possible that you became confused by some of the items, or you may have had difficulty understanding their meaning. In some cases, people get tired and careless or sometimes even angry about doing the test, so they answer randomly. In other cases, some people experience disturbing thoughts that were brought on by some of the items.

True Response Inconsistency (TRIN) Scale

General Descriptors

Complaints

Unmotivated for testing procedure.

Cognitions

Reading difficulties; comprehension problems.

Emotions

Frustration with testing procedures.

Traits and behaviors

Uncooperative; overreporting or underreporting of psychological problems.

Therapist's Notes – TRIN Scale

The TRIN score is based on the test-taker's responses to 33 item pairs, which are keyed such that the raw TRIN score equals the number of pairs (inconsistently) answered True/True minus the number of pairs (inconsistently) answered False/False. Therefore, high raw TRIN scores reflect fixed True responding, while low scores indicated fixed False responding.

T score 50–69

The profile shows no inconsistency in responding True or False, so the profile is interpretable if all the other Validity Scales are valid.

T score 70–79T

There is some evidence that the client answered with a True response set. This could be due to reading difficulties or misunderstanding the double negative items. It would be important to discuss with the client their inconsistent responses since there may be some valid explanation. Scores on the rest of the scales should be interpreted with caution unless there is a valid explanation of these inconsistencies. In that case, the profile may be valid.

T Score ≥80T

The protocol is likely invalid since the individual has answered with a tendency to respond True in an inconsistent manner. Sometimes this is due to reading difficulties or difficulties with double negatives. However, if a number of items are all answered True in a consistent manner that could suggest an angry or uncooperative response to the test-taking. Consequently, the protocol is not interpretable.

T score 70–79F

There is some evidence that the client responded with a False response set inconsistently. This could be due to reading difficulties or misunderstanding double negatives. It is important to discuss with the client the inconsistent responses since there may be a valid explanation. Scores on the rest of the scales should be interpreted with caution unless there is a valid explanation of the inconsistencies. In that case, the profile may be valid.

T Score ≥80F

The protocol is likely invalid since the individual has answered with a tendency to respond False in an inconsistent manner. Sometimes this is due to reading difficulties or difficulties with double negatives. However, if a number of items are all answered False in a consistent manner, that would suggest an angry or uncooperative response to the test. Consequently, the protocol is not interpretable.

Feedback Statements – TRIN Scale

T score 50–69

You answered the items thoughtfully, without answering True or False carelessly. Your test results will likely be valid.

T score 70–79T

You answered some items True in an inconsistent manner. This may have been because you occasionally lost your concentration or had difficulty understanding the items. You also may have wanted me to know how out of sorts you are right now, so you were in a mindset to answer True to items that reflected your symptoms and complaints.

T Score ≥80T

It is hard to interpret your profile because you had a tendency to mark True to many items in a way that was inconsistent. It may be because you lost your concentration periodically or were angry or irritated with the test and so responded True without reading the items carefully. It is also possible that you had good reasons as to why you did this. Let's explore some of the items where you answered True inconsistently. This will allow me to know how to interpret your test results.

T score 70–79F

You answered many items as False. Sometimes, by answering False to a number of items, you appear to be contradicting yourself. Perhaps you occasionally lost your concentration or had difficulty understanding the items. You might have been in a mindset to answer False without fully considering the items that reflected your symptoms and complaints.

T score ≥80F

It is challenging to accurately interpret your profile because you had a tendency to mark False to many items. Possibly, you periodically lost your concentration or were angry or irritated with the testing and so responded False without carefully reading the items. It is also possible that you had good reasons why you did this, so we should explore the items where you answered False inconsistently. Once we have done that, it will be possible to more accurately interpret your test results.

Infrequent Responses (F) Scale

General Descriptors

Complaints

Stressed; dissatisfied; panicked; pleading for help; alienated.

Cognitions

Low self-esteem, self-deprecating, disorganized; possible reality distortions.

Emotions

Moody; unstable; fearful; distressed.

Traits and behaviors

Possible overreporting of problems; genuine psychopathology depending on elevations.

Therapist's Notes – F Scale

The F Scale consists of 35 items rarely answered in the scored direction by the MMPI-3 normative sample. Elevated scores may reflect a deep disturbance across a broad range of psychological, cognitive, and somatic functions. However, elevated scores can also reflect overreporting and, therefore, can suggest that the profile is invalid due to exaggeration or confusion. Normal-range scores indicate a willingness to be open and honest about any unusual experiences and possible freedom from major psychopathology. F Scale elevations are one of the best predictors of valid responding. They can also reflect clients' current levels of pain, fear, and their general level of psychological organization and stability. The scale consists of unambiguous content areas of physical symptoms, paranoid ideation, psychotic traits, family enmity, schizoid under-involvement, psychotic processes, and a compulsion to pathological activity.

F Scale scores above a T score of 85 are not always invalid. While this may indicate overreported psychopathology, it may also reflect severe distress, disorganized, possibly psychotic thinking, or behavior disorders. In some psychiatric settings where clients are extremely disturbed or in cases where young adults have experienced a panic disorder following bad drug reactions, highly elevated, but valid, F scores are not uncommon. However, with F above a T score of 85, other scale elevations are less likely to be stable on retest.

F scores between a T score of 55 and 65 reflect the endorsement of some unusual items and thus may suggest some psychological pain and distress. However, F score elevations in this normal range could also reflect eccentricity, nonconformity, or a situational adjustment reaction. The higher the F Scale score, the more likely the client is experiencing disruptions in cognitive and behavioral efficiency and emotional stability. In the presence of elevated scales, F scores between a T score of 55 and 65 suggest a stable, perhaps ego-syntonic disturbance. F elevations between 55 and 65 in the presence of a non-elevated profile would predict unconventional, although not necessarily disturbed, individuals.

F scores below a T score of 50 could reflect someone who is defensively denying symptoms and complaints, especially if the Uncommon Virtues (L) Scale and Adjustment Validity (K) Scale are elevated. A low F score may also reflect conventional, but stable, psychologically well-balanced individuals who have few complaints and no psychological impairment.

When giving feedback, consider high F elevations as reflecting clients' levels of pain and concern about their psychological state. Even when profiles are exaggerated, it may be useful to tell clients that the F Scale reflects that they may be panicked and pleading for help from the clinician. In cases where malingering or symptom magnification is suspected, discuss that they may have taken the test to ensure that the clinician knew they were experiencing distress and, in the process, magnified many of their symptoms and behaviors.

T score <75

The protocol is valid and there is no evidence of overreporting.

T score 75–79

While F scores in this range may reflect possible overreporting of psychological dysfunction, it is also possible that the profile is valid, especially if the consistency scales are within the normal range and there is clinical evidence of psychopathology. F scores in this range could reflect overreporting if there is secondary gain from a severe disturbance. If the Infrequent Psychopathology Responses (Fp) Scale is not elevated above 80, it would increase the probability that the protocol is valid.

T score 80–89

Scores in this range suggest a possible overreporting of psychological dysfunction as indicated by a larger than average number of infrequent responses. If overreporting is suspected, the motive may have been to draw attention to the individual's distress. In the presence of clinical evidence of bona fide disturbance, this F score would not invalidate the protocol, especially if the consistency scales are valid. Exploring the critical items reflecting severe disturbance would aid in clinical understanding. If the Fp Scale is not elevated above 80, it would increase the probability that the protocol is valid.

T score 90–99

The protocol may be invalid due to a tendency to overreport psychological problems. However, if consistent responding is indicated by valid CRIN, VRIN, and TRIN scores, and there is clinical evidence of severe mental disturbance, the profile could be an accurate reflection of the individual's current condition. If Fp is not elevated above 80, it would increase the probability that the protocol is valid.

T score ≥100

The protocol is likely invalid. However, if the CRIN, VRIN, and TRIN scores do not reflect inconsistency, the extremely high F score could reflect a panicked plea for help or severe psychopathology. Although the scores on the other scales should not be interpreted, the critical items could be used as a basis to explore the psychopathology evidenced by the responses.

Lifestyle and Family Background – F Scale

If the high F is due to a panic or plea for help or a need to appear disturbed for secondary gain purposes, then hypotheses about lifestyle or family background are not warranted. In some cases, however, high elevations of F reflect a stable although disturbed personality organization. In such cases a chaotic, emotionally unstable lifestyle and/or backgrounds of neglect and abuse or psychological trauma are suggested. If the high F is reflecting a response to a recent crisis or trauma with subsequent psychological disorganization, the lifestyle of these individuals can be at least temporally chaotic, with possible psychosis and/or general inefficiency and emotional ability.

Clarifying Scales – F Scale

If Fp, the Infrequent Somatic Responses (Fs) Scale, FBS, and/or RBS are elevated above a T score of 85, consider exaggeration or malingering. If Fp is below a T score of 80, high F scores may reflect a significant mental disturbance.

Therapy and Therapeutic Pitfalls – F Scale

As the F Scale elevates above a T score of 75, the goal of therapy is stabilization. Supportive, practical treatment strategies as well as medication referrals are often appropriate for these individuals. When the high F score reflects a panic or plea for help, therapy should include risk assessment, possible hospitalization, and ongoing monitoring of their condition. Avoid insight-oriented therapies that could overload individuals who may already be emotionally and cognitively disorganized. Moderate scale elevations between a T score of 60 and 65 suggest a more stable disorder. Inspect the scale configurations for diagnostic configurations and possible treatment strategies.

Feedback Statements – F Scale

T score ≤64

You answered the test items candidly without overemphasizing any symptoms or complaints [assuming an inspection of the other MMPI-3 scales does not reflect specific problems].

T score 65–74

You answered the test candidly and openly and you may be experiencing some distressing feelings and thoughts. This may mean you are open to help and psychological guidance.

T score 75–79

Your answers to the test suggest that you are experiencing significant current distress. You wanted me to know that you are knocked off balance and that your psychological symptoms are distressing, and you likely want help. You may have occasionally emphasized your distress, wanting me to know that you are not doing well. Your symptoms may be causing you significant anxiety and you, therefore, may be open to help from someone you trust.

T score 80–89

The way you answered the test reveals that you are feeling very distressed and that you want me to know how badly you are feeling. You may even be feeling panicked by your condition, so you may have gone out of your way to let me know you need help. I may want to explore some of your item responses to determine what you are feeling now versus how you felt at better times in your life. I may want you to retake the test and answer the items in such a way to reflect how you most typically feel rather than how you feel currently.

T score 90–99

The way you answered the test shows that you are experiencing many psychological symptoms and disturbing feelings and thoughts. You may be feeling panicked, perhaps wanting me to understand how distressed you are. Because you answered so many items reporting severe distress it is difficult to determine what you are exactly thinking or feeling. I may want you to retake the test after exploring your answers with you. Generally, even people with a serious medical or psychological condition don't typically answer as many items in such a severe direction. Consequently, it is difficult to interpret your test accurately. However, that doesn't mean your efforts were wasted, as I want to explore with you the concerns you are reporting.

T score ≥100

Your responses suggest that you feel very knocked off balance, with numerous symptoms, disturbing thoughts, and physical complaints. As you answered so many items reporting severe distress, it is hard to have an accurate picture of your personality makeup. It is as if you are saying, "All aspects of my psychological life are broken!" I may ask you to retake the test after exploring your answers with you. Generally, even people with a serious medical or psychological condition don't typically answer so many items in such a severe direction. Consequently, interpreting your test accurately is challenging, but that doesn't mean your efforts were wasted, as I would like to explore with you the concerns you are reporting.

Lifestyle and Family Background Feedback – F Scale

T score ≥75

Your profile suggests you may have experienced some recent trauma or setbacks that are causing you fear, anxiety, and unhappiness. Perhaps growing up you experienced painful losses, unsupportive adults, or even some kind of neglect and abuse. Recent events may have restimulated old psychological scar tissue, making current painful events even more difficult.

Treatment and Self-Help Suggestions – Elevated F Scale Scores

1. Discuss with your doctor whether medication might help you feel better and more in control.
2. People with your profile feel better in structured, safe environments. Until you feel better, avoid stressful situations when possible, and try to take better care of yourself by being with people around whom you feel safe.
3. If you feel panicked, there are actions you can take to minimize the likelihood that you will experience a panic attack. Try to decrease or eliminate food and beverage ingredients that may be detrimental to your health and wellbeing. Deep breathing and relaxation exercises can be helpful. Should you feel panic, shift your focus onto a relaxing or comforting image and imagine as you breathe deeply that you are in a place, imaginary or real, that could bring you at least some temporary comfort. Some people may imagine being in nature by water on a perfect day or in a cozy favorite hideaway where they feel comfortable and safe.

Infrequent Psychopathology Responses (Fp) Scale

General Descriptors

Complaints

Numerous symptoms; possible substance abuse; inefficiency; anxiety.

Cognitions

Confused; ambivalent; indecisive; negative; possible thought disorder.

Emotions

Depressed; anxious; conflicted; moody; irritable.

Traits and behaviors

Possible exaggeration and overreporting of symptoms; self-defeating; ineffective; possibly psychotic.

Therapist's Notes – Fp Scale

Elevations on the Fp Scale suggest someone who answered the test in a highly unusual fashion. In some cases of extreme disturbance, an Fp T score of 90 could still be valid, although exaggeration is a strong possibility. However, if the F, Fs, FBS, RBS and measures of confusion are elevated, then an Fp score with a T score higher than 90 suggests invalidity. In some rare cases, the Fp Scale can be elevated in the absence of severe psychopathology, reflecting unconventional, unusual individuals with eccentricities and amoral attitudes, but not mental disorder. When Fp is below a T score of 70 and other measures of validity suggest a severe disturbance, the Fp score would imply that the profile reflects genuine psychopathology rather than exaggeration. An Fp T score of 100 or greater, especially if CRIN, VRIN, and/or TRIN scores are significantly elevated, suggests inconsistent responding due to malingering/symptom magnification or mental disorganization or confusion. Therefore, scores on the Substantive Scales (Higher-Order (H-O) Scales, Restructured Clinical (RC) Scales, Specific Problems (SP) Scales, and Personality Psychopathology Five (PSY-5) Scales) should not be interpreted.

T score <70

Scores in this range suggest there is no overreporting, even if F is significantly elevated.

T score 70–79

Scores in this range, in the presence of clinical evidence of psychopathology, do not invalidate the profile. However, should there be secondary gain from a diagnosis of mental illness, the score may indicate a degree of exaggeration. The clinician should examine the Fp items as a rich source of data about how the client wants to be viewed. In the presence of high inconsistency measures, Fp scores in this range would suggest that the protocol could be invalid due to inconsistency.

T score 80–99

Scores in this range suggest possible overreporting or inconsistent responding. In the presence of high CRIN, VRIN, and TRIN scores, scores in this range would suggest confusion. However, in cases with clinical evidence of severe psychopathology, the Substantive Scales could be interpreted with caution. If there is secondary gain from a diagnosis of severe mental illness, scores in this range should be considered as reflecting exaggeration.

T score ≥100

The protocol is invalid as the individual reported psychopathological symptoms and behaviors significantly more frequently than individuals with genuine psychopathology. This noncredible responding could be due to response inconsistency and/or a tendency to significantly exaggerate. The clinician should examine the Fp items and use them as a source of discussion to determine whether the Fp score reflected exaggeration, confusion, or some highly unusual psychological condition. Nevertheless, the scores on the Substantive Scales should not be interpreted.

Feedback Statements – Fp Scale

T score <70

You were candid and open in describing your symptoms and behaviors, so the resulting personality profile is valid and is likely not exaggerated.

T score 70–79

The results of your personality profile reveal that you are experiencing numerous symptoms, anxieties, fears, and concerns that may be distressing you. You clearly want me to understand your state of mind so you may have gone out of your way to alert me as to how knocked off balance you feel.

I may explore some of your responses and might ask you to retake the test in order to have a better understanding of what you are experiencing.

T score 80–99

You answered several items in a way that suggests you are experiencing many psychological symptoms, anxieties, concerns, and perhaps even confusion. You may have wanted me to know that you are in distress. I may ask you to retake the test focusing on how you feel when things are not so severe.

T score ≥100

Your profile is difficult to interpret as you answered many items indicating a great deal of distress and confusion. You may be experiencing panic, so you answered True to numerous symptoms and concerns making it difficult to precisely understand you. We may want to explore your responses further and determine whether you became overwhelmed taking the test or became confused.

Infrequent Somatic Responses (Fs) Scale

General Descriptors

Complaints

Multiple somatic complaints; exhaustion; pain; dizziness; numbness; headaches; nausea; lightheadedness.

Cognitions

Negative thoughts; pessimistic; worry about declining health; preoccupation with medical diagnosis.

Emotions

Helpless; hopeless; irritable; fearful; tense.

Traits and behaviors

Demanding; complaining; lacking drive.

Therapist's Notes – Fs Scale

This scale acts as a Validity Scale for over-declaring somatic symptoms and complaints. This scale consists of 16 items with somatic content uncommonly endorsed by medical patients receiving treatment for various physical diseases. It is based on a similar developmental rationale as the other two MMPI-3 infrequent response indicators, F and Fp. Individuals with a bona fide medical condition without any psychological overlay typically score lower on this measure than individuals overemphasizing somatic complaints. It is important to note, as described in the MMPI-3 manual (Ben-Porath & Tellegen, 2020a, 2020b), that overreporting is not synonymous with faking or malingering. The manual states, "Noncredible somatic complaints may stem from a variety of sources, including external incentives but also the internal psychological factors, underlying a somatic symptom disorder or somatic delusions" (p. 34). Extra-test data, such as a detailed medical and psychological history, are needed to understand the factors for these distinctions.

T score <80

Scores in this range are valid and there is no evidence of overreporting.

T score 80–99

Scores in this range suggest that the somatic complaints scales - Somatic Complaints (RC1), Malaise (MLS), and Neurological Complaints (NUC) - should be interpreted with caution. Generally, people with severe and/or complicated medical conditions, especially ones with multiple organ involvement, could score in this range but there may be a degree of over-endorsed somatic items as individuals with genuine medical conditions do not usually score in this range.

T score ≥100

If the consistency scales of CRIN, VRIN, and TRIN are in the normal range, then T scores of 100 or above reflect a consistent endorsement to numerous physical and neurological symptoms and pains that leave the client exhausted and depleted. However, scores in this range typically reflect overreporting since actual medical patients score significantly lower. Moreover, scores in this range raise scores on the other Somatic/Cognitive Scales, suggesting general somatic overreporting. Scores of 100 or above suggest an overreporting of somatic complaints, which could invalidate the accuracy of scores on the somatic complaints scales – RC1, MLS, and NUC. Individuals with a chronic history of generalized pain or numerous medical or indeterminate diagnoses may overemphasize their symptoms as a way of desperately trying to alert their medical providers that "something is wrong."

Feedback Statements – Fs Scale

T score <80

You answered a number of items that dealt with your physical health. You tried to be accurate, without exaggerating your condition. That suggests your test results could be an accurate description of your current condition.

T score 80–99

Your item responses to several of the statements regarding your physical functioning reflect that you may have multiple medical conditions and concerns. However, the number of items that you endorsed in the area of physical functioning is generally higher than the number most medical patients experience. You may have exaggerated a bit to make sure I understood how badly you feel. Or you may be experiencing a recent worsening of your medical condition. We may want to explore some of your answers to make sure we have an accurate assessment.

T score ≥ 100

You answered many items suggesting you are experiencing a great deal of physical discomfort and numerous physical symptoms, some of which may come and go and others that are constant. These symptoms may frighten you, leading you to feel hopeless and helpless at times. Physical pain likely makes you irritable and constantly concerned with getting an accurate diagnosis. The way you answered the test suggests that in your desire to draw attention to your physical concerns you may have endorsed so many symptoms and concerns that it is not possible to make an accurate appraisal of your condition. The number of items that you endorsed in the area of physical functioning is generally higher than the number most medical patients experience. We may want to explore some of your responses to ensure we have an accurate assessment.

Symptom Validity (FBS) Scale

General Descriptors

Complaints

Concentration difficulties; nightmares; general pain; overwhelmed; stressed; defeated.

Cognitions

Negative; hopeless; defeated; suicidal.

Emotions

Dysphoric; overwhelmed; exhausted.

Traits and behaviors

Feeling negative and defeated with numerous pain complaints; subtly demanding and dependent.

Therapist's Notes – FBS Scale

This 30-item scale is derived from the original 43 items that comprised the MMPI-2 version of this measure. Originally called the "Fake Bad Scale (FBS)," the scale was developed to better understand elevated MMPI-2 F scale scores. It was developed by identifying individuals presenting with noncredible symptoms in the context of civil litigation. The FBS Scale, like the Fs Scale, acts as a validity measure to make sure the other somatic complaint scales (such as RC1, MLS, and NUC) are valid. Though this scale involves somatic and neurological symptoms, it is only moderately correlated with the Fs Scale, so both scales capture different aspects of somatic overreporting. Complaints of pain, exhaustion, and concentration difficulties could be valid but high scores are probably exaggerated.

T Ssore <78

Scores in this range are likely valid and do not reflect exaggeration, especially in the presence of a medical condition.

T score 78–89

In the presence of consistent responding, scores in this range could be valid, especially if there is evidence of a medical condition. However, there is a possibility of exaggeration, perhaps out of a desire to have the symptoms taken seriously.

T score ≥90

Patients with bona fide medical problems do not score this high. Consequently, scores on the somatic and cognitive scales are likely to be artifactually elevated and the protocol itself could be invalid if scores on the other Validity Scales are elevated. If the inconsistency scales – CRIN, VRIN, and TRIN – are elevated, the profile is invalid.

Feedback Statements – FBS Scale

T score <78

The items on this scale appear to have been answered accurately.

T score 78–89

Your item responses to several of the statements regarding your physical functioning reflect that you may have multiple medical conditions and concerns. However, the number of items that you endorsed in the area of physical functioning is generally higher than what most people experience. You may have overemphasized some of the items to ensure that I understand how badly you feel. We may want to explore some of your answers to make sure we have an accurate assessment.

T score ≥90

Your test responses revealed you may have exaggerated the severity of your symptoms, perhaps wanting to make sure I understand how poorly you are feeling. Your responses suggest that you are experiencing pain and find concentrating difficult. You may feel exhausted and often defeated, even hopeless. You may ruminate on whether life is worthwhile, since it is so stressful, painful, and overwhelming. Perhaps you want me to understand how depleted and overwhelmed you feel. It is difficult to accurately understand your current condition because you have endorsed multiple symptoms that most medical patients do not experience. We may want to explore your responses to make sure I have a complete understanding of what is troubling you.

Response Bias (RBS) Scale

General Descriptors

Complaints

Concentration and memory difficulties; stressed; easily knocked off balance; headaches; blank spells.

Cognitions

Possible auditory hallucinations; difficulty thinking and concentrating.

Emotions

Feels emotionally fragile; hopeless; feels out of control.

Traits and behaviors

Dependent; depressed; complaining.

Therapist's Notes – RBS Scale

This scale is composed of 28 items empirically associated with inadequate effort made on cognitive testing, known as performance validity tests. The items on this scale are heterogeneous, ranging from somatic concerns to dysphoria to anxiety to problems of memory and concentration to delusions of control. The scale was originally designed for the MMPI-2 to detect neurocognitive malingering. T scores of 90 or higher would indicate a strong possibility of overreporting of cognitive problems, such as memory impairment. High scores would limit the accuracy of scores on the Cognitive Complaints (COG) and the Neurological Complaints (NUC) Scales. Individuals with severe mental disturbance, such as severe depression and possible psychosis, could also score in the 75–89 T score range.

T score <75

Scores in this range indicate cognitive complaints that are likely valid.

T score 75–89

Scores in this range reflect a reporting of an unusual combination of responses that may be associated with noncredible memory complaints. Assess if the COG Scale is also elevated due to possible exaggeration.

T score ≥90

Scores in this range are likely invalid due to the overreporting of cognitive and other psychological problems.

Feedback Statements – RBS Scale

T score <75

You answered the items thoughtfully without overemphasizing your concerns.

T score 75–89

Your responses show that you possibly have concerns with memory and concentration functions and/or the ability to think clearly and efficiently. You may also be strongly emphasizing other problem areas, such as feeling anxious or demoralized. In order to better understand your responses, I would like to examine and discuss with you the items you endorsed on this particular measure.

T score ≥90

You answered many items in a way that revealed you have numerous problems with memory, concentration, and/or the ability to think clearly and efficiently. Your responses may be accurate, but you appeared to emphasize the severity of your distress. It is important for me to explore some of your answers with you in order to obtain an accurate picture of your current functioning.

Uncommon Virtues (L) Scale

General Descriptors

Complaints

Feeling judged, unfairly criticized, or accused.

Cognitions

Conventional; judgmental; moralistic; lacking in insight; inflexible; psychologically naïve.

Emotions

Self-controlled; denying; constricted emotionally.

Traits and behaviors

Self-righteous; defensive; conscientious; rigid; naïve; perfectionistic; psychologically unsophisticated.

Therapist's Notes – L Scale

The Uncommon Virtues (L) Scale consists of 14 items phrased in a way that a False response denies normal moral imperfections or failings of character. Most people readily admit to many of these common human failings. The scale was originally designed as a validity indicator to detect intentional efforts to underreport problems. The derivation of this rationally developed scale, which has its origins in previous research on honesty and deceit, can be found explicated in the texts by Friedman et al. (2015) and Nichols (2011).

Elevated L Scale scores can occur for a number of reasons. Individuals who are naïve or psychologically unsophisticated, and want to present themselves in a favorable light, may over-endorse L items. In some cases, individuals concerned that their test results may be negatively judged may over-emphasize their moral virtues. This suggests a test-taking stance of wanting to "pass the test," which would suppress the Substantive Scales. Because the items on this short scale are transparently virtuous, it is not difficult for sophisticated and/or educated individuals to avoid endorsing the items on this scale if they are so motivated. In fact, scores are negatively correlated with education, intelligence, and cultural sophistication.

As various MMPI textbooks (Ben-Porath & Sellbom, 2023; Friedman et al., 2015; Levak et al., 2011; and Nichols, 2011) emphasize, there are two overlapping categories for elevations on the L Scale. These categories are (1) worries about how one's responses will be perceived, and (2) impression management in which deceiving the clinician is the principal motive. Elevated inconsistency scales would render the profile invalid. When CRIN, VRIN, and TRIN are all within the normal range, then an elevated T score on the L Scale of ≤80 likely indicates significant underreporting. Elevated L scores do not necessarily invalidate elevated substantive scores though the high L may mean an underestimation of the problems associated with these elevations. As the MMPI-3 manual indicates, an absence of elevation on the Substantive Scales is uninterpretable when there are elevated L scores.

T score <65

The client answered the test honestly and openly, admitting to normal human frailties and moral lapses. Their willingness to do so suggests that they answered the other test items honestly without putting their best foot forward or trying to make themselves look above moral reproach. Therefore, the test is likely valid.

T score 65–69

L scores in this range are not abnormal in divorce custody cases and other legal proceedings, as the perceived threat level for being morally judged is high. Determining whether the L Scale score is situation-dependent or characterological would be important. In the presence of a history of rigid parental values and psychological naïveté in the client, the L score could be determined by character. The Substantive Scales could likely be suppressed with L in this range. Therefore, even 5 T score points above average on these scales could be interpreted as indicating personality attributes that should be interpreted cautiously.

T score 70–79

Scores in this range suggest possible underreporting but could also reflect rigid traditional backgrounds and a belief system that has strict proscriptions about moral behavior. Scores in this range could reflect an individual involved in a legal issue, where the drive to present oneself above reproach is high. If the Substantive Scales are elevated, the high L score would not invalidate the profile though the level of disturbance may be somewhat muted by the defensiveness.

T score ≥80

The protocol may be invalid as the client has denied basic human failings that most people readily admit, such as not always telling the truth. L scores in this range usually suppress the Substantive Scales reflecting the denial associated with the L Scale item endorsements. If, however, any or all of the Substantive Scales are elevated, the L Scale elevation suggests a naïve, perhaps unsophisticated, individual with rigid values and a lack of self-awareness. A L Scale score in this range with elevations on Thought Dysfunction (THD) and Aberrant Experiences (RC8) would support the possibility of psychosis.

Lifestyle and Family Background – L Scale

Without an interview, it is difficult to determine if an elevated L score is due to conscious defensiveness, self-deception, or rigidity of values and a lack of psychological sophistication. High L scores can be obtained from bright and educated people who nevertheless have very rigid values. In the presence of a lifestyle of rigid and judgmental attitudes, look for a history of strict and uncompromising parental values. If the high L is due to fears of being judged and reflects a conscious attempt to "pass" the test, explore the client's fears about how the results of the test may be used as well as the possibility of a future retest.

Clarifying Scales – L Scale

When K is also elevated, the high L is likely due to conscious positive impression management. If K is within normal limits, the L elevation may be reflecting a rigid "black-and-white" personality style.

When the Ideas of Persecution (RC6) Scale is elevated, an elevated L score may indicate fears of being judged and criticized or a paranoid trait disturbance or disorder may be present.

If the Substantive Scales are elevated, the profile could be valid, and the L Scale elevations would suggest rigidity of moral values and a tendency to be judgmental and self-righteous.

Therapy and Therapeutic Pitfalls – L Scale

Validating the client's desire to be above moral reproach would be an important initial alliance-building strategy. Validate that the client has very high standards and others may feel they can't live up to those standards so they may feel judged by the client. Beware of clients feeling judged by the clinician and eliciting countertransference because of their defensiveness and judgmental attitude. Educating clients about how people have different values and how their own rigidity may make others defensive could help them to become more flexible. Also explore early parental demands for strict "goodness" and the pressure to perform and be above reproach to avoid criticism.

Feedback Statements – L Scale

T score <65

Your score on this scale is in the normal range. You were able to achieve an appropriate balance between being honest and the temptation to create an overly favorable impression of yourself. You admitted to normal human failings, showing you have good self-awareness and the confidence to be yourself. You were honest about your strengths and vulnerabilities.

T score 65–69

You answered the items carefully to make sure you came across as a moral and decent person. If you are involved in any legal dispute, it would be understandable and normal to minimize any psychological symptoms or personal eccentricities. That may make it harder to get a complete and accurate picture of your true personality makeup, so I may want to explore some of your responses with you.

T score 70–79

You answered the test in a way that suggests you were concerned about being judged or criticized. This would be understandable if you are involved in legal proceedings, since most people want to look their moral best when being judged. You put your best foot forward and denied basic human frailties that we all have. That may mean I did not get a complete picture of you. I may want to explore certain responses with you to obtain a more complete picture of your personality makeup.

T score ≥80

You answered the test carefully, making sure your answers revealed you to be a moral and decent person with very strong values. Generally, people will admit to minor lapses in moral and ethical behavior since nobody always tells the exact truth without bias. Your results are difficult to interpret as you did such a good job of denying basic human weaknesses or psychological problems.

Lifestyle and Family Background Feedback – L Scale

You may have grown up in an environment where parental figures were critical and judgmental and moral standards were hard to live up to. Perhaps you follow a strict religious code of conduct that does not allow for moral shades of gray. It is also possible that you are wary of how the test results could be used against you, so you were careful to reveal your "best side."

Treatment and Self-Help Suggestions – L Scale

1. Consider discussing the use of cognitive-behavioral techniques to help modify your "black-and-white" and "all-or-nothing" thinking.
2. Explore any early experiences where you felt you had to be above criticism. Once you have identified those experiences, the use of cognitive-behavioral techniques to challenge and modify those early childhood assumptions could be useful.
3. Because you tend to be a perfectionist, "thought-stopping" techniques can help you manage the negative thoughts that you are not doing things "well enough." Whenever you become aware of critical thoughts about others, forcefully say to yourself, "Stop." Some people find it helpful to picture a large red stop sign at the same time. Some critical and negative thoughts tend to repeat themselves, so this is a way to recognize and disrupt unhealthy thought patterns. Repeat the technique until the thought is out of your mind. You can then replace it with a more positive and constructive thought (e.g., "I have felt this way before, and I know I can handle this").
4. People may find your standards of behavior hard to live up to so they may approach you defensively and even want to catch you doing something wrong to prove you are not perfect. When you are frustrated with somebody, stick to the actual event or behavior that is bothering you rather than telling them how their behavior is "wrong" or immoral. That will minimize their defensiveness.

Adjustment Validity (K) Scale

General Descriptors – Low K (T Score <40)

Complaints

Overwhelmed; insecure; sometimes confused; inefficient; vulnerable to stress; possible low self-esteem.

Cognitions

Self-doubting; self-critical; disorganized; jaded or cynical view of others.

Emotions

Fearful; ambivalent; overwhelmed; underregulated; alienated from others.

Traits and behaviors

Direct; non-defensive; easily overwhelmed; cynical; complaining; impulsive; demanding.

Therapist's Notes – K Scale (Low K)

Low scores on the K Scale suggest directness, non-defensiveness, and emotional expression in a blunt manner. When the Substantive Scales are elevated in the presence of low K, this suggests that the personality characteristics associated with the Substantive Scales will be palpable and robust. In some cases, the low K score can point to exaggeration and a "cry for help," especially in highly elevated Validity Scales and elevated profiles (T score ≥80.) When the Substantive Scales suggest a severe disturbance, low K scores may indicate difficulty coping and the need for directly supportive and nurturing therapeutic help; in such cases, avoid insight therapy initially until clients are stabilized. In the absence of Substantive Scale elevations, low K scores may not reflect emotional disturbance but, rather, emotional directness and a lack of regard for social niceties. Individuals with low K scores tend to disregard or rise above others' judgments about their emotional expressiveness.

Lifestyle and Family Background – K Scale (Low K)

The lifestyle of people with low K scores tends to be one in which emotions and stress are likely to cause disruptions in efficiency and productivity. In the absence of any elevations on the Substantive Scales, however, the low K score could reflect open, emotionally spontaneous, and uninhibited individuals. Typically, the lower the K, the more likely it is that the individual feels they are at the mercy of the emotional states revealed by their Substantive Scale scores; this may be associated with family backgrounds of emotional disturbance and trauma. However, this kind of disturbance and possible family background would be revealed by the scale elevations and a comprehensive history.

Clarifying Scales – K Scale (Low K)

If any of the overreporting scales (Fp, Fs, FBS, RBS) are elevated between T scores of 80 to 100, and the F Scale is a T score of ≥85, the low K would confirm a pattern of exaggeration.

When the Substantive Scales are below a T score of 65 and the F score is below a T score of 65, the low K may reflect a brash emotional directness.

Therapy and Therapeutic Pitfalls – K Scale (Low K)

In the presence of high elevations on the Substantive Scales, a low K score would suggest a need for support and ego strength-building interventions. Self-soothing and thought-stopping techniques to deal with the scale elevations are recommended. In the presence of a severe disturbance, a low K score may indicate a collapse of ego defense wherein insight therapy is contraindicated. In such cases, even minor stressors can be disorganizing to the individual's coping abilities.

Feedback Statements – K Scale (Low K)

T score <45

The way you answered the test reveals that you were very open and honest about the way you were feeling and were willing to admit to a number of symptoms and concerns. You may have a tendency to be somewhat self-critical.

T score 45–65

Your score on this scale is in the normal range. This score reflects that you answered the items openly without trying to be too self-critical. Your approach was honest and accurate to the best of your abilities. You are likely to be self-reliant and enterprising and to have good coping skills. You have a wide range of interests and adequate resources. I appreciate your willingness to make yourself vulnerable to this process.

Treatment and Self-Help Suggestions – K Scale (Low K)

The following suggestions may not be applicable if the majority of Substantive Scales are in the normal range.

1. Perhaps learn to meditate or deep breathe as a way to manage stress and to turn off ruminative thinking.
2. Every evening, write a list of a few things you want to get done the next day. When you wake up, begin to work on your list so that you feel some sense of accomplishment. A list will help you feel like you have some control over your thinking and behavior.
3. Learning various types of intentional relaxation can help calm your habitual reactions to stressful situations. One type of relaxation, diaphragmatic breathing, exerts a powerful effect on your physical response to stress. When you feel stressed, your breathing is rapid and shallow, but this exercise can calm the automatic response of your nervous system and reduce reactive thinking and destructive emotions. Consider learning diaphragmatic breathing; practice twice daily for two weeks and then continue to practice on a regular basis.

General Descriptors – High K (T Score >70)

Complaints

Few or no complaints.

Cognitions

Denying; conventional; rational; logical.

Emotions

Defensive; emotionally constricted; underreporting of feelings; guarded; controlled; "stiff upper lip."

Traits and behaviors

Uncomfortable with emotionality; conventional; conforming; socially appropriate; lacking self-awareness.

Therapist's Notes – K Scale (High K)

High K scores are associated with defensiveness, emotional control, and conventionality. As a result, the clinician will have to multiply the intensity of what the client is saying to gain a true sense of empathy for them. High K scores can occur for a number of reasons. Clients who are consciously defensive and attempting to "pass" the test may obtain high K scores. Some individuals tend to espouse a cultural value of control, constraint, and social appropriateness. In some cultures – for example in the United Kingdom – expressing emotions publicly is frowned upon and seen as inappropriate. Approaching emotionally upsetting situations with a "stiff upper lip" and denying extreme emotions is seen as appropriate and desirable. In such individuals, high K scores reflect a cultural bias toward control and poise.

In some situations, high K scores may be better understood as reflecting personality variables rather than test-taking defensiveness. Such individuals are likely to be emotionally controlled, and able to manage stressful situations unusually well. It is important for the clinician to determine if the high K score is attributable to conscious attempts to look good and "pass" the test or is a function of personality attributes.

Lifestyle and Family Background – K Scale (High K)

Elevations on K, whether high or low, may not be associated with any particular lifestyle or family background. However, explore the possibility that high K scores reflect family or cultural norms that value emotional control and poise in the face of emotional stress. For example, an analogy would be British or Japanese cultural norms valuing a stiff upper lip compared to the stereotype of the expressive emotionality of Italian or Latin cultures.

Clarifying Scales – K Scale (High K)

If L is not elevated above a T score of 65, then the high K score may reflect a personality style of emotional poise and control rather than a conscious attempt to appear emotionally stable. In other words, the K elevation is measuring a personality attribute rather than a pure validity construct. If there is clinical evidence of psychopathology and a motivation to be evaluated favorably, then the K elevation may be due to conscious attempts to pass the test by appearing emotionally stable and symptom-free.

Therapy and Therapeutic Pitfalls – K Scale (High K)

Typically, individuals with high K elevations are not amenable to cathartic and insight-oriented therapies. This is partially because they are reporting emotional balance and control but also because they may be threatened by emotional expression. Therapy with these individuals can start by being rationally focused, fostering understanding about how others experience emotions and manage stress. The clinician can help these clients understand how they have learned to modulate their emotion through cultural or learned inhibitions against emotional expressiveness. Once these clients are comfortable discussing emotions, techniques such as Gestalt methods or role-playing can help disinhibit their constricted emotions.

Feedback Statements (High K)

The way you answered the test shows you are a poised and emotionally controlled person. In the face of emotional turmoil or stress you approach matters with a "stiff upper lip." You tend *not* to wear your feelings on your sleeve, so people close to you need to multiply the intensity of what you say in order to have a sense of empathy for you. For example, be mindful that if you were to say you are "unhappy" about someone's behavior or "not too pleased," people may take you at your word rather than realize that you could be quite angry and upset.

Treatment and Self-Help Suggestions – K Scale (High K)

1. Start by learning to recognize your emotions. You and your therapist can work together to identify any feelings you may be experiencing during the therapy session. Think of a positive emotional experience and take some time to identify where in your body you experience the feelings. Do the same for a negative experience. Observe to see if you inhibit emotions to avoid them becoming too intense.
2. Explore any childhood or later experiences where you felt the potential for losing emotional control. Revisit and allow yourself to feel those moments, so you can learn the full range of emotional expression.
3. Be mindful that when you express your emotions you may do it in a muted way, so others don't have a full sense of empathy for you. Occasionally ask others how they perceive you are feeling so you learn how you come across to them.
4. As you begin to feel more comfortable with the idea of expressing feelings, acting classes can help you become more spontaneous and perhaps even more creative.
5. Familiarize yourself with the benefits of "emotional intelligence," which is the ability to identify, assess, and manage your emotions in a healthy way. There are many good self-help books written about developing emotional intelligence to make improvements in both your personal life and in the workplace.

3 Higher-Order (H-O) Scales

Introduction

Development

Personality and psychopathology researchers have long sought to identify meaningful structural models to provide an organizing, descriptive framework for psychological assessments and psychodiagnosis (Ben-Porath and Sellbom, 2023). To this end, a set of Higher-Order (H-O) Scales was first developed for the MMPI-2-RF. As reported by Ben-Porath and Tellegen (2008/2011a, 2008/2011b), factor analyses of the Restructured Clinical (RC) Scales identified a three-factor higher-order structure corresponding to broad dimensions of emotional, thought, and behavioral dysfunction. In the empirical development of the H-O Scales, a set of items was identified for each scale by selecting from the entire MMPI-2 item pool diverse and distinctive item markers associated statistically and conceptually with one, but not the other, two higher-order factors.

The three relatively independent resulting scales were labeled Emotional/Internalizing Dysfunction (EID), a measure of difficulties in the domain of mood and affect; Thought Dysfunction (THD), a measure of disordered thinking; and Behavioral/Externalizing Dysfunction (BXD), which assessed problems associated with under-controlled behavior. For EID, most, but not all, of the items selected were scored on one of the three RC Scales that marked this dimension: Demoralization (RCd), Low Positive Emotions (RC2), or Dysfunctional Negative Emotions (RC7). For THD, all the selected items were scored on either Ideas of Persecution (RC6) or Aberrant Experiences (RC8). All but one of the items selected for BXD were scored on Antisocial Behavior (RC4) or Hypomanic Activation (RC9).

The starting point for updating the H-O Scales for the MMPI-3 was the set of items remaining available for each scale after deleting items that were not carried over from the MMPI-2-RF. The authors calculated correlations between the 72 new items included on the MMPI-3 and the H-O Scales. Any item found to correlate discriminately with an H-O Scale was examined for content and added to that scale if it was judged to be relevant to that domain. Ben-Porath and Sellbom (2023) provide additional information about the conceptual foundations of the H-O Scales and their interpretation.

Application

When an H-O Scale is elevated, it informs the therapist that the individual may experience prominent dysfunction in their emotional regulation (EID), their thinking (THD), or their behavior (BXD), and points to possible defensive adaptations. An analogy would be that the H-O Scales provide the location of a city on a map and the RC Scales and Specific Problems (SP) Scales provide the streets and alleys of psychological adjustment. Sometimes only one H-O Scale may be elevated, which provides an accessible uncomplicated summary of the individual's psychological functioning.

DOI: 10.4324/9781003557920-3

However, if two or more H-O Scales are elevated, this requires integrating possibly differing, even conflicting, behaviors and traits. Within the domain of the elevated H-O Scale(s), the RC and SP Scales provide detailed information about the individual's psychological functioning and makeup. Unless otherwise specified, the following descriptors apply at T scores of 65 or greater.

Emotional/Internalizing Dysfunction (EID) Scale

General Descriptors

Complaints

Feeling depressed, anxious, hopeless, worried, and/or overwhelmed; having difficulties with concentration and memory; poor sleep hygiene; possible appetite and weight disturbances, depending on scores on the RC and SP Scales. May complain of demoralization if RCd is elevated.

Cognitions

Pessimistic; easily guilty; ruminative (sometimes morbidly); self-deprecating; catastrophizing; indecisive; possible suicidal ideation, depending on scores on the RC and SP Scales.

Emotions

Depressed; sad; anhedonic; anxious; overwhelmed; insecure; hopelessness; helplessness; feeling burdensome to others, depending on scores on the RC and SP Scales.

Traits and behaviors

Loss is an ever-present perceived threat as stress and setbacks are internalized; anxiety-prone; dutiful, guilt-prone, passive, and ruminative; procrastination; lack of vitality; countermeasures such as dependence on others; setbacks perceived as catastrophic. Expect conflict avoidance unless an activating scale(s) (RC4, Anger Proneness (ANP), Aggression (AGG), Dominance (DOM), or Disconstraint (DISC)) are elevated.

Therapist's Notes – EID Scale

Elevations on the EID Scale delineate many of the same personality and symptom descriptors as those described in DSM-5-TR for the depressive disorders (disruptive mood dysregulation disorder, major depressive disorder, persistent depressive disorder, and various adjustment reactions) and anxiety disorders (phobias, social anxiety disorder, general anxiety disorder). At higher elevations, with no other H-O Scales elevated, this scale identifies an agitated, anxious depression in a hyper-responsible, overly conscientious, guilt-prone individual. Depending on the elevation of the Substantive Scales, these individuals may exhibit vegetative symptoms of depression and complain of anxiety and difficulties with memory and concentration. Sleep and energy problems with feelings of emotional depletion may be present. General inefficiency due to ambivalence and anxiety can lead to weight gain, or loss, in some people. Suicidal ideation and morbid ruminations are possible if Suicidal/Death Ideation (SUI) is elevated.

Scores in the 55 to 65 T score range in a spike EID profile may reflect a personality style of a hyper-responsible, dutiful, worry-prone individual who may not complain of severe anxiety or depression but can exhibit a seriousness about life and a diminution in spontaneous pleasure-seeking. Even in the high normal range, spike elevations suggest a readiness to feel guilt and self-deprecation and, with it, some passivity. In the absence of symptoms or past losses, normal range elevations may reflect a personality style of dutiful responsibility, perfectionism, and a proneness to worry.

Barring evidence of underreporting, low scores reflect the absence of the traits and symptoms associated with emotional dysfunction. A score below T-38 likely reflects someone who is emotionally well adjusted and capable of managing stress with appropriate levels of arousal, without becoming overwhelmed or emotionally hijacked. These individuals are resilient, tend not to experience regret, and approach life with confidence,

If there are elevations on the BXD, RC4, Impulsivity (IMP), AGG, and/or DISC Scales, a low EID score would suggest the absence of inhibiting mechanisms, increasing the likelihood of impulsive tension reduction, and possibly indicating features of psychopathy.

Lifestyle and Family Background – EID Scale

Individuals with a high EID score may have recently experienced an actual or perceived loss that has caused them to withdraw, perhaps fearful of engaging in life, to protect against further loss. Sometimes the loss may have occurred in childhood, with a loss of age-appropriate carefreeness due to caregiver absence or death, an overload of responsibilities, or severe poverty. Typically, these individuals experience pervasive guilt and self-blame for past failures or losses.

Our hypothesis is that inhibiting hope and restricting motivation and reward-seeking could be an adaptive response to loss. "Nothing ventured, nothing lost" captures the possible adaptive nature of depression. An early history of deprivation and severe losses, followed by a relatively good adaptation that is then interrupted by a recent perceived setback, could be the precipitating event for a depressive reaction. Our hypothesis is that past traumas can leave emotional "scar tissue" that recent similar losses reactivate, leading to a potentially severe reaction that might to others appear exaggerated.

Elevations on the EID Scale in the absence of under-controlled behavioral indicators (BXD, RC4, IMP, AGG, DISC) suggest a lifestyle of anxious preoccupation, guilt, and rigid hyper-responsibility. Depression and the absence of pleasurable activities may lead to friends and family seeing these individuals as negative and sour. These clients tend to focus on past setbacks and losses, rejecting reassurance and focusing instead on the perceived hopelessness of their situation. In the presence of a past history of successful adaptation with an absence of past depression, this elevation could be revealing a reactive depression due to a recent loss. However, with a history of early losses or past depressive episodes, this elevation may suggest a chronic and/or intermittent depressive disorder.

Clarifying Scales – EID Scale

Scales reflecting depression (RCd, RC2), Malaise (MLS), Suicidal Ideation (SUI), Helplessness and Hopelessness (HLP), Self-Doubt (SFD), Inefficacy (NFC), Stress (STR), Worry (WRY), and Behavior-Restricting Fears (BRF) may be elevated, providing depth and richness to the primary picture of a depressed, anxious individual. In some cases, for example, while there may be no suicidal ideation, there may be severe self-doubt, feelings of helplessness, hopelessness, feeling like a burden to others as well as feeling inefficacious. Severe behavior-restricting fears that are the central component of the experienced depression may be present with the BRF Scale elevated.

If all or many of the aforementioned scales are elevated and the Validity Scales suggest overreporting, then the elevations may be an attempt to draw attention to severe depression and general internalizing dysfunction for secondary gain purposes. If Social Avoidance (SAV) and Shyness (SHY) are elevated in the presence of elevations on many of the anxiety or depression Substantive Scales, this would add to the severity of the disturbance. If only SAV and SHY are elevated with the EID Scale, the depression may be due to an extreme social phobia and the loneliness inherent in such a disorder. This may reflect an individual whose social anxiety could be the basis of their depression.

If any of the anger and externalizing scales (BXD, RC4, ANP, IMP, AGG, DISC) are elevated, then the depression and anxiety may be expressed through angry outbursts, perhaps vengeful actions, and impulsive tension reduction that is aggressive, followed by guilt and remorse. The more those scales are elevated, the greater the likelihood of impulsive tension reduction in possibly self-defeating ways. In this case, a disruptive mood dysregulation disorder should be ruled out. If the Substance Abuse Scale (SUB) is elevated, the individual may be self-medicating their mood disorder with substances.

Therapy and Therapeutic Pitfalls – EID Scale

As in all depression profiles, a suicide risk assessment is necessary. This is especially so if SUI and/or HLP scores are elevated with the disinhibiting scales such as RC4, IMP, and DISC also elevated. Evaluation for medication is usually helpful, although energizing antidepressants should be monitored if there are indications of impulsiveness. Research shows that cognitive behavioral treatment is effective, especially if combined with medication. Thought-stopping, assertiveness training, mindfulness, and self-esteem-building therapies can also be useful. Analytical therapies are probably less useful since these clients tend to ruminate and overanalyze, so Gestalt "here and now" therapies are more useful. Finishing grieving over past losses with self-acceptance is also useful.

The therapist should avoid excessive reassurance that "things will turn out fine," or encouragement of gratitude, or focus on the "positives" since this could lead to resistance. In the presence of a history of mood swings, the elevation on this scale, especially if RC9 and/or Activation (ACT) are also elevated, could be reflecting recurring mood episodes, such as in a bipolar disorder.

Feedback Statements – EID Scale

T score ≤38 [if no other scales are elevated and no indications of underreporting]

Your profile suggests you are a resilient, energetic, optimistic person, free from much anxiety or worry. You seem to take setbacks well, without beating yourself up or stewing over past mistakes or losses. You bounce back from adversity and are not plagued by guilt or self-doubt. When something unfortunate happens to you, you do not frame yourself as a victim. If you ever experience sadness or anxiety, it will likely be temporary and should disappear once the stress that elicited it has passed. You probably rarely lose sleep over a concern or a difficult decision and you likely have enough energy to get the things done that you desire. People with your kind of resilience and optimism are generally seen as playful and positive.

T score 55–65 [if no other scales are elevated]

Your profile suggests that you are a thoughtful, serious person who takes their responsibilities seriously. You are cautious about taking risks but, because of your strong sense of duty and accountability, you can sometimes take on too many tasks. You can be your own worst critic, and you are cautious to not "count your chickens before they hatch." People likely see you as earnest and circumspect about being overly optimistic.

- If WRY is a T score 55–65, add: When stress builds, you can be vulnerable to losing sleep or to periods of anxiety and apprehension. Sometimes making decisions can be difficult because you can see all sides of an issue. It is possible that you have always been a more cautious and worry-prone individual, but it is also possible that there has been some recent setback or stress that has left you feeling a little less relaxed and easygoing than you would like. Sometimes people with your profile grew up in environments where they had responsibilities or stresses that inhibited a carefree childhood.
- If SFD is a T score 55–65, add: Big decisions and stressful situations can lead you to doubt yourself and wonder if you are up to the tasks before you.
- If Compulsivity (CMP) is a T score 55–65, add: You take your responsibilities seriously and may experience the need to do things a certain way. It may annoy you if others are less meticulous and diligent than you.
- If ANP is a T score 55–65, add: When stressors accumulate you may become a little sharp or even angry, especially if others don't do what you see as the right thing.

T score 65–78

You report feeling significant emotional distress with a tendency to worry, doubt yourself, and, at times, feel demoralized and defeated. You are quick to be self-critical and feel useless and, at times, feel blue and somewhat depressed. Criticism can be particularly painful since you tend to be your own worst critic. Overall life can feel pretty stressful, and a strain more often than you would like.

T score ≥80

Your answers suggest that you are in quite a lot of emotional distress. You do not experience many positive emotions and feel depressed, anxious and, at times, overwhelmed, helpless, and pessimistic about things getting better. Currently you feel demoralized, and little seems to give you pleasure. You feel helpless and hopeless about things getting better and experience a lot of anxiety and fearfulness about the future. You report feeling useless and even, at times, feel that life is not worthwhile. You are your own worst critic and lack confidence. You have even begun to doubt that you can succeed in the things that you do. It is not surprising that, at times, you feel irritable and grouchy since you feel on edge so much of the time.

- If RCd and/or RC2 are elevated, add: Your profile shows that currently you are feeling down, discouraged, blue, gloomy, hopeless, and sad. It is hard for you to feel positive and hopeful a lot of the time. Sometimes this unhappiness can persist for a long time, so you may have come to accept it. It is challenging to feel optimistic or positive. You may experience a withdrawal from things that in the past you found satisfying. Currently, it seems that almost nothing gives you pleasure. You may be feeling pessimistic and demoralized, perhaps feeling that you are doomed to remain depressed.
- If SFD is elevated, add: You may be doubting yourself and your ability to escape the current depression.
- If NFC is elevated, add: At times, you may feel stuck and unable to think as clearly and efficiently as you would like. Problems can feel insurmountable, so it may be hard to motivate yourself.
- If RC7, Anxiety-Related Experiences (ARX), or Negative Emotionality/Neuroticism (NEGE) are elevated, add: Your profile suggests that you may experience much anxiety, with a pit in your stomach as if anticipating some negative event that is looming. You may experience periods of

dread without really knowing why. You may feel as if you have somehow done something wrong and that whatever you are doing isn't "the right thing." The anxiety may interfere with you getting a good night's sleep and you may find it hard to switch off your mind. It is as if your brain is like a computer with too many windows open, so that it is hard to focus on any one thing.

- If WRY is elevated, add: You may catch yourself constantly worrying about something so even small setbacks or responsibilities become nagging worries.
- If BRF is elevated, add: At times, you may find that your fears about things may restrict you from doing things that others seem to enjoy. You may avoid things you know can't hurt you.
- If HLP is elevated, add: Your profile suggests that your depression and anxiety have been intense enough that you may have given up hope of getting better. You may have come to accept that this is the way you are and that there is no point in being hopeful. You may feel that nobody can help you so reaching out to a therapist may feel useless.
- If RCd, RC2, RC7, HLP, SFD, NFC, STR, WRY, and/or NEGE are elevated, add: Living with this anxiety and depression makes it hard for you to think clearly, to concentrate, and to focus on things since your mind keeps interrupting you with negative thoughts. Small tasks and responsibilities can feel overwhelming, and you might procrastinate, hoping to feel more energetic over time.
- If Cognitive Complaints (COG) is elevated, add: When you experience so much "noise" in your head, it is hard to concentrate and to remember things. You may find that you are forgetting even important things and that it is hard to focus and to assimilate new material. You may experience what some people call "brain fog," a feeling that some describe as similar to jet lag, where you can't think clearly.
- If ANP is elevated, add: You may find yourself easily irritated, since you already feel overwhelmed, so minor frustrations and added responsibilities can lead to impulsive expressions of anger.
- If MLS is elevated, add: When you are anxious and on edge so much of the time, it is hard to get a good night's sleep. You may be waking up at night and not be able to return to sleep. When you experience anxiety and depression, it can affect your diet, so you may lose or gain unwanted weight.
- If Eating Concerns (EAT) is elevated, add: Some people attempt to manage their depression and anxiety by controlling what they eat. Sometimes this can lead to an eating disorder.
- If SUB is elevated, add: Sometimes people will attempt to find some relief from their emotional discomfort by using drugs and/or alcohol. While this may provide some compensatory temporary relief, over time it leads to negative consequences.
- If SFD, STR, and/or WRY are elevated, add: Your depression is likely causing you to feel pessimistic, often feeling guilty, as if you have done something wrong. You may find yourself obsessing about a negative thought and you may see small setbacks as potentially catastrophic. You may find yourself having unwanted morbid thoughts.
- If SUI and/or HLP are elevated, add: Sometimes people with this profile feel so exhausted by their anxiety and their depression that they fantasize about how to escape. Sometimes they think it would be easier if they died and, in some cases, they actually think about suicide. It would be important for you to discuss this with your therapist.
- If SUI is elevated, add: You told me that you have been thinking about suicide a lot and have been considering how to do it. We need to plan how you can feel better but, until you feel better, we should make an agreement that you will reach out to me or a suicide hot line [988 in the United States and Canada] for confidential support should the urge to kill yourself become stronger.
- If SFD, RC2, NFC, WRY, and/or NEGE are elevated, add: Currently you may be feeling very down on yourself and focused on your failings and flaws. You are probably doubting your

abilities, so it is hard to be assertive and ask for what you want. You may be feeling undeserving and unlovable, and you may even feel that life is passing you by.

- If Introversion/Low Positive Emotionality (INTR) is elevated, add: It may be hard for you to reach out to others because you are so self-critical. In new social situations you may feel awkward and self-conscious and sure that others are looking at you critically.

Lifestyle and Family Background Feedback – EID Scale

Typically, people with your profile have either experienced some recent loss or setback or a blow to their self-esteem. It is also possible that you grew up in an environment where you experienced overloads of responsibility without periods of age-appropriate carefreeness. You may have always been a dutiful, responsible, worry-prone individual who was quick to feel guilty and with a tendency to feel defeated when things went wrong. It is understandable that when you feel hopeless or defeated you limit wanting anything to avoid the risk of losing it, since further losses would feel unbearable. Not asserting yourself and not asking for what you want would be understandable responses to having experienced what feel like profound losses. Explore with your therapist any past setbacks or losses and see if you experience them as somehow demoralizing or even catastrophic.

Treatment and Self-Help Suggestions – EID Scale

1. Given your MMPI-3 score(s), you may want to create an action plan with your therapist. Review with your therapist the following seven areas to assess your "psychological temperature." These seven areas are all contributors to positive mental health and reflect resiliency, which can be learned and is helpful in facing setbacks, disappointments, and challenges.
   a. Adaptability/flexibility is your ability to adapt when changes occur. Flexibility helps you to ask for help and adopt new decision-making rules or choices. A strong desire to stick to routine may indicate a fear of making mistakes. Flexibility allows you to be open to new experiences in both your work and your personal life and can be improved by practicing versatility in problem-solving.
   b. During times of stress/crisis, it is important for you to identify ahead of time those on whom you can depend or that you can turn to for help and compassion. Empathic responses from others help reduce distress and contribute to a feeling of belongingness, an important factor in coping and mitigating depressing feelings. Supportive relationships will help bolster your resilience. It is not the number of relationships you have that is most important, but rather the quality of your relationships.
   c. It is important to identify the most meaningful purposes you see in facing life's challenges as well as identifying solutions to problems that may feel insurmountable. Having a sense of purpose and meaning is essential for your sense of wellbeing, adaptability, and happiness. Often, reading about others' plights (i.e., bibliotherapy) helps to reduce feelings of isolation by recognizing that others also experience similar feelings. This can help mitigate your level of despair by normalizing your reactions and seeing that your feelings are universal and part of being human.
   d. The key attitude of optimism allows you to remain hopeful about the future, so it is important for you to examine with your therapist ways for you to improve your outlook when situations appear hopeless or overwhelming. Realistic optimism is different than an optimistic bias, which could impair your ability to realistically assess risk. Realistically expecting good things for the future is linked to better subjective wellbeing and coping

strategies that include social support. Focusing on solving problems with an optimistic view is a buffer against depression. The underlying construct of hope is fundamental for the foundational basis of optimism.

e. Taking the initiative by being proactive allows you to feel that you have agency in your life and contributes to feelings of positive motivation. Proactive involvement means acting *before* an event versus reacting to something after it has occurred. Proactive individuals set goals, take responsibility for their actions, and act in ways to initiate and navigate challenging situations before they take place. This approach can help you to ask yourself "What can I do to help solve this problem?" and create solutions rather than more difficulties. This will allow you to feel "more in control" and contribute to you having stronger feelings of well-being.

f. The level at which you control your emotions in adverse circumstances (versus your emotions controlling you) determines in great part your sense of wellbeing. While it is normal to experience both positive and negative emotions, if that range is restricted to primarily negative feelings and thoughts (such as sadness, distress, fear, anger, worry, helplessness, and other unpleasant emotions), then you should discuss with your therapist how to learn new ways of interpreting events and engage in more rational self-talk. It is the view you take of adverse events, not the adverse events themselves, that will generally determine the outcome of how you cope with difficult situations.

g. Your self-esteem is the most significant contributor to your resiliency, thriving, and overall satisfaction with your life. Self-esteem develops from early experiences of being cared about and treated in consistent and loving ways. If you did not experience these early foundational blocks, you can still learn to improve your self-regard (and efficacy) by finding gratification in loving others and receiving affection and positive affirmations from those whom you value. With the help of your therapist, learn that no one is perfect and that making mistakes does not make you a failure or defective person. Not reaching for perfection to feel important is crucial for feeling balanced and motivated. Reframing your negative self-views will help to correct your self-defeating beliefs.

2. If ARX is elevated: Your therapist may suggest referring you for a trial of medication. Research shows that medication can be quite useful in calming down your anxiety and catastrophizing thoughts to help you sleep and have more energy. Medications often take a little time before they start to work, so try not to approach it feeling defeated.
3. If SUB is elevated: You may be self-medicating your anxiety and depression which can actually aggravate both. Consider going to Alcoholics Anonymous or Rational Recovery to get the support you need to manage your substance use. Your medication may take a while to take effect, but it should help. Mixing medications and drugs or alcohol can potentially be harmful.
4. If SUI and/or HLP are elevated (especially with significant IMP or DISC elevation): If you have been feeling suicidal, your therapist may want to develop a plan to protect you from carrying it out in one of your darker moments. If you are having feelings that worry you (such as hurting yourself), and you cannot reach your therapist, call or text or a suicide hot line [988 in the United States and Canada] for confidential support. The counselors answering your call can also refer you to any mental health resources that you might need. You can also call a national hotline [211 in the United States and Canada] that can help you locate mental health resources and even talk through a problem with a trained counselor.
5. If MLS, STR, ARX, BRF, SAV, and/or Disaffiliativeness (DSF) are elevated (or RC9 and/or ACT are low): It may be hard for you to exercise right now since your energy is low, but

exercise could be helpful because it can ease depression and anxiety by releasing feel-good endorphins, which are natural brain chemicals that can improve your sense of wellbeing. If you can find someone to exercise with you, it could improve your mood somewhat, even if just for a short period. Also, being outside in nature can give you a brief respite from negative thoughts.

6. If SFD is elevated: Work with your therapist to improve your self-esteem. When you have negative self-thoughts, write them down and then try to write a list of some of your positive thoughts to balance them out. Ask yourself if your first impulse is to blame yourself for any minor mistake.
7. If RC2, RC7, MLS, and/or any of the Internalizing Scales are elevated: On a regular basis, try to think of things that you are grateful for, even though it may feel like it will take a lot of effort. Research has shown that completing a daily gratitude diary significantly improves mood and reminds us that not everything is negative and hopeless. When dwelling on an unpleasant and depressing thought, think of an alternative idea that is more positive or neutral.
8. If SAV, SHY, or INTR are elevated: Though it may be difficult, it can be helpful to reach out to others since social isolation increases depression. Perhaps you could join a community such as a religious or civic organization where you could connect with others. Even a phone call to an old friend or relative could improve your mood for a while until your therapy begins to take effect.
9. If RC7, HLP, SFD, NFC, WRY, CMP, and/or ARX are elevated: Once you have made an important decision with careful due diligence, try to not go back to it, like a tongue to a sore tooth. Leave it alone and focus on something in the future.

Thought Dysfunction (THD) Scale

General Descriptors

Complaints

Anhedonia (if RC2 is elevated); poor concentration; feeling unfairly treated, bullied, and criticized; seeing others as malevolent; lack of self-confidence; mental confusion and disorganization under stress; psychotic symptoms; somatic concerns; nightmares; intrusive memories; dissociative symptoms; feeling victimized from perceived or real maltreatment.

Cognitions

Delusional thinking; unusual beliefs; unrealistic thinking; tangential and circumstantial associations; hypervigilance; projection as a primary defense mechanism; hypersensitive to criticism; ascribing malevolent motives onto others; guarded and defensive; resentful; injustice preoccupations ("grievance collector").

Emotions

Defensive; overreactive; easily emotionally wounded; fearful and untrusting; flat, inappropriate blunted affect.

Traits and behaviors

Cognitive disorganization under stress; hypersensitivity to perceived slights; stormy relations with others with possible aggression; interpersonal deficits with high social anxiety.

Therapist's Notes – THD Scale

This scale measures the extent to which an individual's thought processes are disordered and out of touch with reality. While the THD Scale is clearly established as a major marker for the thought disorder spectrum, an elevated score does not always indicate a florid psychosis. In some cases, an elevated score may suggest a fixed, rationalized (well-encapsulated) paranoia, a non-paranoid delusion, or an eccentric, immature individual with highly unusual thinking that becomes more psychotic under stress. This condition could include suspiciousness, and even a frank schizophrenic thought disturbance with auditory and/or visual hallucinations and bizarre behaviors.

Elevations on this scale could reflect a paranoid personality disorder, schizoid personality disorder, schizotypal personality disorder, delusional disorder, mania (if RC9 or ACT are elevated), schizophrenia, or a psychotic episode due to medical-, hormonal-, or drug-induced (if SUB is elevated) reactions. Correlates for these disorders include fantasy proneness, odd thinking, magical ideation, and social and interpersonal deficits with excessive social anxiety.

Highly elevated scores (T score 80 and higher) indicate the possibility of psychosis with delusional thinking, especially if RC6 and RC8 are both elevated. If SHY and/or SAV are elevated, look for extreme social anxiety and withdrawal. If RC2 is elevated, a flat, blunted, and inappropriate affect can mask the level of emotional discomfort these individuals experience. For example, smiling or even laughing when discussing painful or bizarre experiences would not be uncommon. In some cases, paranoid ideation can lead to rationalized self-protective aggression if RC4, AGG, and/or DISC are also elevated.

The well-established association between psychosis and the misuse of substances, perhaps as a way to self-medicate, would indicate further consideration if there are elevations on SUB. If RC4 is elevated along with the other externalizing scales, such as AGG, IMP, and/or DISC, beware of the possibility of confused, rationalized aggression against perceived enemies and foes. Expressions of anger could occur in brief acute outbursts. Elevations on RC6 and Neurological Complaints (NUC) would suggest numerous shifting neurological symptoms that could be incorporated into a paranoid delusion, with complaints of being poisoned or irradiated by space aliens or other conspiracy-fed delusions. If RC9 is elevated, the psychotic and delusional thoughts could be manifestations of bipolar disorder and energized and pushed into action in possibly dangerous ways. If RC6 is elevated, but not RC8, the individual may be more coherently rational in their paranoid delusions rather than floridly bizarre. If Uncommon Virtues (L) is elevated, this would suggest a moralistic and rigid individual, perhaps defending against psychosis.

Moderately elevated THD scores (T score 60–70) with moderately elevated RC6 and RC8 scores could reflect an overly sensitive and easily offended individual who distorts the benign intentions of others and interprets benevolent gestures in an offensive manner. Sensitivity can shade toward more paranoid ideation at times, although without clearly psychotic thought processes. Conflicts with others over perceived unfairness and personal slights would negatively affect these individuals' interpersonal relationships. If RC8 is elevated in the 60–70 range, unusual eccentric behaviors and occasional odd interpretations of reality would alert the therapist to the client's occasional manifestations of cognitive slippage.

Lifestyle and Family Background – THD Scale

Elevated THD, RC6 and RC8, and/or Psychoticism (PSYC) profiles indicate a possible psychosis that could be precipitated by drugs or alcohol, hormonal imbalances, prolonged severe stress, or the onset of schizophrenia. Young adults experiencing an identity crisis aggravated by psychedelics can become psychotic. In other cases, the profile may be reflecting an ongoing psychosis that may not have been previously recognized and treated adequately, or the client may have taken themselves off their prescribed medication regimen.

In some of the aforementioned examples, family history may not have been traumatic or particularly dysfunctional. Our hypothesis is that elevations on THD with RC6 and RC8 also elevated may reflect a genetic predisposition to develop a thought disorder and that, in some cases, a disastrous childhood (i.e., severe maltreatment or neglect) or recent trauma may have led to its expression. In some cases, the individual may have been fearful and insecure as a child, perhaps exhibiting eccentricities and slowness to mature, leaving them vulnerable to ridicule and bullying. In these cases, look for experiences of will-breaking hostility, humiliation, neglect, and even cruelty. They may have had a history of family disruptions, severe economic insecurity, and parental rejection or cold indifference. Regardless of the precipitating circumstances, individuals with high THD are likely to have poor work histories and generally marginal adjustment.

Clarifying Scales – THD Scale

The contribution of some of the other scales has been discussed in the Therapist's Notes above. However, scale elevations can point to additional personality and psychopathology features. If EID is also clinically elevated but lower than THD, the likely primary presentation is with thought dysfunction and possibly psychosis. In this case, the individual may doubt their decisions and feel depressed and defeated by their psychosis. If BXD is clinically elevated but lower than THD, the likelihood of impulsive, possibly dangerous, aggressive behaviors is heightened as psychotic thought processes color and drive the impulse to action. If Self-Importance (SFI) and/or DOM are elevated, this would suggest a surgent, possibly charismatic individual like Jim Jones, the pseudo-religious leader who persuaded his whole sect to swallow poison as part of his religious beliefs. Another example from the late 1960s is Charles Manson, the charismatic, psychotic leader who ignited his sect to go on a killing spree in order to incite a racial war (Roy et al., 2023); (Friedman, 2022–2023).

Since psychosis is so pernicious, understandable family conflicts would be reflected in high scores on Family Problems (FML). If DSF is elevated, the individual may withdraw from life, living a reclusive, perhaps paranoid, psychotic existence preoccupied with injustices or bizarre philosophies that reflect their underlying unresolved conflicts.

Therapy and Therapeutic Pitfalls – THD Scale

Psychosis and paranoia can be expressed in different ways. For example, there is the withdrawn, aloof, paranoid individual who initially may not appear obviously psychotic since they are so reserved. There is the florid, rambling, incoherent psychotic, the giggling, garishly dressed psychotic, or the wooden, stiff, non-responsive type. Elevations on the Substantive Scales could be helpful in determining the type of psychotic reaction. Although medication is clearly helpful in almost all cases, the difficulty is in creating enough of a therapeutic relationship that the individual can be persuaded to try medication. Consequently, approaching these patients with gentle caring without being too insight-focused or intrusive is necessary. Overfamiliarity and warmth from the therapist could arouse suspicion and be disorganizing. However, be aware that even hints of impatience on the part of the therapist would be negatively perceived by the client and lead to either communication shutdown and withdrawal, or anger. Encourage the client to ask questions but avoid any kind of uncovering therapy.

Once medicated and in treatment, even if a therapeutic alliance has been established, these individuals can respond with an acute angry episode occasioned by a therapist's inadvertent insensitivity. A therapist's sensitive apologies can lead to a breakthrough in the therapeutic alliance. An example explicates this dynamic:

> A therapist at a Virginia hospital reported a situation that is instructive about the degree to which a therapist needs to be aware of these individuals' sensitivity and the degree to which a therapist needs to be flexible and even non-traditionally therapeutic. They described treating an obese and unhygienic patient with schizophrenia with whom they had established a tentative beginning toward a trusting relationship. After an unusually productive, though faltering, dialogue, the therapist touched the arm of his client as they were opening the door for him to leave after the session. The client stiffened and, in a hostile manner, glared and said, "Never, ever touch me again!" The therapist apologized and continued to meet with the client, being careful not to violate the client's personal space. After several sessions, the client was complaining that his obesity made it impossible to cut his own toenails. The therapist offered to cut them for him in their session and did so, moving their relationship forward significantly.

Looking for ways to be cautiously giving to the client and building trust are ways to develop a therapeutic alliance. Compliance therapy could be helpful. It combines principles of motivating interviewing, inductive questioning, reflective listening, and reinforcing adaptive behaviors and attitudes in order to explore the client's ambivalence and target medication adherence. Cognitive therapy for the treatment of psychosis can also be useful. High THD scores have been found to predict aggression, especially if AGG and/or ACT are elevated in forensic psychiatric hospital patients and those confined under sexually violent predator laws.

Feedback Statements – THD Scale

T score <38

[If the profile is valid and not defensibly underreported and all other scales are in the 45-55 range.]
Your profile suggests you are a very grounded individual who tends to not take things personally. If people are critical or appear to not respect you, perhaps you respond with a shrug, seeing it as their problem. If someone is angry with you, you may not like it, but it doesn't leave you doubting yourself. You may be a person who doesn't spend a lot of time philosophizing. For you, if there is a problem, you want to find concrete, practical ways to solve it. Under stress you don't seem to lose your ability to think clearly, and you generally expect people will not reject you based on who you are. Generally, people may see you as resilient.

T score ≥ 65

- If RC6 and RC8 are elevated: Your profile suggests that when you feel stressed, unsafe, or vulnerable to criticism or being hurt, you become so tense that you can't think clearly. At these times, you get overwhelmed by confusing thoughts that seem to invade your mind, and others may find you hard to understand because your thoughts are expressed in confused ways. If you use alcohol or drugs, this may aggravate your mental confusion and your difficulty communicating with people.
- If RC6, WRY, and BRF are elevated: Your profile suggests that right now the world is a frightening place for you. You may feel unsure about whom you can trust. You may feel a need to constantly be on guard, fearful that others may hurt you or humiliate you. You may have periods where you feel that others are trying to manipulate and negatively influence you or somehow invade your mind and try to control you. It is hard to ever relax around people and, even when you are alone, your anxiety and fearfulness can be overwhelming. At times, your anxiety may be so high that you hear voices and become confused about what is real and what is not.

- If RC6, RC8, and COG are elevated: Living with constant concern about being judged or hurt by others makes it hard to concentrate and think clearly. Reading or trying to think through a solution to a problem may be particularly difficult right now. The "noise" in your head can be so loud that you can't think clearly. It may feel at times that your mind is being invaded, and you can't resist thoughts that are frightening and confusing.
- If ANP is elevated: You may have always been someone who could escape into fantasy to escape from painful feelings or situations. It is a way for you to create your own inner reality. However, currently you may be in a lot of distress because your inner world is as frightening and uncomfortable as the world around you. You may have angry and hostile thoughts, perhaps fantasizing about ways to punish people who have hurt you. You may get so tense and feel so unsafe that you lash out in anger, especially if you feel someone is threatening you. With the confusion and concerns that someone may harm you, it is understandable that you impulsively vent anger. It would be important to discuss these angry thoughts with your therapist and determine if you are planning to hurt someone, or yourself.
- In rare cases, the following descriptors may apply if a combination of AGG, RC4, and RC8 is elevated: Sometimes your thoughts may be confusing, with violence and sexual images interfering with your ability to think clearly. As you fantasize about ways you can punish people and hurt them the way they hurt you, your angry thoughts can become mixed with sexual imagery.
- If RC2 is elevated: Living in a world that is frightening and confusing means that you almost never experience joy or happiness, and you may often feel emotionally dead inside. You have probably been feeling a sense of disconnection and alienation from people, which leaves you feeling lonely and unable to connect with others.
- If AGG or IMP are elevated: When you get tense or threatened, you may impulsively act in ways that others find odd, even frightening or confusing. You may keep people at a safe distance by scaring them, perhaps by appearing tough, threatening, or very angry.
- If RC6 and RC8 are elevated: You may experience times when you see things and hear things that others do not appear to see or hear. This could be frightening for you and make it hard for you to trust that you can talk to anyone about your inner world. Sometimes you may hear voices inside your head telling you that you need to protect yourself and get rid of your enemies. At other times, the voices may tell you to do something harmful to yourself. Even though you feel alone, confused, and frightened, you can get help since what you are feeling and experiencing is a well-understood condition.
- If SUB is elevated: Feeling the way you do, you may use alcohol or drugs as a way to try to shut off the noise in your head and feel better and safer. However, these substances, while they can give you temporary relief, can actually make you worse over the long run and can be dangerous to your health.
- If RC9, IMP, and SFI are elevated: You may experience periods of very high energy and feelings that you have an important message for the world. You may feel that your ideas and plans to punish people and to get rid of your enemies make great sense. You may try to convince people and become angry and threatening if they don't take you seriously.
- If any of RC6, RC8, ANP, SAV, SHY, and DSF or combinations thereof are elevated: Your profile suggests you are feeling vulnerable and unsafe. You may have developed ways to keep people at a distance by dressing in unusual and weird ways. People may look at you and be frightened by you, which might help you feel protected, but also will add to your loneliness and a feeling that you don't belong anywhere.
- If DSF is elevated: Currently you feel safest alone, so you may spend much of your time isolated and preoccupied with your own thoughts and anxieties. You may avoid looking at people when you are out and may recoil if people try to talk to you. This is because you don't trust people and are afraid that they will hurt you somehow.

Lifestyle and Family Background Feedback – THD Scale

Your symptoms could occur for several reasons. One is a bad reaction to some drugs or severe alcohol abuse. It is also possible that you are experiencing a hormonal reaction. In other cases, you may have been a very sensitive child who has survived a difficult childhood. Your parents or caregivers may have been absent due to mental illness or substance abuse. They may have been critical, judgmental, neglectful, or even cruel. Perhaps they used harsh punishment that you felt was undeserved but left you feeling unlovable and damaged. If you come from this background, you probably remember times a parent or caregiving figure was extremely harsh and dominating. In such circumstances, from an early age an understandable way to protect yourself would be to escape into fantasy. To protect yourself, it made sense that you would refuse to let anyone become close to you. No wonder that now you are so sensitive to being disrespected or anybody trying to control or criticize you. It makes sense that you may spend time thinking cruel and angry thoughts as a way to get rid of anger toward those who have hurt you; it is an understandable way of dealing with some of your pain and resentment about the way you have been treated. To protect yourself now, it is understandable that you have developed a way to feel cold and unfeeling about others, perhaps having cruel fantasies about them, even though they may not have done anything to hurt you.

Treatment and Self-Help Suggestions – THD Scale

1. Learn to recognize the triggers for experiencing your symptoms. There can be internal or external triggers (or both). Internal triggers occur within your mind or body and may involve hearing a critical voice (perhaps even telling you to harm yourself) or having thoughts that don't feel like your own. You might experience strange sensations like smelling smoke or have weird bodily feelings. External triggers may involve your thinking that others are talking about you, laughing at you, or staring at you in an odd way. When this occurs, discuss with your therapist ways in which to cope with these uncomfortable, scary experiences.
2. Make sure you are getting enough sleep, which can give you the energy to cope with difficult feelings and experiences. Oftentimes, certain medications can help you with any sleeping problems or other symptoms.
3. Keep a journal of your setbacks, symptoms, and medications as a record to share with your therapist or caregiver(s). Sometimes, with confusion, it is difficult to report accurately what you have been going through. Keeping a log can help you assist those who want to support you in your recovery.
4. Learn to identify what you experienced as stressful events so you can develop countermeasures or more adaptive responses with the help of your therapist. For example, if your job requires you to interact with large groups of people, and you feel others are staring at you or talking about you, you can learn when to leave the group before you feel overwhelmed. In other words, with your therapist, develop an episode action plan.
5. If you are having feelings that worry you (such as hurting yourself), and you cannot reach your therapist, call or text a suicide hotline [988 in the United States and Canada]. The counselors answering your call provide free and confidential support and can also refer you to any mental health resources that you might need. You can also call a national hotline [211 in the United States and Canada] that can help you locate mental health resources and even talk through a problem with a trained counselor.
6. You may be distrustful of taking medication, but it can help you think more clearly and take away some of the feelings of dread and anxiety without taking away your ability to see what is going on around you.

7. It may be hard for you to trust your therapist. In fact, this feedback might make you suspicious and scare you that you are going to be tricked somehow. This feedback is based on my experience of helping others with your condition, which affects many people. You are not alone.
8. Be aware that you are your own worst critic and that you may have come to believe some of the negative and cruel things that were said to you.
9. If RCd and HLP are elevated: You may be feeling hopeless, helpless, and discouraged, feeling that nobody can help you. It will be hard at first but learning to trust your therapist is important, and you could start by talking about how hard it is to trust them.
10. Avoid substances like marijuana, psychedelics, and alcohol because they will increase your symptoms.
11. Be aware that feeling so vulnerable and unsafe, it will be easy for you to see other people's comments or looks as hostile, critical, or dangerous. Be aware that they may not wish you any harm and that currently you are vulnerable to misinterpreting people's motives and their feelings toward you.
12. If AGG, ANP, IMP, or DISC are elevated, add: Be mindful that you may impulsively verbally or physically attack people, perhaps feeling that you are protecting yourself. Surges of angry impulses are the result of your condition, and it would be important for you to learn to recognize them and find alternative behaviors as a way of reducing tension.

Behavior /Externalizing Dysfunction (BXD) Scale

General Descriptors

Complaints

Easily frustrated and intolerant of others "getting in their way"; restless and bored; often perceives rules as unfair; feels disconnected from others; often disappointed by others; sees people as unreliable and untrustworthy.

Cognitions

Lack of deliberateness; disavowals of responsibility; focus on obtaining immediate gratification; unmindful of consequences and lacking reflectiveness; conspicuous lack of long-range planning; poor or reckless judgment; lacking self-criticality and self-awareness; thinking "off the top of the head"; non-analytical; concrete thinking; Machiavellian; externalizing blame; conscience deficit and proclivity to selective reporting or lying.

Emotions

Lacks empathy; angry; hostile; affective lability; shallow; superficial; boredom leading to restlessness and stimulation seeking; emotionally disconnected from self and others.

Traits and behaviors

Conflicts with authority figures; superficially charming; irritable and argumentative if confronted; immaturity; avoids responsibility for their actions; unreliable and irresponsible; risk-taking and adventurous; may abuse substances; poor self-discipline and lacking perseverance.

Therapist's Notes – BXD Scale

BXD measures the tendency for an individual to move into impulsive action when stressed. Under stress, high EID scorers turn inward against themselves (intro-punitive) and are anxious, self-critical, passive, and insecure. Under stress, high THD scorers become cognitively disorganized, odd, paranoid, and psychotic. On the other hand, high BXD scorers are almost the exact opposite. They are not inhibited by self-doubt or fragmented, cognitive functioning. They are propelled to action when stressed and can turn against others (extra-punitive). They do not doubt themselves nor are they indecisive.

High BXD scorers may exhibit impulsive tension reduction, aggressive behaviors, self-indulgence, antisocial behavior, manipulativeness, and/or substance abuse. They tend not to introspect, lack self-awareness, are excitable, tend not to experience anxiety, and are forcefully opinionated. Some engaged in bullying as children, suggesting a genetic vulnerability. Most question norms, dislike being controlled, and flagrantly or subtly break the rules. They externalize blame, tend not to learn from their mistakes, and rationalize their acting-out behavior, selectively reporting and even egregiously lying when confronted. They tend to be viewed as self-centered and quick to anger and blame. Their anger can get them into legal troubles and/or interpersonal conflicts.

If SFI, DOM, and/or Cynicism (CYN) are elevated, the individual can manifest aggressive leadership, grandiosity, distrust of others, and Machiavellian tactics to win dominance over others. If Aggressiveness (AGGR), ACT, DISC, RC4 and/or RC9 are elevated, the propensity for unmodulated expressions of aggression increases, especially if current substance abuse is evidenced by elevations on SUB.

Often individuals with elevated BXD scores have a history of juvenile conduct problems. Conflict with family is common during their teen years, with school performance becoming increasingly erratic due to behavior problems and conflicts with authorities. This is especially true if Juvenile Conduct Problems (JCP) and (FML) are elevated. In some cases, bright individuals with high BXD scores, low scores on measures of anxiety and self-doubt, and some control over their impulsive acting-out can achieve success in the corporate world through manipulation and astute political maneuvering. Educated individuals scoring high on BXD but with relatively good impulse control can be very successful in the areas of finance, private equity, and high stakes startups. Some achieve great success, but their businesses may disintegrate due to their poor judgment and sporadic conformity to rules and regulations. Some may eventually have spectacular falls from grace due to lapses of judgment and illegal or immoral acts.

Scores in the 55 to 65 T score range suggest many of the same traits and behaviors described above but exhibited at a less extreme level. These individuals can exhibit impulsivity and a tendency to selectively report, especially in psychotherapy or to their significant others. They can manifest disconstraint under stress. If SUB is elevated, they may binge drink or develop addiction problems. Marriage difficulties and conflicts with business partners are often common and likely reflect the presence of narcissistic tendencies. In high normal elevations of BXD, the Substantive Scales identify the degree of acting-out and the level of dominance and self-importance exhibited. If RC4, RC9, ACT, and AGGR are elevated, even in an individual with a high normal BXD T score, there is an increased likelihood that the above descriptors for elevated BXD also fit for the high normal range.

Lifestyle and Family Background – BXD Scale

Studies have suggested that pathological narcissism and self-indulgent rule-breaking are genetically influenced. Family backgrounds often involved a permissive caregiver and an authoritarian one. The permissive caregiver tended to hide the child's maladaptive behaviors from the authoritarian caregiver until frustrated, and then out of frustration allowed the authoritarian caregiver to punish the child. Overindulgence or emotionally unavailable caregivers can also play a prominent role in the development of BXD characteristics. Clients with elevations on BXD consequently distrust authority figures and feel justified in breaking rules. Bright clients often did well in school early on, but later experienced problems and increasing family conflict due to their impulsiveness, resistance to authority, and possible drug use. This would be especially likely if SUB and JCP are elevated.

Clarifying Scales – BXD Scale

- If EID is elevated, the acting-out associated with BXD elevations is tempered somewhat by anxiety and guilt, but without behavior change. Clients may ruminate and obsess about their decisions and past recklessness, but, as tension builds, they likely would still act-out and then experience temporary guilt and remorse. An example would be a compulsive gambler who struggles to avoid gambling but in a stressful moment impulsively decides to gamble, loses money, feels guilt and remorse, but compulsively does it again. The defense of "doing and undoing" and "repetition compulsion" is often associated with such a combination of scales.
- If THD is elevated, the impulsive, self-indulgent, and self-defeating behavior can be expressed in bizarre and possibly dangerous ways. This is especially true if SFI, DOM, RC4, RC6, RC8, and/or RC9 are elevated, energizing possible psychotic thought processes. As noted earlier, a notorious example is Charles Manson, who was described as a charismatic leader with bizarre revolutionary ideas confabulated with sexual aggression. He led his "family" of upper-class young people on a murderous spree, hoping to start a race war that would lead to a utopian society.
- If ACT, AGGR, and/or DISC are elevated, there is an increase in the potential for aggressive behavior, especially if disinhibition due to substance use is indicated with SUB elevated. In some cases, a client with a high score on BXD might be seeking help or involved in legal proceedings due to reckless poor judgment. If RCd, SUI, and IMP are also elevated because of their current predicament, impulsive self-destructive behavior is possible.

Therapy and Therapeutic Pitfalls – BXD Scale

Typically, individuals with high BXD scores do not seek therapeutic help unless involved in a difficult legal or relationship problem caused by their poor judgment and lack of discipline. They tend to be manipulative of the therapist and tend not to trust, so a therapeutic alliance is difficult initially. Therefore, premature termination of psychotherapy is common as well as "no shows." The therapist is seen as a mistrusted authority figure. Individuals with elevated BXD scores tend to see the world as a "dog-eat-dog" place, so they could view therapy as a way to manipulate the therapist to get what they want. The therapist needs to work hard to avoid getting into a power struggle, since this will replicate the client's past negative experiences with authority figures. With accurate but non-judgmental feedback, the therapist can win the client's trust, especially if they portray some of the client's behaviors and traits as potentially useful but requiring some discipline and self-control. For example, the therapist can highlight the client's high energy, charisma and big-picture thinking as positive attributes, but in need of discipline and self-control to gain personal advantages.

Feedback Statements – BXD Scale

T score ≤38 [if no other scales are elevated and no indications of underreporting]

Your profile suggests that you are a steady, non-impulsive individual who generally avoids reckless behavior. You tend to follow the rules. You are likely a conformist with traditional values. You are thoughtful, reliable, balanced, non-confrontational, not impulsive, and you tend not to be manipulative. You may be overcontrolled and have difficulty initiating activities or responding to challenges.

T score 55–65 [if no other scales are elevated]

Your profile suggests that you are an excitement-seeking individual who dislikes being controlled. You have the capacity to be subtly manipulative by selectively disclosing information. When stress builds, you can be somewhat impulsive.

- If RC4 and RC9 are elevated, add: You are an excitement-seeking, live-in-the-moment individual. When excited or upset, you can be impulsive. At times, your impulsiveness can get you into trouble, and sometimes your vulnerability is you "shoot before you aim." You tend to be a big-picture thinker. You may notice details, but attending to them bores you. You have high energy, which can lead to you becoming impatient with a world that moves more slowly than you. When you are involved in a task, you can become irritable and even angry if people get in your way. People with your profile may overlook an important detail in their drive to get what they want and that can get them into trouble. Because you may become easily bored, you need a high level of excitement in your life, sometimes living on the edge.
- If CYN is elevated, add: You are a person who doesn't trust others easily, although you can be friendly and even charming, and it takes a long time for you to let someone get to know you. You may feel comfortable being manipulative to get what you want since you feel others are only looking out for themselves, so why shouldn't you?
- If ANP is elevated, add: Your high energy and impatience may mean that you get easily impatient and irritated and you may express this in sharp, angry outbursts that can knock people off balance. If AGGR is also elevated, add: If you feel blocked in getting what you want or if you feel controlled or judged, you can have a hot temper that can sometimes spill into aggressive behavior. If you feel authority figures are treating you badly, it is hard for you to control your temper, which can backfire.

T score ≥65

Your profile suggests that you are a highly independent person who dislikes being controlled. You tend not to trust people in authority, and you tend to break rules that you disagree with.

- If DISC, ACT, and/or AGG are elevated, add: Your profile suggests that you can be quite impatient with people and easily angered. You can be charming and likable, but if someone confronts you, it is easy for you to become hostile, even aggressive. When angered, you might do impulsive things to hurt someone without thinking through the consequences.
- If RC4 and RC9 are elevated, add: It is hard for you to stay disciplined and follow through on your commitments. You are likely to get bored and restless easily and, when you stir up excitement, it can lead to bad outcomes because you haven't thought through the consequences. It is hard for you to feel other people's feelings, so people close to you may accuse you of lacking empathy. If you are confronted because of your behavior, you are quick to get angry and explain

why the problem is someone else's fault. Because you don't trust others and you assume most people are playing a game rather than being truthful, you find it easy to tell white lies or to selectively report.

- If SUB is elevated, add: Your profile suggests that you are vulnerable to using alcohol or drugs, perhaps to alleviate boredom or just for fun. Alcohol or drugs may decrease your self-control and lead you to impulsive, even reckless behavior.
- If SFI is elevated, add: Your profile suggests that you think that you have something valuable and special to say or to add to the world. You may seek leadership roles where you tell people your ideas and where you can opine on what you see as the right way of doing things. Others may feel you are being dominating in social situations since you feel driven to express your thoughts and ideas in a forceful way.
- If DOM is elevated, add: Your profile suggests that you like to be in control and that your strong personality can come across as domineering. People may attempt to resist your dominance, leading to conflict and arguments. You feel a strong need to be in control and you become irritated and impatient if you feel controlled by others.
- If EID is elevated, add: Even though you appear confident, opinionated, and you are a risk-taker, your profile also shows you can be bothered by worry and anxiety. You may build up stress over a big decision and, after worrying about it, you impulsively make up your mind – and then worry that you made the wrong decision. You may have some habits that you feel guilty indulging in, but it doesn't change your behavior.
- If THD is elevated, add: Your profile suggests that you can become excited by your ideas and beliefs and feel that others would benefit from you enlightening them. When you are excited or stressed, others may find your thinking hard to follow. If SFI and/or DOM are also elevated, add: You probably feel very confident in your view of things and you are not afraid to speak your mind. Others may see you as domineering. They may feel some of your ideas are too eccentric, even frightening, which probably incites you to argue with them to show you are right.

Lifestyle and Family Background Feedback – BXD Scale

People with your profile often grew up in environments where a parental figure was dominating, demanding, and controlling. This likely left you feeling unfairly treated or somehow violated. One or both caregivers may have been inconsistent in showing love and nurturance. From an early age you learned to be manipulative and even lied to cope with your family environment. Consequently, you may feel like you are a survivor of your childhood. This likely led to your becoming cautious about trusting authority figures and people in general, and you have to be convinced by them that they are trustworthy. In some cases, with test results like yours, one caregiver was lenient while the other was strict and punitive. The lenient caregiver may have tried to protect you from harsh punishments but inadvertently allowed you to get away with aggressive and manipulative behavior. One way you may have learned to deal with your family turmoil was to numb yourself to avoid feeling pain.

- If CYN is elevated, add: You probably see the world as a "dog-eat-dog" place where you feel a need to be the "top dog." When confronted or controlled, you can become angry and defensive. You likely see people as selfish and looking out for themselves, so you feel justified looking out for yourself.
- If JCP is elevated, add: As a teen you may have gotten into conflicts with authority and developed problems in school because of a lack of discipline and boredom with some subjects.
- If IMP is elevated, add: You may have been diagnosed with attention deficit disorder (ADD) or attention deficit hyperactivity disorder (ADHD) because you found it hard to stay focused on a topic you didn't find interesting.

Treatment and Self-Help Suggestions – BXD Scale

1. Impulsivity is a tendency to act without thinking about consequences. Spontaneity differs from impulsiveness because it does not cause negative results. People with your profile have several strengths. You are independent and a risk-taker. You are not afraid to try new things. You can be fun and exciting to be around. However, you could benefit from learning to manage your energy and excitability. Impulsivity sometimes leads to your overlooking details that can upend you. For example, if you grow frustrated with a project, you may suddenly quit working on it or even resign from an employment position. When you feel a surge of excitement with a new idea or a surge of anger that makes you want to move into action, take a moment, observe the impulse but don't immediately act on it. Consider talking to someone whom you trust for advice before making an important decision. Take a couple of deep breaths and calmly consider your possible responses. Impulsive behavior can have consequences that are hard to undo. Consider discussing with your therapist if certain medications can help control your impulsive behaviors.
2. Because of your childhood, when you felt you had to be a survivor relying on your own wits to protect yourself, you developed a distrust of people. Consequently, you feel that people are not trustworthy, and they play mind games to try to take advantage of you. In fact, consider that many people *are* trustworthy and not trying to take advantage of you. Remember, over time your behavior is transparent, so avoid selectively reporting or outright lying as a way to get what you want.
3. If ANP and/or AGGR are elevated: Your profile suggests that you have a quick trigger and can easily get angry or blow up. Your anger can get you into trouble with co-workers and life partners. Anger management classes could help you identify the triggers that make you blow up and give you alternate ways to blow off steam.
4. If SUB is elevated: You may be using substances as a way to relax or numb yourself. Stimulant drugs could make you more volatile, impulsive, and suspicious of others. Alcohol may increase the chances of your temper erupting, and depressants may make you lethargic and unproductive. Talk to your therapist to see if an addiction treatment program is right for you.
5. If SFI and DOM are elevated: You are a big personality and not afraid to take center stage and express your opinions. However, people may see you as too intense and dominant. In conversations with others, remain mindful of their reactions. Try not to interrupt them while they are speaking. Watch to see if they are trying to jump in and say something during your conversation. If they are looking away while you are talking, you have lost their attention, so stop talking and ask for their thoughts. Listening carefully before responding is an important skill that will serve you well.
6. Be aware you can come across as selfish and demanding. Consider taking a sensitivity class to develop a sense of empathy for others. If a partner is expressing feelings of frustration or hurt, don't defend yourself until you have heard them out. Try to put yourself in their shoes. Try to feel what they are feeling rather than trying to persuade them that their feelings are "wrong," or your behavior couldn't have caused them pain.

4 Restructured Clinical (RC) Scales

Introduction

Development

The Restructured Clinical (RC) Scales (Tellegen et al., 2003) were developed for the MMPI-2 to address psychometric limitations of the original MMPI clinical scales. Specifically, the original MMPI clinical scales were excessively correlated with each other, which substantially limited their discriminant validity. These excessive correlations were the result of two factors. First, there was considerable item overlap among the scales, which introduced correlated measurement error into the correlations among them. The second factor was an unintended consequence of the empirical keying method used to construct the clinical scales. The MMPI authors selected items for the original clinical scales by contrasting the responses of a sample of non-patients with those of eight inpatient groups corresponding to the diagnostic categories they sought to assess. Consequently, some of the items selected for each scale were specific to the targeted disorder whereas others generally differentiated between psychiatric inpatients and a non-patient sample. Tellegen et al. (2003) labeled this general factor Demoralization. The RC Scales were intended to measure a major distinctive component of each clinical scale, distinctive from demoralization and from the major distinctive components of the other scales. For the reader interested in the rationale for and methods used to develop the RC Scales, detailed coverage is provided in several sources, including Tellegen et al. (2003); Friedman et al. (2015); Ben-Porath and Tellegen (2020a, 2020b); and Ben-Porath and Sellbom (2023).

In addition to excessive correlations among them, the original clinical scales were also limited by internal heterogeneity. Thus, though the RC Scales assess major distinctive core components of the RC Scales, they do not cover all the content domains of the original clinical scales, or for that matter the entire MMPI-2 item pool. When developing the MMPI-2-RF (Ben-Porath & Tellegen, 2008/2011a, 2008/2011b), the authors sought to augment the RC Scales with measures needed to assess the broader array of constructs that could be reliably and validly assessed with the MMPI-2 item pool, resulting in the Higher-Order (H-O), Specific Problems (SP), and Personality Psychopathology Five (PSY-5) Scales discussed in other chapters of this book.

The MMPI-2-RF was comprised of 338 of the 567 MMPI-2 items and standardized using the MMPI-2 normative sample. The primary objective for the MMPI-3 was to introduce new item content and collect new norms for the test. An important secondary goal was for users to be able to rely on the MMPI-2-RF literature (over 600 peer-reviewed studies as of this writing) when using the MMPI-3. Updating the RC Scales for the MMPI-3 entailed deletion of items deemed to be unnecessary for maintaining their empirical correlates while adding new items that could enhance their convergent validity. Details are provided by Ben-Porath and Tellegen (2020b) in the *MMPI-3 Technical Manual*.

DOI: 10.4324/9781003557920-4

Application

RC Scale interpretation is an essential component of understanding an MMPI-3 protocol, as these scales indicate some of the core clinical features of the test-taker. The framework for interpreting these scales is described in detail by Ben-Porath and Sellbom (2023). A summary of this approach follows.

Prior to inspecting the RC Scales, protocol validity must first be established by examining the following scales for (1) evidence of content non-responsiveness: Cannot Say (CNS), Combined Response Inconsistency (CRIN), Variable Response Inconsistency (VRIN), and True Response Inconsistency (TRIN); and (2) content-based invalid responding: (i) overreporting: Infrequent Responses (F), Infrequent Psychopathology Responses (Fp), Infrequent Somatic Responses (Fs), Symptom Validity Scale (FBS), and Response Bias Scale (RBS); and (ii) underreporting: Uncommon Virtues (L) and Adjustment Validity (K). After the validity of the protocol is established (see Chapter 2), inspection of the MMPI-3 H-O Scales (Chapter 3) points the user to the general or overarching psychological constructs pertinent to the test-taker. Specifically, the H-O Scales (Emotional/Internalizing Dysfunction (EID), Thought Dysfunction (THD), and Behavioral/Externalizing Dysfunction (BXD)) serve as a compass for pointing out the likely psychological problem areas that can then be more specifically understood by examining the RC Scales.

Interpretation of the RC Scales will be refined by examining the SP Scales that consist of the Somatic/Cognitive Scales, Internalizing Scales, Externalizing Scales, and Interpersonal Scales, as well as the PSY-5 Scales (covered in subsequent chapters of this book).

While one or more elevated RC Scales likely reflect the cardinal psychological features of the individual's functioning/distress, multiple RC elevations can best be understood by examining the Substantive Scales. The case examples in Chapter 10 illustrate this interpretive approach using the MMPI-3 Interpretation Worksheet.

Demoralization (RCd) Scale

General Descriptors

Complaints

Feeling worthless, hopeless, useless, unhappy, insecure, and that life is a strain; feeling on edge; feeling lonely and isolated; sleep and appetite problems; decreased energy; concentration problems; generalized anxiety; empty and emotionally disconnected from life; low self-esteem; self-critical; lacking in confidence.

Cognitions

Negative self-talk; hopelessness; despair; possible suicidal ideation if Suicidal/Death Ideation (SUI) and/or Helplessness/Hopelessness (HLP) are elevated; thoughts of being incapable of dealing with current life circumstances; pessimistic.

Emotions

Dysphoric affect; anxious; distraught; emotionally depleted; easily overwhelmed; rarely happy.

Traits and behaviors

Low frustration tolerance; self-critical.

Therapist's Notes – RCd Scale

This 17-item scale is a general measure of a client's psychological temperature regarding their sense of wellbeing. It measures a client's experience of feeling defeated, helpless, and hopeless about ameliorating their current distress. Elevated Demoralization (RCd) scores indicate that a person feels worthless, useless, and that life is a strain most of the time. They have lost their confidence in things getting better. While RCd is correlated with the Low Positive Emotions (RC2) Scale and does, therefore, reflect some depressive symptoms such as dysphoria and emotional depletion, it is different from RC2 in that it often arises from specific circumstances and can ameliorate once the situation has resolved. High scorers lack current ego strength and self-esteem, which may be an artifact of living with a chronic mental or physical illness that has not been successfully treated. It assesses an individual's despair about their ability to alleviate their mental and/or physical condition. This demoralization can occur due to various factors, such as prolonged stress, continuous setbacks, or intractable mental or physical problems.

High scorers feel overwhelmed, unhappy, and feel their life is going badly and that they are on the wrong track. They feel pessimistic about their future and are unable to manage their current stress. Lacking the capacity to organize efficiently under stress, they report giving up easily when faced with obstacles. They may exhibit symptoms associated with depression, such as suicidal rumination if SUI and/or HLP are elevated.

RC2 and RCd measure different constructs, namely dysphoria and anhedonia, respectively. It is possible for someone to score high on RCd and THD, for example, but not significantly high on RC2 – reflecting that RCd is measuring feelings of despair associated with different psychological conditions, not just depression. It is intuitively understandable that many mental conditions would lead to demoralization, especially if chronic in nature. Consequently, low scores on RCd could be significant if, for example, an individual scored high on THD as well as Ideas of Persecution (RC6) and Aberrant Experiences (RC8), since it would suggest that the current thought disorder is ego syntonic, or that the individual has accepted their condition.

Elevations on RCd and other Substantive Scales provide insight into the particular dysfunction that may be causing the individual to feel demoralized. If, for example, Neurological Complaints (NUC) and Cognitive Complaints (COG) are elevated with RCd, it would suggest that neurological cognitive issues or concerns had worn the individual out, leaving them feeling hopeless and defeated. The same would be true if Eating Concerns (EAT) was elevated, suggesting possible demoralization related to an eating disorder.

Scores <39 suggest a person who feels competent and confident, experiencing a relatively high level of life satisfaction. If there are elevations on other Substantive Scales with low scores on RCd, the individual is reporting various symptoms and problematic behaviors, but they do not feel defeated and demoralized by them. In a valid profile with no significant elevations, low scores suggest good ego strength, emotional resilience, and higher than average level of morale.

Scores in the 55–64 range reflect occasional feelings of defeat and low self-confidence and periods when situational factors make the individual feel blue. If BXD or scales measuring impulsive or aggressive behavior are elevated, moderate scores on RCd could be due to recent negative consequences from acting-out. Remorse and self-criticism, perhaps following a period of significant acting-out, would be an example. If RCd is elevated in this high normal range and/or Worry (WRY), Anxiety-Related Experiences (ARX), and Behavior-Restricting Fears (BRF) are also elevated, the individual's worrying and anxiety are perhaps leading to concerns about being able to manage them.

Scores in the 65–73 range indicate a person who is feeling sad, unhappy, and dissatisfied with his/her current life circumstances.

Scores at ≥74 strongly suggest significant demoralization, extreme unhappiness, and life dissatisfaction. There may be overwhelming feelings leading to suicidal ideation and/or attempts, especially if SUI and/or HLP are elevated. In this case, a risk assessment for self-harm should be conducted.

Lifestyle and Family Background – RCd Scale

High scores could be associated with a lifestyle that lacks joyful experiences. In the presence of a history of adverse childhood experiences, high scores could reflect a loss of hope due to a life of intractable emotional problems and a lack of stable nurturing parental figures coupled with current adverse events that restimulated past emotional scar tissue.

Clarifying Scales – RCd Scale

Any scale could be elevated with the RCd Scale. The MMPI-3 measures various problem areas (different kinds of distress and behavioral dysfunctions), all of which may lead to demoralization. The specific scale elevation will inform what psychopathology is associated with demoralization. For example, a chronic eating disorder (EAT), a vague but painful or disturbing neurological/ cognitive disorder (NUC and/or COG), chronic social isolation (Social Avoidance (SAV), Shyness (SHY), Disaffiliativeness (DSF)), or negative consequences from acting-out (Impulsivity (IMP), Disconstraint (DISC)) can lead to feeling blue, hopeless, and demoralized.

Therapy and Therapeutic Pitfalls – RCd Scale

The therapist's primary task is to restore morale, hope, meaning, and purpose, and to improve coping. If Somatic Complaints (RC1) is elevated, addressing physical symptom burden can improve morale, helplessness, and coping. Treating comorbid psychiatric disorders such as depressive and anxiety disorders and specific problem areas such as eating disorders or family problems is essential. Psychotherapy is a key intervention for demoralization. Mild demoralization can be addressed with empathic listening and supportive psychotherapy. Clients with moderate to severe demoralization in the presence of a severe physical or mental illness may benefit from referral to targeted interventions such as meaning-centered psychotherapy and dignity therapy. Meaning-centered psychotherapy can be delivered in individual or group format and strives to enhance purpose, spiritual wellbeing, and quality of life.

Allying with the client about how their despair and gloom is understandable given their current situation would be important in therapeutic alliance-building. Also important, if possible, would be coaching ways in which family, friends, or other forms of social support could be mobilized. Psychotropic medication is not typically helpful unless RC2 and/or anxiety measures are also elevated.

Narrative therapy can be useful to help the individual see their current condition as potentially temporary and reframe their negative experiences into stories of hope and resilience. Cognitive behavioral therapy, acceptance and commitment therapy, and/or other supportive therapies could be useful. The therapist needs to guard against their own impatience as the client's demoralization can feel annoyingly negative.

Feedback Statements – RCd Scale

T score ≤39

Your score suggests a higher-than-average level of morale and life satisfaction. You tested as resilient and hopeful, accepting life's challenges without feeling defeated or demoralized. If you are going through any psychological difficulties currently, they do not appear to be knocking you off balance. You feel in control of your life and feel up to handling the stressors facing you.

T score 65–73

Currently you are feeling somewhat down, sad, unhappy, and discouraged. You likely feel dissatisfied with your current life circumstances. Perhaps you feel that your current situation is hard to manage and wonder if you are up to the task of dealing with things. You may feel uncertain about whether you can feel better and uncertain about what to do to get better. At times you may even feel defeated and hopeless. There is probably a good reason for your feelings but remember it is possible that, with help and over time, you are going to feel better.

T score ≥74

Your score reveals that currently you are feeling down, sad, depressed, and demoralized. You are likely feeling defeated, hopeless, and unsure how to escape your current situation. You may have periods when you feel a sense of despair and when you feel incapable of changing your feelings and reducing your suffering.

- If SUI and/or HLP are elevated, add: At times, things may feel so bleak and hopeless you think about dying to escape the pain. You might even think about suicide and how to do it, especially if you have some unforeseen increase in stress or bad news. It is important to discuss this with your therapist so you can develop a plan to have support in a crisis.
- If HLP is elevated, add: Right now, it is hard for you to see how the future could be more positive since your situation feels so bleak and hopeless. It is hard for you to look forward to much since you feel so pessimistic and certain that whatever you try to do to feel better will fail. Most people, when they feel hopeless and helpless, find that even small frustrations can overload them, leading to irritability and even anger.
- If Anger Proneness (ANP), Stress (STR), and/or DSF are elevated, add: When you feel worn out and demoralized, people's rudeness, lack of caring, or demandingness can outrage you, leading to episodic angry outbursts.
- If STR is elevated, add: Since you already feel overwhelmed, new stress can be the "last straw" leading you to respond by withdrawing, shutting down emotionally, and being passive. Even if people suggest things they think can be helpful, it is hard for you to take advice since you feel hopeless.
- If EID, Negative Emotionality/Neuroticism (NEGE), Self-Doubt (SFD), and/or Family Problems (FML) are elevated, add: You are likely your own worst critic. You doubt your ability to make your life better, and you feel that others look unfavorably at you. You seem to have lost confidence in yourself, so you give up easily when things get difficult. You feel you are a burden to others.
- If COG is elevated, add: Currently it may be hard to focus and concentrate, so important details may fall through the cracks. You may experience periods of brain fog, a feeling that is similar to jet lag or being sleep deprived.
- If Inefficacy (NFC) is elevated, add: You feel incapable of dealing with current life circumstances. Even small demands or stressors can leave you feeling overwhelmed and unable to make decisions and problem-solve effectively.
- If WRY is elevated, add: You may find yourself constantly worried and preoccupied with a feeling that something bad is about to happen. You may find yourself fretting about some issue but unable to find a solution. You may avoid doing things that in the past you found rewarding or challenging because you doubt yourself.

Lifestyle and Family Background Feedback – RCd Scale

Your current sense of demoralization and despair is probably tied to some specific problems that have left you feeling defeated. This may be due to recent events, but it is also possible that you suffered adverse experiences in childhood where you often felt helpless, trapped, and alone. Your current feelings may be due to recent events that have robbed you of your self-confidence. People close to you may have difficulty understanding why you get so pessimistic and negative about things getting better, but you probably feel you have tried everything you know to feel better, and it has not worked. Explore with your therapist the disappointments you have experienced when unsuccessfully trying to feel better.

Treatment and Self-Help Suggestions – RCd Scale

Your therapist will likely take a full history to see if you experienced adverse childhood events that made you more vulnerable to feeling defeated and hopeless when negative events happen in your adulthood. It will be important to examine your history to see your life in perspective with a focus on things you have done well and how some things in your life have gone well, so that you don't have to be so self-critical. Cognitive behavior therapy could be helpful to identify when you have negative self-talk and when you feel defeated and give up. Even when things are beginning to get better, it is likely hard for you to trust that good things can continue.

1. With the help of your therapist, identify one behavior that you want to change or one task you want to get accomplished and force yourself to do it. It doesn't have to be a big task or change. For example, go for a walk in nature and take a few moments to look at trees, plants, or some geographical feature to remind yourself that there is a world that is apart from your suffering and the inner noise of your despair. Notice when your inner voice is being self-critical or self-doubting and try to balance those thoughts with a reminder of the things you have done well or the people of importance to you.
2. If RC2 is elevated, add: You are feeling depressed as well as defeated and you are likely having trouble sleeping, concentrating, and effectively problem-solving. Your therapist may refer you for a medication evaluation that could help you with some of these symptoms of depression.
3. Keep a gratitude diary where you can write down one small thing that you are grateful for. It doesn't have to be anything big, just a reminder that life is not completely hopeless and negative.
4. Join a community group so you do not feel so alone. Sometimes volunteering for people who are less fortunate than you can help bring some perspective to your life and make you feel important and feel better that you are contributing.
5. If HLP or SUI are elevated, add: Make a list of reasons why life is worth living and remind yourself of those reasons. If you feel hopeless and suicidal and cannot reach your therapist, call a suicide and crisis hotline [988 in the United States and Canada] for confidential support.

Somatic Complaints (RC1) Scale

General Descriptors

Complaints

Preoccupied with physical health concerns; range of somatic symptoms; perceives physical problems as life-interfering; possible low sex drive; pain; fatigue; decreased quality of life.

Cognitions

Fear of illness and dying; pessimistic; critical of others; preoccupation with physical health concerns.

Emotions

Possible depression and anxiety; dissatisfaction; irritability.

Traits and behaviors

Demanding; stubborn; complaining; rejects psychological interpretation of somatic complaints; prone to developing physical symptoms under stress.

Therapist's Notes – RC1 Scale

The RC1 21-item scale is intended to identify individuals presenting with an unusually large number and variety of somatic complaints that, as a whole, are medically unexplained. The scale is sensitive to somatoform symptomatology without being specific to any one condition. RC1 elevations can be observed in those with anxiety disorders, somatic delusions, and other psychological conditions with physiological symptoms. The content coverage of the scale includes gastrointestinal (GI) symptoms, neurological complaints (such as headaches or dizziness), and general pain. In essence, RC1 is a measure of somatoform psychopathology.

Low scores on RC1 (T score 42 and below) likely reflect an individual who reports a sense of physical wellbeing. They may take their health for granted and be sanguine about their physical health. Individuals with elevations on RC1 with a T score of 42-62 may be health conscious and mindful of their physical wellbeing. However, as scores elevate, expect increasing fears of bodily harm, physical illness, and pain. Individuals with significant elevations on RC1 experience physical sensations as frightening because they fear that they may signal the onset of some disease or physical breakdown. Psychological stress leads to an increase in symptoms, which then becomes a consuming focus. They are often seen as lacking in insight because internal conflicts and external stressors tend to be reduced to physical preoccupations. Their somatic focus tends to shift and change and be shaped by the medical personnel whose attention they frequently seek. Individuals with only elevations on RC1 often have few other complaints except those centered on physical illness and infirmity.

Persevering and stubborn about seeking medical help, these clients' symptoms can be shaped and aggravated by their encounters with the medical system. They tend to "doctor shop," depending on their current somatic focus. These clients are often referred to different medical specialists who conduct numerous medical tests, often without identifying a specific cause for their somatic complaints. In other situations, years of repression, inhibition, and denial lead to actual physical deterioration. However, their level of preoccupation and concern, even in the presence of real physical illness, is often exaggerated, as it provides a focus for their psychological conflicts. In some cases, bona fide medical conditions will contribute to elevations on RC1, but typically there is a psychological component whenever RC1 is at a T score of 65 and above. Clients in this RC1 range tend to be perceived as quite dependent, demanding, and seeking to have others take care of them. Apart from their physical concerns, they can appear almost emotionally bland and even cheerful, reflecting their denial and a lack of psychological insight.

Levak's hypothesis (Levak et al., 2011) associated with RC1 elevations is that these clients are terrified of bodily damage. They experience little pleasure from their bodies, living with a sense of dread that, at any moment, physical symptoms will increase in severity or that they will be plagued by some new physical infirmity. Female clients with high scores may report histories of physical and/or sexual abuse and suicide attempts. Both male and female clients may report symptoms of anxiety.

Lifestyle and Family Background – RC1 Scale

Clients with elevated RC1 scores may have experienced a recent traumatic event or illness that has induced a state of panic and preoccupation with physical symptoms. In other cases, somatic preoccupation is associated with early childhood illnesses, either in the client or in significant family members. They learned from an early age to fear physical infirmity and may have experienced significant losses associated with illness. In other cases, these clients may have experienced a recent physical trauma, which has stimulated their panic about physical infirmity. A recent trauma in the absence of a history of somatic preoccupations would suggest a reactive disorder. Psychologists working with disability claimants may have difficulty determining the contribution of recent traumatic events versus that of a longstanding personality style. A comprehensive history will help in determining the relative strength of these factors and their effects on somatic preoccupation.

Clarifying Scales – RC1 Scale

The 21 items on RC1 are face valid (as are the items on Malaise (MLS), NUC, EAT, COG), so some of these Specific Problems Scales are typically also elevated, with RC1 clarifying the type of somatic involvement. In some cases, the complaints are focused only on a specific set of somatic symptoms.

- If the RC2 and RCd Scales (and scales measuring anxiety and worry, such as Dysfunctional Negative Emotions (RC7), WRY, ARX, SHY, and/or NEGE) are elevated, clients will express depression, fears, and anxieties about their physical condition. They may complain of dizziness and stomach issues. Elective surgery should be carefully considered since these individuals tend to experience numerous side effects and recovery is slow.
- If ANP is elevated, individuals are typically demanding and irritable due to physical concerns and possibly compromised energy and efficiency.
- If BRF and/or ARX are elevated, fears and phobias, perhaps centered around avoiding germs, physical harm, and disease, are likely. A generalized anxiety disorder may be present, although the focus is on physical infirmity.
- If MLS is elevated, complaints of poor health, exhaustion, or feeling weak physically and incapacitated are common.
- If NUC is elevated, complaints of vague neurological symptoms such as light-headedness, vision problems, speech problems, and numbness in the extremities add to the other somatic complaints.

- If EAT is elevated, concerns about being overweight, eating, and dieting are added to preoccupations about physical illness.
- If COG is elevated, the somatoform complaints would include anxiety about, for example: "What is wrong with my mind?"; "Do I have a brain tumor?"; "Why is my memory so bad?"; "I can't focus and read like I used to."
- If HLP is elevated, the test-taker is expressing a loss of hope that things will ever change, and that they will be physically pain- or symptom-free.
- If SUI and/or HLP are elevated, be aware that the client may feel hopeless that their physical issues will be solved. A suicide evaluation is recommended.

Therapy and Therapeutic Pitfalls – RC1 Scale

Levak's hypothesis (Levak et al., 2011) is that a somatic preoccupation can be seen as an adaptive response to past actual or feared experiences of bodily damage in the client or a close family member. The goal of therapy would be to desensitize the traumatic events through various cognitive-behavioral techniques. Reassure the client that their somatic worries will be taken seriously, as they likely have had some negative experiences with the medical system telling them their worries are "in their head." Clients with RC1 elevations are very focused on physical symptoms, so they are vulnerable to becoming anxious and preoccupied about side effects and the effectiveness of medications. Anti-anxiety medications are useful initially if panic about physical infirmity is the presenting problem. The immediate relief that medication provides could aid in helping the client realize that anxiety is a core component of their disorder. They are highly suggestible, so changes in physical sensation tend to be upsetting to them. Since anxiety tends to increase the experience of pain, relaxation training and meditation can help alleviate some of the somatic preoccupation. Once a therapeutic alliance has been established, hypnosis can be useful, not only for deep relaxation but to highlight the body-mind connection.

Attempts to nudge a client to shift their focus of attention away from physical symptoms to other conflicts in their life tend to be met with resistance. Not focusing on their physical problems creates concern in them that others do not understand their physical infirmity. Losing this focus increases their fear that they will be overwhelmed by pain and physical decline and have no one to turn to. Developing a therapeutic alliance involves initially "going with the resistance": helping the client organize their medical treatment to avoid repeating numerous medical tests and to help rule out various disorders. Cognitive-behavioral techniques to alleviate anxiety have received empirical support and can be used in conjunction with psychoeducation to inform the client about how anxiety in their lives may be related to an increase in physical symptoms.

In some cases where there has been a traumatic event(s), stress inoculation training and exposure therapy can help build coping skills. In the presence of early childhood illnesses in a client or their family, the re-engagement of early traumas followed by relaxation training and emotional catharsis can be useful for long-term healing. The goal of long-term therapy is to establish the link between stress and physical symptoms and resulting anxiety. Help the client realize that increased physical symptoms are associated with inner conflicts and anxieties. It is important to validate their physical symptoms as real but also to identify which stressors lead to increases in physical symptoms and to help them develop better coping strategies. These clients are prone to dependency, yet highly resistant to being controlled, especially if Antisocial Behavior (RC4) is elevated.

Gestalt therapies can be useful. Getting clients to have their symptoms "do the talking" could provide a concrete, effective way to express repressed emotions. For example, someone with severe and constant stomach upsets could be asked, "If your stomach had a voice, what would it say right now?" In another Gestalt exercise, clients might be asked, "If you could paint a picture of what your stomach felt like right now, what would the picture look like?" This would allow some emotional engagement and catharsis.

Prolonged psychological stress can lead to physical breakdown in some people and untangling the contribution of psychological and organic factors in their contribution to RC1 elevations is difficult. If RC2 and RCd are elevated, consider a referral for a medication evaluation.

Feedback Statements – RC1 Scale

T score ≤42

Your profile shows that you tend not to worry about physical illness and injury, and you treat physical problems lightly. You may ignore a physical issue, even feeling angry with your body because it has let you down. You may be cavalier about taking care of yourself and you might enjoy physical activity that others see as potentially risky.

T score 46–52

You take care of yourself physically when things go wrong and take care of any illnesses you may have responsibly.

T score 55–62

Your profile shows that you are a health-conscious person who is mindful of your physical wellbeing. You ensure that your illnesses are well taken care of, and you are cautious about taking too many physical risks. You or someone close to you may have had a recent illness, which has made you focus on the importance of physical wellbeing.

T score ≥65

Currently, you are very preoccupied with your physical health and perhaps terrified that something is wrong with you and that others are not taking your symptoms seriously enough. You may find yourself worried about different physical sensations and concerned that they are indicating a severe disease or disorder. Your profile suggests that you may experience vague and shifting pain. When you feel pain, you may fear that it is indicating a severe and deteriorating condition.

In some cases, people with your profile complain of pain in a specific area of their body. In other cases, the pain seems to shift and move around their body, which can be experienced as frightening. You may experience numerous physical symptoms that seem to come and go so it can be hard for your doctor to diagnose what the problem is. Sometimes the pain in one area seems to migrate to another and at other times you experience headaches, stomach upsets, and pain in different parts of your body. Not knowing what is wrong likely causes you much worry and frustration.

People with your profile often experience periods of fatigue, exhaustion, and depletion. Being preoccupied with your body and terrified that something is wrong with you may sap your energy and leave you feeling ill-equipped for the everyday demands of life. People who experience physical illness or who have serious physical concerns tend to have little patience. People may see you as irritable and intolerant. Living with a sense of dread that something is wrong with you understandably gives you little cushioning against stress.

People with your profile may experience low interest in sexual activity. It is challenging to enjoy sex if you are worried about your physical wellbeing. It may be that you experience pain during sex, or perhaps you just lack interest given how poorly you have been feeling.

When people are afraid, they tend to get quite inflexible about doing things a certain way. Anything that takes away the fear and anxiety and gives you some relief will quickly feel essential to you. You may develop some rigid habits, compulsions, and obsessions, especially if they provide you with some relief. You may also be critical of others, especially doctors or people involved in your medical treatment. You may be particularly sensitive to how people are treating you and quick to be critical of them because they do not provide you with enough comfort and relief.

Living with a constant sense of dread about your body and illness is likely leaving you unhappy. While you may not complain of general depression, your unhappiness will be centered upon your physical problems. Even though you may want to be optimistic and positive, you tend to worry that your illness will not get better. Others may see you as pessimistic and negative. Perhaps you are afraid to be positive because you have been disappointed in the past.

People with your profile tend not to express anger easily. When people frustrate you, tension may cause an increase in your physical symptoms. Other people may judge your physical problems as an expression of anger or resentment toward them. This is especially true if your physical problems lead you to cancel events or prevent you from doing things that others want you to do. It is hard for you to express conflict directly. You may worry that expressing anger toward loved ones could lead them to ignore or even abandon you when you are in pain.

Because you are so preoccupied with your body and physical symptoms, others may judge you as self-centered and selfish. They may see you as avoiding responsibility by claiming to feel poorly. It is hard not to be self-centered when you are concerned that something is wrong with you and when you are afraid that physical exertion will lead to a deterioration of your condition. Wanting to make sure that those around you are available to help is understandable when you are frightened of illness or even death. Others may see you as quite demanding. It makes sense that you would want to be taken care of when you are feeling badly.

People may judge you as querulous because of your numerous physical symptoms. Often, people with your profile spend a great deal of time trying to find a diagnosis or cure. Over time, people around you may become impatient with you and define you as difficult. This is probably upsetting and leaves you feeling hurt and resentful.

Dealing with the medical system is often difficult. Because of your fears about your physical condition, you may have learned numerous ways to manipulate the system so you can be better cared for. You may find yourself having to control those around you to provide you with resources to help you feel better. Others, however, may complain and refuse some of your requests and demands – which is frightening to you. They may feel manipulated and perhaps don't fully understand how frightening it is to feel ill and not be sure how to get better.

- If RC2 is elevated, add: Your concerns about your health and the discomfort you feel due to your medical problems make it difficult for you to feel pleasure of any kind. You probably feel that your low mood is mostly due to your physical problems and that it would go away if only you could feel better.
- If MLS is elevated, add: You are currently feeling exhausted, weak, and unable to tackle the stressors in your life. You feel you have difficulty managing daily life.
- If COG is elevated, add: You may be experiencing difficulties with memory and concentration and feel you have brain fog, so making even small decisions and solving problems is very difficult.
- If RC8 is elevated, add: You may be concerned that your physical symptoms are due to someone trying to hurt you or that you have been invaded with germs or radiation from an enemy source. You may feel that you are ill because you are a bad person and deserve to be ill.

- If EAT is elevated, add: You appear to be very focused on your eating and diet, perhaps thinking that controlling your food intake will help you feel better or look better. You may be following a rigid diet hoping to control how you feel.

Lifestyle and Family Background Feedback – RC1 Scale

Your profile suggests that much of your life is preoccupied with your physical health. You worry about the symptoms you are experiencing and worry because doctors don't seem to have a clear diagnosis of what's wrong with you. Your symptoms appear to come and go and shift around your body. When you are stressed, they likely get worse. Typically, people develop this preoccupation with their physical health due to a recent illness that was frightening. It is also possible that you grew up in an environment where a caregiver or someone close to you was very sick. Perhaps you were a sickly child with a number of different physical problems that were frightening. In other cases, people with this profile had caregivers or siblings who were sick, and it may have frightened them as a child. Consequently, when you have physical symptoms, you experience heightened anxiety and more fearfulness than you might have, had you not experienced early physical traumatic experiences.

Treatment and Self-Help Suggestions – RC1 Scale

1. Keep a diary of your physical symptoms to see if they increase when you are stressed or if they change over the course of a day. See if you can link the change in your physical symptoms to anything that happens during the day or to your inner feelings. While your physical symptoms are real, they may be aggravated by stress. Understanding how stress aggravates your physical condition could help you learn how to control it.
2. Even though you may resist physical activity and may be unable to be very active, some form of daily exercise is important in helping you heal. Together with your medical doctor, create a program of acceptable physical exercises that can help you deal with stress.
3. Learn to visualize relaxing and peaceful moments and situations so that you can relax your whole body on a daily basis. Tension can aggravate any kind of physical ailment. [If NUC is elevated, add:] When you experience neurological symptoms like numbness, tingling in your extremities or other vague and shifting symptoms, take a few minutes to meditate or breathe deeply and notice if the symptoms get better.
4. If you are able to stretch, do some of kind of yoga that doesn't increase your pain. Meditating can also help promote physical and emotional healing.
5. Create a daily diary of the various stresses that you experience to discuss with your therapist regarding the relationship between those stresses and your physical symptoms.
6. Discuss with your therapist whether biofeedback (a type of therapy used to help control physical responses to stress) might be helpful for you. By using equipment that gives you visual feedback, you receive information about tensing or relaxing various areas of your body, which, with practice, helps to control pain.
7. If EAT is elevated, add: Notice when you begin to think about food and when you begin to fight the impulse to either restrict eating or binge and purge. Identify what is stressing you so you can address the stress with countermeasures to help you not focus on eating.

Low Positive Emotions (RC2) Scale

General Descriptors

Complaints

Difficulty experiencing pleasure; sadness; possible anxiety; sleep or eating disturbance; possible concerns over poor health; low energy; difficulty starting to do things; problems with attention, concentration, and memory; weight change; social detachment.

Cognitions

Loss of interest; hopelessness; pessimistic; guilty; self-deprecating; feeling worthless; worrying; nervous; thoughts of death or suicide; indecisive.

Emotions

Anhedonia; depressed and sad; hopeless; overwhelmed.

Traits and behaviors

Depressive mood symptoms; socially introverted and withdrawn; possibly tense; insecure; low motivation; lacking confidence in one's abilities; indecisive; conflict avoidant; suicidal attempts or gestures.

Therapist's Notes – RC2 Scale

The RC2 Scale consists of 14 items. A lack of positive emotions is a distinctive core component of RC2. Deriving little or no pleasure (anhedonia) in one's relationships and/or activities, while not always present in depression, does suggest with its presence a clearer biological origin, making it potentially more responsive to antidepressant medication. RC2 is correlated with depressive mood symptoms in a wide domain of settings and populations. Non-specific markers include decreased appetite, sleep hygiene problems, concentration and memory issues, low energy and motivation, suicidal ideation, low self-worth, and hopelessness. RC2 elevations can also be found in individuals with non-depression-related conditions. For example, anhedonia is a negative symptom of schizophrenia.

RC2 below T score 39 suggests an individual who experiences a broad range of positive emotions. They tend to be optimistic, not look backward with regrets, and they don't "cry over spilled milk." They may well have a sense of humor, which is often diminished with depression. Confident and energetic, when setbacks occur, they tend to be viewed realistically and don't lead to a collapse in self-esteem. In the presence of a history of resiliency, the low RC2 score could reflect a genetic predisposition for hardiness.

RC2 scores in the normal range (T score 55–64) reflect thoughtful, circumspect individuals who take their responsibilities and life in general seriously. They are not risk-takers (unless RC4 and/or IMP, ACT, or DISC are elevated), and they tend to worry. When things go wrong, they are guilt-prone and can occasionally lose sleep when faced with stress or a difficult decision. They likely would score moderately on scales of conscientiousness.

When RC2 is elevated above a T score of 65, it is suggestive of current symptomatic anhedonia and social detachment. Elevations on RC2 are associated with the typical symptoms of depression: sad mood, feelings of inadequacy, general inefficiency, low morale, guilt, anxiety, social withdrawal, passivity, conflict avoidance, and in some cases (especially if Compulsivity (CMP) is elevated) obsessive-compulsive thoughts and behaviors. RC2 elevated clients may feel hopeless, pessimistic, and fearful of taking emotional or behavioral risks. Elevations can also indicate vegetative symptoms of depression such as altered appetite, weight change, disturbed sleep, and difficulties with attention, concentration, and memory.

Individuals with a high score on the RC2 Scale may have experienced an actual or perceived loss that has left them fearful to engage in life, perhaps out of fear of experiencing further loss. Sometimes the loss associated with RC2 elevations occurred in childhood, resulting from an overload of responsibilities, restricted opportunities for carefree play and normal unfettered learning, and diverse socialization. In other cases, the depression is associated with early parental death, parental withdrawal, or other losses such as poverty and prejudice. High RC2 individuals may blame themselves for their losses and experience a pervasive sense of guilt. Levak's hypothesis (Levak et al., 2011) is that inhibiting hope, motivation, and general drive as a way to protect against further loss is an adaptive response to such loss. In this context, pessimism and negativity can be viewed as protective.

High RC2 scores (without elevated acting-out scales) may reflect personality traits such as hyper-responsibility, perfectionism, and a tendency toward intro-punitiveness, which can predispose individuals to depression when losses occur. Sometimes a RC2 score significantly below a T score of 50 with an elevated Hypomanic Activation (RC9) reflects the manic phase of a bipolar disorder. Individuals with RC2 elevations at T-79 or greater should be carefully evaluated for possible inpatient or intensive outpatient treatment using extra-test information.

Lifestyle and Family Background – RC2 Scale

Low elevations on RC2 (T score ≤38) suggest a buoyant, resilient, person with quick humor and a positive outlook. This may reflect a stable personality type. Elevations on RC2 are associated with a lifestyle of conscientiousness, guilt, and self-doubt, with a tendency toward taking on responsibilities. These individuals may present as depressed and experience difficulty celebrating life, even when things go well. Friends and family members may see them as critical and negative because of their tendency to focus on what can go wrong. From the client's perspective, such negativity can be understood as an effort to protect oneself from further loss. Reactive depressions would be associated with some actual or perceived recent loss. The depression would be more endogenous in the presence of a history of emotional trauma, long-term feelings of hopelessness, early childhood deprivations or losses, and a lifestyle of hyper-responsibility, self-negation, and chronic depressive symptoms. Look for a history of deprivation or overload of responsibility leading to the adaptive response of limiting purposeful behavior and staying pessimistic to avoid disappointment and further loss.

Clarifying Scales – RC2 Scale

Although it is a distinguishing feature of major depression (anhedonia can co-occur with a variety of psychological disorders), the symptoms manifested associated with RC2 elevations will be determined by a multitude of personological factors. The following scales, if elevated, can point to the thoughts, emotions, and behaviors associated with a prominent RC2 elevation. The prominence or intensity of these symptoms will vary as a function of the RC2 elevation and elevations on other MMPI-3 scales.

- If RCd is elevated, the client feels demoralized and hopeless about dealing with their depression and their overall dysfunction. They may have given up hope of feeling better and accepted a low level of functioning. A possible major depressive episode should be considered.

- If RCd and MLS are elevated, the biological symptoms of depression are heightened with possible complaints of low energy, sleep and eating disturbance, sexual dysfunction, and feeling an overall sense of physical debilitation.
- If NUC is elevated, there are likely complaints of dizziness, loss of balance, peripheral neuropathy, and numbness and tingling in the extremities.
- If EAT is elevated, preoccupation with food and eating occurs and possible eating disorders could be a concrete manifestation of body dysmorphia and depression.
- If COG is elevated, the typical mental fog and concentration and memory difficulties associated with depression are heightened, with a low tolerance for frustration as thinking and problem-solving are so depleting.
- If SUI is elevated, there is a serious risk of self-harm, especially if RC4, ACT, IMP or DISC are elevated. If DSF is also elevated, a lack of community support would increase the danger of impulsive self-harm. It is important to conduct a risk assessment with this combination of scales.
- If HLP is elevated, reflecting feelings of helplessness and hopelessness, descriptors that are associated with elevations on RCd and EID are suggested.
- If SFD is elevated, the insecurity and low self-esteem associated with RC2 is increased, suggesting the individual believes they are a burden to others.
- If NFC is elevated, the individual feels an inability to manage their daily life due to feelings of incompetency. They consequently lack perseverance. They readily feel passive and indecisive.
- If STR is elevated, the individual feels nervous and unable to manage even moderate stress.
- If WRY is elevated, the individual is constantly anxious, as if some disaster is looming. Ruminations about past disappointments and worries can include finances, health, and relationship security.
- If SHY is elevated, a social phobia or social anxiety is possible.
- If CMP is elevated, the anxiety and depression inherent in RC2 elevations may be managed through obsessive defenses, rituals, superstitions, and compulsive behaviors.
- If Substance Abuse (SUB) is elevated, the individual may be self-medicating their depression, anxiety, panic, and fears with alcohol and/or drugs.
- If ANP is elevated, the passivity associated with RC2 is punctuated by angry episodes triggered by minor setbacks or perceived empathic failures by others to caretake effectively.

Therapy and Therapeutic Pitfalls – RC2 Scale

An elevated RC2 T score (when all other scales are below a T score of 65) reflects anhedonia marked by an internal sense of loss and a feeling of being inadequate. Being engaged in a healing, supportive, caring relationship can be therapeutic because these clients do not manifest other self-defeating defenses. This profile is associated with generally favorable treatment outcomes.

If there are other signs of depression, antidepressant medications often provide relatively prompt relief, especially when the depression is severe. Cognitive behavioral therapy has been well researched as an effective treatment for depression. Assertiveness training and Interpersonal therapy are also useful. Exercise, a healthy diet, and avoiding alcohol and recreational substances can also be effective in alleviating depression.

These individuals may have experienced an actual or perceived loss that they have not fully worked through and have not completed their grieving process. The therapist should avoid the temptation to prematurely reassure and "persuade" clients to see the "positives" in their lives, as that may have the paradoxical effect of creating resistance. Explore how past goals and desires have been a disappointment and help clients express their anger and sadness associated with losses in order for them to gain self-acceptance.

Feedback Statements – RC2 Scale

T score <42

You are a person who generally stays positive and optimistic, and you have steady and available energy. You have a wide range of emotionally positive experiences and a high level of psychological wellbeing. Things rarely get you down for very long, and you easily bounce back from adversity. When you experience setbacks, you rarely waste energy unreasonably blaming yourself, and you don't easily lose your self-confidence. Your view of life may be that people can solve their own problems if they work hard. You are able to focus on tasks at hand and are generally free of anxious and negative thoughts. You likely have a playful, positive disposition and a supportive social life.

T score 47–60

You appear to have a healthy attitude on how to deal with setbacks and disappointments. You tend not to sulk when things do go wrong and do not waste time with self-recriminations. If you do get blue once in a while, it is usually over a specific disappointment and then you likely snap yourself out of it.

T score = 65

Your profile is just outside the normal range. It shows that you are a serious and thoughtful person who takes responsibilities seriously. When stressed, you may be vulnerable to episodic sleep difficulty. You are vulnerable to experiencing guilt if things go wrong, even though you might not have been responsible for the problem. You shy away from taking unnecessary risks and are cautious about "counting your chickens before they hatch." You are an earnest person, realistic about life's ups and downs. Recently, you may have experienced a minor setback which has left you feeling careful about being too optimistic in case something goes wrong again. On the other hand, you may simply be a dutiful, responsible, thoughtful, conscientious personality type. Also, some people with this profile grew up having had more responsibility than is normal for a young child. Perhaps you were in a caregiver role, either for a younger sibling or even a sick caregiver or family member. Perhaps you had to take on the role of an adult early, leaving you a little vulnerable to worry, since a child can't be expected to manage adult problems. It might be hard now to give yourself permission to relax, be in the moment, and give yourself carefree moments.

T score >65

Your profile shows that you are currently finding it difficult to experience positive emotions. Sometimes people with this profile feel that almost nothing gives them pleasure. You likely feel depressed and doubt that you can reach your goals. You tend to be your own worst critic and in your dark moments it is hard to find something to pull you out of your blue mood.

Sometimes people with your profile can have difficulty sleeping. In some cases, it is difficult to fall asleep because your mind is agitated, and you are unable to switch it off. In other cases, people with this profile can fall asleep, but then awaken in the middle of the night or early in the morning and are unable to return to sleep. They complain of early awakening with some anxiety that interferes with returning to sleep. When people become depressed, they can experience physical symptoms. Stomach upsets and difficulties with elimination are possible.

People with your profile tend to avoid confrontation. This may be because you doubt yourself and tend to blame yourself if someone is upset with you. It may also be hard to confront others because you lack energy and confidence. You tend to worry that you don't have the right to ask for what you want or to assert yourself.

You may give up on hopes and dreams for the future, feeling that it is useless to have desires because you are likely to be disappointed. People may see you as pessimistic, but this reflects your fear that the future is bleak. Having little to look forward to can be quite distressing. You might have given up planning ahead, feeling that little will give you pleasure.

- If RCd is elevated, add: You may be feeling demoralized and defeated and pessimistic about the future. You are your own worst critic, and you doubt yourself. It is hard to not feel despair.
- If RC1 is elevated, add: You are also experiencing a number of physical symptoms that may increase when you are stressed. Sleep problems, weight issues, dizziness, and other body issues that frighten you are possible.
- If WRY is elevated, add: You probably feel a constant pit in your stomach and a sense of dread that something bad is looming and about to happen.
- If EAT is elevated, add: You may use food as a way of soothing yourself. You may binge and purge or you may restrict food intake because you have body image worries.
- If SFD is elevated, add: You suffer from self-doubt and are your own worst critic. It is hard to ask for what you want or to be assertive since you look at yourself so negatively and you assume other people know better than you.
- If COG is elevated, add: You may experience difficulties with concentration, memory, and general alertness and attention. You may reread the same thing without understanding it, and you may be unable to remember what you did earlier in the day or the day before. You may even become fearful that you are somehow losing your mind. Generally, these symptoms remit once the depression is treated. You may feel like you are suffering from mental fog and are unable to think clearly and problem-solve well.
- If NFC is elevated, add: You feel incompetent and indecisive and easily overwhelmed even by small setbacks.
- If HLP is elevated, add: Currently you feel helpless and hopeless and defeated about getting better.
- If SUI is elevated, add: People with your profile can become very aware of the possibility of death and a declining will to live. Sometimes they become preoccupied with thoughts of ending their lives or simply dying in a passive way such as not waking up from sleep. If you feel like this, share it with your therapist. If you cannot reach your therapist and these feelings are immediately occurring, call a national suicide and crisis helpline [988 in the United States and Canada] for confidential support.

Lifestyle and Family Background Feedback – RC2 Scale

Typically, people with your profile have experienced recent or past losses and disappointments that have left them apprehensive about allowing themselves to enjoy life. Perhaps as a child you experienced the loss of a parental caring figure, leaving you with overloads of responsibility; or for some other reason you may have been deprived of the normal joys of a carefree childhood. In other cases, recent losses (perhaps a job loss, a blow to your self-esteem, or a perceived or actual setback) have made you feel hopeless about enjoying life again. Being negative, pessimistic, and withdrawing from life may be an understandable self-protection from further loss or setback.

Treatment and Self-Help Suggestions – RC2 Scale

1. Your therapist may want to recommend that you consider medication, which could help you to feel better quickly.
2. Research has shown that regular aerobic exercise (if you are medically cleared for exertion) can decrease stress and have a very positive effect in relieving depression. Studies indicate that aerobic exercise has antidepressant and anti-anxiety effects and protects against the harmful consequences of stress.
3. Work with your therapist to change how you view yourself. Notice how quick you are to blame and doubt yourself. In any given moment, when you dislike yourself, attempt to make a list of your positive attributes so that you maintain a balanced view of yourself.
4. Building resilience to learn an optimistic (yet realistic) viewpoint can contribute to a more hopeful outlook on life and to better self-esteem. Optimists explain difficulties as temporary, non-personal, and specific, whereas pessimists explain them as permanent, personal, and pervasive. In other words, optimists see disappointments as setbacks, not failures. For example, in a relationship problem the pessimistic explanation would be, "I'm unlovable" (personal, permanent, and pervasive), whereas an optimistic explanation would be, "We have both been under stress lately" (non-personal, temporary, and specific). Practice learning this new way of explaining difficulties.
5. Assertiveness training can be an effective component of mood regulation. Assertiveness is an honest and direct expression of your own desires and thoughts while still respecting the thoughts and feelings of others. An aggressive response ignores the feelings of others, whereas a passive response is the failure to express your own wants and needs. Think of examples either in your own life or something you have observed that illustrates different styles of communication, and then role-play assertive responses with your therapist.
6. Identify with your therapist what you perceive as past or recent losses. Find ways to forgive yourself for these setbacks and losses so that you can stop beating yourself up for them. Learn to express anger about those losses without self-blame.
7. Feeling depressed can be quite lonely and isolating, but one of the best ways to begin feeling better is to reach out for social support and contact. Joining a sports or activity group is a way to seek out social support while concurrently getting the benefits of exercise. Consider making plans with friends or family, even if it is just by phone or for a brief visit.
8. If you have been thinking of dying as a way out of your pain, discuss it with your therapist and develop a safety plan. If you cannot reach your therapist and these feelings are immediately occurring, call a national suicide and crisis hotline [988 in the United States and Canada] for confidential support.
9. Observe your tendency to catastrophize. When something bad happens, you tend to anticipate the worst outcome and then suffer anxiety anticipating it. Make a list of possible positive outcomes and compare them to the list of dire consequences you have imagined.

Antisocial Behavior (RC4) Scale

General Descriptors

Complaints

Easily antagonized; feels unfairly treated; easily bored; interpersonal relationship problems.

Cognitions

Calculating; externalizing blame; self-importance; thinking of ways for immediate self-gratification.

Emotions

Shallow; superficial; emotionally disconnected.

Traits and behaviors

Superficially charming; conflicts with authority figures; rule-breaking; irresponsible conduct; history of juvenile misconduct; difficulty with intimacy; deceitfulness; aggressiveness; blaming others; acting-out; substance abuse; narcissistic; rebellious; immature; self-absorbed; impulsive; unreliable; irresponsible; risk-taking; assertive; manipulative; demanding; lacking discipline, conscientiousness, and judgment.

Therapist's Notes – RC4 Scale

Although the 14-item RC4 Scale is not intended as a direct diagnostic indicator of a specific psychological disorder, it is in fact empirically related to antisocial behavior and psychopathy. Failure to conform to social norms, lying, risk-taking, impulsivity, irresponsibility, and a history of juvenile misconduct are all well documented in several studies as they relate to this scale. There are also robust RC4 Scale linkages to alcohol and substance abuse across different settings and populations. Aggressive and violent behaviors are associated with scale elevations, not surprisingly so. Elevated RC4 scores are associated with low behavioral control and impulsivity or disconstraint.

To conceptualize the RC4 Scale along a dimension, it is useful to discuss traits and behaviors associated with different scale elevations. Low scorers (T score ≤39) are conventional rule-followers. They avoid risky behaviors, are generally reliable, and don't selectively report or exaggerate. They tend to not be sexually aggressive and generally don't manipulate others. They tend to be honest, and others see them as decent and trustworthy. They report a below-average level of past antisocial behavior.

In the normal range of T score 55–64, RC4 individuals will exhibit some of the personality traits seen in higher elevations, but in a less problematic way. In fact, risk-taking entrepreneurs who bend the rules and achieve momentary success before poor judgment upends them may well score in the high normal range. Scores on the scales measuring impulsivity and aggression (BXD, IMP, DISC, Aggression (AGG)) would likely not be elevated in successful, but Machiavellian, RC4 moderate scorers, since those traits would have led to early failure. However, Self-Importance (SFI) and Dominance (DOM) might be elevated in successful individuals whose self-confidence and "take control" traits help them climb the corporate and political ladder. High normal scores predict individuals who are independent and risk-taking; they like excitement, novelty, and challenge.

They can be superficially friendly, even charming, but have difficulties with long-term emotional trust and intimacy. They feel most comfortable in unstructured situations where others' control over them is limited, though they tend to be impulsive when there is little structure. It is a mistake to assume that all persons with high RC4 scores are necessarily antisocial or act-out aggressively. Individuals going through difficult life transitions such as divorce, job loss, or interpersonal conflicts sometimes obtain elevations on RC4. In response to stress, they may emotionally numb themselves as a way of protecting against feeling vulnerable, almost as if on emotional autopilot, whereby they don't allow themselves to feel. If these individuals have experienced recent severe stresses and do not have a history of antisocial or hedonistic self-indulgence, RC4 elevations may reflect a temporary protective shutdown of empathy and emotional involvement.

Individuals with RC4 elevations above T-65 may have difficulties with authority figures and are uncomfortable with the vulnerability associated with emotional intimacy. Their relationships tend to be shallow, and they are often exploitive of others. High RC4 scorers can be manipulative and lacking in empathy. They have difficulty postponing gratification and tend to act-out in various ways. They lack discipline and tend to give in to impulses without regard for long-term consequences.

With a history of interpersonal difficulties and subtle or overt acting-out, a high RC4 score may reflect a character disorder or trait disturbance. It is also important to consider the profile in the context of cultural milieu and socioeconomic status. For example, a high RC4 profile obtained by the head of a university department may reveal a ruthless Machiavellian, self-centered, highly politicized management style but not necessarily someone who has conflicts with authority. High-level executives who are reckless, take unnecessary risks for their own gain, and manipulate the system could reflect upper socioeconomic status RC4 types. Such individuals are unlikely to be in trouble with the law, unless it is for white-collar crimes, but their manipulation, lack of empathy, and tendency to bend rules for their own benefit can cause interpersonal turmoil, conflict, and even systemic economic risks.

Based on a high RC4 elevation, a psychologist may be tempted to predict antisocial behavior, but in the context of cultural milieu, and perhaps tempered by socioeconomic and educational variables, the manipulations and narcissism associated with RC4 can be moderated and kept in check so that legal consequences are avoided. It should be noted that because many of the RC4 items are worded in the past tense, individuals with elevated scores are describing a past history of antisocial behavior. However, in some cases psychopathy and antisocial personality disorder criteria may be met. A history of acting-out, rebellious behavior, interpersonal difficulties, and self-defeating acts would suggest that the elevation is predicting continued acting-out behavior. These individuals are rebellious and instinctively resist being controlled. Some can be charming and gregarious, especially if SAV and SHY are low. In other cases, they can appear cold and aloof, keeping their emotional cards close to their vest until they feel they have control. Most individuals with an elevated RC4 profile tend to see the world as a "dog-eat-dog" place where they need to exert power over others to avoid it being exerted over them. In some cases, they run into legal difficulties because of poor judgment or poorly controlled impulses. Long-lasting intimate relationships are difficult for them, not only because they dislike being vulnerable but also because they are self-focused. They tend to selectively report, if not overtly lie, to achieve their goals, reflecting their belief that getting their way requires manipulation and deviousness. They show a low tolerance for frustration and an inability to delay gratification.

Sometimes high RC4 scores are found in hedonistic, disorganized, live-in-the-moment, freewheeling individuals who show poor impulse control. Their self-centered goals may be ruthlessly pursued but with a degree of calculated discipline. Some high RC4 individuals are charming, hedonistic, impulsive types whose temper and dangerous aggressiveness can be set off by frustration and aggravated by alcohol and drug use. Sexual promiscuity, drinking, fighting, and trouble with the law would characterize these individuals. Others may be passive, dependent, self-indulgent, and undisciplined.

If RCd is elevated, high RC4 individuals can complain of depression. They experience their depression as feeling trapped and bitter, with blame externalized. This is more reflective of despondency, feelings of defeat, and a sense of self-pity. This is usually associated with a current situation that resulted from poor judgment and self-defeating behavior. Their depression involves less sadness and more glum despondency and self-pity. Sometimes guilt is used manipulatively to engender sympathy or forgiveness for recent acting-out.

Lifestyle and Family Background – RC4 Scale

Individuals with prominent RC4 scores reflect a lifestyle of self-serving, manipulative dependency and impulsive tension reduction. Childhoods in which caregivers were controlling and arbitrary but also indulgent would be typical. In other cases, the emotional underarousal associated with RC4 elevations may be related to both a genetic predisposition and emotional numbing in response to parental abuse, neglect, or self-absorption. As children, such individuals may have often exhibited rebelliousness and difficulties with peers and teachers. As adults, they may have shallow relationships, with a low capacity for empathy. They tend to manipulate others into taking care of them and, when their impulsiveness leads to difficulties, they externalize blame rather than take responsibility. Their lifestyle is punctuated by periods of success, especially if they are capable and bright, but they could experience episodic catastrophic failures as a result of poor judgment and lack of discipline.

Clarifying Scales – RC4 Scale

When scales measuring impulsivity, aggressiveness, and disconstraint are normal or below normal, the individual will be more disciplined and less transparent in their manipulations; they may be quite effectively Machiavellian.

- If BXD is elevated, it would reinforce that the individual is an impulsive, authority-resisting, self-centered, rule-challenging, superficially charming individual who has intimacy difficulties.
- If EID is elevated, but significantly lower than BXD, the individual would likely manifest BXD traits but would also feel anxiety and transitory guilt after impulsive behavior. They might manifest approach avoidance conflicts with "doing and undoing" defenses.
- If SAV, SHY and/or Introversion/Low Positive Emotionality (INTR) are elevated, such individuals can appear cold and self-sufficient, with little need for emotional closeness and physical affection. They can appear aloof, ungiving, and distant, with a noteworthy lack of empathy. Some with this pattern can appear subtly paranoid, reflecting a projection of their own cynicism onto others.
- If FML and Juvenile Conduct Problems (JCP) are elevated, look for family conflict and lack of family emotional support as well as adolescent rebelliousness and drug use.
- If BXD, RC9, IMP, ACT, AGG, Aggressiveness (AGGR), and/or DISC are elevated, look for possible antisocial behavior, acting-out aggressively, and potential legal troubles. This is especially true if SFI and DOM are also elevated, since this predicts a narcissistic, self-important, grandiose, and domineering individual with little constraint.
- If DSF is elevated, and the aggressive, impulsive scales are not, then look for individuals who feel disconnected, alone, and alienated from others. This may be the result of a recent reactive disorder subsequent to some kind of transition or loss.
- If RC8 and/or Psychoticism (PSYC) are elevated, beware of potentially bizarre acting-out behavior that may appear senseless on the surface.
- Elevations on SUB would aggravate impulsive, acting-out behavior, especially when under the influence of substances. Substance addiction or abuse is suggested.

Therapy and Therapeutic Pitfalls – RC4 Scale

Important interpersonal correlates associated with RC4 elevations consist of feeling deficits, resulting in distrust and difficulty with emotional closeness and vulnerability. Although high scorers may appear independent, self-sufficient, and charming, they can be challenging to engage in therapy because they tend to project onto the therapist their own role-playing and manipulations. They are inclined to distrust therapists and to see therapy as "a game" or role-play. Dealing with this transference on an ongoing basis is important to facilitate discussing their fears of trusting.

Recalling moments when they felt unfairly punished or emotionally abandoned with no one to turn to could partially help recognition of their numbed emotional response to these events. Gestalt techniques addressing how clients feel at "this moment," including toward the therapist, could maintain their emotional arousal and involvement in the therapeutic process.

Helping high RC4 scorers understand how they learned from an early age to numb their emotions in response to stress could make it easier for them to re-learn emotional responsiveness. In some cases, it can be productive to explain how switching-off emotional arousal robs them of normal levels of excitement and results in their experiencing life as somewhat boring, emotionally dull, and lacking in richness. Assist them to "try on for size" different emotional states to gauge if they can gain a sense of empathy for how most people feel. Emotionally focused therapy, with its emphasis on attachment behaviors, can be useful in helping clients gain awareness of their feelings. Explore how, given their circumstances, their numbing of emotional vulnerability was adaptive but now leads to reckless excitement-seeking behavior.

Short-term therapy can focus on strategies for improving impulse control and managing stress. Learning how to anticipate stressful situations and developing alternative tension-reducing behaviors can minimize rash, angry, and hedonistic responses to pressure. Developing an inventory of self-destructive events resulting from impulsive behavior and using hindsight to learn new coping strategies could reduce the likelihood of future acting-out.

These clients respond best to a strong, but supportive, therapist who sets limits. Staying open to discussing the therapeutic relationship makes the therapy sessions more immediate and therefore less boring to them. The dynamics and immediacy of group therapy can also keep them more stimulated and involved.

Feedback Statements – RC4 Scale

T score ≤38

Your profile reveals you to be a reliable, honest, conventional, and non-manipulative individual. People likely see you as decent and a rule-follower. You are a straight shooter. If you take a risk, it is only a well-calculated one and you are not reckless or aggressive. You generally are truthful and honest. You don't confront authority figures unless you feel there has been a clear violation of reasonable boundaries. You are not impulsive, and you take time to make important decisions.

T score 39–54

Your profile suggests you strike a healthy balance between following the rules and avoiding impulsive, reckless acts on the one hand and taking calculated risks on the other hand. You are generally a reliable, trustworthy person who can stand up to authority if you feel they have overstepped their boundaries.

T score 55–65

Your profile suggests that you are an independent and self-sufficient person who likes excitement and challenges. You are probably cautious about opening up too quickly with people and letting go of emotional control. You tend to rely on your own judgment in times of stress, since you don't trust others easily. Especially when stressed, you can be impulsive and may bend the rules. Sometimes to get what you want you can selectively report or omit information. Others may see you as a good manipulator to achieve what you want. You can work satisfactorily in structured situations, but you work best when you have independence and your relationship with authority is clearly defined. Authority figures that approach you in a controlling manner probably provoke an argumentative or resistant response from you. Abuse of power tends to anger you, and you don't tolerate it as well as other people might so you may confront a situation impulsively.

T score ≥65

Your profile shows you have a number of strengths. You are willing to challenge the established way of doing things and are not afraid to look at things from a new, different perspective. You are an independent, excitement-seeking, and somewhat risk-taking individual who learned from an early age to be a survivor, not trusting that you can be vulnerable with people.

You may also have learned that being manipulative or clever is how one gets along in the world. You may see the world as a "dog-eat-dog" place where being "top dog" is the only solution. You may find yourself seeking positions of power and control to avoid others having control over you. It is hard for you to trust other people or to let down your guard and ask others for emotional support. Your fear is that if you reveal your weaknesses to others, they will somehow exploit you by using that against you. Others may see you as more manipulative and devious than you see yourself. As you had to learn from an early age to manipulate your caregivers to get your needs met, you may have learned to "selectively report," to tell white lies, and even to openly lie as a way of avoiding people's anger or negative consequences for you.

You probably learned to numb your emotions and not let yourself feel when you are stressed. As a result, you may experience the world as somewhat boring and lacking in intensity and excitement. Small, everyday events, such as a walk in nature, and even things that give other people a sense of excitement, may leave you numb, empty, and unable to enjoy the moment. You may look for stimulation and excitement by doing dangerous and reckless things.

Although people may find your personality initially attractive and charismatic, you may find it difficult to allow yourself to be committed, let your emotional guard down, and be emotionally close. You may become involved with others, and though initially you care a great deal for them, nevertheless you seem to get bored and restless quickly. You may find yourself being promiscuous and having difficulty maintaining long-term, one-on-one relationships.

Sometimes people with your profile have legal troubles or conflicts with authority figures. Perhaps an authority figure was unreasonable and controlling when you were a child, so you have a deep distrust of authority figures. For you to obey the rules, authority figures have to gain your respect. You tend to look for their flaws and weaknesses, perhaps justifying why you won't conform and obey basic regulations. Any kind of structured job or situation where others control you can make you tense and angry if you don't respect them. You may find yourself resisting authority figures and bending the rules.

When you are stressed, you have a tendency to be impulsive. You seem to be able to manage your emotions for periods of time, but as stress builds you may impulsively turn to alcohol, drugs, food, gambling, and sexual acting-out as a way of feeling better. However, this behavior may create serious negative consequences. When your impulses get you in trouble, it is easy to feel like the world has mistreated you. When in trouble you feel quite down and defeated so you may blame other people's behavior for your troubles. At these times you tend to see your problems as due to difficult situations and difficult people rather than as a consequence of your own behavior.

People with your profile can be quick to anger, especially if they feel controlled or unreasonably restrained. They have a tendency to argue their case aggressively and when angered it is hard for them to back off and walk away from a confrontation even if it would help their case.

- If DSF is elevated, add: Currently you may feel disconnected from others and feel a lack of emotional connection with a supportive community. It confirms your view of the world as a place where you can only rely on yourself and not others.
- If SAV, SHY, and/or INTR are elevated, add: You are very self-contained and avoid most social situations. This may be because you don't trust people generally or you feel you can't expose any vulnerability because others will take advantage of you. People will see you as aloof and distant and even avoid you because they can't read you and what you are feeling.
- If RC9, IMP, ACT, and/or DISC are elevated, add: Your profile suggests that you can be quite impulsive. When something excites you or makes you angry, you can move into action without considering all the potential consequences. When your impulses get you into trouble, you may try to manipulate or bend the truth to evade the results.
- If FML is elevated, add: You probably have experienced or are experiencing some conflict with your family, perhaps seeing them as unsupportive and critical of you. Perhaps a parent or caregiver was unreasonable, so you still don't trust them. It is hard to not argue with them when you see them.
- If Cynicism (CYN) is elevated, add: You generally see the world as a place where people look out for themselves and take advantage of one another. Consequently, you feel justified in breaking a rule to get what you want.
- If SFI is elevated, add: You tend to feel that your opinions and beliefs are not only the "right" ones but that you need to let people know what you think and how your way of doing things is best.
- If IMP, ACT, and/or DISC are elevated, add: Your tendency to be impulsive is very strong. You likely respond immediately if you are frustrated or excited about something.
- If SUB is elevated, add: When you use drugs or alcohol, your impulsive behavior, and your judgment, may get worse. You may do things that backfire and cause you severe problems.
- If IMP, ACT, AGG, and/or DISC are elevated, add: Your tendency to approach conflicted situations with a readiness to be impulsively aggressive likely gets you into trouble and leads to people wanting to avoid you.

Lifestyle and Family Background Feedback – RC4 Scale

Perhaps you grew up in an environment where one of your caregivers was controlling or even arbitrary and unreasonable. From an early age, you learned not to trust that person, perhaps because they could be rejecting and abandon you emotionally if they were angry. At other times, one caregiver may have been indulgent and easily forgiving while the other was too strict and quick to punish harshly. You learned to not be vulnerable and to not let your guard down. You have learned to numb your feelings, to rely on yourself for emotional support, and to not let yourself care too much about others' feelings in case you get hurt or let down.

Treatment and Self-Help Suggestions – RC4 Scale

1. Work with your therapist to discover moments as a child when you felt unfairly punished or when you consciously turned off your feelings to avoid being hurt. Your therapist will help you understand how you have numbed your emotions and will also help you understand the role that emotions play in daily decisions, relationships, and a successful career.
2. Work with your therapist to "try on for size" different emotional states that most people feel. Then learn to identify your feelings. Emotional awareness begins with identifying bodily sensations (e.g., clenched fists, racing heart). The next step is labeling the emotion and then finally linking the feeling to a precipitating event. The better you become at identifying your feelings, the more proficient you will be in using countermeasures to control your behaviors and emotions, allowing you to cope more effectively with others while maintaining confidence in your abilities.
3. Explore how you can avoid being impulsive by visualizing stressful situations and rehearsing alternative coping strategies. Find ways to live an exciting and risk-taking life that is not reckless. Avoid substances because they tend to increase your propensity for impulsiveness. Anticipate situations where you might act recklessly and find alternative behaviors so that you don't ruin the things that you have worked for. Work with your therapist to identify a specific problem situation and take an objective look at the consequences. Find alternatives, develop a plan, be specific, and put it in writing. Once you have had a chance to try it out, evaluate the outcome to see if the plan needs revising.
4. Building resilience and making lasting change is hard work, especially under stressful situations. If you are struggling, you may have lost sight of your goals, values, and your passion for what life holds. Reminding yourself about what motivates and drives you helps you to commit to change. Either write or record what you envision your life to be like 15 years from now. Where will you live, who will be with you, and what will life "look" like? This exercise can help you reconnect with your passion and your incentives for making positive changes.
5. If you live a life of selective reporting or lying, it is hard for you to trust what others say to you, even when it is positive. You assume others manipulate and lie because you do. Work on being meticulously honest, telling people what you want and how you feel so that you can learn what it is like to live an authentic life, without having to lie and selectively report.
6. Learn and rehearse ways to express anger so you don't wait until you are hijacked by intense, enraged emotions that can ruin your relationships and derail your life. Some people hold the belief that you need to "vent" your anger or it will build up inside you like steam. Research has actually shown the opposite: simply venting only makes you angrier. Healthy ways of coping with anger involve looking at your responsibility in the situation and learning how to problem-solve instead of dwelling on punishing the other person.

Ideas of Persecution (RC6) Scale

General Descriptors

Complaints

Feels criticized and judged; preoccupied with fears of being harmed by others; feels misunderstood and/or unfairly treated; feelings of wounded pride; interpersonal difficulties and resentments toward family; possible hallucinations.

Cognitions

Suspicious; opinionated; ideas of reference; delusions of persecution; rigid thinking; preoccupied with unfair treatment; unforgiving; possibly vindictive; rationalizes.

Emotions

Highly sensitive and emotionally reactive; angry; anxious and fearful.

Traits and behaviors

Lacks insight; blames others for his/her difficulties; values loyalty; argumentative; stubborn; hypersensitive to criticism; self-righteous indignation; distrustful; paranoid ideations and/or delusions; actions to protect oneself from others seen as malevolent; poor reality testing.

Therapist's Notes – RC6 Scale

The RC6 Scale is comprised of 14 items that are correlated with a broad range of psychotic symptoms, including hallucinations and non-paranoid delusions. However, a range of psychological disturbances can be associated with elevations on this scale that may not be floridly psychotic in nature, such as a hypersensitivity to criticism and interpersonal mistrust and suspiciousness. The RC6 item content reflects a continuum of threat sensitivity. In elevations in the high normal range, threat sensitivity is comparatively "low," though the individual is likely fearful of rejection and concerned about others talking negatively about them. Moderate elevations are associated with individuals who believe others are trying to "get them" or threaten them. High elevation individuals perceive a "severe" threat wherein they think there is an imminent risk to their physical and psychological safety. Inspection of the RC6 item responses can help inform the clinician about the particular concerns reported by the client.

Normal high range RC6 elevations (T score 59–65) suggest a sensitive, rational, analytical individual who values loyalty and meticulous fairness. These clients can be somewhat rigid in their values ("There is a right way and a wrong way to do things, and I act the right way") and they are sensitive to any kind of inferred criticism or to what they perceive as unfair demands. These individuals feel that they must pursue justice. They are not overtly paranoid; rather, they are highly rational, with fixed rationalized resentments that have a paranoid flavor.

RC6 elevations at T score 66–78 may be associated with a recent accusation of wrongdoing, so paranoid item elevation could accurately reflect a current threatening situation. Elevations in this range with no obvious threat, however, reveal a tendency to take things personally and readily feel hurt, misunderstood, and lonely. Elevations also suggest the storing of resentments, difficulties with assertion until they feel above criticism and justified, and a propensity to be vindictive if slighted. They deny hostility, which tends to be expressed as a rationalized resentment.

RC6 elevations generally reflect a need to avoid criticism and judgment and, at higher elevations (T score ≥79), a fear of attack by others and subjugation. At this high elevation, the individual's sensitivity begins to shade toward paranoia, with persecutory ideation and paranoid delusions. These may be very fixed and rationalized, unlike the more disorganized delusions associated with the RC8 Scale. As the RC6 Scale elevates above a T score of 79, the individual's sensitivity toward criticism, derision, or control shades into paranoia. They are preoccupied with fairness to the point of mean-spiritedness. They rationalize their actions, perceive implied disapproval, and pre-emptively defend against it. They do not express their wants, needs, or resentments directly until they feel fully justified in doing so, by which time they are angry and unforgiving. They tend to repress emotions that could lead others to find fault with them. When hurt or slighted, there is a desire to punish, a slowness to forgive, and a desire to label the person who has hurt them as "bad" or "evil." This reflects the intensity of their hurt feelings and their need to justify their anger.

At high elevations, paranoia may manifest itself in preoccupations with powerful agencies (e.g., Central Intelligence Agency (CIA), Federal Bureau of Investigation (FBI)), conspiracies, enemies who are stealing from them, or other manifestations of fear of being subjugated. The individual searches repetitively for confirmation of their suspicions of being targeted, followed, or talked about, resulting in high levels of distress. If information is found contrary to their prejudicial thinking, it is readily dismissed rather than considered. Because significant persecutory thinking may require immediate intervention, it is important to inspect the item responses for further understanding of the person's thought processes.

When not threatened, individuals with elevated RC6 T scores can be empathic and highly emotionally responsive. They value loyalty and are unforgiving of transgressions. Other characteristics include a tendency to remember slights and injustices after others have resolved them, and so old resentments are rehashed during current arguments as a way of rationalizing anger. Even at moderate elevations, guardedness and suspicion can lead to difficulties in work, marital situations, and families. Elevations on the RC6 Scale may also indicate symptoms of dysthymia, depression, and suicide attempts.

Lifestyle and Family Background – RC6 Scale

Levak's hypothesis (Levak et al., 2011) is that high levels of vigilance for criticism, judgment, or actual physical attack reflect an adaptive response to a childhood in which parents or caregivers were critical, shaming, and severely punishing, or had standards that were very difficult to achieve. In some cases, affection may have been withheld due to unrealistically high standards of behavior not being met. Caregivers may have been verbally or even physically abusive as a way of disciplining "bad" behavior. This may have instilled a determination to be above criticism or contempt, identifying with the aggressor, and developing a similarly rigid set of values and beliefs. In turn, these "victim" clients can be quite punitive and harsh with their own children.

Clarifying Scales – RC6 Scale

A combination of various scales, or even a singular scale elevation, can modify the expression of behavior, thoughts, or feelings associated with elevated RC6 scores. In some cases, RC6 elevations can reflect persistent paranoid delusional beliefs that result in psychological dysfunction or at least induce anxiety and/or depression that is debilitating. Less extreme expressions of symptoms and complaints associated with this scale may include interpersonal suspiciousness, alienation, and mistrust that can cause minor to significant impairment for the individual. It is, therefore, important to consider other elevated scales to further define the meaning of an RC6 elevation.

- If RC1 is elevated, the individual may have developed a well-rationalized, paranoid delusion involving their somatic symptoms. Sometimes they develop delusions about people trying to hurt them or implant devices that control them and cause them physical discomfort.
- If RC2 is elevated, consider an affective disorder with subtle, if not overt, projections onto others. Sad moods, crying, worrying, and feelings of inferiority are likely. The client may be feeling trapped, a victim in a current situation, and mistreated. There may be a belief that their depression has been caused by others' unreasonable behavior.
- If RC4 and/or ANP and AGG are elevated, the individual's hypersensitivity can lead to vindictive, angry outbursts toward others. They are argumentative and demanding and, at high levels, a possible paranoid schizophrenia diagnosis could be considered. The combination of elevations on the RC6 and RC4 Scales suggest a childhood of conflict with an opposite sex caregiver and a childhood of temper outbursts and adolescent rebelliousness. This is especially true if JCP is also elevated.
- If RC7 and/or WRY and CMP are elevated, the individual's paranoia is heightened by an obsessive preoccupation with rooting out perceived enemies and the compulsive collection of evidence to prove the rational basis of their paranoia.
- If SAV and/or SHY are elevated with RC6 and RC8, there may be a long history of withdrawal and social isolation. Anger expression tends to come in brief, acute outbursts, and it may involve dangerous assaultive behavior.
- If RC8 is elevated, look for a possible florid paranoid disorder. Anhedonia, bizarre paranoid delusions, inappropriate, immature behavior, flat, blunted, and inappropriate affect, and suspiciousness are all associated with these elevations. THD is likely highly elevated.
- If RC9 is elevated, manic overactivity will mix with paranoid ideation. Projection is a primary defense mechanism, and the individual often focuses on how they have been mistreated.
- If CYN is elevated, the self-referential concerns indicated by RC6 are augmented by a general distrust of others and their motives that goes beyond concerns about specific threats to oneself.

Therapy and Therapeutic Pitfalls – RC6 Scale

High RC6 scorers are often seen as difficult to treat because they are sensitive to criticism and may view insights as shaming. They can be highly rational to the point of being argumentative, possibly replicating their relationship with a punitive and demanding caregiver. Overt paranoid symptoms may require medication, which would likely be resisted. Exploring current feelings of vulnerability to attack or judgment could be validating. Paranoid symptoms are usually fixed and rational rather than diffuse or disorganized. Although perhaps exaggerated by hypersensitivity, there is sometimes a basis for the persecutory ideation. It is important to validate and affirm these clients' reactions without endorsing paranoid beliefs (e.g., "No wonder you are so frightened and self-protective given how attacked, criticized, or judged you feel.") Be mindful to not confront the client with their hypersensitivity directly. Exploring how sensitivity is a trait that not all people possess and how being sensitive is positive, but with a downside, could be a way to validate the client and help them see others' behavior as thoughtless rather than pointedly hostile toward them. Generally, when discussing a client's hypersensitivity to criticism or perceived mistreatment, be mindful to use language that does not threaten them or make them defensive.

Often these clients will express hurt and rationalized resentments toward specific people. Explore childhood episodes of unfair or harsh punishments or criticisms to develop self-empathy and help them understand why they are so defensive now. Consider using Gestalt role-playing techniques in which old injustices, wounds, and repressed anger are vented. Learning to feel empathy for themself as a vulnerable child who wanted to be "above reproach" may help them develop greater empathy for others. Help clients identify their wants and desires, learning to express them without blame or criticism of others. Teaching them to be assertive before resentment develops is a useful cognitive-behavioral tool.

Teaching communication skills can help clients identify their feelings that can be better expressed without subtle blame. Their tendency to subtly blame leads to defensive arguments. For example, saying "I only asked you for one thing …" as a way of asking for something can be argumentative. Another example when discussing a topic might be "We have already discussed this, why are you bringing it up again?" Help them learn to ask for what they want without needing to explain that they deserve it and why the other person owes it to them.

Feedback Statements – RC6 Scale

T score 40–54

Your profile suggests that you don't take things personally easily and are generally able to ask for what you want without waiting until you feel resentment. When upset by someone, you are able to get over your hurt or anger without holding a grudge. You can be direct without being hostile and you don't waste a lot of time fretting about what people think about you.

T score 55–64

Your profile is in the high normal range. It suggests you are a sensitive person who tries hard to be above criticism. You tend to be your own worst critic, so criticism is particularly painful for you. You work hard to "do the right thing" and meeting other's expectations is important to you. You are inquisitive, rational, and analytical. Since you want to be above reproach, you sometimes allow anger or frustration to build until you feel completely justified in expressing it, but by that time you are quite angry and resentful. Anger can come out as sharp rebukes, rather than being expressed directly.

People with your profile are sensitive to being controlled and value their independence. You have high standards and are rational and fair-minded. If people are disloyal or unfairly critical it can be hard for you to forgive them. In an argument, you are acutely aware of who said what to whom and can't let go of a dispute until it has been resolved fairly. You may have had caregivers who could be somewhat critical, with a tendency to use shaming as a parenting tool, so it is no wonder you are sensitive to being controlled or criticized.

You are loyal to those you trust. You have high personal standards and work hard to be above criticism or judgment. You have strong values and may be very strict about the right and wrong way of seeing and doing things.

T score 65–78

Currently you appear to be feeling vulnerable to being criticized, judged, or even physically attacked. Someone may have accused you of something that is humiliating, or you may feel someone has it in for you. Feeling vulnerable, it is hard to know whom to trust right now.

Currently you may feel on edge and tense, as if someone is going to unfairly criticize or attack you. At times, your sensitivity can shade toward paranoia, so that it is hard for you to know whom to trust. These times might be quite frightening because you don't know whether your mistrust of others is due to your sensitivity or whether you are truly seeing things clearly.

People probably see you as having high personal standards, and you work hard to be above reproach. People with your profile have a keen sense of justice. If you feel unfairly treated or if you feel others are mistreated, it makes you angry, and you feel driven to "right the wrong." If people hurt you, even though you may forgive them, it is hard for you to forget what they have done.

You tend not to let others know when you are hurt or angry until you feel you are completely justified in doing so. However, by that time you are angry and have hard feelings about the other person not being sensitive to your needs. You may store and rationalize your resentments without letting people know how you feel and, if they continue their actions, you begrudge them and feel bitter. You don't ask for what you want until you feel you fully deserve it. Because you are so sensitive to the issue of fairness, when you finally express your feelings, you may try to explain why you are feeling hurt or angry and you may have a list of things that you feel were done to you as a way of justifying your anger. This is your way of justifying yourself; however, it makes others feel defensive, so they likely tend to argue back rather than have empathy for you.

If people let you down or you feel unjustly treated, it is difficult for you to forgive people. You may feel a need to punish people because of what they did to hurt you. Since you are so sensitive, you assume other people are also, so when they act cruelly or selfishly, it is easy for you to assume they were hurtful on purpose. As a result, you feel a need to punish them, so they don't "get away with it." Because you experience feelings intensely, painful events sting and cut deeply. When you are angry with people, you tend to see them as evil or bad, and you keep them at a distance and perhaps justify why you need to punish them.

T score ≥79

You are feeling very vulnerable to being mistreated and hurt, perhaps even attacked. This is understandably very frightening. Consequently, you are trying to determine who your enemies are and whom you can trust. It is no wonder you are so vigilant! At times you may feel paranoid. This may lead you to think that others are plotting to hurt, fool, and take advantage of you. You may get so confused that you even wonder if people have implanted listening devices and cameras so they can better hurt or monitor you.

Currently you may be experiencing difficulties in your personal relationships. Your distrust of people right now may lead you to keep people at a distance and you might even push people away if they don't agree with your suspicions. When you perceive people as disloyal you tend to write them off and it is hard for you to forgive them.

You try hard to be above criticism and above blame, so when other people do the wrong thing, you may feel they need to be punished and have blame assigned to them. However, when you blame someone, even if they deserve it, they tend to blame you back, which leads to conflict.

- If RC1 is elevated, add: You may be experiencing a lot of physical problems such as headaches, light-headedness, dizziness, stomach problems, undiagnosed illnesses, or different areas of your body experiencing numbness and tingling. You might feel these symptoms are the result of someone (or some entity) causing them as a way to get to you. You may have difficulty trusting your medical professionals, especially since getting a diagnosis has been difficult.
- If RC2 is elevated, add: You may be feeling trapped in a current situation, feeling mistreated and hurt. It is making you feel sad and unhappy. Crying spells and worry would not be uncommon. You likely feel that your depression is the result of others' behavior and that you can't get better until others change and treat you differently. You feel resentful and even bitter since your current trap is not your fault. You are likely to express your anger as hurt, for example saying, "I'm not angry, I'm just hurt."

- If RC4 is elevated, add: You are very sensitive to being controlled or having demands placed on you. You don't trust people's motives so you are vigilant for anybody who might take advantage of you. Others may see you as demanding, but slow to give, since you go through life suspicious of others' motives, feeling people will take advantage of you. You may feel you have to be constantly self-protective and ready to argue or fight for what you think you deserve. When you are in trouble, it is hard for you to see your contribution to the problem. You tend to see your problems as due to others' behavior and that you are being treated unfairly. You may have grown up with a very controlling and, at times, harsh caregiver who could be severely punishing and humiliating. You may have learned to be on guard and ready to fight back as an understandable defense against unreasonable punishment. Since you go through life ready to be aggressive, small frustrations can lead to angry outbursts and even aggressive behavior. [This is especially true if IMP, ANP, and/or DISC are also elevated.]
- If RC7 is elevated, add: You are feeling so vulnerable to being judged, criticized, and attacked that you feel paranoid and unsure who to trust and know who is against you. You may have developed some compulsive behaviors, such as deep research or analysis of people or institutions you feel have wronged you. You are likely constantly worrying about your safety and reputation and spending a lot of time researching, collecting evidence, and worrying about how to protect yourself and prove that your concerns are valid.
- If WRY and/or CMP are elevated, add: You may feel a compulsion to perform certain behaviors or rituals, thinking they might protect you from danger.
- If RC8 is elevated, add: Your profile suggests that you are experiencing thoughts and emotions that could be frightening. You may feel so tense that you are unsure of who to trust. The distrust may be so deep that you become paranoid, feeling that people or institutions are trying to poison you, invade your mind, implant devices around you or in you, and generally want to hurt you. You may experience hearing voices or even see visions that others don't appear to see. You feel suspicious of people, even if they try to be nice to you, because you have been disappointed before. You likely feel empty and alone and feel you get no pleasure from life. When something stresses you, your mind can easily become confused, so it is hard to think clearly or express yourself the way you want to. You are very sensitive about people's hostility toward you so you may have become preoccupied with guns and weapons as a way to protect yourself. If you feel cornered, you could be explosively angry, even though you may have misread the danger to you.
- If RC9 is elevated, add: You may be feeling highly energetic, driven, and focused on what you perceive as unfairness and injustice toward you. Your energy may be so high that you are exhibiting manic behaviors like intensity, sleeplessness, irritability, aggressiveness, and paranoia. You may be feeling that others or institutions have harmed you or want to harm you, and so you feel a mission to stop them and defeat your enemies. Perhaps you were treated with gross unfairness or injustice and have become mobilized to protect yourself.
- If IMP, ANP, ACT, and/or DISC are elevated, add: When angered you could lose your temper and become aggressive or violent, especially if you feel wronged by someone.
- If SAV and/or DSF are elevated, add: You avoid people and social situations since it is so hard for you to be around others. You may feel people can't be trusted and that they have evil intentions toward you. Being around people makes you feel paranoid since you don't know who is trustworthy. You may feel that you have to isolate and hide to protect yourself against a particular enemy or institution.

Lifestyle and Family Background Feedback – RC6 Scale

Typically, people with your profile had caregivers who were critical, shaming, judgmental, and severely punishing. They may have had high standards, so that you always felt subtly or overtly criticized or judged. Perhaps you had to endure verbal or even physical punishments that were will-breaking and shaming, which made you feel emotionally knocked down and crushed. From an early age, you learned to protect yourself by wanting to be above reproach, by doing everything right, and by making sure that you were not punished. You learned not to express anger because it could lead to retaliation by a parental figure. No wonder you avoid expressing vulnerable feelings. Growing up feeling humiliated and judged, you go through life ready to defend yourself, making notes of others' flaws, and storing them away as ammunition should you need to protect yourself against them.

Treatment and Self-Help Suggestions – RC6 Scale

1. Learn to ask for what you want before you are resentful and angry. You don't have to justify yourself. Avoid trying to explain to others why they "owe" you something because that will make them defensive. You are afraid to ask for things in case other people use it to control you and make unreasonable demands on you. See if you can identify any "cognitive distortions" that are triggering this belief. Because you work so hard to protect yourself, this may trigger "mind reading," where you assume that you know what other people are thinking and how they will act. Work with your therapist to explore where these ideas came from and then develop some alternate ways of thinking.
2. Learn to express anger when you feel it. Don't try to rationalize it or wait until you feel justified in expressing it. By the time you feel justified, you are resentful, and then it is hard for you to forgive the other person. Learn to verbalize your anger assertively but without attacking the other person. Define what it is that you want to express, and don't assume that the other person will know what you want. When practicing assertiveness, it may help to write down what you wish to express. Use "I" statements to communicate how you feel without blaming someone else. For example, try saying "I'm feeling frustrated," instead of "You frustrate me."
3. Explore with your therapist childhood experiences where you felt unfairly criticized and judged. See if you can develop empathy for yourself as a child, exploring specific situations where you felt unfairly treated. Role-play getting angry with the person who mistreated you as a way of gaining empathy for yourself.
4. Forgiveness is not easy or quick, but the ability to do so leads to less anger, less stress, greater optimism, and even better health. An exercise to help with forgiveness is to "rewrite" the offense using a more "positive" approach. Write about any benefits you may have gotten from someone's transgression against you (e.g., a rude salesclerk saved you money because you left the store before you finished the purchase). This can be a creative way to foster a more positive outlook.
5. Be aware that you are quite sensitive, so you might take things personally that were not meant to be so. Your therapist may suggest the option of using medication to alleviate your extreme sensitivity if it has led to you misperceiving others' motives. Be honest with your therapist about any ambivalence you might have about taking your medication. At times, your sensitivity may shade toward unrealistic thinking when you are unsure about who is for you and who is against you. If you are going through such a period, it might be quite frightening because it is hard for you to trust your judgment. Discuss with your therapist if you are feeling unable to trust him or her.
6. During this time of stress, make sure you exercise (if not contraindicated by your physician), eat healthily, and avoid alcohol and recreational and illegal drugs. Exercise, especially aerobic exercise, can help reduce stress and also can help improve your mood.

7. Be aware that you have a tendency to look at life in "black-and-white" terms. That made sense growing up when you tried hard to avoid criticism, judgment, and attacks by meticulously following rules, but discuss with your therapist how you might now inadvertently come across as rigid and judgmental toward others.

Dysfunctional Negative Emotions (RC7) Scale

General Descriptors

Complaints

Anxiety; insomnia; irritability; fears of failure; insecurity; self-consciousness; impaired concentration and memory; lack of confidence; guilt; self-criticism; somatic symptoms.

Cognitions

Obsessive ruminations; self-critical; guilt-prone; preoccupied with fears of failure and criticism; intrusive ideation; indecisive; worries excessively; perceives others as overly critical.

Emotions

Stress reactive; fearful; moody; emotionally inhibited; panicky at times; anxious; apprehensive; insecure; guilty; tense.

Traits and behaviors

State and/or trait anxiety; high-strung; unable to relax; apprehensive; sleeping difficulties, including nightmares; irritable; impatient; obsessive; perfectionistic; compulsive; interpersonally hypersensitive; stress reactive; anger-prone; behaviorally inhibited.

Therapist's Notes – RC7 Scale

Dysfunctional negative emotions are measured by the 19-item RC7 Scale. The negative emotional states tapped by the scale content correlate with a diverse array of psychological conditions, including post-traumatic stress disorder (PTSD) and other anxiety-related psychopathology. Anxiety, fear, and anger are correlates associated with RC7 Scale elevations. Empirical correlates for elevated RC7 scores may include intrusive thoughts, anger proneness and irritability, self-criticality, stress reactivity, sleep hygiene problems (including nightmares), impatience, oversensitivity to criticism, and excessive worry. Inspection of the item responses on this scale can help inform the clinician about the various types of negative emotions the client may be experiencing.

RC7 scores below a T score of 39 have been associated with a below-average level of negative emotional experiences. Positive descriptors applying to low scores include cheerful, relaxed, self-confident, and placid. These clients are also efficient, capable, and able to mobilize their resources easily and effectively. Their low level of anxiety and worry can, however, lead to ignoring important details, taking imprudent risks, and being too relaxed about deadlines. This is especially true if IMP, RC4, and/or RC9 are even only moderately elevated.

In the normal range (T score 39–64), RC7 suggests clients who are conscientious, responsible, and dependable. They have a tendency, when stressed, to become anxious, worried, insecure, and are concerned about disappointing people. They have difficulty making decisions because they examine all possible ways things can go wrong. Traits associated with the construct of conscientiousness are exhibited. They dislike disappointing others and feel guilty and inadequate if they make a mistake. These individuals tend to be reliable, conscientious, dependable, detail-oriented, and trustworthy.

At T scores of 65 or above, the primary complaints are negative emotional experiences, such as worry, anxiety, stress, intrusive thoughts, self-criticality, guilt feelings, and/or dread. These clients feel on edge, as if some unpredictable event will lead to a negative or catastrophic outcome. Any relaxation of intentional or determined activity is experienced as perilous. They are vigilant, scanning their internal and external environment in an attempt to anticipate and prevent something from going wrong. The capacity to predict and manage threats may be survival-related. It would make intuitive sense that the aptitude to anticipate danger would be normally distributed in the general population, with some people highly sensitive and others having a higher tolerance for uncertainty. Guilt serves as a reminder to stay vigilant. They don't trust others' watchfulness for things going wrong because they lack confidence that others will be as thorough and as responsible as they are.

Clients with an RC7 elevation overanalyze their own behavior, the observing ego maintaining control, perhaps in an attempt to pre-empt guilt over failure. Living with a heightened sense of anxiety, they tend to develop superstitions, obsessions, and compulsions. These individuals seek reassurance from others but have difficulty being soothed when it is received. Pervasive apprehension serves as a pre-emptive defense against the possibility of unpredictable events or failure. When they seek advice, they doubt that the advisor has thoroughly understood the problem. Any major decision becomes anxiety-provoking because they tend to see every side of every issue. The more opinions they get, the more anxious and self-doubting they become.

The high level of tension and anxiety associated with RC7 is often manifested as somatic symptoms, especially as muscular tension symptoms. Understandably, dysphoria is a common complaint, as stress and tension crowd out the ability to enjoy life. If clinically significant, the dysphoric affect is typically registered on elevations on RCd and/or RC2 Scales. Irritability is often present as a function of the high tension. As an example, being interrupted, hurried, or made to wait can make them anxious and even angry.

These individuals tend to gravitate toward responsibility out of a compulsive sense of duty and then become overloaded and overwhelmed. Nevertheless, they often procrastinate due to their need for perfection and their fear of being criticized for performing inadequately. They are their own worst critics and find praise difficult to accept. When taxed, they tend to not be assertive or confrontational. Phobias, obsessions, and specific ruminations can serve as a way of binding and reducing anxiety. Unsurprisingly, with this amount of internal "noise" and the constant chatter of self-monitoring and overanalysis of most situations, they have difficulty with concentration and memory. Sometimes clinicians can misdiagnose ADD, rather than anxiety, as interfering with concentration and decision-making. Perceived failure, especially if shame is involved, is experienced by them as catastrophic and can lead to suicidal ideation. This is especially true if SUI is elevated.

The RC7 Scale is rarely elevated on its own. When it is, it reflects a generalized, anxious state without any specific focus. However, elevations on the other RC and SP Scales reflect the focus of the anxiety.

Lifestyle and Family Background – RC7 Scale

In combination with a genetic predisposition, early childhood experiences of clients with elevated RC7 scores often involve an adaptive response to being flooded with anxiety subsequent to an unpredictably frightening childhood event or a series of events. These individuals have modified their behavior through hypervigilance in an attempt to predict any onset of a painful and potentially panicking event. Given this fear, they scan the environment to anticipate how others could be disappointed and to perform rituals and compulsions to reduce anxiety. The anticipation of all eventualities is these individuals' response to protect themselves against the onset of unpredictability. Elevated RC7 scores reflect a strong motivation to avoid disapproval and criticism. Unpredictable losses, humiliations, or setbacks could also increase vigilance to protect against the onset of panic surrounding a recurrence of these events. Fears about relaxing would maintain a high drive state.

Clarifying Scales – RC7 Scale

- Elevation on RC1 would predict panic and anxiety around the possibility of body damage. The anxiety could center on specific bodily functions, fears of general physical decline, and the possibility of impending death.
- If NUC and/or COG are elevated as well as RC1, anxiety may be focused on worries about cognitive decline and impairment and preoccupation with vague and shifting neurological complaints. If CMP is elevated, there may be an obsessive preoccupation with finding a diagnosis and treatment for perceived physical symptoms.
- Elevation on RC2 would predict fear and apprehension about loss, both future and past. The individual is obsessively unhappy and worn out by worry. They are experiencing sad moods, despondency, guilt, and feelings of doom. It also suggests a possible agitated depression that may include suicidal ideation and/or attempts.
- If RC4 is elevated, it suggests an individual who experiences high anxiety and worry. As stress builds, they act-out in some way that serves as an outlet for their anxiety. The acting-out could be substance abuse, gambling, sexual promiscuity, or some other risky, impulsive, tension-reducing behavior. Following the acting-out, the individual likely experiences guilt and anxiety, followed by another cycle of increasing stress. One example is a client, a young woman elevated on RC7, RC4, and BXD Scales. When stressed, she would go shopping and shoplift. Returning home, having shoplifted, she would feel remorse, guilt, and anxiety. She might then go and try to replace the items back in the store without being caught. This reflects the classic ego-defense mechanism of doing and undoing.
- If RC6 is elevated, it would suggest an individual with obsessive ruminations about how others view them and how others have hurt or slighted them. They may be perceived as "grievance collectors."
- If RC8 is elevated, it suggests a preoccupation with avoiding being humiliated and rumination about how others view them. Feelings of being damaged or unlovable are suggested. These individuals experience a great deal of fearfulness but also depersonalization and isolation from affect. Early childhoods have often been associated with eccentricities, temper tantrums, and enuresis, which led to being teased and infantilized. Individuals with these elevations can become involved with esoteric philosophies that reflect their tendency to employ intellectual defenses. They have low self-esteem, so intimacy is difficult for them. As children, some experienced unpredictable humiliations and some had personal eccentricities and were immature, leading to painful social relationships. If PSYC is also elevated, there is a possibility of a psychotic process against which the person is actively defending.
- Elevation on RC9 would suggest anxiety and worry about failure and a fear of missing out on opportunities. The energy and drive suggested by RC9 would increase the anxiety associated with the RC7 Scale. This creates a focus on achievement, success, and a mitigator against worrying about unpredictable loss of approval and others' admiration.

- Elevations on SFD, NFC, STR, and/or WRY would indicate a possible anxiety disorder in a self-doubting, stressed, worried individual who feels inadequate to handle life's vicissitudes.
- If SHY is elevated, consider social phobia due to severe anxiety and self-doubt.
- If ANP is elevated, the high level of anxiety and tension experienced by the RC7 would be easily dislodged into irritability and anger over minor interruptions and delays.

Therapy and Therapeutic Pitfalls – RC7 Scale

Individuals with elevations on the RC7 Scale are amenable to therapy and, in many ways, are compliant clients. They are diligent, responsible, and want to please and follow instructions. However, their tendency is to distrust that people fully understand the complexity of their world or have the discipline and attention to detail necessary to comprehend the problems they experience. Validating the details of their concerns tends to inspire trust. Because these clients value thoroughness, positive therapeutic transference is most likely to occur when the therapist takes careful notes, asks many questions to understand the exact nature of their problems, and does not offer advice or diagnoses prematurely. These clients are highly sensitive to anything that can be construed as criticism or therapist disappointment. When clients start to anticipate therapist disapproval with statements such as "you may be disappointed with me," it can lead to a therapeutic discussion about their transference.

Individuals with elevations on RC7 dread making changes and need reassurance to do so. Validating the disabling effects of anxiety tends to be helpful in establishing trust. Often, didactic information, such as explaining the physiological response to anxiety and how it develops and is maintained, can be helpful. Cognitive behavioral therapy and systematic desensitization have proven successful. Insight-oriented therapies are useful in helping them to understand the origins of their anxiety, although psychoanalytic therapies may aggravate already overly introspective tendencies. Psychotropic medications may help clients to reduce their high levels of ruminations, improve their sleep hygiene, and allow them to relax to a greater degree.

Feedback Statements – RC7 Scale

T score <39

Your responses suggest you are a relaxed person who tends not to worry or doubt themselves. When things go wrong, you don't waste time beating yourself up and worrying that people are going to think badly of you. Your resilience and self-confidence allow you to relax easily, sleep well, and shrug off mistakes. Experiencing low levels of anxiety is healthy but also can have some negative consequences. You may allow tasks and duties to accumulate and be less diligent about timelines and deadlines. You may pay bills "in the nick of time," with occasional slip-ups due to your relaxed approach.

T score 39 to 64

Your profile is in the normal range and shows that you have a number of strengths. It suggests you have a healthy approach to your duties and responsibilities, getting things done in a timely manner without putting enormous pressure on yourself. You don't lose your patience easily and generally you are able to relax and sleep well.

You are a thoughtful, analytical individual who takes responsibilities seriously. You may have a mild tendency to worry and be anxious about things going unpredictably wrong. This may mean that, at times, you make mental lists so you can stay "on top" of your responsibilities. Making decisions can sometimes be difficult for you because you are apt to see everything that can go wrong with any choice you make. Whenever things do go wrong, you are likely to blame yourself and feel guilty. Because you can see all the possible ways things can go badly, you are likely to avoid taking risks. Generally, confrontations are difficult for you, and you worry if you have to confront someone. If you feel you have let someone down, you can experience uncomfortable levels of guilt.

T score >65

Currently, some of your strengths may be working against you. You may spend a lot of time standing back and observing the world, worried that some mistake you make will lead to catastrophe. You often feel a sense of anxiety, even dread, as if something bad is about to happen. Even when things are going well, it is hard for you to switch off your mind to get rid of that feeling of nervousness and pressure that you need to do something or are doing something wrong.

It is hard for you to be spontaneous because you see every side of every issue. When you have to make a decision, you are likely to overanalyze, worrying that you might have missed some important detail. Part of the reason you fret so much about making a mistake is that when something goes wrong you feel so deeply guilty. Not only do you focus on possible future mistakes, but you also spend a lot of time thinking about the past, about oversights you have made, and obsessing about how much guilt you should feel.

You tend to be your own worst critic. Even when things go well, you can't relax and enjoy your accomplishments. When people compliment you, it is hard for you to get pleasure from it because you feel undeserving. Perhaps you are afraid that if you enjoy any successes and pat yourself on your back, you'll make a mistake and regret having celebrated any victories. Staying on edge and not letting yourself enjoy life are ways for you to protect yourself against being disappointed should you fail at something.

Being on edge and obsessing about all the possible things that could go wrong likely makes it difficult to concentrate. Your own inner thoughts often interrupt you, making it difficult to remember things. It is hard to "log in" new information if your mind is preoccupied with everything that might go wrong.

This worry and tension likely tire you out and leave you exhausted. It is hard to relax when your mind is preoccupied, so falling asleep is probably difficult. It is not surprising that you might wake up exhausted in the morning. Sometimes people with your profile use substances as a way of calming down. Be careful, as they may actually aggravate your anxiety.

People who worry a great deal often develop superstitions, obsessions, compulsions, and phobias. If something frightened you in the past, it is easy for you to feel like you have to stay away from it or practice some ritual that you feel protects you from harm.

Because you are so tense and high-strung, when little things go wrong you may feel overloaded, so you get irritated and angry. If people keep you waiting or interrupt you or don't do what they said they would do, you may get quite irritated.

- If COG is elevated, add: You report experiencing some difficulties with memory and concentration and that it is hard for you to pay attention. Sometimes you might worry that there is something wrong with your mind. Anxiety can be responsible for a lot of these symptoms.
- If SUB is elevated, add: You may be using substances as a way to medicate your anxiety. It can have very bad side effects interfering with your sleep and you may have rebound anxiety after the alcohol or drugs wear off.
- If CMP is elevated, add: You might have some compulsions or eccentric ways of doing things to make you feel you have some control. For example, you may make mental lists of everything you need to worry about, or you may need to check things multiple times to make sure you have completed a task.

- If ANP is elevated, add: Irritation can lead to angry outbursts when you feel interrupted or pressured and people around you might complain that you are too volatile.
- If RC1 is elevated, add: You probably have some physical ailments and complaints that may be aggravated by stress. These physical symptoms may cause you a great deal of anxiety and concern. It may be frightening since you often look for "What is the worst health-related thing that can happen?" and assume it will happen to you.
- If MLS is elevated, add: Your anxiety may have drained you to such a degree that you feel spent and exhausted and tired far more than you would like.
- If RC8 is elevated, add: Your profile suggests that you become easily preoccupied and concerned with how others see you negatively. You tend to stand back and observe the world almost as if you are watching a movie, perhaps as a way to avoid getting hurt. You may escape into your own fantasy world, especially during stressful times, and you may find it hard to relate to people and share your inner thoughts.
- If EAT is elevated, add: You may have focused on your eating as a way of managing your worries and concerns. Sometimes this can lead to an eating disorder, so it would be important to discuss this with your therapist.
- If SUI is elevated, add: Your anxiety and worry may at times be so severe that you consider suicide as a way of finding peace. Sometimes that is an escape fantasy but sometimes it is more serious. It would be important to discuss this with your therapist.
- If BRF is elevated, add: Your worry and anxiety may block you in a number of activities that you may have enjoyed in the past or activities that others seem to enjoy. These activities may cause you anxiety and even, in some cases, panic attacks.
- If SAV and/or INTR are elevated, add: You are an introvert, so meeting new people, making small talk with people you don't know, or going to loud parties of mostly strangers can be very difficult. You prefer small groups of people you know. It is possible that you have begun to avoid most people, perhaps because they make you anxious and you expect them to be critical of you even if they try to hide it. Your social phobia can leave you lonely and isolated and lost in your own thoughts.

Lifestyle and Family Background Feedback – RC7 Scale

People with your profile were often tense and high-strung children. Perhaps you were a "late bloomer" or had some personal eccentricities that made you vulnerable to being teased or put down. You may have been sensitive about failing in any way and were quick to feel guilty if you were scolded. A caregiver or authority figure may have been controlling or hovering and inadvertently made you feel like you weren't quite good enough.

In other cases, a major upheaval or series of recent unpredictable events may have put you on alert, always waiting for "the other shoe to drop." You adapted to this stress, scanning your environment to see what could go wrong next. Now you are going through life unable to relax and attempting to protect yourself against some unexpected catastrophe. You have learned to dislike surprises, even those with possible pleasant and happy connotations.

Treatment and Self-Help Suggestions – RC7 Scale

You have likely sought help because your anxiety feels overwhelming and because you are experiencing symptoms of stress. Anxiety and mood disorders are the most common mental health problems in the United States, and many effective and well-researched treatments are available.

The suggestions that follow will outline effective treatments, but in the United States, for general information about anxiety disorders, you can contact the National Institute of Mental Health (NIMH) at (866) 615-6464. The NIMH website is http://www.nimh.nih.gov.

1. Learn to stop your thoughts when they begin to get out of control. Work with your therapist to identify some of the more "intrusive" or anxiety-provoking thoughts that you have. "Thought-stopping" is an effective technique you can practice to help prevent the types of unwanted thoughts that can make you feel anxious. Several forms of thought-stopping are effective. One quick technique involves picturing or saying out loud, "Stop," whenever you experience these types of unwanted thoughts. You then replace the thought with a pleasant image or affirmation that is more positive (e.g., "I have felt this way before, and I know I can handle this"). Some individuals find snapping a rubber band on their wrist is helpful to distract them to more constructive thoughts.
2. Acceptance and commitment therapy uses strategies such as mindfulness and goal-setting to lessen discomfort and anxiety. Learn to meditate for a short time period every day to slow down or even stop your constant stream of thoughts. Many types of meditation practices have been demonstrated to help control distracting thoughts and to improve concentration and focus. One simple meditation technique involves sitting comfortably for 10 to 15 minutes each day with your eyes closed, silently repeating a sound, word, or phrase (called a mantra) to calm the mind and body. Overall, the regular practice of meditation is linked with many long-term positive effects, such as increased positive emotions, attentional abilities, and emotional stability.
3. Learning various types of intentional relaxation can help calm your automatic reactions to stressful situations. One type of relaxation, diaphragmatic breathing, exerts a powerful effect on your physical response to stress. When you feel threatened, your breathing is rapid and shallow, but this exercise can calm the automatic response of your nervous system and reduce reactive thinking and destructive emotions.
4. Work with your therapist to remember an event or series of events in which you felt completely taken off guard. Recall what it felt like. As you think about the frightening, unexpected event, close your eyes, take a deep breath, and use diaphragmatic breathing to relax. After repeating this process several times, you may find that the painful event is less upsetting. As mentioned above, mindfulness is a way to begin to manage your emotional responses; it involves paying attention to the present moment in a non-judgmental way and fostering a quality of curiosity and openness. You can begin by setting aside time to watch the moment without analyzing or judging it. Pay attention to the sight, sound, taste, smell, and feel of the experience. Engaging in a daily practice of mindfulness can help you manage powerful emotions.
5. Cognitive behavior therapy is an example of one type of psychotherapy that teaches different ways of thinking, behaving, and reacting to situations to reduce fear and anxiety. Work with your therapist to identify how automatic negative thoughts (ANTs) influence your feelings and your behavior. With practice, you can change the negative thought patterns that lead to anxiety. Examples of ANTs include, "I will never get this right," "I should have known better," and "I am sure that she doesn't like me."
6. Daily exercise (if permitted by your physician), especially aerobic exercise, can help reduce anxiety and can also help improve your general mood. Avoid caffeine. Try to incorporate a regular program of exercise into your daily routine.
7. Resilience building: If something goes wrong, try not to beat yourself up. Self-forgiveness begins with accepting the fact that you are human and can make mistakes. Instead of feeling remorse, think about what it is you regret, what you wish you had done differently, and what you can change. Make a list of your "signature strengths" that will help you the next time you are in a similar situation. For help identifying your signature strengths go to https://www.authentichappiness.sas.upenn.edu/testcenter.
8. Learn to recognize when you are angry with someone and attempt to deal with it directly. Don't assume that you are always at fault in any interpersonal misunderstanding. Learn to ask for what you want early in the process, so you don't develop resentment.

9. In some cases, your therapist may suggest medications that can help relieve your symptoms. Healthcare providers such as your primary care physician, a psychiatrist, a psychologist (in some states), or other qualified providers with specialized training can identify which medications may be of benefit to you.
10. If you are in a crisis, and unable to reach your therapist, call a suicide and crisis hotline [988 in the United States and Canada] for confidential support.

Aberrant Experiences (RC8) Scale

General Descriptors

Complaints

Confusion; alienation; disorganized thoughts; work and relationship difficulties; difficulties with memory, judgment, and/or concentration; feelings of derealization; bizarre bodily concerns; seeing things others don't; smelling peculiar odors; disturbing and strange thoughts; hearing one's thoughts out loud; hearing voices; believes others can read their mind; believes they have unusual perceptual abilities; believes they have unusual sensory/perceptual abilities.

Cognitions

Disorganized thoughts; imaginative and altered states; bizarre and intrusive thoughts; non-persecutory delusions; visual, auditory and olfactory hallucinations; loose associations; difficulty following conversations; unusual beliefs; concentration and attention difficulties.

Emotions

Dissociative experiences; feeling broken, damaged, or unlovable; outbursts of rage or hostility; feeling strange.

Traits and behaviors

Possibly psychotic; schizoid-like behavior; eccentric; socially withdrawn or reclusive; alienated; unkempt; lack of interests; disorganized speech; difficulty following conversations; problems performing tasks under stress.

Therapist's Notes – RC8 Scale

The 18 RC8 items reflect a variety of deviant sensory, perceptual, cognitive, and motor experiences. RC8 item content consists of aberrant experiences associated with hallucinations, dissociative experiences, and non-persecutory delusions (persecutory delusion item content is in RC6). Unusual thinking and perceptual processes, which are well-established aspects of psychosis proneness, are empirically linked to this scale. However, it is important to note that elevations on RC8 are not always associated with a primary thought disorder. The diagnosis of schizophrenia, for example, requires the exclusion of other conditions that contribute to psychosis (such as a substance/ medication-induced psychotic disorder).

Additionally, while RC8 covers much of the psychological landscape of aberrant experiences for a psychosis diagnosis, many characteristics that may pertain to a diagnosis of schizophrenia are captured on other RC Scales (such as RCd, RC2, and RC6). These scales include items measuring anhedonia, blunted affect, depression, and persecutory delusions. Simply stated, significant RC8 elevations likely reflect aberrant experiences/symptoms that may be associated with psychosis. However, it is important to consider other MMPI-3 scale elevations to refine a differential diagnosis as well as examining non-test data for inclusion of a psychotic diagnosis.

Individuals who fall within a T score range of 65–74 on RC8 have a rich imagination and may be described as creative, whereas those with low scores (T score ≤39) tend to be conventional and concrete in their thinking. Clients in this intermediate range of T score 65–74 are over-ideational, have a rich, at times troubling, inner life, and tend to withdraw into fantasy when stressed. They can become confused and unpredictably brittle and angry when stressed. They are sensitive to hostility and tend to keep others at a cautious emotional distance. These clients may report unusual thoughts and perceptual processes. Elevated scores should be inspected for item responses that may require follow-up questions.

Individuals with an elevated RC8 (at or above a T score of 75) have a number of things in common, including an incongruity of affect and thought content and the tendency for cognitive processing to break down under stress. Isolation of affect is a primary defense, so painful, even bizarre experiences are reported with little obvious emotional expression (unless RCd and/or RC2 and RC7 are elevated.) These clients exhibit negative self-esteem and can feel like "damaged goods." Clients with elevated scores feel isolated, alienated, and disconnected from others. Cold, indifferent, or hostile family relationships, general apathy, and conflicted feelings toward people they care about are common symptoms.

Many individuals who elevated on RC8, even if not overtly psychotic, feel dissociated and report bizarre sensory experiences. Under stress, their thinking can become disorganized, with loose associations, cognitive confusion, and unrealistic thinking. Other aberrant experiences may include auditory and visual hallucinations and non-persecutory delusions such as thought broadcasting and mind reading. Somatic delusions would be predicted if RC1 or NUC have a T score ≥65. If HLP is also elevated, they feel hopeless, helpless, and overwhelmed. Not surprisingly, emotional closeness and long-term relationships are difficult. These individuals feel disconnected from others and from a world that appears perplexing and strange. Aloof, tending to be secretive, and fearful of being rejected or humiliated, high scorers likely become cognitively disorganized under stress. Emotions are often experienced as alien and out of volitional control. High RC8 scorers may experience anger or disgust when others might feel love and contentment. They may have a sense of empty deadness in moments when others experience joy. Sexual or aggressive feelings may aggravate the cognitive slippage associated with elevations on RC8. Sexual urges and desires can be interrupted by fears of emotional closeness and vulnerability, eliciting approach–avoidance conflicts. Disturbing or distracting cognitive interruptions impair the processing of everyday reality to the detriment of basic daily activities and even minor decisions. Unable to think clearly, mistrustful, and disturbed by unusual sensory and motor experiences, many live a marginal and emotionally nomadic life. Individuals tend to develop magical ideation such as superstitions, rituals, and eccentric behaviors that serve as a way of keeping people at a distance and perhaps give some sense of control over their environment.

Lifestyle and Family Background – RC8 Scale

Often, as children, individuals elevated on RC8 exhibited peculiarities, eccentricities, or a slowness to mature. Levak's hypothesis (Levak et al., 2011) is that a genetic sensitivity and vulnerability to the disorganizing effects of hostility and a possible deleterious environment of cruel neglect or hateful hostility leads to high RC8 elevations. Withdrawal into fantasy, keeping others at an emotional distance and shutting down emotional and cognitive processes to escape perplexing reality makes adaptive sense. Personal eccentricities, slowness to mature, and being fearful and insecure in the presence of an adverse environment could have provoked humiliations, put-downs, and hostility from others. Developing eccentric, aberrant, and hostile behaviors as a self-protective way of keeping others at a distance would be adaptive in such an environment. The eventual collapse of effective functioning is hypothesized to be a result of being overwhelmed, both cognitively and emotionally.

Clarifying Scales – RC8 Scale

- When RC1 is elevated, clients will likely complain of unusual and even bizarre somatic symptoms that may have some organic neurological basis but could be compounded by delusional ideation.
- If RC2 and RCd are elevated, there is greater likelihood of withdrawal from others and feelings of being hopelessly damaged and demoralized. This is especially true if HLP is also elevated.
- If SUI is elevated, the psychological symptoms are so disturbing that suicide may be the only escape the person can envision for relief.
- If RC4 is elevated, the distrust and lack of empathy already associated with RC8 is increased. These individuals experience profuse, generalized distrust as opposed to the fixed rational paranoia associated with high RC6 elevations. Unpredictability, impulsivity, hostility, and irritability would be likely. Sexual adjustment is difficult, with a tendency for sexual aggression confusion. Relationships are often marginal and highly conflicted.
- If RC6 is elevated, there is an increased probability of psychosis with persecutory paranoid delusions, suspiciousness, and florid schizophrenic thinking. Flat, blunted, and inappropriate affect would not be unusual. If any of AGG, ANP and IMP are elevated, anger expressions could erupt as brief, acute, and possibly dangerous outbursts.
- If RC7 is elevated, distortions in reality testing can lead to anxiety and fearfulness, but also isolation from affect, so the therapist may not observe the physiological signs of severe anxiety.
- If WRY, NFC, or SFD are elevated, clients will manifest chronic worrying, nervousness, fears and anxieties, and feelings of inferiority and inadequacy. They lack basic self-confidence, have difficulties with concentration and problem-solving, and frustrations in maintaining positive interpersonal relationships.
- If RC9 is elevated, episodes of hyperactivity when the individual is seen as confused, demanding, hostile, panicky, and circumstantial are predicted. Delusional thinking may be grandiose, such as receiving special religious messages.
- If SFI is elevated, the individual may feel they are an important messenger of some bizarre entity, organization, or philosophy. This reflects the combination of grandiosity and psychosis. Self-expectations tend to be perfectionistic, so small failures are experienced as confirming the individual's low self-esteem and can precipitate manic overactivity. The psychosis could be associated with a manic episode.
- If DSF, SAV, and SHY are elevated, social avoidance and shyness combined with a sense of being damaged and broken would aggravate the severity of the disturbance.
- If NUC is elevated, the individual likely experiences numerous vague and shifting neurological symptoms as well as the bizarre sensory experiences associated with RC8 elevations.
- If EAT is elevated, an eating disorder that could be intertwined with delusions and paranoid ideation is possible.
- If SUB is elevated, there is the possibility that substance abuse has precipitated or aggravated a psychotic disorder.

Therapy and Therapeutic Pitfalls – RC8 Scale

Clients with high elevations on RC8 are alienated and often mistrustful. Although psychotropic medication is often useful, without the development of trust it is hard to prescribe. Even non-psychotic clients are guarded and exhibit the hostility, coldness, and indifference toward the therapist that they expect from others. An overly familiar and friendly therapeutic attitude may be met with suspicion and discomfort. However, interpersonal warmth, with structure and professional objectivity, can help to establish trust. In "brief therapy," teaching basic social skills, thought-stopping, and relaxation techniques can be useful. It would be challenging for these clients to benefit from relaxation exercise, however, until they have developed some control, usually through medication, over their disruptive internal environment.

Helping clients recognize what types of stress precipitate cognitive disorganization and withdrawal could be useful. During therapy sessions, should clients manifest cognitive slippage or psychotic-like symptoms, therapist awareness of the shift to identify what precipitated the cognitive disorganization would be important. Such moments provide an opportunity to teach clients to recognize when they become disorganized and to rehearse self-calming exercises. For example, the therapist might observe, "Right now, I'm not able to follow you. Did something frighten you, upset you, or make you angry? Did I say or do anything that made you feel that way?" Giving the clients accurate feedback about what is happening in the "here and now" can help them to recognize when they experience stress and can teach more socially appropriate responses.

Long-term supportive, structured, and measured nurturing therapy can help repair damaged self-esteem and teach the management of cognitive disruption and emotional panic. Discussing how the client is feeling in the moment and discussing the therapist–client interactions (as long as the therapist is authentic and not hostile) is a way to repair damaged identity and teach social skills. Building social skills and helping the client with social support systems and collateral contact with family and friends is also often helpful.

Feedback Statements – RC8 Scale

T score 55–64

Your profile suggests that, when stressed, especially when people are angry with you, it can cloud your thinking and lead you to withdraw to protect yourself.

T score 65–74

Your profile suggests that you may be a creative person and readily able to escape into a rich fantasy world. Others may see you as eccentric because of some of your ideas and they may find you somewhat difficult to get to know on a deep level since you are cautious about trusting people with your inner life. You are sensitive and may become knocked off balance if you perceive hostility from others. There are other times when disturbing, unwanted thoughts can interrupt your concentration. You may periodically experience bad moods, unsure what precipitated them, when you feel empty, isolated, and disconnected from others. At these times you may withdraw from others and feel annoyed if they attempt to discover what is upsetting you. You are careful to avoid being open or vulnerable with others until you are certain that they harbor no hostility toward you. When you sense that someone is angry with you, your thinking can become confused, and you may respond in ways that others find difficult to understand.

People with this profile often grew up in environments where a parent or caregiving figure sometimes treated them with hostility, coldness, or even cruelty. Therefore, it is not surprising that you are particularly sensitive to antagonism from others. You likely feel out of sorts if you experience hostility or coldness from others. You have learned to be cautious, keeping an emotional distance from people until you can really trust them.

T score ≥75

Currently you may be knocked off balance and confused. The world may be a somewhat frightening place right now because it is hard for you to read people and to know how they're feeling toward you. You may feel disconnected from others, as if you are looking at the world from a distance. Perhaps you feel as if you are outside of your body, looking in on a world to which you feel you don't belong. This feeling of apartness from yourself is called depersonalization. Feeling as if things are not quite real (as if you are watching them in a movie) is called derealization. These feelings may be a way for you to escape from what you feel is an uncomfortable or scary situation. Watching the world from an emotional distance rather than being spontaneously involved is a way to protect yourself from being hurt.

Even when things are going well, or in a tender or sweet moment, you may find yourself feeling strangely cold or even angry or disgusted. Moments that others find happy or tender might leave you untouched. You may experience dark moods where you suddenly feel angry, empty, and irritable, and you might not know where the mood comes from. In fact, these dark moods may sweep over you even when things are going relatively well. You may know you are experiencing a lot of emotion, yet you may feel strangely disconnected from the feelings, able to observe them but not feel them.

It is hard to trust people because you feel as if most people are wearing a mask. You find it difficult to trust people who appear to be sincere, as it seems like they are hiding behind a facade. You may be afraid that if you let down your guard and show vulnerability, people will take advantage of you or be cruel. It is challenging to be around people because you feel uncomfortable. Your profile suggests that you are sensitive to others' moods toward you. At times, you may feel paranoid, afraid that people are out to get you and that you can't trust anyone. You may find yourself coming up with conspiracy theories about what people or institutions are trying to do to you and how they want to hurt you.

It is hard for you to focus and plan effectively because it is strenuous to control your thoughts and organize them in a meaningful way. When you are attempting to concentrate, you may experience interruptions to your thinking, as if you don't have control over your mind. Sometimes the intrusive thoughts that invade your mind may be disturbing and may frighten you.

You have a tendency to daydream, spending time inside your mind fantasizing; sometimes these daydreams may be disturbing. Spending time in your own thoughts may make it hard for you to get things done. Life must feel somewhat gray, empty, and at times meaningless. It is laborious to get motivated and to have goals and ambitions because nothing seems worthwhile or rewarding.

You could get so tense that you may be unable to decide what is real and what is not. Sometimes you may hear your thoughts spoken out loud, as voices talking to you. In some cases, people with your profile actually have hallucinations where they see, hear, and even feel things that others don't experience. Some of these frightening hallucinations and thoughts may get so intense that you withdraw and hide. In some stressful situations you may feel as if things are not real. You may have blank spells where your activities are interrupted and you don't know what is going on around you. At times, you may feel as if someone has control over your mind and is hypnotizing or controlling you to make you do things you may not want to do.

- If RCd is elevated, add: You appear to feel pretty discouraged about your current psychological condition, perhaps because it has gone on so long or because it has been so exhausting and frightening. Perhaps you have had unrewarding experiences with mental health practitioners or bad experiences with medications that have left you feeling that you can't get better very easily.

- If RC2 is elevated, add: You lack positive emotional experiences. You may experience difficulties with sleep, or waking up too early and not being able to return to restful sleep. You may find that little gives you pleasure and may have difficulties with memory and concentration.
- If HLP is elevated, add: You may feel defeated, helpless, and hopeless, feeling that your condition can't get better no matter what you do.
- If SUI is elevated, add: Thinking of ending your life may be a way for you to escape the bad thoughts and feelings that you are having. In some cases, people with your profile actually develop a plan on how to end their life. In either case, please discuss these thoughts and feelings with your therapist. If you are in a crisis, and unable to reach your therapist, call a crisis helpline [988 in the United States and Canada] for confidential support.
- If RC4 is elevated, add: Right now, it is very hard for you to trust anyone, so you feel alone and self-protective. You may even feel suspicious of people and their motives. Consequently, you may approach people with a demanding, angry stance, feeling that you have to fight for what you need, since you assume people are against you. You may be impulsive in the way you deal with stress, becoming aggressive quickly if you feel mistreated or misunderstood. Since you don't trust others, you may want to come across in a way that frightens people, so they don't approach you. Wearing clothes that suggest you are dangerous, having tattoos and piercings that reveal you to be a rebel, even a dangerous rebel, could be your way to keep people away.
- If RC6 is elevated, add: Your profile suggests that you may be experiencing disturbing paranoid thoughts and feelings, so you don't feel safe. You likely feel deeply suspicious that others are out to harm you, control your thoughts and your behaviors. You might feel a need to protect yourself with weapons, even though that would be dangerous. When stressed, you might find yourself unable to think clearly, with bizarre, unpleasant thoughts invading your mind. You may be so stressed that you hear your own thoughts and experience visual hallucinations.
- If RC7 is elevated, add: People probably can't see how anxious and fearful you feel since you are not able to reveal it or talk about it. Yet inside, you appear to live on edge as if something bad might happen at any moment.
- If WRY, NFC, and/or SFD are elevated, add: Worry appears to be a constant companion with you feeling fearful, constantly on edge, waiting for something terrible to occur, and doubting yourself whatever you do. Decisions can be difficult since you don't trust your problem-solving skills, so you might let others take charge even though, at times, that can be humiliating.
- If RC9 is elevated, add: Your energy level right now is very high, so you may experience racing thoughts and periods where you are extremely active, perhaps believing that you have a special mission to fulfill or a big idea that you need to convince people is workable. You may find that you have periods where you feel very agitated, even panicky, and at times get demanding, irritable, and hostile since you feel intense pressure to be heard and achieve your goals. You may feel you have the right answer to various conspiracy theories, or that you have a religious message that people need to hear. You are your own worst critic, so if you have recently had a setback, you likely perceived yourself as failing disastrously. This may have led to you experiencing a manic episode, as if mobilizing all your energy to undo what you see as a big failure. The high energy may be disorganizing your thoughts. Imagine a computer that keeps flicking through numerous windows so you can't focus on any one window. That is perhaps an analogy to how your mind is currently racing.
- If SFI is elevated, add: You likely feel that you are a very important person and have monumental things to say that people need to hear. You may become intense, even loud, trying to get others to pay attention to your ideas.
- If SFD, SAV, SHY, and/or INTR are elevated, add: Currently you are doubting yourself and feeling very insecure around others. You avoid people, not even wanting to look at others, since you dread strangers talking to you. You probably try to be as invisible as possible, drawing as little attention to yourself as you can.

- If NUC is elevated, add: You may be experiencing some physical symptoms such as numbness, tingling in your extremities, headaches, dizziness, and other shifting symptoms that come and go, especially when you are stressed.
- If ANP or AGG are elevated, add: Your profile suggests that you are vulnerable to episodes of impulsive anger and even aggression, especially if you feel threatened or humiliated. Most people experience anger sometimes, but it appears that you are often on the edge of being explosive.

Lifestyle and Family Background Feedback – RC8 Scale

Perhaps you grew up in difficult financial circumstances, so you did not feel secure. Many with your profile grew up in homes with caregivers whose anger could become hostile, even cruel. It is possible that you didn't get parental attention and affection. They may have treated you at times with contempt or cold hostility. This was very painful, so now when you need support, it is difficult to know where to turn because you are afraid that the people around you will be cruel and rejecting. You may have protected yourself by retreating into daydreaming and fantasy. You may have fantasized about how to pay others back and treat them cruelly to punish them for what they were doing to you.

You may also have had some habits (such as stuttering or nervousness) that left you vulnerable to being teased and humiliated. Because of your sensitivity, you may have experienced your childhood as particularly painful. It could be that you are going through a similar period right now, feeling vulnerable to being disliked or rejected.

Treatment and Self-Help Suggestions – RC8 Scale

1. Often, medication can help to take away the disquieting thoughts, dark moods, and the feelings of unreality. It can also aid you in thinking more clearly and not feeling so empty and alone. It is important that you and your therapist talk openly about any uncertainty or concerns you have about taking medication.
2. If you find yourself daydreaming or having cruel, angry, or hostile fantasies, learn how to switch off your thoughts and focus on more positive things. Work with your therapist to identify some of the most distressing and negative intrusive thoughts that you have. "Thought-stopping" is an effective technique you can practice to help prevent you from having the types of unwanted thoughts that can make you feel anxious. Several forms of thought-stopping are effective. One quick technique involves picturing or saying out loud "Stop" whenever you experience these types of unwanted thoughts. You then replace the thought with a pleasant image or affirmation that is more positive (e.g., "I have felt this way before, and I know I can handle this").
3. When you feel dark moods sweep over you, don't give into them. Because you anticipate the worst and have difficulty focusing on the positive, keeping a daily "gratitude journal" can help instill a sense of hope and can help to replace some of your negative thinking with more positive thoughts and feelings.
4. Don't assume that people are going to hate you and that you are unlovable. Your tendency is to think that all reactions by others toward you are negative. You may feel so self-conscious that you believe people are looking at you critically. Remember that you are knocked off balance right now and that you may be misinterpreting others' motives.
5. See if you can become aware of negative, self-critical thoughts such as telling yourself that you are unlovable or somehow defective. This type of harsh self-judgment can cause a great deal of pain. Work with your therapist on ways to increase your self-esteem. There are a number of good techniques, including personal wellness, setting goals, self-expression, looking at "core beliefs," and monitoring your "self-talk."

6. Work with your therapist to identify your positive traits and "signature strengths." Write them in a list and read them every day.
7. If people are nice to you, don't assume that it is a trick. Work with your therapist to identify people or agencies that you have difficulty trusting. See if the two of you can discover any fear-based types of "distorted thinking," and then work to challenge those old beliefs that are not helpful to you right now. One type of distorted thinking is called "overgeneralization" (e.g., assuming that because someone was cruel to you in the past all people will be cruel). A more helpful way of thinking would be that just because one person was cruel does not mean that no one will ever be kind again.
8. Role-play with your therapist to develop your social skills, foster your relationships, and help you create new ones.
9. Get enough sleep and ask your therapist for techniques to achieve better sleep hygiene.
10. Exercise, if your physician permits it, as this can relieve tension for you.
11. Keep up good hygiene which will help you to feel more comfortable around others.
12. If you are not working or in school, ask your therapist about social services to help you get back into work or study.
13. Importantly, stick to your treatment plan even if your symptoms lessen.
14. Have a plan in place should your symptoms worsen so that you can get the right help as soon as possible.
15. If you are comfortable enough to join a support group of others with similar challenges, this will facilitate you learning helpful new coping strategies.
16. If you are in a crisis, and unable to reach your therapist, call a crisis helpline [988 in the United States and Canada] for confidential support.

Hypomanic Activation (RC9) Scale

General Descriptors

Complaints

Irritability and/or temper outbursts; sometimes acts aggressively; racing thoughts; concentration problems; feels misunderstood; sleep hygiene issues; poor frustration tolerance; easily bored; readily disappointed.

Cognitions

Overly optimistic; grandiose ideas; enterprising; flight of ideas; tangential thinking; overinclusive; easily distracted; ebullient; possible delusions; self-aggrandizing; opinionated.

Emotions

Emotions alter quickly; cheerful and/or easily aggravated; optimistic; impatient; enthusiastic; excitable; episodically irritable; hostile; aggressive; depressed and/or elated.

Traits and behaviors

Upbeat; positive; highly energetic; sensation-seeking; narcissistic; manipulative; dominant; possibly antisocial or psychopathic; overexcitable; mood instability; possible hypomanic or manic episodes; ambitious; driven; jocular; approval-seeking; garrulous; exuberant; overcommitted; unrealistic; irritable or aggressive; disorganized; possible sexual promiscuity; poor judgment; antagonistic.

Therapist's Notes – RC9 Scale

The 15 items on the RC9 Scale are designed to identify the main construct of hypomanic activation which, at its core, includes two temperamental traits: aggression and overexcitation (i.e., activation). While most individuals with hypomanic personality traits do not develop a bipolar disorder, elevations on RC9 are associated with an increased risk for this disorder. Because elevated RC9 scores can reflect a state of manic activation or the more stable trait of hypomanic characteristics, it is important to examine other MMPI-3 scales to better refine an accurate interpretation of the individual's RC9 score. These scales include IMP, ACT, AGG, AGGR, CYN, SFI, and DOM as well as DISC. Mania and hypomania are multifactorial, and the inherently transient nature of its core manifestations may not be captured by the RC9 score alone. However, in most cases, elevated RC9 scores likely reflect the underlying features of these disorders and personality traits.

Elevations on RC9 (T score 65 and above) are associated with a high level of energy, activity, and possible aggression. Even if appearing relaxed, individuals will report a great deal of internal cognitive activity. High RC9 scores suggest individuals who can appear buoyant, cheerful, and charismatic; however, when frustrated or confronted, they can quickly become hostile, angry, demanding, and confrontational. Hypomania or mania are possible diagnoses at T scores of 65 or above. Overactivity, overcommitment, unrealistic goal-setting, and irritability are common in this T score range. Flight of ideas, pressured speech, a hostile joking humor, and grandiosity are characteristics of elevations on RC9. These elevated scores are associated with individuals who are highly competitive, threatened by the successes of others, and have strong needs to achieve. Elevated scores reflect individuals who work in spurts of energy and become highly energized in the face of a possible failure; becoming productive in a demanding, irritated, and controlling fashion.

Increased RC9 elevations reflect disorganization, distractibility, and grandiose, unrealistic goal-setting. A reduced need for sleep, rapid weight changes, and the use of substances as a way of medicating and managing energy are associated with high elevations. These elevated scores reflect an increased energy that can manifest itself in flight of ideas and significant grandiosity, increased sexual drive, and overcommitment. Elevations do not always reflect mania, and elevations do not correlate perfectly with the degree of disturbance. Sometimes moderate elevations (T score 65 to 74) may reflect a manic episode and, in other cases, higher elevations of RC9 are a sign of hypomania rather than mania. Examining other associated scales and the history of the individual can help determine a differential diagnosis. Precipitating circumstances are often a perceived or actual failure or a grandiose overcommitment. Individuals with elevated scores tend to have poor judgment, poor frustration tolerance, and intimidate others with their temper and the intensity of their demands. Many bright individuals with elevated RC9 scores can be extremely successful, blazing new trails in business, finance, and politics. Their success improves when they surround themselves with methodical, detail-oriented types to protect them from hasty, poorly thought-through actions. In other cases, their heightened activation is clearly evident, with occasional disastrously poor judgment.

Elevated scores on RC9 are seen in individuals who are easily bored, impatient with details, and strongly resist being controlled. These scores suggest individuals who are liable to be narcissistic and opportunistic and tend to exploit situations created by others' mistakes and vulnerabilities. Elevated scores do not necessarily indicate antisocial or psychopathic traits, unless RC4, JCP, and AGGR are also elevated. Although often highly social, individuals with high RC9 scores have difficulty being vulnerable and intimate. As partners, non-manic individuals are initially seen as attractive and charismatic. However, if the elevation increases, the person is seen as controlling, irritable, and demanding when stressed.

Individuals with low T scores (T <39) exhibit some of the opposite attributes associated with RC9 elevations. In the presence of RC2 elevations, a low RC9 score may reflect the depressive side of a bipolar disorder. Sometimes, medical problems (e.g., thyroid) may be the source of low energy. In the absence of any other RC elevations, a low T score may reflect a reliable, orderly individual who is careful not to overcommit and is protective of their energy level.

Lifestyle and Family Background – RC9 Scale

Levak's hypothesis (Levak et al., 2011) is that RC9 reflects a combination of a genetic predisposition to overactivity and high needs for stimulation and excitement, together with possible early demands from caregivers for success and achievement. Individuals with elevated RC9 scores have been described by caregivers as having been active, energetic, and hard-to-manage overly excitable and demanding children. Some may have been diagnosed as hyperactive in childhood and medicated with psychostimulants. Caregivers may have attempted to control a demanding, high-energy, distractible child by restriction, thus increasing the child's drive state.

In some instances, parental, social, and economic striving meant that parental approval was contingent upon getting good grades, winning competitions, and earning prestige through continuous accomplishments. The hypothesis is that parental approval was under a partial reinforcement schedule, often only for spectacular success. This maintained the child in a constant high-drive state and led to feelings of vulnerability to rejection around failure.

Clarifying Scales – RC9 Scale

- If RC1 is elevated, there is a significant focus on physical ailments that may be shaped by the stress imposed by hypomanic overactivity on the individual's musculoskeletal and organ systems. Typically, the person is lacking insight into the psychological component of their somatic symptoms.
- If NUC is elevated, vague and shifting numbness, tingling in the extremities, blurred vision, and/or headaches could be reflective of these individuals' overall stress due to hypomanic overactivity.
- If COG is elevated, complaints of difficulty with concentration and memory are likely, with an intense focus on diagnosis and treatment.
- If RC2 is elevated, the euphoria and expansiveness of RC9 will be mitigated by the dysphoria and fears of loss associated with RC2. The result is moodiness, emotional lability, agitation, tension, anxiety, irritability, and episodes of hypomania.
- Elevations on RC9 are associated with energized behaviors, thoughts, and emotions associated with other scale elevations. For example, elevations on RC4, without an elevation on RC9, would predict cold, calculating, aloof, and emotionally distant traits. With the addition of RC9, RC4 behaviors are "energized," suggesting impulsive, hedonistic, rule-breaking acting-out.
- Even in the absence of significant RC4 elevations, if IMP, ACT, and/or AGG are elevated with RC9, there is an increased likelihood of impulsive aggressive behavior.
- If RC6 is elevated, there is a strong possibility of highly rationalized delusions and fixed ideas of being mistreated. Abrupt angry reactions are predicted since these individuals have difficulty with expressing anger. They tend to be morally rigid and judgmental toward others, and they have a strong need for approval. Criticism or judgment toward them leads to angry defensiveness and agitation.
- If RC7 is elevated, the anxiety, worry, and self-doubt are energized, predicting panic attacks, restlessness, and preoccupations about being a failure.
- If RC8 is elevated, the individual is likely to be confused, hostile, hyperactive, circumstantial, panicky, high-strung, and evasive, yet talkative.

- If SFI is elevated, grandiose religious or conspiratorial content is possible. Self-expectations are perfectionistic, so perceived failures are seen as disastrous blows to self-esteem.
- If DISC, ANP, ACT, AGG, and/or AGGR, are elevated, the irritability and impulsive anger expression associated with RC9 elevations are heightened. This is suggestive of angry outbursts and possible aggression when the individual feels blocked or frustrated in their goal-directed behavior or if they feel criticized.
- If DOM is elevated, the individual will present as forceful, opinionated, and dominating. The individual confidently takes a position on topics that interest them and possibly takes an argumentative stance in their interpersonal relationships.
- If SAV and SHY are elevated, the individual will likely present as aloof, overly confident, self-absorbed, possibly grandiose, but also taciturn and reclusive.
- If SUB is elevated, there is a strong likelihood that the individual may be self-medicating with substances, increasing the risk of impulsive, possibly dangerous, highly energized, and aggressive behavior.

Therapy and Therapeutic Pitfalls – RC9 Scale

Impulsive and reckless conduct is likely in a manic state. High RC9 suggests self-defeating and self-destructive behavior, such as driving at excessive speeds, abuse of substances, promiscuous sexuality, and irritable aggression. Suicide risk increases if clients move from a euphoric to a dysphoric state subsequent to perceived catastrophic loss. Medication is usually necessary to control a manic state, although it is often resisted as it interferes with the experience of elation and control. Rarely is treatment sought voluntarily, and often only after legal, interpersonal, or family difficulties.

These clients typically are resistant to insight therapy because of the taxing emotional demands, the slow pace, and the lack of external focus. Coaching can be less threatening to clients in less manic states because of its practical "here and now" focus. It may help clients manage their overactivity and may provide "reality-based," practical guidelines on how to manage daily activities, goals, and the tendency to be impulsive and overcommitted. One analogy that may resonate for these individuals is to suggest that their "engine" goes from 0 to 100 miles an hour with little modulation.

Understanding the drawbacks of euphoria and using cognitive behavioral therapy to teach emotional-behavioral control can be useful. Relaxation training and daily physical exercise can be helpful in managing high levels of energy.

Therapists who are relaxed but set limits, and who exhibit a sense of humor, will work well with clients who experience wide mood swings: charming and likable one minute but irritable and angry the next. These clients tend to be evasive, so feedback from collateral sources is useful if permitted by the client.

Secondary paranoia is not unusual, so a misdiagnosis of schizophrenia is a danger. Not all individuals with RC9 above a T score of 65 are necessarily manic or even disorganized.

The degree of disorganization and pathology is not always well correlated with elevations, so moderate scores can predict hypomania. The interview and history determine the level of disturbance.

Feedback Statements – RC9 Scale

T score <39

Your profile suggests that you approach life with a steady, slow pace, careful not to overcommit to too many tasks and activities. You generally dislike feeling pressured or hurried and you generally take care not to wear yourself out. After bursts of activity, you generally need time to recuperate, and you don't need to be "always on the go."

- If RC4 is low, add: You are likely seen by others as reliable and dependable, completing things that you committed to.

T score 39–64

Your profile is in the normal range. You have a ready supply of energy and do not drive yourself unrealistically to achieve and succeed. You generally do not overcommit to too many tasks and activities. Things get done in an orderly manner without your being driven by unrealistic competitive needs to prove yourself.

T score 65–74

Your current scores suggest that you are energetic and optimistic. People generally see you as cheerful, positive, driven, and happy. You have a need to prove yourself and are motivated to achieve. Tending to be a big-picture thinker, you can easily become distracted, bored, or restless. You can become irritable and angry, perhaps even explosively so, especially when people get in your way, frustrate you, or block your goals. People with your profile tend to be somewhat distractible, and when excited about something, you can easily become overcommitted and unrealistic. Because your pace and energy are greater than average, you may get frustrated when others cannot keep up with you. Feeling that the world moves too slowly, it is easy to become impatient with how long it takes others to do things. You like to handle a number of projects at the same time and sometimes will take on more than you can possibly finish on time. Preferring a life that is filled with projects and excitement, routine may be boring, and you will likely seek novelty and some risk.

T score >75

Your profile reveals you have a number of strengths. You are an energetic, driven, ambitious individual who is able to think and move quickly and get a lot done. You generally are seen as positive, optimistic, and sunny. You have boundless energy and are able to see the connections between things, so you think quickly. People with your profile are often highly social, engaging, and interesting.

Some of your strengths may actually work against you at times. You may have periods where you are so optimistic that you overcommit and take on so many tasks and activities that it is very difficult to complete them all. Sometimes your energy may be so high that you feel a reduced need for sleep and feel impatient and angry with a world that moves too slowly. During these periods, your moods may quickly shift from positive to negative. You may be upbeat and cheerful one moment and angry and irritated the next, feeling that people are blocking you from getting what you want.

Sometimes your optimism may shade toward euphoria. During these times, you may feel that you can accomplish anything and may engage in behavior that later is seen as reckless, even dangerous. You may come up with grand ideas that later prove to have been unrealistic. You may feel so energized that you don't feel a need for sleep, so you go for many hours without rest. When you exhaust yourself, you may "crash land" becoming depressed and self-critical.

You may feel so much energy that you can become irritated with people for not keeping up with you. When your energy is high, working on a single task can be difficult. You have a tendency to see the connections between things, so it is easy for you to become distracted and sidetracked. At other times, you may become so focused on a particular idea or activity that you keep at it when others feel you should let it go. At these times, when people try to persuade you that you are being unrealistic, you can become quite angry or irritated, even explosive and aggressive.

People with your profile tend to need excitement, adventure, and a challenge – so without such stimulation you can become easily bored. You tend to go for the big, grand, idea rather than taking a slow, steady approach toward solving a problem. Daily routine and details can be difficult for you. Your high level of energy may have been productive in the past, but your judgment may be currently impaired and could get you into difficulties.

During times of high emotional arousal, you may get so wound up and your mind may work so quickly that you actually distort reality. In some cases, people with your profile can experience reality distortions, reflecting your intense energy and internal pressure.

- If SFI is elevated, add: You may feel you have very important things that you need to tell people and you may become intense, demanding that people listen to you. Others may feel bullied by your intensity.
- If ACT, ANP, DISC, IMP, AGG, and/or AGGR are elevated, add: When you become frustrated by what you perceive as other peoples' stupidity or if you feel impatient or blocked in getting what you want, you may become quite aggressive and angry, and your intensity may frighten people. Your surges of high energy, confidence, and need to achieve may lead to you being impulsive, jumping on opportunities, promising things to others, overcommitting, and jumping to conclusions that can backfire.
- If ACT, DISC, IMP, AGG, and/or AGGR are elevated, add: When you become frustrated by what you perceive as other peoples' stupidity (or if you feel impatient or blocked in getting what you want) you may become quite aggressive and angry, and your intensity may frighten people.
- If THD and/or PSYC are elevated, add: You may think you see all the ways the world is connected, and believe your reality makes sense. You may think you see conspiracies or religious messages, but this might be the result of having excessive energy.
- If SUB is elevated, add: People with your profile often use alcohol or some other substance as a way to either medicate the intense energy and euphoria or keep it going. You may feel that alcohol is not affecting you, so you keep drinking until you become quite inebriated or even black out. You may be trying to self-medicate your moods, to manage the high energy, or keep it going since you don't want to slow down; however, this can be quite dangerous and will actually increase your mood instability.

Lifestyle and Family Background Feedback – RC9 Scale

People with your profile were often energetic, driven, and rambunctious children. Perhaps you have always been adventurous, excitement-seeking, and risk-taking. Sometimes, as children, people with your profile were diagnosed with attention deficit hyperactivity disorder. Your need for novelty and stimulation might have led to struggles with your caregivers over being controlled. In some cases, your need to do extremely well came from a childhood where you felt you had to achieve high levels of success to prove that you or your family were worthwhile. Now, you strive to excel through overcommitment, overactivity, and achievement.

You may have recently experienced a setback or loss that makes you feel you have failed and will never be successful enough. This might have pushed you into an increased level of activity, driving you to strive to accomplish great things in a short period of time.

Treatment and Self-Help Suggestions – RC9 Scale

1. When other people are speaking, observe your tendency to interrupt or become distracted and think about other things. When you catch yourself interrupting or becoming distracted, take a deep breath and try to listen, slow your thoughts, and stay in the present moment.

2. Learn with your therapist how to recognize when you have racing thoughts. The practice of mindfulness is a way for you to channel your high levels of energy and to increase your focus and productivity. Mindfulness involves paying attention to the present moment in a non-judgmental way and fostering a quality of curiosity and openness. Try to intentionally bring an open and accepting attention to everything you do. Engaging in a daily practice of mindfulness can help you redirect your attention instead of going on autopilot.
3. At times, your energy may work well for you, so you have a great deal of confidence and infectious energy, quickly getting the big picture, but you can also have trouble concentrating on details. Work with your therapist to develop habits that will help you stay focused. For example, morning is often the best time to take on tasks that require attention. Although many people need a quiet environment to stay on task, you may find it more helpful to turn on a sound machine or play non-distracting background music so that you have some "white noise." Giving yourself breaks every hour can also help you to stay focused.
4. You may feel that you are seeing reality clearly and that most people are unable to appreciate your insights and goals. You may have a lofty goal in mind and may feel others block you because they are not very bright, or because they are jealous. Be aware you are so energized that you are speeding too fast and likely missing the road signs of possible danger ahead.
5. Because of your high-energy, racing mind, and your tendency to overcommit, you may need medication to slow you down enough so that you can be productive. Although you may be successful in the short term, eventually something is likely to go wrong if you continue to move so quickly. It is important that you and your therapist talk openly about any uncertainty or concerns you have about taking medication.
6. In your therapy, see if you can identify any recent events that may have pushed you into this state of heightened activity. Did you experience a recent setback or loss? Have you lost someone important in your life? Did someone else's success lead you into thinking that you were not successful? Did someone criticize or judge you? Or are you anticipating that you are going to fail at something?
7. As you have a tendency to overcommit, you may be unrealistic about what you can actually accomplish. There are many software applications for the computer and cell phone that could help you manage tasks, set priorities, and track important dates. A useful software application can be found at http://www.mylifeorganized.net.
8. It is important that you engage in physical exercise during this period of high energy. Daily exercise, if allowed by your physician, can help you to become more relaxed, but don't overdo it.
9. Avoid recreational drugs as a way of medicating your energy. They may actually aggravate your mood swings and lead you to making unpredictable and even dangerous decisions.
10. When you experience surges of irritability and rage, take a moment to stand back from the situation in order to calm yourself down. Practicing some type of relaxation exercise on a regular basis can help reduce irritability, stress, and anger. Relaxation can lead to a decrease in heart rate, blood pressure, respiration, and muscle tension. Yoga, meditation, biofeedback, and progressive muscle relaxation are all methods that can help you achieve a state of deep relaxation.
11. Adhering to a structured daily routine can be pivotal for you in promoting emotional stability, resilience, and overall wellbeing. A regular schedule can help you to avoid potential triggers that could set off your symptoms.
12. Common triggers include lack of sleep, abusing alcohol or drugs, financial stressors, relationship conflicts, and stress. Discuss with your therapist ways to address these triggers so you can better cope with them.

5 Somatic/Cognitive Dysfunction Scales

Introduction

Development

The Specific Problems (SP) Scales were developed to identify more narrowly focused issues and characteristics assessed by the Higher-Order (H-O) Scales and Restructured Clinical (RC) Scales as well as those that are not directly measured by any of the RC Scales, such as suicidal ideation or shyness. The empirical literature and *MMPI-3 Technical Manual* (Ben-Porath & Tellegen, 2020b) indicate that SP Scale scores are sufficiently reliable and valid to be interpreted as stand-alone independent measures, regardless of elevations on higher-level scales. The relatively short SP Scales range from 5 to 15 items; 19 scales have less than 10 items; and 7 scales are comprised of 10 or more items.

The 26 SP Scales are categorized into 4 groupings: Somatic/Cognitive, Internalizing, Externalizing, and Interpersonal. These groupings were classified through both conceptual reviews and correlation analyses with the H-O and RC Scales.

Within the somatic/cognitive domain are four scales: Malaise (MLS), Neurological Complaints (NUC), Eating Concerns (EAT), and Cognitive Complaints (COG). MLS, NUC, and COG are related to specific expressions of somatic symptoms as categorized in the *Diagnostic and Statistical Manual, Fifth Edition, Text Revision* (American Psychiatric Association, 2022).

The *MMPI-3 Technical Manual* (Ben-Porath & Tellegen, 2020b) presents supportive reliability data for all these scales, indicating that these measures are reliable sources of information about psychological functioning. Empirical correlates for each of the 26 SP Scales are generally consistent with the scale names, reflective of the underlying constructs. There is empirical support for both convergent and discriminant validity for these scales.

Application

The Somatic/Cognitive Scales should be examined after protocol validity is established. Threats to validity may contraindicate a valid interpretation of Somatic/Cognitive Scales.

Following validity considerations, the H-O and RC Scales will serve as a compass, pointing to specific Somatic/Cognitive Scales for further interpretive clarity. However, there may be instances wherein a Somatic/Cognitive Scale is notably elevated without H-O and/or RC Scale elevations. In such a case, a full interpretation of the Somatic/Cognitive Scales would still be indicated.

DOI: 10.4324/9781003557920-5

Malaise (MLS) Scale

General Descriptors

Complaints

Feels weak; tired; sluggish; worn out; worries about poor health; sleep disturbance; sexual dysfunction; distressed; self-perceived functional incapacity.

Cognitions

Pessimistic; preoccupied with perceived loss of health or concerns over poor health; inattentive.

Emotions

Unhappy; long suffering; dysphoric mood.

Traits and behaviors

Lives with a sense of physical decline; protects energy levels to avoid exhaustion; seen as negative and passive.

Therapist's Notes – MLS Scale

Feeling malaise and feeling demoralized are related concepts, but they differ in their nature, causes, and manifestations. Demoralization refers to a loss of hope and confidence. The individual feels discouraged and defeated by their challenges and perceived failures. Demoralized individuals exhibit decreased goal-motivated behavior and diminished self-confidence.

Malaise is a broader term that encompasses a feeling of discomfort and unease and a lack of physical well-being. It includes a deep sense of exhaustion that is not improved with rest, a feeling of weakness, and a loss of vitality. In its extreme, it may be similar to the complaints of people suffering from fibromyalgia or chronic fatigue. Daily life feels like a struggle to find the energy to get ordinary things accomplished.

This scale will generally not be elevated as a "spike" without other scales measuring mental distress also being elevated, but this is a possibility. Like all the SP Scales, it can be used to highlight characteristics associated with a particular RC and/or H-O Scale but can stand on its own without being an auxiliary to a "parent" RC Scale.

This 7-item scale measures an individual's self-perceived level of energy, vigor, and overall health, or lack thereof. It measures how they perceive their health status. High scorers compare themselves unfavorably with their peers in regard to overall physical health. People elevated on this scale feel tired and unrested, even after a night's sleep. They may experience sexual dysfunction, which could be an artifact of feeling worn out and depleted. They feel that their physical health has evaded them for a long time. It is common for depression to be associated with elevations on this scale.

This scale may be elevated due to genuine chronic physical ailments and/or temporary conditions like chemotherapy or post operative complications. If the somatic validity scales are elevated with MLS, rule out malingering or symptom magnification by an examination of other testing or extra non-test data suggestive of a strong incentive to appear infirmed. Even though the reported somatic symptoms may not have a clear medical explanation, the client may experience genuine distress and impairment. Note that individuals with elevations on this scale may have difficulty participating in psychotherapy due to their malaise. If a physical cause for the somatic complaints has been ruled out, consider a diagnosis of a somatic symptom disorder.

Lifestyle and Family Background – MLS Scale

This scale is sensitive to an individual's genuine physical ailments and involvement in the medical system. It is understandable that medical problems requiring numerous visits to see medical professionals, long waiting room waits, uncertain and shifting diagnoses, pain, financial concerns, and exhaustion could lead to experiencing malaise. However, if Fs and FBS are also significantly elevated, malingering or symptom magnification is possible. Otherwise, childhood experiences of illness and severe infirmity in the client, close caregivers, or death of loved ones due to illness could have created in the client "scar tissue" regarding somatic symptoms, with a readiness to become discouraged and panicked by physical symptoms, with resulting psychic and physical depletion.

Clarifying Scales – MLS Scale

- If F is elevated but still valid (T score 75-79), chronic psychological distress may have contributed to the development of malaise and discouragement.
- If EID is elevated, it suggests that anxiety, self-doubt, and exhausting ruminations about possible disasters may have led to discouragement and depletion.
- If THD is elevated, it suggests that the hypersensitivity, paranoia, and cognitive slippage associated with THD elevations may have led to exhaustion and psychic depletion.
- If BXD is elevated, it is possible that impulsive, aggressive, self-aggrandizing behavior has led to negative consequences, with transitory malaise as a consequence.
- If RCd is elevated, the level of demoralization, discouragement, and psychic depletion is increased. Elevations on the other scales can identify the possible causes of the malaise and demoralization.
- If RC1 is elevated, the individual's generalized malaise and depletion are associated with a broad range of specific somatic complaints.
- If RC2 is elevated, the malaise may be associated with a severe depression marked by vegetative symptoms that leave the individual energy-depleted and enervated.
- If RC4 is elevated, there is a possibility that the impulsivity, distrust, rule-breaking, and lack of intimacy associated with this scale's elevation have led to a setback with resulting temporary emotional depletion.
- If RC6 is elevated, the malaise may be associated with a recent accusation of malfeasance, or interpersonal strife.
- If RC7 is elevated (with WRY), the individual may be experiencing cognitive and emotional depletion due to the emotionally draining result of constant anxiety, obsessive rumination, and self-criticism.
- If RC8 is elevated, emotional depletion and malaise may be due to feelings of alienation, poor communication, and dysfunctional problem-solving as well as possible psychotic delusions.
- If RC9 is elevated (with ACT), it is possible that the hypomanic overactivity associated with this scale has led to physical and psychic exhaustion.
- If any of the Internalizing Scales are elevated, the malaise may be related to the energy-robbing effects of feeling suicidal, helpless, self-doubting, worried, and/or inefficacious. For example, if SFD and WRY are elevated, the malaise may be precipitated by the energy depletion of constant worrying and enervating self-doubt.

Therapy and Therapeutic Pitfalls – MLS Scale

The individual scoring high on this scale is admitting to feeling depleted, weak, and tired. They are likely to respond to empathic reflection by the therapist about how difficult life is under these conditions. This would be especially true if they are an individual with a limited support group. A holistic approach involving sound sleep hygiene, healthy eating, and exercise (as well as guidance in navigating the process of obtaining an accurate diagnosis) is most useful if the malaise is related to medical issues. The therapist has to guard against the counter-transference view of the client as self-defeating, lacking in insight, and somehow psychologically lazy. Keeping a diary of when the depletion is particularly salient and linking it to possible psychic conflict could allow the client to start to understand their mind-body connection.

Feedback Statements – MLS Scale

T score <39

Your answers indicate that you are not concerned about your overall health.

T Score 65-74

You may worry that your health is not as good as that of your peers or that it is not as good as it once was. This may be because during the past few years, or maybe recently, you have not been feeling as well as you might like. This could be due to a physical problem that might have been hard to diagnose or treat or it may have been due to a lingering emotional issue that has been hard to resolve.

You likely feel tired more often than you would like and sometimes wake up without feeling fully refreshed. You likely feel like your strength and vigor are diminished. When you feel tired and not well, sexual activity is much less desirable.

T score ≥75

You are reporting that you rarely feel well compared to your peers. This may be due to a chronic physical problem that has been hard to treat or an emotional condition that has not been resolved. You likely feel tired almost all the time and rarely wake up feeling refreshed. You mostly feel physically depleted, drained, and weak much of the time. You are concerned that your health will not improve.

Lifestyle and Family Background Feedback – MLS Scale

In the presence of a family history with adverse childhood experiences, such as parental indifference or cruelty, your current malaise may have been precipitated by a recent loss or setback that has re-stimulated past emotional scar tissue. In the absence of such a history, the current malaise could be hormonally precipitated by medication side effects or an illness. It could also be associated with a current depression that has exhausted you.

Treatment and Self-Help Suggestions – MLS Scale

1. You probably are not eager to engage in physical activity since you feel tired and in poor health, but if you are able to go for a short walk and be in nature, you may find your energy and mood will improve.

2. Develop a healthy evening bedtime ritual by avoiding screen time before bed and going to bed at the same time every night, allowing for about 8 hours of sleep each night.
3. If you are dealing with a challenging medical condition, ask a friend or family member to act as an advocate by attending medical appointments with you and helping you to navigate the medical system.
4. Even though comfort foods are tempting when you aren't feeling well, avoiding junk food and staying hydrated will help you feel better and have more energy. Smoking and drinking alcohol can also contribute to feelings of malaise.
5. Finding a friend or community to support you can be uplifting and help you when you feel tired and depleted.
6. Meditation, yoga, deep breathing, and mindfulness exercises can help you feel better physically and emotionally.
7. Shift your focus from negative to positive by practicing gratitude. Try to identify the things in your life for which you are grateful and take time to appreciate them.

Neurological Complaints (NUC) Scale

General Descriptors

Complaints

Dizzy spells; fine motor clumsiness; difficulties with balance; numbness; paralysis; twitching muscles and weakness; trembling hands; fatigue.

Cognitions

Catastrophizing about illness; preoccupied with neurological complaints.

Emotions

Worrying about neurological symptoms or incongruent lack of worry about these symptoms.

Traits and behaviors

Restricting physical activity; frequent medical visits; developing physical symptoms in response to stress; possible pain disability; decreased quality of life.

Therapist's Notes – NUC Scale

This 10-item scale describes a number of vague, physical complaints that may be associated with a neurological condition. A neuropsychological and/or neurological evaluation may be indicated. Complaints such as feeling dizzy, trouble with balance, numbness and tingling in the extremities, and difficulty controlling fine motor movement are associated with NUC elevations. If the Infrequent Somatic Responses (Fs) and/or the Symptom Validity Scale (FBS) are elevated in the overreporting range, then NUC elevations would indicate possible exaggeration. At the same time, it is possible that the individual is undergoing medical treatment, with resulting medication side effects or neurological symptoms that can elevate the scale requiring a medical history. Vague and shifting neurological symptoms, no matter what the cause, create significant alarm in the client since they are hard to predict and may mimic serious medical conditions. People can easily become convinced that they have serious medical conditions based on some of these neurological symptoms. These beliefs often lead to a decreased quality of life.

T scores of 65–87 reflect someone who is reporting vague neurological complaints. In the presence of a medical diagnosis, elevations in this range could be reflecting the condition. T scores equal to or greater than 88, however, suggest the strong possibility that there is a psychological component to the numerous complaints of disturbing neurological symptoms. If Cynicism (CYN) and Shyness (SHY) are equal to or less than a T score of 39, explore the possibility of a functional neurological symptom disorder (conversion disorder).

Lifestyle and Family Background – NUC Scale

It is unlikely that a client would have a "spike" NUC profile with no other scales elevated. In such a situation there is a possibility that the neurological symptoms are medically related, so there is no hypothesis about lifestyle and family background. On the other hand, if CYN and SHY are below a T score of 39, they suggest an extroverted, trusting, denying individual who possibly represses their emotions, leading to tension-related somatic symptoms.

Clarifying Scales – NUC Scale

- If Somatic Complaints (RC1) is highly elevated, especially if SHY and CYN are below a T score of 39, consider a functional neurological symptom disorder (conversion disorder).
- If Low Positive Emotions (RC2) and Aberrant Experiences (RC8) are both elevated, a neurological examination is suggested, especially if the neurological symptoms are recent.
- If COG is elevated and there is no medical diagnosis, the client's neurological complaints are combined with reported difficulties with concentration and memory.
- If Worry (WRY) is elevated, it is possible that the neurological complaints have led to worry, agitation, and anxiety about the possibility of a medical condition.
- If Demoralization (RCd) and MLS are elevated, consider that the client has tried to find a medical explanation for their neurological symptoms and has felt discounted by suggestions that their symptoms are "in their head."
- Elevations on the other SP Scales would clarify possible co-morbid symptomatology.

Therapy and Therapeutic Pitfalls – NUC Scale

If an NUC score is the only significant elevation and a medical condition has been ruled out, therapy could focus on identifying when the neurological symptoms increase in intensity and determine if they could be related to tension, stress, and the unconscious repression of conflicted emotions.

Relaxation training to observe what thoughts elicit tension could be useful in determining the locus of internal conflict. Meditation training, if the client is not opposed to it, could also help them learn to monitor their response to stress and their inner dialogue.

Clients with neurological complaints by the time they seek therapy are usually extremely anxious and often feel discounted by the medical profession. Consequently, therapy should focus on determining when the symptoms worsen and how they might be alleviated through biofeedback and possibly anxiolytic and/or antidepressant medications.

Feedback Statements – NUC Scale

T score 65–87

You occasionally experience concerning vague and shifting body symptoms such as numbness, tingling, dizziness, or loss of balance. These symptoms may come and go or be a source of constant discomfort. These symptoms may also increase during periods of stress. People often find these symptoms worrying and distracting. It is also possible that you have gone through some medical procedures or medical problems that have affected your neurological system, leading to these symptoms. You may be the kind of person who responds physically to stress, tensing your back, neck, and stomach muscles without being fully aware of it. That could restrict nerves leading to numbness and tingling in the extremities.

T score >88

You are experiencing many neurological symptoms with worries about your balance, dizziness, weakness, and numbness in your extremities. You may have even experienced moments where you felt unable to move and you may feel clumsy in your coordination generally. These symptoms may be very concerning to you, or you may have brushed off concerns, learning to live with the symptoms. You may be the kind of person who responds physically to stress, tensing your back, neck, and stomach muscles without being fully aware of it. That could restrict nerves leading to numbness and tingling in the extremities. It is easy to get demoralized if you have constant neurological symptoms. Talk with your therapist about how you can stay hopeful and not be defeated.

- If RCd and/or MLS are elevated add: Often medical professionals will attempt to diagnose your symptoms, but when they are unsuccessful, they refer you on to another specialist. It can feel discouraging and defeating to be told you have no clear diagnosis.

Lifestyle and Family Background Feedback – NUC Scale

Sometimes people with your concerns have recently experienced a medical condition or are suffering from a medication side effect. In other cases, people with these neurological complaints are physical responders to stress.

When stress occurs, you might unconsciously tense up around your neck and shoulders, even your stomach muscles, and may breathe shallowly, leading to pinched nerves, numbness, and dizziness. If, in your childhood, you or a family member experienced a serious illness, it might have left you with a vulnerability to becoming tense and knocked off balance by illness of any kind.

Treatment and Self-Help Suggestions – NUC Scale

1. Monitor your neurological symptoms by keeping a diary for a week or two. Observe when your symptoms are worse and what you were doing and thinking about at that time.
2. Learn techniques to help you relax such as deep breathing, guided imagery, progressive muscle relaxation, and meditation. These can be very effective.
3. Try to get some exercise, if your physician approves, to help relieve some of the symptoms and avoid stimulants which can increase anxiety.
4. Talk to a neurologist to help you better understand your condition and ask if medication is indicated to help alleviate your symptoms.

5. Find regular time in your daily routine for relaxation, self-care, and activities that give you pleasure. Make sure you get enough sleep.
6. Rely on your medical providers or other reliable sources for information rather than the internet. It can be tempting to surf the internet looking for information about your symptoms, but this can result in an overload of information.

Eating Concerns (EAT) Scale

General Descriptors

Complaints

Complains about eating problems, although may not report these issues in a clinical interview because denial is often associated with eating disorders; may complain about attempts by others to control eating behavior; physical self-image; depression and tiredness.

Cognitions

Preoccupied with food and eating; possibly body dysmorphic; concerned about weight gain and weight loss.

Emotions

Dysphoric; self-critical; poor self-image.

Traits and behaviors

Perfectionistic; often driven; lacks self-awareness.

Therapist's Notes – EAT Scale

This 5-item scale is new to the MMPI-3. Any response in the scored direction of True is potentially meaningful since each item reflects possibly problematic eating behaviors or at least internal conflicts about food and body image. Since eating disorder clients are often in denial of their condition, scored responses suggest they may be open to treatment or a discussion of eating and body image issues.

Lifestyle and Family Background – EAT Scale

Family dynamics play a significant role in development, maintenance, and recovery from eating disorders. These disorders do not develop from a single cause and are influenced by many factors, including genetics, personality, and social factors. However, family dynamics can play a part. For example, highly enmeshed families without clear boundaries and families with highly controlling, perfectionist caregivers with high expectations have been associated with children who have eating disorders. A caregiver's overinvolvement in an individual's weight and appearance (for example, regularly weighing the client or criticizing their appearance) has also been associated with eating disorders.

Clarifying Scales – EAT Scale

- If Emotional/Internalizing Dysfunction (EID) is elevated, the client's eating disorder may be serving as a tension reducer from a high level of anxiety, stress, and depression. This is especially true if Impulsivity (IMP) is elevated, suggesting a cycle of building tension and anxiety, followed by the impulsive reduction of tension through either eating or purging, followed by guilt and anxiety setting up the next cycle.
- If Compulsivity (CMP) is elevated, the individual's eating disorder may reflect a coping strategy, a focused outlet to deal with compulsive drives.

Therapy and Therapeutic Pitfalls – EAT Scale

Treating eating disorders requires specialized training involving individual, didactic, family, and group modalities. Applying cognitive behavior therapy to challenge distorted beliefs and attitudes around food, weight, and body image can help in developing healthier eating habits. Dialectical behavior therapy has also been useful in teaching mindfulness and emotional regulation to help clients manage stress and the emotional triggers that lead to dysfunctional eating patterns. Usually, family therapy is beneficial, especially if caregivers are too enmeshed. Individual insight therapy may be useful to teach coping strategies and self-awareness. As in most therapeutic situations, moving slowly to build trust in the eating disorder client is important to avoid becoming seen as another parental figure that focuses on weight and food. The client may elicit caretaking empathic behavior from the therapist, then resent the control that is implied. Build self-empathy initially, helping the client realize the joy-blocking habit of constant food and eating preoccupation. Regardless of the treatment modality, the individual needs to learn new coping mechanisms for dealing with emotions and stressors that may trigger disordered eating behaviors. In some cases, psychotropic medications may be prescribed to address co-occurring mental health issues, such as anxiety and/or depression.

Feedback Statements – EAT Scale

[Feedback should focus on the answer to individual EAT items as well as the T score elevation.]

- If Item 51 is True: You said that you go on eating binges several times a week. Do you do that because you restrict food at other times or because you love food? Tell me about the binges. Tell me about the last one? What was going on in your life before the last binge?
- If Item 100 is True: You said you have used purging as a way to control your weight. Is that something you occasionally do now? When was the last time? What prompted you to do it? Was it your concern about how you look or something someone said about your appearance?
- If item 111 is True: You said there are times you can't stop eating. Is that because you starve yourself until you are ravenous or because there are certain foods you love? When was the last time you were unable to control your drive to eat? What was going on in your life around that time?
- If item 130 is True: You sometimes vomit after eating. Is that to control your weight or because you feel too full? When was the last time and what was going on in your life around that time?
- If item 209 is True: You said you are willing to starve yourself to be thinner. Do you ever go a long time not eating? When was the last time? When you do finally eat are you able to keep the food down or do you feel a need to purge?

T score = 56

You answered an item that suggests that eating and body image are areas that concern you. You may feel that restricting food, even starving yourself, are reasonable ways to control your weight. You may occasionally focus on eating and weight as a way to control anxiety and stress.

T score ≥65

- Your responses indicate that you are experiencing several concerning patterns related to eating, weight control, and body image. Together, these behaviors suggest a challenging relationship with food and your body that might be significantly affecting your wellbeing.
- Your responses indicate periods where you feel unable to control your eating and times when you may take measures like self-induced vomiting or significant food restriction to manage your weight. This combination of binge eating episodes and compensatory behaviors (vomiting, restriction) represents a pattern that can be harmful to your physical and emotional health.
- These experiences often come with significant emotional distress, including feelings of shame, guilt, or being out of control. Many people with similar patterns report that these behaviors develop as ways to cope with difficult emotions or situations but, over time, they can become their own source of distress.
- These patterns can impact your physical health, including potential issues with your digestive system, electrolyte imbalances, nutritional deficiencies, and dental problems. They can also affect your emotional wellbeing and social life.
- It is important to know that you are not alone in experiencing these challenges, and effective, compassionate support is available. Speaking with a healthcare provider who specializes in eating disorders could provide you with appropriate assessment and care options. Many people with similar experiences have found relief and recovery with professional support.

Lifestyle and Family Background Feedback – EAT Scale

Sometimes people with your profile come from a background where they felt they had to be perfect in order to obtain love and approval. You may have felt controlled by caring but hovering caregivers, but you didn't want to disappoint them by your physical appearance or your behavior. You may have learned to use food as a way to control your environment or as a way to vent built-up frustration and anxiety. You are likely a perfectionist, especially about your physical appearance. It is possible someone close to you was critical of your weight or was very involved in coaching your eating habits and now you have internalized their critical voice.

Treatment and Self-Help Suggestions – EAT Scale

1. Individual therapy, group therapy, and even family therapy can all be effective in treating eating disorders.
2. Cognitive behavioral therapy can be helpful in understanding your thought patterns and behaviors around food and body image.
3. Dialectical behavior therapy can be useful in helping you recognize, label, and manage your emotions. Since eating can often be a way to release bottled-up emotions, this therapy can be effective in reducing the desire to eat in unhealthy ways.

4. Mindfulness therapy can help you to learn to be in the moment and in touch with your feelings.
5. Keep a food journal to help you identify the connections between your feelings and urges to eat, and what you are feeling when you feel the urge to binge and purge. Try to identify if your eating issues are tied to inner emotional conflicts and tensions.
6. Take a moment before you act on an impulse and take some deep breaths, relaxing your body slowly from head to toe. Consider taking a yoga class or going for a walk, if your health permits, when you begin to feel the urge to act on eating disorder impulses.
7. Try to eat slowly and recognize your hunger cues.
8. Seek support by consulting a nutritional expert for information about a balanced diet and consider joining a group with others who are focused on healthy eating behaviors.

Cognitive Complaints (COG) Scale

General Descriptors

Complaints

Concentration difficulties; attention problems; comprehension problems; memory problems; easily confused.

Cognitions

Unfocused; easily distracted; forgetful; easily confused.

Emotions

Possibly depressed, anxious and distressed; easily frustrated.

Traits and behaviors

Challenged to stay task-oriented; possible multiple symptom clusters associated with depression, anxiety, feeling overwhelmed, psychotic thought processes, and/or under-controlled behaviors such as substance abuse and poor impulse control.

Therapist's Notes – COG Scale

This 11-item scale identifies reports of difficulties with concentration, memory, attention, comprehension, and general cognitive inefficiency. Items also reflect problems with confusion and concerns about something being wrong with one's thinking. If the validity scales FBS and Response Bias Scale (RBS) are significantly elevated, high scores on COG may reflect overreporting of cognitive impairment. At the same time, with valid highly elevated RCd and high RC2 profiles, high scores on COG could reflect the mental fog and cognitive sluggishness of severe depression. With cognitive impairment it is understandable that daily life is stressful, so elevated scores are associated with low frustration tolerance and difficulties dealing even with minor stress. Irritability and the avoidance of stressful responsibilities are likely.

The COG content can also capture the sequelae following a traumatic brain injury, stroke, or seizure. Certain medications can also cause cognitive difficulties, so a review of current medications may be indicated. Individuals with an attention deficit disorder may also endorse items on this scale, so it is important to evaluate for this condition.

Lifestyle and Family Background – COG Scale

Elevations on COG could be due to a number of causes. Since many psychiatric conditions, such as severe depression, anxiety disorders, or psychosis, can interfere with efficient cognitive functioning, the elevations on the H-O Scales would provide the backdrop for the interpretation of elevations on COG. It is important to determine the etiology of the cognitive complaints. If the individual has a history of vague somatic complaints with no clear diagnosis, scale elevations may reflect a somatic symptom disorder. A recent onset of cognitive difficulties could require a neurological evaluation to determine the possibility of a neurological/medical disorder. It is important to assess whether the individual is abusing substances that can impair cognitive functioning. Note that a range of medications can also affect cognitive efficiency.

Clarifying Scales – COG Scale

- If RCd is elevated, the client's cognitive difficulties may have resulted in demoralization and despair.
- If RC1 is elevated, the cognitive complaints may be part of a somatic symptom disorder.
- If EID and/or Dysfunctional Negative Emotions (RC7) and RC2 are both elevated, the cognitive complaints may be due to severe depression and anxiety.
- If Suicidal/Death Ideation (SUI) and/or Helplessness/Hopelessness (HLP) are elevated, the client may be feeling desperate about their cognitive difficulties, especially if they are longstanding.

Therapy and Therapeutic Pitfalls – COG Scale

Cognitive scale elevations can be a function of multiple medical and psychological conditions. Therapeutic recommendations will rely heavily on the H-O and RC Scales for understanding the potential sources of cognitive difficulties. Given the etiological heterogeneity of COG elevations, an examination of the MMPI-3 relevant item pool is indicated. Therapy would depend on what other scales are elevated together with COG. In the absence of clear depression and anxiety, a neuropsychological evaluation is suggested.

Feedback Statements – COG Scale

T score <50

When it comes to concentration, memory, and the ability to understand what you are reading, you can keep your mind on one thing and don't lose your focus easily. Your memory seems to work well, and you have little or no trouble concentrating.

T score 65–75

You report that you have some difficulty with concentration and memory. You may find it hard to concentrate and it might be hard to keep your mind focused on one thing. You may occasionally worry about your memory – for example, forgetting where you leave things.

T score ≥76

You report having difficulty with memory, attention, and concentration. You likely are finding it hard to keep your mind on a task or job and may have significant difficulty in understanding what you read as well as you used to. You might forget where you leave things or get confused or forget what you wanted to say in a conversation. You might worry that something is wrong with your mind since your memory is not what it used to be. Consequently, you may have a low tolerance for frustration and even moderate levels of stress can knock you off balance.

- If FBS or RBS are elevated, add: You answered a number of items in a way that suggests you have numerous physical complaints and difficulties with memory, concentration, and focus. It is possible that you have been very concerned about your physical and mental condition, so you went the extra step to let me know how severely affected you are. Typically, people with even more severe symptoms do not endorse so many items. Consequently, your therapist may want you to retake the test answering how you feel most of the time rather than when you are in an acute crisis.
- If RCd is elevated, add: Your profile suggests that your concentration, memory, and general mental efficiency may be causing you to feel demoralized and defeated. You may have tried many ways to deal with your difficulties with focus and comprehension and now may feel hopeless about things getting better.
- If RC1 is elevated, add: Your profile suggests that you are experiencing a lot of uncomfortable physical symptoms together with focus, concentration, and memory difficulties. Your symptoms may shift and change, occasionally getting better and then worse. People with your profile are vulnerable to developing physical and mental symptoms when they experience stress. This can affect different muscle groups as well as leaving you feeling foggy and less able to think clearly.
- If RCd and RC2 are elevated, add: Your profile indicated that you are currently feeling quite down, quite anxious, and, at times, quite depressed. Your depression is likely affecting your ability to focus, concentrate, and think clearly. You may have become more forgetful and may misplace things and have difficulty keeping your mind on one task or job. It appears that your memory and concentration difficulties may be due to your depression and anxiety.
- If Hypomanic Activation (RC9) and/or Activation (ACT) are elevated, add: You have an unusual profile in that you test as energetic, driven, ambitious, and self-confident. However, at the same time, you are complaining of difficulties with concentration, memory, and general focus. Your therapist may want to refer you for a neuropsychological evaluation.
- If SUI and/or HLP are elevated, add: Your difficulties with memory and concentration and your ability to read, remember, and understand things has disheartened you to the point that you may be considering ending it all. It would be important to tell your therapist how you are feeling hopeless about your cognitive difficulties ever changing. If you feel hopeless and suicidal and cannot reach your therapist, call a suicide and crisis 24/7 hotline [988 in the United States and Canada] for confidential support.

Lifestyle and Family Background Feedback – COG Scale

In some instances, individuals with your type of cognitive dysfunction may have experienced a traumatic brain injury or illness contributing to problems with thinking, concentration, and attention. In other cases, a person may have a family history of cognitive dysfunction such as Alzheimer's disease which may be a contributing genetic factor. It is important for you to consult with a neurological specialist to evaluate possible causes of your thinking problems.

Treatment and Self-Help Suggestions – COG Scale

For most people, having difficulties with memory, comprehension, concentration, or thinking clearly is very frightening. Often, these difficulties are due to a combination of depression and anxiety and are responsive to medication. In some cases, these symptoms could be the result of a recent concussion or a number of concussions in early life from playing sports. Your therapist will likely want you to have a neuropsychological evaluation if these symptoms are not due to depression or anxiety. Before you have a full diagnosis, it might be useful to keep a diary to monitor what time of day you seem to function best and what kind of situations seem to aggravate the concentration and memory problems.

If you are struggling with concentration and memory problems, there are several strategies and techniques that might help.

1. Develop a nightly bedtime routine, limiting screen time and having about eight hours of quality sleep to help with mental clarity.
2. Research shows that regular physical activity can help sharpen focus and improve memory. If your physician approves, try engaging in activities like aerobic exercises, yoga, or even brisk walking.
3. Concentration and memory can be improved by mindfulness techniques and meditation.
4. Brain health is enhanced by a healthy diet, including foods rich in omega-3 fatty acids, antioxidants, and vitamins. Stay hydrated, as concentration is impacted by dehydration.
5. Keep your mind active by engaging in puzzles and memory games. Try brain-training apps that stimulate different parts of your brain. Other activities such as learning new skills, reading, or completing challenging tasks help to keep your mind active.
6. Break large tasks into smaller, manageable tasks, completing one at a time to keep you from feeling overwhelmed. Limit your work to shorter, focused intervals, taking breaks in between.
7. To reduce distractions, work in a quiet, organized space and try blocking social media or unnecessary notifications. Noise-canceling headphones can minimize distracting noise. Limit visual distractions by keeping only essential items on your desk.
8. Some memory tools include mnemonic devices, visualization techniques, repetition, and actively recalling information.
9. Use to-do lists, planners, or apps to write things down to keep track of important tasks or information.
10. Short naps or rest periods can help you to stay fresh. Fatigue can impact memory, concentration, and acuity.
11. Discuss with your therapist if medication might be indicated. Many types of medication are available for different kinds of cognitive problems and can help to improve your concentration and focus.

6 Internalizing Scales

Introduction

Development

The Specific Problems (SP) Scales were developed as a way to identify individual issues and characteristics that comprise the population of problems assessed by the Higher-Order (H-O) and Restructured Clinical (RC) Scales as well as relevant issues that are not directly measured by any of the RC Scales, such as suicidal ideation or shyness. The empirical literature and *MMPI-3 Technical Manual* (Ben-Porath & Tellegen, 2020b) indicate that the SP Scales are sufficiently valid to be interpreted as stand-alone independent measures. The relatively short SP Scales range from 5 to 15 items; 19 scales have less than 10 items; and 7 scales are comprised of 10 or more items.

The 26 SP Scales are categorized into four groupings: Somatic/Cognitive, Internalizing, Externalizing, and Interpersonal. These groupings were classified through both conceptual reviews and correlation analyses with the H-O and RC Scales.

The Internalizing Scales comprise 10 domains: Suicidal/Death Ideation (SUI), Helplessness/Hopelessness (HLP), Self-Doubt (SFD), Inefficacy (NFC), Stress (STR), Worry (WRY), Compulsivity (CMP), Anxiety-Related Experiences (ARX), Anger Proneness (ANP), and Behavior-Restricting Fears (BRF).

The *MMPI-3 Technical Manual* (Ben-Porath & Tellegen, 2020b) presents supportive reliability data indicating that these measures are reliable sources of information about psychological functioning. Empirical correlates for each of the 26 SP Scales are generally consistent with the scale names, reflective of the underlying constructs. There is empirical support for both convergent and discriminant validity for these scales.

Application

The Internalizing Scales should be examined after protocol validity is established. If the profile is invalid, it cannot be interpreted, although inspection of scale elevations may still yield valuable information about the test-taker.

Following validity considerations, the H-O and RC Scales will serve as a compass, pointing to specific Internalizing Scales for further interpretive clarity. However, should an internalizing scale be elevated without H-O and/or RC scale elevations, the scale can nonetheless be interpreted.

DOI: 10.4324/9781003557920-6

Suicidal/Death Ideation (SUI) Scale

General Descriptors

Complaints

Depressed; feeling helpless and hopeless; feeling burdensome to others; death ideation.

Cognitions

Negative thoughts; defeated; preoccupied with death/suicide; pessimistic.

Emotions

Demoralized; depressed; possible agitation; negative; hopeless.

Traits and behaviors

Pessimistic; possibly self-defeating; suicide attempts and/or gestures.

Therapist's Notes – SUI Scale

The items in this face-valid 7-item scale are all keyed in the True direction. Any endorsed item indicates a need for the client to be assessed for suicide risk. The item content of the SUI scale is critical, and any endorsed items should be reviewed with the respondent. SUI scores are associated with suicidal ideation, depression, hopelessness, negative thoughts about one's life, as well as feeling like a burden to others.

A raw score of 1 yields a T score of 58, which is considered clinically elevated for the SUI scale (Ben-Porath & Tellegen, 2020). Elevations are empirically associated with suicide attempts. Some therapists feel cautious about exploring suicide ideation directly, perhaps out of concern that verbalizing it might somehow give the client permission to put it into action. Generally, clients with suicidal ideation are willing to talk about their feelings and preoccupations and welcome discussions about their psychic pain and their feelings of defeated hopelessness. However, for some individuals, it is easier to admit suicidal intent/ideation on an inventory rather than in a face-to-face interview. There is no evidence that discussing suicidal ideation or suicide plans increases the likelihood of precipitating an attempt. In some cases, endorsement of some suicidal items reflects an escape fantasy from a current trapped situation without the determination to die by suicide. However, endorsement of items that signify a clear plan for suicide necessitates an immediate safety plan. Note that hopelessness and disconstraint coupled with item endorsements on SUI are particularly strong predictors of suicide risks.

Lifestyle and Family Background – SUI Scale

In some cases, clients with a personality disorder have experienced a number of suicide attempts and other kinds of self-harm. In the presence of this past history of self-harm, especially if drugs and alcohol are currently heavily involved, the danger of suicide is increased. If a severely depressed, suicidal client had a caregiver who had attempted suicide, the danger of suicide is also increased. If the client has recently experienced what they perceive as a catastrophic loss and if they have a limited support system, live alone, and/or have a suicide plan, then there is a need for an immediate intervention.

Clarifying Scales – SUI Scale

- If Emotional/Internalizing Dysfunction (EID) and/or Low Positive Emotions (RC2) are elevated, suicidal ideation is clearly a reflection of the depth of the demoralization and depression the client is experiencing.
- Demoralization (RCd) has the strongest association with current suicidal ideation and recent suicide attempts. If RCd is elevated, suicidal ideation is associated with a deep sense of defeat and discouragement about one's current condition. The client feels helpless and frustrated and unsure of how to deal with their current problems, so suicidal ideation could be an escape plan from what they perceive as an intractable situation.
- If Somatic Complaints (RC1) and Malaise (MLS) are elevated, the client's numerous physical complaints and lack of a specific diagnosis could be contributing to feelings of despair, perhaps even anger, and resulting suicidal ideation.
- If Antisocial Behavior (RC4) is elevated, there is a heightened risk of an impulsive, angry suicide attempt, especially if drugs or alcohol are involved. Often, in SUI and RC4 elevations, the client is in a difficult legal or emotional situation due to poor judgment, impulsive behavior, or violence. The suicidal impulse, which is serious, likely reflects a desire for immediate relief, but also anger at the world.
- If Ideas of Persecution (RC6) is elevated, especially if RC4 is also elevated, SUI elevations could be associated with a desire to punish others for mistreating them. Suicidal impulses and gestures would be an expression of rage and hurt.
- If Dysfunctional Negative Emotions (RC7) is elevated, the component of agitation (WRY, ARX, STR) can exacerbate the distress, leading to suicide attempts.
- If Aberrant Experiences (RC8) is elevated, suicidal ideation could be part of a psychotic episode, with voices telling the client to self-harm. It could also be an attempt to escape the disturbing and frightening inner voices that torment the individual.
- If Hypomanic (RC9) and/or Activation (ACT) are elevated, there is a possibility of a manic episode followed by a severe depression. Activating scales can fuel the energy needed to attempt or complete suicide.
- If Cognitive Complaints (COG) and/or Neurological Complaints (NUC) are elevated, the client may be responding to feelings of impending cognitive decline, perhaps fearful that they are developing dementia or Alzheimer's disease.
- If HLP, SFD, NFC, and/or WRY are elevated, the client is reporting feeling that they have no confidence in their ability to manage daily stress or agitation or deal with overwhelming worries. Routine problem-solving feels overwhelming. Suicidal ideation may be a reflection of lost self-confidence and, with it, a feeling of defeat and anger directed at the self.

Therapy and Therapeutic Pitfalls – SUI Scale

In assessing suicide risk, interpretation of the MMPI-3 should be combined with multiple sources of data, including a clinical interview, comprehensive psychosocial history, and results from a variety of other psychometric instruments, The prediction of suicide is too complex a task to be measured reliably by any single variable or even a combination of measures on the MMPI-3.

Numerous factors influence a person to think and behave in a suicidal manner including, but not limited to, changes in personal circumstances, such as a loss of support from significant others, irreversible business losses, or the worsening of a medical condition, perhaps with intractable pain. Severe psychiatric symptoms such as command hallucinations, intolerable depressive symptoms, or alcohol and/or drug intoxication may also increase suicide risk.

Inspection of the SUI endorsements can help inform and guide a risk management strategy. If the client is actively suicidal, an inpatient psychiatric hospitalization can provide a safe holding environment until the acute crisis abates. Managing acute active suicidal ideation is difficult with only outpatient individual psychotherapy. An intensive outpatient program can better serve as a therapeutic milieu (versus individual therapy sessions) while emotional stability is restored. If abuse of substances is part of the clinical picture, this exponentially increases the risk of suicide. Dual diagnosis substance-abuse programs are often indicated for these types of at-risk cases.

Feedback Statements – SUI Scale

[Regardless of the T score elevation, if any of the SUI items are endorsed, the therapist needs to explore safety precautions for the client. Since each item is potentially critical, feedback will be tied to items endorsed as True.]

T score 58–79

You reported that you spend time thinking about how to kill yourself and you may have attempted it in the past. Suicidal thoughts may serve as a way of escaping from what you have perceived as an intolerable situation.

T score ≥80

Your profile suggests that you are very preoccupied with suicide and death. This may be the result of a severe depression, an intolerable situation, or a prolonged medical condition for which you have given up hope that it will ever improve. If you are using substances, you may be vulnerable to impulsively wanting to end your life. It would be important to discuss with your therapist how you are feeling to help you gain emotional support and develop better coping skills.

If you feel hopeless and suicidal and cannot reach your therapist, call a suicide and crisis 24/7 hotline [988 in the United States and Canada] for confidential support.

ITEM 38: THOUGHTS ABOUT WAYS TO END ONE'S LIFE

You stated that you have spent some time thinking about how you might kill yourself. This may be an episodic desire to escape from your current pain or a difficult situation. But it could be a reflection of how desperately trapped and unhappy you feel. It is important that you discuss this with your therapist.

ITEM 93: RECENT THOUGHTS OF SUICIDE

You answered that you have recently considered killing yourself. This may have come up as an escape fantasy from what you perceive as an intolerable and painful situation. Whether this was a passing thought or if you have seriously considered a plan, it is critical that you talk to your therapist.

ITEM 120: FREQUENT WISHES TO BE DEAD

You answered that most of the time you wish you were dead. You are likely feeling trapped in an intolerable situation or are in great and inescapable pain. Typically, people who feel this way are severely depressed. It is important to discuss this with your therapist.

ITEM 126: PLANS TO COMMIT SUICIDE

You stated that you have made a plan for killing yourself. You likely see your situation as intolerable, and you might perceive yourself as being in inescapable, intolerable pain. It is important for you to share this plan with your therapist to obtain emotional support and alternative ways to cope with your stress.

ITEM 149: LOW MOTIVATION TO LIVE

You answered that you have lost your will to live. This may be because you are exhausted by your current situation or completely depleted by physical and/or emotional pain. It is important to discuss with your therapist how you might get some emotional support and some relief from the overwhelming pain.

ITEM 164: FREQUENT THOUGHTS ABOUT DYING

Lately you have been thinking a lot about killing yourself. This may be because of some recent stress or what you perceive as overwhelming burdens or pain. It is important to discuss this with your therapist since it is possible you could get some relief and emotional support.

ITEM 251: HIDDEN ATTEMPTS AT SUICIDE

You said that you have tried to kill yourself. It is hard to know whether this was in the past, when you felt trapped or in what you felt was inescapable pain, or it could be a recent attempt because of recent overwhelming stress or pain. It is important to discuss this with your therapist as it is likely you would get relief, emotional support, and new coping strategies.

- If EID and RC2 are elevated, add: Your answers reveal that you have been suffering from significant depression. Sadness, feelings of loss, and a constant lack of joy or positive excitement may have left you feeling that life is not worthwhile and you may have escape fantasies about killing yourself. It is important you share these feelings with your therapist.
- If RCd is elevated, add: Your suicidal thoughts may be aggravated by your feelings of discouragement and defeat about not being able to feel better.
- If RC1 and MLS are elevated, add: Your physical symptoms and worries about the right diagnosis appear to have made you feel despairing and even angry with your body. Your thoughts about suicide may be your way of escaping what you see as an impossible situation.
- If RC4 is elevated, add: You may be in a difficult situation because of some action on your part that backfired or was too impulsive. You may feel angry with others, or even yourself, and may think of suicide as a way of escaping from what you see as a difficult situation. It may be hard for you to trust others emotionally, which aggravates your feelings of being alone and with no one to turn to.
- If RC6 is elevated, add: You appear to be feeling very vulnerable to criticism, blame, or judgment coming from others. It may feel humiliating or very unfair. You may think people are out to get you, hurt you, or humiliate you so it is hard to trust right now. You may be thinking about suicide to escape the pain you feel right now, or you may fantasize about punishing others with your own death.
- If RC8 is elevated, add: You appear to be thinking about suicide. It is possible that you want to escape disturbing and frightening inner voices or thoughts. It is also possible that your thoughts about suicide are coming from inner voices telling you that you need to do it. You may think you need to kill yourself, but it is likely that these thoughts are part of a current illness that can be treated.

- If RC9 and/or ACT are elevated, add: Your thoughts about suicide may have welled up recently after a period of very high energy that has left you feeling depleted and depressed about some of your actions when you were in a manic state. It is also possible that you are in a manic phase where killing yourself makes some kind of sense to you and you feel obligated to do it.
- If COG and/or NUC are elevated, add: Your thoughts of suicide may be related to your complaints about your neurological conditions or some of the cognitive issues that you struggle with. Perhaps you are afraid that you are in decline and that you need to end your life before things get more severe.
- If HLP, SFD, NFC, and/or WRY are elevated, add: You appear to have lost confidence in your ability to manage the stresses of everyday life and the burden of what you feel are overwhelming worries. Routine problem-solving may feel overwhelming. Losing confidence in yourself may have led to you feeling like you have to consider suicide as an option.

Lifestyle and Family Background Feedback – SUI Scale

Sometimes people with your profile have had previous episodes of deep depression and despair and have either thought about suicide or attempted it. This may be because you are vulnerable to mood swings and episodes where life feels just too overwhelming to keep going. In other cases, people with your profile have had caregivers who experienced severe depression and possibly attempted suicide. This may have instilled in you a feeling that suicide is always an option when things get too tough. If, in fact, you had a caregiver, friend, or close acquaintance who was suicidal, try to remember the enormous pain that people around them suffered because of their behavior.

Treatment and Self-Help Suggestions – SUI Scale

If you are feeling suicidal, it is crucial to recognize that you are not alone, and there are steps you can take to help yourself in this moment. While you should seek professional help if you are feeling suicidal, here are some self-help strategies to manage your thoughts and emotions.

1. If you are feeling suicidal, it is important to recognize that you are not alone and there are steps you can take to help yourself. Identify a therapist, friend, family member, or someone else with whom you feel safe to share your feelings. If you are not ready to talk to someone you know, consider calling a suicide and crisis 24/7 hotline [988 in the United States and Canada] for confidential support.
2. If you are considering acting on your suicidal thoughts, remove or avoid access to dangerous items such as medications or weapons. Find a safe place to go, since changing your environment can help shift your mindset, even temporarily.
3. Deep, slow breathing and mindfulness techniques to help you focus on your immediate senses can help you to stay present, reduce anxiety, and calm your mind. Set short-term goals such as getting out of bed or brushing your teeth and focus on the next minute or the next hour. These small, manageable actions can help you feel a sense of control.
4. Activities that require concentration, such as writing or drawing, can offer a constructive release of emotions. Other activities such as reading, watching a movie, doing puzzles, or taking a walk can also provide a distraction from painful emotions. Sometimes seeing your thoughts written out helps reduce their intensity.
5. Replace negative thoughts with more realistic or compassionate ones. Instead of thinking you are worthless, remind yourself that you are doing your best. If you are in pain, focus on the possibility of a medical solution. Remind yourself that you are valuable. Think about your reasons to live, whether it is loved ones, pets, goals you would like to achieve, or a desire to experience the future. Be kind to yourself, treating yourself with the same compassion you

would give others in a similar situation. Remind yourself that it is okay to struggle and ask for help.

6. Find a therapist to help you work through these feelings in a safe environment. Sometimes medication prescribed by a licensed professional can help brain imbalances that cause depression and suicidal thoughts.
7. Make an effort to stay connected to friends, family, and your community. Try to keep from isolating yourself, even if it feels exhausting. Join a support group, since talking to others who have faced similar struggles can offer some relief and reduce the sense of loneliness.
8. Develop a "no harm" contract plan with your therapist, including the steps you would take if you are ever feeling suicidal. Document specific steps to take if you feel unsafe, including phone numbers of friends, hotlines, and professionals, as well as safe places you can go. Commit to *not* acting immediately. Suicidal thoughts often pass, reducing in intensity and giving you a buffer. While feelings of hopelessness and pain may cloud your ability to see options, help is available. Please reach out to a professional immediately or go to an emergency room if you are feeling overwhelmed. You don't need to go through this on your own. If you feel hopeless and suicidal and cannot reach your therapist, call a suicide and crisis 24/7 hotline [988 in the United States and Canada] for confidential support.

Helplessness/Hopelessness (HLP) Scale

General Descriptors

Complaints

Feeling hopeless about the future; feeling unhappy and powerless to change; feeling life's goals are out of reach; feeling trapped.

Cognitions

Pessimistic; negative thoughts; self-critical; lacking self-efficacy; low motivation to change.

Emotions

Feeling unhappy, hopeless, helpless, and like a burden to others; demoralized.

Traits and behaviors

Passive; defeated; easily overwhelmed; lacking motivation to initiate change efforts; lack of resilience.

Therapist's Notes – HLP Scale

This 7-item scale includes items reflecting pessimism about one's future prospects and ability to change for the better, leading to feelings of hopelessness and helplessness. The constructs of hopelessness and helplessness are important risk factors for assessing suicide risk. Thwarted psychological needs and emotional pain that reach intolerable levels can lead to suicidality. Hopelessness about ever experiencing a meaningful connection to others as well as feeling burdensome is often a proximal cause of suicidality. While the HLP item content is clearly of a demoralized nature, feelings of defeat and a sense of being victimized by life and difficult circumstances capture the essence of this scale. The quality is more of a trapped depression than a communicative sense of sadness. Elevations on this scale could also predict a client's negativity toward therapy, with a possible stance of "I've tried all your suggestions, they don't work." Therapists will need to guard against wanting to convince the client that things can be better and then perhaps becoming annoyed as the client points out how their therapeutic suggestions won't work.

Lifestyle and Family Background – HLP Scale

It is important to determine why the person feels hopeless and helpless. It is possible that there has been a recent history of setbacks and perceived losses that have precipitated a sense of hopelessness and helplessness. In the presence of a childhood history of difficult, inescapable privation and negative childhood experiences, the client may have learned a passive, self-defeating mindset. Exploring childhood events that were experienced as inescapably painful could be useful in helping the client develop self-empathy. Redefining their helplessness and hopelessness as an understandable response to intractable circumstances could help in creating a therapeutic alliance.

Clarifying Scales – HLP Scale

- If EID is elevated, the client has become discouraged and defeated by the severity of their depression and anxiety.
- If Thought Dysfunction (THD) is elevated, the client may have become discouraged and defeated by the constant intrusions of psychotic thought processes. Elevations on HLP might lead them to discontinue medications since they have given up feeling that anything they do to ameliorate their condition will work.
- If Behavioral/Externalizing Dysfunction (BXD) is elevated, it is possible that the individual's sense of hopelessness and helplessness is the result of some impulsive, poorly thought-through actions that have led to serious negative consequences. The individual then feels like giving up and turns anger at their circumstances into self-defeating hopelessness.
- If RCd is elevated, this would add to the general picture of defeat, demoralization, pessimism, and lack of drive toward making any possibly beneficial changes. If SUI is elevated, there is a significant danger of self-harm since the client feels hopeless and helpless and has lost self-confidence in their ability to change their life circumstances.
- If RC1 is elevated, look for a history of physical complaints with no reliable diagnosis and no decrease in physical symptoms. The person may feel hopeless and ineffectual about the possibility of reducing their level of pain and discomfort.
- If RC2 is elevated, this increases the possibility of a severe depression and hopelessness about it ever being ameliorated. It would be particularly significant if SUI were also elevated, since the quality of the depression is predicted to be negative, self-defeating, and potentially self-destructive.
- If RC4 is elevated, it is possible that the sense of defeat, helplessness, and hopelessness is the result of some hasty, impulsive, rule-breaking act. Individuals with this combination might verbalize self-criticism and hopelessness as a way of avoiding responsibility to change their behavior.
- If RC7 is elevated, the client's experience of overwhelming anxiety has likely left them feeling discouraged about making positive changes and left them feeling hopeless and defeated. The associated agitation, especially if coupled with items endorsed on SUI, increases the risk for suicidality.

- If SFD, NFC, STR, WRY, Negative Emotionality/Neuroticism (NEGE), and/or Introversion/Low Positive Emotionality (INTR) are elevated, the individual is reporting that their anxiety, self-doubt, constant worry, and feeling overwhelmed by stress have left them feeling that they are unable to make any positive changes and that the future feels bleak and hopeless.
- If CMP is elevated, explore how compulsive behavior is leading to feelings of defeat and hopelessness. A combination of these two scales might be seen in an individual who has a serious negative compulsion such as gambling or sex addiction that they feel helpless about changing.
- If Substance Abuse (SUB) is elevated, especially with Impulsivity (IMP), RC4, and/or Disconstraint (DISC), examine for any endorsed suicide items on SUI.
- If IMP is elevated, especially with item endorsements on SUI, a suicide risk assessment is important.
- If ARX and BRF are elevated, the person's life may have become so constricted by anxieties, fears, and phobias that they feel incapable of improving it.

Therapy and Therapeutic Pitfalls – HLP Scale

The items on this scale reflect a defeated, hopeless person who feels helpless to change their life for the positive. These individuals invite the therapist to persuade them not to feel so defeated and hopeless, but this can lead to therapist frustration since such individuals tend to be negative about any therapeutic strategies. In some cases, the negativity about the possibility of change may frustrate a therapist, leading to countertransference. Cognitive behavioral strategies are probably most useful, since a large proportion of the individual's feelings of hopelessness involve irrational and negative beliefs. Exploring past failed therapeutic strategies and validating the client's frustration and consequent hopelessness could encourage emotional catharsis and self-empathy. Hopelessness may serve as a protective function to avoid feelings of disappointment. It may feel safer to have low expectations with pessimism.

Feedback Statements – HLP Scale

T score 51–58

You can occasionally feel that life is difficult and at these times you might feel a little negative about your ability to change things.

T score 65–75

You are currently feeling quite pessimistic, hopeless, and defeated by your current circumstances. It appears that you are doubting your ability to make positive changes in your life. It is hard for you to believe that anyone can help you, so your motivation to seek help is low. At times, it is easy for you to feel helpless, feeling that you don't have the tools to make life better.

T score ≥80

You appear to have lost hope in your life improving and lost faith in yourself and in being able to change your circumstances. Life feels like a strain, and you often feel overwhelmed. You don't seem to believe anybody can help you, so it is easy to feel that life is unfair. You likely don't believe any kind of therapy will help, so you probably have low motivation to seek help. It is hard right now for you to believe that you can achieve any of your life goals. At times, you may feel like you don't belong and are a burden to others.

- If EID is elevated, add: Your depression and anxiety appear to have worn you out and drained you of optimism that things can get better. You likely have been feeling chronically depressed and anxious without much relief, so you are feeling hopeless and helpless about feeling better.
- If THD is elevated, add: You appear to be feeling defeated and hopeless, perhaps because you have been struggling with mental health problems. Sometimes people with your profile feel unsafe and vulnerable to people being hostile or mean. Perhaps you have been feeling paranoid, unsure who to trust, or perhaps you have been hearing voices or having feelings of unreality. It is possible you have felt that medicine has not helped, leaving you feeling discouraged and defeated.
- If BXD is elevated, add: People with your profile can run into conflict with authority figures since they are sensitive to being controlled and dislike rules inhibiting their behavior. Your impulsive behavior or rule-bending may have gotten you into trouble, which now feels overwhelming. You now appear to be feeling hopeless about your current situation and may have lost some trust in your ability to deal with things.
- If RCd is elevated, add: You are reporting feeling very discouraged, defeated, and hopeless about ever feeling better. Your confidence is shaken, and you have difficulty getting things done. You are very self-critical and give up quickly on tasks, especially if you think they are not improving quickly enough. You seem to feel that you will never amount to much and that making significant life changes is almost impossible.
- If SUI is elevated, add: Feeling discouraged, hopeless, and having lost confidence in yourself, you are reporting that you are thinking about suicide to escape what you see as a hopeless situation. It is very important that you share these feelings with your therapist. If you feel hopeless and suicidal and cannot reach your therapist, call a suicide and crisis 24/7 hotline [988 in the United States and Canada] for confidential support.
- If RC1 and/or MLS are elevated, add: Your physical problems and worries about your health appear to have worn you out, leaving you feeling hopeless and helpless about ever feeling better. In some cases, when people feel so defeated, they want to look for new medical treatments, diagnostic examinations, and medicines.
- If RC2 is elevated, add: You appear to have been struggling with depression and are experiencing sad moods, low energy, and difficulties with brain fog, concentration, and memory. Sleep problems and eating and weight disturbance are likely also of concern. Currently, you may have lost confidence in your ability to get better, so you have been feeling hopeless and helpless, feeling that your life goals are out of reach.
- If RC4 is elevated, add: Currently you are feeling hopeless, and you appear to have lost confidence in your ability to make your life better. You may be in trouble because of a hasty or impulsive act, or you may have bent the truth and that got you into trouble, so now you feel glum and defeated, and that you are getting a "raw deal" out of life.
- If RC7 is elevated, add: Currently you are often on edge, anxious and preoccupied with avoiding what feels like a constant threat of something bad happening. Most of the time you feel a sense of dread without always knowing why and you easily feel guilty that you have done something wrong. These feelings appear to have worn you out, so you are feeling hopeless about ever feeling relaxed and at peace. This anxiety has robbed you of your self-confidence and you now doubt that you can get what you want out of life.
- If SFD, NFC, STR, WRY, NEGE, and/or INTR are elevated, add: Your constant worrying, self-doubt, and self-criticism appear to have worn you out. You seem to have lost confidence that you can make life better since you feel constant stress and getting even small tasks done feels overwhelming. It is hard to make decisions since you second-guess yourself constantly and see every side to every problem. Now you are reporting feeling hopeless that anything can be better. You also feel helpless, feeling that making changes is almost impossible.

- If CMP is elevated, add: Your compulsive behavior has worn you out, leaving you feeling helpless to change it. You have lost confidence in your ability to make positive changes in your life, so you are feeling hopeless and defeated. The compulsions likely are seriously affecting your life, but you appear to feel powerless to control them.
- If IMP is elevated, add: Your impulsive actions and behaviors may have led to consequences that you regret and feel helpless to correct. Discuss with your therapist new ways to reassess straightening out your life circumstances.
- If ARX and BRF are elevated, add: Your anxiety and worry about impending disaster, your fear of the unknown, and your fears and phobias have restricted your life much more than you would like. Now you are reporting that you have lost confidence in your ability to make positive changes. You feel hopeless and helpless. You have given up hope that you can get what you want out of life, since making any positive change feels almost impossible.

Lifestyle and Family Background Feedback – HLP Scale

Your feelings of being defeated, hopeless, and helpless could be due to a recent traumatic or very upsetting event that has left you feeling trapped in a current situation. In other cases, the feelings you are experiencing may have been caused by a long period of constant inescapable stress, worry, or physical infirmity that have made you feel worn out, believing that nothing is ever going to get better. In still other cases, childhood experiences of severe psychological pain, strain, and stress may have predisposed you to feel that any current psychological pain can never be escaped and that you are powerless to ameliorate it.

Treatment and Self-Help Suggestions – HLP Scale

Feeling hopeless and helpless can be overwhelming, but there are steps you can take to regain a sense of control, hope, and resiliency. It is important to remember that these feelings are not permanent, even though they may feel that way. Progress may take time, but small steps can lead to big changes. Here are some self-help suggestions.

1. Recognize and validate how you feel, because denying or suppressing these feelings can make things worse. Keeping a journal or talking to a friend, family member, or therapist can help release these feelings.
2. Accomplishing even minor tasks can provide a sense of achievement and momentum. Start with small, manageable tasks to make it easier for yourself.
3. Shift your focus to what you can change when things feel out of control, even if it is only a small change to your daily routine or immediate environment.
4. Limit your exposure to "doom scrolling" negative news or influences that can reinforce feelings of helplessness, and seek positive and inspiring content instead. Monitor your time on social media as it can amplify feelings of inadequacy.
5. Deep, slow breathing and mindfulness techniques to help you focus on your immediate senses can help you to stay present, reduce anxiety, and calm your mind. Consider trying an app such as *Headspace* or *Calm*.
6. Make an effort to stay connected to friends, family, and your community. Try to keep from isolating yourself, even if it feels exhausting. Consider joining a support group, since talking to others who have faced similar struggles can offer some relief and reduce the sense of loneliness. If you feel that you are a burden to others, talk with your therapist to help you with these negative self-perceptions.
7. Physical movement can help, and exercise, even a short walk, releases endorphins that improve mood.

8. Keep a gratitude journal with things that you are grateful for each day, no matter how small. This will refocus you on more positive aspects of your life.
9. Set small, achievable daily or weekly goals, instead of focusing on long-term goals, to help build your confidence.
10. A therapist or counselor can help if your feelings of helplessness and/or hopelessness persist. Sometimes, professionals can offer deeper insights and coping strategies. If you have suicidal thoughts and feel vulnerable to harming or killing yourself, discuss this immediately with your therapist. If you cannot reach your therapist, call a suicide and crisis 24/7 hotline [988 in the United States and Canada] for confidential support.
11. Replace negative thoughts with more realistic or compassionate ones. Instead of thinking you are worthless, remind yourself that you are doing your best. If you are in pain, focus on the possibility of a medical solution. Remind yourself that you are valuable. Be kind to yourself, treating yourself with the same compassion you would give others in a similar situation. Reassure yourself that it is okay to struggle and ask for help.

Self-Doubt (SFD) Scale

General Descriptors

Complaints

Feeling worthless; lacking confidence; feeling like a burden to others; feeling ineffective and inferior.

Cognitions

Lacks self-confidence; feels inferior and useless; self-critical; ruminates how others view them.

Emotions

Self-disparaging; intro-punitive; dysphoric.

Traits and behaviors

Passive; easily wounded; takes few, if any, risks; low motivation for achievement; struggles to make important decisions; low self-esteem.

Therapist's Notes – SFD Scale

This 7-item scale is saturated with low self-esteem variance. The individual is reporting feeling useless, worthless, a burden to others, and lacking in any desirable abilities. Typically, this scale will be elevated together with EID, RCd, MLS, RC2, and/or other SP measures of self-esteem such as NFC. These scale combinations may reflect a vulnerability to, if not actual, significant depression and damaged self-esteem. Self-doubt has been implicated as a risk factor for suicidal ideation, borderline and avoidant personality disorders, eating disorders, and PTSD. One source of chronic self-doubt can be a result of the individual internalizing significant others' perceptions and treatment of them.

Elevations on EID, RCd, RC2, and/or MLS (especially if SUI is elevated), would reflect a severe, potentially self-destructive depression, so suicide potential should be evaluated. Self-esteem building would be a primary goal of therapy, together with self-acceptance and self-forgiveness for past mistakes. Cognitive behavioral therapy to shift the person's negative self-image into more realistic thinking would be indicated.

Lifestyle and Family Background – SFD Scale

The self-doubt and intro-punitiveness could be due to a recent ego-damaging setback resulting in the client becoming profoundly self-critical. It could also reflect a lifestyle of passivity and self-doubt conditioned by caregivers who were demeaning, critical, identity-damaging, and rarely, if ever, validating. In the presence of a history of childhood abuse, neglect, and rejection, the self-doubt and self-negation could reflect a long-term adaptation of self-denigration as a way of pre-empting the pain of others' critical judgments. By being self-critical the client is attempting to take some control over the unpredictable onset of pain.

Clarifying Scales – SFD Scale

- If EID is elevated, the client's emotional dysfunction may be related to profoundly low self-esteem, with feelings of being unlovable and unworthy.
- If THD is elevated, clients often feel like "damaged goods," so elevations on SFD increase the likelihood of self-loathing and the strong tendency to keep people at a self-protective emotional distance.
- If BXD is elevated, the SFD elevation may be due to a recent negative event caused by impulsive self-centered behavior or conflict with authority. The self-negation associated with SFD may be a manipulative gesture attempting to signal remorse.
- If RCd is elevated, the SFD elevation adds profoundly low self-esteem to the demoralization and dysphoria.
- If RC1 is elevated, it is possible that the somatization is a manifestation of low self-esteem and self-doubt. Somatization could be a way to elicit sympathy and care since the individual does not feel deserving of love and approval.
- If RC2 is elevated, the self-negating, self-doubting intro-punitiveness may be a manifestation of the severity of their depression.
- If RC7 is elevated, it is possible that the anxiety, fears, and phobias, with resulting dysfunction, could be increasing self-doubt.
- If RC8 is elevated, the damaged self-esteem and cognitive disorganization under stress could be leading to the client's profoundly negative self-esteem.
- If MLS is elevated, the client's complaints of exhaustion and poor health could be associated with general dysphoria and self-negation.
- If NFC is elevated, the client's low self-esteem may be aggravating difficulties with decision-making and general competence. In this case, individuals avoid difficult decisions and then second-guess themselves and ruminate about past decisions. They miss opportunities out of low self-confidence and give up easily when confronted with even minor setbacks.
- If Eating Concerns (EAT) is elevated, the client's preoccupation with food and eating could have led to self-doubt and insecurity. It is also possible that the self-doubt and fears of being useless and a burden to others could have led to an eating disorder as a form of control and psychological catharsis.
- If Social Avoidance (SAV), Shyness (SHY), and/or INTR are elevated, the individual's self-doubt and low self-esteem may aggravate their constitutional disposition toward shyness, leading to the development of a social phobia and withdrawal from others.

Therapy and Therapeutic Pitfalls – SFD Scale

Extreme self-doubt often leads to passivity since the individual avoids making decisions and avoids taking proactive steps toward defined goals. Even setting goals is difficult, since defining a goal risks self-loathing for having failed to complete it. Self-doubt can lead to "analysis paralysis" and to a vicious cycle of low self-esteem, guilt, and self-recrimination due to lost opportunities. In therapy, the client will likely be self-denigrating, and the natural therapeutic reflex is to reassure and want to identify the client's strengths and minimize their missed opportunities. While reassurance and supportive listening are often temporarily soothing, it is generally not the most efficient strategy. Cognitive behavioral therapy is likely the most effective therapeutic modality for educating the client in how to modify cognitions to a more adaptive perspective. This avoids the trap of therapist reassurance and a client's reluctance to believe it, followed by therapist frustration.

Inspection of the item endorsements on this scale can yield valuable information about the client's self-views.

Feedback Statements – SFD Scale

T score 53–59

You are vulnerable to self-doubt and self-criticism, especially if things go badly in your life. At these times you may feel your actions are pointless or useless.

T score 65–78

You are quick to lose self-confidence and compare yourself negatively to others. You likely believe that you are not very good at most things. You doubt your abilities, and you are quick to feel worthless. You tend to be your own worst critic and around other people it is easy for you to feel inferior and insecure. You are probably spending time ruminating about how others see you, worrying that they are critical of you. You may feel like you are a burden to others.

- If EID is elevated, add: You have been feeling depressed and anxious, and very self-critical, feeling unlovable and unworthy. Your extreme self-doubt may make it hard for you to do what is necessary to get out of this negative, depressed state.
- If THD is elevated, add: Your self-doubt and worry that you are not good enough and that you are a burden to others is likely aggravating your fears and anxieties that people are going to hurt or reject you.
- If BXD is elevated, add: Your current self-doubt and preoccupation with feeling that others see you as a burden and are critical of you may be due to some recent negative events caused by your impulsive and poorly thought-through behavior. You may be extremely self-critical as a way of showing remorse or you may be self-doubting because of past decision-making that you regret.
- If RCd is elevated, add: You are feeling defeated, down, and very self-critical. You are having difficulty persevering at things, giving up quickly when things go wrong and feeling that you are not as good as others and a burden to them. Your self-doubt may make you reluctant to take risks and make changes that could help you feel better.
- If RC1 is elevated, add: Your self-doubt, feeling useless, and feeling that you are a burden to others may be related to a medical condition, and you may question whether you will ever feel better. You may be blaming yourself for your physical symptoms or thinking that you are somehow defective because your body is letting you down.

- If RC2 is elevated, add: You have been experiencing depression and self-doubt, wondering if you are as good as other people and worrying that you are a burden to others. Your low self-esteem and your self-doubt may make it hard for you to get motivated to make the changes you need to so that you will feel better and less depressed.
- If RC7 is elevated, add: You are reporting feeling a lot of self-doubt, wondering whether you are a burden to others, and feeling useless compared to others. Your anxiety and tendency to worry and feel guilty may have left you feeling badly about yourself, since the anxiety can, at times, be overwhelming. Your sleep may be difficult, as your worries, which are hard to turn off, may keep you awake.
- If RC8 is elevated, add: You are doubting yourself, feeling that you are a burden to others, and that you are not as good as other people. You may also feel that somehow you are damaged and, therefore, unlovable, so you feel a need to keep people at an emotional distance to protect yourself. Your self-doubt and feeling that you are not good enough could affect your motivation to make changes and to stop being so self-punishing.
- If MLS is elevated, add: Perhaps your feelings of being constantly tired and often feeling unwell has sapped your confidence. This has likely led you to doubt yourself, wondering if you are a burden to others, and not as good as most other people. Your low self-confidence may make a hard for you to make an effort to change the way you see things in order to become less self-critical.
- If EAT is elevated, add: Your preoccupation with food and eating may have contributed to your self-doubt and feelings that you are a burden to others and not as good as most people. Once you have worked on your eating behaviors, it is very possible that you will have more confidence and be less self-critical.
- If NFC is elevated, add: You have been experiencing difficulty making decisions, tending to see every side of an issue and worrying that you are not going to make the right decision. This is aggravated by your self-doubt. You are your own worst critic, and you worry that you might be a burden to others and that you are not as good as other people. This leaves you feeling insecure, with a tendency to give up quickly, as you are sure you are going to make bad decisions. Consequently, you can be passive, hanging back, and feeling insecure and not worthy to be around people who are successful.
- If SAV, SHY, and/or INTR are elevated, add: Your self-doubt and feelings that you are not as good as others is likely aggravating your natural shyness. Consequently, you are vulnerable to developing a social phobia, afraid to go out and meet new people because you doubt that you are good enough to be liked by others. Being in new social situations is possibly making you feel very insecure and sure that people are looking at you negatively. In fact, most people are oblivious and are not looking at others critically.

Lifestyle and Family Background Feedback – SFD Scale

There may have been some recent events that went badly, and you have responded by beating yourself up, losing your self-confidence and experiencing profound self-doubt. It is also possible that self-doubt and insecurity came from your childhood. It is possible that you grew up in an environment where a parental caregiver was critical and demeaning. Perhaps they put you down in ways that robbed you of self-confidence. It is also possible that you were a shy child or maybe you had some eccentricities or learning differences that made you feel that you are not as good as others, leaving you to feel rejected. It is understandable that you developed caution about ever being too confident, hanging back before you make decisions, wanting to avoid criticism and judgment from others.

Treatment and Self-Help Suggestions – SFD Scale

Self-doubt is a common response to experiencing some recent setbacks or having had parental figures who were critical, demeaning, and judgmental. The way you think about yourself tends to be self-perpetuating. You doubt yourself so you hang back. You avoid making decisions because you don't want to get it wrong. You give up on a task because you think it is not going well enough. Later, you feel guilty and bad about yourself for having given up and then you doubt yourself all over again. Learning to see yourself more clearly and in a more balanced way could help you become less self-critical. Even very successful professionals may experience "imposter syndrome" where they doubt their abilities and accomplishments compared with others, despite evidence to the contrary.

Overcoming self-doubt is a journey that many people face. Here are some strategies that might help.

1. Self-doubt is very common, and it is okay to feel unsure at times. You may have become fearful of taking risks if you had some failures or setbacks. Small steps will help you to build your confidence. When you begin to doubt yourself, challenge those thoughts. Are they based on facts or assumptions? Try to substitute these thoughts with more positive ones.
2. To build your confidence, break larger more challenging goals into smaller, achievable tasks – and celebrate your progress, even if it is small.
3. Remind yourself that you are valuable. Be kind to yourself, treating yourself with the same compassion you would give others in a similar situation. Remind yourself that it is okay to struggle and ask for help.
4. Talk to your therapist, friends, family, or a mentor about your feelings. Sometimes, an outside perspective can help you see things more clearly. Consider joining a group such as a religious organization or a "meet-up" group to meet like-minded people.
5. Take a break from or reduce your time on social media as it can amplify feelings of inadequacy.
6. Choose a task and visualize yourself succeeding at it, even a small task like going for a walk or tidying a messy desk. Visualization can help you feel confident in your abilities. You may experience negative self-talk as you visualize but concentrate on switching off this inner voice.
7. Try keeping a journal of your thoughts and feelings to help you process your emotions and identify self-doubt patterns.
8. Doing things that boost your confidence and emphasize your strengths will empower you.
9. A therapist can help you with feelings of self-doubt. Don't assume that your therapist is being critical of you and try to not play a role to please them. Overcoming self-doubt takes time, and it is okay to seek help in this process.

Inefficacy (NFC) Scale

General Descriptors

Complaints

Difficulty starting things; troubled in making decisions; lacks perseverance.

Cognitions

Thoughts of inadequacy; "analysis paralysis;" overthinks decisions; pessimistic.

Emotions

Anxiety about making decisions; feelings of helplessness; low frustration tolerance.

Traits and behaviors

Shrinks from responsibility; gives up easily; procrastinates and has difficulty starting things; small decisions can feel overwhelming.

Therapist's Notes – NFC Scale

This 9-item scale measures feelings of indecisiveness, passivity, and difficulty making decisions. Assertiveness is challenging, even in inconsequential matters. These individuals feel insecure about making even small decisions and are incapable of dealing with crisis situations. Even minor matters can knock them off balance and lead to "analysis paralysis," seeing every side of an issue, and being driven by a fear that they are incapable and not as smart as other people. Consequently, their subjective incompetence means that they tend not to be self-reliant and tend to hang back rather than assert themselves in life generally, with the result that they can be easily controlled by others. Feeling inefficacious – that is, feeling incompetent – such individuals often feel ashamed and guilty. Their lack of perseverance toward goals leaves them feeling inadequate compared to others. If SFD is significantly elevated, it is possible that self-doubt and inefficacy are primary, resulting in depression and anxiety.

Lifestyle and Family Background – NFC Scale

If the individual's history reveals a lifestyle of passivity and inefficacy, look for an early childhood of severe stress and adverse experiences without a stable, validating caregiver. In some cases, the caregivers could have been demeaning and invalidating, robbing the client of self-confidence and eliciting self-protective passivity. In the absence of a traumatic childhood, the elevated NFC scale may reflect a recent threatening experience that has negatively impacted the client's confidence and self-esteem.

Clarifying Scales – NFC Scale

- If EID is elevated, the client is reporting considerable emotional distress and may be in a crisis mode. They will likely express a significant depression with sadness and even despair. They feel overwhelmed and unable to deal with minor stresses and life's daily vicissitudes.
- If RCd is elevated, the client is reporting having lost hope and feeling like they are incapable of reaching their life goals. They feel hopeless, pessimistic, overwhelmed, and that life is a strain.

They don't believe anyone can really help and experience self-pity, feeling that they are getting an unfair deal out of life.

- If RC1 is elevated, the inefficacy and withdrawal from active problem-solving may be the result of acute or chronic somatic problems that have shaken the client's confidence in their body's ability to heal and return to some kind of normality.
- If RC2 is elevated, the client may manifest symptoms of depression, with sad mood, concentration and memory problems, disturbance in eating and sleep patterns, as well as feelings of pessimistic despair. The NFC elevation could be an artifact of their depression since low confidence and inefficacy are associated with depression. It is possible that their depression could be the result of a lifestyle of chronic difficulties in making daily life decisions and feelings of inadequacy in managing daily life.
- If RC4 is elevated, the person's impulsive actions, which may have led to negative consequences, likely have created hesitancy in taking the initiative or making decisions. The items on these two scales are seemingly contradictory, since inaction and self-doubt are central to NFC and acting without sufficient deliberation is associated with RC4. If both scales are elevated, item inspection and further probing with the client can help clarify the meaning of these elevations.
- If RC6 is elevated, the person may be suffering from paranoid delusions and fears of being judged or criticized by others, which has led them to doubt their ability to make effective, reality-based decisions. The inefficacy may reflect a "freeze" reaction in response to perceived threats.
- If RC7 is elevated, the client is reporting chronic anxiety, worry, and a pervasive sense of impending catastrophe. Although there is no item overlap between the RC7 and NFC scales, they both reflect feelings of inadequacy, anxiety, self-doubt, and difficulties with decision-making. RC7 adds additional correlates, such as stress reactivity, anxiety, anger-proneness, and impaired sleep hygiene.
- If RC8 is elevated, the feelings of inefficacy may be aggravated by a thought disorder and profoundly negative self-esteem. The individual may have difficulty thinking clearly, and therefore, has doubts about their ability to problem-solve. Misinterpreting others' motives and exhibiting eccentric and disorganized thoughts likely hamper the individual's self-confidence in their problem-solving ability.
- If SUI is elevated, the client is reporting suicidal ideation and strong suicidal urges. This may be because they feel inadequate, inefficacious, and unable to manage daily life tasks. They feel overwhelmed by making even small, inconsequential decisions. It is also possible that they have experienced a major setback or even catastrophe due to their difficulties making decisions, which has led them to thoughts of suicide.
- If HLP is elevated, the client is reporting feeling hopeless, unable to reach their goals, and unable to make any positive changes. This is against the backdrop of feeling unable to make effective decisions and giving up quickly at the slightest provocation. The combination of these scales suggests significantly low self-esteem.
- If SFD is elevated, as well as feeling inefficacious, the individual has significant self-doubt about their abilities. They compare themselves negatively to others, feel worthless, and think they are a burden to others. It is possible that elevations on SFD are manifesting severe difficulties in managing daily life, which has led to extreme self-doubt. There may be a feedback loop, whereby observing themselves being inefficacious, they develop severe self-doubt, leading to problems making basic decisions, aggravating their self-doubt, and decreasing their self-confidence in their ability to make effective decisions.
- If STR is elevated, the client is experiencing constant stress and high anxiety. It is hard to know to what degree the high levels of experienced stress have led to a breakdown in the individual's effective decision-making and self-confidence, or whether their lowered ability to manage daily

life has increased their perception of being severely stressed. Nevertheless, the picture emerges of a person who feels inefficacious, extremely stressed, constantly on edge, unable to think clearly, and passively observing life due to anxiety and self-doubt.

- If WRY is elevated, the client's feelings of incompetence and inability to make decisions are likely aggravated by their constant worry that an impending disaster is looming. This combination of scales, especially if RC7 is also elevated, reflects an individual living with constant anxiety who is possibly preoccupied with money and security and overwhelmed by regrets and fears of misfortune.
- If CMP is elevated, in addition to self-doubt, difficulty making decisions, and feeling ill-equipped to deal with daily stressors, the individual has also developed compulsions, perhaps as a way to develop some sense of control and competence over their lives. The type of compulsions may reflect particular aspects of their anxiety and would somehow relate to their attempts to feel competent. For example, repetitive checking and counting could serve as a soothing habit, allowing the individual who is feeling inefficacious to have a focus and a sense of control.
- If ARX is elevated, the addition of elevations on this scale would suggest that severe generalized anxiety, constant intrusive thoughts, and sleep difficulties could be contributing to the individual's lack of confidence in their ability to make effective decisions and take responsibility for their life. It is hard to feel efficacious if an individual is "bombarded" by internal "noise," meaning a backdrop of anxiety and worry about disaster looming. In such circumstances, it would be difficult to think clearly, effectively leading to avoidance of decision-making.
- If ANP is elevated, the addition of this scale would indicate a person whose tolerance for frustration is compromised, so small setbacks or frustrations lead to irritability and even temper outbursts. Most people would find feeling inefficacious very stressful, since basic competence is crucial to maneuver through life. If a person already feels incompetent and shrinks from assertive decision-making due to self-doubt, then it is understandable that they have little patience, are quick to catastrophize and express irritability, even rage, over minor frustrations.
- If BRF is elevated, unrealistic fears further restrict the client in their ability to feel a sense of agency. These fears may include claustrophobia, fear of being away from home, fear of dirt, or even anxiety about using a knife.

Therapy and Therapeutic Pitfalls – NFC Scale

Feelings of inefficacy are associated with a sense of being unable to achieve desired and important outcomes. These individuals feel unable to make any real difference in their lives – they have given up trying. They can be challenging to manage therapeutically because they have a fixed, deep-seated, negative view of their problem-solving capacity. Therapy should address these beliefs by examining their causes. For example, the individual may have experienced a recent traumatic or difficult event where they have perceived themselves as failing, and their adaptive response has been to label themselves as incompetent and lacking agency. It is also possible the scale is reflecting a childhood that was traumatic, without caregivers to model good problem-solving skills or coach the client in self-discipline and self-confidence in their own abilities.

Cognitive behavioral therapy approaches are the most effective in changing negative self-views and they help to teach the client to switch off their intrusive negative thoughts. Assigning small tasks as homework to begin the process of convincing them that they are capable of making some decisions is also useful in building confidence. Anticipate robust resistance, with the client persuading the therapist that they are incapable of changing and that the therapist has an unrealistic view of their positive qualities. Self-esteem building is important, but it cannot be "given" by the therapist as the client has to feel they have earned it. Analyzing early childhood experiences could be important to help the client understand where the negative self-image was first formed.

Feedback Statements – NFC Scale

T score = 37

Your answers suggest you are a person who can be quite decisive and approach even difficult decisions with self-confidence and an ability to think clearly, even under stress. You likely enjoy situations where you are in charge.

T score 44–48

Your answers suggest that while you may occasionally have difficulties making decisions, generally you are able to act without overly obsessing about your choices. Like most people, when decisions seem critical, you will analyze your options carefully and not make impulsive decisions.

T score 65–77

Your answers suggest that you can be very indecisive, worrying about whether you are capable of seeing problems clearly and making wise decisions. You are generally quick to doubt yourself and often feel that you don't have what it takes to take charge of your life and make changes, even if they're good for you. Even small decisions loom large for you, and you may spend a lot of time thinking about every side of every issue. You likely worry that you have missed something important and that your decisions will lead to failure. Since you doubt yourself, others may see you as passive, hanging back, and not making decisions, even when that leads to negative consequences. When your self-doubt leads to you missing opportunities or allowing negative events to occur, you are quick to feel ashamed. Because you think that any mistake you make is a reflection of not being good enough, when things become difficult, it is hard for you to persevere at them, and you are quick to give up on a task if you think you are failing or might fail.

- If EID is elevated, add: Your profile suggests that you can get quite down, depressed, anxious, and feel easily knocked off balance by even minor stressors. You are quick to doubt yourself, and can become depressed, especially if you miss out on opportunities because you have been passive out of fear of making a mistake. Your depression and anxiety may have led to you becoming immobilized and unable to make even small decisions. It is also possible that you have become depressed because you feel that you have lost your ability to take charge and take care of problems and make difficult decisions.
- If RCd is elevated, add: You appear to be demoralized. Since life has been feeling like a strain most of the time, it is easy for you to feel hopeless, and alone. You are your own worst critic and are quick to give up on a task if you think it is not going well since it is so painful to feel like you are going to fail again.
- If RC1 is elevated, add: Your profile suggests that you have been experiencing numerous physical symptoms that come and go, and under stress you may actually feel worse. This may have sapped your confidence and affected your ability to make decisions and to trust that you are capable of taking charge over your life. It is also possible that your self-doubt, difficulty in asserting yourself, and lack of trust in your decision-making have put stress on your body, leading to numerous physical symptoms.

- If RC2 is elevated, add: Your profile indicates that you have been feeling depressed. Making decisions is difficult for you since you see all sides of an issue. You are afraid to make a bad decision since you already feel quite depressed and making a mistake would lead to further self-criticism and feelings of hopelessness. When people experience depression, they often also experience guilt and self-doubt. They think that they are incapable of making meaningful changes in their lives. They also tend to become passive and are afraid to take risks in case they incur further losses. Do you think you became depressed because of recent or past losses, leading you to feel incapable of making changes?
- If RC4 is elevated, add: Your profile suggests that you are currently feeling unable to make even small decisions effectively. You may have recently been in trouble because of past behavior or impulsive actions and you now doubt yourself and second-guess your decisions. It is also possible that you feel defeated because you are in trouble and you feel that the consequences of your behavior are unfair to you, so you have "thrown in the towel."
- If RC6 is elevated, add: Your profile suggests you are feeling very vulnerable to criticism or judgment, or even to being personally attacked by others. This may have left you feeling "frozen" in your behavior, unable to make decisions because you are afraid that they will lead to further attacks and possible humiliations.
- If RC7 is elevated, add: Your profile suggests you suffer from a great deal of anxiety. Your mind seems to be working constantly, looking at every possible thing that could go wrong and trying to pre-empt what you perceive as possible disaster. You live with a constant knot in your stomach, as if you are in a war zone, anticipating that you are going to set off an explosion because you have missed some important detail. You live with a sense of urgency, as if you are somehow behind or running late, even when there is no objective urgency. Because of your anxiety, you also have a lot of difficulty making decisions and feeling competent to make changes in your life, even if they're good for you. You are quick to feel ashamed. If you make a mistake by being passive, you can miss opportunities and later feel guilty.
- If RC8 is elevated, add: Your profile suggests that when you are stressed, it is hard to focus and keep your mind grounded in reality. People with your profile have difficulty trusting others. If you perceive others as hostile, it is easy to feel panic and want to escape, either by shutting down or being verbally aggressive as a way to warn people to back off and leave you alone. Sometimes you may feel that others see the world so differently from you that you experience the world as alien and difficult to understand. Even when you are alone, you may experience periods when your mind plays tricks on you, and you see and hear things that others do not appear to experience. It is no wonder that you have difficulty taking charge of your life and avoid making decisions, even small ones, because you are afraid that you don't really understand what is important.
- If SUI is elevated, add: Some of your answers have indicated that you are feeling pretty defeated and hopeless and that you may be thinking about suicide. It is hard to know what has kicked off these feelings. There could have been some recent or longstanding events that have left you feeling hopeless and defeated. Your difficulties in taking charge of your life, being assertive, and making decisions may have contributed to your feelings of hopelessness. Perhaps being passive and indecisive has made you miss opportunities or led to losses that seem catastrophic and that can only be resolved by dying. If you feel hopeless and suicidal and cannot reach your therapist, call a suicide and crisis 24/7 hotline [988 in the United States and Canada] for confidential support.
- If HLP is elevated, add: Your answers suggest that you have been feeling helpless, hopeless, and pessimistic. It appears that you have lost some hope and belief that you can make changes. Life feels overwhelming and stressful. Feeling this way, it is understandable that you have become passive, hanging back from making decisions, doubting that you are able to make good decisions, and giving up quickly when things go wrong.

- If SFD is elevated, add: Because you feel inferior to others and insecure, it is understandable that you hold back and avoid making decisions out of fear of negative consequences. You are quick to put yourself down and you can easily feel useless. Having such self-doubt hinders decision-making. Even small decisions can loom large, so you hesitate to make them. Others are likely to see you as passive. You may end up missing opportunities because of self-doubt and feelings of unworthiness.
- If STR is elevated, add: Your answers indicate that you constantly have high levels of stress and anxiety. Much of the time you operate as if you are in danger, with a pit in your stomach. Stress makes it hard for you to make decisions, leading you to become passive out of fear that something you do, or decide, will lead to catastrophe.
- If WRY is elevated, add: Your profile suggests that you live in a constant state of worry. You fret about possible misfortune, finances, or about something happening to your loved ones. It is difficult to focus and think clearly if you are constantly thinking about what can go wrong. It is understandable that you have challenges in making decisions. You are afraid that if you make an incorrect choice, it could lead to severe consequences. It is as if you are constantly seeing the world as a dangerous place where a decision you make will lead to bad consequences Avoiding decisions makes sense as a way to protect against something bad happening.
- If CMP is elevated, add: Your profile suggests that you have developed some compulsions, behaviors that you feel you have to keep doing in order to somehow protect yourself from something bad happening. Because you have such self-doubt and you avoid making decisions because you don't think they will be good ones, you may have compensated by finding a compulsion that gives you a sense of control over your life, even though others may see your compulsions as unnecessary and annoying. Even though your compulsions may make you feel temporarily better, they don't actually help you in making decisions and taking charge.
- If ARX is elevated, add: Your profile suggests that you have many anxious experiences, with sleep difficulties, nightmares, sometimes feeling that you are outside your body, and intrusive thoughts that occur at unexpected times. You might be in an objectively pleasant situation, and suddenly have a thought about something ugly, painful, or catastrophic. You may have moments where you suddenly feel panicky, but you are not sure why. It is not surprising that this has caused you to feel incapable of making big decisions or even small ones. You likely are passive since you are unsure when one of these intrusive thoughts or panic moments will crop up.
- If ANP is elevated, add: Your profile suggests that you have problems with anger and irritability. People may see you as argumentative and impatient with others. It is hard for you to forgive others if they hurt or disappointed you. If people bother you or make demands on you when you are trying to think clearly or concentrate, it is easy for you to become quite angry and irritable, even explosive.
- If BRF is elevated, add: Your profile suggests that you have a number of fears that restrict your daily activity. You likely avoid making decisions and feel incompetent at managing your life since these fears block you from doing many things, even things you might want to do.

Lifestyle and Family Background Feedback – NFC Scale

People with your profile sometimes grew up in environments where parents or caregivers were not good coaches in helping you to feel competent and modeling wise decision-making. Perhaps your caregivers were hostile or critical, or so controlling that they robbed you of self-efficacy. Perhaps you consequently have a history of tending to be passive, afraid to take charge, and afraid to make decisions. It is also possible that you have recently had a major setback that eroded your confidence and left you standing back, observing life rather than jumping in and taking charge.

Treatment and Self-Help Suggestions – NFC Scale

Feeling ineffective can be really challenging, but there are strategies you can use to regain a sense of control and productivity. Here are some self-help tips that might help.

1. Set small, achievable daily or weekly goals. Start with something simple, like going for a short walk or tidying up a drawer, and celebrate these small accomplishments.
2. Take time to prioritize tasks by their urgency and importance. You may not be able to easily identify the key items, since you focus on every side of an issue, but starting one task and focusing on it can help you build momentum.
3. Engage in mindfulness techniques, such as meditation or deep breathing, to help you remain present, reduce anxiety, and increase focus. Take a few moments daily and think about something you are grateful for to refocus on the more positive aspects of your life.
4. Keep a journal where you note daily accomplishments, no matter how small, to remind you of your successes and help shift your focus from what you haven't done to what you have done.
5. Establish a daily routine that includes time for work and yourself. Structure and consistency can help improve your effectiveness. Try this for at least a day to see if it helps you feel better and more capable.
6. Try volunteering, taking a class, or trying a new hobby that interests you to boost your confidence and sense of accomplishment. Find something easy to start with that gives you pleasure and build from there.
7. Practice self-compassion by being kind to yourself. Treat yourself as you would treat a friend experiencing something similar. Recognize that everyone has periods of feeling ineffective. Try not to compare yourself to others. Everyone moves at their own pace.
8. Regular exercise, even a short walk, can release endorphins that will improve your mood and energy levels, and make you feel more capable and focused.
9. Visualize achieving your goals to motivate you and reinforce a positive mindset. Be aware of any negative self-talk you experience. Focus on your visualized goals rather than any past failures.

Stress (STR) Scale

General Descriptors

Complaints

Often feels nervous; low stress tolerance; functions poorly under stress; feels pressured.

Cognitions

Catastrophizes; has ruminative thoughts.

Emotions

Feels anxious and on edge.

Traits and behaviors

Nervous; feels incapable of managing stress; on edge; constantly worries; reacts to minor events in a major way.

Therapist's Notes – STR Scale

Every item on this 6-item scale is face-valid and reflects difficulty managing stress. The individual is reporting functioning poorly under stress, constantly feeling pressured, and incapable of controlling their anxiety. They admit that their stress reactivity is problematic. Elevations on this scale may suggest acute or chronic stress, with anticipatory anxiety likely dominating the individual's life. In some cases, this scale will be elevated only with other measures of anxiety such as RC7, ARX, and WRY, reflecting a generalized anxiety disorder. In other cases, depression may be more salient, so the STR scale could be elevated along with depression indicators, such as EID, RCd, and RC2, reflecting the co-morbidity of anxiety with depression.

Lifestyle and Family Background – STR Scale

It is difficult to predict what kind of family background is likely associated with elevations on this scale. In some cases, individuals with a vulnerability to be easily knocked off balance by stress were anxious and nervous children. With a history of anxious attachments in childhood, inconsistent parenting, or early childhood adverse experiences, elevations on the scale could be reflective of these past events. In other cases, early childhood insecurities and inconsistent, unsupportive caregivers would have led to the adaptive response of constantly anticipating problems, with the resulting experience of anxiety. It is also possible that elevations on this scale reflect a current difficulty or even a traumatic incident, leaving the individual feeling overwhelmed and incapable of managing their stress. Acute or chronic stress is a risk factor in the etiology of several mental disorders.

Clarifying Scales – STR Scale

- If EID is elevated, the individual's nervousness and experience of severe stress is probably part of a depression and/or anxiety constellation. Elevations on STR would support that the individual is experiencing severe stress.
- If THD is elevated, the client's stress level and nervousness may be associated with an awareness that their cognitive processes are somehow impaired. The stress associated with the scale may also reflect the individual's fears about other people's hostility toward them, and perhaps an awareness that paranoid or psychotic thought processes are negatively impacting their reality testing. Though there are situations in which a person with a thought disorder does not experience anxiety, it is unusual. A therapist would expect somebody with paranoid ideation to feel somewhat anxious and stressed since the world would appear unsafe and uncertain to them.
- If RCd is elevated, the individual's level of stress and nervousness would be part of a general experience of demoralization, feeling defeated and hopeless about making positive changes in their lives. Feeling insecure as compared to others as well as constantly on edge and pressured, this combination of scales suggests a client who is worn out, defeated, and feeling incapable of managing their stress.
- If RC2 is elevated, clients who are experiencing severe depression generally also complain of anxiety, low self-esteem, stress, and self-doubt. Elevations on the scale would support that the individual is experiencing chronic severe stress, as well as depressive symptomatology.
- If RC7 is elevated, the client is exhibiting symptoms associated with a generalized anxiety disorder. They are complaining that they are anxious, nervous, on edge, constantly stressed,

preoccupied with avoiding loss and failure, feeling readily guilty, and constantly insecure. The addition of this scale supports the severity of their generalized anxiety.
- If MLS is elevated, the client is reporting feeling weak, unwell, tired, and unrested as well as nervous, anxious, and constantly stressed. They feel that they are more stressed than most people and they do not feel they are capable of managing the stress effectively. They feel unmotivated and enervated and are likely to be somewhat passive, given that they do not feel well.
- If NUC is elevated, the client is reporting numerous neurological symptoms, with dizzy spells, fits or convulsions, difficulty with balance, and vague and shifting somatic symptoms, such as numbness in the extremities and involuntary muscle twitches, as well as feeling constantly stressed, on edge, and nervous. It is possible that the high stress level is due to concern, even panic, about the neurological symptoms, but it is also possible that the neurological symptoms are reflecting a physiological response to constant stress and anxiety.
- If EAT is elevated, preoccupation with food and purging could be an attempt at getting some control over the experience of intense stress and anxiety by focusing on controlling food. It is also possible that the high stress level is reflecting the individual's awareness that the eating disorder is potentially a problem and dangerous.
- If COG is elevated, the concerns over memory impairment, episodic confusion, difficulties with concentration, and focus may be causing the individual an extreme stress response. It is also possible that the client's high stress level is leading to cognitive inefficiency that may not be organic.
- If HLP is elevated, the client's feelings of hopelessness and helplessness may be aggravating their experience of stress.
- If SUI is elevated, it is possible that the experience of constant stress is leading to suicidal escape fantasies.
- If RCd, RC2, and HLP are elevated, the client may feel hopeless about ever feeling at peace.
- If NFC is elevated, the client is feeling incompetent at basic life skills, and this also likely increases their stress level.

Therapy and Therapeutic Pitfalls – STR Scale

Often, STR will be elevated with other scales measuring dysfunctional negative emotions, such as maladaptive anxiety, anger, irritability, and depression. If ACT is elevated, it could reflect an individual who becomes stressed, tense, and anxious, and then behaves impulsively, followed by guilt and anxiety. If the scales measuring introversion and shyness are elevated, the client may feel constant stress due to social anxiety. Each issue would need a different therapeutic strategy. Stress management could help the client deal with the experience of stress and learning healthy stress relievers such as exercise. Identifying the triggers for stress is important. The other elevated scales could aid in identifying the possible causes of the stressors. If STR is <39, the individual experiences less stress than most people and appears resilient in the face of negative events. This could be significant if, for example, the client is elevated on acting-out aggression scales such as RC4, ACT, and DISC. The lower score might suggest lessened constraints on the acting-out.

Feedback Statements – STR Scale

T score < 39

You appear to be free from feelings of stress and pressure, and few stressors interfere with your functioning.

T score 65-75

You appear to be feeling quite a lot of stress currently. You report feeling pressured and that you experience more stress than you think others feel. You don't work as well under stress as you would like.

T score = 76

You appear to be feeling significant stress, with little patience. You report not functioning well under stress and feel that you are more stressed and nervous than most people. Waiting for people or events likely makes you nervous and high-strung and you feel unable to control your anxiety level.

- If EID is elevated, add: You report feeling anxious, depressed, and constantly stressed. You feel a lot of pressure and feel nervous and unable to function under stress. Your depression may be aggravating your stress level.
- If THD is elevated, add: You report feeling nervous and unable to manage your stress levels. This may be aggravated by your fears about how others are viewing you and your concern that others harbor hostile and cruel intent toward you. If you feel the world is somewhat frightening, it is understandable that you would feel nervous and stressed.
- If RCd is elevated, add: You appear to feel very demoralized, defeated, and even hopeless, and at the same time very stressed and pressured. You report feeling nervous and unable to work under stress. Perhaps prolonged stress has left you feeling hopeless about changing your life in a positive direction.
- If RC2 is elevated, add: You report feeling quite down and depressed. Depression may be affecting your sleep, appetite, and ability to enjoy life. You also appear to feel a lot of stress and pressure and are more nervous than most people. It is hard for you to work under stress. Did you become depressed after a period of intense pressure and stress, or did you become more stressed because depression has affected your energy levels and general efficiency? Discuss this with your therapist.
- If RC4 is elevated, add: Your profile suggests that currently you are feeling pressured and stressed by your life. You may have recently had some setbacks due to what you consider to be impulsive or poorly deliberated decisions resulting in stress because of the consequences. It will be important to follow the rules in resolving your current stressful situation, since trying to manipulate your way out could lead to further negative consequences.
- If RC6 is elevated, add: Your profile suggests that you are feeling stressed currently, perhaps because you feel so unsafe and vulnerable to others' criticism and judgments. When we feel unsafe, it is very stressful, since we are unsure which behavior could lead to exposing more vulnerability to others.
- If RC7 is elevated, add: You reported feeling anxious, constantly living with a knot in your stomach as if something bad is about to happen. You easily feel guilty and your hyper-responsible, dutiful personality means that you take on too many tasks and responsibilities that end up overwhelming you. It is not surprising that you are reporting you feel constant stress, pressure, and nervousness most of the time. You find it hard to function under stress, yet it is hard for you to not feel responsible and commit to tasks.
- If MLS is elevated, add: Your experience of constant stress and pressure may be wearing you out, so you feel weak, tired, and never fully rested. You may avoid doing things because you don't feel well enough.

- If NUC is elevated, add: You are experiencing life as very stressful right now. You are also experiencing a number of neurological symptoms such as dizzy spells, fits, difficulties with balance, and other vague and shifting body symptoms. This might even include numbness in your hands and feet and involuntary muscle twitches. It may be that these physical symptoms frighten you and stress you, leading to more internal pressure. Perhaps the stress increases the physical symptoms. It is possible that you have developed these physical symptoms in the recent past and they are frightening you, causing you greater stress.
- If EAT is elevated, add: You report that you are having preoccupations with food and eating and are also experiencing a lot of stress, pressure, and nervousness. It may be that you are stressed because you feel you have an eating problem. It is also possible that, because you are high-strung and can get stressed by even ordinary events, you have focused on food as the one area in your life you can control. It would be important to discuss with your therapist the connection between your stress and eating habits.
- If COG is elevated, add: You are reporting a number of concerns about your memory and episodic confusion as well as difficulties with concentration and focus. It is possible that these symptoms are due to the high level of stress that you are currently experiencing. Sometimes people respond to stress by shutting down internally, which can lead to cognitive problems. On the other hand, it is possible that you have developed these cognitive problems due to a medical condition, and they are stressing you because of your fears that something is wrong with you.
- If SUI is elevated, add: You report thinking a lot about suicide lately. You also report that you are experiencing a great deal of stress and that you feel more nervous and more stressed than most people. It is possible that you are feeling hopeless about feeling better, so you are having escape fantasies that involve suicide. It is also possible that you have been thinking about suicide, and you realize that is not positive, so you have felt very stressed about it. It would be important to discuss this with your therapist. If you feel hopeless and suicidal and cannot reach your therapist, call a suicide and crisis 24/7 hotline [988 in the United States and Canada] for confidential support.
- If HLP is elevated, add: You have been experiencing high levels of stress, and it has left you feeling helpless and hopeless.
- If NFC is elevated, add: Your current level of stress may make it hard for you to feel that you are able to handle life's difficulties and it has left you feeling unable to make decisions and take charge of things.

Lifestyle and Family Background Feedback – STR Scale

It is hard to know whether you have always been someone who is vulnerable to developing stress or whether your current stress is due to some recent difficult event. Sometimes, people who are high-strung and easily stressed had childhoods in which they experienced setbacks and losses that led to their adaptive response of constantly being on guard for any negative events. Feeling guilty and constantly scanning the environment for danger is an understandable response if you have been in situations where things went wrong and weren't prepared for them. If your current high level of stress is due to a recent event, it is important to put things in perspective and find ways to self-care.

Treatment and Self-Help Suggestions – STR Scale

Stress is a normal human response to situations where we feel we don't have full control or when we are afraid something bad is going to happen. We experience stress mostly in our bodies. As stress increases, we are likely to become progressively more aware of it as it affects our muscle tension and other bodily functions. When you are stressed, it is hard to focus on anything other than the situation that is stressing you. Following any of these recommendations may be difficult, so it is important you don't put pressure on yourself to do them all. If you can do one every so often, that can help.

1. Perform deep breathing exercises to calm your nervous system when you feel overwhelmed by stress. Research shows that slow, deep breaths work. Inhale for four counts, hold for four, and exhale for four.
2. Make time for exercise, even if it feels like another burden. Taking a walk around the block or doing yardwork can help you shift your focus and relieve stress by releasing endorphins.
3. Spend time outdoors, such as in a park or garden. Nature can be very soothing. It may be difficult to think about spending time outdoors when you are feeling stressed but try to do so and notice whether you experience any relief.
4. Mindfulness techniques and meditation can help you relieve stress by focusing on the present moment for a few minutes. Apps like *Headspace* or *Calm* can help guide you through this.
5. Share your feelings about what you are going through with a trusted friend or family member.
6. Engage in creative activities like drawing, music, or writing to relieve stress.
7. A healthy diet with limited caffeine, alcohol, and sugar intake can help with anxiety levels.
8. Healthy sleep habits are helpful in managing stress. Taking a warm bath or shower before bed can help you to fall asleep.
9. Keep a gratitude journal to remind you about the positive things in your life.
10. Learn to set boundaries with others by not overcommitting yourself.
11. When managing your daily tasks, be realistic about allocating sufficient time. Prioritize important tasks and avoid getting distracted by non-important items. Limiting time crunches can allow you to feel more in control and less stressed.

Worry (WRY) Scale

General Descriptors

Complaints

Frequent worries; feels overwhelmed; possible money worries.

Cognitions

Preoccupation with disappointments; worries about future misfortunes; ruminations about future financial security.

Emotions

Constant apprehension; tension.

Traits and behaviors

High-strung; high anxiety; worrier; possibly guilt-prone; security preoccupied; often dutiful and responsible; intro-punitive.

Therapist's Notes – WRY Scale

Individuals with elevated scores on this 7-item scale may have difficulty letting go of past failures and disappointments. They are extremely security conscious and may worry about money matters but almost any circumstance could elicit worry. Generally, they do not act-out aggressively, especially if RC4, RC9, ACT, Aggressiveness (AGGR), and DISC are low. Elevations on WRY would suggest a responsible, dutiful individual who is quick to feel guilty over minor mistakes. Typically, the scale will not be the only elevated scale, since worry is often co-morbid with other experiences of anxiety and general distress. For example, hypothetically, a client could be elevated on RC9 and Self-Importance (SFI) as well as WRY. The clinician's hypothesis might be that the client is driven to be productive and prominent, and their self-importance is driven by anxiety and fears of losing status or failing. People who are prone to worry are usually amenable to cognitive behavioral therapy, thought-stopping, relaxation training, and other behavioral interventions.

Lifestyle and Family Background – WRY Scale

It is difficult to infer whether elevations on this scale reflect a client who has been worry-prone for most of their lives or one whose worrying is a response to a new frightening situation. A chronic ruminator could have been an anxiously attached child or someone who had difficulties separating from a caregiver and was easily overwhelmed by the stresses of school, such as exams and homework. There could be a genetic component to chronic worriers, but their apprehensiveness could also be aggravated by a childhood where their caregivers were inconsistent or where there were adverse events and traumas.

Worrying is an adaptive response to trauma, such as an unpredictable negative event that is perceived as potentially catastrophic. Trying to anticipate all eventualities would be an adaptive response. On the other hand, it is possible that this scale elevation could reflect a client who has had recent causes to worry, whether due to a medical condition, the illness of a child or close friend, or a recent financial setback. Worrying is an attempt to anticipate an unexpected event to avoid the onset of an anxiety response. Constantly expecting a catastrophe provides the belief to the individual that they won't be taken by surprise by an unpredictable negative event.

Clarifying Scales – WRY Scale

- If EID is elevated, it suggests that the client's mood and affect are colored by constant generalized worrying as well as concerns about specific issues, like financial security. It is possible that worrying is a cognitive aspect of an anxious depression predicted by the EID elevations. It is also possible that the prolonged worry has developed into a depression due to the serotonin and dopamine enervating effects of constant worry.
- If THD is elevated, the individual's worrying could be associated with their understanding that they are impaired by psychotic thought processes and are worried about how to ameliorate their condition. The worrying could also be part of a paranoid delusion – for example, a client who is constantly worried that the CIA is bugging their house and following them.
- If RCd is elevated, the client is admitting to feeling defeated, dysphoric, useless, and fearful of "falling to pieces." The individual experiences withdrawal, sadness, and despair. Elevations on WRY add energy in the form of diffuse worry. In a sense, demoralization suggests passivity and worrying is activating, albeit dysfunctionally so. If a person is fretful, they are still engaged and concerned about outcomes. In that sense, WRY suggests that the individual has not completely given up.

- If RC1 is elevated, the focus of the worry may be physical illness and infirmity. It could also mean that the individual's preoccupation and concern with somatic symptoms has generalized to worry about many different things or non-specific things.
- If RC2 is elevated, depression is mixed with generalized worry, which may be deepening the depression. Alternatively, the worry may be a manifestation of depression and, therefore, may possibly be ameliorated by antidepressant medications.
- If RC7 is elevated, the generalized diffuse anxiety suggested by RC7 is combined with constant worrying and nervousness. Adding agitation to the clinical picture elevates suicidal risks if SUI is elevated.
- If RC8 is elevated, the individual is anxious, possibly obsessive compulsive (if CMP is elevated), and possibly schizoid. There may be reality distortions and depersonalization. If SFD and/or NFC are elevated, the client manifests chronic worrying, nervousness, feelings of inferiority and inadequacy, and low self-confidence.
- If ANP is elevated, the irritability, impatience, and volatility associated with this scale may reflect a client who is nervous and high-strung. Small frustrations lead to irritability, since the individual's level of resting arousal is already high.
- If SAV, SHY, and/or INTR are elevated, the individual may have social anxiety and constantly feel nervous about interacting with other people.

Therapy and Therapeutic Pitfalls – WRY Scale

In the absence of more severe psychopathology, worrying as a specific symptom is relatively amenable to cognitive behavioral therapy. Sometimes chronic worrying is part of a depression and/or generalized anxiety disorder. Typically, psychotropic medication can attenuate the symptoms of chronic worrying and tension. In some cases, elevations may reflect a client with a lifelong vulnerability to worry. A full history should reveal whether the client was an anxious child or if the current brooding was precipitated by early trauma or neglect. In the presence of an adverse childhood, therapy should combine insight to help the client understand how worrying may have been an adaptive response to uncertainty and unpredictable trauma. Once the client has accepted that there is a cause, then a therapeutic alliance can be developed. Cognitive behavioral therapy should help the client switch off negative thoughts and learn to manage the tendency to catastrophize. The client has probably often heard people say "stop worrying" and, therefore, would resist any pushing by the therapist to give up their habitual "overthinking." Helping them to understand how negative thinking has been an adaptive response is the best approach to dealing with resistance.

Feedback Statements – WRY Scale

T score <44

Your answers suggest that you are unusually free from worry. You don't lose sleep over a worry, and you don't worry about possible misfortunes. You trust that your financial security and important relationships will work out and you don't beat yourself up over past mistakes. You are mostly able to relax without worried thoughts intruding and probably make decisions pretty easily.

T score 44–49

Your profile suggests that generally you don't worry a great deal. However, like many people, you may have some occasional worries, perhaps being preoccupied about finances or beating yourself up over a past disappointment. Nevertheless, you are still able to let go of worries and allow yourself to relax most of the time, though you may occasionally have trouble sleeping because you have something on your mind.

T score =54

Your profile suggests that your worrying may occasionally interfere with your sleeping or cause you some distress. You may find yourself worrying about something that makes it hard for you to relax and switch off your mind. You may also have worry-free periods where you are able to relax and not be preoccupied with other matters.

T score ≥65

Your profile suggests that you are a worrier. You fret about many things, possibly future misfortunes or financial insecurity, and ruminate about past losses and disappointments. You may feel a constant nagging worry, a pit in your stomach, sometimes without even knowing what you are concerned about. Worrying is likely affecting your sleep. It is hard to switch off your mind when you go to sleep, and it is challenging for you to ever fully relax without worried thoughts invading your mind.

- If EID is elevated, add: Your profile suggests that you have been feeling quite depressed, with sad moods, difficulties with concentration, memory, and letting go and enjoying life. You often worry that something bad is about to happen. You overthink about financial security and are quick to beat yourself up over past losses or disappointments. You dread possible misfortunes even though you have no control over the future.
- If THD is elevated, add: Your profile suggests that you experience a constant nagging worry and anxiety about possible future misfortunes. Sometimes it is hard for you to sleep because your mind is so preoccupied with concerns about money and security. These intrusive thoughts may also be related to the way you have been feeling. You appear to be feeling vulnerable to being criticized, judged, or even attacked by others. When stressed, it is hard for you to stay focused. Constantly worrying may be your adaptive attempt to try to gain control over what feels scary to you right now.
- If RCd is elevated, add: Your profile suggests you have been feeling quite demoralized, unhappy, even depressed. You are very self-critical, feeling worthless, and feeling that life is a strain most of the time. You also seem to be worrying a great deal. In spite of feeling demoralized, the worry suggests you are still trying to problem-solve, trying to anticipate everything that can go wrong in the future, and wanting to make sure your finances or affairs are taken care of.
- If RC1 is elevated, add: Your profile suggests you have many physical symptoms that may trouble you. Vague and shifting physical symptoms that are hard to diagnose can cause a person a lot of worry. You also seem to be constantly anticipating that some bad event is about to happen. You stress about finances and how you could have done things differently in the past. Fretting about your physical wellbeing can be exhausting and might actually aggravate your physical symptoms because of the stress you put on your body.
- If RC2 is elevated, add: Your profile suggests that you have been feeling quite depressed. Depression causes difficulties with thinking, concentration, and memory, but it can also create anxiety. Your profile suggests that you have been experiencing much worry about how bad things could happen in the future. You may worry about your financial security, and you may fret over past mistakes or disappointments. Feeling a constant pit in your stomach and constant nagging worry can add to the feeling of being drained and unhappy.
- If RC7 is elevated, add: Your profile indicates that you suffer from a great deal of anxiety and tension. You are likely a responsible, dutiful person who takes life seriously. You live with a constant sense that something bad is going to happen and you easily feel guilty, even for minor

mistakes. You tend to try to anticipate all future eventualities constantly, so making decisions can be quite difficult. As well as feeling anxious, your test results suggest you obsessively ruminate, sometimes causing you to lose sleep. You can particularly feel stressed about money and financial security and may find it hard to let go of past disappointments or losses.

- If RC8 is elevated add: Your profile suggests you are a chronic worrier and that you easily feel nervous with fears and anxieties. You are quick to feel inferior and inadequate. You may have some difficulties with concentration and memory. Because you are your own worst critic, it might be hard for you to find meaningful relationships with people who really get to know you.
- If ANP is elevated, add: Your profile suggests that you worry a great deal, sometimes you are even not quite sure what you are worried about. You worry about financial security and often have difficulty letting go of a past disappointment or loss. You may lose sleep fretting over possible future misfortunes. You also report having trouble with irritability, anger, and even explosiveness. When you are constantly worried, it is understandable that minor irritations can set you off since you are already very tense. People may find it hard to be around you, since they feel your tension and know that small frustrations can make you blow up. You can react with irritability to stressful situations.
- If SAV, SHY, and/or INTR are elevated, add: Your profile suggests that you are uncomfortable in large groups of people you don't know. Your profile also suggests that you are a worrier, constantly on edge, anticipating something bad happening. It is possible that your worry is precipitated by having to be around people you don't know. It is also possible that you feel awkward around people you don't know well and may be concerned they might see your anxiety.

Lifestyle and Family Background Feedback – WRY Scale

Tendencies to worry may be genetic in some people. In some situations, people who are worriers may have grown up in an unpredictable environment with unreliable people caring for them. Perhaps you were a sensitive and high-strung child who tended to suffer from anxiety. You may have had an anxious attachment to a caregiver because you couldn't quite trust that they would be there when you needed them. If that is the case, then as a child you would have felt worried constantly. If you have experienced worrying most of your life, it could be genetic or due to adverse childhood experiences. It is also possible you experienced a recent setback that triggered your worrying, so you are now constantly on edge, anticipating that something awful may happen unpredictably.

Treatment and Self-Help Suggestions – WRY Scale

Feeling constantly worried is exhausting and crowds out your ability to think clearly and make decisions easily. Worry is often an adaptive response. If at some point in your life a trauma took you by surprise, you may have responded by worrying and trying to learn to predict the future as one way to protect yourself against a negative unpredictable event. However, worrying is rarely an effective strategy. Initially you may feel insecure giving up worrying, even for a short while, perhaps fearing that something bad will happen unless you stay vigilant. Here are some strategies that may help. By practicing these techniques regularly, you may find it easier to manage worry.

1. Practicing mindfulness techniques and meditation to focus on the present moment can be helpful in calming your mind. When you are constantly worried about past regrets or future anxieties, you are not able to enjoy life fully. Try to distract yourself with an activity or find something in nature that you can observe and enjoy for a moment.
2. Worry often comes with "what if" thinking that tends to be exaggerated or unrealistic. Challenge these thoughts by considering what evidence supports or contradicts the worry, what the "worst case" scenario might be, and how likely it is to happen. Ask yourself if you have

successfully managed similar situations in the past. Make the case against the need to worry by reminding yourself that there are alternative positive views. Substitute positive affirmations for negative thoughts and remind yourself that you are better able to handle challenges than you think.

3. Allow yourself a short, scheduled period of time to focus on your worries, writing them down and then letting them go for the rest of the day. Also write down any actions you could take to make the worry go away, even temporarily, to help you feel more in control. Take proactive steps where you can and try to accept the rest. Break down big worries into smaller steps, since small actions can reduce your anxiety. For example, if you are worried about money, develop a budget and put a small amount of money away every week.
4. Deep breathing can ease tension and refocus you away from worrying. Breathe in slowly, hold, then exhale.
5. If your worries center around world events, choose a few trusted information sources and limit your exposure to this, including social media. Set aside time to check the news or your social media to prevent overload.
6. Regular physical exercise releases endorphins, which are natural mood lifters. Even a short walk can be helpful.
7. Adhere to a regular healthy sleep schedule. Since it is hard to sleep when you are worried, write down your concerns before you go to bed and put them in another room, allowing yourself to revisit them the next day.
8. Share your worries with a trusted friend or family member, or with a therapist, in order to gain a fresh perspective and emotional support. Consider joining a support group with individuals who have similar concerns as a reminder that you are not alone and to provide you with comfort and helpful information.
9. Obsessional thinking or worry can often be treated effectively with medication. Consider asking your therapist for a referral to someone who specializes in this area.

Compulsivity (CMP) Scale

General Descriptors

Complaints

Compulsive need to check and double-check; nervous if things are out of place; inefficient. (Usually, complaints are made by family members rather than the compulsive person.)

Cognitions

Obsessional and rigid thinking; overattention to details.

Emotions

Anxiety; tension.

Traits and behaviors

Loss of self-control over certain behaviors; rigid, compulsive, and ritualistic behaviors; perfectionism.

Therapist's Notes – CMP Scale

The 8 items on the scale are face-valid, so even moderate elevations suggest an obsessive-compulsive propensity. High scorers are rigid, compulsive, perfectionistic, and controlling; they become anxious if things are not done in a certain ordered and structured way. Generally, they do not seek treatment if they are suffering from a simple compulsion or obsession unless friends or relatives find their behavior controlling and restricting. As parents, they can be difficult because they demand that their children conform to their rigid compulsions and obsessions. If measures of anxiety are elevated, compulsions could be ego-defense measures for regulating affect. The cognitive style of the compulsive individual may lend itself to successful work tasks requiring repetition and scrutiny to detail until it is necessary to adapt to changed circumstances. Compulsivity may severely restrict a person's ability to shift their attention smoothly, reflecting restricted flexibility.

Lifestyle and Family Background – CMP Scale

Their lifestyle is one of strict adherence to certain compulsive behaviors. These individuals tend to be rigid about doing things in a highly specific way to avoid becoming irritated and anxious. An early childhood history of chaotic circumstances would suggest that the compulsions developed as a way to maintain control in an environment that was uncertain and potentially harmful. In some cases, the client was anxious and compulsive as a child, perhaps developing severe food finickiness, germ phobias, and various compulsions that made parenting them difficult. If their compulsive behavior had a recent onset, it may have been precipitated by some anxiety-provoking incident and developed as a defense against feeling overwhelmed.

Clarifying Scales – CMP Scale

- If EID is elevated, an individual's compulsive behavior may have developed as a way to manage depression and anxiety. Compulsions may have developed as a way for the client to feel some control over feeling inferior, anhedonic, and worthless. It is possible that the individual became depressed after an exhausting, prolonged period of compulsive behaviors.
- If THD is elevated, the compulsions may be part of a thought disorder and serve to give the individual some sense of control. The client may feel that their actions are somehow protecting them from the dangerous and intrusive thoughts that they have difficulty controlling. For example, one client, believing that things belonging to a difficult stepfather were cursed, began throwing out all the stepfather's personal possessions from their home each day at sunset, feeling that they needed to be burned in order to protect her from their malevolent power. People with elevations on THD are vulnerable to developing certain rituals and compulsions as a function of their psychotic thought processes.
- If BXD is elevated, the individual may have developed acting-out compulsions. Compulsive shoplifting, sexual behavior, and/or drug addiction could be examples of how CMP is associated with under-controlled behavior.
- If RC1 is elevated, the individual may have developed compulsions as part of their attempt to deal with numerous somatic symptoms that are both frightening and uncomfortable. They may believe that these compulsions protect them from further physical deterioration and keep them healthy. For example, some people with severe dietary restrictions may, in fact, be exhibiting a compulsion, especially if there is no medical basis for their restrictive behavior.
- If RC2 is elevated, it would suggest that certain compulsive behaviors have become soothing, giving the individual a feeling of control that they are doing something toward ameliorating their depression. Elevations could also reflect depression that is being funneled into

compulsions. One could argue that a compulsion exhibited by a depressed person is hopeful, in that the individual is still involved in purposeful behavior rather than being passively hopeless.

- If RC6 and/or RC8 are elevated, the compulsions may be a manifestation of the client's paranoid ideation. These compulsions might serve as a way of providing the person with protection from what they perceive as evil spirits, evil people, and malevolent forces that are threatening them.
- If RC7 with WRY and ARX are elevated, the compulsions may not be effectively controlling the person's anxiety. These elevations would suggest a generalized anxiety disorder that is pervasive and likely interfering with basic functioning.
- If EAT is elevated, the individual may be suffering from a compulsive eating disorder. Generally, there will be underlying unresolved issues that have led to the rigid control necessary to maintain an eating disorder. It would be important to identify what the client is experiencing and thinking about when anticipating eating or purging.
- If SUI is elevated, the individual may be suffering from a compulsive pressure to commit self-harm acts or suicide. In rare cases, powerful, suicidal compulsions have been associated with a traumatic brain injury, often the result of sports injuries or motor vehicle accidents. In other cases, severe depression or traumatic losses have led to suicidal compulsions.
- If STR, ARX, and/or WRY are elevated, PTSD symptomatology may be present, with compulsions potentially acting as an outlet and a sense of control.
- If ANP is elevated, it would suggest that the individual becomes irritable, angry, and explosive if their compulsions are blocked or if others do not conform to their rigid way of doing things.
- If SAV, SHY, and/or INTR are elevated, the individual may be struggling with social anxiety and may have developed rituals to help them feel more in control in social situations. Look for any conditioning experiences (for example, an event in which the client was socially embarrassed) that led to a compulsion related to the event to avoid the embarrassment recurring. In one example, an accomplished professional had been embarrassed as a shy teenager by having a tendency to spill food on his shirt as he ate, and he was teased by his peers for being sloppy. He developed a compulsion lasting into adulthood to constantly check his shirt to make sure that nothing had been spilled on it when he was in social settings.

Therapy and Therapeutic Pitfalls – CMP Scale

Elevations suggest a rigid, perfectionistic individual. Compulsions likely developed as adaptive responses to a particular event or series of events. We see the compulsion as lowering the individual's anxiety, allowing them to feel a sense of control. For example, a mature individual whose caregiver was perfectionistic and punitive may have developed a compulsion to be meticulously clean in an attempt to cope with the emotional turmoil of displeasing their caregiver. The compulsion is adaptive and, once established, hard to displace without training in other self-soothing behaviors.

Therapeutic interventions could combine insight therapy (understanding how the compulsion became an adaptive response) with cognitive behavioral techniques to help the individual identify when the compulsion is triggered. Relaxation training would be important, since taking away the compulsion would increase anxiety. Medication is generally quite effective for an obsessive-compulsive disorder (OCD), especially when combined with cognitive behavioral therapy as well as exposure and response prevention therapy. Many people with OCD find support groups helpful since they provide reassurance and coping advice from peers, which reduces feelings of isolation. Groups can also provide educational information and advice for family members and friends.

Feedback Statements – CMP Scale

T score 46–56

You have a tendency to be somewhat rigid in your habits and a tendency to be perfectionistic. You may have developed some compulsive behaviors that you engage in during times of stress. You may feel irritated if others don't do things the "right" way, so others may see you as somewhat critical. You may find yourself performing small compulsions, like checking and rechecking something or feeling that you need to do things a certain way each time.

T score 65–76

Your score suggests that you have a tendency to be compulsive, feeling the need to act in a precise manner and do things a certain way every time you do them. Others may see you as rigid and perfectionistic, and critical of them, especially if they don't do things the "right" way. Your compulsive behaviors may include checking and re-checking, counting and re-counting, or engaging in behaviors that others see as inefficient and irrational. Your compulsions may interfere with your life and may annoy those closest to you. You may be embarrassed by your compulsions and may avoid certain people so that they do not see them.

- If EID is elevated, add: Your profile suggests that you feel quite down and sad, and that you may suffer from generalized anxiety. You have developed some compulsions, perhaps as a way to feel less anxious or depressed. At one time your compulsions may have made you feel temporarily better but they have now become something that controls you. These compulsions may also provide you with the feeling that you are doing something to protect yourself against further loss and emotional turmoil.
- If THD is elevated, add: Your profile suggests you have developed some compulsive behaviors that make you feel safer and more in control. Perhaps you think these behaviors protect you from what you see as dangerous or cruel people. You may find yourself counting things, doing and undoing things, or perhaps feeling that you have to adhere to a rigid and inflexible way of doing things to avoid feeling vulnerable.
- If BXD is elevated, add: Your profile suggests that, when stressed, you move into action and you can be impulsive and show poor judgment. You scored highly on a scale that suggests that you have a compulsion or a number of compulsions. Perhaps these compulsions are ways to relieve tension so that, as stress builds, you feel driven to do something impulsively to feel better. These compulsions could get you into trouble with the authorities or with those closest to you. The compulsions could involve sexual behavior, gambling, shoplifting, or using drugs. While some compulsions could be harmless, they might deplete your energy. Possibly after you have acted impulsively, you may deal with your guilt by some compulsive act.
- If RC1 is elevated, add: You may be experiencing many physical symptoms that probably concern you. You may have developed compulsions as a way to manage your physical symptoms. Perhaps you have rituals, special foods, or repetitive habits like counting things that give you a sense of control. Others may see you as perfectionistic and rigid about doing things your way. It makes sense that you do anything you think will help you feel better physically, even if some of your compulsions don't make sense to others.
- If RC2 is elevated, add: Your profile suggests that you are feeling down. You may have developed compulsions as a way of managing your current depression. Perhaps you feel compelled to count things, or do something and then undo it, or other rituals that give you a sense of control and may temporarily make you feel better. Those closest to you may see you as perfectionistic and rigid about doing things your way.

- If RC6 and RC8 are elevated, add: Your profile suggests that you may have developed behaviors and compulsions that you feel protect you or somehow give you control over an environment that you see as dangerous and frightening. Perhaps you feel that you have to perform certain rituals that will protect you, like counting things, avoiding touching certain things, or walking carefully to avoid cracks. If you have been feeling afraid that people are out to get you, you may have developed some compulsions to protect your safety, such as making sure that you travel different ways to avoid giving your enemies information about your whereabouts. While these compulsions may temporarily make you feel better, they may also interfere with your getting things done.
- If EAT is elevated, add: Your profile suggests that your eating behaviors have developed into a compulsion. Perhaps you feel that unless you do things a certain way something bad will happen. These compulsions drive you and may interfere with your general productivity, health, and wellbeing.
- If SUI is elevated, add: Your profile suggests that you have been feeling a strong drive and compulsion to harm yourself. Perhaps you feel trapped in a current situation or have experienced depression for a long time, feeling defeated and hopeless that it will ever get better. If you feel hopeless and suicidal and cannot reach your therapist, call a suicide and crisis 24/7 hotline [988 in the United States and Canada] for confidential support.
- If STR and WRY are elevated, add: Your profile suggests that you have developed compulsive behaviors. Perhaps because you have felt so stressed, constantly worried, and apprehensive that something bad was about to happen, counting things or practicing various rituals make you feel in better control. Feeling constant stress and having a pit in your stomach, it would make sense that you might develop certain rituals or behaviors that give you the comfort that you are somehow taking care of yourself.
- If SAV, SHY, and/or INTR are elevated, add: Your profile suggests that you are someone who finds being around people, especially people you don't know, difficult and stressful. You prefer either being alone or with small groups of people who you know. Small talk with strangers likely stresses you. You have developed compulsions that perhaps make you feel better if you have to meet people or attend a social function. These compulsions could be counting things, engaging in a behavior and then undoing it, walking in a certain manner, or some other compulsion that gives you a feeling of better control when you are dealing with people.

Lifestyle and Family Background Feedback – CMP Scale

Compulsions develop as a way of dealing with anxiety and stress. For example, someone who has been anxious about becoming sick may start compulsively washing their hands, giving them a sense of control and temporarily soothing their anxiety. It is possible that you grew up in a difficult environment where you didn't feel much sense of control and things were frightening. It is also possible that you grew up in an environment where your caregivers were rigid and strict, with a tendency to make you conform to very high standards. One way you might have coped with that situation was to develop compulsions as a way of dealing with your anxiety.

It is also possible that these compulsions have only begun recently after a traumatic or significantly distressful event. You may catch yourself counting things and feeling anxious if you don't, or performing other repetitive behaviors. Discuss with your therapist whether you are suffering from some underlying anxiety or fear about some looming event. People close to you may label you as difficult and controlling because of your perfectionism.

Treatment and Self-Help Suggestions – CMP Scale

Managing compulsions can be challenging, but there are self-help strategies that may help you reduce their intensity and frequency.

1. Observe your behavior and recognize your specific compulsions. The first step in controlling them is to note when and where they happen and what events seem to trigger them, along with any thoughts you have at these times.
2. Compulsions are often the result of anxiety or fear, so try to challenge this response by asking yourself whether the behavior is necessary and based on a valid fear. After you act on your compulsion, try to understand what it is about doing it that makes you feel better.
3. One therapy, exposure and response prevention, involves gradual exposure to the things that trigger your compulsions while you resist the urge to respond with your compulsion. This is a process where you begin to increase your response gradually and slowly. Start with small steps, perhaps begin the compulsive behavior and quit halfway, then work your way up. For example, if you bite your nails, you might put a finger in your mouth but then remove it without biting your nail. To reinforce your action, reward yourself for resisting a compulsion when you are successful.
4. If you are having trouble making progress, try managing how often you act on your compulsion. Reducing the frequency or intensity over time can reduce the drive to act on the compulsion. Resisting a compulsion once means it can be resisted twice.
5. Once you have understood the source of your compulsion, you can focus on solving the underlying problem rather than distracting yourself with the compulsion.
6. Mindfulness exercises, like deep breathing or progressive muscle relaxation, can help ground you in the present, reducing the anxiety and tension that can contribute to compulsive urges, and give you a respite from the intensity of the driven compulsion.
7. If you feel compelled to act on your compulsion, try distracting yourself to delay the action briefly. Over time, the urge will often weaken. Even a delay of a minute or two can remind you that you can survive without it.
8. Regular exercise, healthy sleep habits, and a balanced diet can increase your resilience and reduce anxiety.
9. Start slowly and celebrate each small success, and they will add up over time. Plan rewards for yourself to reinforce your actions.
10. Talking to a trusted friend or family member about your compulsions can reduce the shame or isolation you might feel. Support groups and online communities can also help you to connect with others facing similar challenges. Remember, your compulsions came about for an adaptive reason. Some event or series of events led you to develop these compulsions as a way of managing your anxiety. Now you can find better ways to manage your feelings so that you are not controlled by the compulsions.
11. Compulsive behaviors can be effectively treated with medication in some cases. Consider asking your therapist for a referral to someone who specializes in medications for treating compulsions.

Anxiety-Related Experiences (ARX) Scale

General Descriptors

Complaints

Anxiety that feels out of control; nightmares; sleep interruptions; intrusive painful memories; easily startled and panicked; feelings of dread; racing heart, sweating, and rapid breathing.

Cognitions

Uncontrollable ruminations about past and/or recent painful experiences; thoughts of impending disaster; intrusive thoughts.

Emotions

Dread; anxiety; fear; panic.

Traits and behaviors

Fearful; worried; high-strung; constantly on edge; easily startled and panicked; stress reactive; social and occupational impairment.

Therapist's Notes – ARX Scale

With the publication of the MMPI-3 in 2020, the MMPI-2-RF scale for anxiety (AXY) was renamed as Anxiety-Related Experiences (ARX). There were 10 new items added to this anxiety measure resulting in a 15-item face-valid scale. This expanded anxiety scale captures more trauma-related stress symptoms, sensitizing the scale to better detect post-traumatic distress and anxiety-related symptoms, such as panic, worry, intrusive thoughts, nightmares, marked startle responses, and increased arousal. These symptoms are all consistent with the different anxiety disorders. In essence, ARX captures generalized anxiety- and trauma-specific symptoms.

Clients who score high on this scale are high-strung and worried, anticipating a future threat or recurrence of an emotional response to a real or perceived imminent threat. If they score high on measures of anxiety only, this would suggest a generalized anxiety disorder. Elevations on other scales, however, change the focus of the anxiety. For example, if RC2 and WRY are elevated, the anxiety may be related to an agitated depression with a focus on past losses and avoiding further loss. Often it is the partner or family member of the ARX client who pushes them into therapy, since their anxiety can feel controlling and overwhelming, readily ensnaring family members in codependent support.

Lifestyle and Family Background – ARX Scale

Vulnerability to developing anxiety disorders may be moderately heritable. It is also possible that a client had a history of uncertainty, unreliable caregivers, and unpredictable, traumatic fear-inducing events. Being constantly on edge and anticipating the next negative unpredictable event, the person feels vulnerable to being startled and therefore they remain in a chronic state-of-readiness tension. In one example, a client reported a history of being the oldest child living on an avocado farm in California with his parents. His father died when he was eight and he became the man of the house. Part of his duties involved getting up at four in the morning to water the avocado trees. Too many mistakes in the watering schedule would damage the crop and the family's livelihood. From an early age, he could never relax, even after successfully watering the trees, and was constantly vigilant, checking the time, even when it wasn't relevant, at different times of the day. This anxiety then generalized to him being constantly anxious well into his adult life. The anxiety was adaptive initially but developed into constant vigilance.

It is possible that an anxiety disorder developed due to some recent unpredictable traumatic event, such as a serious accident or being accused of sexual abuse. Their anxiety could also be manifesting some underlying repressed emotion, an inner conflict that is too difficult to bring to consciousness. For example, a young man in his 20s from a deeply religious family developed severe anxiety, panic attacks, and nightmares even though there had been no previous symptoms. There was no history of traumatic early events, but, while in college, he and his roommate became good friends, and one time while they were drunk, had a sexual experience. It became clear in therapy that he was struggling with his sexual identity and, since he came from a very religious background, was tortured by awakening sexuality. The anxiety was signaling that he was in severe conflict.

Clarifying Scales – ARX Scale

- If EID is elevated with RC7 and WRY, high scores on ARX would suggest an agitated depression. Typically, these individuals are hyper-responsible and tend not to act-out aggressively. They can be passive and withdrawn, and they report feelings of exhaustion, guilt, self-criticism, and perfectionism. Examine for item endorsements on SUI, indicating a suicide risk assessment.
- If THD, RC6, and/or RC8 are elevated, the client's severe anxiety may be related to paranoid ideation and conspiracy theories that render them feeling unsafe and vulnerable to being attacked, hurt, or humiliated.
- If RC7 is elevated, there are only three overlapping items, so elevations on both scales would suggest they accelerate each other. Severe anxiety, hyper-responsibility, low self-esteem, perfectionism, and guilt would be predicted.
- If RC8 is elevated, the anxiety could be reflecting a developing psychosis that the client is attempting to defend against.
- If RC9 is elevated, hypomanic individuals could suffer from severe anxiety around high stakes career events or performance setbacks. It is also possible that anxiety and fear of failure can be driving hypomanic activity.
- If MLS is elevated, the dysphoria and depletion may be combined with severe generalized anxiety.
- If NUC is elevated, the client may be experiencing neurological symptoms due to their stress. If the NUC symptoms ebb and flow or shift around the body, they may be tension-related. If the NUC symptoms are stable and persistent, severe anxiety may be related to a neurological condition. For example, anxiety has been found to occur in the early stages of Parkinson's before the condition is clearly manifested.
- If SUI is elevated, suicidal ideation may be at least partly related to the depleting hopelessness of severe anxiety. SUI coupled with an elevated ARX score indicates a need for a suicide risk assessment as anxiety and agitation is an accelerator for impulsive actions.
- If EAT is elevated, the eating disorder may be a way for the client to take control and discharge some of the anxiety through purging.
- If COG is elevated, the client's severe anxiety may be causing difficulties with memories and concentration. It is possible that both are elevated due to a neurological condition, so if there are any other soft signs of neurological impairment, a neurological evaluation is suggested.

- If HLP is elevated, the client is feeling drained and defeated, riddled with anxiety, and losing hope that things can be different.
- If SFD is elevated, the anxiety may have eroded the client's self-confidence, especially if involved with a demanding career which may have led to their overwhelming anxiety.
- If NFC is elevated, the anxiety is likely interfering with the client's ability to make decisions and take charge of their lives. Their constant anxiety leads to their dwelling on every side of each issue and becoming immobilized by even small decisions which renders them highly inefficient.
- If STR is elevated, the client is likely feeling very stressed as well as overwhelmed by anxiety. It is possible that a period of prolonged stress has led to a severe generalized anxiety disorder, but it is also possible that the client suffers from so much anxiety that even small tasks are experienced as extremely taxing.
- If WRY is elevated, this adds to the picture of a person who is, at times, immobilized by anxiety, paralyzed about making decisions, and constantly inundated by intrusive, catastrophizing thoughts.
- If CMP is elevated, the client may have developed a compulsion or a series of compulsions as a way to take control over the anxiety and make it manageable. As anxiety builds, the client likely feels increasingly overwhelmed, so engaging in some compulsion could provide an outlet for their energy and temporarily make them feel that they are managing their anxiety.
- If ANP is elevated, the client's anger, which is close to the surface, belies their severe generalized anxiety, so that small frustrations or setbacks can lead to irritability and, in some cases, explosiveness.
- If BRF is elevated, the anxiety suggested by elevations or ARX is manifested in fear of knives, the dark, open spaces, being away from home, and small restricting spaces.
- If SAV or SHY are elevated, it is possible that the individual is suffering from a social phobia. It is also plausible that they are avoiding social engagements because of their anxiety or embarrassment about the visibility of their anxiety.

Therapy and Therapeutic Pitfalls – ARX Scale

As in most therapeutic interventions, a psychosocial history should be obtained to identify whether early traumas, abandonments, or cruel rejections have contributed to the client's lifelong pattern of feeling insecure and vulnerable in a world where catastrophes may have occurred. Often, while psychically depleted and ashamed of their severe anxiety, clients are reluctant to relax since their anxiety serves a protective function. Identifying early events that may have precipitated an adaptive, constant vigilance would be helpful. Catastrophizing about possible outcomes serves as a way to keep the client vigilant and mobilized. Since the anxiety is labeled as adaptive by the therapist, the client can develop empathy for themselves, and then other therapeutic strategies can be utilized.

Cognitive behavioral therapy, acceptance and commitment therapy, and dialectical behavior therapy, as well as relaxation training, can all be useful. Cautiously providing the client with a time-contingent dose of panic-reducing medication is often helpful as it provides reassurance to them as they live in dread of having a panic attack away from helpful resources. Having medication can help assure a client that they are less vulnerable to experiencing an out-of-control panic attack. Many of the symptoms associated with the scale elevations are similar to symptoms of PTSD. Constant vigilance and intrusive disturbing thoughts, as well as startle responses and sleep difficulties including nightmares, are all associated with PTSD. However, elevations on the scale do not necessarily indicate a diagnosis of PTSD.

Feedback Statements – ARX Scale

T score <44

Your profile suggests that you do not experience periods of severe anxiety. You generally don't experience physical manifestations of anxiety even when you are stressed or if things are going badly. You don't lose sleep even when you are distressed and do not constantly revisit past mistakes and regrets. Consequently, your profile suggests that you are resilient, letting go of mistakes, living in the moment, and not allowing negative events to knock you off balance.

T score 44–54

Your profile suggests that, when you experience stress, like most people you occasionally respond by losing a little sleep or experiencing moments where you worry about what could go wrong in the future. Generally, however, your ability to manage anxiety is well within the normal range.

T score 56–62

Your profile suggests that there are times when you are stressed and experience periods of anxiety, perhaps losing sleep or feeling jumpy and nervous. Generally, however, you seem to manage your anxiety as well as most people.

T score 66–73

Your profile suggests that, when stressed, you can become quite anxious, losing sleep, and experiencing periods of dread as if something bad might happen unexpectedly. You might experience uncomfortable, physical effects of anxiety, such as a racing pulse and periods when you have nightmares.

T score 77–81

Your profile suggested you experience periods of substantial anxiety. Your sleep is affected, so you may wake up with nightmares and cold sweats. You are likely experiencing intrusive negative thoughts, with worries about what catastrophe lies around the corner and what can go wrong next. Stressful events can cause you to feel panicked since you are always on edge, as if you are living in a war zone.

T score 85–88

Your profile suggests that you are experiencing a great deal of anxiety and probably feel as if you live in constant danger waiting for disaster to strike but are unsure where it could come from. The feeling of dread and anxiety is with you almost all the time. Painful memories seem to intrude into your mind and can be hard to switch off. You can easily feel panicked by events that later don't seem as disastrous as you experienced at the time.

- If EID is elevated, add: You are experiencing severe anxiety most of the time as well as feeling down and depressed. Painful memories probably keep entering your mind and you often feel exhausted and defeated by your anxiety and depression. Your sleep is likely affected, and you probably suffer from poor memory and concentration difficulties. Your appetite, general energy level, and sex drive may all be diminished due to this agitated depression.

- If THD, RC6, and/or RC8 are elevated, add: You are currently suffering from a great deal of anxiety as well as feeling fearful that something terrible is about to happen. You may have many intrusive thoughts that bring up painful memories, and you may find it hard to think clearly. At times, you may feel quite paranoid, fearful that others are out to hurt you. You may have developed a whole way of thinking about the anxiety, trying to understand who is to blame and how to protect yourself. There may not be people who wish you harm, but your thinking may be confused due to the severe anxiety that you are experiencing, so you may be interpreting things the wrong way.
- If RC7 is elevated, add: Your profile suggests that you are a person who lives with a constant sense of dread, as if anticipating something bad happening. You constantly feel anxious, easily panicked, and startled. Sometimes you find it hard to control your thinking, so negative thoughts, maybe even painful thoughts, seem to invade your mind and cause you anxiety. You are your own worst critic and easily feel guilty. It is hard for you to say "no" or set boundaries with people, so you may find yourself getting overworked and taking on too many responsibilities that then overwhelm you. You likely experience the physical symptoms of anxiety, such as a racing pulse, profuse sweating, difficulty sleeping, and nightmares.
- If RC9 is elevated, add: Your test results suggest that you are going through a phase of very high energy and drive, with periods of almost unrealistic optimism. You may be overcommitting yourself and taking on too many tasks and activities. The test results suggest that some of your energy is coming from your anxiety about failure and fears of not succeeding to a spectacular level. You may go through mood swings where you are anxious and fearful, experiencing nightmares, and living with a pit in your stomach. At other times, you may feel buoyant, optimistic, even manic. People with your profile generally do not experience much anxiety. When they do become anxious, it is usually around a fear of failure in a situation where they perceived the stakes as very high.
- If MLS is elevated, add: You answered the test in a way that suggests that you feel blue, depleted, unhappy, and very anxious. You are exhausted by the anxiety, the sleep difficulties, the nightmares, and the constant pit in your stomach waiting for a disaster that you are convinced will happen.
- If NUC is elevated, add: You appear to be experiencing a number of neurological symptoms, which could be frightening you. These symptoms may be the result of the severe anxiety that you have been experiencing. Long periods of anxiety can leave its toll on the body and mind, leading to vague neurological symptoms reflecting the extreme stress on the muscular skeletal system. On the other hand, it is possible that you have developed anxiety due to the neurological symptoms that you are experiencing. Perhaps the symptoms have frightened you and now you are living with a pit in your stomach, anticipating what can go wrong next.
- If SUI is elevated, add: The way you answered the test suggests that you are suffering from a great deal of anxiety that may be robbing you of happiness and leaving you feeling a constant sense of dread, as if waiting for a disaster to happen. Disturbing images and thoughts, perhaps due to some past trauma, keep invading your mind, even though you try to switch those thoughts off. The anxiety may have led you to think of suicide as a way to escape. It is also possible that your anxiety has developed because you are trapped in some difficult situation and you don't know how to get out of it other than by death. If you feel hopeless and suicidal and cannot reach your therapist, call a suicide and crisis 24/7 hotline [988 in the United States and Canada] for confidential support.
- If EAT is elevated, add: The test suggests that you have a great deal of preoccupation with eating and purging. You also tested as very anxious, living with a constant sense of dread as if anticipating a looming disaster. You may experience nightmares and have disturbing images and

thoughts invading your mind, and you find it hard to switch them off. You may turn to eating and purging or may restrict your eating as a way to feel in control of your emotions. It is also possible that you realize that your eating disorder is potentially harmful, so your anxiety could reflect your constant inner battle about whether to eat or not to eat and whether to purge or not to purge.

- If COG is elevated, add: The way you answered the test suggests that you are experiencing a lot of difficulties with concentration, memory, and focus. You are finding it hard to pay attention and remember what you were just saying, and you may have a tendency to lose things. You are also suffering from severe anxiety, living with a constant pit in your stomach, and fearful that some disaster is looming in the future. It is possible that the anxiety is affecting your memory and general cognitive efficiency. If we suffer from constant anxiety, it is hard to focus and remember what we were just doing. The anxiety seems to crowd out all the other information.
- If HLP is also elevated, add: Your constant anxiety and dread may be wearing you out and leaving you feeling hopeless that you can ever be free of it.
- If SFD and/or NFC are elevated, add: Your profile suggests that you are suffering from a great deal of anxiety, with a constant knot in your stomach and a sense of dread that something terrible is about to happen. You are also your own worst critic and quick to doubt yourself. You assume that you are somehow going to fail, and things are not going to work out. It is possible that self-doubt has arisen because you have lived with so much anxiety for so long. The anxiety probably interferes with your making decisions easily and robs you of your confidence.
- If STR is elevated, add: Your profile suggests that you feel a lot of pressure and stress as well as a great deal of anxiety. It is possible that you feel stressed because you are so anxious, living with a constant sense of dread and anticipating a looming disaster. It is hard to manage stressful situations when you are already feeling anxious, on edge, and unable to think clearly and focus because of the anxiety.
- If WRY is elevated, add: Your profile suggest that you live with constant anxiety, worrying that something bad is about to happen. Your sleep is likely disturbed by nightmares and at times you may feel that your anxiety is out of control. You suffer from anxiety, but also worry about specific things like money, safety, and your past mistakes or disappointments.
- If CMP is elevated, add: You may have developed a compulsion or a few compulsions, perhaps as a way of dealing with your anxiety. Living with a constant sense of dread and being on edge because you are afraid something dreadful is about to happen is exhausting. You may have developed rituals or compulsions that you feel protect you from the things that you are anxious about. Being compulsive might reassure you that you are disciplined and might make you feel that you are at least doing something to manage the anxiety.
- If ANP is elevated, add: Your severe anxiety, living with a pit in your stomach and a constant sense of dread is exhausting. Feeling constantly on edge, it is understandable that, when small irritations or frustrations occur, you don't have the resources emotionally to deal with them and you likely get angry, irritable, or even blow up.
- If BRF is elevated, add: Your profile suggests that you experience constant dread and anxiety. You also live with fear that some disaster is around the corner, ready to take you by surprise. Consequently, you may have developed fears and anxieties about ordinary things like knives, heights, or driving since they can trigger your darkest thoughts.

Lifestyle and Family Background Feedback – ARX Scale

Sometimes people with your profile grew up in environments where they didn't feel protected by caring and supportive caregivers. In some cases, people who suffer from severe anxiety grew up in an environment that they experienced as unpredictable, with setbacks, losses, and a lack of emotional support. Sometimes their caregivers were so dysfunctional that they were completely unreliable or even cruel. In some cases, the anxiety you are experiencing developed as an adaptive response to a difficult and frightening situation. Living constantly on edge and trying to anticipate every possible eventuality is an adaptive response when a child is in a frightening or emotionally painful situation without support. In other cases, people with your profile have experienced some recent trauma or setback – for example, experiencing combat or the unpredictable and catastrophic death of a loved one. These negative events are dealt with adaptively by trying to stay alert and always on guard to try to predict and prevent a possible disaster. However, this can be depleting and exhausting and it actually interferes with your ability to think clearly. The good news is that anxiety is one of the easiest things for psychologists to treat.

Treatment and Self-Help Suggestions – ARX Scale

Anxiety can be overwhelming, yet it is an understandable human response after a trauma or frightening, painful event has occurred. Trying to anticipate all possible negative eventualities makes sense if a person has been surprised by a severely negative event in the past. We try to control the onset of something painful by anticipating how it might feel. Unfortunately, the anticipation becomes a constant sense of dread that generally interferes with joy and with life.

1. Anxiety can create a loop of stress; the more we try to control it or avoid it, the more it can strengthen. The first step is to identify your anxiety so you can better understand what triggers it. Then you can consider how to respond better emotionally to these triggers or cues. Ask yourself if your anxiety is tied to actual events or ones that you anticipate or imagine. Often, we catastrophize outcomes when the situation does not warrant it.
2. Anxiety often comes with "what if" thinking that tends to be exaggerated or unrealistic. Challenge these thoughts by questioning them. Consider what evidence supports or contradicts the fear, what the "worst case" scenario might be, and how likely it is to happen. Ask yourself if you have been able to get through similar situations before.
3. Begin gradually exposing yourself to situations that anxiety has led you to avoid in small, manageable steps. Successful encounters will build your confidence, while continuing to avoid anxiety-producing situations can make the fear grow stronger over time. For example, if you are afraid of public speaking, start by talking informally to a couple of people, then work your way up to larger groups.
4. Breathing techniques, mindfulness, and grounding techniques can help with feelings of panic. While facing a fear or anxiety-producing situation, try focusing on your breathing. This can help you stay grounded and calm your body's physical response to stress. 5-4-3-2-1 grounding is another technique where you identify 5 things you see, 4 things you feel, 3 things you hear, 2 things you smell, and 1 thing you taste.
5. Be kind to yourself and show yourself some compassion. Remind yourself that you are a good person, it is okay to feel anxious, and you are doing the best that you can. Remember that everyone experiences fear and you are not failing or weak because you feel anxious.
6. Anxiety can often be treated effectively with medication. Consider asking your therapist for a referral to someone who specializes in this area.

Anger Proneness (ANP) Scale

General Descriptors

Complaints

Easily irritated; impatient; loses temper; hot-headed; easily upset; angered when interrupted.

Cognitions

Judgmental; perceives others as irritating.

Emotions

Easily upset; impatient; easily irritated and overcome with anger; low frustration tolerance.

Traits and behaviors

High-strung; tense; impatient; irritable; demanding; hostile; argumentative.

Therapist's Notes – ANP Scale

The 12 items on this scale address irritability, impatience, low frustration tolerance, emotional reactivity, and difficulties controlling anger. The ANP items emphasize the experience of anger rather than aggressive acting-out. (The latter is better captured by the Aggression (AGG) scale described later.) The emotional volatility measured by ANP results from being tense, high-strung, and easily knocked off balance. The anger expressed in the items reveals an individual stressed by life, living on edge emotionally, with no cushion for frustration, so small frustrations and setbacks lead to anger and irritability. Elevations on the other scales would provide a clue as to what the sources of irritation and anger could be.

Note that chronic and episodic anger is associated with many different mental disorders, including intermittent explosive disorder; disruptive mood dysregulation disorder; various personality disorders; neurocognitive disorders; substance intoxication or withdrawal; and impulse control disorders, such as oppositional defiance disorder or even autism spectrum disorder.

Lifestyle and Family Background – ANP Scale

High scorers on this scale admit to feeling constantly tense and easily perturbed. Their response to stress or pressure is anger and irritability. They lack resilience and experience small setbacks as big ones. Explosiveness comes as a result of frustration rather than a manipulative attempt to use anger for their own ends. Often people who are depressed and anxious can elevate the scale. Since they feel depleted and live with a high-level of anxiety and worry, minor stresses are experienced as potentially catastrophic. Sometimes people with a relatively good psychological adjustment can be placed in stressful situations that are beyond their ability to manage. For example, an introvert who proves herself extremely competent in a particular job is promoted to a managerial role. She is uncomfortable, dealing with people who she does not know, and feels she lacks the interpersonal skills necessary to manage group tensions. Within a few weeks in her new job, she became irritable and even explosive, surprising everyone since she had been so placidly competent. She was being stretched beyond her abilities – not technical abilities but interpersonal ones – and it manifested as irritability and anger. In this case, it would be situation-specific. In other cases, a person with a history of explosive anger may have had a childhood in which a caregiver was unpredictably explosive. Consequently, the individual lived with constant apprehension which manifested later in life as high stress and tense irritability.

Clarifying Scales – ANP Scale

- If EID is elevated, the irritability and explosiveness associated with ANP is co-morbid with depression and anxiety. Feeling blue, anhedonic, useless, and that life is a strain most of the time, small frustrations lead to irritability and anger. In some cases, depressed, anxious people are passive, insecure, and tend to withdraw intro-punitively. In other cases, their depression may be masked and expressed as anger and irritability, especially in men.
- If THD is elevated, the heightened sensitivity to criticism shading toward paranoia and psychosis suggests that the anger expressed could be self-protective or psychotically driven to deal with demons and imaginary enemies.
- If BXD is elevated, anger and irritability likely reflect a lack of impulse control and immediate tension reduction. The client may consciously use their anger manipulatively to intimidate people into giving them what they want in order to avoid their temper.
- If RCd is elevated, demoralization, resigned passivity, and low self-esteem would suggest that the individual has very little emotional cushion or resilience, so small setbacks lead to anger and irritability. The client may have lost the will to control their emotional impulses.
- If RC1 is elevated, the client's preoccupation with pain, illness, and their medical condition can make them irritable and demanding. An individual who complains of physical pain, doctor shops, and is preoccupied with avoiding body damage may eventually become angry and impatient. Family members may, over time, become frustrated or passively aggressive in meeting the constant demands of a RC1 elevated client.
- If RC2 is elevated, the client's depression has likely eroded their resilience, so small problems and impediments are experienced through the prism of seeing the world as potentially fraught with possible further catastrophic losses. Life feels sad and stressful, so small events could lead to angry outbursts.
- If RC4 is elevated, the client is self-centered, manipulative, and impulsive. They likely express anger without much self-control and can become angry and demanding if their needs are not met. Their irritability and outbursts would likely manifest whenever they don't get their way or if they feel frustrated, since they act-out their feelings without much self-control.
- If RC6 is elevated, the client's irritability and anger may come as a breakdown of brittle control, especially if they feel they are being treated unfairly or feel vulnerable to humiliation. In the presence of a paranoid episode, their anger may serve as a way of keeping people at a safe distance.
- If RC7 is elevated, the client may feel tense about living in a world that feels potentially dangerous, with catastrophic, unforeseen consequences. The client may have developed rituals and compulsions as a way to manage their anxiety and so might become angry if others don't adhere to their way of doing things. The client is likely high-strung, so small irritations or setbacks are experienced as potentially dire and, therefore, very destabilizing.
- If RC8 is elevated, anger and irritability may be due to a thought disorder, with distortions in reality testing and the resulting anxiety, which serves to keep people at a distance.
- If RC9 is elevated, manic overactivity, pressured speech, and an intense drive state predict an individual who is impatient and demanding. Irritability and loss of emotional control would not be uncommon. The addition of ANP would predict difficulty with frustration tolerance and possible explosive anger.

- If MLS is elevated, with the client feeling tired, weak, and unwell, small stressors can lead to irritability and anger.
- If NUC is elevated, the client's concerns about their neurological symptoms can lead to brittle irritability and anger. However, in the presence of a possible bona fide neurological disorder, the recent occurrence of irritability and anger could be part of a neurological condition.
- If EAT is elevated, the client's anger and irritability may be due to a restricted diet and lack of appropriate calories. Their anger and irritability could also be occurring because the client knows on some level that they have a serious disorder and so feels defensive. As a great deal of psychic energy goes into controlling their diet, the client has few rewarding experiences and likely has little resilience for dealing with common stress.
- If COG is elevated, the client is reporting that their cognitive abilities are compromised. Forgetting where they put things, difficulty focusing and concentrating, and difficulty comprehending things are likely extremely stressful to them, so small irritations, such as needing others to repeat what they just said, could lead to anger and irritation. This is especially true in relationships where only one partner has cognitive difficulties. The other person understandably can become frustrated with repeating themselves or reminding the individual that they had been told something a few days earlier.
- If SUI is elevated, ANP might act as an energizer for suicidal ideation. The linkage between anger and suicidal ideation and/or behaviors may be mediated by a sense of thwarted belongingness and perceived burdensomeness to others. Higher levels of anger are associated with increased levels of suicide risk.
- If HLP is elevated, irritability and anger are mixed with defeated hopelessness. Perhaps the loss of hope has led them to give up emotional self-control, as if "there is nothing left to lose, I give up."
- If SFD and NFC are elevated, intuitively one would expect anger to be turned inward since the individual lacks self-confidence and feels like a burden to others. However, their irritability may be defensive. For example, if others make a request that the client doubts they can perform, then they may respond angrily or defensively.
- If STR and WRY are elevated, the individual likely feels constantly stressed, worried, and burdened by life, so minor irritations, setbacks, or demands can lead to frustrated irritability and outbursts of anger.
- If CMP is elevated, the client's compulsions serve as anxiety reducers, so if others impede them or interfere with them the client can become irritated and angry.
- If ARX is elevated, the client's anxiety, fears of the future, and quickness to panic means that their base level of arousal is very high. Small negative surprises, last-minute changes in plans, and others' inattention to a perceived important detail can lead to outbursts of anger.
- If BRF is elevated, the client may experience irritability and anger if they are pushed to face their behavior-restricting fears. One usually docile client was in a line to explore the control room on a decommissioned aircraft carrier. It was a hot day, and the guide suggested that once inside the cramped space there was no turning back since the stairs were narrow and full, so the line had to proceed to the exit slowly. The client, realizing this would engage her fear of small spaces, panicked, and angrily demanded she be let out the line, to the embarrassment of her family since there was no going backward. Less obvious situations could also cause anxiety and resulting anger.

Therapy and Therapeutic Pitfalls – ANP Scale

The experience of occasional anger is universal. Anger is a normal human response that may be expressed or suppressed to at least three categories of experience: (1) if someone is caused to be fearful, (2) if they are blocked in getting what they want, or (3) if they are caused pain. The normal response to these experiences is anger, which can either be expressed or repressed. A person who is constantly irritable or angry is clearly not getting what they need, which may result in emotional pain or fearfulness. The expression of anger is not a diagnostic category but cuts across many different, psychological conditions as noted earlier.

Exploring with the client what could be causing their pain, fear, or what is blocking them from getting what they want could be a starting therapeutic strategy. Explaining that anger is understandable and that it comes from a legitimate source could build the therapeutic alliance to help the client focus on their triggers and learn better self-control. Countertransference can be an issue with angry, irritable clients since they are intimidating and challenging to work with. It can be especially difficult if the irritable, angry individual is with a partner and there is a natural tendency for the therapist to feel protective of the partner who experiences the other's anger. Seeing the angry irritable client as a frightened, needy, or insecure child and showing empathy to them can help develop a therapeutic alliance. Other scale elevations can help the therapist determine the triggers for the angry client.

Feedback Statements – ANP Scale

T score 49–51

Like most people you feel angry occasionally, but you seem to have good control over how you express it. Perhaps when stressed you, like most people, can become a little irritable.

T score 53–56

Your profile suggests that you are prone to feeling and expressing irritability, and occasionally, as stress builds, you might be prone to angry outbursts. You are probably high-strung and may be perfectionistic and prone to worry. You may dislike being interrupted when you are working. You generally don't have much patience with people, especially if you think they are doing the wrong things. People may be a little intimidated by you and see you as a hot-headed person with a short temper.

T score 58–78

Your profile shows that you have a low tolerance for frustration. You may be a perfectionist or may be high-strung, living constantly on edge, as if something bad is about to happen. Consequently, you have a short fuse, and small stressors can make you quite irritable. It is challenging for you to approach tasks in a relaxed manner and, when things go wrong, it is hard for you to control your temper. Anger can hijack you, so that you end up exploding over matters that you later realize weren't important. There may be times when you feel you cannot control your anger, and it overwhelms you. If people get in your way or frustrate you, it is hard for you to forgive them and you may sometimes hold a grudge, perhaps wanting to teach them a lesson.

- If EID is elevated, add: Your profile suggests that you are experiencing some depression and anxiety, often feeling a pit in your stomach as if something bad is about to happen. You may be having trouble sleeping and may feel tired with low energy. Feeling depressed, anxious, and worried is exhausting, so small irritations and stresses may cause you to be irritable and angry. At times, unreasonable demands on you or feeling that you are not being helped might even lead you to have explosive outbursts since you are already feeling so depleted.
- If THD is elevated, add: Your profile suggests that you are feeling somewhat unsafe, perhaps fearful that other people wish you harm. It is possible you feel you have lost some control over

your mind because images and thoughts seem to invade, and it is difficult sometimes to know what is real and what is your imagination. You may experience periods where you feel things are not real, or when you feel that you are outside of your body looking at life from a distance. You may hear things or voices and then wonder if they are real or if it was just your thoughts. It is not surprising that sometimes you feel irritable and angry, since you already feel stressed and alone. At times, your anger may feel out of control, especially if you feel someone is being hostile or trying to control you.

- If BXD is elevated, add: Your profile suggests that you are easily angered and have a low tolerance for frustration. You generally want what you want when you want it since you are impatient. It is hard for you to discipline yourself, so when people get in your way, it is easy for you to feel irritable, even angry and explosive. You may feel that your anger is a way to get things done because people likely are intimidated by it. On the other hand, impulsively expressing anger can get you into trouble, especially with authority figures.
- If RCd is elevated, add: Your profile shows that you are experiencing a lot of irritability and, at times, even explosive anger. This is understandable, given that you have been feeling demoralized, down on yourself, and hopeless. Since you feel so depleted, small irritations and setbacks can lead to irritability and anger that you have trouble controlling.
- If RC1 is elevated, add: Your profile suggests you have been on edge, irritable, and at times even explosive. There are times you feel that your anger overcomes you and you can't control it. This is understandable given that you are also feeling unwell and worried about your physical symptoms. Experiencing headaches, dizziness, stomach problems, and pain in different parts of your body can all contribute to your feeling unwell and stressed. It may be that you haven't had a favorable prognosis which concerns you a great deal. Your irritability and anger may arise when you feel others are not sympathetic or don't help you when you need it. You may find yourself blowing up if you feel demands are made of you that you are unable to meet.
- If RC2 is elevated, add: Your profile suggests that you are currently experiencing depression with sad mood, low energy, and difficulty concentrating and thinking clearly. Your profile also suggests that you perhaps have a shorter fuse now than you had in the past. You feel easily irritated and impatient with others. At times, your anger may overcome you, making you prone to outbursts. It is understandable when someone is feeling depressed that much of life feels like a burden, so small stressors or demands on you at times overwhelm you, leading to angry frustration.
- If RC4 is elevated, add: Your profile suggest that you have been irritable, easily frustrated, and, at times, explosive. Your profile also suggests that you can be impulsive and sometimes bend the rules to get what you want. In some cases, people with your profile actually use their anger as a way of getting what they want since people tend to be intimidated by anger. In other cases, people with your profile express anger and irritability impulsively. You do not control your emotions as much as they control you. Sometimes your irritability can backfire and get you into trouble.
- If RC6 is elevated, add: Your profile suggests that you have been feeling irritable, impatient, and, at times, explosively angry. This may be because you have been feeling vulnerable to being criticized or judged by others, perhaps even being accused of things that you feel are unfair. Perhaps you have felt that other people are out to get you or somehow ruin your reputation, and you have been quite vigilant and suspicious of people in order to protect yourself. Going through life feeling vulnerable to criticism or attack is stressful, so your fuse is shorter, and you might be quick to anger or get irritable. You may direct your anger toward those you think are treating you unfairly, or you may just be so tense that it leaks out toward anyone in your life who is being demanding or stressing you.

- If RC7 is elevated, add: Your profile suggests that you have been feeling impatient with others, on edge, irritable, and perhaps even, at times, explosive. Your profile also reveals that you are generally a worrier, feeling a knot in your stomach as if anticipating some disaster coming around the corner. You are a responsible individual who can take on too many responsibilities and duties, and, once you have committed to them, they may stress you, leading you to have a shorter fuse and be more irritable. People with your profile tend to be perfectionistic. They demand a lot from themselves, and so they expect others to be diligent, productive, and follow the rules. When you perceive others are not doing the right thing, it may lead to you become very frustrated. It is also possible that living in a world where you think you can see disaster around the corner can be very difficult for those living with you, since they likely accuse you of exaggeration.
- If RC8 is elevated, add: You may be going through a frightening time where the world does not seem real to you. Perhaps you feel as if you are standing back, observing the world as if it is a movie you are watching from the outside. You may worry that people look at you critically or that they are somehow out to get you or that they could hurt you. You may experience periods of suspiciousness when you are unsure who you can trust. You may even experience some visual or auditory hallucinations. It is not surprising then that you are irritable and possibly even explosively angry. Likely, the irritability comes when you feel pressured or experience people as hostile, and the explosive anger may come when you feel threatened.
- If RC9 is elevated, add: Your profile suggests that you are quite irritable, impatient, and, at times, prone to emotional outbursts. People see you as hot-headed, with a low frustration tolerance. This may be because you are so high energy, and the world moves too slowly for you. You think quickly, move quickly, and tend to see the big picture, being bored by dealing with details. If people get in your way when you are on a mission, or if people move too slowly, perhaps driving slowly or poorly, you can get irritable and angry.
- If MLS is elevated, add: Since you have been feeling unwell, tired, and weak, small stressors can loom large. No wonder that you have a short fuse, finding yourself getting irritated and impatient easily. If you are particularly depleted and someone makes a demand on you or you are very stressed, you might become quite angry and prone to emotional outbursts.
- If NUC is elevated, add: Your profile suggests that you have become irritable and impatient and, at times, explosively angry. You are also experiencing some neurological symptoms, possibly dizzy spells, feeling clumsy and, at times, having trouble walking. It is possible that your anger and irritability are due to you feeling stressed by some of your neurological symptoms. It could also be that your anger and irritability are relatively recent and occurred at the same time as you developed these neurological symptoms. A neurological examination would help you determine whether the irritability is due to your stress or whether it is part of the same neurological issue that is troubling you.
- If EAT is elevated, add: Your profile shows that you are struggling with an eating disorder. You also appear to have a short fuse and often feel irritable. This may be because you are not eating enough calories or because you are so preoccupied with your eating habits that you have little resilience to deal with stress. Your anger and irritability might also be occurring because you feel defensive, feeling that those around you are judging you because of the way you eat. At times you might even express emotional outbursts, perhaps when you feel others are trying to control how you eat.
- If COG is elevated, add: Your profile suggests you have been feeling impatient and irritable. At times you get so frustrated, you may explode in anger and feel like you can't control yourself. You may also have been experiencing some difficulties with memory, concentration, and staying focused. It may be hard for you to read, remember, and comprehend as easily as you have in the past. You may be worrying that something is wrong with your mind. Your anger and

irritability may be due to the fact that you are worried about how you are functioning. It is also possible that the difficulties with concentration and memory have stressed you, so you are less resilient and get impatient with people more easily. Perhaps, people remind you of things you forgot about or get irritated with you for not remembering things and that makes you feel angry and defensive.

- If SUI is elevated, add: You report feeling pretty down, hopeless, and suicidal. You have been thinking a lot about suicide. You have also been quite irritable, impatient, and high-strung. At times, you feel like exploding and it is difficult for you to control your anger. If life has become so difficult for you, you may think about suicide as a way of escaping. It is possible that you are thinking of suicide because you are angry with others and want to punish them by killing yourself. If you feel hopeless and suicidal and cannot reach your therapist, call a suicide and crisis 24/7 hotline [988 in the United States and Canada] for confidential support.
- If HLP is elevated, add: You have been feeling hopeless and defeated, thinking that it is impossible for your life to change. You have also been feeling irritable and impatient with people. At times, your anger may feel out of control, as if you may explode. This anger and irritability may be due to the fact that you have been feeling so defeated and hopeless that you have given up the will to try to change your life. Consequently, little gives you much pleasure and when things go wrong or there is stress, you just don't have a long fuse.
- If SFD and NFC are elevated, add: The profile shows that you are quick to doubt yourself, and find it hard to make decisions since you are afraid you'll miss something important. You are your own worst critic and feel like you are a burden to others. Consequently, when people make demands, you assume you are not going to succeed, so you likely get irritated and impatient. When things go wrong or you have an important decision to make and you don't know what you should do, it is easy for you to get irritated and even, at times, explosively angry. Living with self-doubt and constantly feeling that you are not as capable as others, it is understandable that small setbacks lead to anger and explosiveness.
- If STR and WRY are elevated, add: Your profile indicates you are stressed and tend to worry a great deal. Living with that level of worry and stress leaves you with less resilience than you would like. Consequently, small setbacks and frustrations can lead to irritability and anger. If people are too demanding or discount your worries and how stressed you are, it could lead to anger and even explosiveness.
- If CMP is elevated, add: Your profile suggests that you have developed compulsions, perhaps as a way to deal with anxiety. Counting things, doing things a certain way, and creating other kinds of rituals are a way for you to feel in control and sometimes help you to feel less anxious. Other people in your life, however, may be annoyed by your compulsions and may criticize some of your rituals. People may feel that your demands that they do things a certain way are controlling, and so they resist you. This may lead you to feel irritable and impatient with people and, at times, when you are stressed and feel the need for your compulsions to be accepted, you might even get explosive when they are resisted.
- If ARX is elevated, add: Your profile indicates that you are anxious, with your mind invaded by thoughts of past painful events or possible future negative outcomes. You feel constantly on edge, anxious, and easily startled since you are already tightly wound. No wonder that small frustrations, surprises that you were not prepared for, or people being late or changing plans unpredictably can set you off into irritability and even, at times, explosive anger.
- If BRF is elevated, add: Your profile suggests that you have been feeling irritable, impatient, and, at times, explosively angry. Your profile also suggests that you have a number of fears that prevent you from being as spontaneous and uninhibited as you might like. Since a number of things frighten you, it can inhibit your behavior. You probably get irritable and angry if people try to push you to do things that frighten you. Living with fears that restrict your behavior can be difficult, and so it can leave you with less of a cushion to manage stress.

Lifestyle and Family Background Feedback – ANP Scale

In some cases, people with a tendency to be irritable and anger-prone come from a background where they experienced an explosive and irritable caregiver. Children observing such a person can often become conditioned to repeating that behavior. Over time, it can become part of the way you deal with stress. It is also possible that you have become irritable and angry more recently due to an accumulation of stressors and the feeling that you are not getting what you need out of life. You might feel overwhelmed and unable to cope easily so small frustrations irritate you and occasionally, if you are frightened by an event, you can become explosively angry. Unfortunately, people around you will experience your irritability and anger more intensely than you might realize. They may try to protect themselves from your anger by withdrawing from you or walking on eggshells around you. You may have some behaviors that irritate those closest to you and their reactions might make you angry. Fortunately, there are many ways you can get help for your anger and irritability and develop better emotional control.

Treatment and Self-Help Suggestions – ANP Scale

1. Cognitive behavioral therapy is a common therapeutic approach that helps you identify and challenge the harmful thought patterns that encourage anger. It shows you how to reframe irrational beliefs into more objective perspectives and how to recognize triggers and automatic reactions. Cognitive behavioral therapy provides tools to change your thought patterns and respond more calmly. By identifying the kinds of situations that trigger you, you can develop alternate strategies to respond, rather than acting-out in anger.
2. Mindfulness techniques can help you increase your awareness of anger before it escalates, allowing you to de-escalate and choose a more balanced response. It can also reduce overall stress, which may reduce irritability. In progressive muscle relaxation therapy, you alternately tense and relax various muscle groups. This process can reduce the physical tension that often accompanies anger and can help calm you and make it easier to stay composed when you are stressed.
3. Deep breathing helps calm your nervous system, lower your heart rate, and can prevent the physical symptoms of anger, such as increased heart rate or muscle tension, from spiraling. It helps you center yourself when you are triggered, giving you a chance to pause before reacting.
4. When you begin to feel angry, take a break to pause and reflect. If possible, physically remove yourself from the situation. A brief break allows you to cool down, avoid saying or doing things you will regret, and helps you return to the situation with a clearer, calmer perspective.
5. Keeping a journal of your thoughts, feelings, and experiences around anger can help you process pent-up emotions constructively and gain insight into their underlying causes. This may help you to uncover triggers or patterns that you can address proactively.
6. Exercise is a great stress-reducer, releasing endorphins that are natural mood boosters. These can help reduce frustration and irritability and serve as an outlet for releasing stress when anger builds. If the idea of exercise is not appealing, try starting slowly, perhaps just going for a short walk.
7. You may be angry because of a problem you are facing or a perceived injustice. If you are overloaded, worn out, or depressed, it may be difficult to deal with stress. When you are already stressed, your response to people making demands on you is to be irritated. It is also possible that you are self-critical and become angry with yourself when you see you are doing something poorly. Instead of focusing on what is frustrating you, try to develop better problem-solving skills to find a solution and solve issues in a more productive way. This will help you feel more in control.

8. Set clear boundaries with others to reduce situations where you feel disrespected or overloaded. Assert your needs respectfully to reduce conflicts and prevent frustration from building up.
9. Find a trusted friend, family member, or support group to talk to about your feelings. This can help you gain perspective, offer emotional relief, and give you a safe way to vent.
10. Discover with your therapist how your childhood might have been frightening if a caregiver was explosive or irritable. It is possible that your tendency for irritability and anger was conditioned years ago as a child. Learning to have empathy for your childhood self could pave the way for you to give up anger and irritability as a coping strategy.
11. Practice gratitude by taking time each day to reflect on things you are grateful for. This can help you focus on positive aspects of life and manage the intensity of your anger by instilling a more appreciative, balanced outlook.
12. Learn assertiveness and conflict resolution skills to prevent misunderstandings and help you express anger in a healthy way. As you become aware of your inner feelings, it will be easier for you to ask for what you want rather than waiting until you are angry. You can learn to express anger without blame or judgment. Telling people that you are frustrated or angry is not going to alienate or frighten them.
13. You can help prevent outbursts or impulsive reactions by reducing or eliminating the use of chemical substances that affect mood. Alcohol, for example, lowers inhibitions and can increase aggression.
14. There are medications designed to stabilize your mood and decrease your emotional reactivity. Consider asking your therapist for a referral to someone who specializes in this area.
15. Online and in-person anger management classes are available to teach you how to de-escalate anger and manage your distress. Ask your therapist for a referral if interested.

Behavior-Restricting Fears (BRF) Scale

General Descriptors – BRF Scale

Complaints

Fear of closed spaces, dirt, the dark, sharp knives, open spaces.

Cognitions

Fearful; avoidant.

Emotions

Generally fearful; apprehensive.

Traits and behaviors

Preoccupied with avoiding frightening things; events and objects trigger anxiety and panic.

Therapist's Notes – BRF Scale

The 7 items on this scale are face-valid and all scored in the True direction. The item content includes fears of being away from home, being confined to a small, closed space, being in the dark, or using a sharp or pointed object such as a knife. These items describe fears that significantly restrict normal activities inside and outside the home. Highly specific phobias such as fear of animals, blood injection injuries, and other subtypes are not covered within this scale. However, fear-related disorders such as social anxiety disorder can be assessed with other scales such as SHY. BRF is empirically associated with agoraphobia and, more generally, fearfulness. When BRF is elevated, the clinician should evaluate for anxiety disorders and focus on behavior-restricting fears as a target for intervention. One explanation for the development of a behavior-restricting fear is an actual event that became associated directly or indirectly with the person's experience. Alternatively, it is possible that the development of a fear of an object or situation is related to the client's repressed emotions associated with the object or event. For example, a fear of knives might be associated with repressed feelings of anger or desire for revenge, and so a knife elicits those feelings, which are deemed frightening or unacceptable. One woman who was extremely angry with her husband and was in a marriage governed by religious beliefs and practices became phobic of large windows. Upon further exploration, she became aware that she was extremely angry with her husband and the restrictions imposed on her by her religion. Large windows seemed to beckon the possibility of smashing them and so venting repressed rage. To engage that possibility was too frightening, so large windows were avoided. Fear of dirt could be associated with a fear of illness and germs. Closed spaces may elicit in the client fears of being trapped and controlled. Clients with multiple fears tend to be passive, lack insight, and are controlling, since they build routines around avoiding certain objects and events.

Lifestyle and Family Background – BRF Scale

Behavior-restricting fears may be recent or longstanding. They can arise across a number of different diagnostic conditions. In some cases, a client may have no other diagnosable conditions except for fears and phobias. In the presence of a background of early trauma, abuse, or neglect, the fears may have developed as a response to a difficult situation. For example, one client grew up in a poor neighborhood and when her father died unexpectedly, her mother put her in an orphanage, separating her from her brother, until the mother could mobilize resources to take care of her children. The client had presented with an overwhelming fear of spiders, restricting her life to the point where she was housebound and constantly looking for spiders to eliminate. One of her frightening memories was being punished for misbehaviors by being made to work in the basement laundry of the orphanage. She could remember the smell of soap, the heat, and the claustrophobia. She recalls the nuns in their habits (as she put it) "scurrying around," making sure she was working hard, and often being unpredictably punitive with more time in the laundry as punishment. Insight therapy revealed that spiders reminded the client of her negative experiences with the nuns. If the fear has developed recently, look for a possible trigger, exploring how the fear symbolizes an understandable but repressed emotion. Developing a fear is not restricted to one type of diagnosis since it arises as a way to deal with mixed feelings or repressed emotions across many conditions. Conditioning experiences, such as a traumatic event, can lead to avoidant behaviors such as fear about being in a car after a motor vehicle accident. Classical conditioning paradigms can often help explain the development and maintenance of a behavior-restricting fear.

Clarifying Scales – BRF Scale

- If EID is elevated, the fears and phobias may be associated with anxiety and depression. The event or object feared may represent some aspect of the client's anxiety. For example, one client at age 16 had become a caretaker for her ill mother who was immuno-compromised. The mother recovered after a lengthy illness. As an adult, the woman developed a severe anxious depression post-partum and became phobic of dirt. Insight therapy revealed that she had never fully engaged the loss of her adolescence as a caregiver and the fears that she had experienced for a number of years about possibly losing her mother. When her child was born, it elicited in her fears of losing the child since she had been traumatized by the fear of losing her mother. The fear of dirt was a symbol of her adolescent fear of getting her mother sick by careless housekeeping. Look for ways that the fears are a symbol of some aspect of the events that led to the depression and anxiety.

- If THD is elevated, the specific fears may be symbolically incorporated into psychotic thinking. For example, a client may feel that dirt is radioactive and that it is contaminated by the CIA, or they may feel that they are unsafe traveling away from home or being in wide open spaces. These fears reflect the overarching fear that they are not safe.
- If BXD is elevated, consider how the particular fear is symbolic of the client's fear of being controlled or their fear that their impulses will overcome their control. For example, one client with elevated BXD was extremely fearful of heights. Upon further exploration, it was his fear that he would have the impulse to jump off a high place that was scaring him.
- If RCd is elevated, determine how a particular fear is symbolic and expressive of demoralization and depletion. For example, if an individual scoring high on demoralization develops a fear of knives, it could be a good prognostic sign, perhaps reflecting they are angry with their condition.
- If RC1 is elevated, the fears and phobias could be part of the client's preoccupation with avoiding illness and reflect fears and anxieties about physical decline and a catastrophic somatic diagnosis.
- If RC2 is elevated, the client likely fears further loss and guilt about past mistakes. One severely depressed client had a fear of driving since he was afraid he had run over people without realizing it. He was also struggling with guilt that he had not been kind to his dying mother.
- If RC4 is elevated, assess how the fear may be symbolic of the client's fear of being controlled or losing control of their impulses. For example, one client with an elevated RC4 score was generally impulsive, self-serving, and hedonistic. Yet he had a severe phobia of heights and of driving across bridges. These likely represented his fear that he could not control an impulse to jump off or drive off the bridge.
- If RC6 is elevated, a particular fear may be part of a paranoid construction. The fear of knives, for example, could represent a fear of being attacked. Fear of open spaces could reflect a client's fear that they don't feel safe and feel exposed.
- If RC7 is elevated, a particular fear could reflect some aspects of their generalized anxiety.
- If RC8 is elevated, a particular fear could be part of a psychotic condition. Given that individuals scoring high on RC8 often suffer from intrusive, paranoid, and confusing thoughts, a particular fear could be readily incorporated into their psychotic construct.
- If RC9 is elevated, look for a particular fear that is expressive of their fears of failure and their striving for great achievement and approval.
- If MLS is elevated, a particular fear could be symbolic of their general malaise and feeling tired and weak. For example, a fear of closed spaces might reflect how trapped they feel in their current condition. A fear of knives might reflect their underlying sense of defeat and unconscious escape fantasies through suicide, but without conscious expression of suicidal ideation.
- If NUC is elevated, a particular fear may reflect the client's concern with neurological decline. The fear could encapsulate the client's concerns. For example, one client developed a fear of walking in a dog park or being around any dogs. With insight therapy it became clear that he was afraid that a dog would run into him, and, since his balance was unsteady, he worried he might fall over, hurt himself, and die.
- If EAT is elevated, a particular fear may hold the clue to the underlying dynamic that is driving the eating disorder. Alternatively, the fear could reflect the client's concern that their condition is potentially dangerous.
- If COG is elevated, a particular fear could likely reflect the client's fears of cognitive decline.

- If any of the internalizing, anxiety, low self-esteem scales are elevated (HLP, SFD, NFC, STR, WRY), then the fears likely would be symbolic and expressive of the client's condition.
- If CMP is elevated, the client's compulsion and fear are likely linked by the same drive to control and alleviate the underlying conflict and anxiety.

Therapy and Theraputic Pitfalls – BRF Scale

A combination of therapeutic strategies is suggested. Initially, empathy for how the client's fears interfere with their life can facilitate a therapeutic alliance. This can be followed by insight therapy to help the client understand how the fears developed understandably, given the events that precipitated them. Initially, the client may resist a psychodynamic interpretation, but once they understand the link between a trauma and the development of a fear, they are more likely to be amenable to cognitive behavioral therapy techniques to help them manage the impulse to avoid the fearful object or situation.

Feedback Statements – BRF Scale

T score 65–83

Your profile suggests that you have a number of fears that can restrict your activities. You may be fearful of dirt, sharp objects, enclosed small spaces, or even wide-open spaces. Usually when somebody develops a fear, it arises, understandably, from an event or trauma. Your fear may also symbolize other underlying conflicts. Work with your therapist to understand how the particular fear you have reflects something deeper. Once you have understood that it will be easier to gradually diminish the fear.

T score ≥91

Your profile indicates that you have a number of fears and phobias that severely restrict many of your life activities. You may have periods of panic around open spaces, crossing bridges, dealing with dirt, or being near sharp objects. You are likely embarrassed to experience these fears, since others will probably become impatient with you, especially since your activities may be restricted. In many cases, fears like yours have developed for good reason, precipitated by a recent or past trauma or painful event. The particular fears that you experience may be symbolic of a deeper fear. Understanding that deeper fear will help you make an alliance with your therapist to better understand how these fears developed. This will enable you to learn techniques to manage your anxiety as you gradually confront those fears.

- If EID is elevated, add: Your profile suggests that you are currently experiencing depression and anxiety, and may have developed fears that reflect your preoccupation with avoiding further loss. It is possible that one of the fears you developed reflects your vulnerability to feeling guilty, especially if you feel angry toward someone.
- If THD is elevated, add: Your profile suggests that you are going through a confusing time and are concerned about how others are going to treat you or possibly hurt you. You may have periods when you are so confused that you might even get paranoid, wondering if people are out to get you. You may have developed some specific fears and phobias, perhaps as a way to protect yourself. You might have decided that being in wide-open spaces or leaving home could be dangerous and may have developed theories as to how your enemies are trying to hurt you.

- If RCd is elevated, add: You have developed some phobias that possibly reflect your low self-confidence, low self-esteem, and your attempts to deal with them.
- If RC1 is elevated, add: Your preoccupation with avoiding a new medical condition might have led to you developing some fears around specific things, such as dirt or certain places where you are afraid you might get sick.
- If RC2 is elevated, add: Your fears may reflect your current depression and anxiety. You might be avoiding certain objects or places. These fears likely reflect your depression and your fear of further loss.
- If RC4 is elevated, add: You likely have developed fears reflecting how concerned you are about ever being controlled and you realize you can be reckless and impulsive. For example, if you fear handling knives, it is possible that you are afraid that your anger can sometimes get out of control. If you are afraid of heights, perhaps you are afraid of your impulse to jump. If you are afraid of being in a small space, it might reflect your fear of being controlled, loss of freedom, or even death.
- If RC6 is elevated, add: Your current fears or phobias may reflect how unsafe you have been feeling. Because you feel so vulnerable to criticism or judgment, or even being attacked by others, you may have developed a fear that encapsulates and reflects your concern that you are going to be badly treated.
- If RC7 is elevated, add: You may have developed a fear about handling knives or dirt, being in open spaces, or another type of fear that reflects your anxiety that something bad is looming and you need to be constantly on guard. The fear will likely be symbolic of your generalized anxiety.
- If RC8 is elevated, add: You may have developed fears that limit the things you can do. These fears may be part of your general fear that the world is an unsafe place, and that you have to protect yourself against bad things happening to you.
- If RC9 is elevated, add: You may have developed fears that are symbolic of how pressured you feel to achieve great things, and yet concerned that somehow you might fail.
- If MLS is elevated, add: You may have developed fears that reflect your deeper concerns that you are unwell and often feel tired and depleted.
- If NUC is elevated, add: You may have developed a fear or fears that reflect your deeper concern that there is something wrong with you neurologically.
- If EAT is elevated, add: Your fears may hold a clue as to what is driving your eating disorder. The fear could also reflect that you are concerned you are harming yourself with the way that you deal with eating.
- If COG is elevated, add: You may have developed a fear or fears that reflect your deeper concern that something is wrong with your mind. Perhaps something bad happened because you weren't focused or because you forgot something important, and you developed a fear or phobia as an adaptive response to make sure it doesn't happen again.
- If CMP is elevated, add: You have developed a fear as well as a compulsion, and the two are probably linked. Some of your compulsions may be an attempt to deal with your fears – for example, doing things a certain way, avoiding dirt or sharp knives, or going out of your way to avoid open spaces. You likely feel temporarily calmer and less fearful if you can act on your compulsion and see your compulsive behavior as somehow protecting you, even though it restricts your life a great deal.

Lifestyle and Family Background Feedback– BRF Scale

You have developed some fears that can control aspects of your life and restrict your behavior. Sometimes these fears develop as part of another psychological issue. Often, the fear reflects a deeper issue and is symbolic of that. For example, somebody being afraid of sharp knives may be repressing anger, so sharp objects elicit feelings of anger that could be frightening. In other cases, when people are depressed or anxious, the fears they develop reflect depression and low self-esteem. In some cases, a person may develop fears in childhood because of early trauma or adverse childhood experiences. Perhaps you witnessed a frightening event or something bad happened that was not only painful but very frightening. The fears that developed after these events were an adaptive response to avoid the frightening event. It is possible that your fears developed recently, and, in that case, they likely reflect some recent traumatic event that has motivated you to avoid certain things or places.

Treatment and Self-Help Suggestions – BRF Scale

Overcoming fears that restrict your behavior involves self-awareness, gradual exposure, and the development of coping mechanisms. Here are some suggestions to help manage and reduce behavior-restricting fears.

1. It is important to identify your fear. It may be a fear of failing, being rejected or judged, or being physically harmed. It may be a very specific fear, such as of knives, dirt, or wide, open spaces. Try to analyze how that fear reflects a deeper fear, perhaps being angry or trapped, or that something terrible is going to happen. Learn to identify your triggers by noting situations or thoughts that cause your fear to intensify. You may have become used to avoiding fearful situations or may not feel it is valuable to address if it doesn't significantly affect your life.
2. Document your fearful thoughts to help you to see patterns and question their validity. Your fears may have arisen for valid reasons but may no longer apply. Ask yourself if the situation you are afraid of is likely to happen and if you are being realistic. Or is this just an instinctive habit you have developed. Replace your fearful thoughts with rational, balanced ones. For example, "If I touch dirt, I'm going to get sick" becomes "Many people touch dirt and don't get sick."
3. Take small steps toward confronting your fear in manageable increments. Desensitize yourself by gradually increasing the duration or frequency of these situations. Take time to celebrate small wins to build your confidence and resilience and see that fear isn't insurmountable. Be patient if progress is slow or setbacks occur, and avoid self-criticism. Visualize yourself confidently overcoming your fear and remind yourself of past successes.
4. Mindfulness, meditation exercises, and deep breathing can help you to stay present and to calm your nervous system, which can help alleviate your anxieties.
5. Share your fears with a trusted friend or family member for emotional support. Support groups can help you connect with others sharing similar challenges and provide encouragement and insight.
6. A therapist can employ cognitive behavioral therapy techniques to help you address deep-rooted fears.
7. Consult with your therapist to learn if certain medications might be effective. Some antidepressants, for example, can help treat anxiety by regulating levels of serotonin, which is a neurotransmitter responsible for mood.

7 Externalizing Scales

Introduction

Development

The Externalizing Scales assess seven constructs: Family Problems (FML), Juvenile Conduct Problems (JCP), Substance Abuse (SUB), Impulsivity (IMP), Activation (ACT), Aggression (AGG), and Cynicism (CYN).

The *MMPI-3 Technical Manual* (Ben-Porath & Tellegen, 2020b) presents data indicating that these measures are reliable sources of information about psychological functioning. There is also empirical support for both convergent and discriminant validity for these scales. Empirical correlates for these scales are generally consistent with the scale labels, reflective of the underlying constructs. As explained in the technical manual, the seven Externalizing Scales measure aspects of two Restructured Clinical (RC) Scales: Antisocial Behavior (RC4) and Hypomanic Activation (RC9). FML, JCP, and SUB measure facets of RC4 while IMP, ACT, AGG, and CYN gauge facets of RC9.

As described by Ben-Porath and Sellbom (2023) in their MMPI-3 textbook, externalizing psychopathology is a higher order construct that diverges into two specific realms: disinhibited externalizing and antagonistic externalizing. The disinhibited-externalizing dimension includes JCP, SUB, and IMP, which align with problematic impulse control, irresponsibility, sensation-seeking, and risk-taking. The antagonistic-externalizing dimension captured by AGG and CYN correlates with components of callousness, deceitfulness, suspiciousness, interpersonal aggression, and hostility. These traits are prominent in antisocial (psychopathic), narcissistic, and paranoid personality disorders.

As noted in the Ben-Porath and Sellbom (2023) textbook, the ACT scale does not specifically measure externalizing behaviors. This scale's items include racing thoughts, elevated mood, overexcitation, and cycling moods, and may reflect a thought and/or bipolar one disorder. The ACT scale has been shown to be particularly relevant in the assessment of manic symptoms and can be useful in differentiating a bipolar disorder from a major depressive disorder and schizophrenia. The correlates of ACT do, however, include a range of externalizing behaviors.

Application

The Externalizing Scales should be examined after protocol validity is established. If the profile is invalid, it cannot be interpreted, although inspection of scale elevations may still yield valuable information about the test-taker.

Following validity considerations, the Higher-Order (H-O) Scales and RC Scales will serve as a compass, pointing to specific Externalizing Scales for further interpretive clarity. However, should an Externalizing Scale be elevated without elevations on the H-O and/or RC Scales, the scale can nonetheless be interpreted. Alternatively, if a test-taker generates a moderate elevation on RC9 and

DOI: 10.4324/9781003557920-7

an elevated score on ACT, but no elevation on FML or SUB, interpretation of the elevated RC9 score would emphasize heightened excitation and energy levels but de-emphasize features related to family problems and substance abuse.

Family Problems (FML) Scale

General Descriptors

Complaints

Family conflicts; feeling discounted and unappreciated by family members; annoyed by and disliking family members; feels family isn't supportive; possible partner distress.

Cognitions

Feels infantilized by family; believes family cannot be counted on in a crisis; dislikes family members.

Emotions

Alienated; feels a victim of family's lack of support; blames family; conflicted mixed emotions toward family members.

Traits and behaviors

Blames family for difficulties; problems with significant partners; feels unappreciated; angry with family; frequent family conflicts.

Therapist's Notes – FML Scale

The 10 items on this scale describe negative family experiences that may apply to one's current family or family of origin. Individuals scoring high on this scale view their family as quarrelsome and annoying. They have trouble liking family members, feeling mostly unappreciated and discounted by them. They feel alone and, in times of need, do not see their family as supportive. They feel their family is highly critical of them and not functioning well. They may experience internal conflict, so while they express occasional love toward their family, they also feel intense anger and even hatred toward them. In some cases, a client's family experiences could reflect a realistic understanding of their family, which in fact may be quite dysfunctional. In other cases, the individual may have depleted their family's goodwill toward them through dysfunctional behavior, drug addiction, rebellious antisocial acts, or financial profligacy. Consequently, the family may well be critical of them and try to set limits, which result in the client's negative, blaming feelings toward the family. If any of the other Specific Problems (SP) Scales are elevated, it is possible that the empirical correlates reflected in those scales are associated with having come from a family who are experienced as unsupportive, critical, argumentative, and dysfunctional. A low score (T <39) would suggest that the client has experienced or may be experiencing, a stable, supportive, non-critical, relatively conflict-free family background.

Lifestyle and Family Background – FML Scale

It is well understood in psychology that a nurturing, supportive family who foster trustworthy stable bonds is important in building good self-esteem and psychological resilience. Some people have managed to thrive in spite of unsupportive, critical parenting. However, in many cases, negative parenting can lead to a greater incidence of anxiety, self-doubt, inefficacy, and generalized anxiety. Elevations on other SP Scales would provide information on the consequences of living in an unsupportive, demeaning, critical, and argumentative family.

Early life chronic stress, such as adverse childhood familial events, has been shown to have long-term neurobiological effects associated with an increased risk of developing anxiety and mood disorders. The earlier these conditions emerge in childhood or puberty, the greater the likelihood that mental health problems in adulthood will emerge. These early adverse events can condition a child to view non-threatening situations as dangerous and conversely view an unsafe situation as safe. A lack of vigilance or hypervigilance is often the result of misinterpreting social cues as a function of early familial discord.

It is difficult to understand without a clinical interview whether the client is experiencing family conflict due to their own behavior, resulting in the family becoming unsupportive, critical, and angry. It is also possible that the client is accurately reporting the results of a dysfunctional family dynamic, perhaps due to drug addiction or alcohol abuse in family members. In other cases, the client may have grown up in an unsupportive, critical, fault-finding, dysfunctional family with little emotional support or positive guidance. A clinical history will determine the provenance of the individual's resentment and anger toward their family and perhaps identify why the family has been so critical and unsupportive. This would provide clues for helpful psychological interventions.

Clarifying Scales – FML Scale

- If Emotional/Internalizing Dysfunction (EID) is elevated, the depression, anxiety, and demoralization associated with that scale may be a consequence of a dysfunctional family dynamic. The client may be feeling guilty and self-recriminatory, feeling that family issues are related to their unlovability and past mistakes. It is also possible the client is depressed and anxious because of a history of unsupportive, critical, or even abusive caregivers. The way the client is currently responding to their family would suggest that they may be perpetuating the familial discord with their blaming and quarrelsome stance, even if the original emotional scars were created by bad caregiving.
- If Thought Dysfunction (THD) is elevated, the client's family conflict and their view of their family as unsupportive, critical, and demeaning may be part of a thought disorder with paranoid ideation and hypersensitivity to criticism.
- If Behavioral/Externalizing Dysfunction (BXD) is elevated, family conflict could be the result of acting-out behavior on the part of the client. A history of impulsive acts, rule-breaking behavior, reckless finances, and/or substance abuse could have led to a family being critical, angry, and distanced. It is also possible that the impulsive, hedonistic behavior associated with BXD is the result of growing up in a family who were critical and unloving, leading to the development of antisocial and anti-authority behavior. Finally, it is also possible that the individual was raised by caregivers who themselves were prone to engage in externalizing behavior.
- If Demoralization (RCd) is elevated, the client is reporting feeling worthless, defeated, lacking in self-confidence, and lonely. They likely complain about an unsupportive, critical, and dysfunctional family. It is possible that their demoralization is the result of absent nurturance and support and/or the presence of negative caregiving.

- If Somatic Complaints (RC1) is elevated, explore the possibility that the development of somatic complaints is related to anxiety that may develop if a client feels that their family is unsupportive, critical, and demeaning. It is also possible that their bodily complaints and somatic responses to stress could be an attempt to win support and care from a dysfunctional family. At the same time, it is possible that a family has become angry and resentful because the client appears to be dysfunctionally preoccupied with physical symptoms and avoids dealing with the normal demands and stresses of life.
- If Low Positive Emotions (RC2) is elevated, low positive emotions and low self-esteem may be related to feeling alone and unsupported by family members.
- If Antisocial Behavior (RC4) is elevated, it is possible that the family is or was critical, unsupportive, and discounting due to the client's problems with relationships, substance abuse, authority issues, or financial profligacy. It is also feasible that the client grew up in a dysfunctional family and their acting-out and hedonistic behavior is a response to feeling unsupported and constantly criticized.
- If Ideas of Persecution (RC6) is elevated, the client could view their family as critical, unsupportive, and argumentative as part of a persecutory worldview. It is also possible that growing up in a dysfunctional, unsupportive family has contributed to the development of a psychotic condition in which the client feels vulnerable to criticism, attack, and judgment.
- If Dysfunctional Negative Emotions (RC7) is elevated, the client's experience of anxiety, dread, and self-doubt is perhaps related to growing up in a critical, unsupportive family. This may have contributed to the client's low self-esteem and self-doubt.
- If Aberrant Experiences (RC8) is elevated, psychotic thought processes could be related to growing up in a dysfunctional, critical, and unsupportive family. It is also possible that the client is delusional about the level of criticism and lack of emotional support coming from their family. Poverty, family dysfunction, hostility, and lack of emotional support are associated with an increased risk for psychosis.
- If RC9 is elevated, the hypomanic activation, ambition, and need for attention and approval could be associated with wanting to prove oneself to a critical and neglectfully unsupportive family.
- If Malaise (MLS) is elevated, the exhaustion and feelings of depletion could be the result of a history of unsupportive, critical, and judgmental caregiving figures.
- If Eating Concerns (EAT) is elevated, an eating disorder might reflect the client's attempt to elicit caretaking behavior or an attempt to exercise some psychological control over the dynamics of a dysfunctional family.
- If Suicidal/Death Ideation (SUI) is elevated, the client's suicidal ruminations could be an escape fantasy from an unsupportive family. Suicidal ideation and/or actions might also be an expression of rage toward a critical family or an expression of trapped hopelessness.
- If Helplessness/Hopelessness (HLP), Self-Doubt (SFD), Inefficacy (NFC), Stress (STR), Worry (WRY), Anxiety-Related Experiences (ARX), and/or Behavior-Restricting Fears (BRF) are elevated, explore the possibility that the elevations are associated with the conditioning experience of growing up with critical, unsupportive, argumentative caregivers. This could have contributed to anxious or compromised attachments resulting in stress, vulnerability, and a lack of resiliency. Feelings of helplessness, hopelessness, chronic worry, and ineffectual decision-making likely are a result.
- If Compulsivity (CMP) is elevated, compulsions may have evolved as an attempt to control the anxiety that might understandably develop growing up in an environment of critical, unsupportive, and dysfunctional caregiving figures.
- If ARX and BRF are elevated, the severe anxiety, fears, phobias, and quickness to startle may reflect the insecurity and low self-esteem that result from unsupportive, critical caregiving.

Therapy and Therapeutic Pitfalls – FML Scale

With only FML elevated, therapy should focus on identifying the dynamics between the client and family members. Has there been a history of unsupportive parenting or is it recent? What could have caused it? To what degree could the client be creating conflict with family members by their own behavior? Elevations on this scale suggest that the client tends to see themselves as a victim of their family interactions. If other scales are elevated, therapy should explore the relationship between early conditioning experiences of unfair and unreasonable criticism and current symptomatology as manifested by other scale elevations. Once a therapeutic alliance has been established, family therapy may be useful. However, in cases where the family is clearly too dysfunctional, individual therapy can help the client emancipate and develop an identity separate from the one imposed on them by their family. A potential pitfall is engaging in family therapy before a firm therapeutic alliance has been formed, since family criticisms in front of the therapist may make the client feel ganged up on. On the other hand, the family may judge the therapist as indulging the client and not holding the client accountable if the therapist is client-supportive.

Feedback Statements – FML Scale

T score <39

Your profile suggests that you are reporting little conflict with your family, either in the past or currently. You may have grown up in a family who resolved conflicts peacefully and effectively, and that generally got along well with each other. You likely feel that your family is supportive and not unreasonably critical of you. You probably feel that you can turn to them for help should you need it.

T score 43–51

Like most people, you can occasionally have issues and conflicts with your family, and, at times, they might even be critical of some of your decisions. Generally, however, you feel you can depend on them. Most of the time your family members get along well with each other.

T score 55–59

Your profile suggests that you are currently experiencing some family conflict and feel that your family is somewhat unsupportive and unduly critical. There are times when you may have intense mixed feelings toward your family, feeling angry with them or perhaps even that they are hateful even though you also feel love toward them. Getting together with them might be difficult, at times, since you see them as quarrelsome and fault-finding. If you really need their support, you might find it hard to ask for it.

T score 65–79

The family conflict that you have experienced recently and/or in the past has caused you to have ongoing negative feelings toward family members. This has likely left you feeling unsupported and even unloved or cared about. It is hard for you to like members of your family since you experience them as critical and quarrelsome. You may feel criticized and avoid family members, as contact leaves you feeling bad about yourself.

T score ≥80

Your profile suggests that you are experiencing your family as very critical and unsupportive. You see your family as quarrelsome and often in conflict. At times, their behavior has frightened you. In a time of need, you would not turn to them for support. You often feel that they discount you and treat you like a child. You find them annoying and experience mixed feelings toward them, sometimes hating some of them even though you might also feel love toward them.

- If EID is elevated, add: Your profile suggests that you are currently feeling quite down, depressed, anxious, and insecure. You are reporting that you cannot rely on your family and that you see them as too critical and unsupportive. You feel constantly on edge, looking for what can go wrong next. It is possible that growing up in a family who were critical, quarrelsome, judgmental, and did not get along well with each other robbed you of self-esteem and self-confidence. It is painful when you feel that you have no one you can rely on in times of need. This could aggravate your depression and anxiety.
- If THD is elevated, add: Your profile suggests that currently you do not feel that you can trust your family since you see them as critical, judgmental, and unsupportive. You may have grown up with a family who you saw as demeaning and critical of you, or they may have become this way recently. It is also possible that you are feeling very vulnerable and even, at times, confused about who you can trust and who is against you. It is hard for you to trust anyone, and you see your family as unsupportive, so you do not want to reach out to them for any help or support.
- If BXD is elevated, add: Your profile suggests that you see your current or past family as unsupportive, critical, and discounting of you. You may have grown up with a family who you saw as fault-finding and argumentative. They may have been a quarrelsome family and overly critical of you. It is also possible that some of your behavior has led to them being angry, critical, and negative toward you. It is possible that you have acted impulsively and gotten into trouble, which has led to them being unsupportive and negative toward you.
- If RCd is elevated, add: Your profile shows that you see your current or past family as unsupportive, critical, and negative toward you. You do not feel you could turn to them in times of need, and you report feeling depleted and that life is a constant strain. Feeling alone, useless, and blue, you cannot trust your family for support. Perhaps your demoralization comes from growing up with a family who were not there for you, or recent events may have occurred that led them to become more difficult and unsupportive. Feeling alone and unsupported may make you feel like giving up on things.
- If RC1 is elevated, add: You are reporting a number of physical symptoms and worries about your health. You feel your family is unsupportive and critical of you and you find them difficult to be around. You see them as quarrelsome, fault-finding, and demeaning. Their lack of support may cause you stress and worry and aggravate some of your physical symptoms, which are likely to increase your experience of pain and discomfort. Your family may be judgmental of you, feeling that your physical symptoms are "in your head." On the other hand, it is possible that you developed physical symptoms after years of the stress of living with a critical, unsupportive family.
- If RC2 is elevated, add: You report that you are currently feeling depressed and unhappy. It could be related to your experience of your family since you report you see them as unsupportive and critical of you. You would not turn to them in a time of need since you find them judgmental, annoying, and demeaning. Perhaps you became depressed after a number of years of feeling that you did not have a family to turn to. It is possible your depression was precipitated by an unrelated event, though family issues likely make it worse. You likely experience intense, mixed feelings toward family members, sometimes hating them as well as loving them. Perhaps realizing that you do not have a family to turn to has contributed to your depression.

- If RC4 is elevated, add: You currently see your family as quarrelsome and negative toward you. You see them as generally unsupportive. They annoy you and you do not feel you could turn to them in a time of need. It is possible that they have recently become critical and unsupportive, perhaps in response to some of the things that you have done. Or it is possible that you grew up with such a family and so, from an early age, you became a survivor, turning to your own resources in times of stress rather than trusting your family. To this day, you do not see them as people you could go to for support. You may have responded by becoming self-centered or self-reliant. You live in the moment, doing things impulsively and, at times, regretting the consequences.
- If RC6 is elevated, add: Currently you see your present or past family as unsupportive, critical, and negative toward you. You feel you cannot trust them to provide you with emotional support. You also feel quite vulnerable to being judged, criticized, or even attacked, and may now see your family as emotionally dangerous. It is possible you are seeing things accurately, but it is also possible that the feelings of mistrust and suspiciousness you are experiencing could be aggravated by things that have recently stressed you.
- If RC8 is elevated, add: Your profile suggests that you see your family as critical, unsupportive, and demeaning. You may have grown up in such a family, so that, from an early age, you felt that they were hostile toward you and you could not trust them. It is also possible that they have recently become critical and judgmental of you, perhaps for something that they think you have done. It is also possible that you are going through some very difficult stress, which is affecting your judgment and the way you see your family. You may see them as more threatening than they actually are.
- If RC9 is elevated, add: You tested as having a lot of energy, drive, and ambition. You think and move quickly, and you are impatient with a world that moves too slowly for you at times. You feel a strong need to do something important, perhaps because you came from a family who were critical and unsupportive. Perhaps some of your drive is motivated by a desire to prove to them that their criticism and judgment of you were unfounded. Or it is possible that you feel a need to work hard so that you can support yourself, since you do not feel you can turn to your family for support.
- If MLS is elevated, add: You report feeling exhausted, depleted, and weak much of the time. You may have developed some of these feelings because you see your family as critical, judgmental, and unsupportive of you. Having to go through life depending on only yourself can be emotionally and physically exhausting.
- If EAT is elevated, add: Your responses suggest that you may have a conflicted relationship with food, eating, and your weight. At the same time, you reported that your family is critical and unsupportive of you, and you often feel annoyed and even hateful toward them, even though you love them. You do not feel you could go to them for emotional support when you are stressed. It is not surprising that you have developed some habits around food as a way to manage your anxiety and feelings of loneliness.
- If SUI is elevated, add: Your responses suggested you have been having thoughts about suicide and ways to end your life. Things have become very desperate for you to be thinking this way. Your profile also suggests that you see your family as unloving, unsupportive, and ungiving toward you. You see them as finding fault with you and do not feel you could turn to them when you are feeling really down. Your thoughts about suicide might be a way of escaping the pain of being unhappy and alone. Your thoughts of suicide might also be due to some anger you feel toward them and your belief that killing yourself might wake them up to what they have done and how unsupportive they have been. If you feel hopeless and suicidal and cannot reach your therapist, call a suicide and crisis 24/7 hotline [988 in the United States and Canada] for confidential support.
- If HLP is elevated, add: You report that you have lost hope in your ability to change things for the better and your ability to reach your goals. This could be because you feel alone and unsupported by your family so it is understandable that you feel that you could never achieve any of your goals. It is hard to be optimistic when you feel alone and unsupported by your family.

- If SFD is elevated, add: You report that you have little self-confidence and there are times you think you are no good at all. You see yourself as not as good as others and sometimes feel worthless. This may be related to feeling that you do not have a family who you can rely on, perhaps because they have been critical of you, robbing you of self-esteem and confidence.
- If NFC is elevated, add: You report that you have difficulty making decisions and are quick to doubt yourself. When things go wrong, you give up on the task or project quickly because of your self-doubt. This may be partially due to coming from a family who you see as unsupportive and quick to criticize you. It is hard to have good self-confidence when you feel your own family sees you negatively and is not there for you should you need them.
- If STR is elevated, add: You report functioning poorly under stress and that you see yourself as more nervous than most people. It appears that stress is a constant companion for you these days. This may be related to some of the issues you have with your family since you see them as generally unsupportive and quick to criticize you. In a crisis you do not feel you could turn to them for support. It is understandable that you would experience stress more intensely since you do not have your family to fall back on.
- If WRY is elevated, add: You report living with a constant background noise of worry. You may worry about money and think that some unpredictable event in the future is going to cause a disaster. Sometimes it is hard to sleep because you are worried about something and often feel a sense of looming misfortune. You report your family as being critical and generally unsupportive. You do not have them to turn to, which may be aggravating your worries. It is also possible that you grew up in a critical and non-supportive family, which increased your tendency to worry, since you do not have anyone to fall back on.
- If CMP is elevated, add: You report experiencing a number of compulsive behaviors. Your tendency to be compulsive may be at least partially related to the fact that you feel alone because your family is quite critical and fault-finding. You report that they are not people you could turn to for emotional support in the event of a crisis. That is generally anxiety-provoking for people, so one way you might be controlling your anxiety is by engaging in compulsive behaviors.
- If ARX is elevated, add: You report feeling anxious and often preoccupied with worrying that something bad is about to happen. You can panic easily and often experience nightmares. Your tendency to worry and keep reliving past painful experiences may be related to feeling that you have no one to rely on because your family is unsupportive and critical of you. You report that you would not turn to them in a crisis, which likely leaves you feeling vulnerable and alone.
- If Anger Proneness (ANP) is elevated, add: You report that you have a short fuse and can easily become impatient and angry with people. Sometimes it is hard for you to control your anger, so you might get explosive with difficult people or irritating events. This could be related to having grown up with an unsupportive family who were critical and demeaning toward you. You report that you could not turn to them for support in a crisis. Perhaps that is why you are so high-strung and quick to anger, since you do not have a family to fall back on.
- If BRF is elevated, add: You report experiencing some fears and phobias, such as being afraid to be in a small, enclosed place or afraid of being in a wide-open space. Leaving home can make you anxious, and dirt may frighten or disgust you. It is possible that you have developed some of these fears and phobias as a reaction to having a family who you see as very critical and unsupportive of you. In a time of crisis, you do not feel you could turn to them for support. This could have made you more vulnerable to developing fears and phobias, since you do not have a family to lean on.

Lifestyle and Family Background Feedback – FML Scale

Your answers suggest that you see your current or past family as very critical and unsupportive of you. When the family gets together, you see them as quarrelsome and quick to argue with one another. Some of your family members may really bother you, so you find it hard to be around them. You feel demeaned when they treat you as a child. In a crisis, you do not feel you could turn to them for support. It is possible that your family has been this way for a long time, even since you were a child. Growing up with an unsupportive family, especially one that is critical and fault-finding, can lead to a person becoming anxious, insecure, and self-doubting. Children develop self-confidence by being guided into making good decisions. If you lack confidence in your ability to make good decisions, it becomes more likely that you make bad decisions, which further decreases your self-confidence.

Treatment and Self-Help Suggestions – FML Scale

Family conflicts can be challenging, but with the right self-help strategies, you can navigate them constructively and foster healthier relationships. Here are some practical suggestions.

1. Keep a journal to help with self-awareness and identifying your feelings. This can also help you recognize stressful family dynamics, and what your part in them may be, so you don't completely blame others.
2. Develop good communication skills with your family by listening and understanding rather than just responding. To demonstrate this, you can wait to respond until others have finished speaking and then repeat what you heard them say. Be sure to listen carefully, rather than preparing your response while they are still speaking, and let them finish, even if you disagree. Instead of judging and blaming, use "I" statements (e.g., "I feel upset when...").
3. Decide what behaviors and topics are not acceptable and communicate those boundaries clearly and respectfully. Honor these boundaries and those set by other family members.
4. If family conflicts arise, use techniques like deep breathing, meditation, or grounding exercises to avoid impulsive responses. You are allowed to step away when emotions run high to regroup and avoid escalation. Exercise self-care and try to engage in physical activity or hobbies to manage stress and frustration. Talk to trusted friends or join support groups to help you process family conflicts.
5. When facing difficulties with family members, look for underlying problems that may be driving surface arguments and try to find compromises that accommodate everyone's needs. Recognize that it is okay if some differences are not resolved.
6. Put yourself in the other person's shoes to better develop empathy and understanding. It may not feel like it, but most families want love and harmony. Try to let go of resentments and grudges for your own peace of mind.
7. Educate yourself by reading, listening to podcasts, or attending workshops or online courses about family dynamics and conflict resolution.
8. Consider family therapy to address underlying issues and improve communication. Individual counseling can help you to work on strategies to cope with family dynamics, as can support groups where you can connect with others facing similar challenges.
9. Exercise patience, kindness, and respect for others, which might encourage them to do the same. Focus on how you respond to situations rather than trying to manage things out of your control. Acknowledge any improvement in your family relationships, no matter how small.

Juvenile Conduct Problems (JCP) Scale

General Descriptors

Complaints

Reports a history of juvenile conduct problems; difficulties with authority figures; conflicted interpersonal relationships; possible consequences for criminal or antisocial behavior.

Cognitions

If no other behavioral dysfunction indicators are elevated, acknowledgment of history of juvenile misconduct.

Emotions

Disinhibited; impulsive; callous; insensitive toward others.

Traits and behaviors

Possible history of antisocial behavior and juvenile delinquency; aggressive behaviors including possible violence; conduct disorders; ADHD; possible substance abuse; possible externalizing disorders, such as antisocial personality disorder.

Therapist's Notes – JCP Scale

While elevations on this 7-item scale can also be associated with current acting-out behavior, elevations could reflect purely historical behavior. If scores on all the behavioral dysfunction indicators (BXD, RC4, RC9, FML, SUB, ACT, AGG, CYN, and Disconstraint (DISC)) are in the normal range, the elevated score on JCP may be characterizing a test-taker who is acknowledging past juvenile misconduct but no longer engages in acting-out behavior. Moreover, since BXD, RC4, and DISC include items not shared with JCP, but which assess past antisocial behavior, it is possible that these scales could also be elevated, to some extent, based on past behavior. Consequently, elevations on JCP may only be associated with current acting-out. However, in the presence of a juvenile history of acting-out, current manipulative, devious, and antisocial behavior, as well as elevations on the behavioral dysfunction indicators, JCP elevations could be indicating an antisocial personality disorder.

High scorers, especially if RC4 is also elevated, are sensitive to being controlled, tend to disparage authority figures, and have difficulties with emotional trust and being vulnerable. With other behavioral dysfunction indicators being elevated, these individuals can be very manipulative, selectively report, impulsively act-out, and have conflicted interpersonal relationships. These individuals have difficulty trusting a therapist and tend to see the world as "dog-eat-dog," assuming their therapist is playing a role and being manipulative with them. Gaining the client's trust is important and usually involves dealing with the transference on an ongoing basis. Confronting the client with the fact that they may not trust their therapist can open the door to talking about trust in general and the client's experience with authority figures who were not trustworthy.

Scores below a T score of 48 would suggest a trouble-free adolescence, conformity to rules and regulations, and a lack of hedonistic, impulsive behavior. T scores of 52 to 56 suggest normal adolescent questioning of authority and occasional impulsive behavior. Higher T scores likely suggest that the client has a history of juvenile conduct problems with difficulties conforming to school rules, conflicts with caregivers, and perhaps drug use. Look for a history of problems and potential conflicts with the law due to stealing, being arrested, and/or drug or alcohol use.

Lifestyle and Family Background – JCP Scale

Often, people who have experienced juvenile problems with authority figures, conduct problems at school, stealing, and getting arrested, have backgrounds where caregiving figures were either overly authoritarian, indulgent, or under-involved. Alternatively, caregivers may have been inconsistently indulgent or unpredictably severe. From an early age, these individuals may have learned to act on an impulse, be manipulative, discard conventions and rules, and not trust authority because they saw authority figures as unreliable and hypocritical. If other behavioral dysfunction indicators are elevated, the client is reporting currently living a life of hedonistic acting-out, with resulting interpersonal problems and possible conflicts with authority figures. These clients are perceived as self-serving and lacking in empathy.

Clarifying Scales – JCP Scale

- If BXD and /or RC4 and RC9 are elevated, the client is reporting a broad range of externalizing, acting-out, self-serving, and manipulative behaviors. The juvenile acting-out behavior appears not to have matured, and the client is continuing what appears to be a lifestyle of self-serving, energized, hedonistic, devious, and impulsive behavior.
- If SUB is elevated, the client is reporting current substance abuse and possibly a history of substance abuse, perhaps from adolescence.
- If IMP is elevated, the likelihood increases that the juvenile conduct problems never really matured, and the individual's impulses are likely to still get them into trouble.
- If ACT is elevated, the client is reporting heightened excitation, possible hypomanic episodes, and mood swings. The concurrent elevation on JCP suggests that juvenile, impulsive, and hedonistic behaviors may have been predictive of a mood or conduct disorder.
- If AGG and/or Aggressiveness (AGGR) are elevated, it is probable that other scales measuring behavioral dysfunction are also elevated, confirming that the juvenile dysfunction was a precursor to the development of an acting-out, aggressive, self-centered personality.
- If DISC is elevated, the client is reporting that they are continuing to act like a rebellious juvenile, abusing drugs and alcohol, being impulsive, doing dangerous things for the thrill of it, and breaking rules which can all result in their getting into trouble with the law.

Therapy and Therapeutic Pitfalls – JCP Scale

Psychotherapy depends on which other scales are elevated with JCP. If only JCP is elevated, the client is reporting historical data that may no longer apply to them. In the presence of elevations on scales associated with behavioral dysfunction, such as impulsivity, recklessness, rule-breaking, or drug and/or alcohol abuse, the focus of therapy is usually on dealing with current consequences of reckless behavior. The essence of this constellation of acting-out scales is a profound distrust that impairs both empathy and intimacy. Typically, these individuals do not trust their therapist, often seeing them as part of the "system" that they oppose. It would be most helpful for the therapist to give feedback about how the client has become cautious about trusting, perhaps for good reason – for example, due to early childhood adverse experiences with authority figures. Predicting the transference early on can also be useful. Suggesting to the client that they will have difficulties trusting and will put the therapist through "trust tests" could be a good way to start tackling the transference issues. When the client's compliance with regular sessions starts to break down with late cancellations and excuses, dealing with the transference would be a more useful strategy than being punitive or critical.

Feedback Statements – JCP Scale

T score ≤56

Your responses suggest that you had a normal upbringing, rarely questioning authority, generally following the rules, and not being reckless and impulsive.

T score = 61

Your responses suggest that you occasionally questioned authority if you felt that they were being unreasonable. Sometimes, like most teens, you could be a bit impulsive, occasionally bending the rules.

T score = 68

Your responses suggest that you had a tumultuous adolescence because you questioned authority, at times, and were impulsive and even a little reckless. Sometimes you broke the rules and were manipulative to avoid consequences. You likely experimented with alcohol and drugs, which was bad for your health and may have gotten you into trouble with your family.

T score 74–80

Your responses suggest that you had a history of juvenile delinquency and perhaps even behavior that got you in trouble with the law. You disliked being controlled and you questioned authority figures. You would break the rules if you thought they were unreasonable or stupid and you have a tendency to be impulsive, acting without fully thinking through all the consequences. People with your profile often have conflicts with family or loved ones. Your family likely viewed you as acting selfishly and may have lost trust in you since you can selectively report or even lie. You may have outgrown some of your early rebelliousness, but it is possible that some of those behaviors have continued into adulthood.

- If BXD and/or RC4 and RC9 are elevated, add: Your responses suggest that you are somewhat of a rebel, distrusting authority figures and bending the rules when they get in the way of getting what you want. You can be manipulative and are comfortable selectively reporting or even lying in order to avoid negative consequences. You may use drugs or alcohol, which can increase your tendency to be impulsive. It appears that you have not changed much from the fun-loving, living-in-the-moment, rule-breaking juvenile you once were. However, living in the moment now, being reckless at times, using drugs and alcohol, and upsetting the people who care about you likely leads to a lot of conflict with family and friends.
- If SUB is elevated, add: Some of your responses suggest that you are currently using drugs and/or alcohol. You may have continued to use substances, which you likely started in adolescence, or it could be something you have returned to recently. Alcohol and drugs are going to make you more impulsive and could lead to conflicts with authority figures, family, and friends.
- If IMP is elevated, add: Your profile suggests you were a rebellious juvenile who got into some trouble because of impulsive behavior. It appears that you currently have a tendency

to be impulsive, perhaps because you have so much energy. When you want something, you sometimes just go for it rather than thinking through all the consequences. This probably got you into trouble as a teenager and can still cause you problems, especially with authority figures.

- If ACT is elevated, add: Your responses suggest that you have a lot of energy and can get quite excited about a new idea or project that you are involved in. As a juvenile, you may have been diagnosed as hyperactive and likely got into trouble with authority figures because of your tendency to be impulsive and even reckless. Sometimes your high energy may get you into trouble because you get too excited and impatient with people. You also may have a vulnerability to mood swings, getting excited and overcommitted and then disappointed and depressed.
- If AGG and/or AGGR are elevated, add: Your responses suggest that during your juvenile years you were quite rebellious and, at times, reckless and impulsive. Currently you are reporting having trouble with your temper, which can lead to aggression toward others and maybe even violence. You may actually enjoy intimidating others, and you might even resort to some kind of violence when you do not get what you want.
- If DISC is elevated, add: You reported your juvenile years were marked by impulsive and, at times, reckless behavior. You also report that you have continued to act impulsively and are attracted to immediate gratification. You like excitement and sensation, and you seek it out, whether it is using drugs and alcohol, or some other behavior that might get you into trouble.

Lifestyle and Family Background Feedback – JCP Scale

People with your profile often grew up in an environment where, from an early age, they had to rely on themselves during times of stress. Perhaps your caregivers were very strict, and you saw them as unreasonable. At other times they may have been permissive, letting you get away with things but then coming down hard on you when you did something they did not like. From an early age you appear to have learned not to trust fully, since you could not trust your caregivers to manage you. One of them might have been indulgent and hidden things that you did from the other caregiver because the other was too harsh. At other times, the caregiver that protected you might have also threatened you with consequences from the stricter caregiver. You may have learned from an early age to be impulsive and manipulative in order to get what you want. Unfortunately, that lifestyle can catch up with you, since people stop trusting you and authority figures want to punish you. People with your profile generally do not seek out therapy unless they are ordered to or recognize a need for change. You have trouble trusting authority figures and may have a tendency to want to manipulate the therapist. It is important that you discuss your feelings toward your therapist so you can practice developing trust by understanding that they will not abandon you or treat you harshly.

Treatment and Self-Help Suggestions – JCP Scale

Rebuilding and growing up after a history of juvenile delinquency or a difficult upbringing can be a powerful and transformative journey. Here are some self-help suggestions tailored for someone seeking to move forward positively.

1. Keep a journal to help develop your self-awareness and uncover the root causes of past rebelliousness. Learn what kind of situations motivate you to act without thinking through all the consequences. Use the journal as a tool to practice gratitude as well, by focusing on progress and good things.

2. Taking responsibility for your behavior is an important step in growth and regaining the trust of others. This will help you to let go of the past and forgive yourself and others. Accept responsibility even if you believe your rebellious behavior was due to difficult caregivers or tension and difficulties at home, as is often the case with teenagers.
3. Create a support network to help you repair family relationships. Seek out positive influences by volunteering and finding role models to inspire and guide you. Giving back can build self-worth and a sense of purpose, and you can inspire others facing similar challenges by sharing your story.
4. Build healthy lifestyle habits to help you manage stress and control your impulses. Exercise helps build discipline and improve mood, as does a healthy diet and self-care routines, like meditation, deep breathing exercises, and consistent sleep hygiene.
5. If you experience legal conflicts, seek support from organizations that rehabilitate former offenders.
6. Avoid people and settings that may tempt you to act-out. Before you make any big decisions, take time to consider all the possible outcomes.
7. Be kind to yourself, be patient with your progress, and celebrate small achievements.

Substance Abuse (SUB) Scale

General Descriptors

Complaints

Strained and/or broken interpersonal relationships; vocational failures or academic problems; legal problems such as drinking under the influence offenses (DUIs) and illegal possession of drugs; medical problems and possible withdrawal symptoms; chronic fatigue; memory and concentration problems; guilt and shame.

Cognitions

Belief that substance use is essential for functioning; denial of an addiction; disbelieving that treatment can be helpful.

Emotions

Feeling helpless to stop/curb cravings for using; despair over one's addiction; excited about next opportunity to use substance; disinhibited restraints.

Traits and behaviors

Increased tolerance to receive pleasurable effects; irritability, anxiety, and nausea when not using; struggle to limit amount or frequency of substance use; neglecting obligations for school, work, and personal relationships; risky behaviors while under the influence; preoccupation with obtaining, using, or recovering from substance effects; minimizing severity of abuse (denial); emotional instability with mood swings and anxiety.

Therapist's Notes – SUB Scale

Elevated scores on the 9-item SUB scale reflect a high risk for substance abuse, including alcohol, drugs, and prescription medications. It directly assesses the disinhibited-externalizing component of psychopathology constructs. Problematic impulse control, irresponsibility, sensation-seeking, and risk-taking are at the core of this scale. Antisocial personality disorders, conduct disorders, ADHD, and alcohol and/or other substance use disorders are consistent with the disinhibited-externalizing construct. Elevations would suggest that the individual has impaired functioning due to substance abuse, and, in some cases, legal problems associated with abuse. Substance misuse serves as a risk factor for interpersonal violence in a variety of contexts. Rarely would there be a solo elevation on the SUB scale, but if so, it may reflect a generally well-functioning individual with a drug and/or alcohol problem. It is possible that an elevated score reflects past substance abuse, so careful review of items answered in the keyed direction is warranted. Usually, other elevated scales provide indications as to what thoughts, feelings, and personality attributes the substance abuse is attempting to medicate.

If any of the four SUB items reflecting current usage are answered in the keyed direction, follow up on these items with the client. If only past use is endorsed, rule out current usage. Even one item answered in the keyed direction may signal a current issue warranting clinical attention.

Lifestyle and Family Background – SUB Scale

It is generally accepted among psychologists that there is a strong genetic component to addiction-proneness. Substance abuse in the family of origin or the extended family would suggest that genetics are playing an important role in the client's substance abuse. In the absence of such a history, the client may have developed alcoholism or drug abuse in an attempt to medicate post-operative or post-injury pain or the psychic pain of depression and anxiety. Drug and alcohol abuse may also have developed in an attempt to medicate another underlying psychiatric condition, such as mania or schizophrenia. In other cases, for example when BXD and/or RC4 and RC9 are elevated, hedonistic pleasure-seeking and self-indulgence drive the abuse of drugs and alcohol.

Clarifying Scales – SUB Scale

- If EID is elevated, the substance abuse may be related to the client's depression and anxiety. They may find that substances alleviate some of their anxiety when they are in social situations, using substances to boost their self-confidence and numb their anxiety. Alcohol is generally experienced as an effective anxiolytic, though with potential severe negative side effects. People who go through life constantly stressed and tense may turn to substances to be able to relax.
- If THD is elevated, the client's psychotic thought processes may lead them to use substances as a way of trying to dampen their disturbing thoughts and feelings. This can lead to serious negative effects on people with psychosis. In some cases, certain drugs induce persecutory ideation (i.e., amphetamines) and can lead the individual into destructive actions.
- If BXD is elevated, the client may be reporting using drugs and alcohol recreationally. This is another aspect of their acting-out, impulsive, hedonistic lifestyle. These individuals live in the moment and tend to ignore the possibility of future negative consequences. They are sensation-seeking and generally resist attempts to control them. Consequently, inpatient treatment programs have limited success with this group of people unless they have voluntarily admitted themselves.
- If RCd is elevated, the client's alcohol or drug abuse may be related to underlying demoralization. Feeling worthless and useless, they feel life is a constant strain, so substances may be an attempt to self-medicate.

- If RC1 is elevated, the client may use substances as a way of self-medicating a perceived or actual medical condition or the experience of pain.
- If RC2 is elevated, the client may be using substances as a way of self-medicating their depression.
- If RC4 is elevated, the client's use of substances tends to be recreational and is part of their hedonistic, self-indulgent lifestyle. These clients tend to impulsively seek immediate tension reduction, so they are particularly vulnerable to substance abuse when stressed, infirm, or recovering post-operatively.
- If RC6 and/or RC8 are elevated, the client may be self-medicating their psychotic thought processes. The use of certain drugs could be particularly harmful since it may increase their paranoia and likelihood of acting-out.
- If RC7 is elevated, the client's substance abuse is likely self-medicating severe anxiety and their tendency toward guilt and self-recrimination.
- If RC9 is elevated, the abuse of substances may be related to the client's attempts to manage their surges of hypomanic energy and overexcitability. In some cases, they may have begun to use alcohol or substances as a way of shutting down their energy and falling asleep. In other cases, using stimulants may have developed as a way to maintain manic energy levels.
- If DISC is elevated, the person's abuse of substances may reflect their generally impulsive personality with little restraint over their urges.
- If MLS is elevated, substance abuse may be related to feelings of exhaustion and depletion. The client may have begun to use substances as a "pick-me-up" to counter feelings of malaise. The substance abuse could then further contribute to feelings of malaise, robbing the individual of energy and drive.
- If NUC is elevated, the vague and shifting neurological symptoms may be causing the client severe anxiety, which they medicate with substances. Given that some of the complaints involve dizziness and balance problems that are aggravated by alcohol, intuitively it seems unlikely that they self-medicate with alcohol, although that is possible. They may use prescription medicines if they feel that they help with some of their neurological symptoms.
- If EAT is elevated, there is a possibility that they may use stimulants as a way of controlling their eating habits and appetite. Intuitively it would seem that people with an eating disorder would not develop a dependency on alcohol, but they could.
- If Cognitive Complaints (COG) is elevated, the individual's complaints of becoming easily confused, unable to focus, and having poor concentration and memory suggest that they would not seek substances that could further interfere with cognition. However, should the scale be elevated, they may be using stimulants or some other substances that they believe are improving their cognitive ability. Alternatively, their neurological complaints could be a consequence of their excessive substance abuse.
- If SUI is elevated, the risk of an impulsive suicide attempt increases. The substance abuse may be related to severe depression, hopelessness, and/or loneliness.
- If HLP is elevated, the client has lost hope, feeling that they are unable to make changes in their life. The future seems hopeless to them, and they have given up on ever feeling better. Feeling "I have nothing to lose," they may have turned to substances as a way of numbing themselves or to experience temporary euphoria.
- If SFD is elevated, substances may be abused to help the client relieve their severe lack of self-worth and self-confidence.
- If NFC is elevated, the client may be abusing substances to self-medicate their difficulties in making decisions and tendency to shrink from a crisis or challenge. Perhaps they began to use alcohol when faced with very difficult decisions as a way to calm themselves, and it then became an ongoing crutch.

- If STR and/or WRY are elevated, the client is particularly vulnerable to using anti-anxiety medicines such as benzodiazepines. They may also abuse alcohol as a way to de-stress.
- If CMP is elevated, the client's compulsions reflect the externalization of anxiety and attempts to manage and control it. Consequently, these individuals may turn to substances as a way to manage their anxiety and lessen their compulsions.
- If ARX is elevated, the client is experiencing severe anxiety. They are easily panicked, have nightmares, and are easily startled. They tend to relive bad experiences. Consequently, they are vulnerable to abusing any substance that soothes their anxiety, even temporarily.
- If ANP is elevated, elevations on SUB predict an increased likelihood that using alcohol or drugs could increase explosiveness and lack of impulse control. It is also possible that the individual could be attempting to medicate their high-strung, angry outbursts by numbing themselves.
- If BRF is elevated, the individual may be using substances to manage their fears – for example, of dark closed spaces, of dirt, or of being out in the open.
- If IMP is elevated, the individual's impulse control is further compromised under the influence of substances. They are more likely to behave recklessly and in self-defeating ways.
- If ACT is elevated, substance abuse increases the likelihood of mood swings and manic overactivity.
- If AGG and/or AGGR are elevated, the use of substances lowers the threshold for hostile and potentially physical aggression.
- If Self-Importance (SFI) and Dominance (DOM) are elevated, the client may become more dominating and argumentative under the influence of drugs or alcohol, extolling their own virtues, forcefully opining, and demanding attention.
- If Disaffiliativeness (DSF) is elevated, the client may be using substances to deal with their extreme withdrawal from others and their potential loneliness. Since they report preferring to be alone, substances may act as a companion.
- If Social Avoidance (SAV) or Shyness (SHY) are elevated, the client may be using substances as a way of dealing with social anxiety and/or extreme introversion. They may use alcohol before going to a social event and drink heavily at the event as a way of managing social anxiety.

Therapy and Therapeutic Pitfalls – SUB Scale

Treatment for substance abuse has evolved. There was a time that the main treatment for substance abuse was abstinence. Currently other treatment modalities have become more common. Although there are situations where people can be taught to drink or use substances responsibly, it is currently understood that, for most people with a substance-abuse problem, abstinence is still the best treatment. However, it is important to identify the reasons for the substance abuse and what is driving the individual to self-medicate. For long-term success, the client must learn alternative responses to stressful and triggering events. The combination of individual cognitive behavioral therapy and group support through either Alcoholics Anonymous or Rational Recovery therapy are the most efficacious treatment modalities. The most difficult part of dealing with substance abuse is convincing the client that they have a problem. In many cases, an intervention is necessary to confront the client with the negative consequences of their use. In some situations, family therapy together with gentle but direct support from their therapist is necessary to cajole the individual into treatment.

Feedback Statements – SUB Scale

T score 65–79

Your profile suggests that you have abused substances in the past or are doing so currently, which is causing problems with family and/or others.

T score ≥80

Your profile suggests you have abused substances in the past and are probably still using them. You may have started to use alcohol or drugs as a way of opening up and relaxing, but it appears from your answers that substance use is currently a significant problem.

- If EID is elevated, add: Your profile suggests you may be using drugs or alcohol as a way to deal with your depression and anxiety. Perhaps when you are in social situations, you believe substances give you more confidence and manage your anxiety. While substances can make you feel better temporarily, they have serious side effects. Your use of them may have led to conflicts with others and even legal problems.
- If THD is elevated, add: Your profile suggests that you are experiencing some disturbing thoughts and emotions. Perhaps, at times, you even feel confused about what exactly is reality. You may have moments where you are fearful that other people are hostile toward you or out to harm you. You may be using substances as a way of medicating the "inner noise" that could be frightening at times. There are certain substances that you may think help you feel better, but they are likely to make you more suspicious and confused. Alcohol and drugs can actually worsen your symptoms. In some cases, it could lead to you hearing voices directing you to do harmful things.
- If BXD is elevated, add: Your responses show that you may be using alcohol and/or drugs in a way that is potentially harmful. You may have gotten into trouble with authorities because of things you did when using substances. You generally dislike being controlled and distrust authority figures. When you are stressed, you tend to move into action impulsively, and if you are in any kind of discomfort, it is hard for you to problem-solve patiently, so you may end up turning to substances as a way to get immediate relief or reward. You test as a sensation-seeker, so you may have experimented with substances as a way to get high, and this may have led you to continue to abuse them.
- If RCd is elevated, add: Your answers suggest that you may be using substances as a way to relieve your sense of demoralization. It appears that you feel life is a constant strain and you are quick to feel worthless and useless. You may have turned to substances as a way to relieve some of that pain, either to numb yourself or just to get a high to feel better. While using, you might temporarily feel better, but over time you are likely to feel more demoralized and even worse about yourself.
- If RC1 is elevated, add: Your profile suggests that you are very concerned about your physical wellbeing. You seem very focused on finding out what is wrong with you since some of the symptoms you are experiencing cause your anxiety. You may have already spent a lot of time talking to doctors and trying to find the right treatment. Your responses suggest that you may have turned to substances as a way to medicate some of your symptoms and your anxiety. Using alcohol and drugs can aggravate your symptoms and can cause more problems, especially with family and friends.
- If RC4 is elevated, add: Your responses suggest that you may be using substances that may have caused problems with your family and even with authority figures. People with your profile have difficulty postponing gratification, so if you are in any pain or discomfort, you are likely to use anything you can to feel better, even if it has negative consequences. You may have started using substances recreationally or because you were in pain after an injury or surgery, but, since you have difficulty disciplining yourself, you might have become dependent on them. Consider talking to your therapist about your use of drugs and alcohol since it likely will begin to cause you numerous interpersonal and even legal problems.

- If RC6 and/or RC8 are elevated, add: Your profile suggests you are currently using substances as a way of feeling better. You may have started to use drugs and/or alcohol to manage your anxiety and your preoccupation with avoiding others' criticism, judgment, and hostility. Your profile suggests that you do not feel safe with most people and might, at times, even feel suspicious, unsure of whom to trust. It is understandable that you began self-medicating with drugs or alcohol as a way to manage the mistrust that you occasionally experience. There are certain drugs that will aggravate your distrust and actually drive you to do things that are irrational, self-defeating, and destructive. Stimulants, in general, are bad for you and can increase your feelings of persecution and your sense that you have to do something to protect yourself.
- If RC7 is elevated, add: Your profile suggests you may be abusing substances, perhaps as a way to manage your anxiety, which appears to be constant. You are quick to feel guilty and beat yourself up for any mistakes, and this likely exhausts you. You may have started to use substances as a way to "switch off the noise" in your head of self-recrimination and self-doubt. You may have begun using substances to get temporary relief from your anxiety. While substances can help temporarily with anxiety, the long-term consequences are serious and, over time, will increase your anxiety.
- If RC9 is elevated, add: Your profile suggests you have a lot of energy. You appear to go through life with two speeds: either "full on" or "full off." You likely work in spurts of energy, and, when you have an idea, you tend to rush into action. You can be excitable and impulsive. You may have begun to use substances as a way to maintain your high energy because you felt that stimulants could make you more productive. On the other hand, you may use substances to manage your energy, which can be overwhelming at times. Perhaps you began using alcohol or downers to try to switch off the intensity of your drive so you could sleep. The danger is that your impulses may become more destructive under the influence of substances.
- If MLS is elevated, add: Your profile suggests you are currently feeling exhausted and depleted. It also reveals that you have been using drugs and alcohol, perhaps as a way to medicate your feeling of malaise. You may have thought that substances would be a "pick-me-up" to counter feelings of exhaustion. The problem is that, over time, substances tend to increase malaise as well as interfering with judgment.
- If Neurological Complaints (NUC) is elevated, add: Your profile indicates that you may be abusing substances. You have reported experiencing a number of neurological symptoms that may be causing you anxiety. You may have started to use alcohol and drugs as a way to try to self-medicate your neurological symptoms. However, since you may be experiencing dizziness and balance problems, alcohol will certainly make them worse. Any drugs you might be taking could also be aggravating neurological symptoms.
- If EAT is elevated, add: Your test scores indicate that you are preoccupied with food, eating, and your weight. You also indicate that you have been using substances and that they may have caused trouble with your family and even authority. You may have started to use stimulants as a way of controlling your weight and hunger. It is also possible that you use substances as a way to numb yourself so that you can continue to restrict your food intake.
- If COG is elevated, add: Your responses suggest that you are having some cognitive difficulties, with an inability to focus and becoming easily confused. You report poor concentration and some memory problems. It is surprising that you report using drugs and alcohol since they likely aggravate some of these cognitive symptoms. You may have begun to use substances as a way to control your anxiety around your cognitive issues, or perhaps you believed that they might help you think more clearly and improve your concentration and memory. Over time, any substances you are using could potentially make your cognitive difficulties worse.

- If SUI is elevated, add: Your test results suggest you have been thinking about suicide and that you have lost your will to live. You may have begun to use substances as a way to medicate your sense of loneliness and desperation. The problem with using substances is that you may feel better temporarily, but they also can lead to depression and impulsive self-harm. If you feel hopeless and suicidal and cannot reach your therapist, call a suicide and crisis 24/7 hotline [988 in the United States and Canada] for confidential support.
- If HLP is elevated, add: Your profile suggests that you have lost hope and feel unable to make any changes in your life for the better. Perhaps because you have been feeling hopeless, you appear to have turned toward substances as a way of self-medicating. However, drugs and alcohol could increase your desperation and will sap your motivation and energy to change your life.
- If SFD is elevated, add: Your profile suggests that you are very self-critical and do not feel good about yourself. It is easy for you to lose your confidence, so you shrink from difficult situations, thinking that you are not going to be able to problem-solve. This may be why you have turned to drugs and/or alcohol, as a way of getting some courage and self-confidence or to numb yourself to escape the feelings of low self-worth.
- If NFC is elevated, add: You reported that you have difficulty making decisions and starting new projects. When things go wrong, because you doubt yourself, you tend to give up quickly. Making big decisions makes you nervous. This may be why you have turned to substances as a way to feel more confident and assertive. While substances may make you feel stronger or better temporarily, over time they will lead to errors of judgment and problems with family and authority.
- If STR and WRY are elevated, add: Since you often experience stress as overwhelming, and because you have a tendency to worry, you might have turned to substances as a way to handle stress and shut off the constant worrying. You might be using alcohol or unprescribed medications that may make you feel better temporarily, but this can quickly become addictive and negatively affect your decision-making and judgment.
- If CMP is elevated, add: Your profile suggests that you have developed a number of compulsions that you act on, perhaps as a way of dealing with some of your anxieties and fears. You may also have begun using substances as a way to manage your anxiety. However, they will likely aggravate your anxiety over time and will not help with your compulsions.
- If ARX is elevated, add: Your profile suggests you have turned to substances as a way of dealing with your severe anxiety and episodic panic. Perhaps you have chosen to use substances to stop nightmares and the reliving of past negative experiences. However, over time, substances will increase your symptoms and lead to further problems.
- If BRF is elevated, add: You may have begun to use substances as a way of dealing with some of your fears and phobias. While substances can temporarily make you feel less anxious or fearful, over time they may actually increase your symptoms.
- If IMP is elevated, add: Your profile suggests you can be impulsive, jumping into things quickly without always looking at possible negative consequences. Your profile also suggests that you are currently using drugs and/or alcohol or have used them in the past. Substances are likely to increase your impulsiveness, which can lead you into hasty and even self-defeating acts.
- If ACT is elevated, add: Your profile suggests that you are excitable and highly energetic. Sometimes your energy may shade into manic hyperactivity, so you overcommit to many tasks and activities. You are reporting that you are currently using or have used drugs and/or alcohol. Using substances can increase your mood swings and manic overactivity.
- If AGG and/or AGGR are elevated, add: Your profile suggests you have some trouble managing your anger and aggression. Perhaps you get aggressive and hostile with people, or perhaps things frustrate you, causing you to become angry and even explosive. When intensely

frustrated, you might become physically aggressive. Your profile also suggests that you are currently using substances or have used them in the past. Substances will likely increase your aggression, so things easily dealt with when not under the influence could instead become big deals, leading to aggression that could develop into physical violence.

- If SFI is elevated, add: Your test results suggest you are very confident in your abilities and talents. You see yourself as an important person and feel people should pay attention to what you have to say. Your profile also suggests you are currently using substances or have in the past. When under the influence, you may come across to people as a braggart, extolling your own virtues. You might not notice that people resent you for coming across as feeling you are better than them.
- If DOM is elevated, add: You are someone who is not afraid to take on a leadership role, stand up for yourself, and offer people your opinions. You likely come across as assertive and direct. You also reported that you are using or have used drugs and/or alcohol. When under the influence, you might come across as more loud, brash, and opinionated than usual. You may upset people by dominating the conversation and not letting others speak. Or you might get argumentative, pushing your views onto people. People at parties might avoid you, perhaps concerned that when you have had a few drinks you will dominate the conversation.
- If DSF is elevated, add: You report that you like time alone and are cautious about getting close to people. It appears that you have begun using substances, perhaps experiencing them as a companion that you can turn to in order to feel good.
- If SAV or SHY are elevated, add: Your profile suggests that you are quite introverted, enjoying small groups of people you know while avoiding and disliking large groups of people who you do not know. You may have started to use substances as a way to gain social self-confidence, or you may use them as a way to numb any feelings of loneliness.

Lifestyle and Family Background Feedback – SUB Scale

Research has shown that vulnerability to developing substance abuse is at least partly genetic. Consequently, if you had a parent, sibling, or extended family member who experienced addiction problems, it suggests that you may have a vulnerability to developing an addiction. However, there are a number of reasons why people begin to use substances. Sometimes it is prescription medications that have helped with post-operative pain or were prescribed to help with anxiety. Sometimes people use alcohol to deal with social anxiety and low self-confidence. While alcohol can be a good anti-anxiety substance, it has terrible side effects and can lead to severe physical and even mental problems. Once you have begun to develop a substance-abuse problem, you will find yourself constantly thinking about how to procure substances. You may even start to hide bottles or drugs to avoid family and/or friends voicing concerns or criticism. If you grew up with someone who was a substance-abuser, you will remember the severe family problems that it likely caused.

Treatment and Self-Help Suggestions – SUB Scale

Seeking help for substance abuse is a courageous and commendable step. Overcoming substance abuse requires patience, effort, and support. Here are actionable steps you can take to help yourself.

1. Be honest with yourself and acknowledge how substance use is affecting your health, relationships, and wellbeing.
2. Define clear goals that are realistic, measurable, and specific. Ask yourself if you want to quit entirely or reduce use, and, if so, in what ways. Keep a journal to track your progress, noting successes and setbacks, and celebrate small milestones.

3. Identify your triggers for substance use, whether it is stress, specific people, or certain places. Develop a plan to cope with or avoid these triggers. Consider therapy to address underlying emotional issues, such as anxiety or depression, which may contribute to substance use.
4. Build healthy habits to manage stress, improve mood, and reduce cravings. Adhere to a consistent bedtime routine with sufficient sleep and a regular exercise program. Practice mindfulness techniques, meditation, deep breathing, or yoga, and adopt a healthy diet.
5. Create a support system with trusted friends or family members. Join a support group, such as Alcoholics Anonymous, Rational Recovery, or Narcotics Anonymous, with like-minded members who focus on accountability and can offer shared experiences.
6. Engage in volunteering or creative activities such as art, music, or writing to replace unhealthy habits and to develop a sense of purpose.
7. Practice self-compassion by forgiving yourself for past mistakes. Focus on the present and what you can do now. If you should relapse, remember that it is part of recovery and can be a growth opportunity.

Impulsivity (IMP) Scale

General Descriptors

Complaints

Legal/vocational and/or interpersonal problems; lacks restraint over emotions; risky behaviors lead to negative consequences; frequent loss of emotional control.

Cognitions

Lacking confidence for self-control; insufficiently deliberates actions.

Emotions

Regret and/or guilt after impulsive actions; frustration about feeling helpless to control impulses.

Traits and behaviors

Impulsive behaviors lead to unfavorable consequences, such as self-harm, risky behaviors, legal difficulties, and/or vocational and interpersonal relationship disruptions; recklessness.

Therapist's Notes – IMP Scale

This 6-item scale measures the very core of disinhibition and is evident in all forms of disinhibited psychopathology, including antisocial personality disorder, ADHD, intermittent explosive disorder, borderline personality disorder, alcohol use disorders, and others. Clients with low scores report not engaging in impulsive behavior and are generally thoughtful and considerate of consequences. High scorers likely exhibit impulsivity, impatience, and acting-out traits and behaviors.

Clients with impulsivity problems might not seek therapy, except when referred by the courts, frustrated family members, or self-referred due to workplace and/or academic difficulties. Complaints could reflect the tendency to externalize and blame others for one's own misfortunes.

However, some self-aware clients may complain of difficulty controlling their impulses and seek help in this area.

Impulsivity is defined as acting without forethought and restraint, sometimes resulting in destructive and self-defeating outcomes. Whims, urges, cravings, and immediate desires are acted upon, and gratification is rarely delayed. No one condition, however, drives impulsivity. It may originate from a number of psychological and neurophysiological (e.g., tic disorder) conditions and drives. For example, it is possible for highly anxious people to act impulsively. As they wrestle with trying to make a decision and become depleted seeing every side of every issue, they may make an impulsive decision to relieve stress. A hypomanic individual may be impulsive due to being overactivated. Self-centered, narcissistic individuals may act impulsively because they lack self-control. Elevations on other scales can provide clues as to what could be driving the impulsivity.

Lifestyle and Family Background – IMP Scale

The lifestyle of people who manifest impulsivity is one of poor decision-making, conflict with family and/or co-workers, and potentially conflict with authorities. In the presence of a childhood history of ADHD, the client's current impulsiveness could be the result of a longstanding neurological condition. In the presence of a childhood diagnosis of a conduct disorder, adult impulsivity could be the result of a lack of maturity and self-discipline. Clients in a manic episode can also be highly impulsive. In some cases, people become impulsive only in certain situations that are particularly stressful because they activate old psychological "scar tissue."

There is no evidence of a particular family background associated with impulsivity, although early childhood overactivation would suggest a genetic component. Clients scoring high on the SUB scale could also be impulsive due to the disinhibition caused by substance misuse.

Clarifying Scales – IMP Scale

- If EID is elevated, the impulsivity is likely driven by anxiety and depression, which could be depleting the client's psychological resources. During times of stress, the depressed, anxious client may impulsively give up, even if things are getting better. It is also possible that they impulsively get angry when frustrated, since their threshold for frustration is lowered by anxiety and depression.
- If THD is elevated, the client may be experiencing psychotic thoughts, hypersensitivity, and mental confusion. It is possible that they impulsively vent or engage in self-protective behavior that appears bizarre and unpredictable to others.
- If BXD is elevated, an elevation on IMP would predict an individual who impulsively reduces tension in ways that could cause problems interpersonally and with authority figures.
- If ANP is elevated, impulsive rage is possible. The need for instant gratification and use of substances together with impulsivity would predict that the client has severe difficulties with family and friends because of reckless, poorly thought-through behavior.
- If RC4 is elevated, impulsive acting-out when stressed is predicted. Whether it is expressing anger, using substances, or manipulating others, the client acts on impulse without considering possible consequences.
- If RC6 or RC8 are elevated, the client may show abrupt, brittle, angry, or impulsive reactions when feeling threatened. Hypersensitivity shading toward paranoia could lead to conspiracy theories and an impulsive lashing out at perceived enemies.
- If RC7 is elevated, the client's anxiety, fears of failure, and self-criticisms can lead to impulsive tension reduction that might involve abruptly giving up on a project, out of concern that they are not good enough. Impulsive behavior would be in the service of reducing anxiety and tension, though it likely could lead to guilt and self-recrimination.

- If RC9 is elevated, mood swings, intense overactivity, and excitability can lead to impulsive overcommitments and expressions of anger and frustration.
- If EAT is elevated, the client may not resist their urges to overeat or purge to relieve tension. This behavior, however, will likely lead to guilt, shame, and self-recrimination.
- If SUI is elevated, the danger of an impulsive suicide attempt increases.
- If SUB is elevated, the client is likely using substances impulsively as a way of managing stress and frustration, and substance abuse increases the likelihood of impulsive behavior.
- If any of these scales are elevated: HLP, SFD, NFC, or STR, the client is stressed, self-doubting, and feeling hopeless and helpless. They likely impulsively reduce tension in self-defeating ways, such as withdrawing from problem-solving or exaggerated self-criticism.
- If ANP is elevated, the client is reporting that they have a problem with the impulsive expression of anger. This could cause interpersonal and workplace problems.
- If AGG and/or AGGR are elevated, the client is reporting impulsive, angry, and aggressive reactions to stress and frustration of needs. There is a possibility that this could lead to physical altercations, name-calling, and/or hostile argumentativeness.
- If SFI is elevated, the client views themself as important, interesting, and worth listening to, so they are comfortable impulsively arguing their point, interrupting alternate views, and stating their firmly held beliefs.
- If DISC is elevated, it suggests that the client has a significant problem with impulse control. They admit to problems with authority figures due to a lack of impulse control and admit to drug and alcohol abuse if SUB is also elevated.

Therapy and Therapeutic Pitfalls – IMP Scale

Managing impulsivity requires self-awareness, self-discipline, and practical strategies for self-control. Impulsive behavior takes many forms and is not associated with any one mental condition. Impulsive spending, stealing, substance abuse, anger expression, sexual behavior, and gambling are examples of behaviors that occur as tension-reducers.

A clinical example is that of a woman who was elevated on anxiety, impulsivity, and acting-out scales. She developed a habit of shoplifting when she was extremely anxious. After a successful shoplifting event, she returned home and became anxious and guilty. Subsequently, she went back to the store and surreptitiously brought back the stolen merchandise. In another example, a successful professional, with a high standing in his community and a successful and happy marriage, would occasionally feel overwhelmed by the stress of his high-paced job. Impulsively, he would visit prostitutes and then become guilty and self-recriminating. This would lead to more stress and then he would act-out again as tension accumulated.

Impulsive behavior is associated with a number of different mental conditions. The first task of psychotherapy is to help the client become aware of impulse pressures and triggers and then learn alternative coping strategies. Dealing with the underlying mental condition that leads to impulsive behavior would be important. Addressing possible transference is important in the first sessions, suggesting that if the therapy feels stressful the client may impulsively leave. Agreeing on how to address premature termination would be an important initial step in psychotherapy.

Feedback Statements – IMP Scale

T score <39

Your responses suggest that you are not an impulsive person. You tend to consider your options carefully even under stress and do not allow yourself to impulsively reduce tension by behaviors that could backfire.

T score 45–52

Although you are generally thoughtful and careful not to be impulsive, like most people you occasionally allow yourself to do something impulsively that maybe later you wish you hadn't.

T score ≥65

Your responses suggest that you have difficulty managing your impulses. When you are stressed or somehow frustrated, you act impulsively and then probably regret it.

- If EID is elevated, add: Your responses suggest that when your anxiety and depression overwhelm you or when you feel defeated, you can do something impulsively to feel relief. You might give up on a task or person because you feel depressed or anxious. You may withdraw from someone or impulsively give up on exercise or doing things that have helped you in the past. When you feel depressed and act impulsively, you end up feeling more guilty and badly about yourself.
- If THD is elevated, add: Your responses suggest that you are feeling vulnerable to being criticized, judged, or even attacked by others. The world does not feel safe to you so you may act impulsively to protect yourself from what you perceive as danger. You may impulsively withdraw from others or lash out against them. This can lead to negative consequences since currently you may not be thinking as clearly as you would like.
- If BXD is elevated, add: You are a person who tends to live in the moment, dislikes being controlled, and is comfortable breaking rules. Your profile suggests that you are quite impulsive in the way you express anger and deal with frustration. You have difficulty disciplining yourself, whether it is how you deal with food, drugs and/or alcohol, or authority figures.
- If ANP is elevated, add: It may be hard for you to manage your temper when people block you from getting what you want or you feel unreasonably controlled. You tend to express anger impulsively without considering consequences.
- If RCd is elevated, add: Your profile suggests you have been feeling that life is a strain much of the time. When stress accumulates, you might impulsively want to give up and walk away from a project that you have started. You are quick to beat yourself up, often feel useless, and lack self-confidence. It is not surprising that you occasionally impulsively reduce tension by withdrawing from life. You often feel as if you are about to collapse, so it is hard for you to feel happy and confident. You may impulsively give up on a project that you feel is not going well. Sometimes when you act on an impulse it can be self-defeating.
- If RC4 is elevated, add: Your profile suggests that you have difficulty controlling your impulses. When you want something, you might pursue it without thinking of possible negative consequences. Whether it is spending money, using substances, or expressing anger and frustration, when you have an impulse, you tend to act on it. If confronted with a difficult situation, you might selectively report and impulsively distort the truth.
- If RC6 and/or RC8 are elevated, add: Right now you may be feeling vulnerable, concerned that other people are critical and judgmental of you. You might even be concerned that somebody could possibly harm you. You may experience periods of intense suspiciousness, when you are not sure whether you are seeing things clearly and if you can trust your view of what's happening. You may lash out impulsively at people you think are going to hurt you or do things impulsively that you think could protect you.
- If RC7 is elevated, add: Your profile suggests that you live with a lot of anxiety, constantly feeling on edge, as if something bad is about to happen. You tend to worry and are your own worst critic. Being anxious much of the time likely saps your energy, so you have less patience

and "bandwidth" to deal with stress. Consequently, even small frustrations can sometimes lead you to get angry or run away impulsively from a stressful situation. If you act impulsively, you likely feel guilty afterwards.

- If RC9 is elevated, add: Your test results show that you are very energetic and excitable. You can get very enthusiastic about your projects and ideas and are not afraid to speak your mind. Perhaps, because you have such high energy, you can overcommit to tasks and activities impulsively and wear yourself out. You might commit to things that are unrealistic or be irritable and even explosive when people get in your way.
- If SFI and ANP are elevated, add: You feel that you have a significant mission to accomplish and think it is important that people listen to you. If people are not supportive, it can make you impulsively angry, or even explosive.
- If MLS is elevated, add: Since you have been unwell and have felt tired and weak, you might impulsively give up on things or withdraw from life in ways that can backfire.
- If SUI is elevated, add: Your profile suggests you can be an impulsive person and have been thinking a lot about suicide, often wishing you were dead. It is important that you discuss this with your therapist so that you can discover what triggers you into wanting to commit self-harm impulsively. If you feel hopeless and suicidal and cannot reach your therapist, call a suicide and crisis 24/7 hotline [988 in the United States and Canada] for confidential support.
- If HLP, SFD, NFC, STR, and/or WRY are elevated, add: Your profile suggests that, when you feel helpless and hopeless or stressed and worried, you do something impulsive to escape the negative feelings. Acting impulsively can actually aggravate your anxiety since you likely feel guilty or concerned about how others could judge you.
- If ACT is elevated, add: Your profile suggests that you are excitable and have so much energy at times that it is hard to sleep. Sometimes your thoughts race ahead faster than you can speak them, and the world may seem like it moves too slowly. With all that energy, it is not surprising that you can be impulsive and let your excitement overtake you. If people interrupt you or get in your way, you may be impulsively irritable or angry. Perhaps in your excitement you overcommit or get involved in projects that are unrealistic.
- If AGG and/or AGGR are elevated, add: Your test results suggest that you have a short fuse. Frustrations, setbacks, or people doing things that annoy you can lead to you having angry or even violent reactions. It is hard for you to control your impulses, especially your anger, which can frighten people and make them avoid you. Your impulsive expressions of anger can even lead to physical altercations.
- If SFI is elevated, add: You have a high opinion of yourself and believe that your ideas and abilities are somewhat exceptional. You may feel that people should listen to you and take you seriously since you have a lot to say that you think is important. You may interrupt people impulsively when you think they are on the wrong track and may impulsively remind people of your own special abilities.
- If DOM is elevated, add: You are very comfortable taking charge and being in control. You tend to have firmly held opinions and can be quite assertive and direct with people when you feel strongly about something. You may expect to be in leadership roles since you are confident and like to take charge, but others may shrink from your assertiveness. With your confidence and "take charge" attitude you can impulsively offer your opinion or take on leadership roles without considering how others are seeing you.
- If DISC is elevated, add: You answered items in a way that suggest you are a sensation-seeker and tend to act on your impulses without thinking through the consequences. You enjoy the adrenaline rush of bending the rules and do not like to be controlled or restricted in your behavior. Your impulsive behavior may get you into trouble with people and even with authorities.

Lifestyle and Family Background Feedback – IMP Scale

Your tendency to act impulsively to reduce tension or get what you want may have arisen for a number of reasons. It is possible that you were diagnosed with ADHD as a child and some of that early excitability and impatience may have continued into adulthood. It is also possible that you are currently going through stress, whether it is physical, medical, or emotional, and have little capacity to deal with further stress. Therefore, you may do something impulsively to feel better, even though it may have negative consequences.

Treatment and Self-Help Suggestions – IMP Scale

Impulsivity can be managed effectively with self-help strategies that promote self-awareness, self-regulation, and healthier decision-making. Here are some practical approaches.

1. Keep a journal to help identify triggers that lead to impulsive behavior. Recognizing these situations, settings, and feelings will help you to anticipate and manage your feelings before you respond impulsively. Learn to count to ten, take a deep breath, or step away momentarily before responding.
2. Practice mindfulness or meditation techniques to stay present. When you feel impulsive, try describing what you see, hear, or feel in your surroundings to distract you and curb impulsive tendencies.
3. Set clear goals before taking action. Take a moment to think about any decision's long-term effects and decide if this will help you achieve your goals. Give yourself a "24-hour rule" before making any major decisions. Choose a trusted friend or family member to share your goals with and gently remind you when you are acting impulsively.
4. Manage your energy level by engaging in exercise or hobbies. Practice yoga, deep breathing, or progressive muscle relaxation to keep your emotions in check.
5. Practice delaying gratification in small ways to improve self-control. Reward yourself for small victories to reinforce your self-control.
6. Build healthy habits and routines that reduce the need for last-minute decisions.
7. Consider psychotherapy such as cognitive behavioral therapy to explore deeper personality issues if impulsivity is impacting your life. Certain conditions like ADHD, anxiety, or mood disorders can aggravate impulsivity.
8. Impulsive behaviors can be effectively treated with medication in some cases. Consider asking your therapist for a referral to someone who specializes in medications for treating impulsivity.

Activation (ACT) Scale

General Descriptors

Complaints

Sleep difficulties; racing thoughts; hyperexcitability; hyperactivity; mood swings; fits of uncontrollable laughing and crying.

Cognitions

Racing thoughts; possibly grandiose.

Emotions

Excitable; energetic; possibly euphoric; moody.

Traits and behaviors

Garrulous; manic or hypomanic; excitable; uncontrollable mood swings; loquacious; pressured speech; behaviors possibly substance-induced.

Therapist's Notes – ACT Scale

This 8-item scale highlights the externalizing behavior sequelae of hypomanic and manic symptomatology. Seven of the eight items on this scale are also scored on the RC9 scale, a measure of hypomanic activation. Both ACT and RC9 capture overexcitation and the expansive mood aspect of hypomania or mania.

High scorers on ACT exhibit many of the symptoms associated with mania, such as mood swings, garrulousness, and a decreased need for sleep. Such individuals are excitable and report surges of exuberance not necessarily tied to reality. They report racing thoughts and fits of laughing and crying that they cannot control. In the presence of a history of manic and depressive episodes, the scale may be measuring the manic side of bipolarity. With a history of impulsive behavior driven by manic optimism and then depressed episodes, elevations would suggest ruling out a bipolar diagnosis. Often, sleep is disturbed due to the heightened arousal associated with elevations on this scale. In the presence of a history of childhood hyperactivity, elevations may reflect a genetic predisposition to hypomania. If the surges of excitability are recent, hormonal imbalances may be contributors. If substances are involved, the excitability and mood swings may be associated with substance abuse or medications. Often, clients resist medication to help them modulate their energy levels since they enjoy the heightened energy and exuberance associated with mania or hypomania.

Lifestyle and Family Background – ACT Scale

Elevations on ACT are associated with a history of manic or hypomanic episodes. In some cases, the vulnerability to activation may have been expressed as childhood ADHD. In such cases, genetics clearly play a role and activation may be longstanding, with resulting difficulties. In some cases, the hypomanic activity is associated with more recent substance abuse or a panic over some perceived catastrophic setback that induces a hypomanic response.

In bipolar disorders, epigenetic factors could be involved in the neurobiological consequences of childhood trauma. Traumatic events are risk factors not only for developing bipolar disorders, but can lead to alterations of affect regulation, impulse control, and even cognitive functioning. These factors can decrease coping strategies in adult life. In the presence of adverse childhood events, current activation occasioned by a recent perceived loss may be a manifestation and reactivation of early trauma. A complete psychosocial history is therefore recommended.

Clarifying Scales – ACT Scale

- If EID is elevated, the client is reporting depression, anxiety, feeling worthless, and feeling overwhelmed by stress. At the same time, they are reporting feeling episodic or ongoing activation, racing thoughts, and surges of non-reality-based exuberance. This combination of scales may be indicating a rapidly cycling bipolar disorder with sudden mood shifts triggered by external events. The agitation/activation component coupled with EID should alert the clinician to assess for impulsive behaviors and suicide risk.
- If THD and/or Psychoticism (PSYC) are elevated, the client is reporting thought-disordered symptomatology, paranoid ideation, and hypersensitivity to anything that can be construed as criticism, at the same time as reporting excitability, hypomania, and racing thoughts. It is possible that the paranoid thought disorder is related to a manic episode or a manifestation of a schizoaffective disorder.
- If BXD is elevated, it would increase the likelihood of impulsive acting-out, substance abuse, aggressiveness, and generally reckless behavior. The reckless behavior and impulsivity may occur during exuberant mood swings.
- If RCd is elevated, feeling blue, demoralized, having low self-worth, feeling lonely, and that life is a strain most of the time co-exists with periods of hyperexcitability, euphoric mood swings, and unrealistic activation. The possibility of a medication side effect, hormonal imbalance, or a bipolar disorder should be explored.
- With RC1 elevations, intuitively, one would not expect activation, which involves energy and drive. Typically, a clinician would think of an RC1 elevation as reflecting an individual who is protective of their bodies, perhaps slowed down, and unlikely to manifest hypomanic behavior. However, in the event that these two scales are elevated, it is possible that the individual's psychosomatic presentation also involves mood swings, excitability, and unrealistic exuberance that may be incorporated into the somatization disorder. For example, one client with an elevation on RC1 complained that episodically she would experience mood swings, with surges of energy and optimism that led to a gambling addiction. She claimed that her adrenal burnout from workplace stress was causing numerous physical symptoms and mood swings.
- If RC2 and RC9 are elevated, the likelihood of a bipolar disorder increases.
- If RC4 is elevated, the likelihood of impulsive acting-out, substance abuse, and/or conflict with authority is increased. When the client experiences exuberant mood swings, they may become involved in risky behavior, especially if substances are involved.
- If RC6 is elevated, the heightened activation of paranoid ideation could lead to potentially aggressive and dangerous behavior. Periods of exuberant self-confidence in the presence of distorted thought processes could lead to the individual acting on their paranoid suspicions.
- If RC7 is elevated, it is possible that periods of anxiety, self-doubt, and guilt are followed by, or interspersed with periods of exuberance and excitability. The resulting behavior may appear to a clinician as a bipolar disorder, but anxiety could be driving the energized component of the behavior.

- If RC8 is elevated, the client likely manifests the symptoms of a schizoaffective disorder with mood swings and possibly psychotic thought processes that are energized, but confused and unrealistic. An individual with schizophrenia may manifest the symptoms associated with the elevations on RC8 and ACT, with inappropriate giggling, nonsensical and colorful language, and emotional lability.
- If RC9 is elevated, there is an increased likelihood of impulsivity, grandiosity, and emotionally labile episodes. Sleep will likely be disturbed due to increased arousal, and speech will be rapid and pressured. Irritability and even aggressiveness, especially if goal-striving behavior is blocked, are likely.
- If MLS is elevated, the client is reporting feeling weak, tired, and in poor physical health. Consequently, a clinician would not intuitively expect elevations on ACT. However, if these two scales are elevated, it is possible that they reflect a mood disorder. Alternatively, a hormonal problem or medication side effect could contribute to these hypomanic mood swings. Certainly, periods of excited exuberance, emotional lability, and garrulousness followed by exhaustion and weakness would appear to the clinician as possibly manic depression.
- If NUC is elevated, the hypomanic symptoms associated with ACT would blend well with the symptoms associated with the NUC scale. Dizzy spells, numbness in the extremities, fits, and convulsions are NUC complaints, and ACT symptoms of laughing and crying at the same time, racing thoughts, and unrealistic exuberance could be interpreted by the clinician as part of a neurological condition.
- If EAT is elevated, it is possible that the episodic eating issues are related to hypomanic activity. In some cases, hypomanic activation might lead to stress, and purging could be utilized as a way of relieving it. In other cases, hypomania may provide the determination and drive to restrict eating.
- If COG is elevated, complaints about cognitive inefficiency, memory problems, and difficulty focusing and concentrating may be associated with a highly activated hypomanic state. The co-existence of these two sets of symptoms may indicate a hormonal imbalance, or the result of substance abuse or a neurological condition.
- If SUI is elevated, the elevation on ACT would heighten the risk of a successful suicide attempt, especially if SUB is also elevated. A suicide risk assessment would be indicated.
- If HLP, SFD, and/or NFC are elevated, the client may experience periods of hypomanic activation and excitability, interspersed with periods of severe self-doubt, hopelessness, and feeling that making positive changes in life will be impossible. Likely, other scales will be elevated, suggesting a bipolar diagnosis.
- If STR and/or WRY are elevated, complaints about feeling constantly stressed, worried, and nervous would alternate between periods of hypomanic excitability, exuberance, and unrealistic optimism. While all these symptoms could be associated with a bipolar diagnosis, it is also possible that they are the results of substance abuse, side effects of medication, or hormonal imbalances.
- If CMP is elevated, the compulsion to do things in a certain way could be part of a hypomanic episode. It is also possible that the compulsions arise out of an attempt to manage and direct the hypomanic activation.
- If ARX is elevated, the severe anxiety and sense of impending doom, episodes of panic, and nightmares could be part of a hypomanic episode in which periods of exuberance and unrealistic optimism collapse into anxiety and self-doubt.
- If ANP, AGG, and/or AGGR are elevated, difficulties controlling anger and irritation are predicted. One would expect a hypomanic client to exhibit some impatience, given their high

drive state, but with elevations on ACT, impatience and irritability may be expressed as anger and aggression.
- If FML is elevated, it is possible that the client's hypomanic activities and mood instability has alienated their family. On the other hand, it is possible that alienation from the family has caused a reaction in the client leading to hypomanic activation.
- If SUB is elevated, it is possible that the activation is a result of substance abuse. It is also possible that the client is seeking out substances as a way of managing their hyperexcitability and the difficulties they have controlling their energy level.
- If IMP is elevated, the likelihood of impulsive, poorly thought-through behavior is significantly heightened. Risky behaviors may lead to negative consequences.
- If SFI and/or DOM are elevated, the client will come across as dominating and self-important, expressing themselves in an exuberant, hyperexcited fashion.

Therapy and Therapeutic Pitfalls – ACT Scale

Overactivation can be caused by a number of different conditions. In some cases, people have a genetic vulnerability to mood swings. In other situations, activation can be caused by medication side effects, such as the long-term use of certain medications (i.e., Prednisone). In some other cases, activation can occur as a defense against an impending depression due to a perceived severe loss. The use of high-tetrahydrocannabinol (THC) marijuana can produce a schizomanic episode, especially in young adults and teenagers. The clinician would need to examine associations between elevations on the ACT scale and other elevated scales. The relationship between the scales would give a clue as to what could be driving the activation or how the activation is causing other problems. Sometimes, people are reluctant to seek therapy to lower their level of activity and exuberance. Generally, they seek therapy when problems have accumulated due to reckless behavior. A medical referral is often necessary to determine the provenance of the heightened activation and help control it.

Feedback Statements – ACT Scale

T score <39

Your answers suggest that you approach life with a steady and even energy level. You test as non-excitable and tend to conserve your energy, so you do not overcommit. You approach tasks in an orderly and disciplined manner.

T score 41–49

Your responses suggest that your energy level is normal, without surges of excitability. You approach life with a fairly steady and even manner although, like most people, things can excite you and quicken your pulse.

T score 53–58

Like many people, you can have periods when you are highly excited, perhaps finding it hard to get to sleep because something has stimulated you, and sometimes your ideas can occur almost faster than you can speak them.

T score 65–80

Your profile suggests that you are highly excitable. Ideas and projects can feel so exciting that it is hard for you to sleep or switch off your thoughts. At times, your thoughts might race, making it difficult to sleep. Your thoughts may also race faster than you can speak them. At times, your energy level may lead you to overcommit to many tasks and activities. Medication can often help even out surges of energy and help you to balance out your mood swings.

- If EID is elevated, add: Your responses suggest that you may be experiencing mood swings, when you go from feeling depressed, anxious, and pessimistic about the future to episodes when you feel elated, excited, optimistic, and exuberant. During periods when you are in an excited mood, your thoughts might race, and you may find it hard to sleep. It appears that you could cycle between excited, energetic moods and periods where you are quite down and depressed.
- If THD and/or PSYC are elevated, add: Your profile suggests that you are currently feeling preoccupied with protecting yourself against what you perceive as enemies or people out to hurt, criticize, or judge you. You may experience energized periods when you do not know whom to trust. You may have a fixed idea about who your enemies are and whom you need to protect yourself from. Your profile also suggests you have periods of high energy and excitability, when your thoughts race, making it difficult for you to sleep. When you are in a highly activated mood, you may become convinced that you know who is responsible for your troubles and may feel energized to somehow protect yourself or even punish people whom you feel might hurt you. During these periods of high energy, you may experience disturbing thoughts that might frighten you.
- If PSYC is elevated, add: You may experience hearing voices, perhaps hear people calling your name, or feel that people are looking at you critically, which may feel confusing and frightening. It is important that you realize you may be distorting reality and feeling highly suspicious without clear evidence.
- If BXD is elevated, add: Your profile suggests that you are experiencing mood swings where you feel "on top of the world," excited, and optimistic. Your thoughts may be racing and sometimes you may find it hard to sleep because you are so excited. It is possible that during these periods you can engage in impulsive and reckless behavior, feeling sure your behavior is justified. You may seek out substances in order to feel even better and may break rules and get into conflict with anyone who tries to set limits with you.
- If RCd is elevated, add: Although your answers suggest that you have been feeling demoralized, blue, that you have low self-worth, and often believe that life is a strain, your profile also shows that you have moods where you feel exuberant, "on top of the world," optimistic, and highly energized. When you are feeling in a highly activated mood you may do things impulsively that you could later regret.
- If RC1 is elevated, add: Your profile suggests that you are concerned about physical symptoms that cause you pain and discomfort. You are also reporting that you have mood swings where you feel excited and optimistic, and your thoughts race so that you cannot sleep. You may be concerned that all these symptoms are caused by a physical infirmity.
- If RC2 is elevated, add: Your answers suggest that you experience periods of depression and sadness, but also experience moods where you are extremely excited, energetic, and optimistic. Your thoughts may race so you find it hard to sleep. It may be that you cycle between depression and hypomanic moods.
- If RC4 is elevated, add: Your profile suggests that you dislike being controlled and can be impulsive and even manipulative in order to get what you want. It also appears that you have

moods where you feel exuberant, optimistic, and full of energy, where your thoughts race and you cannot sleep. It is possible that during these times of heightened activation you get involved in impulsive and risky behavior. You may also use substances that would likely increase your reckless behavior.

- If RC6 is elevated, add: Your profile suggests you are feeling vulnerable to people hurting, judging, or criticizing you. You may have periods when you are not sure whom you can trust. Your profile also indicates that when you become excited, optimistic, and full of energy your thoughts race and it is difficult to sleep. Perhaps, during these times of heightened energy, you can become somewhat suspicious and unsure about whom to trust. At these times, you may become convinced that you are seeing things clearly, and it might drive you into behavior that you feel is protective but may actually work against you.
- If RC7 is elevated, add: Your profile suggests that you have periods of worry and anxiety interspersed with periods where you feel exuberant, optimistic, full of energy, and have racing thoughts and difficulties sleeping. It is possible that these mood shifts are due to a medical condition. However, it is also possible that you can become so anxious that it drives you into a hyperactive mood where you feel driven and excited to deal with all your anxieties and worries.
- If RC8 is elevated, add: Your profile suggests that you are experiencing disturbing thoughts and experiences, perhaps hearing voices or feeling that someone has control over your mind. You also experience mood swings when you feel very energized, your thoughts race, and you are unable to sleep. At these times, your thinking may become even more confused and frightening. You may even become very suspicious, wondering if there are enemies who wish to harm you, or worry that someone is controlling your mind. Your therapist may suggest medicine to help you feel better and think more clearly.
- If RC9 is elevated, add: Your profile suggests you are a very energetic, driven, and ambitious individual. Your profile also suggests that you can experience moods when you feel even more exuberant, optimistic, and full of energy and big ideas. At these times, your thoughts can race so quickly that it is hard for you to speak them, and you may have trouble sleeping. During these times you may also overcommit to many tasks and activities, and perhaps impulsively do things without fully thinking them through.
- If MLS is elevated, add: Even though you report feeling tired and unwell most of the time, you are also reporting that, at times, you feel excited, exuberant, optimistic, and full of energy. During these mood swings your mind might race, making it hard for you to sleep. If you experience a mood shift from feeling depleted and tired to highly energetic and excited, it might reflect a mood disorder that medication could help.
- If NUC is elevated, add: You are reporting experiencing a number of neurological symptoms such as dizzy spells, numbness in your extremities, even fits and convulsions. At the same time, you are reporting experiencing mood swings where you feel exuberant, optimistic, and excited for no particular reason. At these times, your thoughts may race, and you may find it difficult to sleep. All these symptoms likely concern you.
- If EAT is elevated, add: You report that you have difficulties managing your eating habits, so that sometimes you restrict your food intake and other times you might purge. You report experiencing moods where you feel extremely energetic and excited for no particular reason. At these times, your thoughts might race, and you may find it difficult to sleep. It is possible that during this hypomanic mood, you restrict eating. It is also possible that you become aware of how hungry you are, and you gorge. Your energized mood could also be due to the side effect of starving yourself.
- If COG is elevated, add: Your answers suggest that you have been feeling concerned about your memory and are having difficulty focusing and concentrating. You are also reporting having heightened moods for no reason. Your thoughts race and you likely have difficulty sleeping.

These symptoms may be somehow connected, perhaps due to a hormonal imbalance or a side effect to using substances. It is possible that you have a neurological condition that your therapist will evaluate.

- If SUI is elevated, add: Your responses reveal that you have been thinking about suicide, and you often wish you were dead. Your profile also indicates that you have periods of high energy and excitability. During these periods, your thoughts race and you find it difficult to sleep but also feel excited for no particular reason. It is possible that during these highly energized mood swings, you do not think about suicide. It is also possible that it is at these times you think about ending your life. It would be important for you to discuss with your therapist what happens during these mood swings and when your thoughts about suicide occur. If you feel hopeless and suicidal and cannot reach your therapist, call a suicide and crisis 24/7 hotline [988 in the United States and Canada] for confidential support.
- If HLP, SFD, and/or NFC are elevated, add: Your profile suggests that you may experience periods of excitability and hypomania, where you feel happy for no particular reason. Your thoughts might race, and you may find it difficult to sleep. Then you experience periods when you feel hopeless, worthless, and doubt yourself, finding it hard to make decisions and get things done. You and your therapist should discuss what precipitates these mood swings. Are they triggered by an event where you feel excited because you have been successful and then you crash? Or do your moods switch without knowing what triggered you?
- If STR and/or WRY are elevated, add: Your answers suggest that you often feel stressed and worried that something bad is going to happen. You may worry about money and possible future misfortunes. However, you also reported that you can experience periods where you are very excited for no particular reason, with racing thoughts and difficulty sleeping. Sometimes these mood swings can be precipitated by hormone imbalances, medication side effects, or substance use. You suggested that you experience periods of severe anxiety and a sense of impending doom, but you also have periods where you feel extremely energized, optimistic, and excited for no reason. During these high-energy times, your thoughts race and you likely find it difficult to sleep. It is hard to know whether the periods of anxiety occurred during your hypomanic episodes or whether you get exhausted by anxiety and something switches so that you suddenly feel exuberant and happy. It is possible that these mood switches can be due to hormonal problems, substance use issues, or even medication side effects. In some cases, these mood swings can occur because of a chemical imbalance.
- If CMP is elevated, add: Your profile suggests that you have some compulsions or behaviors where you feel you have to do things in a certain way or something bad will happen. Your answers also suggest that you have periods of a heightened energy level when you feel excited for no particular reason and your mind races so you cannot sleep. It is difficult to know during these episodes whether you become compulsive as a way to manage your energy. Or do you give up your compulsions when you are in an excited, energized mode?
- If ARX is elevated, add: Your answers suggest that you experience periods of severe anxiety, with a sense of impending doom. At the same time, you have periods where you feel extremely energized, optimistic, and excited for no reason. During these high-energy times, your thoughts race and you find it difficult to sleep. It is hard to know whether the periods of anxiety occur during your hypomanic episodes or whether you get exhausted by anxiety and something switches so that you suddenly feel exuberant and happy. It is possible that these mood swings can be due to hormonal problems, substance use, or even medication side effects. In some cases, these mood swings can occur because of a chemical imbalance, causing a mood disorder.
- If ANP is elevated, add: You reported having periods of excitability where you feel exuberant and happy for no particular reason. At these times, your thoughts might race, and you may find it hard to sleep. At the same time, your profile suggests that you can be irritable and easily angered, perhaps holding a grudge when someone upsets you. You may have episodes when you

are energized and excitable but easily knocked off balance by frustration. You might become angry and irritable with people if they do not move as quickly or as efficiently as you would like. Once you have expressed anger or thrown a temper tantrum, you might then switch to being excited and exuberant. It is also possible that, given your high energy, the world moves too slowly for you and so you become irritable when people do not do things at the same pace as you would like.

- If AGG and/or AGGR are elevated, add: Your answers suggest that you have periods of intense high energy, when your mind races, you find it difficult to sleep, and you are easily excited for no apparent reason. Your profile also suggests that you can become angry and irritable easily and may be impatient with a world that moves more slowly than you would like. You might use your anger to get people to do the things you want done and even intimidate people into giving you what you want with the threat of your temper.
- If FML is elevated, add: Your profile suggests that you experience conflicts with your family and cannot count on them for support. It is possible your episodes of high energy and excitability have concerned them, so they may come across as critical or controlling, attempting to show you that your mood swings could be hurting you.
- If SUB is elevated, add: Your answers suggest that you have periods when you are highly excitable, with your mind racing and difficulties with sleep. It is possible that these hypomanic episodes are the result of your use of substances. Many substances can have side effects of high energy, excitability, and racing thoughts. It is also possible that your hypomania came before you started using substances and that you turned to substances as a way to self-medicate your episodic mood swings.
- If IMP is elevated, add: Your profile suggests that you can be quite impulsive, responding to situations without really thinking through consequences. You also report having periods when you feel excited for no real reason. At these times, your thoughts might race, and you may find it difficult to sleep. During these times you may also become even more impulsive than usual. This might lead you to engage in reckless behavior that could have severe negative consequences.
- If SFI is elevated, add: Your profile suggests you have periods when you are highly excited and exuberant for no particular reason. You may have a lot of energy, with racing thoughts and difficulties sleeping. Since you feel that you have something important to say to people during periods when you are particularly energized, you may dominate the conversation and come across as extolling your own virtues.
- If DOM is elevated, add: When you are in your excited, high-energy mode, you may come across as domineering, telling people what you think in direct or even harsh terms. Sometimes you may come across as bossy, imposing your will on others. You may not mean to do that, but if people see you as domineering or self-centered, they likely will resist giving you what you want.

Lifestyle and Family Background Feedback – ACT Scale

It is not always easy to know what precipitated your periods of high energy and excitability. If either your caregivers or members of your extended family have experienced mood swings, that would suggest a possible genetic component. It is possible that you were a highly energetic child, perhaps even diagnosed with ADHD. If you have experienced periods of intense energy and mood swings throughout your life, you may be diagnosed with a bipolar disorder for which medication can be helpful. It is also possible that your mood swings are the result of a medication side effect, the use of substances, or the result of a long period of intense stress. Your therapist would likely want to take a history to determine how to help you utilize your energy and excitability so that it does not work against you.

Treatment and Self-Help Suggestions – ACT Scale

Self-help strategies for managing hypomania can be effective when paired with professional support. Here are some approaches.

1. Learn your triggers and early symptoms, such as increased energy, reduced need for sleep, or impulsivity. Keep a journal or use an app to track your mood, energy level, and sleep patterns to help you take control over your mood swings.
2. Maintain a consistent routine. Prioritize a regular sleep schedule, even when you are feeling like you do not need as much sleep. Eat a healthy, balanced diet with regular mealtimes to stabilize your energy level. Limit caffeine, alcohol, and other substances that can exacerbate overactivity. Moderate exercise can help alleviate excess energy, but when you are in your excitable mood, be mindful not to overdo exercise.
3. In an excitable mood you may feel "anything is possible" and be vulnerable to making impulsive decisions, so avoid taking on too much and limit your commitments. You may also seek out intense, exciting environments that could overstimulate you.
4. Practice mindfulness techniques, meditation, or deep breathing to ground you and calm your thoughts.
5. Share your experiences with trusted friends or family to help you manage your moods or join online or in-person support groups for people with similar challenges.
6. Set clear goals before taking action. Take a moment to think about any decision's long-term effects and decide if it will help you achieve your goals. Give yourself a "24-hour rule" before making any major decisions.
7. Be sure to take any medications as prescribed and discuss concerns with the professional who is treating you.
8. Consider therapy, such as cognitive behavioral therapy, to help if your overactivity becomes a challenge.
9. If overactivation leads to risky behavior, contact a mental health professional or crisis service immediately. If you feel hopeless and suicidal and cannot reach your therapist, call a suicide and crisis 24/7 hotline [988 in the United States and Canada] for confidential support.

Aggression (AGG) Scale

General Descriptors

Complaints

Concerns about a violent temper, including explosive behavior and physical altercations; interpersonal, work, or legal problems related to losing control.

Cognitions

Blaming; externalizing; indifferent to others' feelings.

Emotions

Volatile; vindictive; callous; possible feelings of remorse; anger; short-tempered.

Traits and behaviors

Interpersonally abusive; possibly physically aggressive; manipulative, using the threat of bad temper; easily agitated or aggravated.

Therapist's Notes – AGG Scale

The 6 items on this scale describe physically aggressive behavior and having a callous attitude about engaging in such conduct. Aggressive behavior can be manifested across a number of mental disorders captured by the DSM-5-TR, such as intermittent explosive disorder (IED). The cardinal feature with IED is a deficiency in controlling impulsive aggressive behavior in response to subjectively experienced triggers.

Elevations on the AGG scale predict an individual who can resort to aggression without obvious provocation and with aggression that is not particularly instrumental. Unlike elevations on AGGR, which measures the threat of aggression as a manipulation to obtain a goal, individuals with high AGG scores approach life aggressively in general. They can be vindictive, wanting to punish others for any perceived transgressions. They may enjoy making people afraid of them without having a goal in mind. These individuals can resort to physical violence when frustrated. Certain scale elevations are more likely to be associated with aggression reflecting a personality disorder. It is theoretically possible that other psychological conditions can lead to aggressive behavior. There have been, for example, situations when an individual with severe physical problems and chronic pain became violent with healthcare providers. For example, a combat veteran with PTSD may develop severely aggressive behavior even though their profile predicts severe depression and anxiety. Consequently, the elevations on other scales will provide clues as to what could be driving physical aggression and whether it is reflecting a stable personality type or a reactive disorder.

Because problems associated with AGG item endorsements may require immediate attention, it is important to explore with the test-taker the meaning of any endorsed items.

Lifestyle and Family Background – AGG Scale

Family backgrounds can vary with elevated scores on this scale. High scorers may have experienced caregivers as being bullying and abusive toward them. This may have led to an identification with the aggressor who modeled self-control poorly. From an early age, they may have developed an angry "chip on the shoulder" attitude, ready to argue their case either verbally or physically. Some may have been bullies or been bullied as children, and so they approach others with defensive, aggressive attitudes and behaviors.

In terms of lifestyle, these individuals may anticipate resistance or frustration in their lives and so approach things in a ready-to-react stance. They lack insight and their frustration leads to aggressiveness.

Clarifying Scales – AGG Scale

- If EID is elevated, conceptually it may be hard to imagine that anger would also be elevated. Depression is often considered as "anger turned inward" with resulting withdrawal and passivity. However, aggression could counter feelings of helplessness and hopelessness. Should the depression manifest as aggression, antidepressant medication could mitigate it.
- If THD and/or PSYC are elevated, there is concern that paranoid and thought-disordered thinking, combined with aggression, could lead to episodes of unprovoked aggression. An aggressive individual, ready to do battle and driven by paranoid ideation, could potentially be dangerous.
- If BXD is elevated, the client is rebellious, impulsive, self-serving, and expresses anger or the threat of their bad temper manipulatively to get what they want from others. Although they may be charming until frustrated, they can also show flashes of anger and even violence when confronted or frustrated.

- If RC1 is elevated, although unlikely, it is possible that the client has developed a bullying aggressiveness in response to the medical system that they find frustrating. It is also possible that an aggressive individual has developed somatic symptomatology and may navigate the medical system using their traditional response style of immediate aggressiveness when feeling frustrated or disrespected.
- If RC4 is elevated, it predicts substance abuse and impulsiveness. This, combined with aggressiveness, suggests the possibility of unpredictable, impulsive, violent outbursts that can lead to interpersonal problems and, potentially, legal problems.
- If RC6 is elevated, combined paranoid ideation and aggressiveness would suggest an individual who is vulnerable to explosive outbursts that they perceive as justified and self-protective, given that they feel vulnerable to criticism and attack from others.
- If RC8 is elevated, aggressiveness may be self-protective as a way to keep people at a distance and may include bizarre clothing and piercings that reflect alienation from others.
- If RC9 is elevated, the individual's hypomania suggests impatience and irritability, especially if blocked in goal-oriented activity. Impatience and irritability could manifest as vindictive or even violent, abusive behavior.
- If NUC is elevated, it is possible that the explosive anger could be part of a neurological condition. However, in the presence of a history of anger and aggressive behavior, the two conditions may be uncorrelated.
- If ANP is elevated, it confirms that anger is a serious problem. The individual is reporting that anger is very close to the surface much of the time. They feel easily irritated and impatient. The combination of ANP coupled with elevated AGG suggests the potential for violent behavior.
- If FML is elevated, the client may have become alienated from family due to their explosive and violent behavior. It is also possible that their conditioning experiences with their family were violent and abusive.
- If IMP and/or ACT are elevated, the likelihood of impulsive aggression, intimidation, and mood swings that could lead to violence is increased.
- If SFI is elevated, the client may use violence and intimidation with the justification that they feel important, special, and deserving of being taken seriously.
- If DOM is elevated, the client's need for dominance and to be in a leadership role is punctuated by explosive anger or even violence, perhaps when the client feels they are not being taken seriously.
- If AGGR is elevated, the client is reporting that their explosive, at times violent, behavior is instrumental in trying to get what they want. They use the threat of their bad temper to manipulate others into acquiescing and giving them what they want. They enjoy intimidating others and can be vindictive.

Therapy and Therapeutic Pitfalls – AGG Scale

When dealing with high scorers, the therapist should predict the transference by suggesting that the client may, at times, experience aggressive feelings toward the therapist. Articulating the boundaries early on in therapy would be important. The therapist could explain to the client that they understand that, at times, the client is going to feel angry and even aggressive, and that threats toward the therapist cannot be tolerated. Articulating aggressive impulses could be permitted, as long as there is no direct threat. The setting of boundaries should be done in a caring, rather than in an authoritarian manner, since any suggestion of authoritarianism toward the client will likely lead to immediate anger toward the therapist. Since therapists are generally empathic and caring people, dealing with someone who is potentially a bully and intimidates others can be difficult, so dealing with countertransference is essential. Attempting to see the client as a frightened child rather than an abuser of others is important.

Cognitive behavioral therapy is usually the most appropriate therapy. The client should learn to recognize what triggers them and find behavioral ways not to act on their impulses. Exploring childhood conditioning experiences of abusive caregiving could also be useful. Helping the client to develop empathy for those that they have intimidated could be constructive, especially if it involves close family members. Explore possible insecurities and fears of inadequacy that could be driving their need to intimidate others and be vindictive. Once a client can express anger toward their therapist without it breaking the therapeutic relationship, therapy can move forward on a deeper level.

Feedback Statements – AGG Scale

T score = 39

Your profile suggests that you control your temper and do not intimidate others with aggressive statements or tendencies. You do not lose your cool easily.

T score 49–55

Like most people, you can get frustrated and irritable, and you occasionally show flashes of temper.

T score 62–70

You can have a short fuse and blow up when stressed. Sometimes you can lose control and become aggressive and even violent.

T score 78–86

Your profile suggests that you can become physically aggressive, even violent, when frustrated. It reveals that you can be explosive, possibly get into physical altercations, and actually enjoy intimidating others.

- If EID is elevated, add: Your answers suggest you have been suffering from depression, feeling “less than” others and that life is a strain much of the time. Your profile also indicates that you have a temper and can get quite aggressive with people. Perhaps because you feel badly about yourself most of the time, feeling blue and unable to enjoy life, you occasionally intimidate others, getting aggressive or even violent. Perhaps you feel unfairly criticized or so stressed that you have little cushion to deal with frustration. You may blow up and get aggressive or even violent when frustrated. Perhaps your moods swing from feeling depressed and withdrawn to being angry and confrontational with others.
- If THD and/or PSYC are elevated, add: Your profile suggests that perhaps you are going through a frightening time right now, unsure of whom you can trust and fearful that you might be criticized, judged, or even attacked. You may have periods when you get confused and/or periods where you are sure you know who your enemies are. Your profile also suggests that you can get very angry, perhaps because you get frightened. You may intimidate people as a way of protecting yourself. At times, you may get so frustrated or frightened that you get explosive or even physically violent.
- If BXD is elevated, add: Your profile indicates that you are a rebel. You dislike being controlled and can be impulsive and reckless. People with your profile often use substances for the thrill of it. Your profile also suggests that you can be quick to anger and, at times, can be explosive

or even physically violent. If you feel controlled or that authority figures are coming on strong, you might respond with anger, sometimes intimidating people for the thrill of it. You are easily triggered by frustration or not getting what you want from people. When you use substances, you get triggered easily. Your anger and violence could get you into trouble with family, friends, and authority figures.

- If RC1 is elevated, add: Your profile indicates that you are experiencing a number of physical symptoms that may frighten you, especially since the symptoms may be hard to diagnose. You also have a temper and can be quite aggressive or even violent at times. You may enjoy intimidating others, perhaps to make yourself feel more powerful. It is hard to know whether you have developed this aggression because of a long history of physical symptoms that frightened you and made you lose faith in the medical system. Perhaps you lose your temper because you have felt powerless within the medical system to get your problems resolved. It is also possible that you have been a somewhat explosive and angry person for most of your life and these physical symptoms are relatively new.
- If RC4 is elevated, add: Your profile suggests that you are a rebel, dislike being controlled, and can be impulsive and aggressive. You may be using substances, likely increasing your vulnerably to being impulsive, breaking the rules, and getting you into conflict with authority figures. Your profile also suggests that you are easily frustrated, going through life with an aggressive stance toward others. When frustrated, you might blow up and even get physically violent. If you are using drugs or alcohol, your vulnerability to aggression increases. At times you may enjoy intimidating others, perhaps as a way to feel in control or powerful.
- If RC6 is elevated, add: Your profile suggests you feel vulnerable to being judged, criticized, even attacked by others. At times, your sensitivity may shade toward suspiciousness, when you are not sure whether to trust people. You may also judge some people as out to hurt you or malign your reputation. Perhaps your temper and desire to intimidate others is intended to keep people away from you. You may become so convinced that you are vulnerable to being harmed that you get explosively angry or even aggressively violent.
- If NUC is elevated, add: Your profile suggests you are experiencing a number of neurological symptoms that may be hard to diagnose, which may frighten you. You are also reporting that you have a temper and can be explosive and, at times, even physically violent. You may have been an aggressive, explosive person before the neurological symptoms began, but it is also possible that your temper has developed at the same time as the neurological symptoms developed. If your explosive temper is recent, it would be important to discuss all your symptoms with a neurologist. It is also possible that you have been an aggressive person for quite a while and the neurological symptoms may be associated with the fact that you are so high-strung.
- If ANP is elevated, add: Your profile suggests that your anger is very close to the surface, so small frustrations can lead to anger. At times, that anger may become explosive and violent, and you may become physically aggressive with people. At times, your anger may drive you to want to intimidate people, perhaps to prove a point or make you feel more powerful.
- If FML is elevated, add: Your answers suggest you have a family who you cannot rely on and see as quarrelsome and unsupportive. Your profile also indicates that you have a temper, and frustrations can lead to explosiveness or even physical violence. Perhaps because you felt discounted in your family or had a caregiver who was very controlling, unreasonable, or abusive, you developed a tendency to intimidate people. When you feel frustrated, you can become physically violent. Perhaps you and your family do not get along because they are frightened of your temper. It is also possible that you are responding with anger to a family who you felt were unsupportive and unreasonable.
- If IMP is elevated, add: Your profile indicates that you can be quite impulsive, which can get you into trouble. Whenever you experience a strong emotion, your tendency is to act on it. From

some of your answers, it appears that you can impulsively blow up and even get violent when frustrated. At times, you like to intimidate others, perhaps to make yourself feel powerful. You might impulsively become aggressive and even hurt someone.

- If SFI is elevated, add: Your profile suggests that you have a very good opinion of yourself, and you feel that your ideas and opinions should be shared with others since you think they are valuable. You have a temper and can be abusive or even physically aggressive. You also can intimidate others, sometimes for the thrill of it and to show that you can. Perhaps you are aggressive and blow up if you think others are not listening to you or if you feel they are discounting your valuable opinions.
- If DOM is elevated, add: Your profile suggests that you like to be in control, in the driver's seat, and enjoy positions of authority and power. The profile also suggests that you have a temper and can blow up and be aggressive and, at times, potentially violent. Since you like being in control, that may be why you enjoy intimidating others – as a way of asserting your power and control. When people do not acquiesce to your authority, that could be when you are the most aggressive and potentially violent.
- If AGGR is elevated, add: Your profile suggests that you have a lot of difficulty dealing with anger and aggression. It appears you are going through life with a lot of anger that can easily bubble over into aggression and even violence. You may have learned to use aggression as a way of getting what you want, perhaps using the threat of your bad temper as a way to manipulate people. It is possible that this worked for you in the past, even though it can get you into trouble with people and make them fear and mistrust you. You are likely aware that your anger and potential for violence frightens people and you may use that to manipulate people into giving you what you want. The threat of your bad temper may lead people to avoid you and/or give in to your demands even though they may resent it.

Lifestyle and Family Background Feedback – AGG Scale

You may have grown up with caregivers who were bullying and abusive toward you. This may have led to you adopting this style as well. From an early age, you may have developed an angry "chip-on-the-shoulder" attitude, ready to argue your case either verbally or physically. You may have been bullied as a child, or you may have been a bully, and so you approach others with a defensive, aggressive attitude and behavior. You may anticipate resistance or frustration in your life and therefore approach things in a ready-to-react stance, which can lead to your aggressive behavior.

Treatment and Self-Help Suggestions – AGG Scale

Managing aggressive behavior involves recognizing triggers, developing coping strategies, and practicing self-regulation. At times, aggression can be a natural response, but learning to manage it can help you to build healthier relationships and improve your overall sense of wellbeing. Here are steps you can take to address aggressive behavior constructively.

1. Keep a journal to document situations or people that provoke aggressive feelings. These feelings often stem from stress, fear, frustration, or unresolved issues. When you are feeling aggressive, take a moment to try to identify what may be contributing to these feelings.
2. Challenge yourself to use words to describe your feelings instead of acting aggressively. Be aware of changes in your body that signal anger, such as an increased heart rate or clenched fists.
3. Practice techniques such as deep breathing, pausing for a moment, or walking away to defuse a situation. Mindfulness techniques and progressive muscle relaxation can reduce physical tension and help you stay calm in stressful situations.
4. Practice communicating effectively by expressing your feelings without judging or blaming others. Use "I words" (e.g., "I feel angry when …"). Use active listening, where you repeat

back what you heard, and pay attention to others' perspectives to minimize conflict and misunderstanding.

5. Establish a routine for stress management by ensuring adequate rest and a balanced diet to build emotional stability. Dedicate time to activities that make you feel peaceful and fulfilled and engage in physical activities to release built-up tension.
6. Share your feelings with a trusted friend, family member, or therapist to develop a support system. Join groups where people share strategies for managing anger and aggression.
7. Therapy such as cognitive behavioral therapy can help you identify and modify thought patterns that lead to aggressive behavior.
8. If your aggressive behavior has hurt others, acknowledge it and make amends.

Cynicism (CYN) Scale

General Descriptors

Complaints

Antagonistic interpersonal interactions and behaviors; sees others as selfish and not to be trusted; disappointed by others' imperfections and failings.

Cognitions

Cynical; sees people as selfish, self-serving, untrustworthy, prevaricating, and unfair; mistrusts others' motives.

Emotions

Emotionally cold; distant; aloof; lacks empathy.

Traits and behaviors

Sees relationships as transactional; low emotional investment in relationships; distrusts others; expects people to be self-serving and dishonest; avoids emotional vulnerability.

Therapist's Notes – CYN Scale

This 13-item scale measures the client's highly negative and cynical view of human nature. However, the content does not reflect that the client feels personally persecuted. High scorers view relationships as transactional, and they avoid emotional investment in them. They see people as lying, cheating, self-serving, unreliable, and prevaricating. They do not necessarily report distress since the scale is non-self-referential but are likely to be seen by others as aloof, if not cold, and hard to get to know. They likely come across as subtly, if not overly, critical, and not readily enthused or optimistic. Consequently, they have negative interpersonal experiences, since others will view them as sour, lacking empathy, and angry or even hostile. Socially alienated, the individual may be isolated, aloof, cold, or emotionally constricted. The *MMPI-3 Technical Manual* (Ben-Porath & Tellegen, 2020b) reports positive correlations with different aspects of interpersonal mistrust and psychopathic personality traits. An individual with elevations on the scale is unlikely to seek therapy unless a frustrated partner has threatened separation or there have been complaints from work colleagues that their aloof negativity is disruptive. Blame externalization is observed in high scorers with relationship problems.

Low scorers (T <39) are trusting, approval-seeking, tend to turn a blind eye to things that might bother others, and are vulnerable to using denial and repression as primary defenses. They are likely seen by others as agreeable and trusting to the point of being naïve. They may bottle up emotions repressing negative feelings which may then manifest in subtle ways.

Lifestyle and Family Background – CYN Scale

Childhood experiences of cynical people can vary, but certain early conditioning events may contribute to the development of a mistrustful worldview. Cynicism may have a genetic component. There may be a feedback loop whereby an individual approaches others with distrust, which leads others to view the individual unfavorably as negative and cynical. This reinforces the individual's cynical outlook, leading to a self-perpetuating pattern. Certain events in childhood may strengthen temperamental vulnerability to cynicism. Early betrayal or disappointment by trusted figures can condition the individual to be cautious about trusting. Promises that were repeatedly broken or situations where trust was exploited could have led to the client developing an adaptive response of incredulity. An early environment that was negative, with critical and pessimistic caregivers, may have reinforced a cynical attitude. Growing up in a family with adults constantly critical of each other and viewing the world through cynical lenses may have normalized cynicism as a way of approaching life to avoid disappointment and hurt. It is also possible that emotional neglect or the child's emotions being invalidated may have conditioned in the client caution about experiencing empathy for others. Experiencing or observing blatant injustices could also have led to the development of cynicism. Hearing a caregiver complaining about dishonesty, selfishness, and a lack of integrity in others may have modeled cynicism for the client. Consequently, cynicism could have been learned as an adaptive defense to avoid disappointment and vulnerability.

Family backgrounds of low scorers are likely varied. In some cases, an agreeable, suggestible, and naïve disposition could be genetic. In other situations, a sheltered upbringing in which individuals have been raised in overprotective households with a lack of exposure to deception or manipulation could have led to naïveté. It is also possible that an authoritarian and strict rule-based background might have led them to develop the trait of acceptance of authority without skepticism. It is also possible that caregivers who were nurturing, warm, generous, and democratic may not have developed children who were skeptical of others' intentions. There is some evidence that people who rely heavily upon others for decision-making may be highly suggestible. Social isolation and a religious background may also contribute to individuals underdeveloping healthy skepticism and cynicism.

Clarifying Scales – CYN Scale

- If EID is elevated, the individual is reporting low positive emotions, feeling depressed, pessimistic, overwhelmed, and constantly stressed. At the same time, they are reporting feeling cynical and distrustful of others. They maintain a self-protective emotional distance from others, which may aggravate their depression and lead to people avoiding them. Their depression is likely manifested as angry, critical, and negative toward others, without the communicative sadness that could promote empathy and support from others.

- If THD is elevated, confused, paranoid thinking is combined with a cynical, distrustful attitude. The individual will likely present as very reserved, aloof, suspicious, and feeling victimized and persecuted. They could be grievance collectors, meticulous chroniclers of perceived injustices, accumulating resentments and harboring smoldering resentments.
- If BXD is elevated, the client likely rationalizes their self-serving, manipulative behavior as justified, given their skeptical view of others. Seeing the world as a place where people lie, cheat, and steal rationalizes their own devious behavior.
- If RCd is elevated, the client's feelings of demoralization and defeat are likely aggravated by their feeling that the world is a place where no one can be trusted, and everyone selfishly takes care of their own needs. It is possible that the client blames their current distress on the way they feel others have treated them, but their cynicism would hamper any therapeutic attempts to deal with demoralization.
- If RC2 is elevated, their depression is likely angry and bitter rather than obviously sad. The client's distrust of others, negative view of people, and low empathy hampers them in developing sensitivity for themselves. This reduces their ability to process their sadness regarding past losses. They may view their depression as inevitable given that they see others as selfish and unfair.
- If RC1 is elevated, they may alienate healthcare providers with their negative and cynical attitude toward them. They may view their medical condition as not being treated adequately due to healthcare providers who they see as self-centered, unwilling to accept responsibility, and willing to lie to protect themselves. With the combination of these two scales, the client may be a poor risk for elective surgery since they are likely to approach treatment with a highly cynical attitude. Their cynicism toward medical professionals may actually lead to them receiving less warm and nurturing treatment, which further reinforces their maladaptive beliefs.
- If RC4 is elevated, it would confirm that the individual is highly distrustful of others and has difficulty with emotional vulnerability. They likely rationalize their acting-out, self-centered, and manipulative behaviors as justified, given that "everybody else is doing it, so why shouldn't I?"
- If RC6 is elevated, the individual mistrusts people, believing they are self-centered, selfish, manipulative, and devious. They feel that people are intentionally trying to hurt and mistreat them. They may be self-protectively preoccupied with collecting proof of others' malevolence toward them.
- If RC8 is elevated, confusion and thought dysfunction is combined with cynicism and a profound distrust of others. The individual will likely keep an emotionally guarded distance from others and be suspicious of any goodwill shown toward them. Their cynicism could be incorporated into psychotic symptoms whereby they view most people as potentially harmful to them.
- If RC9 is elevated, hypomanic behavior with racing thoughts and impulsive acts combines with an intensified cynical view of others. The individual would likely be opportunistic and demanding, viewing interactions as one coming out ahead and the other losing.
- If MLS is elevated, the individual is reporting feeling general malaise, tired, unwell, and weak. The client sees the world as a place where people lie, cheat, and are selfish. It is possible that their malaise is precipitated to some degree by a worldview that is distancing from others and does not promote social connections. It is also possible that, over time, feeling unwell has led to the client becoming grumpy and cynical, aggravating the physical experience of malaise.
- If NUC and/or COG are elevated, the client's cynical attitude may hamper their mental health treatment. Medical professionals may be less supportive, especially if the expressed complaints do not have an obvious medical explanation. It is more challenging for a medical professional to have empathy for a cynical, distrustful patient whose diagnosis is elusive.

- If SUI is elevated, the client's cynicism may aggravate their suicidal ideation. Lacking trust limits others' ability to provide support to the client when they are in need. It is possible that current stressors and difficulties have become unbearable as the client has few trusting, supportive relationships to rely upon.
- If HLP is elevated, the client's sense of helplessness and hopelessness is aggravated by feeling that people cannot be trusted, as they are malevolent and selfish. This likely adds to the client's sense of hopelessness. They have lost faith in themselves and others.
- If ANP is elevated, the client is reporting having a short fuse and being hot-headed, perhaps because they have little faith in others and distrust people's motives. They likely have difficulty interacting with people as they approach others with distrust and, consequently, fail to receive emotional support. Their resulting frustrations could then lead to angry temper outbursts because they view others as uncaring or even aggressive.
- If SUB is elevated, the client's use of substances may be a way to medicate their cynicism, which likely keeps them alienated from others.
- If AGG is elevated, the client's cynicism and distrust of others could make them vulnerable to explosive episodes, since they readily read self-serving motives into others' behaviors. They likely have little emotional control when they assume they are being lied to or unfairly treated.
- If AGGR is elevated, the client's cynicism rationalizes the need to use aggression and the threat of their bad temper in order to get what they want. Seeing the world through cynical eyes, and assuming that most people lie, cheat, and steal to get ahead, gives them permission to use aggression, or the threat of it, in order to further their own ends.
- If DSF and/or SAV are elevated, the client's cynicism has led them to avoid people or avoid building a community, instead preferring to be alone.
- If SHY is elevated, the client is reporting shyness, with a propensity for social anxiety. They are also reporting that they do not trust people and doubt their honesty. It is possible that the client developed cynicism because of a genetic propensity to shyness. However, it is also possible that they are genetically predisposed to shyness and, due to conditioning experiences, have learned to be cynical.

Therapy and Therapeutic Pitfalls – CYN Scale

Since therapy involves trust, the fact that cynical people do not generally trust can make it challenging to develop a therapeutic alliance. The client will likely project onto the therapist that the therapist is playing a role and being self-serving. Initially, warmth or enthusiastic validation from the therapist would likely be seen by the client as role-playing and telling the client what they want to hear. Positive affirmations likely will be met with, "But you are supposed to say that to try to make me feel better."

A clinical history looking for early childhood conditioning experiences that could have led to cynicism could be helpful in explaining to the client how their cynicism is an adaptive response, given what they experienced as children. In the presence of a history of caregivers letting them down, consistently breaking promises, or abusing authority, it would be helpful for the client to understand how their cynicism developed as an adaptation. Experiencing their caregivers as cynical, talking negatively about people, and appearing to praise people who take advantage of others could also have led the client to learn cynical behavior. In the initial sessions, perhaps when giving feedback from the testing, the therapist should predict the transference and develop a contract with the client so that when they experience feeling cynical and distrustful of the therapist, they have the courage to bring it up in therapy. The therapist should check in with the client on an ongoing basis to see if the client is experiencing the therapist as inauthentic, role-playing, or insincere.

With low scorers, validate that they are agreeable and conflict avoiders, liking to please, generally being non-aggressive, and instinctively wanting to see the best in people. Should naïveté and repression be an issue, use cognitive behavioral therapy to help the client set more effective limits without needing to be hostile. Explore possible conditioning experiences that could have led to the adaptive response of repression and denial.

Feedback Statements – CYN Scale

T score <39

Your responses suggest that you are a person who trusts others and generally sees the best in people. You do not assume that people are selfish or believe they are going to lie or take advantage of you. At times, others may see you as so trusting that they wonder if you are a little naïve. To avoid conflict, you may repress anger or irritation without even realizing it. Over time that irritation may leak out as subtle, joking sarcasm. While your agreeableness and good nature is positive and helps you get along with people, at times it may come at the expense of asserting yourself and setting effective boundaries.

T score 42–51

You have a realistic view of people, expecting them to be self-serving but generally wanting to do the right thing.

T score 55–60

Your profile suggests that you are somewhat cynical and may have trouble quickly trusting people. You likely see people as somewhat selfish, self-centered, and willing to lie or do things only in their own best interests. Before you completely trust anyone, they have to prove that they are trustworthy.

T score 66–79

Your profile shows that you have a cynical and negative attitude toward people. You see people as self-centered, looking out for themselves at the expense of others and willing to lie to protect themselves or get ahead. It is hard for you to trust or let your guard down since you assume that people are untrustworthy. You assume that most relationships are unhappy, and that people only make friends who are useful to them. It takes a lot for you to allow people to get close to you. When people share emotions with you, it is hard for you to trust that they are not role-playing for some manipulative reason, so you may not allow yourself to have empathy for them.

- If EID is elevated, add: You are reporting feeling depressed and lacking in self-confidence. You feel that life is a strain most of the time and that little gives you pleasure. You also report that you do not trust people. You feel people are self-serving and that most relationships are unhappy. You think that people look out for themselves and are willing to lie to get ahead or protect themselves. It is going to be hard for you to feel better since you do not trust people, which leaves you deprived of emotional support and feeling disconnected from others. You have built up a wall because you do not trust. You might have experienced a childhood when people let you down or betrayed your trust. Keeping a wall up from people may aggravate your current depression.

- If THD is elevated, add: It is difficult for you to trust people. Your answers suggest that you are fearful that people are judging you, critical of you, and maybe even going to hurt you. You see others as untrustworthy since you think most people lie to get ahead or avoid taking blame. You might think relationships are generally unhappy, and that people make friends only because it benefits them. You may be feeling self-protective, afraid that you are not safe and cannot trust anyone. You may find yourself collecting evidence against people you think might be your enemies and, perhaps, planning how to protect yourself.
- If BXD is elevated, add: Your answers revealed that you see the world as a "dog-eat-dog" place where most people are willing to lie to protect themselves or get ahead. You are quite cynical about people, feeling that they are generally not trustworthy. You believe that most people make friends to benefit themselves and that relationships are mostly unhappy. Consequently, since you do not trust others' motives, you do not open up and allow people to get close to you. Because of your view of the world, you rationalize that it is all right for you to bend rules to manipulate others and impulsively get what you want, since you think most people are doing that anyway.
- If RCd is elevated, add: You have been feeling unhappy and lack confidence. At times, you want to give up when things get difficult. You also have difficulty trusting people, feeling that they are selfish and willing to bend the truth to get what they want or get out of trouble. You likely see others as self-centered, uncaring, and self-serving. You may think most people make friends because it benefits them and that many relationships are not happy. This likely makes you feel demoralized since you do not think happiness is possible.
- If RC2 is elevated, add: Your answers suggest that you are depressed, feel blue, and sometimes wonder if life is worthwhile. You have developed a cynical attitude toward others, feeling that people are not to be trusted and are self-serving, and you are willing to lie to get ahead or avoid responsibility. It is hard for you to believe that people could be happy in relationships or that people could be generous because it gives them pleasure. It is possible that you have become depressed because you have been let down, so your cynicism has arisen from your past experiences. Seeing people as dishonest and self-serving may aggravate your depression, though, since it robs you of the chance to develop a caring support system.
- If RC4 is elevated, add: Your profile suggests that you can be a rebel, breaking rules to get what you want. You likely see the world as a "dog-eat-dog" place, so you rationalize your impulsive, self-centered behavior because you think you are behaving just like everyone else. You have developed a cynical attitude toward people, believing they lie to get ahead or avoid negative consequences. Your cynical attitude helps you rationalize that your own behavior is not so bad and believe that you have to look out for yourself, since everybody else is looking out for themselves.
- If RC6 is elevated, add: Your answers suggest that you feel vulnerable to being criticized, judged, or even attacked by others. You likely feel you have to protect yourself and be very vigilant for what others might do to you. Your profile also suggests that you have developed a cynical attitude toward people. You may think that most people will lie to get ahead or avoid negative consequences. It is hard for you to imagine that people can make friends because they enjoy them rather than because they can exploit them. You likely feel especially cautious about letting down your guard since you see most people as untrustworthy. You may feel that you have to collect evidence against people you see as potentially harmful.
- If RC8 is elevated, add: Your answers suggest that currently you feel very cautious about trusting others. You probably feel you have to keep a distance from others and not let them get to know you, since you fear they could use that knowledge against you. At times, your sensitivity to people might verge toward suspiciousness, where you are unsure about whether you are seeing them clearly and fear that they might hurt you. You do not trust people, seeing them as dishonest and feeling they look out for only themselves, so you likely avoid them. You might even have

ways to keep others at a distance, perhaps by wearing clothes that might frighten them or by staring them down as a warning not to get close.

- If RC9 is elevated, add: You are a high-energy individual and tend to think quickly, move quickly, and feel impatient with people who move too slowly. You are likely quite ambitious and driven. At the same time, you have a cynical view of the world. You feel that people are self-serving, dishonest, and cannot be trusted. Consequently, you may feel justified grabbing what you can get in life and manipulating others by bending the truth to get what you need. Since you assume everybody is looking out for themselves, you rationalize that you can pursue your own interests without feeling a need to look out for other people.
- If MLS is elevated, add: You are reporting feeling unwell, often tired, and weak. You also report that you see people in a somewhat cynical manner. It is hard for you to trust people because you think most of them lie to get ahead or avoid consequences. You perceive that few relationships are happy, so it makes you doubt that real happiness is possible. You think most people are self-serving and selfish, so you are cautious about letting others get close to you. This view of people may aggravate your malaise, since it will limit your development of a support system, leaving you feeling alone. It is possible that you have experienced some recent events when you felt let down and where your trust was broken. This may also have led to your feeling of malaise.
- If NUC and/or COG are elevated, add: Your profile suggests you have been experiencing some cognitive problems affecting your concentration, memory, and general efficiency. You might experience a number of physical symptoms that concern you. It is probably hard dealing with a medical system when specialists do not come up with realistic diagnoses of what is troubling you. Perhaps you have always been somewhat cynical about people and cautious about trusting others because you see most people as willing to lie to get ahead or avoid consequences. You may have become cynical because the medical system has not solved your problems, and you may feel that most medical professionals are self-serving and do not care about you. However, if you approach your medical providers with aloof caution and distrust, they may become less helpful.
- If SUI is elevated, add: You have reported having thoughts about suicide and have been thinking about how to do it. You also report that you do not trust people because you see them as self-serving and untrustworthy. You likely avoid being vulnerable with others because you feel that most people do not care about you and only care about themselves. You may have developed this cynicism as a protection against disappointment. However, viewing people as selfish and untrustworthy leaves you feeling very alone and probably magnifies your feelings that connecting with people isn't worth it. When you feel lonely and disconnected from others and afraid to be vulnerable, it likely aggravates your depression and feelings that you would be better off dead. If you feel hopeless and suicidal and cannot reach your therapist, call a suicide and crisis 24/7 hotline [988 in the United States and Canada] for confidential support.
- If HLP is elevated, add: You reported currently feeling hopeless and helpless to change things. At the same time, you feel that reaching out to people for emotional support is not worth it. Your answers suggest that you see people as selfish and self-serving and it is hard for you to believe that others can be caring, without ulterior motives. You appear to have lost hope in yourself and have also lost hope in others. That leaves you very lonely and likely aggravates your negative feelings.
- If ANP is elevated, add: Your answers suggest you have little faith in others, seeing people as selfish, self-serving, and willing to lie to get ahead and avoid consequences. Since you have this negative view of people when they frustrate you or when you perceive them doing something that you disagree with, you are quick to anger. You may be quick to get angry because you view people negatively and assume the worst in them. People may view your irritability and anger

negatively, so they avoid you or resist you in passive-aggressive ways. Thus, your anger may backfire.

- If SUB is elevated, add: Your answers suggest that you are vulnerable to abusing substances. Your answers also suggest that you have a negative, cynical view of people and see them as self-serving, selfish, and untrustworthy. It is hard for you to develop a support system to help you with substance abuse if you view most people negatively and anticipate that they are going to let you down or lie to you. It is also possible that your substance abuse has led people to withdraw from you and that you have developed a cynical attitude to protect yourself from being hurt. Perhaps they might have withdrawn from you because they felt that to continue to be connected with you was enabling you.
- If AGG is elevated, add: Your answers suggest that you have developed a cynical attitude toward others. You see people as lying, selfish, and self-serving. Since you have little faith in people, when frustrated you appear to have a short fuse, becoming angry or perhaps even explosive. Your negative view of people may be noticeable to them and may lead them to respond to you in rejecting ways.
- If DSF and/or SAV are elevated, add: You view people in a negative light, seeing most of them as selfish, self-serving, and willing to lie to get ahead or avoid consequences of their behavior. Since you view people this way, it makes sense why you avoid them and avoid being part of a supportive community. You likely feel that you are better off alone, where you cannot be let down or taken advantage of.
- If SHY is elevated, add: Your profile suggests that you are socially anxious. With new people, it takes time for you to warm up, since you likely dislike small talk. Your caution about opening up may also be due to the fact that you are cynical about people. You see them as willing to lie to get ahead and willing to take credit for work that others have done. It is hard for you to trust others, so it takes a while for you to let your guard down. Consequently, you are reluctant to meet new people since it takes so much energy to role-play being friendly when you feel cautious about being vulnerable.

Lifestyle and Family Background Feedback – CYN Scale

Your profile suggests that you have a cynical, distrustful view of people. You assume people are going to lie to get ahead and avoid consequences, and that they are generally self-serving and selfish. It is possible that you grew up in a family where you watched your caregivers disparage people, talk behind people's back, or behave in ways that revealed they thought that lying or taking advantage of others was a good way to get ahead. It is also possible that you experienced caregivers who betrayed your trust consistently and were not reliably supportive. They may have often been selfish, thinking of themselves rather than you. You may have developed a cynical attitude as a way to protect yourself against being disappointed. It would make sense that if you experienced caregivers who bent the rules, lied to you, and were willing to cheat to get ahead, that you would be cautious about trusting others, assuming that most people behave that way. The problem is that going through life suspicious and mistrustful of people's motives will lead them to resent that they are being judged negatively. They will then likely respond by being argumentative or negative toward you.

Treatment and Self-Help Suggestions – CYN Scale

You may be seeking therapy because a family member, friend, or co-worker in your life told you that you are too cynical. You may have noticed that your cynicism keeps you separated from others and may want to try to understand it better. It will be important for you to discuss with your therapist how you might see them as self-serving and that you think their being warm or supportive of you is a role-play to keep you as a client. Since from an early age you developed cynicism, perhaps as a way to protect yourself against disappointment in people, it is understandable that you may see your therapist through that same lens. Discover with your therapist how you have learned to view the world cynically and find small incremental steps to begin to trust others. You do not have to immediately trust people, but you could take small steps to try to find something positive about people's behavior so that you do not immediately judge them negatively.

Here are steps and self-help strategies to address and manage cynicism.

1. Identify the root cause of your cynicism by reviewing past emotional experiences, which may have included betrayals, disappointments, or unfulfilled expectations.
2. Keep a daily gratitude journal and observe and document the positive things in your life for which you are thankful, including instances of kindness in others. This trains your brain to notice the positives.
3. Notice when you tend to expect the worst and challenge that expectation. Question whether evidence supports your belief or if you are overgeneralizing. Consider whether there is a more positive way to view the situation.
4. Try giving others the benefit of the doubt, understanding that everyone has their own challenges that may not be readily apparent. Lowering your expectations can minimize disappointments and reduce your cynicism.
5. Limit time spent with pessimistic or critical people and add inspirational content on your social media feed. Consider volunteer work to remind you of others' kindness and compassion. Join a community group with positive goals.
6. Find the humor in life's absurdities rather than becoming disillusioned.
7. Engage in meditation or mindfulness exercises to stay present and observe your thoughts without judgment. Breathing exercises can help detach from cynical spirals.
8. Prioritize books, talks, and leaders who foster hope and optimism.
9. Consider therapy to help uncover underlying causes of your cynicism and develop strategies to foster trust and optimism.

8 Interpersonal Scales

Introduction

Development

The five MMPI-3 Interpersonal Scales have relational functioning as the central measurement focus. These five scales are Self-Importance (SFI), Dominance (DOM), Disaffiliativeness (DSF), Social Avoidance (SAV), and Shyness (SHY). All but DSF have interpretable low scores. As discussed in Ben-Porath & Sellbom (2023), these five interpersonal Specific Problems (SP) Scales include updated versions of DSF and SAV with the SHY scale remaining unchanged. The newly named DOM scale is modified from the MMPI-2-RF interpersonal passivity scale with a reversal of its scoring key.

The *MMPI-3 Technical Manual* (Ben-Porath & Tellegen, 2020b) shows normative test-retest coefficients ranging from .72 (DSF) to .91 (SHY) and internal consistency coefficients ranging from .65 (DOM) to .81 (DSF). The correlation between SAV and SHY, and between SAV and DSF, in both the normative and clinical samples are reliably the largest, consistent with the common theme of social isolation.

Convergent and discriminant validity for the Interpersonal SP Scales is extensively reported in the *MMPI-3 Technical Manual* as well as in the MMPI-2-RF literature supporting the construct validity of these scales.

Application

The Interpersonal Scales should be examined after protocol validity is established. If the profile is invalid, it cannot be interpreted at face value, although inspection of scale elevations may still yield valuable information about the test-taker.

Following validity considerations, the Higher-Order (H-O) Scales and Restructured Clinical (RC) Scales will serve as a compass pointing to possible specific Interpersonal Scales for further interpretive clarity. However, should an Interpersonal Scale be elevated without H-O and/or RC scale elevations, the scale(s) can nonetheless be interpreted. The Clarifying Scales sections of this chapter explicate which additional scales may help interpret elevated scores on the Interpersonal Scales.

DOI: 10.4324/9781003557920-8

Self Importance (SFI) Scale

General Descriptors

Complaints

Feels underappreciated; complains they are undervalued.

Cognitions

Sees themself as exceptional, brilliant, and unique with special talents; natural leader.

Emotions

Confident; self-important; feels superior.

Traits and behaviors

Seeks acclaim; sense of superiority; in some cases, delusions of grandeur; possible grandiose narcissism.

Therapist's Notes – SFI Scale

These 10 face-valid items give the client an opportunity to extol their own virtues and endorse themselves as exceptional. They believe they have unique talents, excellent leadership skills, and possess a brilliant mind with abilities unequalled by most people. The scale's development was intended to improve upon the coverage of grandiosity. However, high scorers may either be well-adjusted and self-confident or have narcissistic personality disorder traits or psychopathy. In the context of psychosis or mania, high scorers may be manifesting grandiose delusions.

Data collected with the original MMPI revealed that, in the 1950s and 1960s, the item reflecting the belief of being an important person was rarely endorsed. By the 1990s, the majority of people endorsed that item as True on the MMPI-2. Cultural values have changed, with caregiving emphasis on validating children's self-esteem in early childhood and encouraging children to see themselves as special, unique, and equal to others, regardless of performance. Recently, reality television has rewarded contestants whose confidence shades into grandiosity and narcissism. Culturally, therefore, it has become acceptable to claim exceptional abilities, with modesty sometimes labeled as a weakness. Thus, endorsement of some of the items on this scale would not necessarily mean the individual is narcissistic, it could suggest a high self-opinion or healthy self-esteem.

Elevations on this scale are unlikely to occur if elevations on scales measuring Self-Doubt (SFD), Inefficacy (NFC), Worry (WRY), or most of the Internalizing Scales are elevated. Intuitively, one would expect many of the Externalizing Scales, including Activation (ACT) and Impulsiveness (IMP), to correlate with elevations on the scale. Consequently, the rest of this chapter will explore the combination of scales that are most likely to occur.

Low scorers describe themselves as lacking in positive qualities. They likely present as modest and self-effacing, possibly with depressive feelings and ideation.

Lifestyle and Family Background – SFI Scale

Inflated self-importance may be one symptom of a manic disorder and, therefore, is transitory as the mania subsides. On the other hand, there are people whose inflated self-worth is an enduring narcissistic personality attribute. In some cases, their self-aggrandizement is based on actual remarkable accomplishments. Certain sports figures and politicians are good examples of people who can extol their virtues publicly and receive acclaim without apparent embarrassment or self-doubt.

Some cultures, for example the Japanese culture, value modesty and self-effacement in the interest of community cohesion. In the United States, brimming self-confidence and adamant statements of one's special skills and attributes is regularly exhibited in political debates, so a modest elevation on the scale may not be pathological and would need to be interpreted in the context of culture and the individual's actual accomplishments. Nevertheless, high elevations are likely associated with an unrealistic self-image that could cause problems interpersonally, as some people would likely find the individual's self-importance annoying.

Childhood experiences that might contribute to grandiosity and self-importance involve a dynamic interaction of emotional, cultural, and psychological factors. Children who were excessively praised and treated as special may develop a sense of entitlement or superiority. Caregivers who, for example, show off the children's accomplishments to their friends and relatives on an ongoing basis may instill in children a sense of their superiority and model for the child that extoling virtues is acceptable as a way of obtaining approval. In one example, a woman grew up in a family where achievement was essential as a way of obtaining love. She had a talent for playing the piano and whenever anyone visited, her parents would insist that she play the piano for the guests. She recounted how her parents would show disappointment and withdraw from her if she made mistakes or did not play exceptionally well. Her self-importance was, thus, compensatory for underlying feelings of unworthiness unless she was performing.

Messages that a child is better, smarter, or more talented than others can reinforce unrealistic self-perceptions. This is aggravated if caregivers demonstrate affection largely based on the child's achievements. A child may then equate self-worth with performance and external validation. Caregivers who overindulge a child and overly prioritize their needs may create an elevated sense of self-importance in the child. This could be aggravated by caregivers who pressure the child to excel in academics, sports, or other achievements, which could lead the child to internalize the need to be exceptional. It is also possible that early trauma could lead some children to develop a grandiose self-image as a protective defense against feeling vulnerable.

Clarifying Scales – SFI Scale

- If Behavioral/Externalizing Dysfunction (BXD) is elevated, the client is likely narcissistic and self-indulgent, rationalizing their manipulative, self-serving behavior as justified, given how unique, special, and deserving they believe themselves to be. An archetype would be a typical reality TV contestant who feels no shame in selfishly manipulating and being devious while, at the same time, telling the camera that they are exceptional leaders and deserve attention and approval.
- If Low Positive Emotions (RC2) is elevated with a low SFI score, the client likely feels depleted, lacking in vitality, and chronically depressed. If RC2 is elevated with a high SFI score the individual may report having exceptional talents and abilities, natural leadership skills with many brilliant ideas, and being both important and unique. They may be mirror-hungry personalities impelled to display themselves to elicit attention and admiration from others. This may likely be an attempt to counteract low feelings of self-worth.
- If Antisocial Behavior (RC4) is elevated, rebelliousness, antisocial behavior, impulsivity, and hedonism may be present, with brash overconfidence in their uniqueness and brilliance. Their self-image rationalizes their self-indulgence.

- If Hypomanic Activation (RC9) is elevated, the client may be exhibiting a manic state with hyperactivity, impulsiveness, and grandiosity. They likely offer an opinion on almost any matter, believing that their unique abilities and brilliance deserve to be listened to. They typically have a hard time listening, often interrupting others with their own thoughts and advice, even if it is not welcome.
- If Family Problems (FML) is elevated, the individual views their family as unsupportive and quarrelsome. They may have alienated their family with their inflated self-importance or may have a counterphobic response to having been put down and criticized as children. It is also possible that the individual's family, after years of over-rewarding them for being special and unique, has begun to set limits, which has led to family conflict. If SFI is low, high FML suggests familial degradation and lack of support in developing and fostering the person's self-esteem.
- If Substance Abuse (SUB) is elevated, the client is admitting to using substances that may have pushed them into a manic episode, expressing grandiose self-importance. Substances may increase grandiosity, which could be dangerous since the client has limited internal checks. If SFI is low, substance abuse may be used as a remedial self-stimulant to ameliorate and ward off painful feelings of deadness and boredom. Drug usage can be an attempt to shore up crumbling self-esteem.
- If IMP and/or Disconstraint (DISC) are elevated, the client's grandiosity and self-importance may be expressed impulsively without regard to social niceties and social mores. Bragging and forcefully expressing their thoughts, uniqueness, and ideas is likely.
- If ACT is elevated, the client may experience mood swings during which they become grandiose, self-important, and willing to extoll their own virtues and uniqueness. It is also possible that they manifest the attributes of self-importance, regardless of whether they are in a hypomanic state or not, and they increase their self-aggrandizing verbalizations if they are in a hypomanic state.
- If Aggression (AGG) is elevated, it predicts that the client may have a short fuse, with a tendency to become easily irritated, angry, and possibly explosive. At the same time, the client likely tells people about their own unique and talented attributes and how important they are. Perhaps the aggression is manifested when they feel disrespected or discounted. It is also possible that they do not control their aggressive behavior because they feel it is their right to be irritated with people who are less capable, less bright, less unique, and less special than they are. A very low SFI score with elevated AGG may indicate frustrations with others and a hostile attitude.
- If Cynicism (CYN) is elevated, the client sees people in a misanthropic manner and tends not to trust others, viewing their behavior as generally self-serving and dishonest. At the same time, they see their own behavior as unique, talented, and deserving approbation. They likely come across as "preachy," aloof, and judgmental.
- If DOM is elevated, the client's self-importance and inflated self-image blends with their sense of entitlement to be in charge, direct people, and boldly stand up for their own opinion. The client may be seen by others as a verbal bully or at least overbearing, and people may avoid them. They are likely seen as non-compromising and disagreeable.
- If SHY is elevated with a low SFI score, the individual may lack ambition and drive.
- If Aggressiveness (AGGR) is elevated, the client may approach others in an aggressive, argumentative manner, perhaps using aggression to get what they want. They likely come across as bullying to others with the threat of their bad temper, although they likely see their aggression as necessary to get through people's resistance. They may judge others negatively, believing people need to be treated aggressively to combat their stupidity, laziness, and inefficiency.

Therapy and Therapeutic Pitfalls – SFI Scale

Therapy with high-scoring SFI individuals would depend on how successful the therapist is in winning the client's trust and respect, fostering comfort for entering into a therapeutic relationship. As high scorers are sure of their uniqueness and brilliance, they likely will develop transference quickly, evaluating the therapist critically. Some may ask probing questions about the therapist's education, their standing in the mental health community, and any books or articles produced by the therapist to demonstrate their exceptionalness. Predicting the transference right from the start could be helpful. For example, start therapy by saying, "You have excellent self-esteem and exude self-confidence about your abilities. It is probably hard for you to respect people unless they are as smart and capable as you. You might put me through a number of tests initially to see if I am capable of dealing with you. Maybe we could start with you telling me your view of therapy, and what you would look for in order for me to prove that I am capable of helping you. What tests might I need to pass?" Therapy could progress to understanding the client's history to determine what early childhood conditioning experiences have led the client to believe they have to be exceptional, and that others need to recognize their exceptionalism for them to feel accepted and loved.

Low-scoring SFI individuals may show poor self-esteem and low positive emotions. On the other hand, they may be self-effacing people who do not feel a need to stand out from the crowd and are comfortable working behind the scenes in an organization.

Feedback Statements – SFI Scale

T score ≤40

Your answers suggest that you do not have many positive things to say about yourself. Perhaps you learned at an early age not to brag or even admit to your positive qualities.

T score 42–46

Your profile suggests that your self-confidence and self-esteem are somewhat positive. You may think your ideas are worth listening to and generally feel confident and important. When you feel something is important, you are not afraid to assert yourself and speak your mind.

T score 49–54

Your profile suggests you are self-confident. You feel you have something to contribute to others. You appear to be comfortable in your leadership skills, expressing your opinions with confidence and extolling your virtues to others.

T score 63–72

Your answers suggest that you brim with self-confidence about your abilities and talents. You see yourself as an exceptional and extraordinary person who is brilliant and a great leader. It is hard, perhaps, for you not to see yourself as a somehow superior person.

- If BXD is elevated, add: Your profile suggests you have very high self-esteem and feel that you are exceptional, brilliant, a natural leader, and a special person. Perhaps that is why you feel entitled to break rules that you deem stupid or think should not apply to you. You may feel justified in manipulating people and impulsively doing what you want. Perhaps because you believe that you have exceptional talents, you may feel the rules do not apply to you and so you justify taking advantage of people since they are less capable than you. While you probably get away with things, the downside is that people will see through you and lose trust in you, and some may even want to find a way to punish you.

- If RC4 is elevated, add: Your profile suggests that you are impulsive and can be manipulative and self-centered. You may justify these behaviors because you see yourself as special, unique, and brilliant, with great ideas, so you feel rules do not apply to you.
- If RC9 is elevated, add: Your profile suggests that you can have periods of excitability, high energy, exuberance, and surges of intense high energy. Your profile also suggests that you have exceptional self-esteem, and see yourself as unique, special, brilliant, and a great leader. Perhaps you episodically experience feelings of being gifted and special and then might crash at some later point. It is also possible that you feel unique and special most of the time and are not afraid to tell people about your talents, especially when you are in an energized mood.
- If FML is elevated, add: You report that you view yourself as having special talents and abilities as well as many brilliant ideas. You see yourself as extraordinary and a natural leader. At the same time, you view your family as unsupportive, quarrelsome, and unappreciative of you. It is hard to know whether conflict with your family has arisen because they do not value and validate your exceptionalism or whether you developed your high self-esteem in response to dealing with a family that was critical, negative, and judgmental of you. It is also possible that your family does not appreciate your talents because they may be jealous of your successes.
- If SUB is elevated, add: Your answers suggest you have very high self-esteem, seeing yourself as exceptional, brilliant, unique, and a natural leader. The profile also indicates that you are likely using substances, which may elevate your self-confidence and sense of self-worth. It is hard to know whether your strong belief in your exceptionalism is fed by substances or whether you have seen yourself as unique and exceptional even before you began using substances. The danger is that substances may be elevating your opinion of yourself, which could lead you to making rash or unrealistic decisions. For example, you may think that you have the capability to use drugs without them negatively affecting you.
- If IMP and/or DISC are elevated, add: Your profile suggests that you can be impulsive, acting on your feelings without always thinking through the consequences. Your answers also suggest that you see yourself as a unique and exceptional person. You think you have brilliant ideas and would make a good, natural leader. The profile suggests that you may impulsively express how exceptional you are to people, without thinking through whether it will lead to others judging you or seeing you as a braggart.
- If ACT is elevated, add: Your profile suggests that you may experience highly energized mood swings when you feel excited and "on top of the world." Your profile also suggests that you have a very high opinion of yourself, seeing yourself as exceptional, brilliant, unique, and an excellent leader. Perhaps when you are in one of your energized moods, you express to others your positive qualities and that you see yourself as exceptional. In some cases, when people have been on a high note with brimming self-confidence, they may crash and see themselves negatively. Or you may not have mood swings and may stay energized and excitable most of the time. In that case, your self-esteem and self-opinion are elevated most of the time and you enjoy telling people about your exceptional skills and talents without much concern about how they might view you.
- If AGG is elevated, add: Your profile suggests that you may become explosive if others fail to give you the recognition you believe you deserve. This may be because you see yourself as exceptional, with special talents and abilities. You see yourself as brilliant and a natural leader, so you may quickly become irritated when people do not value you appropriately, or if they are getting in your way with objections when you believe you have a good idea. You may feel entitled to be aggressive if people do not afford you the respect that you feel is due you.

- If CYN is elevated, add: Your answers suggest you see most people as untrustworthy, self-serving, and willing to lie to get ahead and avoid consequences. There is a big disparity between how you see people and how you see yourself. You see yourself as exceptional, with great talents and abilities, and you see others in a negative light. You might be tempted to give people your opinion, tell them how they should change, and maybe remind them of your exceptional qualities. People might resist that and become argumentative with you since they might see you as bragging and resent you for coming across as somehow superior to them.
- If DOM is elevated, add: Your answers suggest that you are comfortable stating your opinion and letting people know where you stand on things. You are not afraid to correct people if you think they are on the wrong path. If someone opposes you, you are willing to go out of your way to win the point. Since you also see yourself as exceptional, perhaps even brilliant, and a good leader, you might feel that it is your responsibility to correct people and let them know when they are on the wrong path. You may be resisted because others see you as too dominating and sure of yourself.
- If AGGR is elevated, add: Since you see yourself as exceptional, unique, and a great leader, you may sometimes feel a need to be aggressive with people to get done what you need done. Since you have self-confidence in your abilities and talents, you rationalize that sometimes using the threat of your bad temper is a reasonable way to deal with people that you see as less intelligent or capable than yourself.

Lifestyle and Family Background Feedback – SFI Scale

Having a high opinion of yourself is not necessarily a bad thing. There have been many people who have done exceptional things and been truly unique and outstanding. You may identify as one of them and so, understandably, want people to know your abilities. The danger is that when you extol your virtues, perhaps as a way of proving to people that you are worth listening to and being taken seriously, they may feel threatened and resent you. Sometimes people who have a sense of superiority grew up in an environment where caregivers continually praised them for performing and achieving. Perhaps you were outstanding in some aspects of your life, and your caregivers may have shown you off to family and friends – for example, by having you perform in certain ways for praise. You may have learned from an early age that the best way to get love and approval was by being very successful and exceptional. It is also possible that you grew up in an opposite type of environment, where caregivers were absent and did not reward you for success and achievement. Perhaps you are completely self-made, so you feel you are entitled to let people know how unique you are since you achieved a great deal on your own. You believe that one way for you to get love is to perform well. Perhaps you were able to be successful at performing well and so now you might feel justified in letting people know your exceptional qualities. The problem is that people may resent you and become passive-aggressive about helping you since they might see you as bragging.

Treatment and Self-Help Suggestions – SFI Scale

Here are some actionable self-help suggestions that focus on cultivating humility, empathy, and perspective.

1. Shift the focus from yourself by keeping a gratitude journal and note 3–5 positive thoughts about others every day.
2. Work on your communication skills by listening more and talking less. Show that you are interested in others' thoughts and experiences by asking open-ended questions.

3. Volunteering will remind you of the importance of empathy and community.
4. Apps like *Headspace* or *Calm* can help you observe your thoughts and guide you in developing self-awareness and humility.
5. Solicit honest feedback from trusted friends or colleagues about how you come across, how your behavior changes when you are under stress, and what opportunities you may have for improvement.
6. Read books like those by Ryan Holiday, the Dalai Lama, Desmond Tutu, or Nelson Mandela to appreciate the value of humility in creating growth and joy.
7. Encourage team success over your receiving individual recognition in the workplace and highlight the contribution of others.
8. Build humility and patience by learning from others when beginning a new hobby or activity.
9. Take a break from social media or set limits on your use of it in order to reduce your focus on external affirmation.
10. Acknowledge your own imperfections and try not to take yourself too seriously.
11. Surround yourself with people who value authenticity to help build self-awareness and encourage humility.

Dominance (DOM) Scale

General Descriptors

Complaints

Conflicted relationships.

Cognitions

Sees self as a good leader; prefers to be in charge; thinks of self as the right person to correct people; opinionated; assertive; blunt and direct.

Emotions

Self-confident; frustrated if rebuked.

Traits and behaviors

Domineering; controlling; persuasive; competitive; self-confident; blunt; rude; antagonistic; decisive.

Therapist's Notes – DOM Scale

This 9-item scale was originally labeled Interpersonal Passivity (IPP) on the MMPI-2-RF but the keying has been reversed for the MMPI-3 to reflect the more common dysfunctional correlates linked with maladaptive dominance. Low scores reflect sub-assertiveness and possible dependency traits. High scores pertain to dominance, including in its maladaptive forms, such as narcissistic and histrionic personality disorders, psychopathy, and trait disturbances.

Dominance traits can be manifested in a number of personality types. Intuitively, one might view dominance as a trait manifested mostly by hypomanic, highly activated individuals or egocentric, narcissistic, self-important individuals scoring high on RC9 and RC4. One would not expect dominance to be elevated on scales measuring worry, self-doubt, anxiety, shyness, or depression and, in fact, they are negatively correlated. However, conceptually it is possible that a highly anxious, insecure, or depressed individual can become domineering as a way of controlling their environment in order to deal with their anxiety or low self-esteem. The traits previously described certainly will make someone appear dominant, but the way those traits are expressed can vary, with some people being more aggressively dominant and others combining dominance with empathy or diplomacy.

People exhibit domineering behavior due to a number of dynamics, including psychological, social, and biological. For example, some people are naturally more assertive and extroverted, making them more likely to take charge in situations. Biologically, higher testosterone levels are linked to dominance and assertiveness. Some people have a strong desire to control their environment due to anxiety or insecurity. For example, a highly anxious, compulsive person could appear controlling and domineering. In other cases, dominance can be associated with exceedingly high self-esteem manifested by a very skilled expert in a particular field. In many cases, however, dominance can arise as an overcompensation due to insecurity. Some cultures, as in the United States, encourage assertiveness as a desirable leadership skill. Other cultures (for example, the Japanese) discourage it. People who are highly competitive with a need to win can manifest competitiveness as domineering behavior. Understanding what drives their dominance would be an important part of the initial evaluation. Maladaptive dominance would likely lead to conflict and resistance from others as well as conflicted relationships. Establishing a therapeutic alliance can be challenging with an overly domineering client.

Lifestyle and Family Background – DOM Scale

Since domineering behavior can arise for a number of reasons, there is not one particular lifestyle or family background associated with it. Individuals with low dominance may have been punished for expressing themselves early on and learned to conceal their wishes and desires, resulting in passive-submissive traits. Clients with a genetic predisposition to assertiveness may develop dominance, enhanced by authoritarian and strict caregivers. In other cases, dominance could have developed in response to overly indulgent caregivers who rewarded aggressive, assertive behavior, leading to the individual believing they are naturally deserving of authority. Alternatively, a childhood history of neglect may have led to dominance as a defense mechanism to regain a sense of control and as emotional self- protection. Obtaining a childhood history would help tease out if the individual was a domineering child, suggesting a genetic predisposition, or developed dominance in response to caregiving styles.

Clarifying Scales – DOM Scale

T score 27–38

These individuals are unassertive. They allow others to take control in various situations and can be passive and submissive. They avoid leadership roles and tend to be self-effacing. If SAV, SHY, and/or Introversion/Low Positive Emotionality (INTR) are also elevated, the client will likely come across as quiet and needing encouragement to speak up in a group discussion. Elevations on SFD, NFC, and/or Anxiety-Related Experiences (ARX) would support that the individual's passivity is partly related to extreme self-doubt, inefficacy, and anxiety.

T score 40–49

These individuals can express their ideas or positions on matters without inhibition and are not likely to be perceived as sub-assertive.

T score ≥58

These clients describe themselves as having strong opinions and a need to express them. They are seen as assertive and direct, seeking leadership roles, which they feel ideally suited for. They do not "back off" or "lean in" during an argument – they feel a need to win the point and let others know where they stand on things. These individuals can manifest excessively assertive domineering behavior.

- If BXD is elevated, the archetype of an opinionated, impulsive, potentially substance-abusing "blowhard" comes to mind. Self-confident in their abilities and the correctness of their opinions, the client is easily drawn into an argument since their communication style is argumentative and self-promoting.
- If RC4 is elevated, the client will be quick to stand their ground and argue their point of view. They may become even more assertive and opinionated when using substances. They are vulnerable to impulsively express their anger and forcefully express their opinions.
- If RC9 and/or ACT are elevated, hypomania associated with elevations on these scales energizes the expression of dominance and self-importance. The client may be loud, excitable, and opinionated, readily and impulsively expressing themselves in blunt, direct, possibly grandiose ways.
- If Anger Proneness (ANP) is elevated, the individual is quick to express anger, impatience, and general irritability at the same time as verbalizing firmly held beliefs in a direct, blunt, self-confident way. Irritability and anger expressed toward people might be followed with explanations of why the anger is justified and why the other person is "wrong."
- If SUB is elevated, the use of substances may lower the threshold of the client's tendency to be opinionated, direct, and dominant. Thus, the individual could be disinhibited and more likely to be argumentative and domineering.
- If IMP is elevated, the client may impulsively express opinions and be overly assertive and dominant, with a tendency to take leadership roles without taking stock of the appropriateness of their behavior. They likely will miss social cues that might inhibit their expression of dominance.
- If AGG is elevated, the expression of dominance is mixed with anger and aggression. The client's anger may be expressed in an argumentative, domineering manner with a veiled threat of aggression.
- If SFI is elevated, this would suggest a dominating, opinionated, narcissistic individual who believes they have exceptional qualities and abilities that they are willing to extol to others. Believing in their own brilliance, they have almost no constraints on being assertively dominant and usurping leadership roles.
- If AGGR is elevated, the client is likely to use the threat of aggression as a way to intimidate others into doing things their way. Overly assertive and opinionated, they likely express their opinions against the backdrop of possible aggression should they not be taken seriously or respected.
- If DISC is elevated, the client's dominance and opinionated assertiveness will impulsively manifest itself, without taking into consideration how socially appropriate it is. This would be especially true if RC9, ACT, IMP, and/or SFI are also elevated. In one example, an employee in his late 20s was referred for psychological coaching by his manager. The manager observed that the employee, when sitting in on high-level meetings, would impulsively jump in and offer his opinion when it was not appropriate. He had been tasked with observing and learning, so the manager had not thought to tell him to stay quiet, believing that the employee would read the room correctly. The employee found it hard to understand why his behavior was being questioned.

Therapy and Therapeutic Pitfalls – DOM Scale

Engaging in psychotherapy involves developing a trusting relationship with a therapist and the willingness to abdicate control to some degree, allowing a therapist to function as an emotional and psychological guide. The client needs to at least internally acknowledge that they do not know all the answers. An individual scoring high on DOM is likely approaching therapy with a somewhat defensive, argumentative stance, finding it difficult to accept information and advice from someone else. This dynamic should be explored early on in therapy, thus managing the possible transference, and pre-empting the client's need to be assertive with the therapist out of a need to be dominant. It is also important to validate the client's strengths, potential leadership skills, and decisiveness, since this will possibly pre-empt, initially at least, negative transference, while later challenging behaviors that can alienate others.

Once trust has developed, therapy should help the client explore the underlying reasons for their behavior. An inherited predisposition to dominance and/or conditioning experiences such as caregiving dominance could be factors in its development. The goal of therapy is to help the client develop self-awareness of how their behavior affects others. Gestalt therapy can be helpful in role-playing with the client how they might come across to others. Examine childhood dynamics for trauma and/or how a caregiver's dominating and overly assertive behavior was impactful. Dominance could be a defense mechanism, hiding deep-seated insecurity. However, it could also be the manifestation of a narcissistic, self-centered individual. Role-playing exercises to help the client step into another person's shoes could be helpful. Once the client has developed some self-awareness and behavioral techniques, joining a group would be useful. Group therapy would be especially useful since the client is likely to manifest the tendency toward dominance in group settings, which could elicit feedback from group members. Help the client to distinguish between healthy assertiveness and dominance. Cognitive behavioral therapy is probably most useful once psychodynamic therapy has uncovered possible conditioning dynamics.

Feedback Statements – DOM Scale

T score ≤38

Your profile suggests that you are not an assertive person. You are comfortable letting others take control while you take a more passive role. You tend not to actively compete for leadership positions, although you might accept a leadership role if you feel particularly competent. You tend to be self-effacing and do not feel a need to convince people of your opinions. [If any of the Internalizing Scales are elevated, add:] You may withdraw from taking leadership roles and not assert yourself because you doubt yourself and feel anxious and incompetent.

T score 40–49

Your profile suggests that you are willing to assert yourself and tell people your opinion and where you stand on things. You are confident in your leadership skills and your ability to make a good argument about your point of view.

T score ≥58

Your profile reveals that you have described yourself as a person with strong opinions and are comfortable expressing those opinions to others. People likely see you as assertive, direct, and wanting to take leadership roles. You tend to not back off in an argument nor "lean in" in order to preserve the peace. Rather, you feel the need to win the point and let others know where you stand on things.

- If BXD is elevated, add: Your profile suggests you are impulsive and, at times, rule-breaking. You may impulsively tell people your opinions. You are ready to confront people if you think that they are wrong about something. You likely think you will make a good leader and do not shrink from asserting yourself. You may come across to people as somewhat undisciplined and dominant. If you are using substances, you may get into more arguments with people because you tend not to back down in a confrontation, as these substances will decrease your self-control.
- If RC4 is elevated, add: Your answers suggest that you are impulsive, live in the moment, and are willing to break rules if they do not work for you. You also are quite dominant – comfortable with asserting yourself and telling people your opinion. Seeing yourself as a leader, you are not afraid to take charge in a situation, even if you do it impulsively. If you are using substances, they likely disinhibit your impulse control, which could create conflicts with people, since you do not back down from disagreements.
- If RC9 and/or ACT are elevated, add: Your answers suggest you have a lot of energy and drive and are excitable. You likely experience surges of energy where you feel optimistic and excited for no particular reason. Being highly energized, you are willing to tell people your opinions and take a leadership role. You do not back down in an argument easily. Others likely see you as dominant and assertive, willing to confront people if you disagree with them. You likely feel that you need to correct people if you think they are on the wrong track and might feel it is necessary to go out of your way to win a point with someone who has opposed you.
- If ANP is elevated, add: Your answers suggest that you have a short fuse, things easily irritate you and make you angry. At the same time, you express your opinions in direct, blunt ways, perhaps feeling a need to correct people. You are not afraid to take control in situations and can go out of your way to win a point with someone who has opposed you. When you get impatient or angry with people, you may justify it by explaining what, in your opinion, they did wrong. People might resist you, feeling that your anger and dominant personality are intimidating.
- If SUB is elevated, add: Your profile suggests that you may be using substances. Since you also scored high on a scale measuring dominance, assertiveness, and a willingness to forcefully express your opinion, substances may disinhibit you meaning you may express yourself in ways that backfire. People may avoid you when you are impaired, concerned you will get on your "high horse" and argue your opinion.
- If IMP is elevated, add: You admitted to being somewhat impulsive. You also reported that you are comfortable being dominant and assertive, telling people what you think and forcefully arguing your point. You are willing to go out of your way to win a point with someone who has opposed you and you will confront people if they have made you angry. You may have a tendency to speak your mind impulsively, assume a leadership role, or correct people, which could lead to people resisting you or becoming argumentative and angry.
- If AGG is elevated, add: Your profile suggests that you are a person who tends to be dominant, assertive, direct, and blunt with people. You are not afraid to speak your mind or go out of your way to win a point with someone who has opposed you. However, your answers also suggest that you can do this with anger and even aggression, perhaps raising your voice in an argument, getting emotionally upset, or correcting people for what you see as their mistakes.
- If SFI is elevated, add: Since you believe that you are an exceptional person with unique abilities, you are not afraid to speak your mind and assert yourself. You tend not to back down in an argument and can go out of your way to win a point with someone who has opposed you. You might come across as domineering and self-confident to the point that people may judge you as narcissistic. You may feel that you have a special talent, so people should respect you and be open to your opinions and insights.

- If AGGR is elevated, add: Your answers suggest that you can be quite dominant and assertive, expressing your opinions and thoughts in a blunt, direct way. Your profile also suggests that you can come across as aggressive, perhaps even using the threat of aggression as a way to manipulate others into doing what you want. People may avoid getting into discussions with you out of concern that you can get wound up, angry, and loudly argumentative.
- If DISC, RC9, ACT, and/or IMP are elevated, add: Your answers suggest that you are impulsive and, when you become emotional, you tend to move into action without thinking through all the consequences. At the same time, you test as someone who is dominant and assertive, willing to speak their mind and not afraid to correct people if you feel they are wrong in their beliefs. You go out of your way to win a point with someone who has opposed you and are willing to tell people when they make you angry. Sometimes you may confront others impulsively or feel the need to correct them, which could lead to people becoming angry with you and argumentative if they feel that you embarrassed or humiliated them.

Lifestyle and Family Background Feedback – DOM Scale

Dominance as a personality trait can occur for different reasons. Sometimes people with your profile grew up in an environment where a caregiving figure was dominant, assertive, and perhaps overly strict. It is possible you learned from an early age that being assertive, speaking your mind, and standing up for yourself was the right way to get along. It is also possible that your caregivers encouraged your dominance, perhaps rewarding you for being more assertive with your peers and validating that you deserved to speak your mind and take a leadership role. In some cases, people with your profile had caregiving figures who rewarded success, accomplishment, and winning, so you learned to approach others with a dominant, assertive manner, as if life is a constant competition. In still other cases, people with dominance are genetically predisposed to being assertive and easily taking leadership roles. You may have been that way as a child. In other cases, a person could have developed dominance from having survived early childhood trauma, instilling in them a self-confident desire to speak their mind and get what they want, since they excelled in spite of early adverse experiences.

Your current lifestyle suggests that the ease with which you tell people your opinions and fill leadership vacuums may be a successful strategy if you do it delicately and are mindful of how you are coming across to people. It is also possible that people might avoid you so as not to deal with your opinionated views and your direct and brusque manner.

Treatment and Self-Help Suggestions – DOM Scale

Addressing domineering behavior involves self-reflection, developing better communication skills, and building healthier relationships. Here are some self-help suggestions to work on this behavior.

1. Keep a journal to help you identify situations where you might have been domineering. Document each event and how you felt as well as how others responded. Ask trusted friends or family members about your behavior and listen non-defensively to their input. Identify the triggers that led to these behaviors, like stress or fear of losing control.
2. Develop active listening skills by focusing on listening to the perspectives of others without interrupting. Repeat back what they have said to confirm your understanding. Put yourself in the other person's shoes to gain empathy for them. Remind yourself that you don't always have to correct people, even if they made a mistake or you have the right answer.
3. Practice communicating effectively by expressing your feelings without judging or blaming others. Use "I words" (e.g., "I feel angry when …"). Practice active listening, where you

repeat back what you heard, and pay attention to the perspectives of others to minimize conflict and misunderstanding. Be willing to engage in a back-and-forth discussion and don't feel you need to have the final say. Prioritize achieving a solution that benefits everyone.

4. When you feel the urge to dominate a situation, wait a moment before jumping in. Even if there is a leadership void, don't feel that you need to fill it.
5. Use mindfulness techniques, meditation, or exercise to reduce stress and minimize impulsive behaviors.
6. Trust in other people's capabilities so you don't feel a need to control every detail. Delegate tasks and responsibilities with the understanding that things may not be done exactly as you would have done them, and that's okay. Make an effort to acknowledge the efforts and achievements of others.
7. Classic books such as *How to Win Friends and Influence People* (Carnegie, 2009) and *Leadership: The Power of Emotional Intelligence* (Goleman, 2011) offer valuable lessons in emotional intelligence and interpersonal relationships, as do podcasts, courses, or workshops on the subject.

Disaffiliativeness (DSF) Scale

General Descriptors

Complaints

Complains about other people wanting to get close to them.

Cognitions

Sees people as bothersome; dislikes others; little interest in others.

Emotions

Emotionally disconnected; may have extinguished need for tactile responding; emotionally constricted; inhibited humor reflex.

Traits and behaviors

Avoids and dislikes people; asocial; cold; aloof; uncommunicative; avoids social relationships; possibly schizoid; takes no pleasure in activities with others.

Therapist's Notes – DSF Scale

This 7-item scale focuses on an individual's aversion to being with others and assesses for a noxious aspect of introversion. Disaffiliativeness measures the potentially schizoid aspect of introversion. The individual claims to actively dislike people, prefers to be alone, and wants to avoid emotional relationships with others. They may dislike being touched or surrounded by people and recoil at unexpected expressions of physical or emotional affection toward them. They generally do not respond favorably to praise or criticism from others. They likely avoid eye contact and may dress as inconspicuously as possible. Sudden unexpected attention can be distressing. and these clients avoid expressing warmth and intimacy, even to family members. They generally will avoid psychotherapy since the trust and intimacy involved might be threatening to them. They are unlikely to be impulsive, aggressive, manipulative, self-important, or dominant. Rather they are quiet, retiring, and likely passive.

People who score high on disaffiliativeness tend to be at higher risk for depression and anxiety disorders as well as schizoid personality disorder. It is also possible that the extreme withdrawal from others expressed in the scale may be a reactive disorder due to a recent or past trauma. In the absence of a history of withdrawal from others, the elevation may be a symptom of PTSD or other disorders involving lack of interest in close relationships. Developmentally, individuals with elevated DSF scores should also be assessed for deficits in social-emotional reciprocity as seen in those on the autism spectrum.

Lifestyle and Family Background – DSF Scale

Symptoms of extreme withdrawal from others often begin when a person is a young adult, although some symptoms might be noticed as developmental deficits in childhood. The symptoms may make it hard for the individual to do well in school or in social situations, but they may do well if a job can be completed while mostly working alone. Extreme social withdrawal is probably a result of a combination of biological, psychological, and environmental factors. Environmental factors vary, but there are some common themes in the childhood of individuals with extreme social withdrawal or detachment. From a young age, many of them may have had difficulty forming close relationships. They likely felt socially awkward, misunderstood, and out of sync with their peers. Signs of social withdrawal can be evident early, since as children they likely had few, if any, close friendships, preferring solitary activities rather than group interactions. Some had eccentricities that could have made them targets for bullying and exclusion. Some likely exhibited eccentric thinking, with creative or unique interests. They may have had difficulty accurately perceiving social cues. In some cases, these individuals grew up in neglectful, unstable, or traumatic environments. A lack of consistent emotional warmth and caregiving may have interfered with the development of secure attachment and trust. A genetic predisposition could also be a factor if there is a history of family schizophrenia spectrum, developmental, or mood disorders. On the other hand, it is possible that the individual grew up in a family where emotions were not discussed, where there was adequate caregiving but without emotional connection. In other words, elevations on the scale may not necessarily indicate psychopathology, but could just point to extreme social detachment.

Clarifying Scales – DSF Scale

T score 55–58

The client dislikes people and dislikes being around them.

T score 65–78

The client is definitive about not wanting to be around others, enjoying time alone, and finding being around others tedious and unpleasant.

- If Emotional/Internalizing Dysfunction (EID) is elevated, the individual is socially isolated and dislikes being around people, but at the same time is reporting depression, anxiety, and negative emotional experiences. People exhibiting disaffiliativeness are more vulnerable to depression and anxiety since they avoid community support and opportunities to connect with others. The depression treatment may involve building social skills.

- If Thought Dysfunction (THD) is elevated, consider schizotypal personality disorder or, potentially, schizophrenia. The individual is socially isolated but also possibly paranoid, with unrealistic thinking and a possible thought disorder.
- If Demoralization (RCd) is elevated, the individual's social isolation and withdrawal from people is co-morbid with experiences of sadness, pessimism, low self-esteem, and helplessness. Since the individual has difficulty relating to others when experiencing trauma or stress, they have no one to turn to, which could increase their feelings of demoralization.
- If RC2 is elevated, the individual presents with anhedonia, is socially disengaged, pessimistic, and lacks energy. Low positive emotions may be an artifact of the individual's dislike of being around people and so, in times of stress, they have no emotional support systems, which increases the chance of depression.
- If Ideas of Persecution (RC6) is elevated, the individual is socially isolated and has persecutory beliefs. The client is likely suspicious and distrustful, seeing themselves as a victim. The isolated, paranoid individual, rarely seen by neighbors except when they are threatening people for crossing their lawn, is an archetypal example. In some cases, the individual may feel a need to collect weapons to protect themselves.
- If Dysfunctional Negative Emotions (RC7) is elevated, the socially isolated individual is also anxious, extremely stress reactive, and has difficulties with sleep. They tend to worry excessively and are self-critical, guilt-prone, and tend to obsessively ruminate. Their reality testing is impaired by their uncommunicative relationship with others. It is possible that their anxiety and self-doubt are factors in keeping them socially isolated.
- If Aberrant Experiences (RC8) is elevated, the social isolation, together with thought-disordered unrealistic thinking, would suggest a possibility of schizophrenia. The individual may have psychotic delusions aggravated by social isolation. The client likely lives in a chaotic inner world with marginal self-care and a cold rejection of others.
- If Suicidal/Death Ideation (SUI) and/or Helplessness/Hopelessness (HLP) are elevated, the individual may experience suicidal ideation and attempts, reflecting their difficulties with social relationships, loneliness, and sense of isolation. They may feel defeated in being able to develop social skills.
- If SUB is elevated, the socially isolated individual is likely to experience impairment in social functioning resulting from substance abuse.
- If CYN is elevated, the client's social isolation is rationalized and justified by their belief that people are self-serving, untrustworthy, ungiving, and look out only for their own self-interest. The client likely comes across as sour, aloof, and suspicious.
- If SAV is elevated, it would suggest that the client is profoundly socially isolated, actively avoiding any kind of social interactions. It could reflect a socially avoidant personality disorder.
- If SHY is elevated, the individual may be avoiding social interactions because they feel inhibited, anxious, and nervous about social situations. They may feel awkward and experience panic in social situations if they are called upon to speak. Or they could feel taken off guard by a social interaction for which they were not prepared.
- If Psychoticism (PSYC) is elevated, it would suggest the possibility that the client is manifesting a schizotypal personality disorder or other psychotic condition. The individual is reporting unusual thought processes and reveals unrealistic thinking with impaired reality testing. The client likely avoids people and may manifest paranoid ideation. They may be preoccupied with their safety and may seek weapons to protect themselves.
- If INTR is elevated, it would confirm the picture of someone who prefers to be alone and dislikes parties, big social events, and meeting new people. They generally do not experience many positive emotions.

Therapy and Therapeutic Pitfalls – DSF Scale

Since psychotherapy is essentially a social interaction, individuals who score high on this scale would likely avoid it. These individuals may not see social detachment as a problem and may be reluctant to seek help. The initial goal of therapy would be to develop a therapeutic alliance, which would involve the therapist being careful not to invade the individual's very strict boundaries. A simple handshake or even an acknowledgment without physical contact might be appropriate. The therapist should move somewhat slowly and not explore any emotional experiences the client may have. The first order of therapy would be to normalize the individual's behavior, providing a non-judgmental space for them to feel understood and accepted, giving them permission to accept that they are uncomfortable around most people, and that the therapist would like to understand how that arose. Was it a genetic trait? Was the individual as a child most comfortable being alone, and how did that affect their experience of school, which is a social experience? Therapy should avoid attempting to have the client emote over painful experiences. The therapist needs to dial down the intensity that they would normally anticipate in a therapeutic relationship. Should the client want help to better connect with a loved one or others, cognitive behavioral therapy is most appropriate. This could help identify and potentially challenge any negative beliefs about relationships and the downside of emotional vulnerability. Therapy could encourage gradual exposure to social interactions and address any beliefs reinforcing isolation. Should the client be open to it, psychodynamic therapy could explore the root causes of emotional detachment, such as having had a distant and emotionally disconnected caregiving figure.

Feedback Statements – DSF Scale

T score 48–52

Your answers suggest that you are quite self-sufficient and feel comfortable being alone. You find it difficult to be around people, generally preferring to be alone.

T score 55–58

Your answers suggest that while there may be some people you enjoy being around, generally you prefer alone time and are cautious about getting too close to people.

T score 65–78

Your answers suggest you are very much a loner. You like to be alone and actively dislike being around most people. You likely find small talk very difficult and dislike it. You likely feel emotionally self-sufficient, so opening up and sharing emotions with people is something you do not enjoy doing.

- If EID is elevated, add: You like being alone and avoid being around people. However, you also report periods where you feel quite down, unhappy, and blue. It is hard to know whether your current depression has made you want to withdraw from people or whether being socially isolated has left you feeling somewhat down and anxious.
- If THD is elevated, add: Your answers suggest that you are quite isolated, living in your own inner world. You may be experiencing some paranoid thoughts, feeling vulnerable and insecure. You likely find being around people difficult, preferring to be alone. It is hard to know whether you have withdrawn from people because you see them as dangerous, or whether you have always been somewhat of a loner, preferring your own company to being around others.

- If RCd is elevated, add: You report that you prefer to be alone and dislike being around people in general. At the same time, you are reporting feeling demoralized, sad, pessimistic, and, at times, helpless and hopeless. You are also reporting that you are your own worst critic. It is hard to know whether you have withdrawn from others because you have been feeling unhappy and dissatisfied with life. It is also possible that your sense of demoralization has arisen because you are so isolated, having difficulty being around people, so you don't experience social support.
- If RC2 is elevated, add: You report that you prefer to be alone and not around people. You also report that not much gives you pleasure these days, that you often feel drained of energy, and that you lack positive emotional experiences. At times, you might feel quite sad, even depressed, and pessimistic about the future. It is hard to know whether you have withdrawn from people because you have been feeling down and believe that you are not good company to be around or whether you have always been somewhat of a loner and that depression has caught up with you.
- If RC6 is elevated, add: Your answers suggest that you are very much a loner, keeping away from people and preferring to be alone. You also may be experiencing some suspicious thoughts, perhaps concerned that other people are going to hurt you and are out to get you. You might be feeling victimized and, therefore, think you need to protect yourself. It is hard for you to trust anyone right now and that may be why you prefer to be alone.
- If RC7 is elevated, add: Currently you report feeling most comfortable being alone and avoiding being around other people. It is possible that you have withdrawn from people because you experience so much anxiety and are so self-critical and guilt-prone. Perhaps worrying constantly about what people think and wondering if they are being critical of you has made you want to withdraw and just be alone.
- If RC8 is elevated, add: Some of your answers suggest that you are a loner, preferring to be alone rather than being around other people. You may be avoiding people because you feel scared they have bad intentions toward you or you think that they are saying cruel and mean things about you. You may have periods when you are not sure what is reality, and whether you are being overly suspicious or are seeing things clearly. You may be preoccupied with finding ways to protect yourself in case you are in danger.
- If SUI is elevated, add: Your profile indicates that you have been thinking a lot about ways to end your life. You also report that you are a loner, tending to prefer your own company rather than being around people. It is possible that your social isolation has gotten to you, and you are feeling suicidal because you cannot see a way to be with other people. Perhaps you doubt that you have the social skills to reach out to others. It would be important to talk to your therapist about these feelings. If you feel hopeless and suicidal and cannot reach your therapist, call a suicide and crisis 24/7 hotline [988 in the United States and Canada] for confidential support.
- If CYN is elevated add: You report that you are a loner and dislike being around people. You feel happier being alone. This may be because you have a cynical view of people and see them as self-serving, lying to get ahead, ungiving, and untrustworthy. You see people as only looking out for their self-interests. Consequently, you feel justified in staying away from others, since you feel relationships are far too much trouble.
- If SAV is elevated add: Your answers suggest that you avoid social interactions and generally do not like most people, preferring to be alone. Perhaps this is because you have trouble opening up emotionally and trusting that you can let down your guard with others.
- If SHY is elevated, add: Your answers suggest that you are a loner, preferring time alone rather than being with other people. You may avoid people because social interactions are stressful since you feel inhibited, anxious, and nervous in most social situations. If people begin to talk to you or call on you by surprise, it is very uncomfortable for you. You might even experience

occasional social anxiety and social panic attacks. It is understandable that you try to avoid being with others.

- If PSYC is elevated, add: Your answers suggest that you avoid people and prefer to be alone rather than around others. Your profile also suggests that you may be feeling unsafe right now, preoccupied with how people are treating you and concerned for your safety. When alone, you may get caught up in your inner world and may develop fantasies that you have difficulty distinguishing from reality.
- If INTR is elevated, add: You report being a loner, preferring spending your time alone rather than being around people. You dislike parties and social events, and you do not like to meet new people. You probably find small talk tedious. At the same time, it may be hard for you to watch people having fun, being engaged, and appearing to enjoy life when you do not enjoy much in life. It is possible that you have withdrawn from people because you feel awkward in new social situations.

Lifestyle and Family Background Feedback – DSF Scale

People develop a preference for being alone for a number of reasons. Perhaps you were a somewhat shy, retiring child, finding it more comfortable playing alone in your room rather than having sleepovers or being with large groups of friends. Or perhaps you were the type of kid who had one best friend with whom you shared a special hobby. Because you were somewhat shy, other kids may have teased you, further convincing you to stay away from people. It is also possible that you grew up in a family with caregivers who did not socialize and who took care of you but were not emotionally expressive. Perhaps you grew up in a family that did not value emotional connections. They may have placed more value on practicalities. From an early age you may have learned to avoid feeling connected to others with a preference for the safety that you felt when you were alone.

Treatment and Self-Help Suggestions – DSF Scale

While professional help, such as therapy and possibly medication, is often helpful for those who are uncomfortable being around others, there are self-help strategies you can adopt to improve your quality of life and manage symptoms more effectively. Explore with your therapist whether you were a shy, introverted child and how that might have affected you and your view of relationships with others. Also explore whether your caregivers were somewhat emotionally aloof and did not nurture you with a lot of physical affection. Here are some self-help strategies for managing your discomfort being around others.

1. Since you prefer to be alone, you may feel justified in keeping your distance from others. However, should you want to feel a little closer to others, there are some things you can do. People often feel awkward in social situations, perhaps because they are suspicious or mistrusting of others or they experience social anxiety. To improve your social interactions, you can start with brief, low-pressure encounters, like saying "hello" to a neighbor or asking a co-worker about their weekend. To gain confidence, you can practice with a therapist, trusted friend, or family member. In social situations, if you focus on listening without feeling a need to speak, it can reduce pressure on you.
2. You may have a tendency to interpret situations in ways that further isolate you or contribute to your mistrust by viewing things in an overly negative or unrealistic manner. Try to identify and challenge these distorted thoughts. When you catch yourself thinking negatively or suspiciously, replace those thoughts with more balanced ones.
3. You probably have lost interest in emotional connections with others. By focusing on what you are feeling, you may be able to develop some empathy for others. Mindfulness can help you

to stay grounded in the present moment and reduce anxiety. This can be especially useful if you tend to feel overwhelmed by intrusive thoughts. Mindfulness practices like deep breathing and progressive muscle relaxation can help you stay calm and manage the physical tension associated with stress.

4. Develop a structured daily routine, with time for work and relaxation, to reduce the unpredictability that leads to feelings of confusion, anxiety, or discomfort. Although you may not be interested in developing close friendships, you can take small steps, such as greeting neighbors or making eye contact with a cashier when you check out. Notice what you are feeling at those times so you can determine whether your anxiety is warranted.
5. Though you may not enjoy being around people, even a small amount of social interaction could be good for your overall health. If you are open to low-key socializing, consider joining a class or group that fits your interests, like an art class or book club. You can begin interacting very gradually by just smiling initially and, when you are comfortable, making brief comments.
6. Start slowly and celebrate each small success, and they will add up over time. Plan small rewards for yourself to reinforce your actions. Treat yourself kindly and try not to be too harsh with yourself. Remind yourself that you are doing the best you can.
7. Understanding your personality style can help increase self-acceptance. There are a number of books and articles that can help you understand your thoughts and behaviors. Online communities can offer support, provide validation, reduce isolation, and allow you to stay connected with people.
8. You may have trust issues and feel suspicious of others, so build trust gradually with close friends or family members. You may wish to find a therapist who is patient and supportive. If you are in therapy, focus on building a trusting relationship with your therapist.
9. Cognitive behavioral therapy or schema therapy can help you address your social challenges. You may benefit from medication, especially if you are also experiencing another condition like depression or anxiety. A qualified professional can help evaluate whether medication might be appropriate.

Social Avoidance (SAV) Scale

General Descriptors

Complaints

Dislikes crowds; dislikes meeting strangers; difficulty making friends; self-conscious.

Cognitions

Anticipates social discomfort; rationalizing social avoidance; belief in their social ineptitude; ruminations over interactions.

Emotions

Social anxiety; insecurity; emotional sensitivity; loneliness; possible anhedonia.

Traits and behaviors

Avoids social situations; fearful of rejection; avoids novel experiences; compares self unfavorably to others; ruminates over interactions; possible avoidant personality disorder.

Therapist's Notes – SAV Scale

There are 9 items comprising this scale, which measures the degree of interest in socializing with others. High scores reflect social introversion, emotional constriction, and challenges in forming close relationships. Low scores reflect social extroversion and gregariousness. Introversion and extroversion are both linked to genetic predispositions and environmental influences. For example, post-traumatic stress disorder can cause social avoidance, and people with autism spectrum disorder experience difficulty with social communication and may avoid people.

Individuals scoring high on SAV avoid social interactions because they experience discomfort, anxiety, and self-consciousness around people. They may desire more social connection and may not actively dislike people but find being around people anxiety-provoking. They may experience anticipatory anxiety before social interactions, imagining "worst case" scenarios such as the possibility of being embarrassed by being unable to think of things to say. They may rationalize social avoidance, thinking it is easier to stay away from others. Their self-image is of lacking social skills and dreading small talk. Elevations on the scale do not suggest that the client does not want to connect with others, but rather that they are conflicted out of fear of being rejected and embarrassed. They likely ruminate over any recent interactions, analyzing their responses and assuming they "messed up," especially if SFD, NFC, Stress (STR), WRY, or ARX are elevated. High scorers avoid people to the point that it can be disruptive to their lives. Unlike shy people who enjoy relating to others and are comfortable once they know someone, people with an elevated score on SAV avoid others.

Social avoidance can occur for a number of reasons. Depression, with its low energy and low confidence, can lead to withdrawal from social activities. People with low self-esteem who have experienced bullying, abuse, or neglect may have learned to feel very uncomfortable when near others. Cultural and religious norms, such as the prohibition of male and female interaction, might lead individuals to avoid social interactions. Medical conditions, such as hearing or speech impediments, can lead to social avoidance and, in the later stages of substance abuse, people can withdraw socially.

Social avoidance is different from shyness. It is stronger, more persistent, and often tied to deeper issues like avoidant personality disorder or past negative social experiences. Social avoidance is motivated by a desire to minimize social contact, avoid fear or stress, and can lead to isolation, interfering with daily functioning. Shy people generally want to engage but feel inhibited, while those who engage in social avoidance actively choose to withdraw. Shyness is often situational and can improve over time as the person gets to know other people. Social avoidance is a behavioral response wherein the individual forcefully steers clear of social interactions. Determining the contribution of these various factors would be important in identifying effective treatment strategies.

Lifestyle and Family Background – SAV Scale

There is no typical background experience that leads to social avoidance. The individual's lifestyle is one of social avoidance and inner conflict, desiring social connections but anxious about the possibility of being embarrassed or rejected. Genetic studies on introversion have shown that social avoidance is a stable trait, tending not to change much over time. In some cases, high scorers may have been socially avoidant children who would experience anxiety, for example, when going on sleepovers with peers or separating from caregivers. They were probably socially retiring children who shunned the limelight and avoided getting into trouble. In some cases, they might have been "only" children in a family with caregivers who were socially avoidant with few social interactions. In some cases, children might have been withheld from interacting with peers for cultural or religious reasons and, so, never learned basic social skills.

Clarifying Scales – SAV Scale

T score <44

The client enjoys parties, describes themselves as highly social, enjoys meeting new people, makes friends quickly, and is energized and excited to be around crowds. Others will likely see them as outgoing, gregarious, and fun to be around. They likely score low on DSF, SHY, and INTR.

T score 44–55

The client can enjoy parties and meeting people but is also comfortable being alone and does not need to be constantly stimulated by others.

T score = 60

The client does not enjoy social events with large groups of people and does not see themselves as making friends easily. They do not find crowds exciting and do not find meeting new people easy and stimulating.

T score ≥66

The client is introverted and dislikes crowds, parties, and meeting new people. They are cautious about "opening up" and are emotionally constricted. They have difficulty forming close relationships since they tend to be "standoffish." They may have a diagnosis of avoidant personality disorder and may admit they are not sociable.

- If EID is elevated, the individual is acknowledging feeling depressed, overwhelmed, helpless, and having low morale. They are also uncomfortable with people and tend to avoid them, perhaps as a symptom of their depression and low self-esteem. It is also possible that their emotional internalizing dysfunction is partly a result of a lifelong discomfort with social interactions. This could have led to loneliness, low self-esteem, and depression.
- If THD is elevated, the individual is reporting distorted thinking with possibly paranoid and non-paranoid delusions. In some cases, paranoid and psychotic individuals may avoid interactions with others due to their paranoia. Social isolation, together with disordered thinking, could lead to bizarre behavior, possibly including conspiracy theories and eccentric rationalizations for their behavior. In the presence of conspiracy theories, an evaluation for dangerousness would be helpful.
- BXD is unlikely to be elevated when SAV is elevated. However, one could hypothesize a situation in which an antisocial, rebellious, substance-using individual is isolated and angry enough to plot antisocial activity in isolation.
- If RCd is elevated, the individual is reporting feeling lonely, demoralized, useless, worthless, blue, and inefficient; having difficulty starting things and giving up when things are difficult. They also avoid other people, perhaps due to their low self-esteem and self-confidence. The person may be genetically predisposed to social avoidance, which then led to the development of demoralization. Perhaps their social avoidance is the result of general demoralization.
- If RC2 is elevated, social avoidance may be an artifact of their depression, with anhedonia and low self-esteem. It is also possible that their depression is a result of a lifetime of social avoidance and, therefore, loneliness and self-doubt.

- If RC6 is elevated, the individual may be avoiding others because of paranoia. They may have developed elaborate conspiracy theories. Their social avoidance suggests they have few corrective experiences that could modify their paranoid ideation.
- If RC7 is elevated, the client may be avoiding social events because of their anxiety, self-doubt, and preoccupation with avoiding criticism and embarrassment. It is possible that social avoidance preceded their anxiety, and they developed ruminations and preoccupations with how others see them because of their social anxiety. On the other hand, their social avoidance could be co-morbid with anxiety, self-doubt, and extreme sensitivity to criticism and rejection.
- If RC8 is elevated, social avoidance as well as disordered thinking would suggest a schizoid personality disorder or a diagnosis of schizophrenia.
- If Malaise (MLS) is elevated, the individual is reporting feeling exhausted and not in good physical health. They may be avoiding people because they do not feel well and may anticipate rejection since they are not currently feeling at their best.
- If SUI is elevated, suicidal preoccupation could be a result of extreme loneliness and a lack of social skills. On the other hand, it is possible that being constitutionally socially avoidant has led to loneliness and despair about ever being able to create relationships and a community.
- If NFC, STR, WRY, and/or ARX are elevated, the client is socially avoidant, perhaps because they feel incompetent, stressed, worried, and/or anxious. They may feel unworthy to be around people since they may assume they are unattractive to others because they find daily life so difficult.
- If DSF and/or INTR are elevated, it would support the likelihood of a schizoid personality disorder diagnosis. The individual is reporting being socially avoidant but also dislikes being around people in general.

Therapy and Therapeutic Pitfalls – SAV Scale

By definition, people who are socially avoidant would likely resist seeking therapy. A clinical history identifying whether their social avoidance was a lifelong pattern and genetically driven or whether it was a learned behavior due to early trauma or social isolation would be an important first step in therapy. As with any of the scales measuring social withdrawal, it is important that the therapist move slowly, without being too exuberant or prematurely expressing warmth. Generally, these individuals would be more open to behavioral approaches, such as cognitive behavioral therapy, since it would not tax them emotionally. Therapeutic strategies would depend on the reasons for referral. In some cases, one person of a couple in marital therapy who is high on social avoidance might be referred because they avoid social events, which is upsetting to the more socially outgoing spouse. In another situation, an individual may have reached a management position, but their social avoidance is inhibiting their management capabilities, so they are seeking help to develop better social skills.

Therapy for social avoidance typically involves addressing the underlying causes of the avoidance. Often it is anxiety and fear of judgment as well as negative self-perceptions. Cognitive behavioral therapy is effective in identifying and challenging negative thought patterns. Practicing gradual exposure to social interactions can help desensitize anxiety over time. Practicing social talk in the therapy session so that the client can learn conversation skills could also be useful. Acceptance and commitment therapy can help the individual accept that they have a tendency toward social avoidance and stop being self-critical because of it. In some cases, group therapy can provide a safe environment to practice social skills with others who may have similar issues. If social avoidance is co-morbid with depression or with anxiety, medication can also be useful.

Feedback Statements – SAV Scale

T score = 37

Your answers suggest that you very much enjoy parties, are a highly social person, and enjoy meeting new people. You tend to make friends quickly and are excited and energized when you are around crowds. People likely see you as very gregarious and fun to be around.

T score 44–50

Your answers suggest that you enjoy parties and meeting new people but are also comfortable being alone and do not need constant social interaction.

T score 53–60

Your answers suggest that, while you can occasionally enjoy being around people, you are comfortable with time alone and dislike being in large crowds and meeting strangers.

T score 66–77

Your answers suggest that you do not enjoy social events with large groups of people you do not know. You tend to make friends slowly and it takes a while for you to feel comfortable with new people. You do not find crowds exciting and meeting new people is not easy.

- If EID is elevated, add: Your answers suggest that you are currently feeling down, somewhat overwhelmed, and defeated. You also report that you have difficulty dealing with social situations where you do not know people. You have learned to avoid many social situations since they likely make you anxious and uncomfortable. It is possible that your current depression, anxiety, and low self-esteem have led to you wanting to avoid people because you do not feel your best. It is also possible that you have been a somewhat self-contained private individual who has not made friends easily.
- If THD is elevated, add: You report feeling fearful right now, unsure of whom to trust, and perhaps, at times, you feel suspicious of people's motives. You are someone who tends to avoid people, and a loner who relies on yourself. Feeling a little suspicious and unsure of whom you can trust, while at the same time feeling unsafe reaching out to people, might make you feel very vulnerable.
- If BXD is elevated, add: Your answers suggest that you are a rebel, dislike being controlled, and tend to resist authority and rules. You like to stir up excitement and are willing to take risks. You may use substances and may be impulsive. At the same time, you are someone who avoids large groups of people you do not know. Being around people makes you uncomfortable, so you are likely a loner, relying on yourself rather than trusting others for any kind of emotional support.
- If RCd is elevated, add: You are reporting that you feel lonely, useless, and may even think of yourself as worthless at times. You also report that meeting new people can be difficult for you and you avoid large groups of people you do not know. Perhaps because you are so tough on yourself and are your own worst critic, you feel insecure being around other people. You may anticipate that they will be critical or judgmental of you and, so, that is why you avoid them.
- If RC2 is elevated, add: Your answers suggest that you have been feeling blue, with not much giving you pleasure. Your answers also suggest that meeting people you do not know is anxiety-provoking and awkward for you. It is understandable that you avoid social situations, since you

get anxious and feel like people might be judgmental or critical of you. Being alone, however, may aggravate your current depression since you do not have a support system to count on.

- If RC6 is elevated, add: Your answers suggest you feel vulnerable to being criticized, judged, and somehow picked on by others. At times you may wonder whether you are overly suspicious or whether you are seeing things clearly. At the same time, your answers suggest that you avoid people, especially in social situations where you do not know anyone. Parties, social events, and small talk cause you discomfort, so you avoid them. Perhaps you are currently feeling quite isolated, since it is hard to know whom to trust. You might become preoccupied with how you are going to defend yourself and, since you do not reach out to people to get feedback, you may not be seeing reality clearly.
- If RC7 is elevated, add: Your answers suggest that you are your own worst critic and suffer from anxiety and self-doubt. You tend to constantly self-observe, wondering if people are being critical or if you have somehow let them down. Your answers also suggest that you avoid meeting new people and avoid large groups of people you do not know. You may avoid others because you worry about how they might see you or if they are going to judge you. It is possible that some of your anxiety is social anxiety, making it hard for you to build friendships or a supportive community.
- If RC8 is elevated, add: Your answers suggest that being around people you do not know or being around large groups of people is difficult for you. Consequently, you avoid social situations. You tend to live in your own world of ideas, perhaps at times feeling suspicious, wondering if you can trust people or if they are going to cause you harm. Perhaps that is why you avoid people, because you do not trust them and are fearful that they can somehow harm you.
- If MLS is elevated, add: You reported that you generally do not feel well and often feel exhausted. That may be why you avoid people, perhaps because you are concerned that you cannot perform well in front of others. It is also possible that you have always had difficulty meeting new people and being in new social situations, so you have tended to avoid people. It is possible that your difficulty meeting people has led to you feeling lonely and depleted.
- If SUI is elevated, add: You reported that you spend a lot of time thinking about suicide and how to escape from your present despair. You also reported that you tend to avoid people because you find meeting people you do not know anxiety-provoking and unrewarding. Perhaps your social isolation has led to you feeling desperate and having suicidal escape fantasies. If you feel hopeless and suicidal and cannot reach your therapist, call a suicide and crisis 24/7 hotline [988 in the United States and Canada] for confidential support.
- If NFC, STR, WRY, and/or ARX are elevated, add: You reported that you generally avoid people. You find meeting new people or being in large groups of people you do not know very stressful and anxiety-provoking. You also reported you often feel very stressed, worried, anxious, and doubt your ability to handle life. Perhaps you avoid people because you are afraid that they will judge you. It is also possible that you have had trouble socially for a long time and your social anxiety has led to increased stress and worry.
- If DSF is elevated, add: Your answers suggest that you dislike people and try to avoid them. You could be described as a loner, finding more comfort in being alone than being with other people. This may be because you expect people will be critical of you, so being around them makes you uncomfortable. You tend to approach people guardedly, not allowing yourself to get close to anyone.

Lifestyle and Family Background Feedback – SAV Scale

In some cases, people with your profile grew up in a family where, for some reason, they did not experience a lot of social interactions. Perhaps your caregivers avoided entertaining or socializing and were typically self-sufficient and independent. It is also possible that you were a shy child and being around people made you anxious and uncomfortable. If you were a socially awkward child, you may have never learned how to reach out to people to develop a peer group, which could leave you feeling lonely. In some cases, people with your profile avoid other people because they have been hurt or traumatized and their trust in people has been broken. They avoid people because they do not trust them, expecting people to be critical, judgmental, or even take advantage of them. Avoiding social situations may make you feel safer and more comfortable in the short run, but over time it may negatively affect you, since you will not have a community to rely on should you need support or help.

Treatment and Self-Help Suggestions – SAV Scale

You may be seeking treatment because of social problems or work-related problems. If you would like to feel a little more socially comfortable, there are simple techniques you can learn to help you. Once you have identified the causes of your social avoidance, whether due to past negative experiences or your own predisposition, you can work on techniques that could enhance your social skills. Here are some self-help suggestions.

1. Start with low-stakes interactions, perhaps saying "hi" to a neighbor, engaging in brief small talk with a cashier, or attending a social gathering for a short time. Over time, as you get more comfortable, you can gradually challenge yourself to stay in social situations longer or engage with more people.
2. Being kind to yourself is key. Understand that social avoidance is often rooted in fear or anxiety, and it is okay to take things slowly. Instead of criticizing yourself for avoiding situations, acknowledge the effort you are making when you do engage.
3. If you find yourself frequently overthinking social situations or imagining "worst case" scenarios, cognitive behavioral therapy can help. It involves identifying negative thoughts, challenging them, and reframing them in a more realistic or positive light. It can also help you to gradually expose yourself to social situations in a controlled manner.
4. If you are feeling quite anxious about a situation, it can be helpful to bring a friend or family member along. This can give you a sense of security and make socializing feel more manageable.
5. Try focusing on listening to others instead of worrying about how you are being perceived. You don't have to worry about saying the perfect thing, just be present and engaged with the person to whom you are talking.
6. Set small, specific goals for yourself, for example, "I'll attend this social event for 20 minutes" or "I'll talk to one person at this gathering." Achieving these goals can build confidence and reduce your fear of future social situations.
7. When you start feeling anxious, practice mindfulness or relaxation techniques. Deep breathing or progressive muscle relaxation can help ground you and calm your nerves before or during social interactions.
8. Consider joining a group that aligns with your interests (such as a book club, art class, or hiking group) as a low-pressure way to connect with others. The shared focus on an activity can make interactions feel less daunting.
9. Working with a therapist, especially one who specializes in social anxiety or avoidance, can be helpful. Therapy can help you understand the root causes of your avoidance and provide structured support as you work through it.
10. Understand that every step forward counts. Whether you attend a party for a short time, start a conversation with a stranger, or push through an uncomfortable situation, give yourself credit. Your social skills will get better with practice.

Shyness (SHY) Scale

General Descriptors

> **Complaints**
>
> Initial difficulty meeting strangers; self-conscious in social situations; wants to engage but initially feels inhibited.
>
> **Cognitions**
>
> Fear of judgment; discomfort of showing embarrassment; conversational reticence; self-effacement; low self-confidence.
>
> **Emotions**
>
> Social anxiety; possible depression; inhibited; passivity.
>
> **Traits and behaviors**
>
> Non-assertive; initially inhibited or anxious in social interactions; forms relationships slowly and deliberately; seen as socially awkward; quick to make concessions; conflict-avoidant.

Therapist's Notes – SHY Scale

This 7-item scale, when elevated, reflects social anxiety. There is a hereditary predisposition to being shy, as studies of introversion and extroversion show little change over time. Individuals scoring high on SAV avoid social interactions because they experience discomfort, anxiety, and self-consciousness around people. Over time they increasingly withdraw from people which can impair daily functioning. In other words, SAV clients might experience avoidance as ego-syntonic. People who score high on SHY, on the other hand, may enjoy social interaction but their initial response to new people is to feel awkward, embarrassed, and anxious about performance. Once they are comfortable, they can be quite social. They form relationships slowly and deliberately but, once formed, these relationships may be highly stable, loyal, and intimate.

Shyness is typically not debilitating unless the individual has a career that involves speaking extemporaneously and/or being called upon to speak without an opportunity to prepare. Shy people can be quite comfortable if they have a specific role that provides them with interpersonal structure. For example, some salespeople can manage their shyness and become successful. Some people may experience anticipatory anxiety before social interactions, imagining "worst case" scenarios, such as the possibility of being embarrassed by being unable to think of things to say.

Shyness is different than social avoidance. Social avoidance is stronger, more persistent, and often tied to deeper issues, such as avoidant personality disorder or past negative social experiences. Social avoidance is motivated by a desire to minimize social contact entirely and can lead to isolation and interfere with daily functioning. Shy people generally want to engage, but feel inhibited by the initial contact, while those who engage in social avoidance actively choose to withdraw. Whereas shyness can improve over time as the person becomes more comfortable, social avoidance is more consistent and can be debilitating.

Lifestyle and Family Background – SHY Scale

Shyness is partly genetic. Shy children become shy teenagers, who become shy adults. Shyness is likely normally distributed, with most people being in the middle; and a small percentage of people being extremely shy or extremely socially disinhibited. Shy children may have had difficulty moving to a new school and leaving an established group of friends with whom they might have been quite comfortable and sociable. People with shyness can enjoy going to parties and meeting new people once they have dealt with their initial anxiety about being embarrassed or unable to think of what to talk about. High scorers on this scale are not pushy or aggressive. They can be somewhat awkward and initially appear distant or cold, until they feel comfortable. They can appear confident with public speaking, but only if they can overprepare and are not subjected to spontaneous dialogue. While introversion and extroversion are not, in themselves, pathological or disruptive of happiness, conditioning and social experiences can accentuate the less adaptive aspects of both ends of the continuum.

Clarifying Scales – SHY Scale

T score = 38

The test-taker reports no social anxiety. They do not experience initial awkwardness when meeting new people nor are they embarrassed by not being able to think of what to talk about. They can engage people spontaneously, without anxiety, and are not intimidated by walking into a room where people are already relating to one another.

T score 45–52

This range reflects mild or situational social discomfort.

T score 55–77

The test-taker is reporting feeling shy and easily embarrassed when meeting new people. They are uncomfortable with small talk and can become tongue-tied. They tend to be somewhat passive, waiting for others to engage them, and may appear standoffish and aloof to people. They would experience anxiety should they be called upon to give a speech or a talk spontaneously without having prepared for it. The higher the T score, the more socially inhibited the individual is likely to be.

- If EID is elevated, the individual is acknowledging feeling depressed, overwhelmed, and helpless. They are initially uncomfortable in unstructured situations and when meeting new people. Although shyness is fairly common and not usually labeled as psychopathology, it may have inhibited these individuals from reaching out to others for social support. If there was a recent change in their work environment or a significant move, shyness may have increased the stress of forming new relationships and led to anxiety and possible depression.
- If THD is elevated, the individual is reporting distorted thinking, with possible psychotic delusions. In some cases, psychotic individuals may avoid interactions with others due to their paranoia. However, shyness would further hamper their forming supportive bonds that may provide reality testing. Their disordered thinking could lead to bizarre behavior, possibly with conspiracy theories and eccentric rationalizations for their behavior. In the presence of conspiracy theories, an evaluation for dangerousness would be helpful.

- BXD is unlikely to be elevated if SHY is elevated. However, it is possible that genetic shyness, together with adverse childhood experiences and a genetic predisposition to antisocial behavior, could have increased the propensity for antisocial behavior expressed in isolation.
- If RCd is elevated, the individual is reporting feeling lonely, useless, worthless, blue, and inefficient. They have difficulty starting tasks and give up when things are difficult. Their demoralization may be aggravated by a genetic shyness that inhibits their social relationships. Their low self-esteem and self-confidence would add to their shyness and, with it, increased social reticence. It is difficult to know whether they are genetically predisposed to shyness, which adds social stress to demoralization, or if shyness has been a learned trait, not relevant to the development of demoralization.
- If RC2 is elevated, shyness may inhibit the individual from reaching out for social support and so may inhibit the treatment of depression. It is possible that a vulnerability to depression was aggravated by shyness, with resulting loneliness and low self-esteem.
- If RC6 is elevated, the individual may be avoiding others because of severe mistrust/paranoia. They may have developed elaborate conspiracy theories and may collect weapons as a way to protect themselves from what they perceive as imminent danger. Shyness would increase the drive for self-protective isolation. Isolation would suggest they have few social corrective experiences that could modify their paranoid ideation.
- If RC7 is elevated, the client may have intense mixed feelings about social events because of their anxiety, self-doubt, and preoccupation with avoiding criticism and embarrassment. It is possible that childhood genetic shyness may have led to the development of anxiety with ruminations and preoccupations with how others see them. A social anxiety disorder may be indicated.
- If RC8 is elevated, shyness as well as disordered thinking would suggest a schizoid or schizophrenic diagnosis, especially if THD, SAV, PSYC, and/or DISC are elevated.
- If MLS is elevated, the individual is reporting feeling exhausted and not in good physical health. Since they are currently not feeling their best, they likely want to avoid people. Shyness would aggravate that tendency, perhaps increasing the malaise.
- If SUI is elevated, suicidal preoccupations could be a result of extreme shyness and a lack of social skills. On the other hand, it is possible that being genetically shy has led to loneliness and despair about ever being able to create relationships and a community.
- If NFC, STR, WRY, and/or ARX are elevated, the client's shyness, as well as feeling incompetent, stressed, worried, and/or anxious, would hamper the development of supportive social relationships. The client may feel unworthy of being around people and feel unattractive to others because they find daily life so difficult. Being shy increases the stress of reaching out to others and increases feelings of incompetence.
- If DSF, SAV, and/or INTR are elevated, the individual is reporting being shy and socially avoidant but also dislikes being around people in general.

Therapy and Therapeutic Pitfalls – SHY Scale

By definition, people who are shy might initially find it stressful to meet with a therapist. A clinical history identifying whether their shyness was a lifelong pattern and genetically driven or whether it was a learned behavior pattern due to early traumas and social isolation would be an important first step in therapy. It is essential to assess the nature and severity of a client's shyness to determine if social anxiety is the issue or whether introversion is limited to certain specific situations (e.g., public speaking). Typically, these clients do not seek treatment for shyness unless they find themselves in situations that demand them to act in ways that are contrary to their introverted personality type.

As with any of the scales measuring social withdrawal, it is critical that the therapist move slowly, without being too intense and prematurely expressing warmth. A structured approach with a clinical history would probably work best to establish a therapeutic relationship. Individuals scoring high on SHY without other pathognomonic indicators can let down their guard relatively quickly and be open with the therapist once trust is established. Unlike the client who scores high on DSF, once the initial discomfort has passed the shy individual can be quite comfortable interpersonally. The therapist will have to multiply the intensity of what the individual says to get a true sense of empathy for them, since their responses, while authentic, might be somewhat muted.

Cognitive behavioral therapy focusing on identifying and challenging negative thought patterns that could aggravate shyness is a useful approach. Rehearsing social skills through role-playing, such as coming up with questions for the client to initiate a conversation with others, could be beneficial. Daily affirmations could help boost their self-confidence. Learning to switch off negative thoughts and painful self-consciousness could also be helpful. People with high SHY scores work better with directive coaching styles of psychotherapy.

Feedback Statements – SHY Scale

T score = 38

Your responses suggest that you are someone who is socially quite comfortable. You do not experience initial awkwardness when you meet new people and do not worry that you might get tongue-tied and not know what to say to someone. Social interactions are probably easy for you, and you enjoy socializing and meeting new people. You are comfortable engaging in spontaneous conversations without feeling that you are not prepared or worrying that you are not going to be interesting.

T score 45–55

Your profile suggests that you may be somewhat shy. Meeting new people can feel a little awkward at first and you may dislike having to talk in front of people without being prepared. Small talk might be uncomfortable for you.

T score 61–77

Your answers suggest that you are quite shy and meeting new people is initially difficult for you. You likely can get easily embarrassed or tongue-tied, unsure what to say to someone. In new social situations you may hang back and wait for others to engage you. People may misunderstand your shyness as aloofness but, once you are comfortable with people, you can be quite socially engaged. You likely dislike being called upon to speak spontaneously or suddenly being made the center of attention without being prepared for it. Your responses suggest that it is uncomfortable for you to interact with people you do not know, and your shyness is present in most social situations. You may desire a social connection but feel inhibited by fears of social embarrassment and rejection. You may be self-critical and assume that you will not be easily liked by others.

- If EID is elevated add: Your answers suggest that currently you are feeling depressed, overwhelmed, stressed, and anxious. Your answers also suggest that you are a somewhat shy person, comfortable with people once you have gotten to know them, but you feel stressed and tense when you meet someone new. It is possible that your shyness has made it difficult for you to meet people and create a community., If you have recently moved or lost the community you developed, it might have led to your current depression. It is also possible that your shyness is genetic, and you have been shy most of your life.

- If THD is elevated, add: Your answers suggest you are quite shy, feeling uncomfortable when you first meet new people. You may find it hard to know what to say in social settings, especially since you are reporting feeling vulnerable and preoccupied with how people might mistreat you. Currently you may be isolated, lost in your own inner thoughts, feeling overly suspicious at times, afraid that people might hurt you or damage your reputation.
- If BXD is elevated, add: You are unusual in that you report being a rebel, disliking being controlled and wanting to live in the moment and go with your impulses. People like you are generally quite extroverted. You are also shy, finding meeting new people difficult and awkward. You also have some difficulty trusting others and letting your emotional guard down with them. Your shyness probably increases your distrust, so it takes a while before you are comfortable enough to let your emotional guard down with people.
- If RCd is elevated, add: Your answers suggest that you are currently feeling blue, lonely, inefficient, and bad about yourself. You test as a shy person, finding it difficult to meet new people and feeling awkward in new social situations. Once you get to know people, you are quite comfortable and can even take a leadership role. You may have been shy most of your life and became used to it. On the other hand, if you have recently moved or lost your group of trusted friends this could have led to your current demoralization and depression.
- If RC2 is elevated, add: Your test results suggest you are feeling somewhat depressed. You also tested as somewhat shy and uncomfortable meeting new people, especially when in large groups of people that you do not know. Once you get to know people, you can be quite comfortable and enjoy social interactions. However, when you first meet someone, you can get tongue-tied and unsure of what to say. You have probably been shy most of your life and have become used to it. It is possible that your current depression is the result of losing your social support system or due to another reason and has nothing to do with your shyness.
- If RC6 is elevated, add: Your profile suggests you are quite shy, so meeting new people is awkward. Being in a large group of people you don't know is quite stressful. You have probably always been shy, but you are currently feeling concerned about how others see you and whether you are being criticized, judged, or even plotted against. Your shyness may have inhibited you from comfortably reaching out to people and developing trusting relationships.
- If RC7 is elevated, add: Your profile suggests you tend to worry and experience anxiety, wondering whether people are being critical or judgmental of you. You are quick to doubt yourself and live with a nagging feeling that something bad is about to happen. You also tested as shy. Shyness is common and generally not a problem unless it interferes with your daily life. It is possible that, having been shy most of your life, you have developed some anxiety and self-doubt because you feel awkward meeting new people. Being shy and anxious makes it hard for you to initiate social contact so you would likely hang back, waiting for others to approach you. After social interactions you might start to worry that you did something wrong.
- If RC8 is elevated, add: Your profile suggests you are shy, finding it hard to talk to people you don't know and anxiety-provoking to be in large groups of strangers. Your profile also suggests you can get caught up in your inner thoughts and sometimes can feel vulnerable, wondering if people are being hostile or somehow dangerous. Your shyness probably stops you from reaching out to people but currently your anxieties and fears that you are not safe probably hinder you from connecting with people.
- If MLS is elevated, add: You are reporting feeling exhausted and in poor health. Since you are not currently feeling your best, you likely find it hard to socialize. You also tested as shy which would aggravate your tendency to withdraw from people, perhaps because you feel you cannot be at your best.

- If SUI is elevated, add: Your profile suggests you are quite shy, so meeting new people is difficult for you and being in large crowds of people you do not know is anxiety-provoking. Perhaps your shyness has inhibited your social life, so you have found it difficult to develop a group of friends and a supportive community. Since you have been preoccupied with suicide, it suggests that you are feeling desperate and hopeless. It is possible that your shyness has led to you feeling lonely and hopeless about ever connecting with others. If you feel hopeless and suicidal and cannot reach your therapist, call a suicide and crisis 24/7 hotline [988 in the United States and Canada] for confidential support.
- If EID, NFC, STR, WRY, and/or ARX are elevated, add: Your profile shows that you suffer from anxiety and stress, tending to worry a lot and feeling that you cannot get things done. Your profile also suggests that you are quite shy, so meeting new people is difficult for you. Feeling shy, unworthy, incompetent, stressed, and worried would likely make it difficult for you to reach out to others to create a supportive community.
- If DSF, SAV, and/or INTR are elevated add: Your profile shows that you find being around people difficult since it causes you anxiety. You prefer to be alone because when you meet new people you feel awkward and easily embarrassed. Getting close to people does not feel good because you dislike letting down your guard and being vulnerable.

Lifestyle and Family Background Feedback – SHY Scale

Shyness is most likely something you inherited. You were probably always a little shy growing up. You may have made friends with a small group in school that stuck together. Being shy is normal but it can make people feel self-conscious and awkward when they meet new people or when at a big party with people they don't know. In some cases, people who are shy were raised with caregivers who were shy and didn't socialize with others. You may have been an only child with caregivers who were shy or socially avoidant and, since you had no siblings to relate to, you never learned social skills. In some cases, caregivers can be overly critical of their child's behavior or appearance and this may instill self-doubt, leading to shyness. If you were ever bullied, teased, or rejected by your peers, that could have made you hesitant to reach out and engage with others. If you were homeschooled, without group activities, you may have become comfortable being a loner and avoiding reaching out to others. Shyness is not necessarily a negative personality characteristic unless it is the result of painful experiences with other people.

Treatment and Self-Help Suggestions – SHY Scale

Shyness is not a negative trait. If you would like to be less shy, there are a lot of ways to get there. Accepting that you are shy and not beating yourself up about it is the first step. If you recall always being a little shy, slow to warm up in social situations, and preferring to be around small groups of people you know, then it is likely genetic. If you have experienced negative events with others, perhaps being bullied, criticized, or rejected by your peers or caregivers, you may have developed shyness as a reaction. If you grew up in a family where there was not a lot of social interaction, you may not have learned the skills of small talk. Learning how to engage in conversation and engage in small talk is not difficult. Here are some things you can work on.

1. Recognize that shyness is a natural response and don't judge yourself.
2. In situations where you feel shy, try to ascertain if it is because the person you are relating to is making you feel insecure or if you are anxious that you are going to come across badly.
3. Set manageable goals, beginning with small social actions, such as smiling at a neighbor or at someone in line at the store. Build on this by making eye contact briefly with someone you meet or saying "hello" to a colleague.

4. Prepare a few conversation starters about topics or questions you are comfortable with so that you won't feel so tongue-tied. For example, you might ask someone about their travel plans or hobbies. You can begin to share something about yourself, when you feel comfortable, which can encourage discussion.
5. Be sure to listen to what others are saying, rather than focusing on how you should respond or how you are coming across.
6. Force yourself to attend a small social function, even if briefly, and even though it will be stressful. One small success will lead to another, and you can gradually expand your social activities. Remind yourself to smile and to try to look like you are enjoying the conversation.
7. Join a support group with other people who struggle with shyness. It can be an opportunity for you to become more comfortable opening up and being vulnerable about your own shyness. It could also provide you with a setting where you can practice how to talk to people that you do not know.
8. Consider working with a therapist who can use techniques such as role-plays, modeling, and instructions to build everyday social skills. Practicing these will help you feel more confident and less isolated.

9 Personality Psychopathology Five (PSY-5) Scales

Introduction

Development

Personality psychologists have focused considerable research efforts on developing dimensional models of normal personality and psychopathology. Eysenck, Wakefield, & Friedman (1983) reviewed the DSM-III's release in 1980 (American Psychiatric Association, 1980) and proposed that categorical diagnosis should be replaced with dimensional assessment. Harkness & McNulty (1994) developed the Personality Psychopathology Five (PSY-5) model based on structural analyses of the DSM-III-R (American Psychiatric Association, 1987) personality disorder criteria. Harkness, McNulty, and Ben-Porath (1995) later developed a set of MMPI-2 scales to assess the PSY-5 constructs, which were subsequently added to the MMPI-2 (Butcher et al., 2001). Next, Harkness and McNulty revised their five scales for inclusion in the MMPI-2-RF (Ben-Porath & Tellegen, 2008/2011a, 2008/2011b) and they updated the scales once more for the MMPI-3 (Ben-Porath & Tellegen, 2020a, 2020b). The five MMPI-3 PSY-5 Scales are Aggressiveness (AGGR), Psychoticism (PSYC), Disconstraint (DISC), Negative Emotionality/Neuroticism (NEGE), and Introversion/Low Positive Emotionality (INTR).

The *Technical Manual* for the MMPI-3 (Ben-Porath & Tellegen, 2020b) and the text by Ben-Porath & Sellbom (2023) provide evidence for the reliability and validity of the PSY-5 Scales. The MMPI-3 PSY-5 Scales "show replicable associations with measures of personality psychopathology, both from the perspective of the traditional categorical DSM model as well as models that align with contemporary personality disorder science" (Ben-Porath & Sellbom, 2023, p. 228).

The *MMPI-3 Technical Manual* reports that the revised PSY-5 MMPI-3 Scales are reliable with test-retest reliability estimates ranging from .72 for PSYC to .93 for DISC. Reliability coefficients for internal consistency in the normative sample range from .67 for men on PSYC to .88 for women. The mental health sample has alpha coefficients ranging from .72 for men on AGGR to .90. More complete psychometric information is provided in the *MMPI-3 Technical Manual* (Ben-Porath & Tellegen, 2020b) and in Ben-Porath & Sellbom (2023).

The PSY-5 Scales overlap considerably with some of the Higher-Order (H-O) Scales and Specific Problems (SP) Scales. This is because, as just described, the PSY-5 model and corresponding scales were developed independently of the remaining sets of MMPI-3 scales, with a focus on underlying dimensions of risk for personality disorder. Consequently, the personality and behavior features described in this chapter, and therapeutic implications thereof, overlap considerably with those found in previous sections of this book.

Application

Inspection of the PSY-5 scores should occur after protocol validity is established. In a valid profile, the PSY-5 Scales will likely align with the H-O Scales, and more specifically with the

DOI: 10.4324/9781003557920-9

Restructured Clinical (RC) Scales and SP Scales. The MMPI-3 Interpretation Worksheet in Ben-Porath & Sellbom (2023) provides an organizational structure for reviewing all the scales by domains. AGGR is associated with interpersonal functioning; PSYC is aligned with thought dysfunction; DISC is associated with behavioral and externalizing dysfunction; and NEGE and INTR are associated with emotional dysfunction.

Aggressiveness (AGGR) Scale

General Descriptors

Complaints

Easily angered; difficulty controlling temper; interpersonal difficulties due to anger; tendency to externalize and blame.

Cognitions

Sees communication as a zero-sum game; vindictive; self-aggrandizing; views others as adversaries; thinks of ways to dominate.

Emotions

Angry; resentful; easily frustrated; short-tempered.

Traits and behaviors

Verbally and/or physically aggressive; domineering; argumentative; moves against versus toward others; vindictive; rudeness; grandiosity.

Therapist's Notes – AGGR Scale

This 15-item scale measures aggressively assertive behavior. This scale differs from the Externalizing Scale Aggression (AGG) in that AGG focuses on violent behavior, whereas AGGR measures instrumental aggression intended to achieve a desired outcome that can also be verbal. Two items on the AGGR scale indicate a proclivity for physical aggression. A client scoring high on AGGR has an instinct to dominate and uses the threat of aggression to get what they want. High scorers on AGG manifest an explosive temper that comes from frustration and a short fuse; reflecting aggressiveness that may be impulsive rather than instrumental. The aggression associated with AGGR is likely a stable personality trait, revealing a person who dominates, wants to win arguments, and pays people back if they feel mistreated. A history of physical violence, fights in which others have gotten hurt, and threats of violence are prognostically adverse.

To better understand the scale, it is instructive to compare the attributes of low and high scorers. Low scorers can be described as non-confrontational to the point of being passive, submissive, and agreeable, tending to "lean in" and get along with people to avoid making waves. They tend to be conflict adverse. Low scorers are probably described by their peers as nice and easy to get along with. They are not demanding and can walk away from an argument without needing to win. In a leadership role, they likely have a democratic disposition rather than an authoritarian one. The correlates associated with high scores on this scale suggest narcissism, antisocial personality disorder, and traits associated with an authoritarian and antagonistic personality.

Lifestyle and Family Background – AGGR Scale

Research suggests that aggressive individuals often have certain common patterns in their childhood experiences, and physical aggression tends to manifest itself early in life. Aggression as a way of problem-solving could have arisen in early childhood in response to aggressive, authoritarian, or abusive caregivers. Domestic violence, sexual and/or physical abuse, yelling, overly strict, punitive, or demanding caregivers, neglect, and exposure to a caregiver's antisocial behavior are all factors that heighten the risk for aggressive behavior. These experiences will likely have led to feelings of frustration, anger, and resentment. Exposure to physical and/or emotional violence in the home and/or at school can desensitize children to aggressive behavior and normalize it as a way to resolve conflicts. Children who were frequently dismissed, belittled, or ignored may have difficulty managing their emotions, leading to aggressive outbursts. Being bullied or rejected by peers can contribute to feelings of anger, resentment, and aggression. When caregivers are inconsistent in their discipline, children may feel a lack of boundaries and limits, leading to aggressive behavior. Children who struggle with empathy, communication, and problem-solving skills may resort to aggression to manage social situations. Understanding what kind of conditioning experience might have precipitated aggressive behavior as a primary problem-solving technique would be the first order of therapy.

There may be a genetic component to aggressiveness, with some individuals having a tendency to be overly assertive and aggressive. Adverse experiences may aggravate this tendency. Clients scoring high on Impulsivity (IMP), who, as children, may have experienced language delays, been bullied, or bullied others, are more vulnerable to expressing aggression. In some cases, a constitutional predisposition to aggression, together with childhood poverty and authoritarian, aggressive caregivers, could predispose an individual to develop aggressiveness.

The most salient aspect of the client's lifestyle is aggression. They go through life expecting arguments and resistance from others, which they create because of their argumentative, demanding self-importance. They approach people anticipating conflict and, thus, may inadvertently create it. There may be an aspect of grandiosity, since they feel driven to offer their opinion and to tell people off. They have difficulty backing off from an argument because they have a need to win. Since aggressiveness is likely a stable personality trait, they may have conflicted marriages or relationships, unless their partner is submissive. Interpersonal problems at work would not be uncommon.

Clarifying Scales – AGGR Scale

T score <39

These scores suggest an unassertive individual who does not get angry easily and is willing to go along with other people's demands. They are generally seen as agreeable with a vulnerability to be passive in the face of potential conflict.

T score 49–57

These scores suggest an individual who can be appropriately assertive but occasionally experiences flashes of anger that can be seen as aggressive.

T score 63–85

This is a person who approaches life in an aggressive, assertive, demanding, opinionated way and, when frustrated, potentially could resort to violence.

- If Emotional/Internalizing Dysfunction (EID) is elevated, it is possible that the client's severe depression, anxiety, and feelings of helplessness and hopelessness can lead to aggressive, angry outbursts.
- If Thought Dysfunction (THD) and/or PSYC are elevated, the client is expressing thought-disordered, aggressive, paranoid ideation. The client could be dangerous since they are paranoid, confused, and feeling vulnerable, so there is a danger of pre-emptive aggression on their part. Any veiled or direct threats should be taken seriously.
- If Behavioral/Externalizing Dysfunction (BXD) is elevated, the client is impulsive, hedonistic, manipulative, and possibly using substances. Their aggression will manifest impulsively when frustrated, especially if IMP is elevated, and they may use anger manipulatively to frighten people into giving them what they want.
- If Antisocial Behavior (RC4) is elevated, the client's impulsive self-centeredness and manipulativeness is likely combined with aggression, resulting in them bullying people with the threat of their bad temper in order to get what they want.
- If Ideas of Persecution (RC6) is elevated, the client's possible persecutory ideation is combined with aggression. The client may be feeling vulnerable to criticism, judgment, or being physically hurt by their perceived enemies. They may defend against it by expressing aggression and getting others to back off by the threat of their physical violence. Threats should be taken seriously.
- If Aberrant Experiences (RC8) or PSYC are elevated, the client may be experiencing a thought disorder that makes them feel vulnerable, so they may pre-emptively express aggression as part of their confused thinking.
- If Hypomanic Activation (RC9), IMP, and/or Activation (ACT) are elevated, hypomanic overactivity, together with impatience and irritability may lead to aggressive behavior, both as a way of getting what they want and a manifestation of overarousal and overexcitability.
- If Anger Proneness (ANP) is elevated, the client is irritable, has a short fuse, is easily angered, and can also be aggressively assertive, argumentative, and potentially physically aggressive.
- If Juvenile Conduct Problems (JCP) is elevated, it suggests that the client's current aggressiveness is a longstanding trait, with adolescent problems of anti-authority acting-out being indicative of a possible antisocial personality disorder.
- If Cynicism (CYN) is elevated, the client's cynical view of people as untrustworthy, lying, cheating, and self-serving may rationalize their aggressiveness and use of aggression as a way to dominate others.
- If Self-Importance (SFI) is elevated, the client's aggressiveness is emboldened by the feeling that they have something unique and special to offer the world and, therefore, aggression is justified in the service of their superior abilities.
- Dominance (DOM) is elevated when AGGR is elevated as eight of the items on the scale are also scored on the AGGR scale. The DOM items capture an essential quality of the AGGR scale, indicating the tendency to dominate and manipulate with the threat of aggression.
- If DISC is elevated, the client is impulsive, substance-abusing, and acts-out antisocially. They are aggressive and sensation-seeking and can use the threat of their bad temper to intimidate people into giving them what they want.

Therapy and Therapeutic Pitfalls – AGGR Scale

Since aggressive individuals are volatile and unpredictable, establishing a safe environment for both the therapist and client is critical. The therapist should establish an understanding about how aggressivity will be mitigated should it escalate. Aggressive people anticipate counteraggression from others, and it would be natural for the therapist to become defensive, fearful, or counterproductive in the face of the client's verbal aggression. During the course of therapy it might be helpful for the therapist to point out when the client's tone is rising and indicating their anger.

Telling the client "I'm feeling anxious because I can feel you are getting frustrated, and it scares me that you are might become aggressive" could be useful.

Acknowledge the individual's emotions, showing understanding why they might be triggered given their childhood experiences. Cognitive behavioral therapy could educate the client that their aggressive impulses are understandable, though not permissible. The goal of therapy would be to identify and modify negative thought patterns and behaviors that contribute to aggression. This would involve teaching coping strategies and problem-solving skills to manage their triggers. Relaxation training to self-soothe as soon as the individual begins to feel agitated could be helpful. Dialectical behavior therapy could also be helpful to teach the client distress tolerance and emotional regulation. Uncovering therapy to explore past traumas and childhood experiences of abuse could be useful. Group therapy with people who have similar problems can also be effective.

Feedback Statements – AGGR Scale

T score <39

Your answers suggest that you are generally an agreeable, non-pushy person who tries to avoid conflict. You do not need to assert yourself with people and generally prefer resolving conflicts in non-aggressive ways.

T score 49–57

Your responses suggest that you can be appropriately assertive and, when angry, are comfortable speaking your mind. At times, your anger may be experienced by others as overly confrontational.

T score 63–85

You approach life in an assertive stance, as if you expect people to resist you and argue with you. You feel a need to defend your opinions and let people know where you stand on things. If somebody irritates you or makes you angry, you feel a need to confront them. In some cases, your aggressiveness may lead to physical violence. You go through life feeling a need to assert yourself, tell people where you stand on things, and tell people off if you think they have done something wrong. People may judge you as overly assertive, even aggressive. When irritated or slighted, you have a tendency to become aggressive, if not physically, then verbally hostile. You are not easily defeated in an argument and strongly defend your own opinions. People may be cautious around you, fearing that you might get angry and even violent. Driving a hard bargain, you likely will go out of your way to win a point with someone who has opposed you. You may feel a need to punish people for offending or opposing you, which could lead to further conflict.

- If EID is elevated, add: Your answers suggest that you may be experiencing sadness, anxiety, and feelings of helplessness and hopelessness. They also suggest that you can become quite angry and assertive with people, feeling a need to express your opinion and argue your point. At times, your assertiveness can become aggressive or even violent. It is possible that your current depression is being expressed as anger and aggression.
- If THD and/or PSYC are elevated, add: Your answers suggest that you are going through a confusing and possibly frightening time, unsure about whom you can trust and whether people are out to hurt you. At times you may feel mistreated and feel the need to be aggressive with people. It is possible that you get confused about who your enemy is and become argumentative with people, feeling a need to win your point and tell people off if they have upset you.

- If BXD is elevated, add: Your answers suggest you are somewhat rebellious, resisting authority, living in the moment, and being impulsive. You may be using substances, which likely increases your impulsiveness and aggressiveness. You feel a strong need to stand up for yourself, tell people where you stand on things, and tell them off if you feel they have done you wrong. You likely get into arguments with others, which can lead to aggressiveness and even violence.
- If RC4 is elevated, add: You are a person who lives in the moment, acting impulsively, and often breaking rules. You likely use substances, which can increase your tendency for impulsive, angry behavior. You can feel a need to tell people where you stand on things and strongly argue your point. You may use the threat of aggression to get what you want.
- If RC6 is elevated, add: You may be feeling unsafe, currently afraid that people are judging you or are somehow going to hurt you. You may think you are protecting yourself with your anger and aggression, perhaps thinking it will make people back off and stop intimidating you.
- If RC8 is elevated, add: You may be going through a confusing time right now, experiencing disturbed thoughts and concerns about people hurting you. You may have moments where you feel intense anger as well as confusion. Perhaps your anger and aggression toward others is a way of warning them to stay away from you.
- If RC9, IMP, and/or ACT are elevated, add: You appear to be going through a period of intense energy and overactivity, feeling that the world moves too slowly for you. This may lead to you being impatient, irritable and, at times, even aggressive. Your aggressiveness may be your way of getting what you want, but it also reveals that you get overexcited and impulsive.
- If ANP is elevated, add: Your answers suggest that you can often be irritable, with a short fuse, and even minor frustrations can lead to anger. Your profile also suggests that, at times, you can be quite aggressively assertive, arguing your case forcefully and perhaps even resorting to physical aggression.
- If JCP is elevated, add: Your answers suggest that you can be quite forceful when you want something. When you're frustrated, you can be aggressively assertive, even physically violent. It appears that you were a rebel in adolescence and may have developed a lifelong pattern of using the threat of your bad temper to get what you want.
- If CYN is elevated, add: You likely have a negative attitude about people, seeing them as untrustworthy and selfish. Perhaps that is why you rationalize that being aggressive with the threat of your bad temper, at times, is justified. You feel a need to dominate others.
- If SFI is elevated, add: Your answers suggest that you feel that you have special abilities and that others could benefit from hearing your thoughts and opinions. Perhaps that is why, at times, you feel justified in being aggressively assertive, using the threat of your bad temper to get what you want and to get your point across to others.
- If DOM is elevated, add: Your profile suggest that you can be quite direct in expressing your opinions and even aggressively assertive with people, letting them know where you stand on things. Sometimes you use the threat of your bad temper to get what you want and assert control over others.
- If DISC is elevated, add Your profile suggests you can be quite impulsive, whether it is going for what you want or expressing anger. Sometimes you can express anger in an aggressive way, perhaps knowing that it can intimidate people into backing off and giving you what you want. You may also be using substances, which can increase your tendency for impulsive, aggressive behavior.

Lifestyle and Family Background Feedback – AGGR Scale

People who have aggressive tendencies tend to come from backgrounds where caregivers were harsh in their punishments, or even aggressive and abusive. In some cases, people with this profile might have witnessed domestic violence, yelling, and intense, aggressive arguments. If you experienced any of those situations growing up, you likely learned that aggression was a way to problem-solve. Growing up with aggression and violence may have desensitized you so that you do not experience empathy for the people who experience your aggression as frightening and upsetting. In some cases, people are born with a vulnerability to be more assertive and early childhood adverse experiences may have conditioned you so that assertiveness turned into aggression. In other cases, people with your profile were bullied as children. Perhaps you learned as a child to be aggressive to get what you wanted or to deal with bullies. You may now go through life ready to do battle, expecting people to be argumentative and resist you, and so you approach things with an aggressive attitude. It is difficult for you to back off from an argument because you feel that winning is important, but that can sometimes lead to aggression. If you would like to be less aggressive, there are some things you can work on.

Treatment and Self-Help Suggestions – AGGR Scale

1. Keep a journal to track what situations, thoughts, or feelings trigger aggressive behavior. Notice physical signs of anger, like an increased heart rate, muscle tension, or clenched fists. By noticing when your anger is building, you can make an effort to ease up before aggression escalates.
2. Practice relaxation techniques like deep breathing, meditation, and progressive muscle relaxation to calm your physical reaction to anger. Once you have learned to notice when you are becoming angry, practice these relaxation techniques to soothe yourself before your anger escalates.
3. Learn how to communicate effectively by using "I" statements to express feelings without judging or blaming others (e.g., "I feel frustrated when …," rather than "you're always …" or "your problem is …"). Practice listening to others without interrupting or thinking about your response while they are speaking. Stay calm and respectful rather than becoming aggressive. If a conversation is becoming aggressive, try to observe the interaction objectively from a distance, as if it were happening in a movie. Recognize when to step away from situations that may provoke aggression. Take a short break from stressful interactions to cool down before re-engaging.
4. Regular exercise can calm and improve your mood. Develop healthy sleep and diet routines and limit your use of alcohol and illegal drugs. Make an effort to focus on positive aspects of your life.
5. Pursue activities that focus on your more caring and gentle creative side. Painting, writing, or playing music can distract you from anger-provoking situations.
6. Consider therapy to help you manage your emotions. Cognitive behavioral therapy has been found to be effective in helping to replace irrational thoughts with more balanced ones. You can also share your feelings with a trusted friend or family member. Join a support group with others facing similar struggles to help you feel less isolated.
7. Instead of building a case against someone, question whether the situation is truly as one-sided as it seems. Try to understand the other person's perspective and feelings. Don't assume that you are always right or that you are the only one who sees reality clearly.
8. Recognize small improvements in managing your aggression and realize that you will have setbacks but can continue to grow and improve.

Psychoticism (PSYC) Scale

General Descriptors

Complaints

Feels they are being controlled and/or followed; believes their thoughts are being influenced by others; feels persecuted; hears voices; possible visual hallucinations; fearful of being poisoned; bothered by peculiar odors; depersonalized; de-realized; poor memory.

Cognitions

Unrealistic thinking; thinks people are malevolent; thinks people are hypnotizing them, controlling their mind, following them, poisoning them, stealing their ideas; impaired reality testing.

Emotions

Fearful; paranoid; isolated; alienated from others.

Traits and behaviors

Possible psychotic episodes with auditory and perceptual distortions; distorted reality; paranoid preoccupation about being followed, harmed, mind-controlled, and attacked by people intent on hurting them.

Therapist's Notes – PSYC Scale

This 20-item scale contains items that are also scored on RC6, RC8, and THD. The scale measures the different experiences of schizotypal and paranoid disorders. The client is reporting feeling depersonalized, de-realized, unsafe, and preoccupied about being followed, poisoned, harmed, and mistreated. They take things personally and are slow to forgive. They may present with a flat, blunted, and inappropriate affect. Others, although not acutely psychotic, will experience reality distortions, misunderstanding others' motives, and readily taking offense. They will present with a basic lack of self-confidence, tangential associations and, in some cases, inappropriate obsessive ruminations with preoccupations about others' hostile intentions. Elevations could be associated with an underlying thought disorder or a borderline personality organization. Sexuality is likely a problem, given their distrust and difficulties with intimacy, and so may be expressed in unusual and even bizarre ways.

Lifestyle and Family Background – PSYC Scale

Family histories tend to be characterized by traumagenic backgrounds and adverse childhood experiences. Poverty, caregiver mental illness, and, in some cases, physical and sexual abuse are strongly linked to an increased risk of psychotic symptoms later in life. Early childhood eccentricities, a slowness to mature, and learning disabilities, together with severe bullying, have also been associated with paranoia and hallucinations in adulthood. Some individuals who develop psychosis show early signs of social difficulties, such as preferring solitude and having a difficult time making friendships. Elevations on Disaffiliativeness (DSF) and Social Avoidance (SAV) would be expected. In some cases, there is a genetic predisposition to psychosis, and growing up in a family with high levels of hostility or cruelty could lead to psychosis in later life. Some studies have linked early and heavy marijuana and/or psychedelic use to an increased risk of developing psychosis, especially in genetically predisposed individuals. The lifestyle of these individuals tends to be marginal, especially if the psychotic episodes are chronic. In some cases, psychosis can be expressed aggressively, however, mostly isolation and withdrawal from social life is likely, with an erratic work history and few, if any, intimate relationships.

Clarifying Scales – PSYC Scale

T score 67–79

The client is reporting some distortions in their reality testing with unrealistic thinking and sensitivity, shading toward occasional paranoia. Alienated from others and suspicious of the motives of others, they may manifest psychotic thought processes when stressed or under the influence of substances.

T score 83–100

The likelihood of paranoid and overtly psychotic thought processes is increased. These individuals are likely isolated and may be diagnosed as schizotypal, paranoid, and borderline personality disordered.

- If EID is elevated, the profile suggests a psychotic depression. Severe depression, anxiety, self-doubt, and hopelessness, as well as psychotic thought content, would be predicted.
- There is a high degree of item overlap between THD and PSYC. Elevations on both would predict a psychotic disorder with paranoid delusions and possible visual and auditory hallucinations.
- If BXD is elevated, the profile suggests an antisocial, rebellious, impulsive, possibly substance-abusing, and psychotic individual. An example would be Charles Manson who, in the late 1960s, led a group of upper-class young people on a murderous spree in an attempt to start a race war (Roy et al., 2023); (Friedman, 2022-2023). He was described as charismatic and persuasive but was also clearly psychotic and paranoid.
- If Somatic Complaints (RC1) is elevated, the client may have developed somatic symptoms with paranoid delusions. One example might be a client who is convinced that the CIA has implanted various devices in their body that are torturing them and causing severe somatic symptoms.
- If RC4 is elevated, the client is impulsive, possibly using substances, and exhibiting psychotic, possibly aggressive, antisocial behavior.
- If RC6 is elevated, the client's reality distortions are paranoid with fixed, rationalized, paranoid ideas of persecution and mistreatment. Interpersonal difficulties, conspiracy theories, and a perceived need for self-protective measures are suggested.
- If Dysfunctional Negative Emotions (RC7) is elevated, anxiety, worry, and apprehension could be seen as an attempt to manage the underlying thought disorder and possible psychotic episodes. Periods of neurotic anxiety and worry could be interspersed with psychotic preoccupations breaking through the anxiety.
- If RC9 (and possibly ACT) are elevated, hypomanic excitation, mood instability, impulsiveness, and hyperactivity, together with thought disordered content, is likely. The possibility that this is a manifestation of a manic episode should be considered.
- If Neurological Complaints (NUC) is elevated, the client may be complaining of dizziness, numbness, weakness, and involuntary movements, which may be a manifestation of the

underlying psychotic disorder. It is possible that some of the neurological symptoms are part of a paranoid or psychotic condition. An example may be complaints of being poisoned or irradiated with X-rays. It is possible that the tension and anxiety associated with the psychotic condition could be associated with a somatic response to stress.

- If Family Problems (FML) is elevated, the client's psychotic thought disorder may be reflecting a toxic and possibly cruel family background. It is also possible that the psychosis is coloring their current view of their family.
- If Substance Abuse (SUB) is elevated, the client may be experiencing a psychotic episode due to the overuse of substances.
- If IMP, RC4, ACT, AGG, DISC, and/or AGGR are elevated, the propensity for bizarre, impulsive, aggressive psychotic behavior increases. An illustrative example is a case of an innocent bystander being pushed under a train in New York by a young man in his 20s for no reason except a burst of psychotic aggression.
- If DSF, SAV, and/or Shyness (SHY) are elevated, the psychosis is associated with withdrawal, isolation, and suspicion of people.

Therapy and Therapeutic Pitfalls – PSYC Scale

Therapy initially should focus on building trust. When the client expresses psychotic thoughts, it would be important for the therapist to understand the flavor of the psychotic content to gain an insight into the client's emotional state. For example, if the thought content is confused but aggressive, validating the client as being angry or frightened could be helpful in developing trust and empathy. Generally, uncovering psychodynamic types of therapy or the exploration of past traumas are contraindicated with these patients. The goal of therapy should be to help the patient regain practical self-sufficiency and a modicum of self-esteem. Supportive nurturing types of therapy are more helpful than insight therapy. Sometimes basic social work is required to arrange a supportive environment for the client. When the client is stable, cognitive behavioral therapy could be useful to help them recognize the situations that can elicit a breakdown in reality testing. Education about the dangers of substance use for their mental health is important.

Feedback Statements – PSYC Scale

T score 65–79

Your profile suggests that currently you may be feeling vulnerable and unsafe. Perhaps you are feeling that others are plotting against you, trying to hurt you, or trying to steal your thoughts and ideas. You may experience hearing voices or noises without knowing where they are coming from. At times, it may feel like your mind is playing tricks on you so that you become concerned that you may not be seeing reality clearly. When you are stressed it may get worse, and when you feel relaxed you may not feel as knocked off balance.

T score ≥80

Your answers suggest that you are feeling very off balance, confused about whether you are seeing reality clearly, and afraid that others are out to hurt you and steal your ideas. You may feel, at times, that somehow you are not fully inside your body as if you are watching yourself in a movie. Things may feel unreal and sometimes you may hear voices or noises without knowing where they are coming from. You may experience confusion about whom you can trust and feel you need to protect yourself. It can be frightening to feel constantly on edge that someone is trying to hurt you.

- If EID, Low Positive Emotions (RC2), and/or NEGE are elevated, add: Your profile suggests that you are going through some depression, experiencing anxiety, self-doubt, and, at times, hopelessness. Your profile also suggests that, when you are stressed, you may become preoccupied with protecting yourself against what you see as other people's intent to harm you. You may find that when you are stressed your mind plays tricks on you, interrupting your thoughts with ugly, negative, and frightening images and ideas.
- If THD is elevated, add: Your profile suggests you are experiencing a confusing and perhaps frightening time right now. Your mind may be flooded, at times, with negative, ugly, and even frightening thoughts. When you are stressed, you may doubt yourself, wondering if you are just being overly sensitive or whether you are seeing things clearly. At times, you may find yourself preoccupied with protecting yourself since you may feel that people are out to do you harm.
- If BXD is elevated, add: Your profile suggests that you are a rebellious, impulsive person who bends the rules to get what they want. Your profile also suggests that you may experience periods when you feel suspicious, wondering who is for you and who is against you. You may distort reality without realizing it and so justify impulsive and possibly dangerous antisocial acts. At times, you may have an impulse to do something dangerous or harmful to yourself or others.
- If RC1 is elevated, add: Your profile suggests you are experiencing a lot of physical symptoms that are uncomfortable or maybe painful. Your profile also suggests that you may have confusing and even frightening thoughts, perhaps preoccupied with how your physical symptoms are somehow due to outside forces or other people's hostility toward you. You may experience mistrust, wondering if your physical difficulties have been caused in some way by your enemies.
- If RC4 is elevated, add: Your profile suggests you may be experiencing suspiciousness about other people's motives, and you are preoccupied with how others are treating you, perhaps anticipating that you are going to get hurt and you need to protect yourself. You also test as someone who can be quite impulsive, perhaps turning to substances as a way to feel good. If you are using substances, they likely will increase your impulsiveness and your tendency to do things that could be self-defeating or even self-destructive. They will also increase your suspiciousness and your difficulty deciding whom you can trust.
- If RC6 is elevated, add: Your profile suggests that right now you are feeling very vulnerable to criticism, judgment, and hostility from others. You are generally sensitive to aggression. At times, your sensitivity may shade toward intense suspiciousness, when you doubt people's motives and become easily convinced that there is some conspiracy to hurt you.
- If RC7 is elevated, add: Your profile suggests you are experiencing a high-level of anxiety, worry, and self-doubt. At times, your mind can be invaded by negative thoughts and bizarre, even frightening, preoccupations that you feel you cannot control. You may find yourself experiencing ugly, even bizarre, thoughts and preoccupations about why you have failed or why you feel you are not a good person.
- If RC9 is elevated, add: Your profile suggests that you are very energized and easily overexcited and impulsive. Your high energy means that you think quickly, move quickly, and that life generally appears to move too slowly for you. Along with the high-energy level, you may experience periods where you feel quite suspicious of other people, preoccupied with how they see you and fearful they want to harm you. You tend to become preoccupied with big ideas, but your thinking is likely distorted and unrealistic.
- If NUC is elevated, add: Your profile suggests that you are concerned about some involuntary movements in your body, as well as dizziness, numbness, and weakness. You also may be experiencing some worries, wondering if your physical symptoms are due to other people doing something to you or somehow finding ways to cause you pain.

- If FML is elevated, add: Your answers suggest that you see your family as hard to be around, quarrelsome, and unsupportive of you. This may have been your experience as a child, or your family may have become unsupportive over time. Your profile also suggests that currently you could be experiencing thoughts that you are being mistreated and harmed, perhaps by your family. It is possible that you have experienced a difficult childhood, with hostility or cruelty from your family, which could have led to your current psychological disturbance. Your profile suggests that, at times, you believe you have been invaded by negative, confusing, and perhaps bizarre thoughts that may direct you into possibly negative actions.
- If SUB is elevated, add: Your profile suggests that you have been using substances, perhaps as a way to try to feel less anxious and fearful. You may be having worrisome thoughts, afraid that people are out to get you, hurt you, or destroy your reputation. When you use substances, it may affect the way you think and see the world, so that some of your troubling thoughts may be activated by drugs or alcohol.
- If there are elevations on the activation aggression scales IMP, RC4, ACT, AGG, DISC, and/or AGGR, add: Your profile suggests that you are currently very tightly wound, with a short fuse that could lead to impulsive aggression, especially if you feel threatened. At the same time, you are reporting feeling frightened and preoccupied with protecting yourself against what you perceive as other people's hostility and danger to you. Your irritability and anger can impulsively become aggression, escalated by fear, so you may misunderstand people's motives and see danger when there really isn't any.

Lifestyle and Family Background Feedback – PSYC Scale

Your profile has revealed that under stress your thinking can fragment and become disorganized, and you can become confused and highly suspicious of other people's motives. At times, your mind can distort reality because of fear, anxiety, and overloads of stress. This vulnerability can develop because of a genetic vulnerability, early trauma, or living in a toxic environment. If your parents or first-degree relative was diagnosed with schizophrenia or a mental disorder, your vulnerability may be genetic. In some cases, childhood trauma, abuse, or neglect can be so disorganizing that under stress a child flees from reality by turning inward to a fantasy world to try to escape unbearable reality. If you experienced high levels of family stress, or if you observed cruelty toward you, a sibling, or caregiver, you may have used the defense of depersonalization. This involves numbing your feelings and observing what is happening as if you were watching a movie from outside of your body. You may also have developed an understandable defense of living in a fantasy world to avoid the cruelty of the world that you were dealing with. At times, your mind might feel invaded with dark and unpleasant, even bizarre, thoughts and you may get confused between reality and your inner world. Medication is often quite useful for people who experience some of these symptoms, but you might resist because you are fearful and don't trust the doctors. If you want to control your suspiciousness and your confused thinking, there are some things you can work on.

Treatment and Self-Help Suggestions – PSYC Scale

1. Refer to website resources, such as the National Alliance on Mental Illness (NAMI) or the Center for Disease Control (CDC), to help you learn more about psychosis and minimize any fear or stigma you may feel.
2. Develop a consistent routine each day for meals, sleep, and activities in order to help manage feelings of intense mistrust or confusion.
3. With psychosis, small stressors can upset you, disorganize your thinking, and make you question whom you can trust. In these moments, you may want either to get aggressive or to

withdraw from people. Learn to recognize your triggers and develop self-soothing techniques, such as deep breathing, meditation, or yoga, to help manage stress.
4. Maintain a balanced diet and avoid alcohol and recreational drugs as these can exacerbate your symptoms.
5. Develop a support system of trusted friends or family members to help you to determine if you are seeing reality clearly or if you are distorting it because you are afraid.
6. Maintain a journal to track symptoms and triggers so you can learn which settings or individuals create discomfort and contribute to your confusing thoughts or mistrustful feelings.
7. Try to exercise regularly to improve your overall wellbeing. This should be something you enjoy doing and can be as simple as a walk around the block. This can provide you relief from a preoccupation with protecting yourself against danger.
8. Find a trusted therapist who can help you manage your feelings and decide if you are seeing reality clearly.
9. Call a suicide and crisis 24/7 hotline [988 in the United States and Canada] for confidential support if you are feeling overwhelmed and can't reach your therapist.

Disconstraint (DISC) Scale

General Descriptors

Complaints

Substance-abuse problems; possible legal problems; relationship problems; poor judgment; impulsive behavior.

Cognitions

Self-centered; externalizing; sees world as "dog-eat-dog"; selectively reports; non-deliberative decision-making.

Emotions

Lacks empathy; self-absorbed; sensation/excitement-seeking; excitable; impatient.

Traits and behaviors

Sensation-seeking; excitement-seeking; possibly rule-breaking; substance-abusing; impulsively acts-out; self-absorbed; likely juvenile conduct problems; risk-taking; irresponsibility.

Therapist's Notes – DISC Scale

This 18-item scale measures the core attribute of behavioral dysregulation. The items include adolescent acting-out behavior, which is often predictive of adult acting-out behavior, as well as items admitting to substance abuse and behavioral problems due to poor impulse control. The individual scoring high on this scale is admitting to a history of impulsive behavior that has created difficulties with authority figures and problems with the law due to reckless behavior. The client lives in the moment, is hedonistic, and acts without forethought. They likely are currently abusing substances or have done so in the past, which would have increased their tendency to be disinhibited. Typically, they would not seek counseling unless pushed to do so by a frustrated partner or difficulties at work or in school. They tend to be unreliable in psychotherapy unless the therapist wins their trust. Since they lack the usual deference to authority, they may put the therapist through trust tests by being manipulative or selectively reporting to see if the therapist is "clever enough" to see through them.

Lifestyle and Family Background – DISC Scale

The family background of people who are rule-breaking, substance-abusing, rebellious, and self-centered is varied. Some have experienced early childhood adverse experiences such as neglectful caregiving with a lack of supervision and possible emotional detachment. In some cases, growing up with caregivers who are involved in antisocial behavior and substance abuse can also normalize deviant behaviors. The client may have learned to manipulate and to be deceitful and aggressive as a survival strategy. The research also suggests there is a genetic predisposition to disconstrained behavior. Beginning in childhood, individuals would bend the rules, act-out, and, as adults, continue to be manipulative, self-serving, and substance-abusing. Caregiver discipline as a conditioning experience can be varied. In some cases, extreme punishments by impulsive, undisciplined caregivers could have instilled a reckless disregard for authority. In other situations, a lack of consistent consequences by caregivers who manipulate and break the rules themselves could also be a factor. A family history of antisocial personality disorder or borderline personality disorder increases the likelihood of developing antisocial personality disorder.

The lifestyle of people with this elevation involves lying, conning, and exploiting others for personal gain. Reckless behavior, such as unsafe sex, substance abuse, or thrill-seeking activities, is common. Individuals scoring high on this scale have difficulty maintaining long-term friendships and romantic relationships due to their tendency to manipulate and selectively report and their difficulties with emotional trust and intimacy. The individual is unlikely to feel remorse and may have difficulties with empathy. They likely rationalize their actions or blame their victims for their own reckless behavior. Lack of job stability and a tendency to be reckless can cause short- and long-term financial consequences.

Clarifying Scales – DISC Scale

T score <39

The individual is likely behaviorally overconstrained.

T score 39–50

The individual is generally self-controlled and disciplined.

T score 51–60

The individual is reporting occasional rule-breaking, impulsive thrill-seeking, and potentially self-destructive behavior that could lead to problems with authority.

T score ≥63

The individual is behaviorally disconstrained, acts-out impulsively, and is sensation-seeking and excitement-seeking. There is a strong potential for substance abuse, which could lead to impulsive and hasty acts that might then result in conflicts with authority.

- If EID is elevated, the individual may be acting-out impulsively and using substances as a way to medicate their anxiety and depression, low self-esteem, and lack of self-confidence.
- If THD is elevated, the client may be medicating their thought disorder with substances and, at the same time, exhibiting reckless, impulsive behavior. Their behaviors may appear bizarre since they are likely colored and shaped by a psychotic thought process.
- If BXD is elevated, this confirms that the client is reckless, impulsive, self-serving, possibly narcissistically antisocial, and substance-abusing. Since 16 items on the DISC scale are also on BXD, they will tend to co-vary together.
- If elevated, other scales measuring overexcitability, impulsiveness, anger proneness, and aggressiveness (ACT, IMP, ANP, AGG, AGGR) would support an antisocial personality disorder diagnosis.
- If Demoralization (RCd) is elevated, the client is reporting feeling sad, blue, useless, lonely, and having difficulty becoming motivated and productive. They also may be reporting using substances, being impulsive, reckless, and rule-breaking. The client may be suffering the consequences of their impulsive reckless behavior, feeling demoralized, but probably unwilling to take responsibility for their behavior.
- If RC4 is elevated, it would add to the picture of an unrestrained, impulsive, manipulative, substance-abusing individual. Since many of the items are also on DISC and BXD, these scales co-vary together and so would likely also be elevated.
- If RC6 is elevated, the individual is reporting persecutory ideation, hypersensitivity that can shade toward paranoia, and, if SUB is elevated, possible substance-abusing, impulsive, reckless behavior. It is possible that substances are increasing the paranoia. It is also possible that their substance abuse developed as a way of managing paranoid ideation. The client may impulsively act-out, driven by paranoid thoughts and rationalized resentments.
- If RC9 is elevated, it would add to the picture of overexcitement, hyperactivity, impulsiveness, and reckless behavior. The use of recreational drugs, especially if SUB is elevated, would increase the likelihood of hypomanic overcommitments, grandiosity, and reckless behavior that could have negative consequences.

Therapy and Therapeutic Pitfalls – DISC Scale

Therapy for people with impulse control problems requires a therapeutic alliance to encourage the individual to recognize and restrain their impulses. Treatment depends on the underlying causes and severity of the impulsive behavior. Cognitive behavioral therapy can help individuals recognize what triggers their impulsive behavior. In some cases, it is a desire for immediate gratification and an intolerance for frustration. Learning to recognize when stress or tension is building and teaching the client how to stand back and self-observe the impulse pressure *without* moving into action is a useful approach. Mindfulness and meditation, with practices such as deep breathing and progressive muscle relaxation can help individuals, once they recognize the impulse to act, to release the tension that drives the impulse. If possible, link the triggers for impulsive behavior to any conditioning experiences in childhood when the client was impulsive because the reward system was highly inconsistent or dependent on caregiver whim. Should there be a link to past conditioning experiences, teach new coping strategies to delay gratification and improve decision-making. Dialectical behavior therapy can be effective for individuals with emotional dysregulation because it focuses on distress tolerance, emotional regulation, mindfulness, and effective interpersonal communication. Acceptance and commitment therapy can be useful as it encourages the client to accept that, although they have impulses, they do not need to act on them. Habit reversal therapy can help the client to focus on replacing impulsive behaviors with more adaptive alternatives. The therapist needs to avoid coming across as a parent with the client in the role of a recalcitrant teenager. Since many people with elevations on this scale will have had a troubled anti-authority adolescence, the client could slip into that role if the therapist is viewed as parentally critical versus nurturing.

Feedback Statements – DISC Scale

T score <39

Your profile suggests that you are a self-controlled, non-impulsive, disciplined person who is cautious and avoids being too spontaneous.

T score 43-63

You are reporting occasional rule-breaking, impulsive, thrill-seeking, and potentially self-destructive behavior that could lead to problems with authority. You may use substances, which could further aggravate your impulsive behavior.

T score ≥ 63

Your profile suggests that you are an impulsive, "live in the moment," sensation-seeking, and excitement-seeking individual. You were likely a somewhat rebellious and impulsive teenager and might have been in trouble with authority figures because of your actions. You currently might be using substances, which would increase your vulnerability to impulsive and poorly thought-through behaviors. These behaviors could lead to conflict with authority and loved ones.

- If EID is elevated, add: Although you answered items suggesting that you are currently depressed, feeling hopeless, blue, and defeated, nevertheless you are impulsive, sensation-seeking, and perhaps abusing substances. You may be feeling down currently because your impulsive behavior has gotten you into trouble. Or it could be that you are dealing with your depression by substance use and impulsive, reckless behavior. You may feel, "What the heck, I'm feeling terrible, so screw it, I'll just give in to my impulses."
- If THD is elevated, add: Your profile suggests that you are going through a confusing, perhaps frightening time, feeling vulnerable to being criticized, judged, or somehow hurt by others. You may have moments where you feel suspicious and feel the need to protect yourself. You may be using substances in an effort to manage the way you feel. However, you may act impulsively, even recklessly, especially under the influence of substances, since they increase your suspiciousness and mental confusion.
- If BXD is elevated, add: Your answers suggest that you are a rebel, disliking being controlled and tending to resist authority figures and bend the rules. You can be impulsive and even reckless, acting on an impulse without thinking through the likely consequences. You may be using substances that could increase your vulnerability to impulsive behavior.
- If ACT, IMP, ANP, AGG, and/or AGGR are elevated, add: Your profile suggests that you are very high-strung with a short fuse. Little things can knock you off balance and make you irritable and angry. At times, your irritation can devolve into aggression, and you can try to control people by the threat of your bad temper.
- If RCd is elevated, add: Your answers suggest that you are feeling blue, worthless, lonely, and lacking in self-confidence. At the same time, you are reporting being impulsive and using substances. It is possible that your demoralized feelings are a recent setback due to your impulsive behavior. It is also possible that when you feel bad you turn to substances, throw caution to the wind, and are reckless and impulsive.

- If RC4 is elevated, add: Your profile suggests that you are an unrestrained, "live in the moment," rebellious person who loves excitement and living on the edge. You can be quite impulsive and can manipulate people to get what you want. You may also be using substances, which would increase your vulnerability to impulsive and reckless behavior.
- If RC6 is elevated, add: You are reporting feeling somewhat suspicious and unsure of whom you can trust. You may feel people are out to hurt you or ruin your reputation. At times, it can be quite confusing not knowing who is trustworthy. At the same time, you report that you can be impulsive and are vulnerable to using recreational substances. Drugs and alcohol likely increase your mental confusion and even increase your suspiciousness. It is possible that you began to use substances as a way to manage your sensitivity, which, at times, can shade to misreading other people's intentions. It is also possible that the unsafe feelings that you have been experiencing have led you to use substances as a way to self-medicate your anxiety.
- If RC9 is elevated, add: Your scores suggest that you are vulnerable to getting overexcited and hyperactive, with your mind racing and lots of projects that you overcommit to. You may also be somewhat impulsive, jumping into things without thinking through all the negative consequences. You may be using substances as a way to manage your energy or perhaps to increase it because you like the idea of being super productive.
- If IMP, ACT, ANP, AGG, and/or AGGR are elevated, add: Your profile suggests you are quite impatient and have a short fuse. Your profile also suggests that you experience heightened moods when you get very excited, enthusiastic, and perhaps unrealistic about some of your ideas and projects. When stress builds, you can move into action impulsively without thinking through the consequences. You are easily angered and, at times, your irritability and anger can devolve into aggression. During these times you might intimidate people with the threat of your bad temper.

Lifestyle and Family Background Feedback – DISC Scale

People develop an impulsive and substance-abusing lifestyle for different reasons. Perhaps you grew up in a family where your caregivers were unreliable and where the rules depended on their moods rather than on your behavior. You may have learned to be impulsive, pushing to get what you desired immediately. Perhaps your caregivers were unreliable, and you could not trust them to follow through on their commitments. It is possible that this normalized your behavior of living in the moment and not thinking through possible consequences. Perhaps your caregivers were drug or alcohol users and acted impulsively, so you learned to act like they did. It is also possible that you had stable, decent, parenting but were diagnosed with ADHD as a child which led you to being bullied or feeling isolated in childhood. Perhaps that led to you being angry and rebellious, having difficulties at school, and getting in trouble for misbehavior. If you want to get better, it would be important to find a therapist you trust and perhaps get help with substance abuse. Once you have controlled your substance intake, you can start to work on identifying what triggers set off impulsive behaviors. If you can learn how to relax through deep breathing and progressive relaxation techniques when you feel that you are going to be impulsive, you will have useful techniques to calm yourself down. You may find it hard to open up to a therapist as you may assume people are manipulative. You might think your therapist is somehow "playing a game" and not really being authentic. Discuss that with your therapist and see if they can approach you non-defensively when you bring up your concerns.

Treatment and Self-Help Suggestions – DISC Scale

Managing your impulses versus them managing you is essential for building healthy relationships and achieving personal goals. Here are some self-help strategies you can work on.

1. Learn to recognize situations or environments that trigger your impulsive behaviors. Write down a list of times when your impulsive behavior led to negative outcomes. Try recalling what you were thinking or feeling before you were triggered. Did it relate to any childhood events when you felt that you had to act quickly because you did not trust what would happen next?
2. Consider one negative outcome that was a consequence of your impulsivity. What could you have done differently and what positive results might have occurred?
3. Consider taking a mindfulness class to increase your awareness of your thoughts and urges, which can then help curb your impulsive actions. Deep breathing, yoga, and meditation can all help reduce anxiety and impulsivity. When you feel an impulse to act, use your relaxation techniques to restrain yourself.
4. Regular exercise can help you feel less anxious and volatile.
5. If you feel the urge to act-out in anger, find a way to observe the situation as if you are watching a movie. Tell yourself that you will not act on the impulse and that you will take time to plan a better response.
6. Find a therapist to help you with these issues. Cognitive behavioral therapy can be effective in addressing impulsive behaviors. Dialectical behavior therapy can help you to recognize when you are becoming emotionally hijacked and provide effective coping strategies. You can improve your impulse control with patience and persistence.
7. Discuss with your therapist whether irritability associated with impulse control disorders can be treated effectively with medications and consider asking for a referral to someone who specializes in this area.

Negative Emotionality/Neuroticism (NEGE) Scale

General Descriptors

Complaints

Severe anxiety; nervousness; easily frightened; constantly worried; prone to panic; negative ruminations; sleep problems; easily distracted; difficulty relaxing.

Cognitions

Worrying over possible misfortune; ruminating about past losses; catastrophizing; brooding about having upset others; self-critical; intrusive thoughts.

Emotions

Easily knocked off balance and upset; agitated; constantly anxious; easily panicked; often fearful.

Traits and behaviors

General negative affectivity; high-strung; constantly on edge; apprehensive about possible disaster; panic-prone; fearful; insecure; ruminative; unassertive; guilt-prone; difficulty making decisions; overly conscientious; self-effacing.

Therapist's Notes – NEGE Scale

This 15-item scale identifies clients who are high-strung, easily upset, constantly anxious, on edge, and prone to panic. They ruminate over past losses and mistakes and are self-critical and guilt-prone. They catastrophize and feel anxiety about someone or something almost all the time. They worry about hurting other people's feelings and doubt themselves. Hanging back, because of low self-esteem, they can be self-defeatingly passive. Sleep difficulties, because of worry and a tendency to ruminate over possible misfortune, likely inhibits efficiency and productivity. Worrying and anticipating catastrophe may be an adaptive response to having experienced an unpredictable trauma. In some cases, a perceived catastrophic loss or number of losses might have led to the adaptive response of worrying, trying to anticipate all possible eventualities in order to pre-empt them. Important life changes, such as job loss, a move, the sudden loss of a significant relationship, or other unanticipated events, can all contribute to the development of negative emotions and constant worry.

Clients with elevations on this scale overanalyze their behavior, with the observing ego maintaining control, perhaps in an attempt to pre-empt the guilt of failure. Living with a heightened sense of constant anxiety, there is a tendency to develop superstitions, obsessions, and compulsions. This would be especially true if Compulsivity (CMP) is elevated. Clients may have a compulsive sense of duty. Pervasive apprehension serves as a pre-emptive defense against the possibility of unpredictable failure, while guilt serves as a reminder to stay vigilant. In some cases, the high levels of anxiety may lead to somatic symptoms, especially if RC1, NUC, and/or Cognitive Complaints (COG) are elevated. There is a genetic predisposition to anxiety; for example, a fussy colicky baby might become an anxiously attached toddler, a high-strung, prone-to-worry teenager, and a ruminative, obsessive adult. A clinical history would determine whether the disturbance is longstanding or a recent reactive condition.

Elevations on the other scales would provide a clue to possible conditioning experiences. For example, if scores on scales measuring depression are elevated, the hypothesis is that the individual may be protecting against an unpredictable, traumatic loss in the future by worrying. In some cases, high levels of anxiety may lead to somatic symptoms, especially if RC1, NUC, and/or COG are elevated.

Studies show that various disorders with strong negative emotions are correlated with NEGE, specifically borderline, narcissistic, obsessive/compulsive, schizotypal, paranoid, and dependent personality disorders.

Lifestyle and Family Background – NEGE Scale

In combination with a genetic predisposition, early childhood experiences of people with high negative emotionality might have involved unpredictable, possibly traumatic events. In some cases, they may have experienced caregivers who were unreliable, unpredictable, unavailable, or hostile. They may also have had caregivers who were overly involved, intrusive, controlling, and did not allow the client, as a child, to develop self-efficacy and autonomy. They may have been slow to mature as children, perhaps with some personal eccentricities like stuttering or shyness that might have led them to be teased and unpredictably put down by peers. In some cases, they may have had overloads of adult responsibilities prematurely that were overwhelming. One hyper-responsible, dutiful, severely anxious client reported the death of a breadwinner parent when he was nine years old. His mother was prone to severe depressions and would withdraw to her room for hours on end. He had two younger siblings that he tried to parent and, though he did a remarkable job, his younger sister once fell off a chair that she was climbing and suffered a severe concussion. As an adult he is still haunted by the event since he was blamed for it. As a parent he became suffocatingly controlling, hovering, and overinvolved, unable to stand back and let his children be independent. An adaptive response to being flooded with anxiety, subsequent to an unpredictable frightening event or series of events, is an attempt to be prepared. Hypothetically, highly anxious individuals have modified their behavior by being hypervigilant. in an attempt to predict and prevent the onset of painful and potentially panic-inducing emotions. Individuals elevated on NEGE are on high alert not to disappoint or lose the love and approval of others and to avoid the guilt that comes with failure.

Clarifying Scales – NEGE Scale

T score <41

This score is associated with positive descriptors such as relaxed, self-confident, placid, and emotionally stable. These clients are likely efficient, capable, and able to mobilize their psychological resources easily and effectively.

T score 45-49

Scores in this range reflect minimal, transient levels of worry and negative emotionality.

T score 50–60

Scores in this range reflect moderate and increasing levels of negative emotionality, that may cause distress and emotional difficulties for the client.

T score 64–80

Scores in this range indicate a client who is chronically anxious, feels insecure, is constantly worried, and is inhibited behaviorally. They are self-critical and guilt-prone, and have sleep difficulties, concentration problems, and difficulties making decisions. Emotional difficulties likely motivated the client for treatment.

- If EID is elevated, the client is experiencing severe anxiety and, at the same time, feeling demoralized, unhappy, blue, and depressed. They report feeling overwhelmed, helpless, pessimistic, constantly stressed, and self-critical. Anxiety may be the most salient presenting complaint, but the client is also highly inefficient and emotionally and cognitively disorganized due to feeling incompetent and overwhelmed. They are experiencing considerable emotional distress, likely felt as a crisis.
- If THD is elevated, complaints of anxiety may be associated with attempting to defend against the underlying psychosis. In the presence of a psychotic episode, the elevated NEGE scale could possibly be prognostically positive since the individual may be attempting to defend against the psychosis. Antipsychotic medication and/or psychiatric inpatient treatment for a thought dysfunction may be indicated.
- If BXD is elevated, the unlikely combination of negative emotionality with rebellious acting-out would suggest that the client may be experiencing severe anxiety due to the consequences of that behavior. Their aberrant behavior may have resulted in legal or other difficulties. It is also possible that the client suffers from anxiety and self-doubt and impulsively acts-out in a reckless, antisocial way in order to discharge anxiety. Despite their distress, they may not be motivated for treatment and could be a high risk for superficial compliance.

- If RCd is elevated, it adds demoralization to anxiety, guilt, and worry. With low self-esteem, and feeling blue, worthless, and lonely, the client reports a lack of perseverance, self-doubt, pervasive anxiety, and life dissatisfaction.
- If RC1 is elevated, the client may be suffering from a number of physical symptoms associated with somatic symptom disorders that may be causing them anxiety and worry. Bona fide medical conditions also need to be considered as a cause of their distress. It is also possible that they have suffered from anxiety over a long period of time and the physical symptoms are a manifestation of the stress on the muscular skeletal system caused by pervasive anxiety.
- If RC2 is elevated, low self-esteem, anhedonia, and pessimism about the future, as well as constant anxiety and apprehension about impending catastrophes are suggested.
- If RC4 is elevated, it is important to examine for possible elevations on FML, JCP, and SUB. If any of those are elevated, the individual is expressing negative emotionality associated with past and/or current behaviors that led to troubles. The individual's negative emotionality reflects feeling defeated and experiencing a trapped depression that is somewhat self-pitying rather than accepting of responsibility.
- If RC6 is elevated, the client may be struggling with paranoid ideation, a hypersensitivity to slights or criticisms, and a preoccupation with how others might be critical or judgmental of them. At the same time as they are developing rationalized, fixed, paranoid ideas, they are also reporting feeling constantly anxious, on edge, and apprehensive about impending consequential outcomes. It may be that their anxiety is indicating uncertainty about some of the rationalized ideas or their anxiety may be related to paranoid fears. It is important to examine the item endorsements on RC6 to better understand the need for an immediate intervention.
- If RC7 is elevated, the client is reporting being high-strung, easily knocked off balance, and easily irritated by minor inconveniences. Their anxiety causes impatience and low frustration tolerance. Anxiety-related psychopathology is likely present. This scale is highly correlated with the NEGE scale, so a high elevation on RC7 would confirm the central role of anxiety in the disturbance.
- If RC8 is elevated, an underlying thought disorder is co-morbid with an anxiety disorder. The client could be schizoid, fearful, insecure, self-doubting, and possibly obsessive compulsive. Neurotic anxiety could break down into loose associations and bizarre, anxiety-driven preoccupations. Disorganized thinking may be present, requiring an immediate intervention.
- If Malaise (MLS) is elevated, the individual is reporting poor health, tiredness, weakness, and, at the same time, severe anxiety and self-doubt. It could be that their malaise is the result of prolonged psychological depletion due to anxiety. Or it is possible that exhaustion and poor health has led to a depletion of physical resources and consequent tiredness and the experience of poor health.
- If Eating Concerns (EAT) is elevated, the individual's eating disorder may be activated by severe anxiety. The individual may use food and eating as a way to control or diffuse generalized anxiety. Eating or restrictive food intake may be ways to distract from or soothe severe anxiety.
- If NUC and/or COG are elevated, the client is reporting neurological and cognitive impairment symptoms such as dizzy spells, fits or convulsions, twitching muscles, imbalance problems, and uncomfortable physical sensations. They also report memory and concentration difficulties at the same time as severe anxiety, ruminations, guilt, and sleep problems. It is hard to know whether neurological and cognitive symptoms are the result of profound anxiety or if the individual has become anxious over their neurological, cognitive symptoms.
- If Suicidal/Death Ideation (SUI) is elevated, the client may be feeling suicidal because of prolonged, psychically depleting, enervating anxiety.

- If Helplessness/Hopelessness (HLP) is elevated, the client is reporting feeling defeated and hopeless about making their life work. This could be the result of a prolonged period of constant anxiety, guilt, and worry that has robbed them of confidence in their ability to effect change.
- If Self-Doubt (SFD), Inefficacy (NFC), Stress (STR), and/or Worry (WRY) are elevated, the constant worrying and guilt is combined with self-doubt, feelings of incompetence, and difficulties making decisions and persevering at tasks. Continual worrying affects stress management so that minor stresses can feel overwhelming.
- If CMP is elevated, the individual may have developed a number of compulsions as a way to manage their ongoing worrying and anxiety. Compulsions may provide soothing structure and purpose to generalized anxiety.
- If Anxiety-Related Experiences (ARX) is elevated, the individual is reporting numerous physical manifestations of anxiety and worrying with possible dissociative experiences. They are easily startled, invaded by painful memories, and experience nightmares with fitful sleep. Elevations on the scale support the existence of a generalized anxiety disorder or, in some cases, PTSD.
- If ANP is elevated, the client is high-strung, irritable, quick to anger, and easily frustrated. This may be a result of negative emotionality leading to lowered frustration tolerance and feelings of being easily overwhelmed. Evaluate for the possible presence of an anger-related disorder.
- If Behavior-Restricting Fears (BRF) is elevated, the client is not only anxious and constantly apprehensive, but also afraid of specific situations, closed and open spaces, handling knives, or the dark. The anxiety may have generalized into a number of specific fears and phobias.
- If SUB is elevated, the client's substance abuse may be related to their severe anxiety. They may have begun using prescription medications, street drugs, or alcohol as a way to moderate and manage their anxiety symptoms.
- If DSF, SAV, SHY, and/or INTR are elevated, the client's avoidance and discomfort around people may be related to their anxiety in general. For some people, social avoidance comes from a distrust and even dislike of most people. However, other people enjoy socializing but are initially shy. Experiencing constant anxiety would aggravate any shy or introverted tendencies.

Therapy and Therapeutic Pitfalls – NEGE Scale

Therapy with chronic worriers (i.e., individuals diagnosed with generalized anxiety disorder and excessive rumination), typically involves evidence-based approaches, such as cognitive behavioral therapy, rather than uncovering insight psychotherapy. Cognitive behavioral therapy is likely the most effective treatment for chronic worrying since it helps individuals identify, challenge, and modify negative thought patterns. Cognitive restructuring is useful to teach clients to recognize when their exaggerated worries might be irrational and help replace those worries with more balanced thoughts. Initially, uncovering therapy could identify specific events (childhood or adult) when the individual was taken by surprise by negative, potentially traumatic events. The therapeutic alliance would involve the client learning that their worry and anxiety was adaptive but is no longer necessary. Pushing the client initially by suggesting that their anxiety is irrational could lead to resistance. Instead, validating the client's anxiety as an understandable, adaptive response could help build a therapeutic alliance. The client typically resists redefining their worries as irrational unless the therapist can link specific painful events with the onset of the adaptive response of being vigilant and scanning the environment for danger.

Cognitive restructuring is helpful by having the client recognize when their worries are exaggerated. Behavioral exercises exposing fears in real-life situations to see if the feared outcome actually occurs could also be helpful (i.e., exposure therapy). For some chronic worriers, scheduling "worry time," when they set aside a designated time each day to focus on worries and then place those worries in a box till the next day can be helpful. Relaxation techniques and deep breathing can help relax the client when they experience moments of panic. The therapist has to be aware of their own impatience with irrational anxiety and worries since clients with this elevation are particularly sensitive to displeasing others and feeling judged.

Feedback Statements – NEGE Scale

T score <41

Your profile suggests that you are likely a relaxed, self-confident, and emotionally stable individual.

T score 41–50

Your profile suggests that you have occasional worries and anxieties but, nonetheless, you generally feel effective in your daily life.

T score 51–60

Your scores suggest that you can experience periods of worry and anxiety. Sometimes you may ruminate about a conversation you had, wondering if you offended or hurt someone's feelings. This can cause you to feel distracted from some of your important activities and you may occasionally lose sleep over a worry.

T score 64–80

Your profile suggests that you feel chronically anxious, feeling insecure and constantly worried, as if something bad is lurking and about to happen. You can be self-critical and easily feel guilty. You likely experience sleep difficulties with some concentration problems and difficulties in making decisions.

- If EID is elevated, add: You report feeling a lot of current anxiety while at the same time feeling demoralized, unhappy, blue, and depressed. Life can feel overwhelming, and you may feel helpless about making any changes. Constantly stressed and quick to be self-critical, it is easy for you to feel incompetent and overwhelmed.
- If THD is elevated, add: Your profile suggests that you are experiencing a lot of constant anxiety and dread, anticipating something bad lurking on the horizon. You may have some difficulties thinking clearly and may experience periods of confusion, wondering if people are out to get you or somehow harm you. It is understandable that you feel constantly anxious, which is affecting your concentration, memory, and sleep.
- If BXD is elevated, add: People with your profile generally do not experience a lot of anxiety. You test as a rebel who likes to live in the moment and is impulsive and driven to seek excitement and stimulation. Typically, people with your profile shrug off negative consequences and generally do not feel guilty. However, you are reporting feeling a lot of anxiety which may be the result of having done something impulsive that led to bad consequences. It is also possible that you suffer from anxiety and that every so often you do something impulsive and rebellious as a way of venting built-up tension.

- If RCd is elevated, add: Your profile suggests that you are feeling demoralized, are quick to beat yourself up, and often feel worthless and lonely. You easily doubt yourself and feel like giving up on projects if you feel they are not going well. At the same time, you are reporting feeling a lot of anxiety with a constant sense of dread, as if something bad is about to happen. Worries can interrupt your sleep and, at times, you experience panic. No wonder you get demoralized! It is possible that you have been an anxious person for a long time which has eroded your self-confidence. It is also possible that you have recently become demoralized for some other reason rather than just being an anxious person, and the worry and anxiety are part of the same response to a difficult situation.
- If RC1 is elevated, add: Your profile suggests you are experiencing a number of physical symptoms as well as a lot of anxiety and worry. Sometimes after a number of years of chronic worry people start to develop physical symptoms because of the stress on their body. It is also possible that you have become a worrier because you have been concerned about your physical health.
- If RC2 is elevated, add: Your profile suggests you have been feeling pessimistic about the future, self-critical, and recently have experienced little pleasure. You also report experiencing much anxiety and apprehension, as if something bad is about to happen. You likely have sleep difficulties and feel anxiety about something almost all the time.
- If RC4 is elevated, add: Your profile suggests that you are feeling trapped, sad, and anxious. You may have recently done something reckless or perhaps you broke some rules which got you into trouble, so now you are feeling anxious, on edge, and fearful. You may be losing sleep over your worries and, at the same time, feeling defeated by them.
- If RC6 is elevated, add: Your answers suggest that currently you are feeling on edge and fearful that others are out to hurt you, criticize you, judge you, or somehow ruin your reputation. Your profile suggests you feel constantly anxious, as if something bad is about to happen. There are moments where you feel panic and you might even feel that you cannot trust others, wondering if you are seeing things clearly or if people are out to hurt you somehow.
- If RC7 is elevated, add: Your profile suggests that you are a high-strung person who is easily knocked off balance by interruptions or minor inconveniences. You worry about how people think about you and if you have somehow hurt or offended them. You also report feeling anxious and worried much of the time and often experience a sense of doom, as if something bad is about to happen. You likely have sleep difficulties because your mind is interrupted by negative thoughts. What is probably most disturbing for you is the constant sense of anxiety and worry you cannot seem to control easily.
- If RC8 is elevated, add: Your profile suggests you are feeling anxious, perhaps even suspicious, wondering whom you can trust. At times, it may be hard to know what is reality and whether your mind is playing tricks on you. You might feel that it is hard to organize your thoughts and may even have weird sensory-perceptual experiences. Sometimes people with your profile believe something is wrong with their body and/or they see or hear things that are not actually there. You are likely experiencing a great deal of anxiety, constantly feeling worried as if something bad is lurking on the horizon. It is difficult for you to trust anyone right now, and you likely feel very alone, so your anxiety is understandable. Feeling on edge and worried probably interferes with your sleep and there may be moments when you might experience panicked feelings without being sure where they come from.
- If MLS is elevated, add: Your profile shows that you are feeling in poor health, often tired and weak, and at the same time feeling anxious and worried. Your anxiety could have worn you out since it affects your sleep and your health.
- If EAT is elevated, add: Your profile suggests you struggle with eating and purging. Your profile also suggests you often feel anxious and on edge, worried that something bad is about to happen. Your anxiety may interfere with sleep, and you may experience periods where you feel

panic. Perhaps you turn to food at these times or focus on restricting your food intake as a way to manage your anxiety. It is also possible that, when you get really anxious, you turn to food to soothe yourself and then feel guilty and feel the need to purge.

- If NUC and/or COG are elevated, add: You are reporting some neurological and cognitive symptoms such as dizziness, balance problems, fits or convulsions, numbness, and muscles twitching. You also report being anxious and constantly worrying that something bad is about to happen. You may also find it difficult to concentrate and remember things, and you may have periods when you are easily confused. These symptoms may be the result of experiencing anxiety for a long time. This can affect your whole body because of the tension that comes from constant worry.
- If SUI is elevated, add: Your answers suggest that you have been thinking about suicide and how to end your life. You also report that you feel constant anxiety and apprehension, with a sense of dread that something bad is about to happen. You have trouble sleeping and sometimes have moments of panic. It is possible that some of your suicidal thoughts are escape fantasies because the anxiety is so overwhelming. If you feel hopeless or suicidal and cannot reach your therapist, call a suicide and crisis 24/7 hotline [988 in the United States and Canada] for confidential support.
- If HLP is elevated, add: Your answers suggest you are feeling defeated and hopeless about making your life work. This could be because you have experienced anxiety for so long that you feel incapable of managing it. On the other hand, your sense of hopelessness and anxiety may have occurred at the same time as symptoms of depression or a generalized anxiety disorder.
- If SFD is elevated, add: You are very self-critical and quick to feel like a burden to others. You often feel useless, at the same time constantly worrying that something dreadful is about to happen. At times, you feel a sense of panic without knowing why. Your sleep is probably disturbed because you are having intrusive negative thoughts. You probably doubt yourself because you are so anxious, which makes it difficult for you to function efficiently. On the other hand, it is possible that your self-doubt and anxiety have occurred because of some trauma, recent loss, or setback.
- If NFC is elevated, add: Your test results show that you have difficulty making decisions, starting new projects, and are your own worst critic. You may have become indecisive because of your high level of anxiety and worry. It appears that you live constantly on edge, anticipating something bad happening. It affects your sleep negatively because you are bothered by intrusive thoughts. At times, you can feel panic and give up on projects that may be going well.
- If STR is elevated, add: Your profile suggests you are knocked off balance by stress. You also experience a lot of anxiety, with a constant sense of dread as if something bad is about to happen. You may be high-strung by nature, or you may have experienced some unpredictable, painful, or traumatic event that has put you on guard, constantly scanning the environment for danger. It is not surprising that even minor stress can overload you, since you are already tightly wound due to worry.
- If CMP is elevated, add: You have developed some compulsions that may be a way for you to manage your high level of worry and anxiety. Your profile suggests that you are constantly on edge, experiencing a sense of dread as if something bad is about to happen. Perhaps, as a way of managing anxiety, you have developed some rituals and compulsions, feeling that somehow they could protect you from something negative happening.
- If ARX is elevated, add: Your profile suggests that you have developed a number of physical symptoms associated with anxiety. You may notice your heart pounding, your hands sweating, and that your breathing is fast for no apparent reason. You are easily startled and there are times

you feel a sense of panic. You live with a constant sense of dread, as if something dreadful is about to happen, and find yourself worried about someone or something almost all the time. Worrying can be exhausting and can lead to feeling overwhelmed.

- If ANP is elevated, add: Your profile shows that you are high-strung and that small frustrations can make you irritable and quick to anger. This may be because you are so anxious, constantly worried about something or someone, and constantly feeling a sense of dread as if something bad is about to happen. It is not surprising that you do not have a long fuse since you already live with constant anxiety.
- If BRF is elevated, add: Your profile suggests that your dread and anxiety might have developed into fears of specific situations, such as closed or open spaces, handling knives, or the dark. You live with worry that something bad might happen and often lose sleep because of intrusive negative thoughts.
- If SUB is elevated, add: Your profile suggests you experience a high level of constant anxiety and dread. You may be using substances as a way to manage your anxiety and perhaps to help you sleep. It is also possible that your use of substances has led to the side effect of severe constant anxiety. Sometimes a person develops a substance-abuse problem as a way to manage anxiety, but then when they try to stop using, they experience severe anxiety.
- If DSF, SAV, SHY, and/or INTR are elevated, add: You report that you feel discomfort being around people and that you avoid them. It may be because you are shy, so it takes a while for you to warm up to others. It might also be because you do not trust people or like them and you prefer to be alone. You also report feeling anxious and constantly worried, and that you often feel a sense of impending doom. You report that you have difficulty sleeping and are bothered by intrusive negative thoughts. It is possible that your difficulty being around people is because it makes you more anxious.

Lifestyle and Family Background Feedback – NEGE Scale

Sometimes people with your profile have a genetic vulnerability to developing worries and anxieties. If you were prone to worry as a child (for example, finding it hard to spend the night away from home at friends' houses, or worrying about getting your schoolwork done and having test anxiety), you may have a genetic vulnerability. If for most of your life you would describe yourself as a worrier, concerned about whether you hurt someone's feelings or worried that some negative event is imminent, then the tendency to worry seems to be longstanding. However, there are other situations that can lead to anxiety and worry. You may have had caregivers who were controlling, perhaps even hovering over you too much, not allowing you to develop self-confidence and independence. In this situation, you might have developed anxiety because you lacked self-confidence. Perhaps as a child you were young for your age or perhaps you had some personal habits, like stuttering or shyness, that may have led you to be teased and unpredictably put down by your peers. In this case, being anxious and worrying about the future may have been your adaptive way to predict teasing so that you could prepare for it and not be taken off guard. Adverse events during childhood may have left you feeling insecure and anxious. Whatever the cause, anxiety is often an adaptive attempt to control the unpredictable onset of trauma or a negative event. Discuss with your therapist any situation you recall where you were surprised by a powerful negative event and determine if that could that have been the beginning of your anxiety and worry.

Treatment and Self-Help Suggestions – NEGE Scale

If you feel as though worry and anxiety are affecting your wellbeing, there are several self-help strategies that can help you manage anxiety, overthinking, emotional reactivity, and stress. Here are some suggestions.

1. Keep a daily journal to help you to identify triggers that cause emotional distress. Evaluate your thoughts to see if they might be unfounded. You may anticipate the "worst case" scenario for future events or fret about things you may have done wrong. If you live with constant anxiety, waiting for something bad to happen, you can make the decision to switch off negative thoughts.
2. Breathing techniques, mindfulness, and grounding techniques can help with feeling anxious. While facing a fear or anxiety-producing situation, try focusing on your breath. This can help you stay grounded and calm your body's physical response to stress. 5-4-3-2-1 grounding is another technique where you identify 5 things you see, 4 things you feel, 3 things you hear, 2 things you smell, and 1 thing you taste. Try doing some relaxation exercises before bed, focusing on a pleasant image. If a negative thought intrudes, imagine putting it in a box and closing the lid. Tell yourself you can revisit it the next day.
3. Anxiety often comes with "what if" thinking that tends to be exaggerated or unrealistic. Challenge these thoughts by questioning them. Consider what evidence supports or contradicts the fear, what the "worst case" scenario might be, and how likely it is to happen. Reflect on past challenging situations where you were successful.
4. Regular exercise, healthy sleep habits, and a healthy diet that limits caffeine and alcohol can increase your resilience and reduce anxiety.
5. People with your profile may have a genetic vulnerability to worry and anxiety. Explore with your therapist what kind of child you were. Were you a somewhat sensitive, prone-to-worry child? What childhood events took you by surprise in a traumatic or negative way? Learning to worry and trying to predict the future are adaptive responses. Explore with your therapist the past experiences which led you to become worry-prone so you can now learn to worry less.
6. Surround yourself with supportive people and find activities that boost your self-esteem and sense of accomplishment.
7. Designate a specific "worry time" each day and avoid overthinking at other times. If you catch yourself ruminating, try a "thought-stopping" technique.
8. Spend time enjoying hobbies, sports, social events, or other activities that allow you to get into the "flow," where you are totally absorbed and intrusive thoughts won't bother you. Experiencing these moments can encourage you to keep working on "thought-stopping."
9. Anxiety can be treated effectively with certain medications in some cases. Consider asking your therapist for a referral to someone who specializes in this area.

Introversion/ Low Positive Emotionality (INTR) Scale

General Descriptors

Complaints

Anhedonia; disinterested in life; dysphoria; lonely; low energy; unhappy.

Cognitions

Pessimistic; negative.

Emotions

Dysphoric; anhedonic; disengaged.

Traits and behaviors

Introverted; socially avoidant; romantic disinterest; lacking positive emotional experiences; few hobbies or interests; low energy; socially awkward; possible avoidant or schizoid disorder with detachment traits.

Therapist's Notes – INTR Scale

Elevations on this 14-item scale suggest a socially avoidant, anhedonic, pessimistic individual who experiences few positive emotions. The scale combines items related to both social avoidance as well as introversion. The individual is reporting that they avoid crowds, do not make friends easily, and do not have many recreational interest or hobbies. They admit that life feels dull to them, they rarely feel bursts of positive energy, and they see the world in pessimistic terms. Six of the items are scored on RC2 and eight items are scored on SAV. Thus, there is a depressive quality to the scale. However, the scale does not measure communicative sadness as much as social avoidance and lack of pleasure. There is a range of reasons why people might avoid social events. In some cases, they are genetically shy, needing time to warm up and enjoying small groups of people they know. This kind of shyness/introversion is not seen as psychopathology, but rather a genetic trait that does not cause the individual significant discomfort. There are socially avoidant people and disaffiliated people who are uncomfortable with people in general and dislike being around them. Sometimes their social avoidance is due to a cynical, negative view of people, perhaps believing that people are untrustworthy and self-serving. In still other cases, people may avoid others because of paranoia and psychosis. Elevations on this scale suggest someone who does not find pleasure in social activity. They likely feel awkward around people, have difficulty making friends, and do not enjoy life. They are not necessarily complaining of depression unless other measures suggest depressivity. The scale is measuring a trait that may be ego-syntonic.

Low scores reflect an individual disposed to being socially engaged with a wide range of positive emotions. Extremely low scores could be associated with an overly socialized individual, such as those with a histrionic personality disorder.

Lifestyle and Family Background – INTR Scale

There may not be a single type of family background that is associated with introversion and low positive emotions. Introversion, however, has a strong genetic component, so if either or both biological parents are introverted, the children are more likely to be introverted. Research has shown that brain activity differences, such as higher sensitivity to stimulation in the nervous system, can be inherited. One hypothesis suggests that introverts have a high level of cortical base arousal, so they tend to be arousal avoiders; whereas extroverts have a lower level of base arousal, so they are stimulation-seeking. In other cases, overly protective and restricting caregivers who maintain a highly structured environment or are very protective may raise more introverted children. However, if they are not genetically introverts, their inhibitions due to conditioning experiences may evolve over time into being more socially oriented. In other cases, an only child, with introverted caregivers who do not socialize, may not develop social interests and skills, especially if they have a genetic predisposition to introversion. Caregivers who encourage independence and self-sufficiency, but do not push social interaction, may raise children who are less extroverted and less skilled in social interaction.

Clarifying Scales – INTR Scale

T score ≤50

The client is socially engaged and finds pleasure in social interactions. They might seek out others to bring them out of a glum mood and are likely optimistic and socially comfortable. They generally enjoy life. They are most likely viewed as extroverts.

T score 52–54

The client is likely to enjoy social interactions at times, especially with small groups of familiar people, but is also comfortable being alone. They may complain of occasional social dissatisfaction and discomfort around others, but not to the degree that they are socially avoidant or distressed. They may need time alone after a period of socializing since meeting new people can be emotionally draining.

T score 57–85

The client reports a lack of positive emotional experiences. Social interactions do not feel rewarding to them, and they tend to avoid people. They maintain an emotional distance from others. Although not reporting clinical depression (unless other depression measures are elevated), they report dysphoria, a lack of rewarding interests and hobbies, pessimism, and anhedonia.

Since introversion may be a distinct genetically driven trait, if INTR is elevated with any other scale, it would modify the expression of that scale either by providing an inhibitory or an energizing effect. For example, if the client scores high on acting-out scales but also on INTR, the acting-out would likely be done in a more passive and potentially less aggressively action-oriented way. If INTR is elevated along with scales measuring low self-esteem, stress, hopelessness, and inefficacy, it would have the effect of hampering the possibility of obtaining social support and better reality testing.

- If EID is elevated, the broad range of symptoms associated with low positive emotions such as low morale, depression, anxiety, and feeling overwhelmed and hopeless, is combined with social introversion and an avoidance of people. It is possible that long-standing social avoidance has led to a dysfunctional, lonely lifestyle with resulting depression and anxiety. It is also possible that the client is experiencing a current agitated depression that is not caused by social avoidance. However, social difficulties could hamper overcoming their depression since the client will have few community support systems. A psychosocial history will answer to what degree their social difficulties have contributed to their anxious depression.

- If THD is elevated, a thought disorder, together with social avoidance and low positive emotional experiences, suggests a schizoid, withdrawn, socially isolated, awkward individual.
- If RCd is elevated, the client is lacking in self-confidence and feels demoralized, blue, lonely, and stressed. They are also introverted and socially avoidant, which might hamper them in reaching out to others for community support.
- If RC2 is elevated, the high correlation between these two scales suggests the client is depressed, socially withdrawn, and isolated. Their depression may be associated with social difficulties and resulting isolation. It is possible that their depression has aggravated their tendency to avoid others. Engagement in psychotherapy could be challenging.
- If RC4 is elevated, the individual is exhibiting antisocial traits as well as social avoidance. Because intuitively one would expect a self-absorbed, possibly narcissistic, individual to come across as extroverted and charmingly manipulative, a socially isolated rebel seems unusual.
- If RC6 is elevated, the client is hypersensitive to any criticism and preoccupied with protecting themselves against what they perceive are unfair and unjustified attacks on them. In a socially isolated, avoidant, and withdrawn client, paranoid conspiracy theories can grow and evolve, since the client is not exposed to the reality testing provided by social relationships.
- If RC7 is elevated, the client's social avoidance could be related to a generalized anxiety disorder in which many situations, events, and social interactions cause self-doubt and guilt. The client's social relationships are hampered not only by their social discomfort but also by their general anxiety about being good enough and pleasing enough to others. Avoidant and personality disorders should be considered.
- If RC8 and/or PSYC are elevated, the individual is possibly psychotic, with paranoid ideation, distorted and psychotic thinking, and difficulties with trust. Social withdrawal and social discomfort would increase the severity of the psychosis since the client will have little motivation to seek either emotional support or feedback about their paranoid ideation.
- If MLS is elevated, the individual's experience of malaise, feeling tired, weak, and not in robust, physical health, is aggravated by social withdrawal, pessimism, anhedonia, and isolation.
- If SUI is elevated, the client is reporting suicidal ideation as well as social avoidance and social isolation. It is more concerning that someone who is actively thinking about suicide and how to do it would also be socially isolated, since loneliness, alienation, and lack of social support is prognostically adverse for suicide.
- If SFD is elevated, it is possible that social avoidance, withdrawal, and isolation is associated with low self-esteem since the client is also reporting a lack of self-confidence and feeling like a burden to others. This self-doubt would aggravate any genetic or conditioned propensity to social withdrawal.
- If SAV and SHY are elevated, the individual is reporting being shy, easily embarrassed, and tongue-tied initially in new social situations. However, they are also reporting social avoidance or withdrawal. It is possible that, after failing at social success in dealing with shyness, an individual becomes demoralized, defeated, and then withdraws into social isolation.

Therapy and Therapeutic Pitfalls – INTR Scale

Using cognitive behavioral training to help identify and challenge negative thought patterns related to social interactions is useful. Therapy could then replace some of these negative thoughts (which lead to anticipatory anxiety) and replace them with more realistic ones. Exposure therapy could also be helpful by gradually introducing the client into social interactions. Social skills training is useful to teach skills such as initiating conversations, learning to maintain eye contact, and recognizing social cues. Relaxation training and deep breathing to help the client manage episodic surges of social anxiety could also be useful. When the client is ready, group therapy can provide a safe environment to practice social skills with others who have similar challenges. The group could provide both support and exposure therapy. Psychodynamic therapy could also be useful to explore possible conditioning experiences that may have led to the adaptive response of social withdrawal. The client may have difficulty developing an attachment to the therapist, so premature intimacy would likely lead to early termination. Practical, concrete, social skills training that avoids too much emotional intensity is probably the most efficacious approach.

Feedback Statements – INTR Scale

T score ≤50

Your profile indicates that you are someone who finds pleasure in social interactions and is likely comfortable being socially engaged. If you happen to be in a glum mood, you might seek others out to cheer you up. You are likely an optimistic and socially comfortable person.

T score 52–54

You likely can enjoy social interactions, especially with small groups of familiar people, but you are also comfortable being alone. Occasionally you may feel discomfort around new people and small talk, but not to the degree that you are socially avoidant or too distressed. You may need time alone after a period of socializing since meeting new people can be taxing emotionally.

T score 57–85

You are reporting that generally you do not have a lot of positive emotional experiences. Social interactions do not feel rewarding to you, and you probably avoid people since they make you uncomfortable. You may find that little seems to give you pleasure and that you don't pursue interests and hobbies since they don't hold your interest. You may feel pessimistic and negative about social interactions.

- If EID is elevated, add: As well as withdrawing from people and finding social relationships non-rewarding, you report that you have been feeling somewhat depressed, anxious, overwhelmed, and hopeless. It is difficult for you to reach out to others and get any kind of emotional support from them. You feel alone, anxious, and self-critical, yet may avoid people because they make you feel uncomfortable. Your social avoidance may be due to your current depression. On the other hand, it is possible that you have been a loner most of your life and your current depression has arisen for some reason other than social difficulties.
- If THD is elevated, add: Your answers suggest that you may be feeling distrustful of people, concerned they might hurt you in some way. At times, you might feel very suspicious, unsure whether what you are seeing is real or if your mind is playing tricks on you. You also reported

that you tend to be a loner, avoiding large groups of people you don't know, and that little in life gives you pleasure. You might prefer living alone and not reaching out to others for any kind of support. Sometimes it is important to reach out to people you do trust to get some advice on whether you are seeing reality clearly.

- If RCd is elevated, add: Your answers suggest you are feeling demoralized, with low self-confidence, and feeling blue, lonely, and stressed. You also report that you are quite introverted and tend to avoid people even if you feel lonely. You may have always been uncomfortable with large groups of people you don't know, but avoiding people when you feel down may aggravate your sense of isolation and demoralization. It may be helpful to have a support system to reach out to when you are feeling low or unhappy.
- If RC2 is elevated, add: You report that you are feeling somewhat down, perhaps depressed. At this time, little seems to give you pleasure and you feel pessimistic about the future. You tested as being an introvert, avoiding large groups of people you don't know, and disliking parties and loud social events. It is possible that you are withdrawing more from people because you have been feeling depressed. It is also possible that you have been an introvert most of your life and your current depression was precipitated by some other event and not due to social isolation.
- If RC4 is elevated, add: You are unusual in that you are a nonconformist, perhaps a rebel who dislikes being controlled. You can be manipulative and selectively report in order to get what you want. At the same time, you are reporting that you are an introvert, avoiding large groups of people you don't know and being uncomfortable at loud social events and parties. Consequently, you may be a loner, perhaps angry with authority but expressing it in subtle and not obviously aggressive ways.
- If RC6 is elevated, add: Your profile suggests that you are currently feeling very sensitive to criticism and are preoccupied with protecting yourself against people you worry may want to harm you. There may be times you feel very unsure about whom you can trust and whether you are seeing reality clearly. At the same time, you report that being around people is difficult, so you avoid parties and large groups of people you don't know. Since you don't socialize, you probably don't get a chance to talk to people about some of your concerns. Sometimes being able to discuss your fears with someone can help you put them in perspective.
- If RC7 is elevated, add: Your profile shows that you are quite high-strung, often feeling nervous and anxious that something bad is going to happen. Being on edge likely leads you to be more irritable, so small interruptions or setbacks can make you angry. You tend to be your own worst critic and anticipate that others will be critical of you. You are also introverted and uncomfortable at parties around large groups of people you don't know. You report feeling somewhat pessimistic and that you find little pleasure in hobbies or activities. It is possible that you avoid people because you become anxious and insecure about how you are coming across, concerned that you will let people down.
- If RC8 and/or PSYC are elevated, add: Your profile suggests that you may be experiencing feelings of unreality as well as feeling anxious and unsafe; perhaps you are worried that people are out to hurt you. When stressed, you may actually experience distortions in your perceptions of what is real or not real. Perhaps you hear or see things that others do not. There may be moments where you feel frightened, wondering who is for you and who is against you and wondering if you are thinking clearly. You also report being an introvert, uncomfortable in large groups of people you do not know, and you avoid parties and social events since you are uncomfortable around people. Being isolated may increase some of your mental confusion; you may believe in conspiracy theories and feel that you have to protect yourself. You may see some people as your enemy when in fact they are not.

- If MLS is elevated, add: Your test results suggest that you are feeling tired, weak, and not in robust physical health. At the same time, you report being introverted, so you tend to avoid people, especially large groups of people you don't know. You report feeling pessimistic and that little gives you pleasure in life. Is it possible that some of your malaise is related to your social anxiety and tendency to avoid people? On the other hand, you might have always been an introvert, preferring small groups of close friends, and the malaise you are feeling may be related to some other event.
- If SUI is elevated, add: You report that you have been feeling suicidal and have even thought about ways you would do it. You also report that you are an introvert, disliking being around large groups of people you don't know. It is difficult to know what led you to this feeling. It is possible that you feel lonely and yet are uncomfortable trying to reach out to make friends. You report that you are pessimistic about the future and that little in life gives you pleasure anymore. Perhaps that is why you feel defeated and are considering suicide. If you feel hopeless and suicidal and cannot reach your therapist, call a suicide and crisis 24/7 hotline [988 in the United States and Canada] for confidential support.
- If SFD is elevated, add: You report feeling like you are a burden to others. You lack self-confidence and are your own worst critic. You also report that you are an introvert, so you don't find parties with large groups of people you don't know enjoyable. You doubt yourself and feel pessimistic about the future. Very little in life seems to give you pleasure anymore, so you have probably withdrawn from others.
- If SAV and SHY are elevated, add: You report that you are quite shy, easily embarrassed, and sometimes at a loss for words with new people you don't know. You are also reporting that you avoid people, probably because being around them makes you anxious. Perhaps you have had some bad experiences lately that made you reluctant to reach out and attempt to connect with others. You report feeling pessimistic about the future and that little seems to give you much pleasure these days.

Lifestyle and Family Background Feedback – INTR Scale

Research suggests that introversion is at least partly inherited with neurophysiological correlates. Dopamine is a neurotransmitter produced in the brain that is associated with positive feelings. Although extroverts and introverts have similar levels of dopamine in their brains, extroverts have a more active dopamine reward system. This suggests that extroverts need more dopamine to feel positive emotions. Extroverts seek out stimulation to feel better versus introverts who avoid being overstimulated. Introverts also show brain activity associated with deep thinking and problem-solving, meaning that they tend to be reflective, not impulsive. Consequently, you probably avoid parties and large social events. You may find the small talk and back-and-forth banter that occurs at parties depleting.

Caregiving styles and culture can also shape introversion. If you were raised in a quiet, reflective household with caregivers who provided necessary resources for child rearing, but who were reserved and not particularly affectionate, it could have led to you being a self-sufficient introvert. A genetic predisposition to introversion, together with a childhood without much social interaction and social skill building could have contributed to your introversion. Introversion can become a problem if you are in a partnership with an extrovert. The extrovert may complain that you always want to go home early from social events. You may complain that you cannot get the extrovert out of the party to go home with you when they likely promised they would. You want to avoid social events, leaving your extrovert partner feeling hungry for more social interaction.

Treatment and Self-Help Suggestions – INTR Scale

If you want help with your introversion and low positive emotionality, the key is to find a balance between honoring your natural tendencies to be alone and gently expanding your comfort zone. Here are some self-help strategies to help you navigate social interactions and reduce avoidance.

1. Get to know yourself to determine if you are shy, introverted, or a social avoider. Introverts need "alone time" to recharge. Introversion is probably genetic and not a psychological condition. Social avoiders become that way for a number of reasons. You may feel insecure, distrust people, or feel vulnerable to judgment or criticism. Some people are not genetically introverted but avoid people because of the way they feel about themselves. In your case, your profile suggests that you just don't get excited and energized by being around people.
2. Being introverted is not a weakness and you don't *need* to change. However, if it is a problem for you, you can work on becoming more comfortable around people. Before a social event are you anticipating criticism or feeling awkward and tongue-tied? Observe your self-talk and see if you can consider possible positive outcomes to balance some of the negative thoughts about the event.
3. Set manageable goals, beginning with small social actions such as smiling at someone in line at the store or a neighbor. Build on this by making eye contact briefly with someone you meet or saying "hello" to a colleague. Prepare a few conversation starters about topics or questions you are comfortable with, so you won't feel so tongue-tied. For example, you might ask someone about their travel plans or any hobbies they may have. Being a good listener is a valuable skill. You can begin to share something about yourself when you feel comfortable, which can encourage discussion. Once you have learned some conversation starters and are less anxious in social situations, you will become more comfortable and enjoy being with more people.
4. Build your social skills by joining a small group involved in an activity you enjoy, like a book club or cooking class. An online chat group around a topic that interests you could be a gradual start and help you to develop the confidence to ultimately meet in person.
5. Practice mindfulness to help you enjoy being in the moment and appreciate small things. Deep breathing, meditation, or grounding exercises can help you calm anxiety before and during interactions at an event.
6. If you have negative thoughts, reframe them in a more balanced perspective. For example, instead of assuming people will know you are nervous, shift your thoughts to understanding that most people are focused on themselves, not judging you. If you cannot always tell if someone else is nervous, why would you think others will notice your nervousness?

10 Providing Therapeutic MMPI-3 Feedback

A Step-By-Step Approach

This book is written for clinicians of any school of thought. It is intended for clinicians, who have a solid understanding of the construction, development, ethical uses, and limitations of the MMPI-3 and who wish to learn the therapeutic feedback approach using this instrument. We see our approach as falling within the therapeutic assessment paradigm. It is unique in that our focus is on providing specific feedback statements and treatment suggestions. Our goal is to provide a guide to help clinicians develop non-judgmental and, wherever possible, empirically grounded feedback statements that facilitate a therapeutic dialogue. We believe that even one feedback session can have therapeutic value if conducted in an empathic manner. Where applicable, our feedback is based on empirical correlates but in some cases the feedback statements are informed by our clinical experience and expertise.

Providing feedback is a complex interactive process that can be emotionally healing and can provide a rich source of additional assessment data. In this chapter, we describe the steps of a therapeutic MMPI-3 assessment and how to engage in therapeutic history-taking so that a client's history, and any precipitating circumstances for the referral, can be integrated with the MMPI-3 data to guide a constructive reframing of the client's life story. The first section outlines the pre-assessment phase and discusses developing rapport, taking a psychosocial and/or therapeutic history, introducing the MMPI-3, identifying conditions for testing, and recognizing ethical issues and pitfalls. The second section describes the steps involved in preparing the test results for therapeutic feedback. This includes scoring the test, addressing validity, and composing and delivering the feedback results.

Pre-Assessment

Developing Rapport and Trust

Begin by building rapport and framing the assessment as collaborative. From the moment an interaction with a client begins, transference is developing. Clients will perceive the clinician's personality and professional style by subtle data, such as promptness in returning calls, reassuring answers to questions, and clinician transparency. A trusting client is more likely to produce a valid protocol. Attending to the following points will contribute toward the development of outcome-enhancing rapport with the client.

- Explain that the MMPI-3 involves a number of statements marked as True or False and that there is no right answer. Describe the importance of responding to the test statements in an accurate manner to maximize the benefit of the assessment. Inform the client that their results will be discussed with them and that they do not need to worry that they will be inaccurately characterized without their input. Emphasize that they will actively collaborate in determining how the results actually apply to them. Answer any questions the client may have and determine whether there had been any negative experiences with prior assessments.

DOI: 10.4324/9781003557920-10

- Ascertain what the client hopes the assessment will address. Discuss how the test results are going to be used and clarify who will have access to the test results.
- Take a psychosocial history, being mindful of any possible early learning or recent experiences that might impact the test results. Point out any adaptive responses evidenced in their history as well as any evidence of resilience and psychological strength. Summarize what you have heard from the client, recounting their story and highlighting moments when they experienced difficulties or traumas and their adaptive response to those events. This constructive review of their history builds rapport and trust, increasing the likelihood that they will produce a valid protocol. By validating their responses to past traumas and negative events as adaptive rather than maladaptive, the history-taking can itself be of therapeutic value.
- A hallmark of therapeutic assessment is the view that all interactions with clients are both a source of data and an opportunity for a positive interaction. Rapport established during the initial interview carries on throughout the course of therapy and will diminish client defensiveness during the assessment process.
- MMPI-3 assessments conducted at the request of other professionals will generate client expectations and concerns that may differ from assessments conducted with a clinician's own clients. Rapport can be complicated by cultural issues, with differing expectations of emotional expression and formality from the clinician. For example, direct eye contact, the use of titles, and clinician self-disclosure may not always be appropriate cross-culturally, so a "one-size-fits-all" approach does not work.
- Clients should be encouraged to express any concerns they may have about taking the test and receiving their feedback results. Explore any of the client's past negative assessment experiences or negative preconceptions. For example, some people may express "I don't believe in this personality testing kind of thing" when asked to take a personality test. Reassurance that they will be the arbitrators of the applicability of the assessment results is important. In some cases, clients have a particular question, such as "Why do I keep getting involved in relationships that don't work?" Even when clients are unable to formulate a specific question but rather seek treatment or an assessment as a result of general unhappiness, there is still a rich opportunity for therapeutic feedback to evolve during the dialogue about test results.
- It is also important to reassure clients that the therapeutic feedback process is fluid; that is, the assessor will provide a number of opportunities for questions and clarification as the process uncovers issues not yet articulated. The collaborative process of working together to help clients share their "story" typically tends to be cathartic.

Taking a Psychosocial and Clinical History

The rationale for completing a psychosocial and clinical history prior to administering an MMPI-3 is to allow for the emergence of possible issues and conflicts that can be more directly addressed in the assessment process. The process of clients telling their story in a chronological fashion is often satisfying, enlightening, and therapeutic for them. In taking the client's history, the clinician can demonstrate empathy and understanding by acknowledging important life events as potentially traumatic in nature and their responses as adaptive and understandable. Validating the client's understandable responses to painful events and finding examples of resilience and displays of character in the face of adversity can provide clients with a more positive view of their life story. The assessor should be aware of the emergence of themes such as a series of early destabilizing moves, early losses, or damaging self-esteem events that may have left emotional "scar tissue." Such instances likely have left clients vulnerable to current stressors that may restimulate the scar tissue due to similar past events. An understanding of early conditioning experiences obtained through the history will help the assessor integrate those experiences with MMPI-3 early background hypotheses drawn from scale elevation data. During the MMPI-3 feedback session, the client's background will allow the assessor to select relevant psychosocial factors for integration into the feedback based upon clinical judgment.

In the preceding chapters, a section for each scale titled "Lifestyle and Family Background" provides the assessor with various hypotheses about a client's early conditioning experiences associated with various particular MMPI-3 scale scores. Obtaining the client's history prior to the administration of the MMPI-3 will provide a source of objective verification about the validity of background experiences that may be associated with MMPI-3 elevations.

The clinician should conclude the obtained history by recounting the client's history, perhaps saying, "This is what I heard you tell me today." The clinician should use positive reframing whenever possible, ending with an open-ended question about anything misunderstood, missed, or neglected.

At the conclusion of the history gathering, acknowledge to the client the trust it takes for them to share their story and thank them for being open and forthcoming. It may be prudent to take a break, or even schedule the testing for another day, to allow the client time to process their experience of sharing their psychosocial history.

Introducing the Administration of the MMPI-3

Properly introducing the MMPI-3 can maximize the information gleaned from the assessment. Clients should be informed about the nature and purpose of taking the MMPI-3 and be given an honest and clear indication of how the results will be used. It is useful to explain to the client that, after their completed test is scored, they will participate in a collaborative discussion of the results. If the client does not affirm that certain feedback statements are accurate, the client and clinician will act as a team to hone the interpretation. Consensus may not be possible in all situations, but a client's resistance to feedback statements provides a good opportunity for dialogue.

Sometimes roles can become murky, with negative consequences. Consider the following scenario given by Pope (1992). A therapist was asked by a colleague to test a client. After the assessment, when the client returned to his next therapy session, he shared that the assessment feedback was very helpful, and the referring therapist became angry; it was the referring therapist's intention to use the assessment to provide feedback himself to his client. In this example the roles of all concerned were not sufficiently considered and explicitly clarified at the beginning of the assessment process. It is important that if a therapist receives a referral to conduct psychological testing that it is clear whether the referring clinician or the assessor is the one designated to provide the client with feedback.

Providing feedback to a client referred by a colleague can sometimes interfere with the client's relationship with the referring therapist. Frequently, the feedback is experienced as so validating that the client verbalizes wanting to switch therapists, which causes obvious problems. Consequently, in some instances giving feedback to the client together with the therapist is most useful, even if via phone or on a videoconferencing app.

The following statements and suggestions can be useful as a way to introduce the MMPI-3.

- The MMPI-3 stands for the Minnesota Multiphasic Personality Inventory, Third Edition. Essentially it is a personality measure first developed in Minnesota in the 1940s and extensively modernized since. An advantage of the test being around so long is that it is widely researched and we have a great deal of experience using it to assist individuals seeking or receiving treatment.
- The MMPI-3 is used in a variety of settings with many different types of people. The purpose for you taking the test today is ______________.

- There are 335 statements for which you will be asked to indicate whether they are True or False as they apply to you. Typically, the test takes under one hour to complete. However, you can take as long as you need. You are free to stretch and take short breaks as needed. It is important that you feel comfortable and not distracted, so if at any time you need a break or find the conditions uncomfortable, inform the person who is administering the test.
- It is important for you to be accurate with your answers for us to understand you well. Your focus and attention are important as you take the test.
- If the client is completing the MMPI-3 in booklet form: Please make sure that each item response that you mark True or False corresponds to the correct booklet item number.
- Remember that the feedback session is a two-way process, so you will be actively involved in helping me understand you. If the test results do not describe you accurately or are not helpful, you will have a chance to clarify how you see yourself. You are being asked to take this test because it will help us understand you more fully. It will provide a road map: a beginning point to explore how you feel and what kinds of events may have shaped you.
- Feedback is a vital part of this process and will help determine the accuracy of the results. The value of the assessment depends on a collaboration between us so you will be able to clarify and describe the way you see yourself. It would be ideal if together we could develop a picture of who you are.

These statements are not intended to replace the standard test instructions that appear in the test booklet or on a screen when the test is administered by computer. Once you have gone over these points with the client, inform them that the specific instructions for responding to the MMPI-3 items will appear in the first part of the assessment.

Conditions for Testing

The *MMPI-3 Manual for Administration, Scoring, and Interpretation* (Ben-Porath & Tellegen, 2020a) provides detailed administration instructions designed to standardize the assessment and maximize the utility of test results. The clinician is encouraged to become familiar with these procedures and adhere to them, as they are designed to match the way data were collected for the purpose of scale development, norming, and validation, and to maintain test security as required by the Standards for Educational and Psychological Testing (AERA et al., 2014, p. 142).

A trained proctor should be on hand to monitor the administration process. It is never appropriate to send a client home with the test material, nor is it appropriate to send them a link for completing the test on their own via computer. Proctors should be instructed to respond to any requests for clarification of a test item by indicating that they are unable to do so and to encourage the client to respond to the item as they understand it.

Although the MMPI-3 can be administered in a group setting, for collaborative feedback purposes it is better to individually administer the instrument using either a test booklet or a computer screen. It is permissible to administer the test over more than one session, however the MMPI-3 is typically completed in one testing session.

At the close of testing, offer appreciation for the client's efforts in completing the MMPI-3. Reinforce the idea that it will be interesting to see what light the results shed on their questions about themselves or how they are feeling. Although the results can be obtained quickly with computerized scoring systems, it is advisable to schedule a separate feedback session when the client is rested, and the clinician has had time to reflect and prepare the feedback.

Ethical Issues and Pitfalls

In any assessment situation, the possibility exists that the process will uncover a current or impending crisis that requires immediate intervention. The clinician may be required to report abuse or respond to clients who decompensate during the course of the assessment. The clinician should be prepared to address any immediate problems, from substance abuse to suicidal ideation and/or intent to harm others. Assessment data are sensitive and can be misused, making ethical guidelines particularly important. For example, clinicians should avoid using assessment data collected in the role of marital therapist to later proffer a forensic opinion in support of one spouse against the other. The clinician should always protect the security of the test items and scale composition. For a deeper discussion of assessment ethics, clinicians should consult *Essential Ethics for Psychologists: A Primer for Understanding and Mastering Core Issues* (Nagy, 2010) and *Standards for Educational and Psychological* Testing (AERA et al., 2014).

See Table 10.1 for a summary of the major points in this section.

Table 10.1 Pre-assessment: a summary

1.		**Developing Rapport and Trust**
	a.	Explain the test and its purpose
	b.	Encourage accurate responding
	c.	Elicit what the test-taker wants to know from their results
2.		**Taking a Psychosocial and Clinical History**
	a.	Client shares their life story
	b.	Listen for and affirm client's difficult and resilient life events
	c.	Provide a recounting of the client's important life events to demonstrate understanding and empathy
	d.	Reinforce the client for sharing their important life events
3.		**Introducing the Administration of the MMPI-3**
	a.	Describe when and how the MMPI-3 test was developed
	b.	Explain clearly how the test results will be used
	c.	Advise the time it will likely take to complete the test
	d.	Emphasize the need for candor when responding to the items for useful interpretation results
	e.	Explain that results that do not match the client's self-perception will be discussed with them for clarification after the test is completed
	f.	Stress that while test-taking is part of the process, the discussion following the results will be the most important part of the collaborative process
4.		**Conditions for Testing**
	a.	Adhere to the standard administration procedures detailed in the *MMPI-3 Manual for Administration, Scoring, and Interpretation* (Ben-Porath & Tellegen, 2020a)
	b.	It is recommended that the test be administered individually rather than in group format
	c.	Testing, whether in-person or on-screen, should be proctored
5.		**Ethical Issues and Pitfalls**
	a.	Be aware that the discovery of psychological issues involving possible near-term harm to oneself or others may emerge during the therapeutic feedback process
	b.	Be clear about ethical boundaries regarding the release of assessment data to others
	c.	Consult the recommended standards for educational and psychological testing to understand important assessment liabilities

Preparing the Test Results for Therapeutic Feedback

Scoring

The *MMPI-3 Manual for Administration, Scoring, and Interpretation* (Ben-Porath & Tellegen, 2020a) describes the available standard scoring options and procedures for the MMPI-3. Although these procedures allow for scoring the test manually using templates available from the distributor, to maximize test score accuracy, we encourage use of the computer-scoring options available via Pearson Assessments (www.pearsonassessments.com). If the test is administered by computer, only one item is presented at a time, which eliminates the problem of misalignment of question-and-answer spaces.

Protocol Validity

The first important step after obtaining the MMPI-3 scores is to determine their validity and interpretability; that is, assessing the validity of the resulting test protocol. Clinicians should be familiar with and follow the MMPI-3 protocol validity interpretive guidelines detailed in the *MMPI-3 Manual for Administration, Scoring, and Interpretation* (Ben-Porath & Tellegen, 2020a).

Composing and Delivering Feedback Results

After a determination of protocol validity is made, provided that the resulting protocol is valid and interpretable, scores on the MMPI-3 Substantive Scales are examined and interpreted. The clinician begins by inspecting scores on the Higher Order (H-O) Scales as they provide a broad indication of the client's psychological functioning. The Restructured Clinical (RC) Scales are then examined to identify problematic personality symptoms and traits. The Specific Problems (SP) Scales add richness and specificity to the general description provided by the H-O and RC Scales. The Personality Psychopathology Five (PSY-5) Scales provide information pertaining to possible features of a personality disorder.

In our experience, clients want to view their MMPI-3 profiles. In general, clients prefer to see their graphed results as this lends credibility and scientific merit to the assessment feedback. We have found it beneficial to share their profile graphs with them in the same order the feedback statements are presented. However, it is helpful to begin by explaining: "Your test results are graphed on these pages, with each page representing a different set of scales that reflect your attributes and traits." Then, provide a general statement about the T score demarcations and how higher scores represent more feelings and behaviors in a particular area of psychological functioning. When presented with high scores, clients may react strongly saying, "Oh my gosh, I am so different from a normal score." In response, the clinician should emphasize that their results represent only one point in time. Explain that the more elevated the scale, the more feelings and behaviors they have in that dimension of personality.

Although several scored pages are produced for an MMPI-3 score or interpretive report, we suggest discussing the most important or relevant set(s) of scores to avoid overwhelming the client with too much data. For example, if their Validity Scales scores are all within the normal limit range, a simple statement saying: "As you can see, all of your scores on these scales measuring your approach to the test indicate that you were open and honest and receptive to receiving feedback." This is typically sufficient for the client. If a scale(s) is outside the normal range, referring to that scale's feedback statement in this book will help explain the score and can lead to questions and discussions about the client's feelings and behaviors.

The desirability of providing written versus oral feedback to the client will depend on the preferences of both the clinician and the client. The clinician should consider the sophistication and emotional resilience of clients in determining the format and content of the feedback. In some cases, the clinician may want to avoid a written report in order to maintain control over the intensity and pace of the assessment feedback. In other cases, the feedback statements in a written format may be suitable for clients to distill and report back which statements are applicable or non-applicable to them. We believe that "feedback about the feedback" allows the client and clinician to focus clinical attention on specific areas of functioning.

In many cases, we have found it useful to provide the client with oral feedback, following up with a written report that selectively emphasizes their affirmations and/or rejections from the feedback session. During this interactional feedback session, explain that these feedback statements are discussion points to be affirmed or refined. Explaining that these feedback statements are hypothetical in nature will minimize any defensiveness arising from a client feeling inaccurately portrayed by any particular statement.

A therapeutic feedback report will be made up of the relevant validity statements, the feedback and family background statements, and the treatment and self-help statements. Each statement which is affirmed or rejected can be further elaborated upon in the session. We do not recommend releasing a written feedback report without first having had an interactive feedback session.

Begin the feedback with a focus on the Validity Scales scores (CNS, CRIN, VRIN, TRIN, F, Fp, Fs, FBS, RBS, L, and K) that may indicate content non-responsiveness, overreporting, or underreporting. Refer to the corresponding sections in Chapter 2, "Validity Scales," for detailed interpretive information. If the Validity Scales reflect non-defensive and candid responding, there is no need to review feedback for each Validity Scale with the client. Instead, a simple statement to the client will suffice, such as: "The scales measuring your attitude toward taking the test show that you were open, honest, consistent, and receptive to receiving feedback."

The "General Descriptors," "Therapist's Notes," "Lifestyle and Family Background," "Clarifying Scales," and "Therapy and Therapeutic Pitfalls" sections are provided for the clinician's benefit and are not intended to be shared with the client.

However, the "Feedback Statements," "Lifestyle and Family Background Feedback," and "Treatment and Self-Help Suggestions" sections can be read to the client verbatim as discussion points, modified by the clinician.

To individualize a written or oral report, review the "Feedback Statements" and "Lifestyle and Family Background Feedback" sections in the chapter for the relevant MMPI-3 scales. The feedback should repeat the statements written for the clinician in user-friendly language. The "General Descriptors" section for each scale provides a condensed list of descriptors that are commonly associated with the scale and can be used by the clinician to form their initial hypotheses. Most of the descriptors are empirically based. The "Therapist's Notes," "Lifestyle and Family Background," and "Therapy and Therapeutic Pitfalls" sections can provide additional clinical data to enrich the clinician's understanding of the client.

As many clients produce multiple MMPI-3 elevations and we have described hypothetical background experiences and conditioning experiences for every scale, we recommend the clinician use the "Lifestyle and Family Background Feedback" associated with the highest one or two scales. In the course of providing feedback, the clinician may also use "Lifestyle and Family Background Feedback" experiences from other scales in order to determine which conditioning experiences are most relevant to a particular client.

The "Clarifying Scales" section provides a refinement of the profile interpretation. The "Treatment and Self-Help Suggestions" section provides self-help and other recommendations for the client. Providing the client with treatment and self-help suggestions for all elevated scores may be overwhelming, repetitive, and counterproductive. Therefore, we suggest that clinicians review Chapters 2–9 for the self-help suggestions associated with the relevant scale scores and communicate a parsed version to the client.

As detailed in the final section of Chapter 1, there is considerable redundancy in the recommended feedback statements for various MMPI-3 scales, particularly across the various sets of scales. The sources of this redundancy are explained in Chapter 1. It is the task of the therapeutic feedback provider to sift through these statements and integrate them in a non-redundant manner. This process is illustrated with two case examples at the end of this chapter.

Clinicians who follow the procedures outlined in this chapter should obtain reasonably similar feedback profiles. To begin, the clinician should obtain a scored MMPI-3 report with all the available scale scores.

Figure 10.1 reproduces an example of the "MMPI-3 T Scores (By Domain)" page from the Pearson MMPI-3 Score Report. This page of the report organizes the MMPI-3 data, identifying and grouping the MMPI-3 T scale scores.

If the clinician is not using a computer-generated report, they can construct a similar summary manually by proceeding to the relevant feedback statements contained in Chapters 2–9 of this book. Once this has been completed, the feedback statements can be organized, with the clinician eliminating redundancies to produce a final feedback report. The feedback report can then be integrated with extra-test information from the clinical history, referral questions, and other test data, if available.

The first step in interpretation is to assess the validity of the test protocol. The first section of the MMPI-3 summary presented in Figure 10.1 provides the clinician with Protocol Validity T scale scores. If the profile is valid, the interpretation of scores on the Substantive Scales can proceed. This framework presents the following domains: Protocol Validity, Somatic/Cognitive Dysfunction, Emotional Dysfunction, Thought Dysfunction, Behavioral Dysfunction, and Interpersonal Functioning.

When composing feedback, the H-O Scales are then examined according to their relative elevations and reported to the client after the Validity Scales scores are addressed. For example, if a protocol shows the highest elevation on the EID Scale, the feedback statements associated with this elevation would be addressed first, and then the scores on all the elevated scales listed under this domain in Figure 10.1 would be interpreted. The clinician should then address the Interpersonal Functioning domain scores. If an elevated EID Scale score is interpreted, the Somatic/Cognitive Dysfunction domain elevations, if any, should be examined for its correlates. If there are no reportable elevations on EID, any elevations within the Somatic/Cognitive Dysfunction domain should be addressed before interpreting possible elevations on the other Substantive Scale domains (Thought Dysfunction, Behavioral Dysfunction, and Interpersonal Functioning.)

See Figures 10.2–10.5 for a step-by-step process to build a feedback profile. This MMPI-3 Interpretation Worksheet can be used as the basis for organizing, writing, and delivering feedback.

Feedback statements for each scale based on T scores can be obtained from Chapters 2–9 and are used to complete the worksheet form. Feedback statements for the scales with feedback content, whether low or high, are included. When there are no empirical correlates for low scores, no feedback is generated. Clarifying statements may be omitted to minimize redundancy. "Lifestyle and Family Background Feedback" is also included after each relevant elevated scale. Although it is unlikely that all these "Lifestyle and Family Background Feedback" sections will apply, they can be used as exploratory therapeutic dialogue. Scale feedback is presented by domain, although scales in Chapters 2–9 are organized in the order of the MMPI-3 interpretative report.

Although constructing a written feedback report might be desirable, it would require parsing of the feedback statements to eliminate redundancy and contradictions and prevent flooding the client with too much feedback. Our advice to clinicians is to use this book as a guide to explore a client's life experiences and as a way to help the clinician understand which areas of the person's functioning should be explored. As indicated earlier, it is advised that the clinician only generate

MMPI®-3 Score Report
08/01/2020, Page 7 ID: Mr. J

MMPI-3 T SCORES (BY DOMAIN)

PROTOCOL VALIDITY

Content Non-Responsiveness

CNS	CRIN	VRIN	TRIN
13	39	39	54 T

Over-Reporting

F	Fp	Fs	FBS	RBS
66*	50	47	51	58

Under-Reporting

L	K
36	38

SUBSTANTIVE SCALES

Somatic/Cognitive Dysfunction

RC1	MLS	NUC	EAT	COG
46	59	38	44	46

Emotional Dysfunction

EID 80

RCd	SUI	HLP	SFD	NFC
80	72	86	78	77

RC2	INTR
75	60*

RC7	STR	WRY	CMP	ARX	ANP	BRF	NEGE
55	68	65	49*	59	51	63	68

Thought Dysfunction

THD 49

RC6
50

RC8
44

PSYC
47

Behavioral Dysfunction

BXD 44

RC4	FML	JCP	SUB
55	59*	48	58

RC9	IMP	ACT	AGG	CYN
36	45	41	49	55

DISC
50

Interpersonal Functioning

SFI	DOM	AGGR	DSF	SAV	SHY
37	34*	31	58*	55*	69

*The test taker provided scorable responses to less than 90% of the items scored on this scale. See the relevant profile page for the specific percentage.

Note. This information is provided to facilitate interpretation following the recommended structure for MMPI-3 interpretation in Chapter 5 of the *MMPI-3 Manual for Administration, Scoring, and Interpretation*, which provides details in the text and an outline in Table 5-1.

Figure 10.1 Sample MMPI-3 T Scores (By Domain) Report page (Mr. J, 08/01/2020) from Pearson's product webpage.

MMPI®-3 Interpretation Worksheet

Protocol Validity

Content Nonresponsiveness CNS ____ CRIN ____ VRIN ____ TRIN ____

Over-Reporting F ____ Fp ____ Fs ____ FBS ____ RBS ____

Under-Reporting L ____ K ____

Figure 10.2 MMPI-3 Interpretation Worksheet (page 1).

Substantive Scale Interpretation

Somatic/Cognitive Dysfunction RC1 ____ MLS ____ NUC ____ EAT ____ COG ____

Emotional Dysfunction EID ____ RCd ____ RC2 ____ RC7 ____ NEGE ____

SUI ____ STR ____ INTR ____

HLP ____ WRY ____

SFD ____ CMP ____

NFC ____ ARX ____

ANP ____

BRF ____

Figure 10.3 MMPI-3 Interpretation Worksheet (page 2).

Thought Dysfunction THD ____ RC6 ____ RC8 ____ PSYC ____

Behavioral Dysfunction BXD ____ RC4 ____ RC9 ____ CYN ____

FML ____ IMP ____ DISC ____

JCP ____ ACT ____

SUB ____ AGG ____

Interpersonal Functioning SFI ____ DOM ____ AGGR____ DSF____ SAV____ SHY____

Figure 10.4 MMPI-3 Interpretation Worksheet (page 3).

Diagnostic Considerations

Treatment Considerations

Figure 10.5 MMPI-3 Interpretation Worksheet (page 4).

a written feedback report to the client after their feedback session has taken place. This allows the clinician to fine-tune a written feedback report as needed.

We do not provide diagnostic recommendations as this is primarily a feedback report. Diagnostic suggestions are provided in the Pearson interpretive report, in *Interpreting the MMPI-3* (Ben-Porath & Sellbom, 2023), and in the *MMPI-3 Manual for Administration, Scoring, and Interpretation* (Ben-Porath & Tellegen, 2020a).

See Table 10.2 for a summary of the major points in this section.

Table 10.2 Preparing test results for therapeutic feedback: a summary

1. **Scoring**
   a. Allow adequate time after the testing is completed to review the results prior to providing feedback to the client
   b. Show the profile graphs to the client, selecting the most relevant ones that illustrate their scale scores
   c. It is recommended that the MMPI-3 be computer-scored using Pearson software to save time and avoid manual scoring errors; the interpretive report for clinical settings provides diagnostic considerations that we do not provide
   d. A computer-administered MMPI-3 is an efficient method for preventing recording errors by the test-taker because each item is presented one-at-a-time; a computer administration also typically reduces the time taken to complete the test
2. **Validity**
   a. Review all MMPI-3 Validity Scales to assess for inconsistent responding, overreporting, or underreporting
   b. Review background life experiences that are possibly associated with invalid profiles
   c. Generate hypotheses for possible patterns of MMPI-3 responses that have led to the resulting Validity Scales scores
3. **Composing and Delivering Feedback Results**
   a. Begin interpreting the client's MMPI-3 profile by inspecting the Validity Scales, H-O Scales, RC Scales, SP Scales, and PSY-5 Scales
   b. Share profile graphs with clients for them to visualize their results
   c. Displaying the graphs lends credibility and scientific merit to their assessment feedback
   d. Explain T score elevations and emphasize scores change with therapy
   e. Share only the most pertinent profile graphs to avoid overwhelming the client with data
   f. Determine whether a written report would be useful after an in-person oral feedback session
   g. Consider the psychological sophistication and emotional resilience of the client when sharing oral and written feedback
   h. Explain that the feedback statements are subject to the client's verification in order to minimize defensiveness
   i. The "General Descriptors," "Therapist's Notes," "Lifestyle and Family Background," "Clarifying Scales," and "Therapy and Therapeutic Pitfalls" sections are for the clinician and, generally, are not shared directly with the client
   j. Collect and integrate the feedback statements associated with each scale elevation and parse all redundancies.
   k. The "Feedback Statements," "Lifestyle and Family Background Feedback," and "Treatment and Self-Help Suggestions" sections are meant to be shared with the client

CASE EXAMPLES

To assist in demonstrating the feedback process, we are presenting two cases, a male and a female. A history for each is presented, followed by their MMPI-3 profiles. Their background history can inform and help to expand the feedback statements that are obtained from the relevant sections in this book.

CASE 1 – MR. H.

Background and Current Issue

- 30-year-old software engineer recently promoted to manager who is struggling with interpersonal skills in his new supervisory role.

- Received negative performance reviews due to being perceived as aloof, hard to relate to, and intimidating to his team.
- Self-referred for therapy to understand himself better and develop better people skills.

Childhood and Family Background

- Only child of older, formal parents who were emotionally distant but not abusive.
- Father was frequently absent due to work and somewhat aloof; mother was strict but fair, used withdrawal/silence as punishment.
- Grew up in a socially isolated environment with little opportunity for socialization.
- Described himself as naturally shy and high-strung, with one particularly humiliating incident at school.

Developmental Patterns

- Developed obsessive-compulsive habits around age 15, including repeatedly checking homework.
- Continued OCD behaviors into adulthood (nail biting, checking work, worrying about others' opinions).
- Limited dating experience; one long-term relationship ended because partner found him too passive.
- Primarily socialized through online gaming communities.

Clinical Understanding

- Therapist identified genetic shyness combined with lack of socialization opportunities as key factors.
- Developed adaptive strategy of avoiding criticism/disappointment due to parents' withdrawal pattern.
- Learned to suppress emotions and avoid conflict, making him "hard to read" as a supervisor.
- Team members may interpret his shyness as rejection or dislike.

See Figures 10.6–10.12 for the MMPI-3 test results for Mr. H.

MMPI-3 Sample Feedback Worksheet – Mr. H.

Notes for the feedback provider are described with the italicized statements intended as feedback for the client. The scores for Mr. H.'s scales are reported as T scores except for CNS, which is a raw score.

Validity Scale Interpretative Feedback Statements

Referring to the MMPI-3 T Scores (By Domain), begin to complete the MMPI-3 Interpretation Worksheet (Figures 10.2–10.5) with the Validity Scales scores. Scores for CNS and the 10 validity indicators are recorded on the worksheet first. Next, the clinician turns to Chapter 2 to generate the relevant validity statements.

MMPI® 3

Minnesota Multiphasic Personality Inventory®-3

Interpretive Report: Clinical Settings

MMPI®-3
Minnesota Multiphasic Personality Inventory®-3
Yossef S. Ben-Porath, PhD, & Auke Tellegen, PhD

Name:	Mr H
Age:	29
Gender:	Male
Marital Status:	Not reported
Years of Education:	Not reported
Date Assessed:	05/15/2025

[1.93 / 19 / QG]

ALWAYS LEARNING PEARSON

Figure 10.6 MMPI-3 Clinical Interpretive Report (Mr. H., 05/15/2025 – page 1: Cover page).

MMPI®-3 Interpretive Report: Clinical Settings
05/15/2025, Page 2 Mr H

MMPI-3 Validity Scales

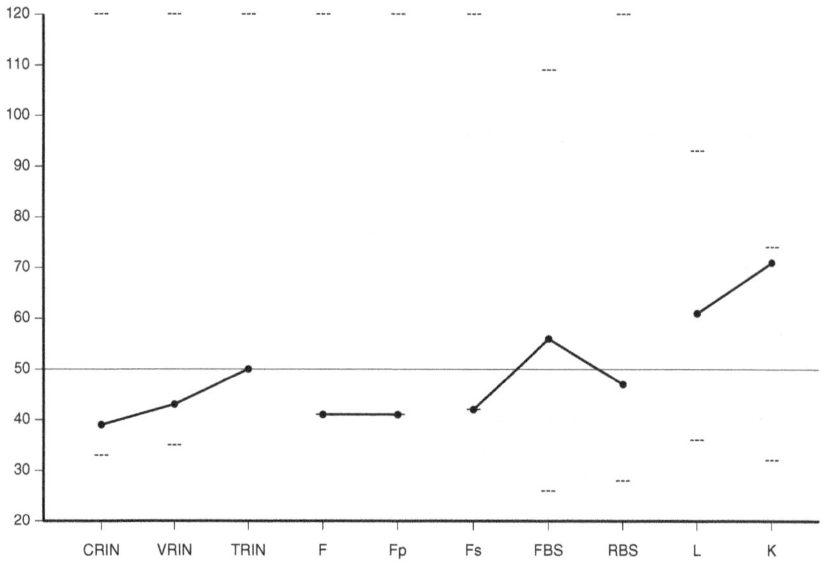

	CRIN	VRIN	TRIN	F	Fp	Fs	FBS	RBS	L	K
Raw Score:	2	2	13	0	0	0	11	5	6	13
T Score:	39	43	50	41	41	42	56	47	61	71
Response %:	99	100	97	100	100	100	100	100	100	100
Cannot Say (Raw):	2									

The highest and lowest T scores possible on each scale are indicated by a "---"; MMPI-3 T scores are non-gendered.

CRIN Combined Response Inconsistency
VRIN Variable Response Inconsistency
TRIN True Response Inconsistency
F Infrequent Responses
Fp Infrequent Psychopathology Responses
Fs Infrequent Somatic Responses
FBS Symptom Validity Scale
RBS Response Bias Scale
L Uncommon Virtues
K Adjustment Validity

Figure 10.7 MMPI-3 Clinical Interpretive Report (Mr. H., 05/15/2025 – page 2: MMPI-3 Validity Scales).

MMPI®-3 Interpretive Report: Clinical Settings
05/15/2025, Page 3 Mr H

MMPI-3 Higher-Order (H-O) and Restructured Clinical (RC) Scales

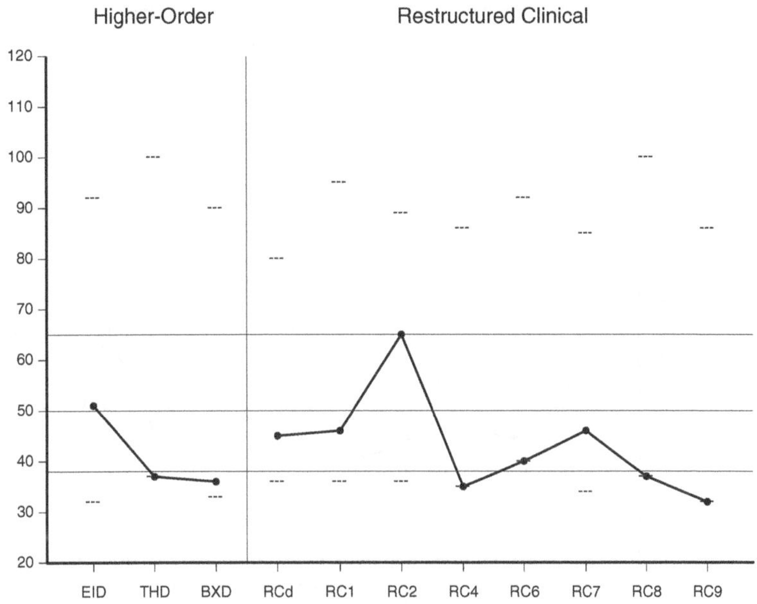

	EID	THD	BXD	RCd	RC1	RC2	RC4	RC6	RC7	RC8	RC9
Raw Score:	11	0	1	2	2	7	0	0	4	0	0
T Score:	51	37	36	45	46	65	35	40	46	37	32
Response %:	98	100	100	94	100	100	100	100	100	100	100

The highest and lowest T scores possible on each scale are indicated by a "---"; MMPI-3 T scores are non-gendered.

EID	Emotional/Internalizing Dysfunction	RCd	Demoralization	RC6	Ideas of Persecution
THD	Thought Dysfunction	RC1	Somatic Complaints	RC7	Dysfunctional Negative Emotions
BXD	Behavioral/Externalizing Dysfunction	RC2	Low Positive Emotions	RC8	Aberrant Experiences
		RC4	Antisocial Behavior	RC9	Hypomanic Activation

Figure 10.8 MMPI-3 Clinical Interpretive Report (Mr. H., 05/15/2025 – page 3: MMPI-3 Higher-Order (H-O) and Restructured Clinical (RC) Scales).

MMPI®-3 Interpretive Report: Clinical Settings
05/15/2025, Page 4 Mr H

MMPI-3 Somatic/Cognitive Dysfunction and Internalizing Scales

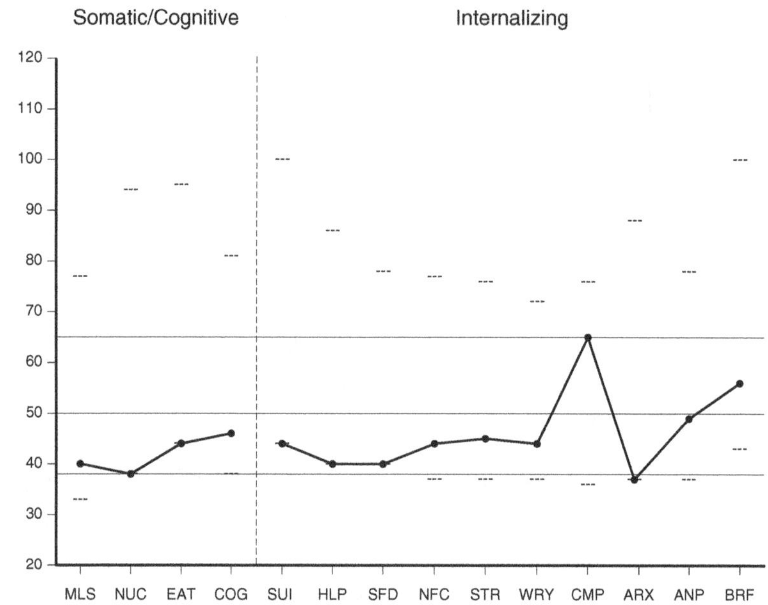

	MLS	NUC	EAT	COG	SUI	HLP	SFD	NFC	STR	WRY	CMP	ARX	ANP	BRF
Raw Score:	1	0	0	1	0	0	0	1	1	1	6	0	2	1
T Score:	40	38	44	46	44	40	40	44	45	44	65	37	49	56
Response %:	**86**	100	100	100	100	100	**86**	100	100	100	100	100	100	100

The highest and lowest T scores possible on each scale are indicated by a "---"; MMPI-3 T scores are non-gendered.

MLS	Malaise	SUI	Suicidal/Death Ideation	WRY	Worry
NUC	Neurological Complaints	HLP	Helplessness/Hopelessness	CMP	Compulsivity
EAT	Eating Concerns	SFD	Self-Doubt	ARX	Anxiety-Related Experiences
COG	Cognitive Complaints	NFC	Inefficacy	ANP	Anger Proneness
		STR	Stress	BRF	Behavior-Restricting Fears

Figure 10.9 MMPI-3 Clinical Interpretive Report (Mr. H., 05/15/2025 – page 4: MMPI-3 Somatic/Cognitive Dysfunction and Internalizing Scales).

MMPI®-3 Interpretive Report: Clinical Settings
05/15/2025, Page 5 Mr H

MMPI-3 Externalizing and Interpersonal Scales

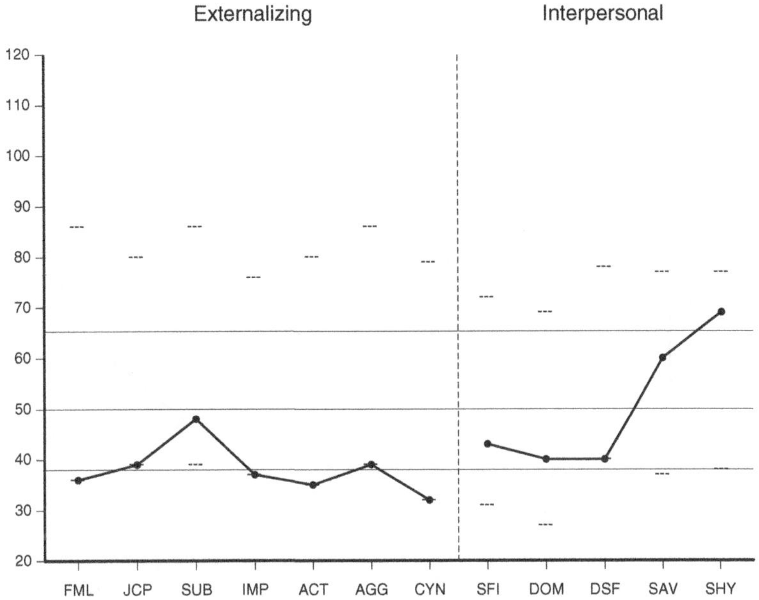

	FML	JCP	SUB	IMP	ACT	AGG	CYN	SFI	DOM	DSF	SAV	SHY
Raw Score:	0	0	1	0	0	0	0	4	3	0	6	6
T Score:	36	39	48	37	35	39	32	43	40	40	60	69
Response %:	100	100	100	100	100	100	100	100	100	100	100	100

The highest and lowest T scores possible on each scale are indicated by a "---"; MMPI-3 T scores are non-gendered.

FML Family Problems
JCP Juvenile Conduct Problems
SUB Substance Abuse
IMP Impulsivity
ACT Activation
AGG Aggression
CYN Cynicism
SFI Self-Importance
DOM Dominance
DSF Disaffiliativeness
SAV Social Avoidance
SHY Shyness

Figure 10.10 MMPI-3 Clinical Interpretive Report (Mr. H., 05/15/2025 – page 5: MMPI-3 Externalizing and Interpersonal Scales).

MMPI®-3 Interpretive Report: Clinical Settings
05/15/2025, Page 6 Mr H

MMPI-3 PSY-5 Scales

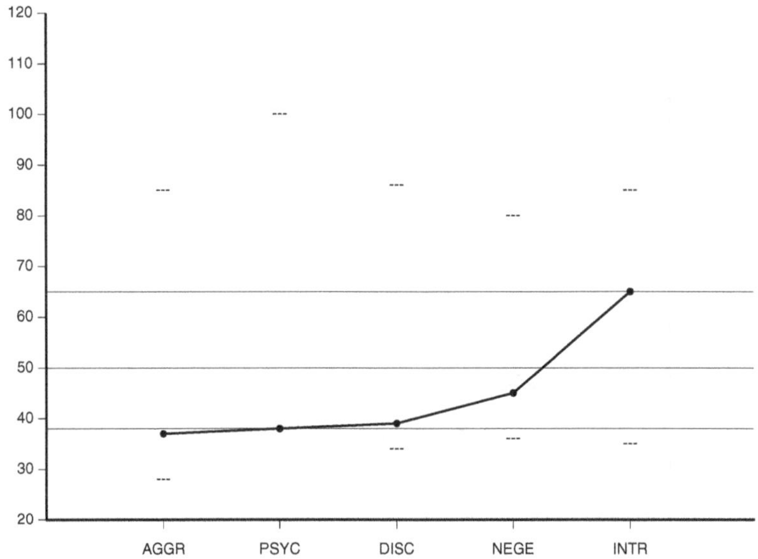

	AGGR	PSYC	DISC	NEGE	INTR
Raw Score:	3	0	1	2	9
T Score:	37	38	39	45	65
Response %:	100	100	100	100	100

The highest and lowest T scores possible on each scale are indicated by a "---"; MMPI-3 T scores are non-gendered.

AGGR Aggressiveness
PSYC Psychoticism
DISC Disconstraint
NEGE Negative Emotionality/Neuroticism
INTR Introversion/Low Positive Emotionality

Figure 10.11 MMPI-3 Clinical Interpretive Report (Mr. H., 05/15/2025 – page 6: MMPI-3 PSY-5 Scales).

MMPI®-3 Interpretive Report: Clinical Settings
05/15/2025, Page 7 Mr H

MMPI-3 T SCORES (BY DOMAIN)

PROTOCOL VALIDITY

Content Non-Responsiveness

CNS	CRIN	VRIN	TRIN
2	39	43	50

Over-Reporting

F	Fp	Fs	FBS	RBS
41	41	42	56	47

Under-Reporting

L	**K**
61	**71**

SUBSTANTIVE SCALES

Somatic/Cognitive Dysfunction

RC1	MLS	NUC	EAT	COG
46	40*	38	44	46

Emotional Dysfunction

EID
51

RCd	SUI	HLP	SFD	NFC
45	44	40	40*	44

RC2	INTR
65	65

RC7	STR	WRY	**CMP**	ARX	ANP	BRF	NEGE
46	45	44	**65**	37	49	56	45

Thought Dysfunction

THD
37

RC6
40

RC8
37

PSYC
38

Behavioral Dysfunction

BXD
36

RC4	FML	JCP	SUB
35	36	39	48

RC9	IMP	ACT	AGG	CYN
32	37	35	39	32

DISC
39

Interpersonal Functioning

SFI	DOM	**AGGR**	DSF	SAV	**SHY**
43	40	**37**	40	60	**69**

*The test taker provided scorable responses to less than 90% of the items scored on this scale. See the relevant profile page for the specific percentage.
Scale scores shown in bold font are interpreted in the report.

Note. This information is provided to facilitate interpretation following the recommended structure for MMPI-3 interpretation in Chapter 5 of the *MMPI-3 Manual for Administration, Scoring, and Interpretation*, which provides details in the text and an outline in Table 5-1.

Figure 10.12 MMPI-3 Clinical Interpretive Report (Mr. H., 05/15/2025 – page 7: MMPI-3 T Scores (By Domain)).

CNS raw score 2: You may have overlooked or intentionally omitted two items related to your self-confidence and physical health. Is there a reason you didn't answer these items?

Next, his low CRIN T score suggests the following feedback statement.

CRIN 39: You answered the test thoughtfully and consistently, clearly reading the items carefully.

The scores on the VRIN and TRIN Scales can be ignored since Mr. H's thoughtful consideration of the test items has been covered by the CRIN feedback statement. Should the clinician want to provide feedback statements for all the Validity Scales scores, they should go to the relevant pages in Chapter 2 and report them. Although, the following VRIN and TRIN feedback statements are redundant, a clinician may want to emphasize the diligence and focus reflected in the Validity Scales scores.

VRIN 43: You answered the test consistently, suggesting that you read all the items carefully and gave much thought to being accurate about how you feel.

TRIN 50T: You answered the items thoughtfully, without answering True or False carelessly. Your test results will likely be valid.

Next, the clinician records feedback statements for the elevations on the following Validity Scales by referring to Chapter 2. In the example of Mr. H., the following feedback statements would be generated.

F 41: You answered the test items candidly, without overemphasizing any symptoms or complaints.

As the feedback statement for Fp is redundant after the F feedback statement, it can be omitted.

Fp 41: You were candid and open in describing your symptoms and behaviors, so the resulting personality profile is valid and is likely not exaggerated.

The clinician should then report the following feedback statement as it covers somatic symptoms not included in the preceding validity statements.

Fs 42: You answered a number of items that dealt with your physical health. You tried to be accurate, without exaggerating your condition. That suggests your test results are an accurate description of your current condition.

As somatic accuracy has been addressed by the Fs feedback statement, the statements associated with FBS and RBS are redundant and can be omitted.

FBS 56: The items on this scale appear to have been answered accurately.

RBS 47: You answered the items thoughtfully without overemphasizing your concerns.

Next, the clinician would look up the relevant feedback statements in Chapter 2 for elevations on the L Scale.

> **L 61**: You were able to achieve an appropriate balance between being honest and the temptation to create an overly favorable impression of yourself, admitting to normal human failings, showing you have good self-awareness and the confidence to be yourself. You were honest about your strengths and vulnerabilities.
>
> **K 71**: The way you answered the test shows you are a poised and emotionally controlled person. In the face of emotional turmoil or stress you approach matters with a "stiff upper lip." You tend to not wear your feelings on your sleeve, so people close to you need to multiply the intensity of what you say in order to have a sense of empathy for you. For example, be mindful that if you were to say you are "unhappy" about someone's behavior or "not too pleased," people may take you at your word rather than realize that you could be quite angry and upset.

Substantive Scale Interpretative Feedback Statements

Review the RC scores next, noting both high and low T scores for applicable feedback.

> **RC1 46**: You take care of yourself physically when things go wrong and take care of any illnesses you may have responsibly.

A clinician may choose to not include the RC1 statement as it may be irrelevant to the main issues dealt with by other elevated scores. On the other hand, some neutral or positive statements may be useful to make the report less negative.

Proceeding to the next Substantive Scale, MLS, Mr. H. omitted one of the seven items. The reason for the omission should be discussed at the beginning of the Validity Scale feedback. Referring to Chapter 5, the clinician could omit the associated MLS feedback statement since it is redundant to the RC1 statement. The low scores on NUC and EAT do not warrant a corresponding feedback statement as there are no meaningful correlates for these low scores.

A score of T = 46 on COG suggests the following feedback statement.

> **COG 46**: When it comes to concentration, memory, and the ability to understand what you are reading, you can keep your mind on one thing and don't lose your focus easily. Your memory seems to work well, and you have a little or no trouble concentrating.

EID and RCd with scores of T = 51 and T = 45 respectively, do not warrant feedback statements as both are in the normal range.

However, an elevated RC2 score at T = 65 leads to the following feedback statement.

> **RC2**: Your score is just outside the normal range. It shows that you are a serious and thoughtful person who takes responsibility seriously. When stressed you may be vulnerable to episodic sleep difficulty. You are vulnerable to experiencing guilt if things go wrong even though you might not have been responsible for the problem. You shy away from taking unnecessary risks and are cautious about "counting your chickens before they hatch." You are an earnest person, realistic about life's ups and downs. Recently, you may have experienced a minor setback which has left you feeling careful about being too optimistic in case something goes wrong again. On the other hand, you may just be a dutiful, responsible, thoughtful, conscientious personality type. Also, some people with this profile grew up having had more responsibility than is normal for a young child. Perhaps you were in a caregiver role, either for a younger sibling or even a sick caregiver or family member. Perhaps you had to take on the role of an adult early, leaving

> you a little vulnerable to worry, since a child can't be expected to manage adult problems. It might be hard to give yourself permission to relax, be in the moment, and give yourself carefree moments.

Since RC2 is high compared to the other scales associated with EID, the clinician should refer to the "Lifestyle and Family Background Feedback" section associated with the RC2 feedback statements in Chapter 4 to obtain further insights about the client.

Lifestyle and Family Background Feedback – RC2

> Typically, people with your profile have experienced recent or past losses and disappointments that have left them apprehensive about allowing themselves to enjoy life. Perhaps as a child you experienced the loss of a parental caring figure, leaving you with overloads of responsibility; or for some other reason you may have been deprived of the normal joys of a carefree childhood. In other cases, recent losses (perhaps a job loss, a blow to your self-esteem, or a perceived or actual setback) have made you feel hopeless about ever enjoying life again. Being negative, pessimistic, and withdrawing from life may be an understandable self-protection from further loss or setback.

As the RC2 "Lifestyle and Family Background Feedback" appears to be redundant with the preceding statements associated with RC2, the clinician may choose not to report one of the feedback statements. If the clinician chooses to look up feedback statements for every scale and report those that have correlates associated with low scores, they can decide whether they add to the feedback dialogue if they suggest positive traits, or whether they are confusing and do not add value to the clinical picture of the client.

An example is RC7 at T = 46. The clinician could look up the following associated feedback statement in Chapter 4.

> **RC7 46**: Your score is in the normal range and shows you have a number of strengths. It suggests you have a healthy approach to your duties and responsibilities, getting things done in a timely manner without putting enormous pressure and guilt on yourself. You don't worry needlessly; you tend to have good self-confidence and are not easily wracked by guilt if things go wrong. You don't lose your patience easily and generally you are able to relax and sleep well.

However, some of the statements associated with a normal range score on RC7 are contradictory to the feedback statements generated by the RC2 elevations, so the clinician may decide to omit the feedback statements associated with a normal T score on RC7.

Omitting feedback about the lower scale scores associated with EID, as they do not provide incremental information, the clinician then focuses on the elevated INTR and CMP Scales. Looking in Chapter 6 for feedback associated with a high score on CMP and Chapter 9 for INTR, the clinician notes down the following.

> **CMP 65**: Your score suggests that you have a tendency to be compulsive, feeling the need to act in a precise manner and do things a certain way every time you do them. Others may see you as rigid and perfectionistic and critical of them, especially if they don't do things the "right" way. Your compulsive behaviors may include checking and rechecking, counting and re-counting, or engaging in behaviors that others see as inefficient and irrational. Your compulsions may interfere with your life and may annoy those closest to you. You may be embarrassed by your compulsions and may avoid certain people so that they do not see them.

As we have provided a "Lifestyle and Family Background Feedback" section for CMP, these statements could also be noted and explored to determine the etiology of the compulsions. The clinician would examine the "Lifestyle and Family Background Feedback" section already reported for RC2 elevations to determine if there are any contradictions between the backgrounds associated with the different elevations.

Similarly, the clinician refers to Chapter 9, noting the feedback statements for T = 65 for INTR reports.

> **INTR 65**: You are reporting that generally you do not have a lot of positive emotional experiences. Social interactions do not feel rewarding to you, and you probably avoid people since they make you uncomfortable. You may find that little seems to give you pleasure and that you don't pursue interest in hobbies since they don't hold your interest. You may feel pessimistic and negative about social interactions.

The clinician would then look up the "Lifestyle and Family Background Feedback" statements associated with elevations on INTR and determine if they are contradictory or redundant given what already has been generated.

As most of the other scales are within the normal or low normal range, the clinician does not need to generate feedback statements for them, unless they choose to do so in order to provide some positive balance to the feedback dialogue. For example, a relatively low score on AGGR suggests a generally agreeable, non-pushy person who is a conflict-avoider. These descriptions might be included to balance out some of the other statements, which may feel negative to the client. We have included some low-score feedback statements as an example of adding positive attribute richness.

The moderately elevated scores in the interpersonal functioning domain for SAV and SHY generate feedback described in Chapter 8. We have included the feedback associated with those scales although the clinician may want to exclude them since they may be redundant, given that there are three measures of social avoidance and shyness.

> **SAV 60**: Your answers suggest that, while you can occasionally enjoy being around people, you are comfortable with time alone and dislike being in large crowds and meeting strangers.

> **SHY 69**: Your answers suggest that you are quite shy and meeting new people is initially difficult for you. You likely can get easily embarrassed or tongue-tied, unsure what to say to someone. In new social situations you may hang back and wait for others to engage you. People may misunderstand your shyness as aloofness but, once you are comfortable with people, you can be quite socially engaged. You likely dislike being called upon to speak spontaneously or suddenly being made the center of attention without being prepared for it. Your responses suggest that it is uncomfortable for you to interact with people you do not know, and your shyness is present in most social situations. You may desire a social connection but feel inhibited by fears of social embarrassment and rejection. You may be self-critical and assume that you will not be easily liked by others.

As we have provided possible treatment considerations and self-help suggestions for every scale, we advise the clinician to adopt whichever self-help suggestions are appropriate and include them in the feedback dialogue. Following are the treatment suggestions that we include regarding this report. These statements are based upon the descriptors for the scales but can be expanded upon using the clinician's own insights and clinical judgment.

High K Suggestions

1. Start by learning to recognize your emotions. You and your therapist can work together to identify any feelings you may be experiencing during the therapy session. Think of a positive emotional experience and take some time to identify where in your body you experience the feelings. Do the same for a negative experience. Observe to see if you inhibit emotions to avoid them becoming too intense.
2. Be mindful that when you express your emotions you may do it in a muted way, so others don't have a full sense of empathy for you. Occasionally ask others how they perceive you are feeling so you learn how you come across to them.
3. Familiarize yourself with the benefits of "emotional intelligence," which is the ability to identify, assess, and manage your emotions in a healthy way. There are many good self-help books written about developing emotional intelligence to make improvements in both your personal life and in the workplace.

RC2 Treatment and Self-Help Suggestions

Mr. H.'s RC2 score suggests mild depression; however, the scale may not be sufficiently elevated to recommend medication. Feedback statements associated with significant, but not highly elevated, scales should be reported as probabilistic, while higher elevations suggest more definitive statements. The clinician should determine the extent of the client's experienced depression before recommending medication. As the treatment suggestions for RC2 are written for all elevations, they need to be modified for profiles that are significant, but not highly elevated. It could be overwhelming to present all the self-help suggestions at once, so the clinician should present the most salient ones.

1. Your therapist may want to recommend that you consider medication, which could help you to feel better quickly.
2. Research has shown that regular aerobic exercise (if you are medically cleared for exertion) can decrease stress and have a very positive effect in relieving depression. Studies indicate that aerobic exercise has antidepressant and anti-anxiety effects and protects against the harmful consequences of stress.
3. Work with your therapist to change how you view yourself. Notice how quick you are to blame and doubt yourself. In any given moment, when you dislike yourself, attempt to make a list of your positive attributes so that you maintain a balanced view of yourself.
4. Assertiveness training can be an effective component of mood regulation. Assertiveness is an honest and direct expression of your own desires and thoughts while still respecting the thoughts and feelings of others. An aggressive response ignores the feelings of others, whereas a passive response is the failure to express your own wants and needs. Think of examples either in your own life or something you have observed that illustrates different styles of communication, and then role-play assertive responses with your therapist.
5. Feeling depressed can be quite lonely and isolating, but one of the best ways to begin feeling better is to reach out for social support and contact. Joining a sports or activity group is a way to seek out social support while concurrently getting the benefits of exercise. Consider making plans with friends or family, even if it is just by phone or for a brief visit.

6. Observe your tendency to catastrophize. When something bad happens, you tend to anticipate the worst possible outcome and then suffer anxiety anticipating it. Make a list of possible positive outcomes and compare them to the list of dire consequences you have imagined.

CMP Treatment and Self-Help Suggestions

As the self-help suggestions for CMP are written for all significant elevations, the clinician needs to choose which ones are most likely to be useful for clients with significant, but not highly elevated, profiles in order not to overwhelm them.

1. Observe your behavior and recognize your specific compulsions. The first step in controlling them is to note when and where they happen and what events seem to trigger them, along with any thoughts you have at these times.
2. Compulsions are often the result of anxiety or fear, so try to challenge this response by asking yourself whether the behavior is necessary and based on a valid fear. After you act on your compulsion, try to understand what it is about doing it that makes you feel better.
3. If you are having trouble making progress, try managing how often you act on your compulsion. Reduce the frequency or intensity over time can reduce the drive to act on the compulsion. Resisting a compulsion once means it can be resisted twice.
4. Mindfulness exercises, like deep breathing or progressive muscle relaxation, can help ground you in the present, reduce anxiety and tension that can contribute to compulsive urges, and give you a respite from the intensity of the driven compulsion.
5. If you feel compelled to act on your compulsion, try distracting yourself to delay the action briefly. Over time, the urge will often weaken. Even a delay of a minute or two can remind you that you can survive without it.
6. Start slowly and celebrate each small success, and they will add up over time. Plan rewards for yourself to reinforce your actions.

SAV Treatment and Self-Help Suggestions

As you are seeking treatment for social problems and work-related problems in order to feel more socially comfortable, these are simple techniques you can learn to help you. Once you have identified the causes of your social avoidance, whether due to past negative experiences or your own predisposition, you can work on techniques that could enhance your social skills.

1. Start with low-stakes interactions, perhaps saying "hi" to a neighbor, engaging in brief small talk with a cashier, or attending a social gathering for a short time. Over time, as you get more comfortable, you can gradually challenge yourself to stay in social situations longer or engage with more people.
2. Being kind to yourself is key. Understand that social avoidance is often rooted in fear or anxiety, and it is okay to take things slowly. Instead of criticizing yourself for avoiding situations, acknowledge the effort you are making when you do engage.
3. If you find yourself frequently overthinking social situations or imagining "worst case" scenarios, cognitive behavioral therapy can help. It involves identifying negative thoughts,

challenging them, and reframing them in a more realistic or positive light. It can also help you to gradually expose yourself to social situations in a controlled manner.

4. Try focusing on listening to others instead of worrying about how you are being perceived. You don't have to worry about saying the perfect thing, just be present and engaged with the person with whom you are talking.
5. Set small, specific goals for yourself, for example: "I'll attend this social event for 20 minutes" or "I'll talk to one person at this gathering." Achieving these goals can build confidence and reduce your fear of future social situations.
6. When you start feeling anxious, practice mindfulness or relaxation techniques. Deep breathing or progressive muscle relaxation can help ground you and calm your nerves before or during social interactions.
7. Consider joining a group that aligns with your interests (such as a book club, art class, or hiking group) as a low-pressure way to connect with others. The shared focus on an activity can make interactions feel less daunting.
8. Understand that every step forward counts. Whether you attend a party for a short time, start a conversation with a stranger, or push through an uncomfortable situation, give yourself credit. Your social skills will get better with practice.

SHY Treatment and Self-Help Suggestions

Shyness is not a negative trait. If you would like to be less shy, there are a lot of ways to get there. Accepting that you are shy and not beating yourself up about it is the first step. If you recall always being a little shy, slow to warm up in social situations, and preferring to be around small groups of people who you know, then it is likely genetic. If you have experienced negative events with others, perhaps being bullied, criticized, or rejected by your peers or caregivers, you may have developed shyness as a reaction. If you grew up in a family where there was not much social interaction, you may not have learned the skills of small talk. Learning how to engage in conversation and engage in small talk is not difficult. Here are some things you can work on.

1. Recognize that shyness is a natural response and don't judge yourself.
2. In situations where you feel shy, try to ascertain if it is because the person you are relating to is making you feel insecure or if you are anxious that you are going to come across badly.
3. Set manageable goals, beginning with small social actions, such as smiling at a neighbor or someone in line at the store. Build on this by making eye contact briefly with someone you meet or saying "hello" to a colleague.
4. Prepare a few conversation starters about topics or questions you are comfortable with so that you won't feel so tongue-tied. For example, you might ask someone about their travel plans or hobbies. You can begin to share something about yourself when you feel comfortable, which can encourage discussion.
5. Be sure to listen to what others are saying, rather than focusing on how you should respond or how you are coming across.
6. Force yourself to attend a small social function, even if briefly and even though it will be stressful. One small success will lead to another, and you can gradually expand your social activities. Remind yourself to smile and try to look like you are enjoying the conversation.
7. Join a support group with other people who struggle with shyness. It can be an opportunity for you to become more comfortable opening up and being vulnerable about your own shyness. It could also provide you with a setting where you can practice how to talk to people that you do not know.

8. Consider working with a therapist who can use techniques such as role-plays, modeling, and instructions to build everyday social skills. Practicing these will help you feel more confident and less isolated.

INTR Treatment and Self-Help Suggestions

If you want help with your introversion and low positive emotionality, the key is to find a balance between honoring your natural tendencies to be alone and gently expanding your comfort zone. Here are some self-help strategies to help you navigate social interactions and reduce avoidance.

1. Get to know yourself to determine if you are shy, introverted, or a social avoider. Introverts need "alone time" to recharge. Introversion is probably genetic and not a psychological condition. Social avoiders become that way for a number of reasons. You may feel insecure, distrust people, or feel vulnerable to judgment or criticism. Some people are not genetically introverted but avoid people because of the way they feel about themselves. In your case, your profile suggests that you just don't get excited and energized by being around people.
2. Being introverted is not a weakness and you don't *need* to change. However, if it is a problem for you, you can work on becoming more comfortable around people. Before a social event are you anticipating criticism or feeling awkward and tongue-tied? Observe your self-talk and see if you can consider possible positive outcomes to balance some of the negative thoughts about the event.
3. Set manageable goals, beginning with small social actions, such as smiling at someone in line at the store or a neighbor. Build on this by making eye contact briefly with someone you meet or saying "hello" to a colleague. Prepare a few conversation starters about topics or questions you are comfortable with so you won't feel so tongue-tied. For example, you might ask someone about their travel plans or any hobbies they may have. Being a good listener is a valuable skill. You can begin to share something about yourself when you feel comfortable, which can encourage discussion. Once you have learned some conversation starters and are less anxious in social situations, you will become more comfortable and enjoy being with more people.
4. Build your social skills by joining a small group involved in an activity you enjoy, like a book club or cooking class. An online chat group around a topic that interests you could be a gradual start and help you to develop the confidence to ultimately meet in person.
5. Practice mindfulness to help you enjoy being in the moment and appreciate small things. Deep breathing, meditation, or grounding exercises can help you calm anxiety before and during interactions at an event.
6. If you have negative thoughts, reframe them in a more balanced perspective. For example, instead of assuming people will know you are nervous, shift your thoughts to understanding that most people are focused on themselves, not judging you. If you cannot always tell if someone else is nervous, why would you think others will notice your nervousness?

Feedback Session Results

Mr. H had a science background and so was very interested in seeing his MMPI-3 profile graphs. He asked many questions about the various elevations. He was non-defensive and was surprised that the feedback was so accurate. He admitted that he was always shy and, at times, tongue-tied in new social situations, especially if he was called on to speak without being prepared. He did not recognize that his social avoidance was problematic until his feedback session. He believed that his anxiety in social situations only became a problem after his promotion, as he had to supervise a group of people and inspire them in motivational meetings. He did recall feeling troubled when a teacher called on him and he froze, after which he was humiliated by his peers. In the feedback session, that event was engaged so that he could relive it and see it from a different perspective and forgive himself for having frozen. He admitted that his compulsions could interfere with his life and were embarrassing to him when he was in a relationship. He was able to acknowledge that he had, at times, felt lonely as a child and had lingering difficulties enjoying life, leading to feelings of anhedonia. He did not feel that he was particularly depressed but was open to joining a group for social skills building. He agreed that exercise and being in nature could be helpful to him. He also wanted help in writing his profile for an online dating app since he had difficulty extolling his own virtues. He found the feedback useful and insightful.

CASE 2 – Ms. N.

This case was adapted and expanded upon from the textbook *Interpreting the MMPI-3* (Ben-Porath & Sellbom, 2023, pp. 431–446). Therapists who want to learn more about this case are encouraged to read Chapter 10, pages 431–446 of Ben-Porath & Sellbom's book.

Background and Current Issue

- 33-year-old woman seeking outpatient treatment for marked depression, sadness, and anhedonia
- Experiencing fatigue, sleep difficulties, and concentration problems.
- Significant anxiety, nervousness, constant worry, and social isolation present.
- Referred by internist for evaluation to determine if depression is primary with secondary anxiety.
- Current crisis triggered by husband's recent erratic behavior and alcohol use.

Childhood and Family Background

- Born in rural Arkansas as middle child of five siblings (two older brothers, two younger sisters).
- Father exhibited binge drinking and violent behavior, including physical altercations with mother.
- Severe financial hardship required periodic placement with maternal aunt when mother couldn't support all the children.
- Family adhered to fundamental Christian beliefs with weekly church attendance.
- Mother maintained strict rules about modesty and forbade rock music.

Developmental Patterns

- Developed as quiet, compliant child who was academically successful but notably passive.
- Consistently followed rules, avoided aggression, and allowed domination by brothers and friends.

- Pattern of dutiful, non-confrontational behavior became defining personality characteristics.
- Advanced from receptionist to management by age 25 due to reliability and responsibility.
- Married fellow employee who shared religious values and appeared stable.
- Initially comfortable in traditional, submissive marital role with two children.

Clinical Understanding

- Current symptoms represent significant departure from previously stable functioning.
- Husband's recent behavior (disappearing for days, returning intoxicated) creates disturbing parallel to childhood trauma with father.
- Childhood pattern of compliance and passivity may have contributed to vulnerability in current crisis.
- Reports difficulty making decisions and avoidance of work problems due to current stress.

See Figures 10.13–10.19 for the MMPI-3 test results for Ms. N.

MMPI-3 Sample Feedback Worksheet – Ms. N.

Validity Scale Interpretative Feedback Statements

CNS Raw Score 0: You completed all the test items without omitting any.

CRIN 48: You answered the test thoughtfully and consistently, clearly reading the items carefully.

Next, the scores on VRIN and TRIN could be ignored since thoughtful consideration of the test items has been covered by the CRIN feedback statement. Should the clinician want feedback statements for all the Validity Scales scores, they should refer to the relevant pages in Chapter 2 and report them. The following VRIN and TRIN feedback statements are redundant and could be omitted.

VRIN 51: You answered the test consistently, suggesting that you read all the items carefully and gave much thought to being accurate about how you feel.

TRIN 54T: You answered the items thoughtfully, without answering True or False carelessly. Your test results will likely be valid.

As the elevation on F adds incremental value to the feedback, it is included.

F 72: You answered the test candidly and openly and you may be experiencing some distressing feelings and thoughts. This may mean you are open to help and psychological guidance.

However, the feedback for Fp is redundant and so can be omitted.

Fp 58: You were candid and open in describing your symptoms and behaviors, so the resulting personality profile is valid and is likely not exaggerated.

As the Fs Scale introduces somatic complaints, it could be included.

MMPI®-3 Score Report
06/21/2019, Page 2

ID: Ms. N

MMPI-3 Validity Scales

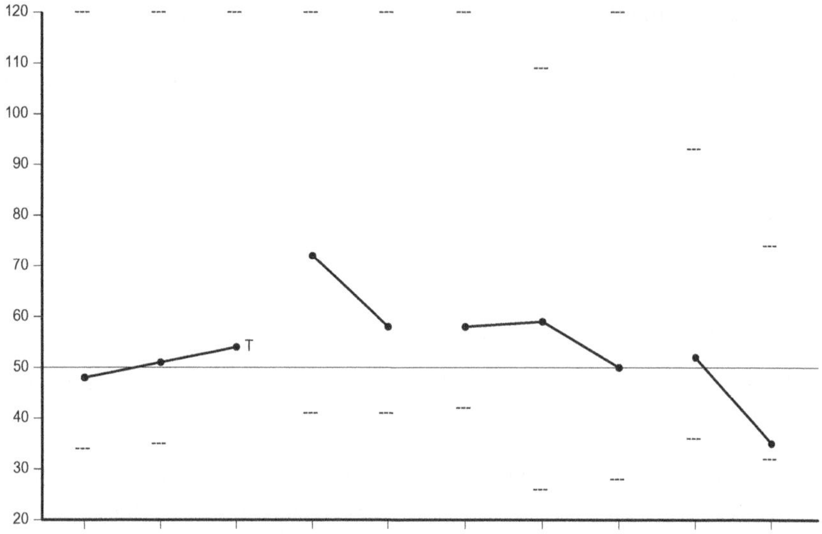

	CRIN	VRIN	TRIN	F	Fp	Fs	FBS	RBS	L	K
Raw Score:	5	4	14	10	2	3	12	6	4	1
T Score:	48	51	54T	72	58	58	59	50	52	35
Response %:	100	100	100	100	100	100	100	100	100	100

Cannot Say (Raw): 0

Percent True (of items answered): 39%

The highest and lowest T scores possible on each scale are indicated by a "---"; MMPI-3 T scores are non-gendered.

CRIN Combined Response Inconsistency
VRIN Variable Response Inconsistency
TRIN True Response Inconsistency
F Infrequent Responses
Fp Infrequent Psychopathology Responses
Fs Infrequent Somatic Responses
FBS Symptom Validity Scale
RBS Response Bias Scale
L Uncommon Virtues
K Adjustment Validity

Figure 10.13 MMPI-3 Score Report (Ms. N., 06/21/2019 – page 2: MMPI-3 Validity Scales).

MMPI®-3 Score Report
06/21/2019, Page 3

ID: Ms. N

MMPI-3 Higher-Order (H-O) and Restructured Clinical (RC) Scales

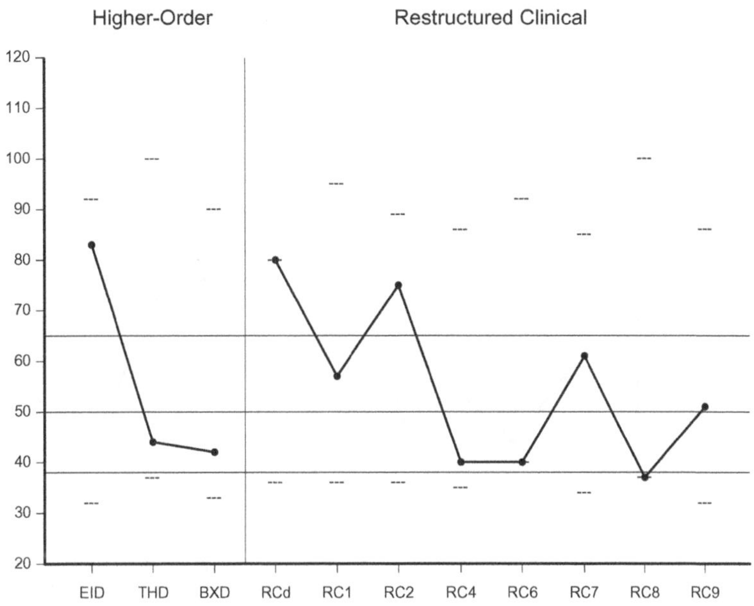

	EID	THD	BXD	RCd	RC1	RC2	RC4	RC6	RC7	RC8	RC9
Raw Score:	36	1	3	17	6	10	1	0	12	0	7
T Score:	83	44	42	80	57	75	40	40	61	37	51
Response %:	100	100	100	100	100	100	100	100	100	100	100

The highest and lowest T scores possible on each scale are indicated by a "---"; MMPI-3 T scores are non-gendered.

EID Emotional/Internalizing Dysfunction
THD Thought Dysfunction
BXD Behavioral/Externalizing Dysfunction
RCd Demoralization
RC1 Somatic Complaints
RC2 Low Positive Emotions
RC4 Antisocial Behavior
RC6 Ideas of Persecution
RC7 Dysfunctional Negative Emotions
RC8 Aberrant Experiences
RC9 Hypomanic Activation

Figure 10.14 MMPI-3 Score Report (Ms. N., 06/21/2019 – page 3: MMPI-3 Higher-Order (H-O) and Restructured Clinical (RC) Scales).

MMPI®-3 Score Report
06/21/2019, Page 4

ID: Ms. N

MMPI-3 Somatic/Cognitive Dysfunction and Internalizing Scales

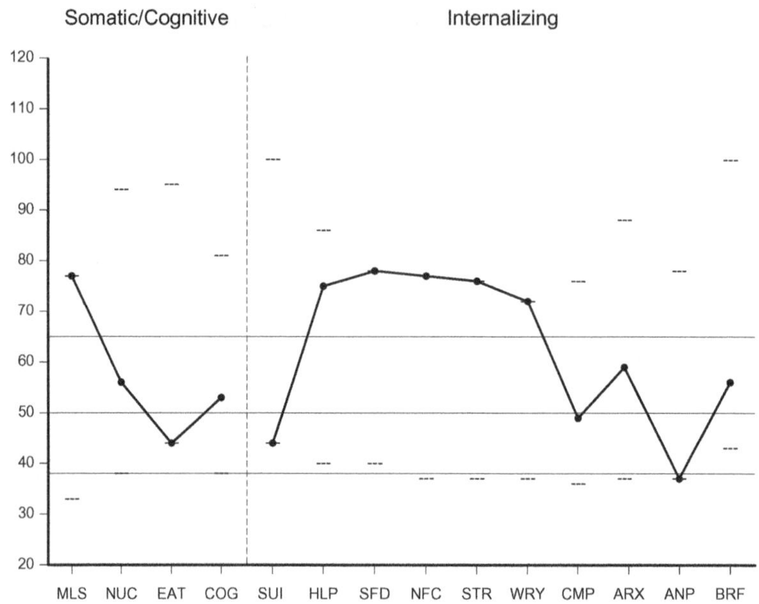

	MLS	NUC	EAT	COG	SUI	HLP	SFD	NFC	STR	WRY	CMP	ARX	ANP	BRF
Raw Score:	7	3	0	3	0	5	7	9	6	7	3	7	0	1
T Score:	77	56	44	53	44	75	78	77	76	72	49	59	37	56
Response %:	100	100	100	100	100	100	100	100	100	100	100	100	100	100

The highest and lowest T scores possible on each scale are indicated by a "---"; MMPI-3 T scores are non-gendered.

MLS Malaise
NUC Neurological Complaints
EAT Eating Concerns
COG Cognitive Complaints
SUI Suicidal/Death Ideation
HLP Helplessness/Hopelessness
SFD Self-Doubt
NFC Inefficacy
STR Stress
WRY Worry
CMP Compulsivity
ARX Anxiety-Related Experiences
ANP Anger Proneness
BRF Behavior-Restricting Fears

Figure 10.15 MMPI-3 Score Report (Ms. N., 06/21/2019 – page 4: MMPI-3 Somatic/Cognitive Dysfunction and Internalizing Scales).

MMPI®-3 Score Report
06/21/2019, Page 5

ID: Ms. N

MMPI-3 Externalizing and Interpersonal Scales

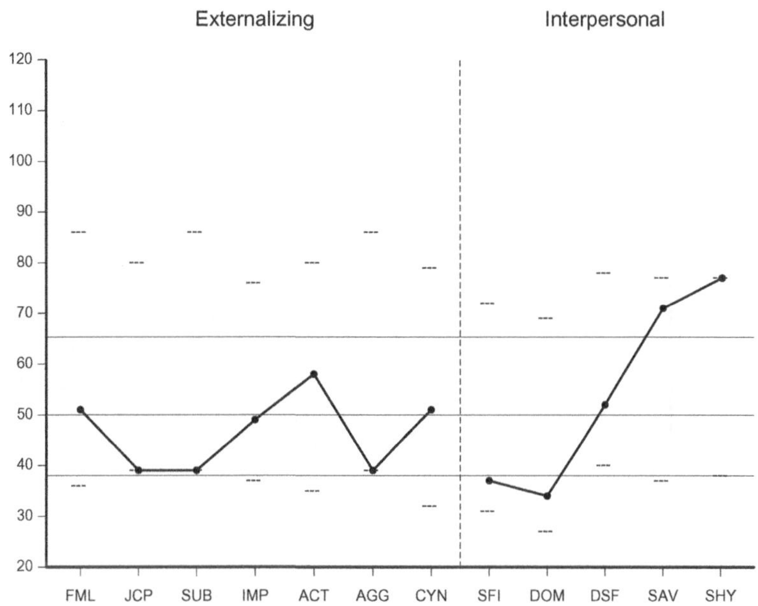

	FML	JCP	SUB	IMP	ACT	AGG	CYN	SFI	DOM	DSF	SAV	SHY
Raw Score:	3	0	0	2	5	0	8	1	1	2	8	7
T Score:	51	39	39	49	58	39	51	37	34	52	71	77
Response %:	100	100	100	100	100	100	100	100	100	100	100	100

The highest and lowest T scores possible on each scale are indicated by a "---"; MMPI-3 T scores are non-gendered.

FML	Family Problems	ACT	Activation	SFI	Self-Importance
JCP	Juvenile Conduct Problems	AGG	Aggression	DOM	Dominance
SUB	Substance Abuse	CYN	Cynicism	DSF	Disaffiliativeness
IMP	Impulsivity			SAV	Social Avoidance
				SHY	Shyness

Figure 10.16 MMPI-3 Score Report (Ms. N., 06/21/2019 – page 5: MMPI-3 Externalizing and Interpersonal Scales).

MMPI®-3 Score Report
06/21/2019, Page 6

ID: Ms. N

MMPI-3 PSY-5 Scales

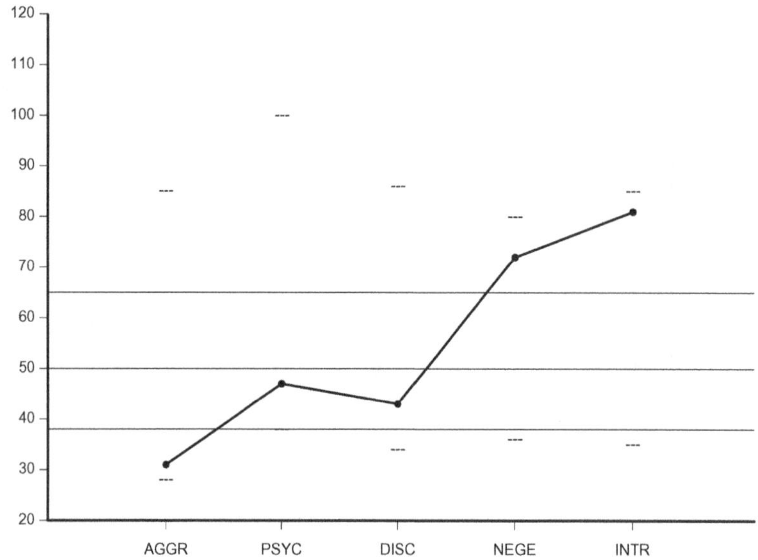

Raw Score:	1	1	2	13	13
T Score:	31	47	43	72	81
Response %:	100	100	100	100	100

The highest and lowest T scores possible on each scale are indicated by a "---"; MMPI-3 T scores are non-gendered.

AGGR Aggressiveness
PSYC Psychoticism
DISC Disconstraint
NEGE Negative Emotionality/Neuroticism
INTR Introversion/Low Positive Emotionality

Figure 10.17 MMPI-3 Score Report (Ms. N., 06/21/2019 – page 6: MMPI-3 PSY-5 Scales).

MMPI®-3 Score Report
06/21/2019, Page 7

ID: Ms. N

MMPI-3 T SCORES (BY DOMAIN)

PROTOCOL VALIDITY

Content Non-Responsiveness

0	48	51	54 T
CNS	CRIN	VRIN	TRIN

Over-Reporting

72	58	58	59	50
F	Fp	Fs	FBS	RBS

Under-Reporting

52	35
L	K

SUBSTANTIVE SCALES

Somatic/Cognitive Dysfunction

57	77	56	44	53
RC1	MLS	NUC	EAT	COG

Emotional Dysfunction

83
EID

80	44	75	78	77
RCd	SUI	HLP	SFD	NFC

75	81
RC2	INTR

61	76	72	49	59	37	56	72
RC7	STR	WRY	CMP	ARX	ANP	BRF	NEGE

Thought Dysfunction

44
THD

40
RC6

37
RC8

47
PSYC

Behavioral Dysfunction

42
BXD

40	51	39	39
RC4	FML	JCP	SUB

51	49	58	39	51
RC9	IMP	ACT	AGG	CYN

43
DISC

Interpersonal Functioning

37	34	31	52	71	77
SFI	DOM	AGGR	DSF	SAV	SHY

Note. This information is provided to facilitate interpretation following the recommended structure for MMPI-3 interpretation in Chapter 5 of the *MMPI-3 Manual for Administration, Scoring, and Interpretation*, which provides details in the text and an outline in Table 5-1.

Figure 10.18 MMPI-3 Score Report (Ms. N., 06/21/2019 – page 7: MMPI-3 T Scores (By Domain)).

MMPI®-3 Score Report
06/21/2019, Page 8

ID: Ms. N

ITEM-LEVEL INFORMATION

Unscorable Responses

The test taker produced scorable responses to all the MMPI-3 items.

Critical Responses

Seven MMPI-3 scales--Suicidal/Death Ideation (SUI), Helplessness/Hopelessness (HLP), Anxiety-Related Experiences (ARX), Ideas of Persecution (RC6), Aberrant Experiences (RC8), Substance Abuse (SUB), and Aggression (AGG)--have been designated by the test authors as having critical item content that may require immediate attention and follow-up. Items answered by the individual in the keyed direction (True or False) on a critical scale are listed below if her T score on that scale is 65 or higher. However, any item answered in the keyed direction on SUI is listed. The percentage of the MMPI-3 normative sample that answered each item in the keyed direction is provided in parentheses following the item content.

Helplessness/Hopelessness (HLP, T Score = 75)

118. **Item content omitted.** (True, 10.9%)
169. **Item content omitted.** (True, 8.7%)
224. **Item content omitted.** (True, 4.6%)
238. **Item content omitted.** (True, 45.4%)
296. **Item content omitted.** (True, 8.4%)

Figure 10.19 MMPI-3 Score Report (Ms. N., 06/21/2019 – page 8: Item-Level Information).

Fs 58: You answered items that dealt with your physical health. You tried to be accurate, without exaggerating your condition. That suggests your test results could be an accurate description of your current condition.

FBS and RBS can be omitted as they are redundant.

FBS 59: The items on this scale appear to have been answered accurately.
RBS 50: You answered the items thoughtfully without overemphasizing your concerns.

Include L as it is the average range and adds new information.

L 52: Your score on this scale is in the normal range. You were able to achieve an appropriate balance between being honest and the temptation to create an overly favorable impression of yourself. You admitted to normal human failings, showing you have good self-awareness and the confidence to be yourself. You were honest about your strengths and vulnerabilities.

Include K since it introduces the client's tendency to be self-critical.

K 35: The way you answered the test reveals that you were very open and honest about the way you were feeling and willing to admit to a number of symptoms and concerns. You may have a tendency to be somewhat self-critical.

Substantive Scale Interpretative Feedback Statements

The RC1 elevation does not warrant feedback as the rest of the profile shows a number of elevated scores that are of greater significance and reveal how the client is presenting psychologically. Moreover, feedback for RC1 could appear to be contradictory with feedback from MLS.

> **RC1 57**: Your profile shows that you are a health-conscious person who is mindful of your physical wellbeing. You ensure that your illnesses are well taken care of, and you are cautious about taking too many physical risks. You or someone close to you may have had a recent illness, which has made you focus on the importance of physical wellbeing.

MLS is included.

> **MLS 77**: You are reporting that you rarely feel well compared to your peers. This may be due to a chronic physical problem that has been hard to treat or an emotional condition that has not been resolved. You likely feel tired almost all the time and rarely wake up feeling refreshed. You mostly feel physically depleted, drained, and weak much of the time. You are concerned that your health will not improve.

We provide hypothetical "Lifestyle and Family Background Feedback" for each elevated scale in Ms. N.'s profile, which has multiple elevations. Providing a "Lifestyle and Family Background Feedback" for each elevation to the client may be overwhelming, contradictory, and/or redundant. The clinician should choose which "Lifestyle and Family Background Feedback" to explore, although it is possible that a number of "Lifestyle and Family Background Feedback" paragraphs are relevant. In some cases, clients have experienced a number of adverse childhood experiences (for example, neglect, abuse, early overloads of responsibility and parental loss) so exploring the relevance of the different "Lifestyle and Family Background Feedback" may add incremental value.

Lifestyle and Family Background Feedback – MLS: In the presence of a family history with adverse childhood experiences, such as parental indifference or cruelty, the current malaise may have been precipitated by a recent loss or setback that has restimulated past emotional scar tissue. In the absence of such a history, the current malaise could be hormonally precipitated by medication side effects or an illness. It could also be associated with a current depression.

General unhappiness and dissatisfaction is revealed by Ms. N.'s elevated RCd score.

> **RCd 80**: Your score reveals that currently you are feeling down, sad, depressed, and demoralized. You are likely feeling defeated, hopeless, and unsure how to escape your current situation. You may have periods when you feel a sense of despair and when you feel incapable of changing your feelings and reducing your suffering.

Lifestyle and Family Background Feedback – RCd: This section may add incremental value to the previous "Lifestyle and Family Background Feedback."

> Your current sense of demoralization and despair is probably tied to some specific problems that have left you feeling defeated. This may be due to recent events, but it is also possible that you suffered adverse experiences in childhood where you often felt helpless, trapped, and alone. Your current feelings may be due to recent events that have robbed you of your self-confidence. People close to you may have difficulty understanding why you get so pessimistic

> and negative about things getting better, but you probably feel you have tried everything you know to feel better, and it has not worked. Explore with your therapist the disappointments you have experienced unsuccessfully trying to feel better.

The clinician may omit HLP feedback since the information is mostly covered by the feedback for RCd, but perhaps consider adding a statement about her low motivation for treatment.

> **HLP 75**: You are currently feeling quite pessimistic, hopeless, and defeated by your current circumstances. It appears that you are doubting your ability to make positive changes in your life. It is hard for you to believe that anyone can help you, so your motivation to seek help is low. At times, it is easy for you to feel helpless, feeling that you don't have the tools to make life better.

Lifestyle and Family Background Feedback – HLP: This next paragraph may be redundant with the previous "Lifestyle and Family Background Feedback," so it could be omitted.

> Your feelings of being defeated, hopeless, and helpless could be due to a recent traumatic or very upsetting event that has left you feeling trapped in a current situation. In other cases, the feelings you are experiencing may have been caused by a long period of constant, inescapable stress, worry, or physical infirmity that have made you feel worn out, believing that nothing is ever going to get better. In still other cases, childhood experiences of severe psychological pain, strain, and stress may have predisposed you to feel that any current psychological pain can never be escaped and that you are powerless to ameliorate it.

Lack of self-confidence and feelings of uselessness are revealed by Ms. N.'s elevated SFD score.

> **SFD 78**: You are quick to lose self-confidence and compare yourself negatively to others. You likely believe that you are not very good at most things. You doubt your abilities, and you are quick to feel worthless. You tend to be your own worst critic and around other people it is easy for you to feel inferior and insecure. You are probably spending time ruminating about how others see you, worrying that they are critical of you. You may feel like you are a burden to others.

Lifestyle and Family Background Feedback – SFD: This paragraph may be redundant with the previous "Lifestyle and Family Background Feedback," so it could be omitted.

> There may have been some recent events that went badly, and you have responded by beating yourself up, losing your self-confidence, and experiencing profound self-doubt. It is also possible that self-doubt and insecurity came from your childhood. It is possible that you grew up in an environment where a parental caregiver was critical and demeaning. Perhaps they put you down in ways that robbed you of self-confidence. It is also possible that you were a shy child or maybe you had some eccentricities or learning differences that made you feel that you are not as good as others, leading you to feel rejected. It is understandable that you developed caution about ever being too confident, hanging back before you make decisions, wanting to avoid criticism and judgment from others.

Ms. N.'s belief that she is indecisive and ineffective likely elevated her score on this next scale.

> **NFC 77**: Your answers suggest that you can be very indecisive, worrying about whether you are capable of seeing problems clearly and making wise decisions. You are generally quick to doubt

yourself and often feel that you don't have what it takes to take charge of your life and make changes, even if they're good for you. Even small decisions loom large for you, and you may spend a lot of time thinking about every side of every issue. You likely worry that you have missed something important and that your decisions will lead to failure. Since you doubt yourself, others may see you as passive, hanging back, and not making decisions, even when that leads to negative consequences. When your self-doubt leads to you missing opportunities or allowing negative events to occur, you are quick to feel ashamed. Because you think that any mistake you make is a reflection of not being good enough, when things become difficult, it is hard for you to persevere at them, and you are quick to give up on a task if you think you are failing or might fail.

Lifestyle and Family Background Feedback – NFC: While this next paragraph may be redundant with the other "Lifestyle and Family Background Feedback" information, it does add information about caregivers possibly being hostile, critical, and controlling.

People with your profile sometimes grew up in environments where parents or caregivers were not good coaches in helping you to feel competent and modeling wise decision-making. Perhaps your caregivers were hostile or critical, or so controlling that they robbed you of self-efficacy. Perhaps, consequently, you had a history of tending to be passive, afraid to take charge, and afraid to make decisions. It is also possible that you have recently had a major setback that has eroded your confidence and left you standing back, observing life rather than jumping in and taking charge.

Ms. N's elevated RC2 score reflects a lack of emotional responsiveness.

RC2 75:

- Your profile shows that you are currently finding it difficult to experience positive emotions. Sometimes people with this profile feel that almost nothing gives them pleasure. You likely feel depressed and doubt that you can reach your goals. You tend to be your own worst critic and in your dark moments it's hard to find something to pull you out of your blue mood.
- Sometimes people with your profile can have difficulty sleeping. In some cases, it is difficult to fall asleep because your mind is agitated, and you are unable to switch it off. In other cases, people with this profile can fall asleep, but then awaken in the middle of the night or early in the morning and are unable to return to sleep. They complain of early awakening with some anxiety that interferes with returning to sleep. When people become depressed, they can experience physical symptoms. Stomach upsets and difficulties with elimination are possible.
- People with your profile tend to avoid confrontation. This may be because you doubt yourself and tend to blame yourself if someone is upset with you. It may also be hard to confront others because you lack energy and confidence. You tend to worry that you don't have the right to ask for what you want or to assert yourself.
- You may give up on hopes and dreams for the future, feeling that it is useless to have desires because you are likely to be disappointed. People may see you as pessimistic, but this reflects your fear that the future is bleak. Having little to look forward to can be quite distressing. You might have given up planning ahead, feeling that little will give you pleasure.

Lifestyle and Family Background Feedback – RC2: The following could be omitted since it is redundant with previous feedback.

Typically, people with your profile have experienced recent or past losses and disappointments that have left them apprehensive about allowing themselves to enjoy life. Perhaps as a child you experienced the loss of a parental caring figure, leaving you with overloads of responsibility; or for some other reason you may have been deprived of the normal joys of a carefree childhood. In other cases, recent losses (perhaps a job loss, a blow to your self-esteem, or a perceived or actual setback) have made you feel hopeless about ever enjoying life again. Being negative, pessimistic, and withdrawing from life may be an understandable self-protection from further loss or setback.

Ms. N.'s elevated score on INTR reflects low positive emotionality, social disengagement, and anhedonia.

INTR 81: You are reporting that generally you do not have a lot of positive emotional experiences. Social interactions do not feel rewarding to you, and you probably avoid people since they make you uncomfortable. You may find that little seems to give you pleasure and that you don't pursue interests and hobbies since they don't hold your interest. You may feel pessimistic and negative about social interactions.

Lifestyle and Family Background Feedback – INTR

- Research suggests that introversion is at least partly inherited with neurophysiological correlates. Dopamine is a neurotransmitter produced in the brain that is associated with positive feelings. Although extroverts and introverts have similar levels of dopamine in their brains, extroverts have a more active dopamine reward system. This suggests that extroverts need more dopamine to feel positive emotions. Extroverts seek out stimulation to feel better while introverts avoid being overstimulated. Introverts also show brain activity associated with deep thinking and problem-solving, meaning that they tend to be reflective, not impulsive. Consequently, you probably avoid parties and large social events. You may find the small talk and back-and-forth banter that occurs at parties depleting.
- Caregiving styles and culture can also shape introversion. If you were raised in a quiet, reflective household with caregivers who provided necessary resources for child rearing, but who were reserved and not particularly affectionate, it could have led to you being a self-sufficient introvert. A genetic predisposition to introversion, together with a childhood without much social interaction and social skill building could have contributed to your introversion. Introversion can become a problem if you are in a partnership with an extrovert. The extrovert may complain that you always want to go home early from social events. You may complain that you cannot get the extrovert out of the party to go home with you when they likely promised they would. You want to avoid social events, leaving your extrovert partner feeling hungry for more social interaction.

Ms. N.'s score on RC7 is relatively normal, but adds to the description of her as self-doubting, which interferes with her capacity to make decisions.

RC7 61: You are a thoughtful, analytical individual who takes responsibilities seriously. You may have a mild tendency to worry and be anxious about things going unpredictably wrong. This may mean that, at times, you make mental lists so you can stay "on top" of your responsibilities. Making decisions can sometimes be difficult for you because you are apt to see everything that can go wrong with any choice you make. Whenever things do go wrong, you are likely to blame yourself and feel guilty. Because you can see all the possible ways things can go badly, you are likely to avoid taking risks. Generally, confrontations are difficult for you, and you worry if you have to confront someone. If you feel you have let someone down, you can experience uncomfortable levels of guilt.

STR 76: You appear to be feeling significant stress, with little patience. You report not functioning well under stress and feel that you are more stressed and nervous than most people. Waiting for people or events likely makes you nervous and high-strung and you feel unable to control your anxiety level.

Lifestyle and Family Background Feedback – STR: The following paragraph describes possible conditioning experiences that could lead to constant scanning of the environment for perceived danger.

It is hard to know whether you have always been someone who is vulnerable to developing stress or whether your current stress is due to some recent difficult event. Sometimes, people who are high-strung and easily stressed had childhoods in which they experienced setbacks and losses that led to their adaptive response of constantly being on guard for any negative events. Feeling guilty and constantly scanning the environment for danger is an understandable response if you have been in situations where things went wrong and weren't prepared for them. If your current high level of stress is due to a recent event, it is important to put things in perspective and find ways to self-care.

The following paragraph could be omitted since it has been covered in previous feedback.

WRY 72: Your profile suggests that you are a worrier. You fret about many things, possibly future misfortunes or financial insecurity, and ruminate about past losses and disappointments. You may feel a constant nagging worry, a pit in your stomach, sometimes without even knowing what you are concerned about. Worrying is likely affecting your sleep. It is hard to switch off your mind when you go to sleep, and it is challenging for you to ever fully relax without worried thoughts invading your mind.

Lifestyle and Family Background Feedback – WRY: This paragraph may be redundant with previous scales, so it could be omitted

Tendencies to worry may be genetic in some people. In some situations, people who are worriers may have grown up in an unpredictable environment with unreliable people caring for them. Perhaps you were a sensitive and high-strung child who tended to suffer from anxiety. You may have had an anxious attachment to a caregiver because you couldn't quite trust that they would be there when you needed them. If that is the case, then as a child you would have constantly felt worried. If you have experienced worrying most of your life, it could be genetic or due to adverse childhood experiences. It is also possible you experienced a recent setback that triggered your worrying, so you are now constantly on edge anticipating that something awful may happen unpredictably.

The next paragraph may be redundant with previous ones describing Ms. N.'s anxiety worries and self-doubt.

NEGE 72: Your profile suggests that you feel chronically anxious, feeling insecure and constantly worried, as if something bad is lurking and about to happen. You can be self-critical and easily feel guilty. You likely experience sleep difficulties and have some problems with concentration and difficulties in making decisions.

Lifestyle and Family Background Feedback – NEGE: As new information about possible genetic predisposition to anxiety is contained in this section, the clinician could report some of the feedback statements.

> Sometimes people with your profile have a genetic vulnerability to developing worries and anxieties. If you were prone to worry as a child (for example, finding it hard to spend the night away from home at friends' houses, or worrying about getting your schoolwork done and having test anxiety), you may have a genetic vulnerability. If for most of your life you would describe yourself as a worrier, concerned about whether you hurt someone's feelings or worried that some negative event is imminent, then the tendency to worry seems to be longstanding. However, there are other situations that can lead to anxiety and worry. You may have had caregivers who were controlling, perhaps even hovering over you too much, not allowing you to develop self-confidence and independence. In this situation, you might have developed anxiety because you lacked self-confidence. Perhaps as a child you were young for your age or perhaps you had some personal habits, like stuttering or shyness, which may have led you to be teased and unpredictably put down by your peers. In this case, being anxious and worrying about the future may have been your adaptive way to predict teasing so that you could prepare for it and not be taken off guard.

THD scores (THD, RC6, RC8, and PSYC) were all within the normal range.

BXD scores (BXD, RC4, FML, JCP, SUB, RC9, IMP, ACT, AGG, CYN, and DISC) were all within the normal limit range.

FML statements could be included, as they convey positive feedback to the client.

> **FML 51**: Like most people, you can occasionally have issues and conflicts with your family, and, at times, they might even be critical of some of your decisions. Generally, however, you feel you can depend on them. Most of the time members of your family get along well with each other.

As Ms. N.'s JCP score is in the average range, it could be included to convey positive information showing an absence of juvenile conduct problems.

> **JCP 39**: Your responses suggest that you had a normal upbringing, rarely questioning authority, generally following the rules, and not being reckless and impulsive.

As previous feedback has described Ms. N.'s difficulties with sleep and anxiety, the next paragraph could be omitted.

> **ACT 58**: Like many people, you can have periods when you are highly excited, perhaps finding it hard to get to sleep because something has stimulated you, and sometimes your ideas can occur almost faster than you can speak them.

Since the next statements are positive, they could be included.

> **AGG 39**: Your profile suggests that you control your temper and do not intimidate others with aggressive statements or tendencies. You do not lose your cool easily.
>
> **CYN 51**: You have a realistic view of people, expecting them to be self-serving but generally wanting to do the right thing.

The following feedback based on low interpersonal functioning scores may be redundant with previous feedback but could be used to describe the client's low self-esteem and low self-assertion more gently than prior feedback.

> **SFI 37**: Your answers suggest that you do not have many positive things to say about yourself. Perhaps you learned at an early age not to brag or even admit to your positive qualities.
>
> **DOM 34**: Your profile suggests that you are not an assertive person. You are comfortable letting others take control while you take a more passive role. You tend not to actively compete for leadership positions, although you might accept a leadership role if you feel particularly competent. You tend to be self-effacing and do not feel a need to convince people of your opinions. You may withdraw from taking leadership roles and not assert yourself because you doubt yourself and feel anxious and incompetent.
>
> **AGGR 31**: Your answers suggest that you are generally an agreeable, non-pushy person who tries to avoid conflict. You do not need to assert yourself with people and generally prefer resolving conflicts in non-aggressive ways.
>
> **DSF 52**: Your answers suggest that you are quite self-sufficient and feel comfortable being alone. You find it difficult to be around people, generally preferring to be alone.

Ms. N.'s SAV score indicates that she avoids social events as she does not enjoy them.

> **SAV 71**: Your answers suggest that you do not enjoy social events with large groups of people you do not know. You tend to make friends slowly and it takes a while for you to feel comfortable with new people. You do not find crowds exciting and meeting new people is not easy.

Lifestyle and Family Background Feedback – SAV: As the following feedback deals with the possible conditioning experiences associated with social avoidance, it could be included in the feedback process.

> In some cases, people with your profile grew up in a family where, for some reason, they did not experience a lot of social interactions. Perhaps your caregivers avoided entertaining or socializing and were typically self-sufficient and independent. It is also possible that you were a shy child and being around people made you anxious and uncomfortable. If you were a socially awkward child, you may have never learned how to reach out to people to develop a peer group, which could leave you feeling lonely. In some cases, people with your profile avoid other people because they have been hurt or traumatized and their trust in people has been broken. They avoid people because they do not trust them, expecting people to be critical, judgmental, or even take advantage of them. Avoiding social situations may make you feel safer and more comfortable in the short run, but over time it may negatively affect you, since you will not have a community to rely on should you need support or help.

Ms. N.'s elevated SHY score indicates that she feels uncomfortable and anxious in the presence of others.

> **SHY 77**: Your answers suggest that you are quite shy and meeting new people is initially difficult for you. You likely can get easily embarrassed or tongue-tied, unsure what to say to someone. In new social situations you may hang back and wait for others to engage you. People may misunderstand your shyness as aloofness but, once you are comfortable with people, you can be

> quite socially engaged. You likely dislike being called upon to speak spontaneously or suddenly being made the center of attention without being prepared for it. Your responses suggest that it is uncomfortable for you to interact with people you do not know, and your shyness is present in most social situations. You may desire a social connection but feel inhibited by fears of social embarrassment and rejection. You may be self-critical and assume that you will not be easily liked by others.

Lifestyle and Family Background Feedback – SHY: As the following feedback deals with the possible conditioning experiences associated with shyness, it could be included in the feedback process.

> Shyness is most likely something you inherited. You were probably always a little shy growing up. You may have made friends with a small group in school that stuck together. Being shy is normal but it can make people feel self-conscious and awkward when they meet new people or when at a big party with people they don't know. In some cases, people who are shy were raised by caregivers who were shy and didn't socialize with others. You may have been an only child with caregivers who were shy or socially avoidant and, since you had no siblings to relate to, you never learned social skills. In some cases, caregivers can be overly critical of their child's behavior or appearance, and this may instill self-doubt, leading to shyness. If you were ever bullied, teased, or rejected by your peers, that could have made you hesitant to reach out and engage with others. If you were homeschooled, without group activities, you may have become comfortable being a loner and avoiding reaching out to others. Shyness is not necessarily a negative personality characteristic unless it is the result of painful experiences with other people.

As we have provided self-help suggestions for every elevated scale, to include all of them would be overwhelming, repetitive, and unmanageable. The clinician should examine the self-help suggestions associated with all the elevated scales to develop an individualized self-help menu. We advise the clinician to choose which ones are most useful given the presenting problem. Focusing on the two or three highest scales and providing self-help suggestions only for those scales would limit redundancy and client overload. In the example of Ms. N, we include parsed self-help suggestions, but the clinician could mix and match self-help suggestions depending on the client's needs. The following is an edited list of self-help suggestions.

MLS Treatment and Self-Help Suggestions

1. Finding a friend or community to support you can be uplifting and help you when you feel tired and depleted.
2. Meditation, yoga, deep breathing, and mindfulness exercises can help you feel better physically and emotionally.
3. Shift your focus from negative to positive by practicing gratitude. Try to identify the things in your life for which you are grateful and take time to appreciate them.

RCd Treatment and Self-Help Suggestions

> Your therapist will likely take a full history to determine if you experienced adverse childhood events that made you more vulnerable to feeling defeated and hopeless when negative events occur in your adulthood. It will be important to examine your history to understand your life in perspective, with a focus on things you have done well and how some things in your life have

gone well so that you don't have to be so self-critical. Cognitive behavioral therapy could be helpful to identify when you have negative self-talk and when you feel defeated and give up. Even when things are beginning to get better, it is likely hard for you to trust that good things can continue.

1. With the help of your therapist, identify one behavior that you want to change or one task you want to get accomplished and force yourself to do it. It does not have to be a big task or a big change. For example, go for a walk in nature and take a few moments to look at trees or plants or some geographical feature to remind yourself that there is a world that is apart from your suffering and the inner noise of your despair. Notice when your inner voice is being self-critical or self-doubting and try to balance those thoughts with a reminder of the things you have done well or the people of importance to you.
2. Keep a gratitude diary where you can write down one small thing that you are grateful for. It doesn't have to be anything big, just a reminder that life is not completely hopeless and negative.
3. Join a community group so you do not feel so alone. Sometimes volunteering for people who are less fortunate than you can help bring some perspective to your life and make you feel important and feel better that you are contributing.

HLP Treatment and Self-Help Suggestions

Feeling hopeless and helpless can be overwhelming, but there are steps you can take to regain a sense of control, hope, and resiliency. It is important to remember that these feelings are not permanent, even though they may feel that way. Progress may take time, but small steps can lead to big changes. Here are some self-help suggestions.

1. Accomplishing even minor tasks can provide a sense of achievement and momentum. Start with small, manageable tasks to make it easier for yourself.
2. Shift your focus to what you can change when things feel out of control, even if it is only a small change to your daily routine or immediate environment.
3. Make an effort to stay connected to friends, family, and your community. Try to keep from isolating yourself, even if it feels exhausting. Consider joining a support group since talking to others who have faced similar struggles can offer some relief and reduce the sense of loneliness. If you feel like you are a burden to others, talk with your therapist to help you with these negative self-perceptions.
4. Physical movement can help, and exercise, even a short walk, releases endorphins that improve mood.
5. Set small, achievable daily or weekly goals, instead of focusing on long-term goals, to help build your confidence.
6. Replace negative thoughts with more realistic or compassionate ones. Instead of thinking you are worthless, remind yourself that you are doing your best. If you are in pain, focus on the possibility of a medical solution. Remind yourself that you are valuable. Be kind to yourself, treating yourself with the same compassion you would give others in a similar situation. Reassure yourself that it is okay to struggle and ask for help.

SFD Treatment and Self-Help Suggestions

Self-doubt is a common response to experiencing some recent setbacks or having had parental figures who were critical, demeaning, and judgmental. The way you think about yourself tends to be self-perpetuating. You doubt yourself so you hang back. You avoid making decisions because you do not want to get it wrong. You give up on a task because you think it is not going well enough. Later, you feel guilty and bad about yourself for having given up and then you doubt yourself all over again. Learning to see yourself more clearly and in a more balanced way could help you become less self-critical. Even very successful professionals may experience "imposter syndrome" where they doubt their abilities and accomplishments compared with others, despite evidence to the contrary. Overcoming self-doubt is a journey that many people face. Here are some strategies that might help.

1. Self-doubt is very common, and it is okay to feel unsure at times. You may have become fearful of taking risks if you had some failures or setbacks. Small steps will help you to build your confidence. When you begin to doubt yourself, challenge those thoughts. Are they based on facts or assumptions? Try to substitute these thoughts with more positive ones.

NFC Treatment and Self-Help Suggestions

Feeling ineffective can be really challenging, but there are strategies you can use to regain a sense of control and productivity. Here are some self-help tips that might help.

1. Set small, achievable daily or weekly goals. Start with something simple, like going for a short walk or tidying up a drawer, and celebrate these small accomplishments.
2. Take time to prioritize tasks by their urgency and importance. You may not be able to easily identify the key items since you focus on every side of an issue but starting one task and focusing on it can help you build momentum.
3. Practice self-compassion by being kind to yourself. Treat yourself as you would treat a friend experiencing something similar. Recognize that everyone has periods of feeling ineffective. Try not to compare yourself to others. Everyone moves at their own pace.
4. Visualize achieving your goals to motivate you and reinforce a positive mindset. Be aware of any negative self-talk you experience. Focus on your visualized goals rather than any past failures.

RC2 Treatment and Self-Help Suggestions

1. Your therapist may want to recommend that you consider medication, which could help you to feel better quickly.
2. Work with your therapist to change how you view yourself. Notice how quick you are to blame and doubt yourself. In any given moment, when you dislike yourself, attempt to make a list of your positive attributes so that you maintain a balanced view of yourself.
3. Identify with your therapist what you perceive as past or recent losses. Find ways to forgive yourself for these setbacks and losses so that you can stop beating yourself up for them. Learn to express anger about those losses without self-blame.
4. Feeling depressed can be quite lonely and isolating, but one of the best ways to begin feeling better is to reach out for social support and contact. Joining a sports or activity group is a way to seek out social support while concurrently getting the benefits of exercise. Consider making plans with friends or family, even if it is just by phone or for a brief visit.
5. Observe your tendency to catastrophize. When something bad happens, you tend to anticipate the worst outcome and then suffer the anxiety anticipating it. Make a list of possible positive outcomes and compare them to the list of dire consequences you have imagined.

INTR Treatment and Self-Help Suggestions

If you want help with your introversion and low positive emotionality, the key is to find a balance between honoring your natural tendencies to be alone and gently expanding your comfort zone. Here are some self-help strategies to help you navigate social interactions and reduce avoidance.

1. Get to know yourself to determine if you are shy, introverted, or a social avoider. Introverts need "alone time" to recharge. Introversion is probably genetic and not a psychological condition. Social avoiders become that way for a number of reasons. You may feel insecure, distrust people, or feel vulnerable to judgment or criticism. Some people are not genetically introverted but avoid people because of the way they feel about themselves. In your case, your profile suggests that you just don't get excited and energized by being around people.
2. Being introverted is not a weakness and you don't *need* to change. However, if it is a problem for you, you can work on becoming more comfortable around people. Before a social event are you anticipating criticism or feeling awkward and tongue-tied? Observe your self-talk and see if you can consider possible positive outcomes to balance some of the negative thoughts about the event.

STR Treatment and Self-Help Suggestions

Stress is a normal human response to situations where we feel we don't have full control or when we are afraid something bad is going to happen. We experience stress mostly in our bodies. As stress increases, we are likely to become progressively more aware of it as it affects our muscle tension and other bodily functions. When you are stressed, it is hard to focus on anything other than the situation that is stressing you. Following these two recommendations may be difficult, so it is important not to put pressure on yourself. If you can do one every so often, that can help.

1. Mindfulness techniques and meditation can help you relieve stress by focusing on the present moment for a few minutes. Apps like *Headspace* or *Calm* can help guide you through this.
2. Engage in creative activities like drawing, music, or writing to relieve stress.

WRY Treatment and Self-Help Suggestions

Feeling constantly worried is exhausting and crowds out your ability to think clearly and make decisions easily. Worry is often an adaptive response. If at some point in your life a trauma took you by surprise, you may have responded by worrying and trying to learn to predict the future as one way to protect yourself against a negative unpredictable event. However, worrying is rarely an effective strategy. Initially you may feel insecure giving up worrying, even for a short while, perhaps fearing that something bad will happen unless you stay vigilant. Here are some strategies that may help. By practicing these techniques regularly, you may find it easier to manage worry.

1. Worry often comes with "what if" thinking that tends to be exaggerated or unrealistic. Challenge these thoughts by considering what evidence supports or contradicts the worry, what the "worst case" scenario might be, and how likely it is to happen. Ask yourself if you have successfully managed similar situations in the past. Make the case against the need to worry by reminding yourself that there are alternative positive views. Substitute positive affirmations for negative thoughts and remind yourself that you are more able to handle challenges than you think.

2. Obsessional thinking or worry can often be treated effectively with medication. Consider asking your therapist for a referral to someone who specializes in this area.

NEGE Treatment and Self-Help Suggestions

If you feel like worry and anxiety are affecting your wellbeing, there are several self-help strategies that can help you manage anxiety, overthinking, emotional reactivity, and stress. Here are some suggestions.

1. Breathing techniques, mindfulness, and grounding techniques can help with feeling anxious. While facing a fear or anxiety-producing situation, try focusing on your breath. This can help you stay grounded and calm your body's physical response to stress. 5-4-3-2-1 grounding is another technique where you identify 5 things you see, 4 things you feel, 3 things you hear, 2 things you smell, and 1 thing you taste. Try doing some relaxation exercises before bed, focusing on a pleasant image. If a negative thought intrudes, imagine putting it in a box and closing it. Tell yourself you can revisit it the next day.
2. Anxiety often comes with "what if" thinking that tends to be exaggerated or unrealistic. Challenge these thoughts by questioning them. Consider what evidence supports or contradicts the fear, what the "worst case" scenario might be, and how likely it is to happen. Reflect on past challenging situations where you were successful.
3. People with your profile may have a genetic vulnerability to worry and anxiety. Explore with your therapist what kind of child you were. Were you a somewhat sensitive, prone-to-worry child? What childhood events took you by surprise in a traumatic or negative way? Learning to worry and trying to predict the future are adaptive responses. Explore with your therapist the past experiences which led you to become worry-prone so you can now learn to worry less.

SAV Treatment and Self-Help Suggestions

You may be seeking treatment because of social problems or work-related problems. If you would like to feel a little more socially comfortable, there are simple techniques you can learn to help you. Once you have identified the causes of your social avoidance, whether due to past negative experiences or your own predisposition, you can work on techniques that could enhance your social skills. Here are some self-help suggestions.

1. Start with low-stakes interactions, perhaps saying "hi" to a neighbor, engaging in brief small talk with a cashier, or attending a social gathering for a short time. Over time, as you get more comfortable, you can gradually challenge yourself to stay in social situations longer or engage with more people.
2. If you find yourself frequently overthinking social situations or imagining "worst case" scenarios, cognitive behavioral therapy can help. It involves identifying negative thoughts, challenging them, and reframing them in a more realistic or positive light. It can also help you to gradually expose yourself to social situations in a controlled manner.

SHY Treatment and Self-Help Suggestions

Shyness is not a negative trait. If you would like to be less shy, there are a lot of ways to get there. Accepting that you are shy and not beating yourself up about it is the first step. If you recall always being a little shy, slow to warm up in social situations, and preferring to be around small groups of people you know, then it is likely genetic. If you have experienced negative events with others, perhaps being bullied, criticized, or rejected by your peers or caregivers, you may have developed shyness as a reaction. If you grew up in a family where there was not a lot of social interaction, you may not have learned the skills of small talk. Learning how to engage in conversation and engage in small talk is not difficult. Here are some things you can work on.

1. Recognize that shyness is a natural response and don't judge yourself.
2. Prepare a few conversation starters about topics or questions you are comfortable with so that you won't feel so tongue-tied. For example, you might ask someone about their travel plans or hobbies. You can begin to share something about yourself when you feel comfortable, which can encourage discussion.
3. Be sure to listen to what others are saying, rather than focusing on how you should respond or how you are coming across.

FEEDBACK SESSION RESULTS

The feedback to Ms. N went well. She was pleasantly surprised and relieved that it validated her experience of intense stress, depression, and anxiety. It also addressed how she felt constantly on edge, as if some impending doom was hanging over her, which robbed her of pleasant experiences. She was able to understand that her husband's recent decline into binge drinking reawakened the trauma of her early childhood. She felt relief that her response of constantly being on edge, worrying, and feeling dread was entirely understandable given her childhood experiences and the recent reawakening of her unhappy childhood memories.

References

Adler, A. (1964). *Problems of neurosis*. Harper Torchbooks.

Allport, G. (1950/1975). *The nature of personality: Selected papers.* Greenwood Press.

AERA [American Educational Research Association], APA [American Psychological Association], & National Council on Measurement in Education (Eds.) (2014). *Standards for educational and psychological testing*. American Educational Research Association.

American Psychiatric Association (1980). *Diagnostic and Statistical Manual of Mental Disorders* (3rd ed.). American Psychiatric Association.

American Psychiatric Association (1987). *Diagnostic and Statistical Manual of Mental Disorders* (3rd ed., revised). American Psychiatric Association.

American Psychiatric Association. (2022). *Diagnostic and statistical manual of mental disorders* (5th ed., text revision). American Psychiatric Association.

APA [American Psychological Association]. (1978). Starke R. Hathaway: Distinguished contribution for Applications in Psychology Award for 1977. *American Psychologist, 33*(1), 63–68. https://doi.org/10.1037/h0078532.

APA [American Psychological Association]. (2017). *Ethical principles of psychologists and code of conduct* (2002, amended June 1, 2010, and January 1, 2017). ASPX. http://www.apa.org/ethics/code/index.

APA [American Psychological Association]. (2020). *APA guidelines for psychological assessment and evaluation.* APA Task Force on Psychological Assessment and Evaluation Guidelines. https://www.apa.org/about/policy/guidelines-psychological-assessment-evaluation.pdf.

Aspinwall, L. G., & Staudinger U. M. (Eds.). (2003). *A psychology of human strengths: Fundamental questions and future directions for a positive psychology*. American Psychological Association. https://doi.org/10.1037/10566-000.

Barron, J. W. (Ed.). (1998). *Making diagnosis meaningful: Enhancing evaluation and treatment of psychological disorders.* American Psychological Association. https://doi.org/10.1037/10307-000.

Ben-Porath, Y. S., & Sellbom, M. (2023). *Interpreting the MMPI-3.* University of Minnesota Press.

Ben-Porath, Y. S., & Tellegen, A. (2008/2011a). *Minnesota Multiphasic Personality Inventory-2 Restructured form (MMPI-2-RF): Manual for administration, scoring, and interpretation.* University of Minnesota Press.

Ben-Porath, Y. S., & Tellegen, A. (2008/2011b). *Minnesota Multiphasic Personality Inventory-2-Restructured Form (MMPI-2-RF): Technical manual.* University of Minnesota Press.

Ben-Porath, Y. S., & Tellegen, A. (2020a). *Minnesota Multiphasic Personality Inventory-3 (MMPI-3): Manual for administration, scoring, and interpretation.* University of Minnesota Press.

Ben-Porath, Y. S., & Tellegen, A. (2020b). *Minnesota Multiphasic Personality Inventory-3 (MMPI-3): Technical manual.* University of Minnesota Press.

Beutler, L. E., & Groth-Marnat, G. (2003). *Integrative assessment of adult personality* (2nd ed.). Guilford Press.

Bonanno, G. A. (2004). Loss, trauma, and human resilience: Have we underestimated the human capacity to thrive after extremely aversive events? *American Psychologist, 59*(1), 20–28. https://doi.org/10.1037/0003-066X.59.1.20.

Bonanno, G. A. (2019). *The other side of sadness: What the new science of bereavement tells us about life after loss* (2nd ed.). Basic Books.

Bonanno, G. A. (2021). *The end of trauma: How the new science of resilience is changing how we think about PTSD* (1st ed.). Basic Books.

Bonanno, G. A., Chen, S., Bagrodia, R., & Galatzer-Levy, I. R. (2004). Resilience and disaster: Flexible adaptation in the face of uncertain threat. *Annual Review of Psychology, 75*(1), 573–599. https://doi.org/10.1146/annurev-psych-011123-024224.

Borgen, F. H., & Betz, N. E. (2008). Career self-efficacy and personality: Linking career confidence and the healthy personality. *Journal of Career Assessment, 16*(1), 22–43. https://doi.org/10.1177/1069072707305770.

Bowlby, J. (1983). Attachment and loss: Retrospect and prospect. *Annual Progress in Child Psychiatry & Child Development*, 29–47.

Brendgen, M., Vitaro, F., Boivin, M., Dionne, G., & Pérusse, D. (2006). Examining genetic and environmental effects on reactive versus proactive aggression. *Developmental Psychology, 42*(6), 1299–1312. https://doi.org/10.1037/0012-1649.42.6.1299.

Butcher, J. N. (1990). *The MMPI-2 in psychological treatment*. Oxford University Press.

Butcher, J. N. (Ed.). (2000). *Basic sources on the MMPI-2*. University of Minnesota Press.

Butcher, J. N., Dahlstrom, W. G., Graham, J. R., Tellegen, A., & Kaemmer, B. (1989). *Minnesota Multiphasic Personality Inventory-2 (MMPI-2): Manual for administration and scoring*. University of Minnesota Press.

Butcher, J. N., & Finn, S. (1984). Objective personality assessment: Present status and future directions. In M. Hersen, A. E. Kazdin, & A. S. Bellack (Eds.), *The clinical psychology handbook* (pp. 329–344). Pergamon Press.

Butcher, J. N., Graham, J. R., Ben-Porath, Y. S., Tellegen, A., Dahlstrom, W. G., & Kaemmer, B. (2001). *Minnesota Multiphasic Personality Inventory-2 (MMPI-2): Manual for administration, scoring and interpretation* (Revised edition). University of Minnesota Press.

Caldwell, A. B. (1976, January). *MMPI profile types*. Paper presented at the 11th Annual MMPI Workshop and Symposium. Minneapolis, MN.

Caldwell, A. B. (1977, February). *Treatment recommendations for patients with different MMPI types*. Paper presented at the 12th Annual MMPI Workshop (sponsored by the University of Minnesota), St. Petersburg, FL.

Calhoun, L. G., & Tedeschi, R. G. (1991). Perceiving benefits in traumatic events: Some issues for practicing psychologists. *Journal of Training & Practice in Professional Psychology, 5*(1), 45–52.

Carnegie, D. (2009). *How to win friends and influence people*. Simon & Schuster.

Chess, S. & Thomas, A. (1977). *Temperament and development*. Brunner/Mazel.

Craddick, R. A. (1972). Humanistic assessment: A reply to Brown. *Psychotherapy: Theory, Research, and Practice, 9*, 107–110. https://doi.org/10.1037/h0086727.

Craddick, R. A. (1975). Sharing oneself in the assessment procedure. *Professional Psychology, 7*(1), 279–282. https://doi.org/10.1037/0735-7028.6.3.279.

Curry, K. T., & Hanson, W. E. (2010). National survey of psychologists' test feedback training, supervision, and practice: A mixed methods study. *Journal of Personality Assessment, 92*(4), 327–336. https://doi.org/10.1080/00223891.2010.482006.

Dana, R. H. (1982). Communication of assessment findings. In R. H. Dana (Ed.), *A human science model for personality assessment with projective techniques* (pp. 217–251). Charles C. Thomas.

Dana, R. H. (1984). Personality assessment: Practice and teaching for the next decade. *Journal of Personality Assessment, 48*, 46–57. https://doi.org/10.1207/s15327752jpa4801_9.

Dickens, W. T., & Flynn, J. R. (2001). Heritability estimates versus large environmental effects: The IQ paradox resolved. *Psychological Review, 108*(2), 346–369. https://doi.org/10.1037/0033-295X.108.2.346.

Domino, B., & Conway, D. W. (2001). Optimism and pessimism from a historical perspective. In E. C. Chang (Ed.), *Optimism and pessimism: Implications for theory, research, and practice* (pp. 13–30). American Psychological Association. https://doi.org/10.1037/10385-001.

Duckworth, J. C., & Barley, W. D. (1988). Within-normal limits profiles. In R. L. Greene (Ed.), *The MMPI: Use with specific populations* (pp. 278–315). Grune & Stratten.

Durbin, C. E., Hayden, E. P., Klein, D. N., & Olino, T. M. (2007). Stability of laboratory-assessed temperamental emotionality traits from ages 3 to 7. *Emotion*, *7*(2), 388–399. https://doi.org/10.1037/1528-3542.7.2.388.

Eagle, M. (1999). Why don't people change? A psychoanalytic perspective. *Journal of Psychotherapy Integration*, *9*(1), 3–32. https://doi.org/10.1023/A:1023254726930.

El-Shaieb, M. (2005). The MMPI-2 and client feedback: A quantitative investigation and exploratory analysis of feedback models. *Dissertation Abstracts International: Section B: The Sciences and Engineering*, p. 2303.

Engelman, D. H., Allyn, J. B., Crisi, A., Finn, S. E., Fischer, C. T., & Nakamura, N. (2016). "Why am I so stuck?": A collaborative/therapeutic assessment case discussion. *Journal of Personality Assessment*, *98*(4), 360–373. https://doi.org/10.1080/00223891.2015.1119154.

Engle, D. E., & Arkowitz, H. (2006). *Ambivalence in psychotherapy: Facilitating readiness to change.* Guilford Press.

Eysenck, H. J., Wakefield, Jr., J. A., & Friedman, A. F. (1983). Diagnosis and clinical assessment: The DSM-III. *Annual Review of Psychology*, *34*, 167–193. https://doi.org/10.1146/annurev.ps.34.020183.001123.

Finn, S. E. (1996). *Manual for using the MMPI-2 as a therapeutic intervention.* University of Minnesota Press.

Finn, S. E. (2007). *In our clients' shoes: Theory and techniques of therapeutic assessment.* Lawrence Erlbaum Associates.

Finn, S. E., & Kamphuis, J. H. (2006). Therapeutic assessment with the MMPI-2. MMPI-2: A practitioner's guide. In J. N. Butcher (Ed.), *MMPI-2: A practitioner's guide* (pp. 165–191). American Psychological Association. https://doi.org/10.1037/11287-008.

Finn, S. E., & Tonsager, M. E. (1992). Therapeutic effects of providing MMPI-2 test feedback to college students awaiting therapy. *Psychological Assessment*, *4*(3), 278–287. https://doi.org/10.1037/1040-3590.4.3.278.

Finn, S. E., & Tonsager, M. E. (1997). Information-gathering and therapeutic models of assessment: Complementary paradigms. *Psychological Assessment*, *9*(4), 374–385. https://doi.org/10.1037/1040-3590.9.4.374.

Finn, S. E., & Tonsager, M. E. (2002). How *therapeutic assessment* became humanistic. *The Humanistic Psychologist*, *30*(1–2), 10–22. https://doi.org/10.1080/08873267.2002.9977019.

Fischer, C. T. (1985/1994). *Individualizing psychological assessment.* Lawrence Erlbaum Associates. (Original work published 1985.)

Fischer, C. T. (2000). Collaborative, individualized assessment. *Journal of Personality Assessment*, *74*(1), 2–14. https://doi.org/10.1207/S15327752JPA740102.

Fischer, C. T. (2006). Phenomenology, Bruno Klopfer, and individualized/collaborative assessment. *Journal of Personality Assessment*, *87*(3), 229–233. https://doi.org/10.1207/s15327752jpa8703_03.

Foster, S. L., & Lloyd, P. J. (2007). Positive psychology principles applied to consulting psychology at the individual and group level. *Consulting Psychology Journal: Practice and Research*, *59*(1), 30–40. https://doi.org/10.1037/1065-9293.59.1.30.

Fredrickson, B. L. (2001). The role of positive emotions in positive psychology: The broaden-and-build theory of positive emotions. *American Psychologist*, *56*(3), 218–226.

Freud, S. (1930). *Civilization and its discontents.* Hogarth.

Friedman, A. F., Bolinsky, P. K., Levak, R. W., & Nichols, D. (2015). *Psychological assessment with the MMPI-2/MMPI-2-RF* (3rd ed.). Routledge.

Gable, S. L., & Haidt, J. (2005). What (and why) is positive psychology? *Review of General Psychology*, *9*(2), 103–110. https://doi.org/10.1037/1089-2680.9.2.103.

Goleman, D. (2011). *Leadership: The power of emotional intelligence.* More Than Sound.

Goosse, M., Martinez Perez, T., & Willems, S. (2025). Communication training for the provision of psychological assessment feedback: An exploratory randomized controlled study. *Training and Education in Professional Psychology*, *19*(1), 14–25. https://doi.org/10.1037/tep0000500.

Gorske, T. T., & Smith, S. R. (2009). *Collaborative therapeutic neuropsychological assessment.* Springer Science and Business Media. https://doi.org/10.1007/978-0-387-75426-0.

Graham, J. R. (2012). *MMPI-2: Assessing personality and psychopathology* (5th ed.). Oxford University Press.

Greene, R. L. (2011) *MMPI-2/MMPI-2-RF: An interpretive manual* (3rd ed.). Allyn & Bacon.

Grossman, L. (1993). The perverse attitude toward reality. *Psychoanalytic Quarterly*, *62*(3), 422–436.

Groth-Marnat, G. (2009). *Handbook of psychological assessment* (5th ed.). John Wiley & Sons.

Handler, L. (2007). The use of therapeutic assessment with children and adolescents. In S. R. Smith & L. Handler (Eds.), *The clinical assessment of children and adolescents: A practitioner's handbook* (pp. 53–72). Lawrence Erlbaum Associates.

Harkness, A. R., & McNulty, J. L. (1994). The personality psychopathology five (PSY-5): Issues from the pages of a diagnostic manual instead of a dictionary. In S. Strack & M. Lorr (Eds.), *Differentiating normal and abnormal personality* (pp. 291–315). Springer.

Harkness, A. R., McNulty, J. L., & Ben-Porath, Y. S. (1995). The personality psychopathology five (PSY-5): Constructs and MMPI-2 scales. *Psychological Assessment*, *7*(1), 104–114. https://doi.org/10.1037/1040-3590.7.1.104.

Harris, T., & Bifulco, A. (1991). Loss of parent in childhood, attachment style, and depression in adulthood. In C. M. Parkes, J. Stevenson-Hinde, & P. Marris (Eds.), *Attachment across the life cycle* (pp. 234–267). Tavistock/Routledge.

Hathaway, S. R., & McKinley, J. C. (1943). *The Minnesota Multiphasic Personality Inventory* (Revised edition, 2nd printing). University of Minnesota Press.

Jacobson, R. M., Hanson, W. E., & Zhou, H. (2015). Canadian psychologists' test feedback training and practice: A national survey. *Canadian Psychology/Psychologie canadienne*, *56*(4), 394–404. https://doi.org/10.1037/cap0000037.

James, W. (1902). *The varieties of religious experience.* Longman, Green & Co.

Jiang, X.-H., & Shen, H.-Y. (2007). Positive psychology in psychological assessment and intervention. *Chinese Journal of Clinical Psychology*, *15*(1), 99–101.

Juffer, F., Stams, G.-J. J. M., & van Ijzendoorn, M. H. (2004). Adopted children's problem behavior is significantly related to their ego resiliency, ego control, and sociometric status. *Journal of Child Psychology and Psychiatry*, *45*(4), 697–706. https://doi.org/10.1111/j.1469-7610.2004.00264.x.

Kunce, J. T. (1979). MMPI scores and adaptive behaviors. In C. S. Newmark (Ed.), *MMPI clinical and research trends* (pp. 1–52). Praeger Publishers.

Kunce, J. T., & Anderson, W. P. (1976). Normalizing the MMPI. *Journal of Clinical Psychology*, *32*, 776–780. https://doi.org/10.1002/1097-4679(197610)32:4<776::AID-JCLP2270320406>3.0.CO;2-P.

Levak, R. W., Siegel, L., Nichols, D. S., & Stolberg, R. A. (Collaborator). (2011). *Therapeutic feedback with the MMPI-2: A positive psychology approach.* Routledge/Taylor & Francis Group.

Lewak, R., Marks, P. A., & Nelson, G. E. (1990). *Therapist guide to the MMPI & MMPI-2: Providing feedback and treatment.* Accelerated Development.

Lindzey, G. (Ed.). (1989). *A history of psychology in autobiography*, Vol. VIII. Stanford University Press.

Linley, P. A., & Joseph, S. (Eds.). (2004). *Positive psychology in practice.* John Wiley & Sons. https://doi.org/10.1002/9780470939338.

Lopez, S. J., & Snyder, C. R. (Eds.). (2003). *Positive psychological assessment: A handbook of models and measures.* American Psychological Association. https://doi.org/10.1037/10612-000.

Marks, P. A., & Seeman, W. (1963). *The actuarial description of abnormal personality: An atlas for the use with the MMPI.* Williams & Wilkins.

Maslow, A. H. (1987). *Motivation and personality* (3rd ed.). Harper & Row. (Original work published 1954.)

May, R. (1989). *The art of counseling* (Revised ed.). Gardner Press. (Original work published 1965.)

McCord, D. M. (2018). *Assessment using the MMPI-2-RF.* American Psychological Association. https://doi.org/10.1037/0000074-000.

McCord, D. M., & Veltri, C. O. C. (2024). The Minnesota Multiphasic Personality Inventories (adult and adolescent versions). https://doi.org/10.1093/oxfordhb/9780190092689.013.13.

McLafferty, C. L., Jr. (2006). Examining unproven assumptions of Galton's nature-nurture paradigm. *American Psychologist*, *61*(2), 177–178. https://doi.org/10.1037/0003-066X.61.2.177.

Meehl, P. E. (1956). Wanted – A good cook-book. *American Psychologist*, *11*(6), 263–272. https://doi.org/10.1037/h0044164.

Meehl, P. E. (1996). *Clinical versus statistical prediction: A theoretical analysis and a review of the evidence.* Jason Aronson. (Original work published 1954.)

Michel, D. M. (2002). Psychological assessment as a therapeutic intervention in patients hospitalized with eating disorders. *Professional Psychology: Research and Practice*, *33*(5), 470–477. https://doi.org/10.1037/0735-7028.33.5.470.

Naglieri, J. A., & Graham, J. R. (2003). Current status and future directions of assessment psychology. In J. R. Graph & J. A. Naglieri (Eds.), *Handbook of psychology: Assessment psychology*, Vol. 10 (pp. 579–592). John Wiley & Sons.

Nagy, T. F. (2011). *Essential ethics for psychologists: A primer for understanding and mastering core issues.* American Psychological Association. https://doi.org/10.1037/12345-000.

Newman, M. L., & Greenway, P. (1997). Therapeutic effects of providing MMPI-2 test feedback to clients at a university counseling service: A collaborative approach. *Psychological Assessment*, *9*(2), 122–131. https://doi.org/10.1037/1040-3590.9.2.122.

Nichols, D. S. (2011). *Essentials of MMPI-2 assessment* (2nd ed.). John Wiley & Sons.

Park, N., & Peterson, C. (2007). Methodological issues in positive psychology and the assessment of character strengths. In A. D. Ong & M. H. M. van Dulmen (Eds.), *Oxford handbook of methods in positive psychology* (Series in positive psychology) (pp. 292–305). Oxford University Press.

Peters, E. J., Handler, L., White, K. G., & Winkel, J. D. (2008). "Am I going crazy, doc?": A self psychology approach to therapeutic assessment. *Journal of Personality Assessment*, *90*(5), 421–434. https://doi.org/10.1080/00223890802248679.

Peterson, C., & Park, N. (2003). Positive psychology as the evenhanded positive psychologist views it. *Psychological Inquiry*, *14*(2), 143–147.

Pope, K. S. (1992). Responsibilities in providing psychological test feedback to clients. *Psychological Assessment*, *4*(3), 268–271. https://doi.org/10.1037/1040-3590.4.3.268.

Poston, J. M., & Hanson, W. E. (2010). Meta-analysis of psychological assessment as a therapeutic intervention. *Psychological Assessment*, *22*(2), 203–212. https://doi.org/10.1037/a0018679.

Purves, C. (2002). Collaborative assessment with involuntary populations: Foster children and their mothers. *The Humanistic Psychologist*, *30*(1–2), 164–174. https://doi.org/10.1080/08873267.2002.9977031.

Riddle, B. C., Byers, C. C., & Grimesey, J. L. (2002). Literature review of research and practice in collaborative assessment. *Humanistic Psychologist*, *30*(1–2), 33–48. https://doi.org/10.1080/08873267.2002.9977021.

Rogers, C. R. (1951). *Client-centered therapy: Its current practice, implications and theory*. Constable.

Rogers, C. R. (1961). *On becoming a person.* Houghton Mifflin.

Rosenthal, L. (1987). *Resolving resistance in group psychotherapy.* Jason Aronson.

Roy, T. A., Mihura, J., Friedman, A. F., Nichols, D. S., & Meloy, J. R. (2023). The last psychological evaluation of Charles Manson: Implications for personality, psychopathology, and ideology. *Journal of Threat Assessment and Management*, *10*(3), 127–150. https://doi.org/10.1037/tam0000197.

Seligman, M. E. P. (1990). *Learned optimism.* Knopf.

Seligman, M. E. P. (1993). *What you can change and what you can't.* Fawcett Books.

Seligman, M. E. P. (1996). *The optimistic child: Proven program to safeguard children from depression & build lifelong resilience.* Houghton Mifflin.

Seligman, M. E. P. (2002). *Authentic happiness: Using the new positive psychology to realize your potential for lasting fulfillment.* Free Press.

Seligman, M. E. P., & Maier, S. F. (1967). Failure to escape traumatic shock. *Journal of Experimental Psychology*, *74*(1), 1–9. https://doi.org/10.1037/h0024514.

Seligman, M. E. P., Maier, S. F., & Geer, J. H. (1968). Alleviation of learned helplessness in the dog. *Journal of Abnormal Psychology*, *73*(3, Pt. 1), 256–262. https://doi.org/10.1037/h0025831.

Seligman, M. E. P., & Weiss, J. M. (1980). Coping behavior: Learned helplessness, physiological change and learned inactivity. *Behaviour Research and Therapy*, *18*(5), 459–512. https://doi.org/10.1016/0005-7967(80)90011-X.

Smith, J. D., & Egan, K. N. (2017). Trainee and client experiences of therapeutic assessment in a required graduate course: A qualitative analysis. *Journal of Personality Assessment*, *99*(2), 126–135. https://doi.org/10.1080/00223891.2015.1077336.

Smith, J. D., Eichler, W. C., Norman, K. R., & Smith, S. R. (2015). The effectiveness of collaborative/therapeutic assessment for psychotherapy consultation: A pragmatic replicated single-case study. *Journal of Personality Assessment*, *97*(3), 261–270. https://doi.org/10.1080/00223891.2014.955917.

Tallent, N. (1992). *The practice of psychological assessment.* Prentice Hall.

Tedeschi, R. G. (1990). Therapeutic listening. In G. McGregor and R. S. White (Eds.), *Reception and response: Hearer creativity and the analysis of spoken and written texts* (pp. 37–51). Routledge.

Tedeschi, R. G. (2020, July 1). Growth after trauma. *Harvard Business Review.*

Tedeschi, R. G. (2023). The post-traumatic growth approach to psychological trauma. *World Psychiatry, 22,* 328–329.

Tedeschi, R. G., & Calhoun, L. G. (1995). *Trauma and transformation: Growing in the aftermath of suffering.* Sage.

Tedeschi, R. G., Moore, B. A., Falke, K., & Goldberg, J. (2020). *Transformed by trauma: Stories of post-traumatic growth.* Boulder Crest.

Tellegen, A., Ben-Porath, Y. S., McNulty, J. L., Arbisi, P. A., Graham, J. R, & Kaemmer, B. (2003). *The MMPI-2 restructured clinical scales: Development, validation, and interpretation.* University of Minnesota Press.

Tharinger, D. J., Finn, S. E., Hersh, B., Wilkinson, A., Christopher, G. B., & Tran, A. (2008, December). Assessment feedback with parents and preadolescent children: A collaborative approach. *Professional Psychology: Research and Practice*, *39*(6), 600–609. https://doi.org/10.1037/0735-7028.39.6.600.

Tyrka, A. R., Weir, L., Price, L. H., Carpenter, L. L., & Ross, N. S. (2008). Childhood parental loss and adult psychopathology: Effects of loss characteristics and contextual factors. *International Journal of Psychiatry in Medicine*, *38*(3), 329–344. https://doi.org/10.2190/PM.38.3.h.

Vaillant, G. E. (1977). *Adaptation to life.* Little, Brown.

Vaillant, G. E., (2000). *Aging well.* Little, Brown.

Veilleux, J. C., Middlebrooks, M., & Schreiber, R. E. (2024). How to communicate a personality disorder diagnosis: The PERSON approach. *Practice Innovations*, *10*(3), 221–236. https://doi.org/10.1037/pri0000269.

Weed, N. C., & Butcher, J. N. (1992). The MMPI-2: Development and research issues. In J. C. Rosen & P. McReynolds (Eds.), *Advances in psychological assessment* (pp. 131–163). Plenum Press.

WHO [World Health Organization]. (2019/2021). *International classification of diseases, Eleventh revision* (ICD-11). World Health Organization.

Williams, P., & Davis, D. (2002). *Therapist as life coach: An introduction for counselors and other helping professionals.* Norton Professional Books.

Index

Notes: Locators in *italic* indicate figures and in **bold** indicate tables.